Rumor in the Early Chinese

This is the first English translation of Lu Zongli's major study of rumor in the early Chinese empires. Zongli explores how rumor, a non-official form of public opinion, formed and spread through non-official channels of early Chinese history. In this careful investigation, Zongli utilizes sources concerning dynastic politics, popular songs, mythology, and prophetic texts, dissecting the nature, function, and impact of rumor on politics and culture. His work demonstrates the ways that historians can examine views outside of mainstream thinking, interpret group mentality, and try to understand the atmosphere of a specific moment in history.

LU ZONGLI is Professor of History at Hong Kong University of Science and Technology.

THE CAMBRIDGE CHINA LIBRARY

The Cambridge China Library is a series of new English translations of books by Chinese scholars that have not previously been available in the West. Covering a wide range of subjects in the arts and humanities, the social sciences and the history of science, the series aims to foster intellectual debate and to promote closer cross-cultural understanding by bringing important works of Chinese scholarship to the attention of Western readers.

Rumor in the Early Chinese Empires

Lu Zongli
Hong Kong University of Science and Technology

With an Introduction by Mark Edward Lewis
Stanford University

Translated by Wee Kek Koon

Sponsored by Chinese Fund for the Humanities and Social Sciences (本书获中华社会科学基金资助)

CAMBRIDGE
UNIVERSITY PRESS

CAMBRIDGE
UNIVERSITY PRESS

Shaftesbury Road, Cambridge CB2 8EA, United Kingdom

One Liberty Plaza, 20th Floor, New York, NY 10006, USA

477 Williamstown Road, Port Melbourne, VIC 3207, Australia

314–321, 3rd Floor, Plot 3, Splendor Forum, Jasola District Centre, New Delhi – 110025, India

103 Penang Road, #05–06/07, Visioncrest Commercial, Singapore 238467

Cambridge University Press is part of Cambridge University Press & Assessment, a department of the University of Cambridge.

We share the University's mission to contribute to society through the pursuit of education, learning and research at the highest international levels of excellence.

www.cambridge.org
Information on this title: www.cambridge.org/9781108749534

DOI: 10.1017/9781108782913

Originally published by Zhejiang University Press as The Rumour of Han Dynasty (ISBN: 9787308091299) in 2011.

First published 2021
First paperback edition 2025

A catalogue record for this publication is available from the British Library

ISBN 978-1-108-47926-4 Hardback
ISBN 978-1-108-74953-4 Paperback

Sponsored by Chinese Fund for the Humanities and Social Sciences
(本书获中华社会科学基金资助)

Contents

Preface

What are rumors?

In Modern Standard Chinese, rumors are defined as "hearsay that is not based on fact; fabricated news";[1] "news that has no basis in fact";[2] and "hearsay that has no basis in fact."[3] Some Chinese writings on popular psychology define rumors as speech that is deliberately fabricated out of thin air and circulated within a specific time and place.[4] Chinese works on social psychology refer to rumors as "news that is erroneous and untrue,"[5] and "imprecise information about people or things that is propagated among people in a society."[6] There are historians who, in their works on rumors in modern history, define rumors as "downright lies that are fabricated out of thin air without a shred of proof," whose "constituent factors are totally bereft of authenticity."[7]

Each of the above popular or academic definitions has its own specific context and academic and social background. A classic Western work on the psychology of rumors argues that rumors are specific statements or those related to current events that people make based on their beliefs, and they are usually propagated among people through word of mouth. In the process of propagation, any rumor could contain some real information.[8]

How do rumors come about? How are they formed? According to Gordon W. Allport and Leo Postman, the formation of a rumor is predicated on two basic conditions: a circulated rumor must contain themes that are "important" to those who spread the rumor and those who receive it; the real information contained in the rumor is secret and processed to render it "ambiguous."[9] Rumors also adhere to a general rule in social psychology: people's perception and interpretation of their environment inevitably involve subjective emotional distortions, and the level of these distortions is determined by the overlapping

[1] *Cihai* (1999), 1 *ce*, p.1094. [2] *Dictionary of Modern Chinese* (2005), p.1583.
[3] *Comprehensive Dictionary of Chinese Phrases* (1993), 11 *ce*, p.382.
[4] Zhang Tiemin (1997), pp.6, 30. [5] Liu Anyan (1993), p.133.
[6] Zhou Xiaohong (1997), p.427. [7] Su Ping (2001), p.5.
[8] Allport and Postman (1965), p.ix. [9] *Ibid.*, p.33.

effects of "importance" and "ambiguity."[10] From these observations, Allport and Postman summarized rumors and their occurrence with a famous formula: Rumor = importance × ambiguity, or R = i × a. "Ambiguity" here refers to the uncertainty of the circumstances or contexts in which the rumor occurs. Based on this formula, the more important the information or theme is, and the more ambiguous the context is, the more impactful the rumor will be.

This formula is quite convincing in its articulation of the prerequisites of the formation of rumors, and helps us to understand the mechanism with which they occur. However, it ignores the importance of interpersonal communication networks in the formation, propagation, and evolution of rumors, as well as the responses and interactions of different groups and individuals. The formula inadvertently considers the groups and individuals who are involved in the occurrence and spread of rumors as "unconsciously reacting" entities.[11]

In their study of rumors, Western sociologists delved into the interpersonal networks and group dynamics at play during the spread of rumors. Tamotsu Shibutani found that different disciplines focused on different things when they studied rumors. Historians and scholars of jurisprudence are concerned with questions of reliability of words and testimonies, while psychologists focus on the accuracy of perceptions and memories. Psychiatrists have a special interest in the repressed impulses that are expressed during the act of communication, whereas sociologists focus on how collective solutions, public opinion, and group responses to disasters take shape when rumors occur.[12] Describing rumors as "improvised news," Shibutani believed that rumors were a collective way of solving problems, a method of communication that repeatedly occurred in groups of individuals and in society. Through this communication method, people in uncertain and unstable social circumstances attempt to pool their intellectual resources to construct an interpretation of their situations that is meaningful to them.[13]

Some scholars believe that while the element of uncertainty is a common impetus in the formation of rumors, it is not the most important one; other environmental factors, such as contradictions and conflicts in the community, are more important.[14] What sets rumors apart from other speech information such as news reports, accounts, and statements is that they are unconfirmed by authoritative sources. This unconfirmed information may be confirmed as real afterward, but of course it could be false.[15] "Rumors are not facts, but hearsay: some rumors eventually prove to be accurate, but while they are in the stage described as 'rumor' they are not yet verified."[16]

Whether or not a rumor can become widespread and accepted by a large audience depends on its themes, opinions, and demands. Shibutani believed

[10] *Ibid.*, p.44. [11] Neubauer (1999), p.167. [12] Shibutani (1966), p.3. [13] *Ibid.*, p.17.
[14] Knopf (1975), pp.90–91. [15] *Ibid.*, p.2. [16] Rosnow and Fine (1976), p.10.

that the interpersonal interaction and group propagation in the course of the formation and spread of rumors should be a dynamic process that went through a conscious "distortion," communication, collective discussion, construction, and reconstruction, before it reached a consensus. For this reason, fabrications and falsehoods are not the essential features of rumors. A rumor may convey false information in the beginning, but in the course of construction and reconstruction, it gradually develops into a self-fulfilling prophecy.[17]

With reference to the above social psychological and sociological theories on rumors, I shall, in this book, define rumors as unconfirmed, but not necessarily fabricated or false, speech information that is spread mainly through word of mouth (of course, the written word can also be a medium), which is constructed and takes shape through interpersonal communication, collective participation, and widespread propagation. This book is not really concerned with whether the original version of a rumor is a fabrication or if the intention of a rumor's originator (if any) was to manufacture something out of thin air. If it cannot enter a channel of propagation and secure some recognition and attention in the course of interpersonal interaction, then the speech is not the type of rumor that this book is concerned with. Rumors discussed in this book are information in the form of speech that enters a channel of propagation and creates considerable social impact, and in its group dynamics is successful in constructing a version that musters a certain level of consensus. This means the rumor is already representing the wishes and demands of the group, and it no longer has anything to do with the subjective intentions of its originator. This book is concerned with rumors that form a ubiquitous social and cultural phenomenon: they exist in all historical periods, all countries and regions, and all cultural forms. "While the content is unique in each historical context, the action pattern itself is recurrent."[18] It is precisely because they are a cultural phenomenon that is universal in its existence and impact that rumors have become an important field of study in modern linguistics, sociology, psychology, anthropology, communications studies, and marketing studies.[19]

Rumors and history are also connected in many profound ways. In fact, most of human history can be seen as a series of responses to and interactions with rumors or rumor-type expressions.[20] In ancient Athens, rumors were considered oracles from Zeus, and altars were erected for Pheme, the goddess of rumors.[21] In the Roman Empire, the goddess was called Fama, which in Latin means fame, public opinion, gossip, and rumors. The imperial capital

[17] Shibutani (1966), pp.14–24, 70–97, 140–181. [18] *Ibid.*, p.17.

[19] For example, in his *Modern Social Psychology* (1997), Zhou Xiaohong discusses the nature of disseminated talk and rumors, the process of their propagation, and the ways of curbing them in his exploration of collective behavior influenced by propagated information. (pp.427–434).

[20] Allport and Postman (1965), p.159. [21] Neubauer (1999), pp.14–16.

Rome was a city of gossip, of hearsay, of rumors.[22] In Europe, rumors were rife in the Middle Ages and early modern period, which is the focus of many works written by Western historians, e.g. *News and Rumor in Renaissance Europe: The Fugger Newsletters* (1959) by George T. Matthews; *The Quest for Eastern Christians: Travels and Rumor in the Age of Discovery* (1962) by Francis M. Rogers; *The Vanishing Children of Paris: Rumor and Politics before the French Revolution* (1991) by Arlette Farge and Jacques Revel; *A Rumor about the Jews: Reflections on Antisemitism and the Protocols of the Learned Elders of Zion* (2000) by Stephen E. Bronner; *A Rumor of Revolt: The "Great Negro Plot" in Colonial New York* (1985) by Thomas Davis; and so on.

Rumors were also a pervasive social and cultural phenomenon in China's past. Many well-known and enduring legends and myths were in fact "rumors" in their original forms. The false and deceitful words that were heavily utilized in military strategy and political conflicts could be considered "rumors." Insincere proclamations of the court, censures by Censors, the many political myths, and popular legends could also be considered "rumors," even if eventually they found their way into official histories.

Chen Hsueh-Ping,[23] the pioneer in the study of rumors in Chinese history, had already written back in 1939 that "essentially, rumors are communicable with all other language- and words-based reports or narratives, such as news reports, legends, history, and so on." If "truthfulness" is the standard with which various forms of speech information are differentiated, then being "unreliable" and "untruthful" are not unique characteristics of rumors. News from newspapers and the radio is an indispensable source of knowledge in modern life; news and rumors should be very different in their respective natures. However, given the complexities of international politics, news censorship, and an era where superstition and fraud are prevalent, news may not be entirely believable. It is widely known that some popular and time-honored folk legends and even historical legends were once rumors that have survived the passage of time. The most valuable and reliable historical sources, and the historical works based on these resources, inevitably contain many unreliable elements. In the remembrance of things past, objectivity is no longer possible.

[22] *Ibid.*, pp.37, 43.

[23] Chen Hsueh-Ping (1901–1999), a native of Yixing, Jiangsu Province, graduated in 1926 from Peking University with a degree in philosophy and a major in psychology. He then headed to the United States, where he studied psychology at Columbia University and obtained a master's degree. After returning to China in the early 1930s, he taught at Northeastern University, Beijing Normal University, Peking University, and then National Southwestern Associated University. During this time, he wrote *The Psychology of Rumors* (1939). In 1948, he was appointed Under Secretary of State for Education and Acting Minister of Education in the government of the Republic of China. In 1953, he began his tenure at Taiwan University as a professor of psychology. His son-in-law is the historian Yu Ying-shih.

What ought to be the most accurate archival materials were often altered or removed altogether because "making them public would not be advisable." The parts removed may well be more important than what remains. The way *Records of the Eastern Flower Gate* was compiled is a good example. Various intended or unintended subjective prejudices that find their way into the sources diminishes the reliability of history. If rumors are defined as "baseless words" and "unverified hearsay," then such speech is surely "ubiquitous in news, testimonies, legends, declarations, and history."[24]

In citing the above, my intention is of course not to equate rumors with speech information whose sources are authoritative, but to explain that in the study of history, all language- and words-based information have their specific value and limitations. In this respect, the following works on Qing and modern history, which begin their narratives with rumors, are excellent works: *Soul-stealers: The Chinese Sorcery Scare of 1768* (1990) by Philip A. Kuhn; chapter 5 of *History in Three Keys: The Boxers as Event, Experience, and Myth* (1997) by Paul A. Cohen; and *A Study of Rumors in Religious Cases in Modern China* (2001) by Su Ping.

Regarding historical sources, researchers of rumors of the Qing and modern period have an embarrassment of riches to refer to. Although there are limited numbers of extant and unearthed texts from ancient China, there are records of rumors and rumor-type expressions from the distant past. Some of the political myths that enjoyed official recognition and "folk stories" that circulated among ordinary people were written down. These narratives are often thought of as false, erroneous, nonsensical, and superstitious. They were taken as baseless hearsay, fabricated information, and weird heresies that devious and unscrupulous types used to mislead and fool the people, rather similar to what Modern Standard Chinese refers to as "rumors." These rumors or rumor-type expressions may appear sporadically in the annals and biographies of historical writings, or they might have been collected, together with *chen* poetry, folk rhymes, and children's rhymes that were popular throughout the realm, and filed under the "Portentous Poetry" category in the various treatises of the Five Agents, becoming the footnotes that scholars use to interpret the past. These Five Agents treatises of various dynastic histories have proved to be a treasure trove.[25] To date, there has yet to be a systematic review and proper discussion of these rumors or rumor-type expressions in the study of China's ancient past, which means that it is difficult to give proper answers to the following questions: What kinds of speech were labeled as rumors in ancient China? Why did rumors start? What forms of expression did they take? How did they spread? How were they constructed? What were the natures and special

[24] Chen Hsueh-Ping (1939), pp.4–9, 13. [25] *Ibid.*, p.8.

features of the information they conveyed? What was the relationship between the information rumors conveyed and truth, falsehood, and fallacy? How were rumors seen by their propagators and receivers? Why did people believe in rumors and spread them? What kind of social and political influence, functions, and limitations did rumors have? How did rulers deal with and respond to rumors? How did intellectuals deal with and respond to rumors?

Given the constraints (including limited historical sources, as well as this writer's limited academic expertise and insights), it is difficult for this book to answer all the above questions, or to provide a complete reconstruction of the rumor-charged social and cultural milieu in the remote past. However, a careful examination and study of the recorded disseminated talk, unverifiable talk, portentous talk, *chen* prophecies, rhymes, political myths, folk legends of the early imperial period, including the Qin, Western Han, Xin and Eastern Han dynasties, and the contexts in which they occurred in, may reveal to us alternative truths or historical views outside the official texts and mainstream thought. It may help us gain an understanding of group mentalities and social psychologies in specific historical contexts, with which we can create multidimensional historical images of many different layers and hues. We can thus offer a more complete interpretation of the relationship between the "historical truth" of such information and their specific historical contexts. This is what this writer has attempted to do in this book.

Chronological Chart of Early Chinese Empires

Qin 秦 (221–206 BCE)
  The First Emperor 始皇帝 (r. 221–210 BCE)
    The Second Emperor 二世 (r. 210–207 BCE)
    King Ziying 子婴 (r. 207–206 BCE)
Western Han 西汉 (206 –8 BCE)
    Emperor Gaozu 高祖 (r. 206–195 BCE)
    Emperor Hui 惠帝 (r. 195–188 BCE)
    Empress Dowager Gao 高后 (r. 188–180 BCE)
    Emperor Wen 文帝 (r. 180–157 BCE)
      Earlier Reign (179–164 BCE)
      Later Reign (163–157 BCE)
    Emperor Jing 景帝(r. 157–141 BCE)
      Earlier Reign (156–150 BCE)
      Middle Reign (149–144 BCE)
      Later Reign (143–141 BCE)
    Emperor Wu 武帝 (r. 141–87 BCE)
      Jianyuan 建元Reign (140–135 BCE)
      Yuanguang 元光Reign (134–129 BCE)
      Yuanshuo 元朔Reign (128–123 BCE)
      Yuanshou 元狩Reign (122–117 BCE)
      Yuanding 元鼎Reign (116–111 BCE)
      Yuanfeng 元封Reign (110–105 BCE)
      Taichu 太初Reign (104–101 BCE)
      Tianhan 天汉Reign (100–97 BCE)
      Taishi 太始Reign (96–93 BCE)
      Zhenghe 征和Reign (92–89 BCE)
      Houyuan 后元Reign (88–87 BCE)
    Emperor Zhao 昭帝 (r. 87–74 BCE)
      Shiyuan 始元Reign (86–81 BCE)
      Yuanfeng 元凤Reign (80–75 BCE)
      Yuanping 元平Reign (74 BCE)

Emperor Xuan 宣帝 (r. 74–49 BCE)
Benshi 本始 Reign (73–70 BCE)
Dijie 地节 Reign (69–66 BCE)
Yuankang 元康 Reign (65–62 BCE)
Shenque 神爵 Reign (61–58 BCE)
Wufeng 五凤 Reign (57–54CE)
Ganlu 甘露 Reign (53–50 BCE)
Huanglong 黄龙 Reign (49 BCE)
Emperor Yuan 元帝 (r. 49–33 BCE)
Chuyuan 初元 Reign (48–44 BCE)
Yongguang永光Reign (43–39 BCE)
Jianzhao 建昭 Reign (38–34 BCE)
Jingning 竟宁 Reign (33 BCE)
Emperor Cheng成帝 (r. 33–7 BCE)
Jianshi 建始 Reign (32–29 BCE)
Heping 河平 Reign (28–25 BCE)
Yangshuo 阳朔 Reign (24–21 BCE)
Hongjia 鸿嘉 Reign (20–17 BCE)
Yongshi 永始 Reign (16–13 BCE)
Yuanyan 元延 Reign (12–9 BCE)
Suihe 绥和 Reign (8–7 BCE)
Emperor Ai 哀帝 (r. 7–1 BCE)
Jianping 建平 Reign (6 BCE)
Taichuyuanjiang 太初元将 Reign (5 BCE)
Jianping 建平 Reign (5–3 BCE)
Yangshuo 元寿 Reign (2–1 BCE)
Emperor Ping 平帝 (r. 1 BCE –5 CE)
Yuanshi 元始 Reign (1–5 CE)
Liu Ying, the Prince Imperial 孺子婴 (r. 6–8 CE)
Chushi 初始 Reign (8 CE)
Xin 新 (9–24 CE)
Wang Mang 王莽 (r. 9–24 CE)
Shijianguo 始建国 Reign (9–13 CE)
Tianfeng 天凤 Reign (14–19 CE)
Dihuang 地皇 Reign (20–24 CE)
Eastern Han 东汉 (25 CE–220)
Emperor Guangwu 光武帝 (r. 25–57 CE)
Jianwu 建武 Reign (25–55 CE)
Jianwuzhongyuan 建武中元 Reign (56–57 CE)
Emperor Ming 明帝 (r. 57 –75 CE)
Yongping 永平 Reign (58–75 CE)

Emperor Zhang 章帝 (r. 75–88 CE)
  Jianchu 建初 Reign (76–83 CE)
  Yuanhe 元和 Reign (84–86 CE)
  Zhanghe 章和 Reign (87–88 CE)
Emperor He 和帝 (r. 88–106)
  Yongyuan 永元 (89–104)
  Yuanxing 元兴 Reign (105)
Emperor Shang 殇帝 (r. 105–106)
  Yanping 延平 (106)
Emperor An 安帝 (r. 106–125)
  Yongchu 永初 Reign (107–113)
  Yuanchu 元初 Reign (114–119)
  Yongning 永宁 Reign (120)
  Jianguang 建光 Reign (121)
  Yanguang 延光 Reign (122–125)
Emperor Shao 少帝 (r. 125)
Emperor Shun 顺帝 (r. 125–144)
  Yongjian 永建 Reign (126–131)
  Yangjia 阳嘉 Reign (132–135)
  Yonghe 永和 Reign (136–141)
  Hanan 汉安 Reign (142–143)
  Jiankang 建康 Reign (144)
Emperor Chong 冲帝 (r. 144–145)
  Yongxi 永憙 Reign (145)
Emperor Zhi 质帝 (r. 145–146)
Emperor Huang 桓帝 (r. 146–167)
  Jianhe 建和Reign (147–149)
  Heping 和平 Reign (150)
  Yuangjia 元嘉 Reign (151–152)
  Yongxing 永兴 Reign (153–154)
  Yongshou 永寿 Reign (155–157)
  Yanxi 延熹 Reign (158–166)
  Yongkang 永康 Reign (167)
Emperor Ling 灵帝 (r. 167–188)
  Jianning 建宁 Reign (168–171)
  Xiping 熹平 Reign (172–177)
  Guanghe 光和 Reign (178–183)
  Zhonghe 中平 Reign (184–188)
Emperor Shao 少帝 (r. 189)
  Guangxi 光熹 Reign (189)
  Zhaoning 昭宁 Reign (189)
  Yonghan 永汉 Reign (189)

Emperor Xian 献帝 (r. 189–220)
- Zhonghe 中平 Reign (189)
- Chuping 初平 Reign (190–193)
- Xingping 兴平 Reign (194–195)
- Jianan 建安 Reign (196–219)
- Yankang 延康 Reign (220)

Introduction to the English Edition

Mark Edward Lewis

The academic study of rumor as a phenomenon began in the early twentieth century among psychologists, notably Louis William Stern in Hamburg, who conducted experiments on how the content of information was altered in the process of passing between individuals. However, it became a topic for historical study only as attention shifted toward examining the conduct of "crowds," the "masses," or the emergence of public opinion. The most important studies of rumor thus appeared in France, where the "crowd" had become a central topic in sociology in the late nineteenth century.[1] Here the study of rumors focused on their contents and significance, specifically on how rumors revealed the fears, hopes, resentments, and other passions of the lower strata who did not otherwise figure in the historical record, notably peasants and urban workers.

These Western studies of rumors, based in France, focused their attention on the crowds of the poor at certain key points in history, especially the French Revolution (and the period immediately preceding it). The role of rumor in spreading fear through the French countryside became the topic of Georges Lefebvre's classic *The Great Fear of 1789: Rural Panic in Revolutionary France*, and rumor's role in disseminating fears or popular panics has subsequently figured in other major studies. Among the most notable are major studies of popular rebellions that were triggered by the spread of rumors in the sixteenth and seventeenth centuries, the account by Arlette Farge and Jacques Revel on the supposed kidnappings or murders of children in Paris shortly before the Revolution, and tales in the late Middle Ages about bands of

[1] For a survey of the crowd in Western thought, see J. S. Mclelland, *The Crowd and the Mob: From Plato to Canetti* (London: Unwin Hyman, 1989). The founders of the systematic study of crowds in modern social sciences were Gustave Le Bon and Gabriel Tarde. See Le Bon, *La Psychologie des foules*, rep. ed. (Paris: Presses Universitaires de France, 1963, originally published in 1895); Le Bon, *La Psychologie politique* (Paris: Flammarion, 1910); Tarde, *L'Opinion et la foule* (Paris: Alcan, 1901). On ideas about the crowd in the age of "mass society," see Serge Moscovici, *The Age of the Crowd*, tr. J. C. Whitehouse (Cambridge: Cambridge University Press, 1985). Psychology and history intersected in the early stages of study in Marc Bloch's essay about rumor in WWI; see Bloch, "Réflxions d'un historien sur les fausses nouvelles de la guerre," *Revue de synthèse historique* (1921).

wandering brigands or evil nobles who kidnapped peasants for ransom or raped their women. These studies show how poor people's perceptions of being powerless and threatened by enemies from other classes or regions manifested themselves in horrifying tales of looming menace. Accounts of Jews murdering Christian children or poisoning wells and tales of the threat of lepers have also been studied under this rubric of fear-inspiring rumors.[2]

Another major aspect of the study of rumor in the West, again especially in France, was the accumulation of gossip about the scandalous lives of great aristocrats, even the king and queen. Tales of a king's impotence, his domination by a queen or mistress, or other effectively pornographic accounts became prominent in the decades prior to the French Revolution, and as Robert Darnton has shown, pornography, gossip, rumor, and philosophy that criticized the monarchy were blended together into a single category in the publishing world of the Enlightenment. Studies on the rise of caricature in this period also show the impact of rumors about the court, and Annie Duprat has argued that the evolution from rumors about the depravity of individual nobles to those about the corruption of the entire regime were crucial to the rise of revolutionary ideology.[3]

[2] Lefebvre, *The Great Fear of 1789: Rural Panic in Revolutionary France*, tr. Joan White (New York: Random House, 1973); Anatoli Ado, *Paysans en révolution: Terre, pouvoir, et jacquerie, 1789–1794* (Paris: Société des Études robespierristes, 1996) has done further work on the background of the "Great Fear" and related incidents. See also Bronislaw Baczko, *Comment sortir de la Terreur, Thermidor, et la Révolution* (Paris: Gallimard, 1989), who argues that understanding the French Revolution would be impossible without taking account of the role that rumor played in shaping the actions of its participants. On the earlier popular rebellions, see Yves-Marie Bercé, *Histoire des croquants: Étude des soulèvements populaires en France au XVII siècle dans le sud-ouest de la France* (Paris, Geneva: Droz-Mouton, 1973); *Croquants et nu-pieds: Les soulèvements populaires en France du XVI au XIX siècles* (Paris: Gallimard, 1974). On popular fears expressed in the spreading of rumors in Paris shortly before the French Revolution, see Arlette Farge and Jaques Revel, *The Vanishing Children of Paris: Rumor and Politics before the French Revolution*, tr. Claudia Miéville (Cambridge, MA: Harvard University Press, 1991); Farge, *Dire et mal dire: L'opinion publique au XVIII siècle* (Paris: Seuil, 1992). In English the pioneer studies of crowds as a historical phenomenon in this period and the role of rumor were George Rudé, *The Crowd in History, 1730–1848* (New York: John Wiley & Sons, 1964); Rudé, *The Crowd in the French Revolution* (Oxford: Clarendon, 1959). On fear and rumor in the late Middle Ages and early modernity, see Jean Delumeau, *La Peur en Occident (XIV–XVIII siècles)* (Paris: Hachette, 1978); Jean Verdon, *Information et désinformation au Moyen Age* (Paris: Perrin, 2010), ch. 3, "La parole indisciplinée: La rumeur."

[3] Darnton, *The Literary Underground of the Old Regime* (Cambridge, MA: Harvard University Press, 1985); *Forbidden Best-sellers of Pre-revolutionary France* (New York: Norton, 1995); *The Devil in the Holy Water, or the Art of Slander from Louis XIV to Napoleon* (Philadelphia: University of Pennsylvania Press, 2009); Bronislaw Baczko, *Les imaginaires sociaux* (Paris: Payot, 1984); Antoine de Baecque, *Le corps de l'histoire: Métaphores et politique, 1770–1800* (Paris: Calmann-Lévi, 1993); Hans-Joachim Neubauer, *The Rumour: A Cultural History*, tr. Christian Braun (London: Free Association Books, 1999); Annie Duprat, *Les rois de papier: La caricature de Henri III à Louis XVI* (Paris: Belin, 2002).

The nineteenth century has attracted less attention, although some scholars have demonstrated that rumor continued to figure prominently in the countryside, while others have examined frequent rumors about a return of Napoleon from Saint Helena, or about political plots and scandals under the Second Empire. The main originality of the period – apart from rich new sources from the popular press and administrative records – is rumor's role in politicizing the people and thereby contributing to the emergence of nation-states. The development of a genre of "war rumors" depicting the savagery of the enemy played a major role in this process of creating the nation.[4] As for rumors in recent times, a substantial literature has emerged dealing with two themes: rumor in the form of "urban legends" and rumor as a form of language circulating on the web. Monographs on these two subjects are too numerous to mention, and they have not yet converged on any common interpretation.

The study of rumor in China has been less rich, probably because the "crowd" has not become a central topic of study, and because the links of rumor and revolution that have been fundamental in Western scholarship remain problematic for a state founded on a peasant rebellion and governed by a party tied to that background. Several important studies *have* been published in English dealing with rumor's social impact in late imperial China, largely focusing on rumors associated with religious movements.[5] As for earlier periods, studies have focused less on rumor's social role than on a distinctive linguistic or literary form in which one subset of rumors circulated, i.e., the doggerel verse sung by children, women, or other parties who were deemed incapable of producing such language.[6] For reasons that will be

[4] Alain Corbin, *Le Village des cannibales* (Paris: Aubier, 1990); *Le Temps, le désir et l'horreur: Essais sur le dix-neuvième siècle* (Paris: Aubier, 1991); François Ploux, *De bouche à l'oreille: Naissance et propagation des rumeurs dans la France du XIX siècle* (Paris: Aubier, 2003); John Horne and Alan Kramer, *German Atrocities, 1914: A History of Denial* (New Haven: Yale University Press, 2001).

[5] Philip A. Kuhn, *Soulstealers: The Chinese Sorcery Scare of 1768* (Cambridge, MA: Harvard University Press, 1990); Barend J. ter Haar, *Telling Stories: Witchcraft and Scapegoating in Chinese History* (Leiden: E. J. Brill, 2006); Paul A. Cohen, *History in Three Keys: The Boxers as Event, Experience, and Myth* (New York: Columbia University Press, 1997), "Part 2: The Boxers as Experience," esp. ch. 5. A Chinese monograph also dealing with the role of rumors in late imperial religious movements is Su Ping 蘇萍, *Yaoyan yu jindai jiaoan* 謠言與近代教案 (Shanghai: Yuandong, 2001).

[6] Lu Zongli 呂宗力, "Han dai de yaoyan yu e yan 漢代的謠言與訛言," *Lishi yanjiu* (2003:2), pp. 14–31; "Han dai 'yaoyan' tantao 漢代妖言" 探討," *Zhongguo shi yanjiu* (2006:4), pp. 39–58; "Lüe lun minjian geyao zai Han dai de zhengzhi zuoyong ji qi xiangguan misi 略論民間歌謠在漢代的政治作用及其相關迷思," *Shehui kexue zhanxian* (2008:9), pp. 106–124; Gao Dianshi 高殿石, *Zhongguo lidai tongyao jizhu* 中國歷代童謠輯注 (Ji'nan: Shandong Daxue, 1990); Lei Qunming 雷群明 and Wang Longdi 王龍娣, *Zhongguo gudai tongyao shangxi* 中國古代童謠賞析 (Changsha: Hunan Wenyi, 1988); Sun Jiazhou 孫家洲, "Han dai 'ying yan' chen yan li shi 漢代'應驗'讖言例釋," *Zhongguo zhexue shi* (1997:2), pp. 82–88; Tian Ying 天鷹, *Zhongguo gudai geyao sanlun* 中國古代歌謠散論 (Shanghai:

discussed below, some of these verses were collected by the state and interpreted as signs of popular feeling. Modern Chinese scholars have consequently argued that Chinese empires invoked public opinion to guide policy. Thus, as in Western scholarship, rumors *are* treated as a phenomenon of crowds, but they are identified not as expressions of anxieties, fears, and hopes that distinguished a peasant or popular mentality, but rather as a form of political thought that influenced elite public discourse.

It is against this background that we can understand the importance of Professor Lu's monograph on rumor in the Han dynasty (202 BCE–220 CE). Unlike previous scholarship, which focused on the popular doggerel gathered by the state and whether it functioned as a form of proto-public opinion, this book comprehensively examines all the forms of rumor, of which the verse represents only one version out of five. The work is comprehensive not only in covering all native categories, but also in conducting a thorough, critical examination of the sources. Finally, it incorporates discussions from the social sciences of the nature and forms of popular opinion, thus developing a comparative perspective. In this Introduction I will briefly sketch the structure of his argument, following his pattern of examining each native term for "rumor," and evaluate what new insights it offers into the Han period.

The first term that he examines, "disseminated words (*liu yan* 流言, a water metaphor, indicating 'flowing,' 'spreading,' or 'adrift')," which is the earliest term for rumors to appear in texts, indicates deliberate slanders spread by hostile parties at the court. It is closely linked to the idea common in the period's poetry of "slander" (as in Darnton's book cited in note 3) and the formation of factions who attacked the virtuous, but isolated, poet. This is *entirely* an elite phenomenon, which is not related to the peasants or poorer levels of society. Later, in the early imperial period, this term sometimes indicated attempts to "delude the masses" by spreading rumors, which still treats the rumors themselves as the product of members of the elite of whom the author of the account does not approve. The closest that one gets to the sense of rumors as an expression of popular sentiment are a few passages that use the term to indicate an inchoate clamor spreading through a crowd, which is interpreted as a hostile response to some political failure. This is of comparative interest, in that Western scholars have noted that the earlier forms of the term "rumor" in Europe indicate precisely such inarticulate noises of the crowd. However, this is still in no sense an articulated "opinion."

Zhonghua, 1959); Wu Chengxue 吳承學, "Lun yao chen yu shi chen 論謠讖與詩讖," *Wenxue pinglun* (1996:2), pp. 103–112; Xie Guian 謝貴安, *Zhongguo chen yao wenhua* 中國讖謠文化 (Haikou: Hainan, 1998); Xu Hualong 徐華龍, *Zhongguo geyao xinlixue* 中國歌謠心理學 (Urumchi: Xinjiang Renmin, 1990); Zhu Ziqing 朱自清, *Zhongguo geyao* 中國歌謠 (Taipei: Kaijin Wenhua, 1994).

The second category is "unverifiable words (*e yan* 訛言, literally 'misguided,' 'deceiving,' or 'swaying,' as in 'to cajole')." This refers to a type of rumor that *is* largely produced by the common people, or that first appears among them. However, it is identified not with the content of the words, but rather as an emotional state that sweeps through a crowd. In this sense it is most commonly a form of contagious fear or panic that *does* resemble the European accounts of mass peasant fears. Elite accounts most commonly treat it as a form of natural prodigy in which some bizarre phenomenon or powerful spirit generates the crowd's emotion. Alternatively, the term also figures in later Han accounts of how tales of supposed miracles led the credulous, usually women and children, to join in collective worship of a divinity that was, in fact, created by the crowd's collective fantasy. The accuracy, or even the content, of such rumors is not an issue in these accounts. To the extent that they effected policy, it was in the same manner as natural prodigies such as droughts, raining blood, or the birth of two-headed calves.

The third category, "portentous words (*yao yan*妖言, literally 'weird' or 'monstrous,' although also in some contexts 'bewitching')," again connects rumors to the spirit world, and like the preceding type it is linked with crowds that generate premonitions of disasters. It survives primarily in legal contexts, where it denounces those who manipulate rumors to conspire against the ruler. On several occasions, it denounces those who spread rumors about the great power of enemy states or armies to sow terror among their own troops. At the end of the Han period, the term *yao* described the religious rebel movements who attacked the dynasty, and their beliefs or texts could be described as "portentous words." In short, this category overlaps with the realm of demonic powers, and it is strictly negative.

It is only with his fourth category, "popular songs or rhymes (*yao yan* 謠言)," that Professor Lu confronts the type of language that had defined rumors in previous studies, and about which he himself has written several articles. These are, as their rubric indicates, rhyming phrases that were sung or chanted by members of the lower classes. The most common type was sung by children, and the inability of their performers, and presumed authors, to understand what they were singing proved the songs' divine origin. While they were generally interpreted as critical reflections on current political affairs, they usually had veiled and prophetic meanings that only became clear after the unfolding of events revealed their hidden import. Their divine origins are also indicated by the fact that the word for these songs was homophonous with the word for "portentous" or "demonic" describing the preceding category, and one graph could substitute for the other.

The reading of these songs as an expression of public opinion was based on a hermeneutic theory that had developed in the late Warring States. This explained the resemblance of many odes in the *Classic of Poetry* to folk songs about rural life with the idea that rulers had collected popular songs to discover the people's moral and emotional condition. While this idea was almost certainly false, it had become so commonly accepted that Han rulers occasionally ordered officials to send up popular songs that they collected in the areas they administered, or those that they visited during official travels. Professor Lu cites these cases, and thus tentatively accepts that these songs might have been used to detect popular sentiment and perhaps adjust policies.

However, he immediately acknowledges that this theory is not very persuasive. The practice of collecting such songs was sporadic, not regular, and the choice of which songs were collected, how they were interpreted, and in what form they were sent up to the emperor all depended on the officials. The emperor, in turn, was free to accept the songs and the proposed interpretation, to offer his own interpretation, or to punish the officials who sent them up for manipulating the people or fabricating the songs. In short, just as the earliest accounts of rumors accepted that they were elite products produced during political conflicts, so these supposedly popular songs only entered elite discourse if some officials found them useful, and they functioned entirely as tools in political conflicts between factions of officials, or between such factions and the emperor.

That these supposed expressions of popular opinion were products and tools of elite conflict is further demonstrated in the fifth category that Professor Lu discusses, the "prophetic words" or "prophetic ditties (*chen yan* 讖言 or *chen yao*讖謠, which the translator simply romanizes)." The *chen* was a type of prophecy that most commonly figured in the *chen wei* texts, "prophetic apocrypha" that were anonymously composed and claimed to be prophetic supplements or esoteric interpretations of the classics. (Professor Lu published an earlier book in English on this phenomenon.[7]) These first appeared in the late Western Han, i.e. the last decades of the first century BCE, and many of them made prophecies about the duration of the dynasty, or its imminent replacement. They figured prominently in the usurpation of Wang Mang (whose Xin dynasty ruled from 9 to 23 CE) and the civil wars that followed, were embraced by the early Eastern Han (25–220 CE) rulers, and reappeared in large numbers in the second century when the end of the dynasty again became an issue. Because these texts were implicated in rebellions, they were repeatedly suppressed and survive only in fragments. The oral *chen*, usually in the form of oracular songs, were less common. Like the other prophetic songs, they were usually understood as products of divine inspiration, and while they sometimes conveyed curses or comments on current politics, they most often were cryptic formulations whose true sense only later became clear.

[7] Lu Zongli, *Power of the Words: Chen Prophecy in Chinese Politics, 265–618* (Oxford: Peter Lang, 2003).

To summarize, rumors in the early empires were most commonly understood in two forms. First, some were the creations of political factions who used them to attack opponents, manipulate the ruler, or stir up crowds. Second, some forms of crowd behavior or popular songs were thought to be inspired by a spirit, whether a positive power like Heaven or a demonic force. These acts, words, and songs were largely interpreted as prodigies such as droughts or raining blood. To the extent that the crowds played any role, it was either as the vehicle through which the spirits acted (these crowds making a particularly good vehicle because of their mental vacuity) or as the generator and disseminator of powerful emotions which themselves could produce other prodigies. Because of the theory that earlier kings had collected popular songs, a handful of Han rulers called for such collecting. However, this simply provided another occasion for the creation or manipulation of rumors by political factions that had figured in the earliest accounts of rumors, and which remained a constant theme of rumor interpretation.

Thus, by undertaking a complete examination of the different terms for rumors and the attributes of these diverse categories, Professor Lu offers a new interpretation of the phenomenon of rumors in the early empires. Freed from the limited vision imposed by the earlier focus on popular songs and their supposed expression of popular opinion, he finds rumors in all their diverse forms, shows how they were politically interpreted and manipulated by elites, and demonstrates how ideas about the relation of rumors to crowds and the lower classes can only be understood through the prism of the religious theory of the period, and the ideas about the contagious power of emotions to sweep through groups. At various points – the emphasis on crowds and the peasantry; the links to crowd noises; the emphasis on the spread of emotions, most importantly fear; and the idea that rumors indicated popular ideas about the court – the early imperial Chinese discourse on rumor overlaps with the modern Western one. Where the two discourses diverge is in their theories for explaining the behavior of crowds, their models of religion and the actions of spirits in the world, their ideas about the emotions, and their focus on different linguistic phenomena as the matrix within which rumors can be understood.

1 Disseminated Talk and Unverifiable Talk

Disseminated Talk

Dictionaries of Modern Standard Chinese usually define *liuyan* as "disseminating baseless talk," "rumors";[1] "baseless talk (usually refers to talk that makes comments on people behind their back, talk that is slanderous, and talk that stirs up disagreements between people)."[2] Chen Hsueh-Ping, a Chinese psychologist in the early twentieth century, averred that "rumors are either referred to as *liuyan* or referred to as *eyan*" – in other words, *liuyan* is rumor.[3] Contemporary Chinese social psychologists may have a different understanding. For example, they believe that both *liuyan* and rumor are "imprecise information," but there are certain differences between the two. The main difference is that "the former is often misinformation that has been disseminated unintentionally, while the latter is fabricated on purpose."[4] Some mass psychologists classify them this way: "*Liuyan* has an origin; a rumor is fabricated from thin air."[5] I have already explained in the Preface that the rumors discussed in this book, be they ancient or modern, are not necessarily speech information that is baseless, false, or fabricated. How then, are *liuyan* and rumor related to each other? What was *liuyan* like during the early imperial period?

We shall begin by looking at how the word *liuyan*, or "disseminated talk," was used in pre-Qin texts, and its expositions offered by famous classics scholars from the early imperial period onward.

An early mention of the word *liuyan* can be found in the chapter "Golden Coffer" in *Book of Documents*: "[Afterward], upon the death of King Wu, [the Duke of Zhou's] elder brother, he of Guan [or Guan Shu], and his younger brothers, spread a report throughout the kingdom, to the effect that the Duke would do no good to the [King's] young son."[6] This passage is extracted from the "New Text" of *Book of Documents*, which is a compilation of historical

1 *Cihai* (1999), 2 *ce*, p.2545. 2 *Dictionary of Modern Chinese* (2005), p.876.
3 Chen Hsueh-Ping (1939), p.4. 4 Zhou Xiaohong (1997), p.427.
5 Zhang Tiemin (1997), p.30.
6 *Annotations and Explanations of the Thirteen Classics: Book of Documents*, *juan* 13, p.197.

texts from great antiquity. It is commonly agreed that *Book of Documents* was compiled during the Warring States Period (fifth to third centuries BCE). After the First Emperor of the Qin Dynasty (Ying Zheng, reigned 221–210 BCE) ordered the burning of forbidden books, parts of *Book of Documents* were lost. In the early Western Han Dynasty, however, Fu Sheng (*c*.260–161 BCE), an Erudit of the preceding Qin Dynasty, orally transmitted its contents, which were then recorded by hand in the Clerical Script. The fruit of this labor was the "New Text." The episode mentioned briefly here was a very popular story during the early imperial period, accounts of which are found in both the "Basic Annals of the Zhou" and "The Hereditary House of Guan Shu and Cai Shu" in *The Grand Scribe's Records.*

Using *liu* as a verb, *liuyan* here refers to openly propagating information. The context of "Golden Coffer" suggests that its compiler was critical of the act of propagation by Guan and his younger brothers, as well as the contents of what they were propagating. The literal meaning of *liuyan*, however, simply refers to the process of openly propagating information. In his annotation of *Book of Documents*, Zheng Xuan (127–200), an erudite classicist of the Eastern Han Dynasty, reinforced the moral judgment implicit in this piece of information, accusing Guan Shu and Cai Shu of "slandering the Duke of Zhou and deluding King Cheng" by their remarks that "the Duke would do no good to the (King's) young son." However, he defined *liuyan* as "releasing information" (*fangyan*), a neutral definition devoid of any judgment. The annotation by Kong Yingda (574–648), an influential medieval classicist, reads: "*Liuyan* means announcing the information; when people hear it, the information will flow like water. *Liu* means to release."[7] His comment is similar to Zheng Xuan's exposition.

Among the pre-Qin historical texts, there are in fact occasions when *liuyan*, or disseminated talk, is linked to false and baseless talk. For example, several lines in "Dang" in the Greater Odes of the Kingdoms section of *Book of Odes* read: "But instead you employ violent oppressors, who trigger many dissatisfactions./They respond to you with baseless stories,/And so robbers and thieves are in your court." The annotation by Zheng Xuan reads: "As royal ministers, you should use good people, but violent oppressors who cause public dissatisfactions are appointed instead. They all use disseminated talk to defame the virtuous. If the King asks, you slander the virtuous by saying that they are treacherous robbers and thieves. Thus, the King believes what you say and appoints the oppressors to his court."[8] Zheng Xuan unequivocally defined disseminated talk as vile talk that "defames the virtuous."

[7] *Ibid.*

[8] *Annotations and Explanations of the Thirteen Classics: The Mao Commentary, juan* 18, p.553.

In his *Collected Commentaries on the Book of Odes*, Zhu Xi (1130–1200), a leading Neo-Confucian of the Southern Song Dynasty, defined disseminated talk in the above poem as "floating and rootless information." "It means you should use good men, but instead you appoint brutal and resentful persons who answer you with disseminated talk. They who are robbers and thieves are instead found in the inner court. Therefore, there is immeasurable resentment and disapproval."[9] Zhu Xi stated that disseminated talk originated from the mouths of "brutal and resentful persons."

The following story is recorded in "Zhao Section II" of *Strategies of the Warring States*. In the sixteenth year (334 BCE) of the rule of Marquess Su of Zhao (Zhao Yu, ruled 349–326 BCE), Marquess Wen of Yan (ruled 361–333 BCE) supplied chariots, horses, gold, and silk to Su Qin (?–284 BCE), ordering him to persuade the State of Zhao into an alliance against the State of Qin. In the course of his lobbying, Su Qin expressed his wish that Marquess Su of Zhao would disregard the influences of slanderous talk (*chanyan*) and disseminated talk and be resolute. "Your servant hears that an enlightened king purges doubts and slander, removes the traces of disseminated talk, and blocks the doors of devious cliques."[10] In this story, disseminated talk was obviously considered undesirable.

That *liuyan* is often defined in Modern Standard Chinese as "disseminating baseless talk" and "talk that makes comments on people behind their back, talk that is slanderous, and talk that stirs up disagreements between people" is due to the influence of the above traditional expositions.

However, talk that was baseless and difficult to verify might not necessarily be slander and defamation.

"On Attracting Scholars" in *Xun Zi* advises that:

> All disseminated talk, disseminated doctrines, disseminated matters, disseminated stratagems, disseminated praise, and disseminated grievances – all things that have been disseminated from elsewhere through improper avenues, the gentleman must treat with caution. When he hears them, he must air them in the open to determine if they are proper. Then he must decide on punishment or reward, and execute his decision at once. In so doing, treacherous talk, treacherous doctrines, treacherous matters, treacherous stratagems, treacherous praise, and treacherous grievances would not dare approach and test him. Instead, loyal talk, loyal doctrines, loyal matters, loyal stratagems, loyal praise, and loyal grievances would be openly expressed and offered without obstruction.[11] (Annotation by Wang Xianqian [1842–1917]: "Disseminated [*liu*] means having no source; grievance means slander." "When the gentleman hears disseminated talk, disseminated doctrines, and so on, and speaks of them openly, he exposes them rather

9 *Collected Commentaries on the Book of Odes, juan* 18, p.203.

10 *Strategies of the Warring States: Collected Annotations and Authentications*, *zhong ce*, *juan* 19, pp.941, 942.

11 *Xun Zi: Collected Explications, juan* 9, p.259.

than keeps them hidden. In this way, evil men would not dare proffer him their schemes.")

According to Xun Zi (*c*.313–238 BCE), a philosopher in the late Warring States Period, on hearing opinions that were the likes of disseminated talk, the gentleman should exercise caution and render the information public and transparent. At the same time, he should carefully verify the information, make a wise judgment, and reward or punish accordingly. In so doing, evil men would find it difficult to peddle their deceit. Xun Zi defined "disseminated" (*liu*) as without source or hard evidence; he did not believe that disseminated talk was necessarily evil talk, evil schemes, or slander.

In pre-Qin texts, "*liuyan*" can also refer to talk that was disseminated by the masses. Confucian scholars in the past had praised maverick scholars who had been able to "hear disseminated talk but not investigate its source"[12] because it was "talk that was disseminated" by the masses.

"The Disseminated Talk of Guan and Cai" as Moral and Political Offense

In the texts written during the early imperial period, "disseminated talk" was often colored with moral overtones, and was equated with defamation, slander, stirring up disagreements between people, and rumor. This was obviously influenced by the way the words were used in the "Golden Coffer" chapter of *Book of Documents*. In classical Confucianism, the Duke of Zhou was seen as the creator of the ideal political system, and the model of perfection in the Confucian ethical tradition. Therefore, the public opinion offensive launched by his older and younger brothers during his power struggle with them, in which disseminated talk was used to garner public support, was naturally defined as a textbook case of deluding the masses with rumors, slandering and defaming the sages, and driving a wedge between the King and his ministers in traditional Confucian-influenced historiography. Although it may be hyperbolic to say that the reign of Emperor Wu of the Western Han Dynasty saw the elevation of Confucianism as the sole state ideology, the preeminent historical status of the Duke of Zhou and Confucius was indisputable. Most historians of the early imperial period also seemed to have accepted such a value judgment. The account of the incident as recorded in "The Hereditary House of the Duke of Zhou" in *The Grand Scribe's Records* was based entirely on "Golden Coffer." "Later, after King Wu had passed away, King Cheng was young and in his swaddling clothes. The Duke of Zhou was afraid that the world would rebel after they heard that King Wu had passed away. The Duke

12 *Annotations and Explanations of the Thirteen Classics: Book of Rites, juan* 59, p.1669.

of Zhou thus ascended the stairs, acting on behalf of King Cheng to take provisional charge of the administration and govern the state. The Prince Guan [or Guan Shu] and some of his younger brothers spread the word throughout the state that, 'The Duke of Zhou will bring no benefits to King Cheng.'"[13] "The disseminated talk of Guan and Cai" thus became an oft-used label in the battle for public opinion in the political struggles during the early imperial period, while historical figures such as King Cheng, the Duke of Zhou, Guan Shu, and Cai Shu became archetypal political symbols.

Emperor Zhao (Liu Fuling, reigned 87–74 BCE), the youngest son and successor of the great Emperor Wu (Liu Che, reigned 141–87 BCE) of the Western Han Dynasty, was eight years old when he ascended to the throne. During Emperor Zhao's thirteen-year reign, Huo Guang (?–68 BCE), an advisor whom Emperor Wu appointed to assist his young heir, dominated the court in his capacity as Commander-in-Chief and General-in-Chief. Although the circumstances in the Western Han Dynasty was different to that of King Cheng, Duke of Zhou, Guan Shu, and Cai Shu a thousand years ago, the renowned historian Ban Gu (32–92 CE) in his *History of the Former Han*, compared Huo Guang to Duke of Zhou and Emperor Zhao to King Cheng.

Ban Gu wrote that in ancient times, King Cheng of the Western Zhou Dynasty succeeded to the throne as a child and there occurred the vicissitudes brought about by the circulation of disseminated talk among the four states of Guan, Cai, and others. Likewise, Emperor Zhao of the Western Han Dynasty took the throne while still a youth and experienced the attempted coup led by his elder brother and sister, the King of Yan and Senior Princess Eyi, together with the Empress's grandfather and father, Shangguan Jie and Shangguan An. However, just as King Cheng had not doubted the Duke of Zhou, Emperor Zhao had confidence in Huo Guang and put him in charge of the government. Each took advantage of the circumstances of their time and thereby made a name for themselves.[14]

It is interesting that such a commendation also became a refutation of the anti–Huo Guang disseminated talk that was making the rounds within and outside the court. Ironically, after Emperor Zhao died without an heir, Huo Guang acted as an "emperor-maker": he chose one of Emperor Zhao's nephews to succeed the throne, and then deposed him and installed Liu Xun, Emperor Wu's great-grandson, as Emperor Xuan (reigned 74–49 BCE). Huo Guang remained politically powerful during the early years of the new reign until his illness and death in the second year of the Dijie reign period (68 BCE). In the following year, the entire Huo family was exterminated by Emperor Xuan for "conspiring against the throne."

[13] Nienhauser, vol. 6 (2006), p.134.

[14] *History of the Former Han, juan* 7, "Annals of Emperor Zhao," p.233.

During the Chuyuan and Yongguang reign periods (48–43 BCE and 43–38 BCE) of Emperor Yuan (Liu Shi, reigned 49–33 BCE), members of the Xu and Shi families, both affinal relatives of the Emperor, and the eunuchs Hong Gong and Shi Xian manipulated power at court. They repeatedly sidelined officials such as Xiao Wangzhi (?–47 BCE), Zhou Kan (?–40 BCE), and Zhang Meng (?–40 BCE). Liu Xiang (77–6 BCE), a member of the imperial clan, formed an alliance with Xiao Wangzhi and others, and submitted a memorial to the throne in the first year of the Yongguang reign period. In it, Emperor Yuan was urged to be King Cheng; Xiao Wangzhi, Zhou Kan, and others were hailed as Duke of Zhou; and Hong Gong, Shi Xian, and their allies were accused of being Guan Shu and Cai Shu. In Liu Xiang's historiographical interpretation, King Cheng had disregarded the many slanders and disseminated talk propagated by the wicked accusing the good, treasured the virtuous services of Duke of Zhou, and had Guan Shu and Cai Shu vanquished. For this reason, his reign was great and his brilliance is still radiant today.[15]

During the reign of Emperor Cheng (Liu Ao, reigned 33–7 BCE), real power was in the hands of one of the Emperor's affinal relatives, Wang Feng (?–22 BCE), the Commander-in-Chief and General-in-Chief cum Intendant of the Masters of Writing, who eliminated those who opposed him and instilled great fear in court. The only person whom Wang Feng trusted and thought highly of was Du Qin, Prefect of the Arsenal under the General-in-Chief. Wang Feng placed Du Qin in his staff and often discussed affairs of state with him. The history books recorded that "many of the good policies today originated from [Du] Qin." Given Wang Feng's overarching manipulation of the court, which had made him many enemies, Du Qin repeatedly reminded Wang Feng to remember "the disseminated talk of Guan and Cai," in the hope that Wang would be prepared and on his guard against the potential damage of disseminated talk. "In times past, the Duke of Zhou had the virtue of a sage and the status of [the King's] uncle, while King Cheng had a singular perspicacity that prevented him from believing in slander. Even then, the Duke of Zhou was fearful of the disseminated talk propagated by Guan and Cai." Du Qin hoped Wang Feng would emulate "the Duke of Zhou's humility and caution" and not allow the wicked to sow words of discord.[16]

Wang Mang (45 BCE–23 CE) came from the most influential affinal clan of the Han imperial house in the latter half of the first century BCE. His aunt Wang Zhengjun (71 BCE–13 CE) was Empress during Emperor Yuan's reign, Empress Dowager during Emperor Cheng's reign, and Grand Empress Dowager during the reigns of Emperor Ai (Liu Xin, reigned 7–1 BCE) and Emperor Ping (Liu Kan, reigned 1 BCE–6 CE). Wang Mang stood out from

[15] *History of the Former Han, juan* 36, "Biography of Liu Xiang," p.1943.
[16] *History of the Former Han, juan* 60, "Biography of Du Qin," p.2676.

among the younger generation of the Wang clan and members of the political and cultural elite, and gained the favor of Wang Zhengjun for his erudition in the Confucian classics, his simple and frugal lifestyle, and his courtly manners and gravitas. In 6 CE, Emperor Ping died without an heir. As the Commander-in-Chief who had manipulated the court throughout Emperor Ping's reign, Wang Mang, with the approval of Grand Empress Dowager Wang, installed the infant Liu Ying (5–25 CE), a descendant of Emperor Xuan, to succeed Emperor Ping as Imperial Heir-Apparent. Wang Mang then named himself Regent.

"The Duke of Zhou feared the aftermath of disseminated talk;/Wang Mang was deferential before he usurped the throne./If they had died before their intentions were revealed,/Then no one would know their true natures."[17] It was this poem by the great Chinese poet Bai Juyi (772–846) that convinced future generations that Wang Mang had a complex and inexplicable link with disseminated talk, so much so that he often styled himself as a latter-day Duke of Zhou assisting King Cheng in gaining the moral high ground. However, it was precisely because of this reason that Wang Mang became more and more sensitive to "disseminated talk that agitated the public." Unsurprisingly, there was an increase in the amount of disseminated talk circulating at both central and provincial levels that questioned Wang Mang's loyalty and sincerity in assisting the young Imperial Heir-Apparent. Under his government, to "spread disseminated talk to agitate the public like Guan and Cai had done" was regarded as one of the most serious offenses, which he used as a serious charge against his political opponents and dissidents. Even his close relatives were not spared.

For example, Wang Mang's eldest son Wang Yu (?–3 CE) did not agree with his father's strategy to separate Emperor Ping from the latter's biological mother, Lady Wei, for fear that the Emperor would bear a grudge when he reached adulthood. Wang Mang, however, refused to listen. So, Wang Yu plotted with his mentor Wu Zhang and brother-in-law Lü Kuan to frighten Wang Mang by staging strange occurrences. When their plot was exposed, Wang Mang ordered the execution of Wang Yu and Wang Yu's wife. In his memorial to the throne, Wang Mang wrote: "Being misled by Lü Kuan and others, [Wang] Yu propagated disseminated talk to agitate the public, which is an offense similar to that of Guan and of Cai. Your servant does not dare to conceal what he has done. He should be executed."

In response, the Grand Empress Dowager issued the edict: "The Duke of Anhan [referring to Wang Mang] occupies the position similar to the Duke of

[17] An alternative rendition of the line "The Duke of Zhou feared the aftermath of disseminated talk" is "The Duke of Zhou feared the days of disseminated talk." See *Collected Works of Bai Juyi*, *juan* 15, third of "Five Candid Poems," p.319.

Zhou and assist your lord [as he assisted] King Cheng. You also execute [your son as he executed] Guan and Cai. You have not allowed your love for those who are close to you to prevail over your honoring of the honorable [i.e., the imperial house]. We approve of it most highly."[18]

Taking advantage of this edict, Wang Mang exterminated Lady Wei's clan and interrogated exhaustively the case of Lü Kuan. Provincial elites were implicated in this case for their previous disapproval of Wang Mang. Those who died were numbered in the hundreds, so that all within the empire trembled before it.

It is interesting that even as Wang Mang styled himself the Duke of Zhou, some people in and outside government, who were disgruntled with the political situation, began writing to reexamine the historical account of the Duke of Zhao, Guan, and Cai. During an interview with the throne, Shentu Gang, who was nominated by the commandery as one of the Capable and Good and the Sincere and Upright, questioned Wang Mang's intentions in isolating Emperor Ping from his affinal relations, the Feng and Wei clans:

> Your servant has heard that when King Cheng was young and the Duke of Zhou was Regent, the Duke listened to the words of the virtuous, and authority and favor were bestowed evenly. It did not matter if they were old or new nobles; the Duke surrounded himself only with the benevolent. His actions were in line with Heaven and Earth, and his policies never failed. But even then, the Duke of Zhao, who was close at hand, was unhappy, and the four states, which were far away, propagated disseminated talk.[19]

The subtext of what Shentu Gang was saying was that even a virtuous man like the Duke of Zhou, who had committed no errors during his regency, would displease the Duke of Zhao, who was also regarded as a virtuous man. The Duke of Zhao was sufficiently unhappy to believe that Duke of Zhou should retire and return authority to King Cheng. Given that Wang Mang's mutinous intentions were known by all at the time, it was little wonder that disseminated talk was spreading throughout the empire. In Shentu Gang's words, disseminated talk was obliquely equated with public opinion; it was not all negative.

When Wang Mang installed the child Heir-Apparent Liu Ying with himself as Regent after the death of Emperor Ping, Zhai Yi (?–7 CE), the Grand Administrator of Dong Commandery, was disgusted. He told his sister's son Chen Feng: "The Marquess of Xindu [referring to Wang Mang] wants to command the whole empire by ruling in the Emperor's place, which explains why he has chosen a toddler from the imperial clan as the child Heir-Apparent. He is taking advantage of the example of the Duke of Zhou's regency during King Cheng's reign. Mark my words: he will overthrow the Han Dynasty. It is

[18] *History of the Former Han*, *juan* 99 *shang*, "Biography of Wang Mang, Part I," p.4065.
[19] *History of the Later Han*, *juan* 29, "Biography of Shentu Gang," p.1012.

gradually becoming apparent." And so, Zhai Yi raised an army in revolt and declared Liu Xin, the Marquess of Yanxiang and a member of the imperial clan, the Emperor. He spearheaded his campaign with a public opinion offensive by "distributing written notices in the commanderies and kingdoms, which said that Wang Mang had committed regicide by poisoning and killing Emperor Ping, and deceitfully heaped the honorific title upon himself."[20]

Wang Mang's regicide of Emperor Ping with poison was an "unverified" and baseless rumor. However, given Wang Mang's intentions in installing the child Heir-Apparent, the reality of him ruling the empire with the imperial house firmly under his control, and the suspicious and devious manner in which he styled himself the Duke of Zhou, the disseminated talk regarding his regicide might have resonated with many people. Initially, Wang Mang became greatly alarmed and raised the elite forces from east of the Pass to put down Zhai Yi's rebellion. He also carried the Child Emperor in his arms to confer with the ministers every day. "When King Cheng was a child and the Duke of Zhou was regent, Guan and Cai held Lu Fu in their hands," Wang Mang said. "Now, Zhai Yi is also holding Liu Xin in his hands and staging an armed rebellion. Even the sages in ancient times had feared this, what more an inconsequential wretch like your servant Wang Mang!" Soon afterward, Zhai Yi's rebellion was put down and Wang Mang was elated. He issued a strongly worded edict: "Zhai Yi, Liu Xin, and their like plotted a traitorous rebellion and propagated disseminated talk that deluded the people. In wanting to harm our Child Emperor, the rebels' crimes are worse than those of Guan and Cai's, and more evil than those of beasts and fowl."[21] Since Wang Mang wrote that "the people" were "deluded," it can be surmised that Zhai Yi's *liuyan* offensive might have had some influence on public opinion.

The above historical examples show that during the political struggles of the late Western Han Dynasty, the moment when openly propagated talk was labeled "the disseminated talk of Guan and Cai," the disseminators were immediately placed in a politically disadvantaged position regardless of whether the discourse was false, seditious, or malicious. Those in positions of authority could also justifiably strip the discourse of any legitimacy. However, whether a *liuyan* should be defined as slander, defamation, or public opinion that sought to right wrongs, the actual historical context and the positions and interests of the people involved must be considered. Sometimes, the label applied by those in power might not completely diminish the level of acceptance of a piece of disseminated talk and its influence on mass psychology. Shentu Gang's reference to history and Zhai Yi's use of public opinion for his cause were examples of this.

[20] *History of the Former Han, juan* 84, "Biography of Zhai Yi," p.3426. [21] *Ibid.*, p.3436.

Talk Disseminated by the People

When "the disseminated talk of Guan and Cai" became a commonly used label or symbol in political struggles, the original definition of *liuyan*, "the open dissemination of information," was often forgotten or ignored. The open dissemination of *liuyan* was not the same as what had been defined in some historical sources as "defamation" or "slander." The subjects and objects of the open propagation of disseminated talk were usually groups or cliques. Certain disseminated talk was propagated across a vast area and it easily became "talk disseminated by the people," whose infiltration into every facet of society was unstoppable. Under certain conditions and within certain limits, such disseminated talk could influence and even shape public opinion. Political theorists during the early imperial period were also aware of this semantic level of disseminated talk and its sociopolitical functions.

Ban Gu commented on the *Book of Odes* in his *History of the Former Han* that the Greater Odes of the Kingdoms section in the former spoke of kings and noblemen, whose virtue reached the common people. The Minor Odes of the Kingdoms section mocked the gains and losses of the self and how they flowed upward. Although they spoke of different things, their virtuous purpose was the same.[22] Here, "flowed" (*liu*) means "to disseminate." In his annotation of *History of the Former Han*, Zhang Yi, an early third-century philologist, interpreted "the self" as referring to the poets themselves, who, being dissatisfied after having made minor gains or losses, wrote poems and propagated disseminated talk to mock those above them.[23] In other words, from the viewpoint of the compiler of *History of the Former Han,* and the classical scholars of the early third century, the poems collected in the Minor Odes of the Kingdoms section of *Book of Odes* could in fact be considered "disseminated talk," which the lower classes composed to mock the upper classes, express themselves, and vent their dissatisfaction.

Du Yannian (?–52 BCE) was formerly a member of Huo Guang's staff. In the early years of Emperor Zhao's reign, he was a great help to Huo Guang in eliminating the latter's political foes by exposing the treacherous schemes of Shangguan Jie; Liu Dan, the King of Yan (?–80 BCE); Sang Hongyang (152–80 BCE); and others. However, when Huo Guang and the Chancellor Che Qianqiu disagreed on the punishments for Commandant of Justice Wang Ping and Privy Treasurer Xu Ren, Du Yannian offered the following advice to Huo Guang:

[22] *History of the Former Han*, *juan* 57 *xia*, "Biography of Sima Xiangru, Part II," p.2609.
[23] *Ibid.*, p.2610.

> I think that as the Chancellor has occupied his position for a long time, and having served the late Emperor, he should not be abandoned unless a grave error has been committed. In recent days, the people have been saying that penalties for offenses are overly harsh, and officials think that this is a spiteful and false allegation. What the Chancellor is arguing with you now also involves legal cases. If the Chancellor is implicated for this, I fear that it will disagree with the people. The masses will holler and the commoners will whisper, and *liuyan* will be disseminated in all directions. I am concerned that you will lose your good name across the empire![24]

For Du Yannian, the hollering of the masses and the dissemination of their *liuyan* would not reinforce Huo Guang's moral advantage by equating Huo Guang with the Duke of Zhou and his opponents with Guan and Cai. They would instead cause Huo Guang to lose the people's allegiance and his good name among them.

During the reign of Emperor Yuan, eunuchs such as Shi Xian repeatedly traduced senior ministers like Zhou Kan and Zhang Meng, prompting Liu Xiang to submit a memorial to the throne, saying: "These lowly persons detect a chasm and use their cunning words to revile, causing disseminated talk to be propagated and words to fly, which results in much clamoring among the people."[25] It can be seen that the "reviling" of Zhou Kan and Zhang Meng by the likes of Shi Xian had exceeded defamatory whispers in the ruler's ears and taken the form of disseminated talk propagated among the people.

Actually, if they were not informed by the personal interest inherent in political struggles, Han Emperors and their ministers might not always label disseminated talk with the "Guan and Cai" tag. Sometimes, they saw it as a kind of public discourse that allowed them to detect public opinion and observe political situations and trends, the kind of talk that served as warning signs. This was referred to as "public criticism" (*wuyi*).

When Emperor Yuan was on the throne, his half-brother Liu Yu, King Si of Dongping, was at loggerheads with his mother, Consort Dowager Gongsun. Emperor Yuan sent Grand Palace Grandee Zhang Zijiao with an imperial edict to warn Liu Yu, reminding him to be careful of the critical talk that was being disseminated. "It has come to our knowledge that there is a failing in your self-cultivation, resulting in disharmony in our court and much disseminated talk being propagated. Slander flourishes from within. We may be presumptuous, but we fear for you."[26] According to Emperor Yuan, the disseminated talk being propagated in the Kingdom of Dongping was due to Liu Yu's own moral

24 *History of the Former Han, juan* 60, "Biography of Du Yannian," p.2663.

25 *History of the Former Han, juan* 36, "Biography of Liu Jiao, King Yuan of Chu (with Biography of Liu Xiang enclosed)," p.1945.

26 *History of the Former Han, juan* 80, "Biography of King Si of Dongping," p.3321.

failings. This was slander that "flourishes from within" and not the seditious rumors started by people with ulterior motives such as Guan and Cai.

Emperor Cheng was the son of Emperor Yuan and Wang Zhengjun. Emperor Cheng's ascending the throne and Wang Zhengjun's becoming Empress Dowager had a profound impact on the politics and fortunes of the Western Han Dynasty in its final years. When Emperor Cheng was Imperial Heir-Apparent, his personal excesses and weak will had given Emperor Yuan cause to consider demoting him and conferring the title of Imperial Heir-Apparent to King of Dingtao, the son of Brilliant Companion Fu, one of Emperor Yuan's consorts. Had there been a change in heirs-apparent, Wang Zhengjun would have lost her political capital and the history of the subsequent decades might have to be rewritten. It is recorded in "Biography of Shi Dan" in *History of the Former Han* that in the first year of the Jingning reign period (33 BCE), Emperor Yuan was seriously ill. As the Emperor had considered replacing the Imperial Heir-Apparent with another one of his sons, there was bad blood between the two. At the time, Shi Dan, an affinal relative of Emperor Yuan, was the latter's favorite and was often attending at his sickbed. One day, when the Emperor was alone in his bedchamber, Shi Dan went straight in and entreated the Emperor in tears:

> The Imperial Heir-Apparent, as the eldest son of the Empress, has been invested for over ten years. His rank and title resonate with the people, all of whom are loyal to him. Yet your servants have recently seen Your Majesty bestow love and favor upon King of Dingtao, thus propagating disseminated talk on the roads and aroused interest in the realm. There is talk that the Heir-Apparent may be removed. If this is indeed the case, the ministers would rather die than obey the imperial command. Your servant wishes to be granted death in the first instance as an example for the other ministers!"[27]

"For this reason, the Heir-Apparent was confirmed as successor to the throne" is of course an oversimplification by the writer of "Biography of Shi Dan." The investiture of the Imperial Heir-Apparent had been made possible with the full support of politically powerful people such as Chancellor Kuang Heng, the Emperor's affinal relatives the Wang clan, and the Prefect of the Palace Writers Shi Xian. Still, Shi Dan's reasons for disseminated talk being propagated "on the roads" and the unease of the people were strong arguments in persuading Emperor Yuan not to replace the Heir-Apparent and destabilize the empire.

[27] *History of the Former Han, juan* 82, "Biography of Shi Dan," p.3377. The last two lines might have been incorrectly punctuated in this reference. The original might have been: "all of whom are loyal to him. Yet your servants have recently seen Your Majesty bestow love and favor upon King of Dingtao" ("*Tianxia mobu guixin. Chenzi jian Dingtao Wang yasu aixing*") instead of "all of whom are loyal to him and regard themselves as his servants. It has recently been seen that Your Majesty bestows love and favor upon King of Dingtao" ("*Tianxia mobu guixin chenzi. Jian Dingtao Wang yasu aixing*").

memorial to the throne, offering a criticism of another flaw in Emperor Guangwu's manpower policies:

According to the *Spring and Autumn Annals*, when the time was out of season, disasters occurred; when abnormal phenomena befell Earth, portents surfaced; when men defied virtue, chaos ensued. When there is chaos, portents and disasters will be upon us. . . . When the state lacks good policies, disasters will affect the sun and the moon. We must be alert to the advent of calamities. The crux lies in yielding to men's hearts and appointing the right men to fill their stations. Yao knew he should not appoint Gun but appointed Gun he did. He suppressed his own sagacity to yield to men's hearts. When Duke Huan of Qi regained power, he made Guan Zhong the Chancellor; when Duke Wen of Jin returned to his state, he appointed Xi Hu. They did not consider their own personal wishes but appointed the right men to fill their stations. Many among the officials are now nominating Guo Ji, Grand Administrator of Yuyang, as the Grand Minister of Works, but the appointment is a long time coming. There are disseminated talk on the roads and all say: "The court wants to appoint those who have served the dynasty with merit." Appointing them will result in the wrong men filling the positions. We implore Your Majesty to learn from Tang [Yao] and Yu [Shun], and consider the examples of [Duke Huan of] Qi and [Duke Wen of] Jin, to embrace the virtue of suppressing the self and yielding to many, thus helping the ministers to promote a good man.[31]

The "disseminated talk on the roads" that said "the court wants to appoint those who have served the dynasty with merit" might have some truth in it, or it might have reflected public concern and speculation. That concern and speculation had given rise to disseminated talk would have been the result of public impressions of personnel appointments made in the early years of Emperor Guangwu's reign. It was recorded that Zheng Xing's memorial was submitted and many suggestions were accepted.[32] Emperor Guangwu's subsequent manpower strategy of "retiring the founding pioneers and promoting civil administrators," which had been favorably regarded throughout history, might have been the result of Zheng Xing's counsel and the public concern reflected by the "disseminated talk on the roads."

During the reigns of Emperor Huan (Liu Zhi, reigned 146–167) and Emperor Ling (Liu Hong, reigned 168–189) of the Eastern Han Dynasty, the affinal relatives of the imperial clan and eunuchs took turns seizing political power. As the Confucian bureaucrats and literati-officials despised the eunuchs, there arose an intense rivalry in court known as *dangzheng* – the struggle between cliques.

Zong Zi, a native of Nanyang and the Grand Administrator of Ru'nan, appointed Fan Pang (137–169) as Bureau of Merit; and Cheng Jin, a native of Hongnong and the Grand Administrator of Nanyang, appointed Cen Zhi as

[31] *History of the Later Han*, *juan* 36, "Biography of Zheng Xing," p.1221. [32] *Ibid.*, p.1223.

his Bureau of Merit. Both Fan Pang and Cen Zhi were well known among the Confucian bureaucrats and literati circles and were entrusted with full authority to handle administrative affairs by their superiors Zong Zi and Cheng Jin. In time, a rhyme became popular in the two commanderies: "The actual Grand Administrator of Ru'nan is Fan Mengbo [referring to Fan Pang]; Zong Zi, the native of Nanyang, just signs his name. The actual Grand Administrator of Nanyang is Cen Gongxiao [referring to Cen Zhi]; Cheng Jin, the native of Hongnong, just practices throat singing."

The rhyme soon turned into disseminated talk that spread into the Imperial Academy, where more than 30,000 students were learning Confucian doctrines to take on the responsibility of running the empire. The students, led by Guo Tai (128–169) and Jia Biao, had a high regard for the leaders of the Confucian bureaucrats and literati, namely, Metropolitan Commandant Li Ying (110–169), Grand Commandant Chen Fan (?–168), and Commandant of the Guards at the Palace of Prolonged Joy Wang Chang. There was much mutual admiration and praise among Guo, Jiao, Li, Chen, and Wang. Encouraged by the literati-officials, as well as the successful examples of Fan Pang and Cen Zhi, the Imperial Academy students had the courage to say what they felt and did not fear the powerful. All the officials in government were afraid of their criticisms and made their way to the students' houses, one after another.[33]

The disseminated talk that spread into the Imperial Academy referred to the "rhyming talk" that sang the praises of celebrated Confucian scholars. Bureaucrats and scholars of the Eastern Han Dynasty were especially good at speaking well of one another and laying down agendas for public discussions. Circulated by the public, this "rhyming talk" steered public opinion during that period.

Liu Li (?–172), King of Bohai,[34] was the younger brother of Emperor Huan. In the eighth year of the Yanxi reign period (165), Liu Li was accused of "plotting immoral schemes." The authorities concerned requested the removal of Liu Li's title. The Emperor could not bear to do it and demoted him instead, making him King of Yingtao, with just one county as his appanage. Later on, Liu Li attempted to get himself reinstated to his former title by bribing Regular Palace Attendant Wang Fu, an influential eunuch, promising the latter 50 million coins if he was reinstated. Just before Emperor Huan's death, he issued a decree reinstating Liu Li as King of Bohai. However, Liu Li knew that Wang Fu had not put in any effort on his behalf and refused to make good his promise. Wang Fu was furious and

[33] *History of the Later Han*, *juan* 67, "Preface to the Biographies of Partisan Prohibitions," p.2186.

[34] The Kingdom of Bohai was a kingdom that was equivalent to a commandery in size. It included parts of the present-day municipality of Tianjin and provinces of Hebei and Shandong.

secretly gathered information about Liu Li's wrongdoings. Shortly after the enthronement of Emperor Ling, who succeeded Emperor Huan, there was disseminated talk on the roads that Liu Li regretted that it had not been him who had been enthroned. Taking this opportunity, Wang Fu falsely accused Liu Li of colluding with two other eunuchs, Regular Palace Attendant Zheng Sa and Palace Attendant of the Yellow Gates Dong Teng, with the latter two "plotting to enthrone Liu Li and committing treason."

Subsequently, Emperor Ling ordered the Inspector of Jizhou Region to arrest and interrogate Liu Li, who then confessed. The Grand Herald, bearing the imperial token, was sent to Bohai, together with the Director of the Imperial Clan and the Commandant of Justice, to harass Liu Li. Eventually, Liu Li took his own life. Eleven of his wives and concubines, seventy of his children, and twenty-four female entertainers all died in prison. His Tutor, Chancellor, and the rest of his staff were all executed for failing in their duties to guide the King. Twenty-five years after the investiture of Liu Li, the Kingdom of Bohai was abolished. All the commoners sympathized with him.[35]

In ancient China, when an emperor died without prior endorsement of an heir who commanded strong support, there would inevitably be intense struggles within the imperial clan and the court in the matter of naming the new emperor. The winner took all, and there was no mercy for those on the losers' side. Emperor Huan passed away without a son. Liu Hong, a ten-year-old boy and a distant cousin of the late Emperor, was chosen by Empress Dowager Dou Miao and her family to succeed the throne, perhaps because of his young age and the ease with which he could be manipulated. As the late Emperor's closest brother by blood, Liu Li was probably not happy with the turn of events. The disseminated talk on the roads that Liu Li regretted that he was not enthroned was a rumor, but it was also a reasonable human response. Disseminated talk such as this often "has a reason for its existence, but real evidence is non-existent"; such talk is accusation based on perceived intent, but the truth is obscure. In times of authoritarian governments, it was used during political struggles as ammunition against enemies. Every time such talk struck its targets, it would create miscarriages of justice and massive numbers of deaths. Liu Li took his own life. His women, children, and staff all died with him. The great tragedy that was the result of this "disseminated talk on the roads" brought out the sympathy of "all the commoners."

[35] *History of the Later Han*, *juan* 55, "Biography of Liu Li, King of Bohai," p.1798.

Disseminated Talk to Mislead People

Given that disseminated talk was a kind of information spread among people at large, it could, naturally, be used as a weapon in propaganda wars. Those in power often used it as a label to demonize their political foes and neutralize the propaganda offensive of opposition groups. On the other hand, opposition groups who were in positions of weakness or outside the system could also ride on the speed and effects of the disseminated talk among the people to shape public opinions that would be advantageous to their side, and to reinforce the legitimacy of their struggle.

In the third year of Wang Mang's regency (8 CE), government troops crushed the armed revolts raised in the northwestern region by the Western Qiang people[36] and in the Central Plains led by Zhai Yi. An elated Wang Mang submitted a report to the throne to claim credit. The report averred that rebels in Dong Commandery[37] disseminated talk, while bandits in the west misled the people.[38] Zhai Yi's propagation of disseminated talk in Dong Commandery and the Qiang's misleading the people in the west would have been the necessary propaganda among opposition groups at the time in their fight for the people's minds.

In the final days of Wang Mang's Xin dynasty, the whole empire was rocked by armed revolts such as those that were led by the Chimei and the Lulin Rebels. Liu Xuan (?–25 CE), a member of the former Han imperial clan, was made Emperor by Lulin rebel commanders, and a new reign period, Gengshi (23–25 CE), was declared. Floating around was all manner of auguries, disseminated talk, and *chen* prophecies regarding the restoration of the Han imperial clan and the imminent demise of Wang Mang's Xin dynasty. Given the mass psychological effect of "the people pining for the Han dynasty," a *chen* prophecy announcing that "a person with the surname Liu will rule" quickly spread far and wide. In his panic, Wang Mang issued an edict claiming that because Liu Yin (16 BCE – 23 CE),[39] the military commander of the Pinglin Army (a branch of the Lulin Rebels), the members of his clan, his relatives by marriage, and his cabal had all falsely disseminated groundless talk to mislead the people into a treasonable rebellion against Heaven's mandate, they had by their own hands killed the General of a New Beginning Lian Dan, Administrator of Qiandui (previously Nanyang) Commandery Zhen Fu, and Chief Commandant Liangqiu Ci. Any person or persons who could capture Liu Yin would be conferred the highest noble ranks, given the income

[36] The Qiang people were an ethnic group that populated northwestern China in ancient times.
[37] The Dong Commandery included parts of the present-day provinces of Hebei and Shandong.
[38] *History of the Former Han, juan* 99 *shang*, "Biography of Wang Mang, Part I," p.4089.
[39] Liu Yin was a member of the former Han imperial clan.

of an estate of 10,000 households, and granted 50 million in precious currency.[40] However, Heaven's mandate was not to be resisted, and disseminated talk was impossible to stop. The misled crowd turned into a united people and Wang Mang's Xin dynasty eventually collapsed. Liu Xiu, the younger brother of Liu Yin, became the founding Emperor of the restored Eastern Han Dynasty.

In summary, disseminated talk referred to information that was spread among the public. The origin of the talk was obscure and its veracity unproven. Whether the disseminated information is true or proven, and whether it should be classified as slander, defamation, public criticism, or public opinion, depended on the historical context and the positions and interests of the persons involved.

Unverifiable Talk

Talk That Was Fraudulent, Erroneous, Changing, and Roving

Dictionaries of Modern Standard Chinese usually define *eyan* as "fraudulent talk," "rumors";[41] "hearsay," "talk that is false, talk that spreads via hearsay."[42]

In ancient historical sources, the word *e* may have multiple meanings. The most common meaning is "false," "fraudulent," and "erroneous." For example, two lines of the poem "Mian Shui" in the Minor Odes of the Kingdoms section of the *Book of Odes* are as follows: "The fraudulent talk of the people [*eyan*]; / Is there no way at all of stopping it?" According to Zheng Xuan's annotation: "Fraudulent. When speaking with ill intent, mean men were prone to fraudulent talk because they wanted to see people grumble after they exchanged words. How could they not be prohibited?"[43]

Another example is in the poem "Zhengyue" of the Minor Odes of the Kingdoms section of the *Book of Odes*: "In the first month the hoar-frost is plentiful, / And my heart is wounded with sadness. / The fraudulent talk [*eyan*] of the people, / Grows greater and greater still." Zheng Xuan annotated that "*E* meant fraudulent. Men ensnared one another with fraudulent talk, causing the King to enact cruel punishments, resulting in natural disasters. Thus, such talk was quite harmful."[44]

40 *History of the Former Han, juan* 99 *xia*, "Biography of Wang Mang, Part III," pp.4180–4181.
41 *Cihai* (1999), 11 *ce*, p.1046.
42 *Comprehensive Dictionary of Chinese Phrases* (1993), 1 *ce*, p.73.
43 *Annotations and Explanations of the Thirteen Classics: The Mao Commentary, juan* 11.1, p.433.
44 *Annotations and Explanations of the Thirteen Classics: The Mao Commentary, juan* 12.1, pp.441–442.

However, in the different contexts of pre-Qin texts, such as *Book of Documents* and *Book of Odes*, *e* had more richness and complexity of meaning, such as "influence" and "change," as well as "action" and "movement."[45]

These meanings of *e* can also be easily found in the historical texts from the early imperial period. For example, in "Biography of Yang Xiong" in *History of the Former Han*: "The flames changed into a yellow dragon and the blaze changed [*e*] into a large *qilin*." Yan Shigu (581–645) annotated that "*E* meant changed."[46]

The character *e* contains the meaning of "change, movement" and *eyan* is also defined as "talk that is moving" and "talk that is changing." For this reason, the kinds of talk that were given the label of *eyan* in historical texts of the early imperial period were often similar to *liuyan*, or disseminated talk. The difference was that disseminated talk usually referred to unverified talk that propagated in the court, or among the elites or the masses, while *eyan* was more often used to label unverifiable talk that spread among the masses.

Talk That Was Weird and Macabre

Perhaps because the word *e* means "fraudulent" and "erroneous," it could also be used to describe the weird and macabre. There was a strange bird in early Chinese mythology. In "Classic of the Mountains: West" in the *Classic of Mountains and Seas*, an early compilation of mythic geography, the bird was described thus: "There was a bird that looked like a crane. It had one leg, a green body with red pattern, and a white beak. It was called Bifang, which was the sound it made. When seen, weird fires [*ehuo*] would break out at the place of its sighting."[47]

It was recorded in "The Hereditary House of Zhao" in *The Grand Scribe's Records* that in the sixth year of the reign of King Qian of Zhao (230 BCE), a great famine occurred. There was unverifiable talk circulating among the people that went: "Zhao is wailing and Qin is laughing. If you don't believe, see if the land is sprouting."[48] The unverifiable talk was expressed in a form similar to a children's rhyme. The line "see if the land is sprouting" described actual facts, while "Zhao is wailing and Qin is laughing" was the people's assessment of the political situation then. It is obviously wide of the mark to

45 See *Comprehensive Dictionary of Chinese Words*, *juan* 6 (1989), p.3948; *Comprehensive Dictionary of Chinese Phrases* (1993), 11 *ce*, p.72.

46 *History of the Former Han*, *juan* 87 *shang*, "Biography of Yang Xiong, Part I," pp.3532–3533.

47 *Classic of Mountains and Seas: Collations and Annotations*, *juan* 2, pp.52, 53.

48 *The Grand Scribe's Records*, *juan* 43, p.1832. The phenomenon of "land is sprouting" was taken as an inauspicious portent in traditional Chinese historical records. There has been a number of hypotheses explaining what it was that was sprouting from the earth, one of which suggests that it might have been some kind of fungus.

interpret this unverifiable talk as a false or fraudulent rumor. For this reason, Zhu Ziqing (1898–1948), an eminent writer and scholar, considered that unverifiable talk and children's rhymes were sometimes interchangeable and similar in nature.[49]

In the many instances where talk was categorized as unverifiable in historical texts dating from the early third century BCE to the late sixth century CE, the information they contained was not necessarily "false, fraudulent, and absurd." However, this talk often included the weird and macabre. Therefore, when Guo Pu (276–324), a prominent early medieval scholar in philology and *fengshui*, interpreted *e* talk as portentous talk,[50] his interpretation explained the reason why disseminated talk was often mentioned in the annals and biographies of the Han histories, whereas unverifiable talk was habitually associated with the treatises of the Five Agents in standard histories beginning in the *History of the Former Han*, and categorized as portentous talk or prophetic poetry. This weird and macabre talk changed and shifted over different times and places. With neither evidence nor a source, its veracity was difficult to prove. Still, it was widely disseminated among the general public, becoming rumor with a touch of strangeness.

Unverifiable Talk in Natural Disasters and Social Crises

It was perhaps due to its weird and macabre nature that the emergence of unverifiable talk was repeatedly accompanied by natural disasters, as recorded in Han Dynasty texts.

Unverifiable Talk Relating to the Great Flood During the transition period between the reigns of Emperor Yuan and Emperor Cheng of the Western Han Dynasty, eunuchs, the Emperors' affinal relatives, and court officials were engaged in a fierce power struggle and much disseminated talk about imperial succession was in the air. Across the empire there were floods and droughts, causing the people much distress. In the fall of the third year of the Jianshi reign period (30 BCE), during the reign of Emperor Cheng, it rained for over forty days within the Pass.[51] A piece of unverifiable talk that the capital would soon be inundated was heard everywhere. At the time, this talk was widely disseminated and made a deep impression on people of all social classes. For this reason, it was mentioned frequently in historical texts. It was recorded in "Annals of Emperor Cheng" in *History of the Former Han* that:

[49] Zhu Ziqing (1994), pp.24, 25.
[50] *Annotations and Explanations of the Thirteen Classics: The Literary Expositor*, *juan* 2, p.2575.
[51] Within the Pass, or Guannei, referred to the area west of the Hangu Pass (located in the present-day city of Lingbao in Henan Province).

> In the fall, there was a flood within the [Hangu] Pass. In the seventh month, Chen Chigong, a little girl who hailed from Sishang, heard that the inundation was coming and ran into the Hengcheng city-gate, trespassed through the side gate of the Imperial Manufactories, and reached [the Office of] the Imperial Parks Products inside the Stables of the Eternal Palace. Officials and commoners had also been frightened and had gone up onto the high places of the city walls. In the ninth month, an imperial edict announced: "Lately, the commanderies and kingdoms have suffered from floods, which have swept away and killed many thousands of people. In the imperial capital, unverifiable talk has been spread without cause that a flood is coming, and the officials and common people are in a panic and terrified, causing them to mount the city walls. This may have occurred because tyrannous and oppressive officials have not yet been curbed and many of the people have cause for complaint because they have lost their occupations. We will send the Grandee Remonstrant Lin and others to travel across and inspect the empire."[52]

Although the talk about the flooding of the capital was later confirmed to be the dissemination of false information, it was irrefutably true that "the commanderies and kingdoms have suffered from floods, which have swept and killed many thousands of people," that the political situation at the time was unstable, and that the administration was brutal and corrupt. The ensuing panic that pervaded the population was completely understandable.

Another account of the unverifiable talk regarding the great flood in "Biography of Wang Shang" in *History of the Former Han* provides us with more interesting details. When the residents of the imperial capital spoke fearful words to one another for no reason, and said that a great flood was imminent, the people ran and trampled one another. The old and the weak cried out and there was great chaos within the capital. Emperor Cheng presided in person in the Front Hall and conferred with his summoned ministers. The General-in-Chief Wang Feng proposed that the Empress Dowager, the Emperor, and the ladies of the palace could get into boats, while the officials and people could be ordered to go up to the city walls to save themselves from the flood waters. All the ministers concurred with Wang Feng's proposal, with the exception of General of the Left Wang Shang, who said, "Since ancient times, even when the state was devoid of morality, flood waters have never breached walled cities. We live in a time of harmonious governance with no armed conflicts, where all within the empire are at peace with one another. Why would a great flood come forth suddenly within a day? This must be a piece of unverifiable talk. It is not advisable to issue the order to go up the city walls and make the people even more frightened." Emperor Cheng accepted Wang Shang's advice.[53]

52 *History of the Former Han, juan* 10, pp.306–307.
53 *History of the Former Han, juan* 82, p.3370.

Wang Shang's judgment regarding the unverifiable talk of the capital's imminent inundation by a great flood was later proved to be correct, and his proposed measures also had the effect of calming the people down. However, "a time of harmonious governance with no armed conflicts, where all within the empire are at peace with one another" was him putting a gloss on the actual situation. Although it was "politically correct," court ministers and the people would not be convinced.

Although everyone in court knew that the unverifiable talk regarding the great flood was not true, no one dared to ignore the alarming signs it had revealed. The court thought that "where there are errors, they must be corrected; where there are none, make sure not to commit one." Emperor Cheng so favored Empress Xu that the rest of his consorts hardly saw him. Empress Dowager Wang and her family were dominating the court at the time and there were murmurings among them. Liu Xiang, Gu Yong (?–9 BCE), and others submitted memorials concerning disasters and unnatural phenomena to the throne, saying that the appearance of the unverifiable talk regarding the great flood was due to the interference in state affairs by palace ladies and their relatives. Emperor Cheng took their advice and trimmed the budget of the Inner Palace. Empress Xu did not give in so readily. She submitted her own defense to the Emperor, to which the latter replied using Liu Xiang's and Gu Yong's treatises on disasters and unnatural phenomena. Various inauspicious omens, such as white mist emerging from the Yingshi Constellation, meteors blazing out of the Wenchang Constellation, "the overflowing well in the Northern Palace, the reverse flow of river waters to the south, the flooding in several commanderies that drowned many people, the spreading of the unverifiable talk that caused great panic, and the girl who trespassed into the palace arousing no vigilance."[54] All these portents were warning signs from Heaven that the Inner Palace was overstepping its boundaries.

The frequent occurrences of natural disasters during the reign periods of Yuanyan (12–8 BCE) and Suihe (8–7 BCE) prompted Li Xun, an expert in the study of *Yinyang* and the Five Agents, to believe that they were signs of the Han dynasty's decline. "In the past, shades of vermillion surfeited the four directions and the earth spewed forth its energy, moving the land and exhausting the people. These were signs of chaos in the world. Comets lit up the sky and great men among the commoners became violent. These are harbingers of powerful rebels."[55] With the appearance of the most menacing omens such as earthquakes and comets, he reckoned that a massive flood would be imminent. This was indicated in the third year of the Jianshi reign period, when "there

[54] *History of the Former Han, juan* 97 *xia*, "Biographies of Imperial Affines, Part II: Biography of Empress Xu, the Empress Xiaocheng," p.3979.

[55] *History of the Former Han, juan* 75, "Biography of Li Xun," p.3181.

was unverifiable talk in the capital about an inundation and the people rushed up the city walls; when the court became panic-stricken and an evil female trespassed into the palace."[56] Although the capital was not flooded in the end, it did not necessarily imply that the unverifiable talk regarding the flood was imagined or made up.

In the spring of the second year of Emperor Cheng's Suihe reign period, the planet Mars was observed to be stationary in the Xin Constellation. Li Xun offered this piece of advice to the Chancellor Zhai Fangjin: "Your Excellency would know the way of meeting emergencies. I said several times in the past that when signs of the sun, the moon, and the stars were observed, they portended the beginning of changes; when convulsions occurred in the mountains and rivers, they reflected the dangers that would plague humanity; when unverifiable talk and folk rhymes were circulated by the people, they expressed the people's truthful feelings about events they knew. Now that all these three portends have come to pass, should we not exercise caution?"[57] It was obvious that Li Xun attached great importance to the warning function of unverifiable talk. It should also be noted that Li Xun believed unverifiable talk and folk rhymes not only had a warning function, they also had the characteristics of *chen* prophecies. "Regarding precedents and examining changes in the past, unverifiable talk always came to pass."[58] In other words, the talk about the flood would be fulfilled; the only question was when. Therefore, rectifications of court politics had to be made quickly to align with the Will of Heaven. Liu Xiang, Gu Yong, and Li Xun were all experts in the *Yinyang* and Five Agents theories expounded in the "Great Plan" chapter of *Book of Documents*. According to the Great Plan Theory of the Five Agents, which was popular during the early imperial period, floods were punishment for an overabundance of the *Yin* element. The interference in state affairs and domination of the court by ladies of the Inner Palace and their relations were the manifestations of the overabundance of *Yin*. Naturally, floods would occur. Thus, while the flooding of the capital might be a piece of unverifiable talk that had yet to come true, its power to warn had not diminished in the eyes of the people of the early imperial period.

By the Eastern Han Dynasty, the warnings contained in unverifiable talk were still frequently interpreted according to the Great Plan Theory of the Five Agents. On the Renzi day of the eleventh month, in the eighth year of the Yanxi reign period (165), it was recorded in "Annals of Emperor Huan" in *History of the Later Han* that fires broke out in the West Pavilion of the Deyang Hall and the Palace Prison of the Northern Office of the Yellow Gates, which then spread to Guangyi Gate and Shenhu Gate. People were burned to

[56] *Ibid.* [57] *History of the Former Han*, *juan* 84, "Biography of Zhai Fangjin," p.3421.
[58] *History of the Former Han*, *juan* 75, "Biography of Li Xun," p.3183.

death. Li Xian (655–684), an imperial prince of the Tang dynasty, in his famous annotation of *The History of Later Han*, provided more details on this episode by citing a sixth-century source, *The Writings of Yuan Shansong*: "There were fires one after another for months, and some offices caught fire several times a day. At night, unverifiable talk was circulated, and drums were beaten everywhere in the palace to drive away the fear. Chen Fan and others submitted a memorial of remonstrance to the throne: 'Only good governance can put a stop to this.' The petition was ignored."[59]

While we do not know the actual contents of the unverifiable talk circulating in the palace, the memorial submitted by Chen Fan and others was quoted in Li Xian's annotation of "Treatise on the Five Agents, Part II" in *History of the Later Han.* In the memorial, Chen Fan, Liu Ju, and Liu Mao argued that in ancient times, fires broke out when a ruler was weak and his ministers strong, indicating the emergency resulting from extreme *Yin*. Earlier in the beginning of spring, punishments for crimes had been harsh; As the Spring Festival progressed, there was uninterrupted cold. The trees froze and snapped in strong winds, and eight or nine regions and commanderies reported simultaneously that premature frost had killed the crops. All the damage suggested the condition of extreme *Yin*, so that the flames of fires did not flare skyward, and the weather became unusually cold. Disasters had already arrived, and abnormal things would follow. "We are afraid that uncertainties may eventually arise. This can only be stopped by implementing good policies beginning in the first day of the first month in the new year. We urge Your Majesty to refer to our previous submissions and not discard our obtuse loyalty. The people will be blessed."[60]

The words of Chen Fan and so on were obviously based on the Great Plan Theory of the Five Agents. During the reign of Emperor Huan, Xiang Kai, an expert in the study of astrology and *Yinyang*, headed to the palace and submitted a memorial: "One night in the third month, an unexplained fiery illumination appeared in the city of Luoyang, causing great disturbance among the people. I divined the sign and determined that within three years, the Son of Heaven will bear the consequences."[61] The appearance of unexplained fires and the unverifiable talk were warnings to rulers. This was exactly what it meant by "in ancient times, fires broke out when a ruler was weak and his ministers strong, indicating the emergency resulted from extreme *Yin*."

Unverifiable Talk Relating to Passing Edict Tokens of the Queen Mother of the West Another piece of unverifiable talk that spread widely in the early imperial period had to do with "passing edict tokens of the Queen

59 *History of the Later Han*, *juan* 7, p.316. 60 *History of the Later Han*, *zhi* 14, p.3296.

61 "Annals of Emperor Huan" in *Annals of the Later Han: Collations and Annotations*, p.615.

Mother of the West," a famous episode in China's religious and mythical history. It is said that records of the Queen Mother of the West had appeared as early as the Yin Dynasty on oracle bones, but sources dating from the Warring States Period were more reliable, such as *Tale of King Mu, the Son of Heaven*; *Bamboo Annals*; and *Classic of Mountains and Seas*. Some scholars believe that during the Western Han Dynasty, the Queen Mother of the West was already worshipped as a deity of well-being and fertility. Images of the goddess were often featured on stones and bricks during the Eastern Han Dynasty. Later on, the Queen Mother of the West became an important deity in the Taoist pantheon. However, the status and function of the goddess in the state cult and folk religion during the Western Han have yet to be determined due to the paucity of historical sources.[62]

Our story began in the spring of the fourth year of Emperor Ai's Jianping reign period (3 BCE), during a devastating drought. This year was marked by unprecedented, nationwide mass hysteria involving "the passing of edict tokens," which went on for the next six months.

Accounts of the event are found in several chapters of *History of the Former Han*. In "Annals of Emperor Ai," it was recorded that "in the east of the [Hangu] Pass, the common people carried in procession the tokens of the Queen Mother of the West. They passed through commanderies and kingdoms and headed west, crossing the [Hangu] Pass toward the imperial capital. The common people [there] also gathered and made offerings to the Queen Mother of the West. Some took fire up to the top of buildings in the night, beating drums and crying out, rousing and frightening one another."[63]

It was also recorded in "Treatise on Astronomy" that "the people agitated one another with fear, shouting as they rushed about to pass the edict tokens of the Queen Mother of the West. They said: 'Men with vertical eyes will come.'"[64]

A more detailed and vivid account can be found in "Treatise on the Five Agents":

> In the first month of the fourth year of Emperor Ai's Jianping reign period, the people ran amok. Each of them passed a bundle of hay or dried hemp to one another, calling it the passing of edict tokens. They met and congregated on the roads, swelling their numbers to several thousands. These people let their hair down and went barefoot, broke through passes in the night, scaled walls to enter buildings. Some dashed about in carriages, or made use of the stage service along postal routes.[65] They traversed

62 For monographs on the Queen Mother of the West, see Loewe (1979), pp.86–126; Cahill (1993); Wang Qing (1998) pp.253–347.

63 *History of the Former Han*, *juan* 11, p.342.

64 *History of the Former Han*, *juan* 26, p.1312.

65 In the Qin and Han empires, non-official trips were restricted. Authorized personnel with the appropriate documentation were permitted to use the stage service, including accommodation and transportation. Other travelers had to show prior approved travel documents with personal

twenty-six commanderies and kingdoms and arrived at the imperial capital. In that summer, the people from the commanderies and kingdoms gathered in the imperial capital's streets and alleys in their thousands. They set up gaming facilities and worshipped the Queen Mother of the West with song and dance. They issued distributed letters with the forewarning: Mother says to the people that "whosoever carries this writing shall not die. Those who doubt my words will do well to look under their door hinges, for behold, there will be white hairs." All of this ended in the fall.[66]

From the scale of the movement, the zealousness of the participants, and the extensiveness of the geographical area covered, it can be surmised that prior to "the passing of edict tokens," the Queen Mother of the West cult had been widespread among the people. When Wang Mang replaced the Western Han with his own Xin Dynasty, he conferred on his aunt Wang Zhengjun, the Empress of the late Emperor Yuan, the title "Grand Empress Dowager, the Gracious Mother of the House of Xin," and claimed that this unverifiable talk–inspired event was an auspicious harbinger of the Xin Dynasty. In Wang Mang's propaganda, both Grand Empress Dowager Wang and the Queen Mother of the West were "Timeless Mothers" of the world; thus, the previous episode of the Queen Mother of the West was obviously an auspicious omen representing Heaven's blessing on his Xin Dynasty. Yet at Emperor Ai's time, the official verdict of the incident by the imperial court and official historians was still one of "unverifiable talk misleading the masses." As to what it was that the unverifiable talk was warning against, there were different responses and interpretations by people holding different positions.

Xifu Gong, one of Emperor Ai's favorites and widely considered one of the triggers that caused unnatural disasters, claimed that the menace was located in the marchlands. He proposed beefing up defenses in response:

information noted in writing, such as physical appearance, at the passes. Those who traveled without valid documents would have to get through illegally, such as breaking through passes under dark of night and scaling walls. Those who were not qualified to use the stage service and could not afford expensive transportation would have to travel on foot. Based on what the "Treatise on the Five Agents" described, we see that the people who were involved in "passing edict tokens of the Queen Mother of the West" were large in number and came from diverse social backgrounds.

66 *History of the Former Han*, *juan* 27 *xia zhi shang*, "Treatise on the Five Agents, Part IV," p.1476. In his annotation of "Annals of Emperor Ai," Wang Xianqian wrote: "When the Son of Heaven went forth, a forerunner would clear the way in front. This was referred to as 'passing the tokens.' Still in practice today, this began in the Han era. This is what was meant by that piece of unverifiable talk, which purported that the Queen Mother would come and that her tokens had to be passed." (*History of the Former Han: Additional Annotations*, *shang ce*, p.138) The way in which this unverifiable talk was spread reminds one of present-day "chain letters" that appear every now and then. Anyone who receives the letter must send a specific number of copies of it to their friends. The chain must not be broken, or misfortune will befall the receiver. Even in the internet age, such psychological games have yet to die out. Sometimes, history can really teach us a thing or two.

Several years ago, the planet Mars was observed to be stationary in the Xin Constellation, the planet Venus was high and emanated rays of light, and the Jiao Constellation was intruded by the star Hegu. It was divined that an armed rebellion would break out. Later on, the unverifiable talk regarding the passing of edict tokens spread across the commanderies and kingdoms, causing great disturbance within the empire. There was fear that unusual changes were at hand. A general-in-chief can be sent to the marchlands and armed defenses fortified, and a commandery administrator can be executed as a demonstration of power to cower the Four Barbarians. Abhorrence can be used to counter the unusual changes.[67]

At the time, Emperor Ai was close to his biological grandmother, Grand Empress Dowager Fu, and his biological mother, Empress Dowager Ding, resulting in the Fu and Ding families dominating the court and many of their men being in high positions. The Emperor also surrounded himself with fawning courtiers. All these caused resentment within the court and among ordinary people, who believed that the unverifiable talk regarding the passing of edict tokens was a reproachful warning against Emperor Ai's placing his affinal relatives and fawning courtiers in important positions. Public opinion was at fever pitch when a solar eclipse occurred on the first day of the first month, in the first year of the Yuanshou reign period (2 BCE). Beset by the portents signaled by earthquakes, the passing of edict tokens, and the solar eclipse, Emperor Ai had no choice but to give in to public opinion. He reinstated his senior minister Kong Guang (65 BCE – 5 CE), who enjoyed great prestige, and dismissed from the court dozens of his favorites such as Sun Chong and Xifu Gong.

The Chancellor Wang Jia thought the various unusual events were a warning from Heaven to Emperor Ai for the latter's excessive love for Dong Xian and the indiscriminate conferring of state honors:

Extravagance, violation of rites, and excesses cause changes and disturbance to the *Yin* and the *Yang*, resulting in a great many unnatural disasters. The unverifiable talk among the people led to panic over the tokens. They walked with their hair down and feet unshod, and those on horses dashed forth in great speed. Heaven had obfuscated their wills and they could not stop themselves. Some say the incident of the tokens was a warning against dire policies. Your Majesty has long been benevolent and perspicacious, cautious in deeds. It is for this reason that I now give my most earnest counsel.[68]

Du Ye, the former Inspector of Liangzhou, was nominated as one of the Sincere and Upright and ordered to submit his frank opinions to the throne. In his interview with the Emperor, he interpreted all the key symbols and signs exhibited in the Queen Mother of the West incident from the perspective of the Great Plan Theory of the Five Agents in his own way.

67 *History of the Former Han, juan* 45, "Biography of Xifu Gong," p.2184.
68 *History of the Former Han, juan* 86, "Biography of Wang Jia," p.3496.

According to him, the tokens were used for counting. The people involved were from below, just like water, thus symbolizing the *Yin* element. Eastward is the correct way for water to flow,[69] yet the people headed west, which meant that it was abnormal and mutinous. The overabundance of portents and the haphazard passing of edict tokens were signs of defying the people's will. The Queen Mother of the West was the symbol of women. Gaming at the capital suggested men's business, and entertaining in the middle of an important event was characteristic of masculine attitude, suggesting the condition of extreme *Yang*.

As for "look under their door hinges, for behold, there will be white hairs," white hairs were the sign of infirm years. The body might be noble, but its constitution was weak, hard to tidy up but quickly disarrayed. The door was where persons must pass, and the hinge was the key to the passage. Being placed where men had to pass and holding the key, white hairs could easily catch people's attention and make their point clearly.

Du Ye accordingly criticized the imperial affinal relatives, the Fu and Ding families, and averred that they should be responsible for the people's resentment and Heaven's condemnation. In their manipulation of the government, criminal and evil persons were not punished, and individuals without achievements and abilities were conferred positions and titles.[70]

Grand Empress Dowager Fu died shortly afterward. Respected Confucian scholar and Grandee Remonstrant Bao Xuan (30 BCE – 3 CE) submitted a memorial to the throne, saying: "Your Majesty serves Heaven as you would your father, serves the Earth as you would your mother, and nurtures the people as you would your children. Since Your Majesty ascended the throne, the father is deficient in brightness, the mother quakes, and the children panic in fear because of unverifiable talk." "It is really something to fear." Although Emperor Ai was now "secreted deep within the palace, castigating himself, and absenting himself from the Audience Hall; although he nominated persons to give honest advice and criticisms of his failings; although he dismissed his relations and those around him who had not worked a day in their lives; although he appointed Kong Guang as Imperial Household Grandee, exposed the excessive evils of Sun Chong and Xifu Gong and had them dismissed and sent down to their own fiefs" – despite all these, "on the Bingxu day of the second month, a worm-like halo was observed around the sun, the sky was continuously overcast but no rain fell. It meant that the sorrows of Heaven had not been soothed, and the resentment of the people had not been

69 The majority of rivers flow west to east into the Pacific Ocean in China due to the country's topography.

70 *History of the Former Han*, *juan* 27 *xia zhi shang*, "Treatise on the Five Agents, Part IV," pp.1476–1477.

appeased."[71] Bao Xuan requested that Dong Xian be dismissed and sent down to his fief, but Emperor Ai refused to listen. Instead, he promoted Dong Xian as Commander-in-Chief, General of the Guards, and Intendant of the Masters of Writing. He even wanted to abdicate this throne in Dong Xian's favor. When Emperor Ai died in the second year of the Yuanshou reign period, Grand Empress Dowager Wang, mother of Emperor Cheng, took over the reins the government and appointed Wang Mang as Commander-in-Chief. Dong Xian was finally ousted and the Ding and Fu clans exterminated.

Unverifiable Talk Relating to Earth-Power Legends and beliefs relating to religion and myths may seem absurd and ridiculous to intelligent people, but they cannot be simply dismissed as superstitions, weird stories, and fallacies. The faith of the believers was informed by their psychosocial background and actual needs. This was what Wang Jia meant when he wrote: "Heaven had obfuscated their wills and they could not stop themselves." One example was the occurrence and spread of the unverifiable talk regarding "passing edict tokens of the Queen Mother of the West." Another was the popular belief during the early imperial period of how the Five Powers cycle directed politics and history.

There was a long tradition in Chinese political thought to formulate a set of political theories for legitimizing rulers and dynasties as far back as the third century BCE. These theories matured with the formulation of the cyclical sequences of historical changes in accordance with the Five Agents Theory in the Han and came to be known as the Theory of the Rotational Changes of the Five Powers. The theory was adopted as a systematic and sociopolitical theory in apocryphal-prophetic texts from late Western Han Dynasty. It was from this that a formal procedure was derived for the legitimate transfer of imperial power. In its early stages, this theory suggested that the Five Powers – wood, earth, water, fire, and metal – overcame one another cyclically. And secular regimes, each represented by one of the Five Powers, replaced one after another following the shift of Heaven's Mandate.[72] Wang Mang, who had the intention to implement a peaceful Mandate transfer between the Han and his new dynasty, adopted a later development of the Rotational Changes Theory. This new theory suggested that the shift of the Five Powers should follow a sequence of generation – wood generating fire, fire generating earth, earth generating metal, metal generating water, and water generating wood. According to this theory, the Han Dynasty's Mandate was supported by the Fire-Power. Subsequently, the next regime should be supported by the Earth-Power. The Eastern Han Dynasty claimed its legitimacy originated from the

[71] *History of the Former Han*, *juan* 72, "Biography of Bao Xuan," pp.3091–3092.
[72] Lu Zongli (2003), pp.84–85.

Fire-Power, and toward the end of that dynasty, would-be usurpers mostly claimed to be supported by the Earth-Power. For this reason, in the periods before the Xin Dynasty replaced the Western Han and the Wei Dynasty replaced the Eastern Han, there were innumerable portents and stories about the color yellow, the designated color of Earth-Power, replacing red, the designated color of Fire-Power, many of which were labeled as unverifiable talk.

In the second year of the Tianfeng reign period (15 CE) of the Xin Dynasty, a piece of unverifiable talk was circulated among the common people living in capital city and its environs: "A yellow dragon had fallen down and died in the Huangshan Palace.[73] Tens of thousands ran there to see it, which incensed Wang Mang." Wang Mang claimed that his legitimacy was supported by the Earth-Power, so naturally he was angry to hear of a yellow dragon falling to its death. He ordered the people involved to be arrested and to have the origin of the unverifiable talk investigated, obviously disregarding the teaching to "hear disseminated talk but not investigate its source," as taught by Confucian scholars in the past. Unsurprisingly, he was not able to trace the source of the talk.[74]

Wang Mang's fear of the possible social consequences of this piece of unverifiable talk should not be seen as an overreaction, but he failed to understand that "stopping the mouths of the people was harder than damming the waters of a river." Public opinion, be it favorable or unfavorable, could not be controlled or swayed by forceful means. As a result, similar stories continued to spread and ferment among the people, eventually bringing about a wave of "loathing for the Xin Dynasty among the populace."

According to "Treatise on the Five Agents," *History of the Later Han*, in the eighth month of the first year of Emperor Huan's Yongkang reign period (167):

It was reported in Ba Commandery that a yellow dragon was seen. Before the commandery submitted the report to the court, the clerk Fu Jian thought it was a joke made

[73] A detached palace located west of the Western Han capital, in the Park of the Supreme Forest north of the Wei River (in present-day city of Xingping in Shaanxi Province). Grand Empress Dowager Wang was encouraged to visit there in the fall when Wang Mang was busy in manipulating the government. See He Qinggu (1998), *Yellow Maps of the Three Metropolitan Areas: Annotations* (*Sanfu huangtu jiaozhu*), p.186, footnote 2.

[74] *History of the Former Han, juan* 99 *zhong*, p.4139. It was recorded in *History of the Later Han, juan* 30 *xia*, "Biography of Xiang Kai" that in the ninth year of Emperor Huan's Yanxi reign period, Xiang Kai submitted a memorial to the throne, saying: "In the second year of Wang Mang's Tianfeng reign period, there was the unverifiable talk about a strange event where a dragon had died in the Huangshan Palace. Later Wang Mang was eliminated and Emperor Guangwu restored the Han Dynasty. With empty talk having such an effect, what more would real events lead to?" (p.1079) Xiang Kai said the piece of unverifiable talk was just empty talk, but empty talk could attract tens of thousands of people to the scene, causing great anxiety to Wang Mang. Its sociopolitical effects should not be underestimated.

by the hirelings and tried to dissuade the Grand Administrator in private. The Grand Administrator did not heed his words. An attempt was made to meet Fu Jian and Fu said: "At the time the weather was hot and some people wanted to bathe in the pond. Seeing that the pond was muddy, however, they joked to one another that 'there is a yellow dragon in the pond.' The story eventually spread among the people. The Grand Administrator thought the story would put him in a good light and he therefore wished to report it."[75]

The spread and resulting transformation of people's "jokes" into popular legends was one typical way in which unverifiable talk and folk beliefs were generated. The many types of folk religion and beliefs in the early imperial period recorded in Ying Shao's *Comprehensive Meaning of Customs and Habits*[76] were often the result of misunderstanding, misinformation, and jokes. (This phenomenon will be discussed in greater depth in Chapter 5.) The story of the yellow dragon in Ba Commandery was originally a joke exchanged among the local hirelings and common people. When the commandery administration got wind of it, the Grand Administrator, knowing what the court liked to hear and wishing to put his administration in a good light, reported it to the court as an auspicious omen and got it into the history books. "Governance was weak and deficient during the reign of Emperor Huan, but there were many auspicious stories of such kind." Emperor Huan was certainly not the only ruler who made use of popular jokes, and spread unverifiable talk on top of previous talk, to create an illusion that he was blessed by Heaven. However, "as Confucian scholars in the past said: auspices that appear at the wrong time are in fact evil. The dragons that were generated by the people's unverifiable talk were in fact evil spawns of dragons."[77] Even if the joke about the yellow dragon were true, it would have been a symbol of the ascendency of the Earth-Power that was supposed to replace the Fire-Power. That Emperor Huan took it to be an auspicious omen for the Han imperial house makes one question his intelligence. This historical account gives us a more concrete understanding concerning the occurrence, dissemination, and creation process of unverifiable talk in the Eastern Han Dynasty.

Unverifiable talk relating to Earth-Power continued to surface during the reigns of Emperor Huan and Emperor Ling.

In the sixth month of the second year of the Xiping reign period [173], the people of Luoyang [the capital of Eastern Han Dynasty] spread the unverifiable rumor that a yellow man sporting a handsome beard and eyebrows was found in the middle of the eastern wall of the Office of the Rapid as Tigers [a contingent of palace guards]. Tens of

[75] *History of the Later Han*, *zhi* 17, p.3344.
[76] A late Eastern Han text that contains various strange and exotic stories of the period, as well as cultural practices, mystical beliefs, and musical instruments.
[77] *History of the Later Han*, *zhi* 17, p.3344.

thousands went to watch it, and those who served in the Forbidden City all came out, causing the roads to be blocked. In the second month of the first year of the Zhongping reign period [184], Zhang Jiao [?–184] and his brothers launched their armed Taoist rebellion in Jizhou Region. Proclaiming their regime the Yellow Sky, the rebels organized their men into thirty-six divisions.[78]

As a Gentleman of the court at the time and a scholar who had great interest in strange stories, Ying Shao paid a personal visit to the Office of the Rapid as Tigers and described what he saw in his *Comprehensive Meaning of Customs and Habits.* He found that "there was no man! There was a spot where filth in the form of a sticky, ocher-colored liquid was seeping out. Another spot on the wall had flaked off in a zigzag line, measuring several *cun.*" His interpretation of the incident was that the sixth month was the last month of summer, the season of the earth's turn, signified by yellow. In the changing of the season, the earth was exactly in the middle of the Five Agents cycle. That was why the "yellow man" was found in the middle of the wall, and walls also represented the earth. As to why it had taken place at the Office of the Rapid as Tigers, it was because the Rapid as Tigers guards were the state's best defenders against aggression. It had to appear on the east wall because "east" (*dōng*) meant "disorder" (*dòng*). This was a sign that armies and generals would be mobilized and all under Heaven would quake. Ying Shao averred that Heaven made things known to men through these omens, much more than employing sight and sound.[79]

Although the "yellow man" that occurred in the Office of the Rapid as Tigers was unverifiable talk, yellow men, yellow earth, yellow skies, and yellow turbans had powerful symbolic meanings in the last years of the Eastern Han Dynasty. The Taoist rebellion troops lead by Zhang Jiao and his brothers were called the Yellow Turban Army. "The linen and clothing of the Yellow Turbans were of pure yellow. They did not carry any weapon and wore long capes covering their shoulders. They walked in gliding, large steps and all the commanderies and counties they went to submitted before them. On that day, the sky turned a rich yellow hue."[80] Obviously, the Zhang brothers chose the yellow sky and yellow turban as political symbols to match the popular beliefs and social psychology prevalent at the time. All the unverifiable talk relating to Earth-Power and the color yellow in the last years of the Eastern Han might have prompted the Zhang brothers to make this choice.

[78] *Ibid.*, p.3346.
[79] Cited by Li Xian in his annotation of *History of the Later Han*, *zhi* 17, p.3346.
[80] Yang Quan's *On the Principle of Things*, cited by Li Xian in his annotation. See *History of the Later Han*, *zhi* 17, p.3346.

Unverifiable Talk in a Chaotic World Unverifiable talk surfaced most readily in the population during natural disasters and times of social crises, as attested by the historical circumstances of the above-mentioned unverifiable talk relating to the great flood, Queen Mother of the West, and Earth-Power. During the early imperial period, there were many occurrences of unverifiable talk being generated and circulating in times of war and in social situations where law and order had broken down.

It was earlier mentioned in the discussion on disseminated talk that Shentu Gang, who was nominated as one of the Capable and Good, Sincere and Upright, questioned Wang Mang's intentions in isolating Emperor Ping from his affinal relatives the Feng and Wei clans. In the same interview with the throne, he also pointed out that:

> After the decline and chaos, following the days that left the world in tatters, the state today is empty and desiccated, and the tax burden is heavy. With harsh officials taking up their time and greedy men raiding their money, the people are in hardship and poverty. Blighted by illnesses, they die. Robbers and thieves band together in their tens of thousands, marching as armies and stationing in hordes. Appropriating spurious honors and titles, they attack the capital and set fire to the counties. They even spread unverifiable talk that they had entered the palace with crossbows, causing great fear to the palace guards. Such has never been seen since the rise of the Han.[81]

It can thus be seen that even palace guards who were close to the center of imperial power would be afraid and swayed by unverifiable talk, when "robbers and thieves banded together in their tens of thousands, marching as armies and stationing in hordes," when they appropriated "spurious honors and titles," "attacked the capital and set fire to the counties."

During the reign of Emperor Zhang (Liu Da, reigned 75–88 CE) of the Eastern Han Dynasty, in the second year of the Jianchu reign period (77 CE), Ma Yan (11–92 CE) was appointed as the Grand Administrator of Chenliu. At the time, there was unverifiable talk in the capital that rebels were approaching from the east. The people were fleeing and frightening one another by spreading the news. The commanderies panicked and informed one another with missives. Ma Yan perceived the news as false and was alone in not putting up defenses. The Emperor demanded an explanation, sending one messenger after another, but Ma Yan insisted that there were no rebels. Eventually, it was as he had said.[82]

Similar incidents took place repeatedly in the Eastern Han. In the fifth year of Emperor Zhang's Jianchu reign period (80 CE), the people of Donghai, Lu, Dongping, Shanyang, Jiyin, and Chenliu spread the unverifiable talk and

[81] *History of the Later Han, juan* 29, "Biography of Shentu Gang," p.1013.

[82] *History of the Later Han, juan* 24, "Biography of Ma Yan," p.861.

frightened each other about how rampant the rebels were. All the people evacuated into walled cities.[83]

During the reign of Emperor An (Liu Hu, reigned 106–125), in the eleventh month of the first year of the Yongchu reign period (107), the people spread unverifiable talk and frightened one another. It resulted in mass movements of people in the regions of Sili, Bingzhou, and Jizhou. Empress Dowager Deng was the dominant force in the court at the time. Historians, observing from the Confucian and the Great Plan Theory perspectives, commented that "the proper way for a woman is to be docile, hence the adage 'submitting to one's son following the death of one's husband.' In conducting herself as a ruler, she [Empress Dowager Deng] was transgressing her station, thus fueling undesirable [talk]."[84]

During the reign of Emperor Xian (Liu Xie, reigned 189–220), in the third year of the Chuping reign period (192), Dong Zhuo (?–192), the notorious warlord of Liangzhou who had manipulated the Emperor and the court with his intrepid Liangzhou Army, was assassinated. Without their commander, Dong Zhuo's men were on tenterhooks. Those who wielded power in court were uncoordinated and indecisive about what to do with the massive and fierce Liangzhou Army. In time, "there was unverifiable talk among the people that all natives of Liangzhou would be executed, which spread and caused fear and disturbance. Provincial leaders within the Pass were all on high alert and readied their troops to defend their territories."[85] The fighting that ensued between Dong Zhuo's men, as well as between them and other armed units, triggered a civil war lasting more than twenty years, leading to the advent of the Three Kingdoms Period.

Official Policies toward Disseminated Talk and Unverifiable Talk in the Early Empires, and Their Theoretical Backgrounds

From the pre-Qin period to the Western and Eastern Han Dynasties, no government would look upon with favor speech information that did not easily lend itself to official controls, such as disseminated talk and unverifiable talk.[86] According to the "Grand Minister over the Masses" section in *Rites of Zhou*, during the Zhou Dynasty "eight types of punishments were employed in the countryside to correct the masses . . . the seventh is the punishment for creating talk." Zheng Xuan, in his annotation, wrote that "creating talk meant confusing

[83] *History of the Later Han*, *zhi* 13, p.3277. [84] *Ibid.*
[85] *History of the Later Han*, *juan* 66, "Biography of Wang Yun," p.2176.
[86] However, the same cannot be said for false information intentionally released by the authorities, or slanderous talk, informants' information, and intelligence that the authorities could use.

the masses with unverifiable talk."[87] Gu Yanwu (1613–1682), the prominent philologist, geographer, and intellectual of late imperial China, thought that the punishment for creating talk was absolutely essential, for "if unverifiable talk was not punished, the Zhou Dynasty would have fallen."[88]

Not being filial to one's parents and not obeying one's older brothers was a heinous crime in ancient Chinese society. That the punishment for fabricating unverifiable talk was just one notch lower than that attested to its seriousness.

The severe punishments meted out by the Qin and Han governments for portentous talk and defamation are well documented. Famous cases included the killing of Confucian scholars by the First Emperor of Qin Dynasty; his killing of all the people who lived next to a fallen meteorite, on which incendiary words had been inscribed; and the execution of Dou Ying (?–131 BCE) and Guan Fu (?–130 BCE) by Emperor Wu of the Western Han Dynasty. There were also countless individuals who were exiled to the borders, jailed, executed, and executed in the marketplaces for crimes of "slander" and "confusing the masses with portentous talk." However, it does not mean that the Qin and Han authorities loathed rumor-mongering, slanderous talk, using flattery to frame the innocent, superstition, and falsehood. It does not mean that the strict prohibitions and severe punishments were purely informed by morality, ethics, and value judgments. In fact, some cases of rumormongering, defamation, slander, and false accusations occurred because of tacit approval, accommodation, and encouragement by those in power. As for the release and dissemination of false information, it was par for the course during political struggles. One would say that the prohibitions against and punishments for portentous talk and slander were implemented for the sake of political stability. At times, it was because those in power had no confidence in controlling the situation due to the intensity of struggles within the government; or they wanted to hide their dirty linen for fear of criticisms.

Having examined the Qin and Han statutes remaining today, we do not find the fabrication and dissemination of unverifiable talk as a crime, nor do they indicate the punishment. Given that unverifiable talk and portentous talk were often used interchangeably in historical texts during the early imperial period, the conviction and penalty for portentous talk can be used as a reference for unverifiable talk. Liu Yu, a member of the Eastern Han imperial clan, was nominated by the Grand Commandant Yang Bing (92 CE–165) as one of the Capable and Good, Sincere and Upright in the eighth year of the Yanxi reign

87 *Annotations and Explanations of the Thirteen Classics: Rites of Zhou, juan* 10, p.707. The origin and authenticity of *Rites of Zhou* is in question. An acceptable dating of the text is the Warring States Period.

88 *Records of Daily Recognitions: Collected Expositions, juan* 5, "Punishment for Creating Talk," pp.280–281.

period (165). When he reached the capital, Liu Yu submitted to the Emperor a memorial of urgent counsel, which included a harsh denunciation of the eunuchs. "Side by side, they were conferred noble titles with enfeoffments. They were vying with one another in adopting boys to be heirs to inherit their names and titles." "As Regular Attendants and Attendants within the Yellow Gate take many women as wives, the miasma of resentment and malevolence gather to bring about evil disasters."[89] "The pent-up mood of the people causes them to join the rebels, while the government is too ready to send troops to crush them. So poor are the people that there are those who sell their heads for recompense, fathers and older brothers mutilate their persons on each other's behalf, and wives and children are taken away before their own eyes."[90] Emperor Huan ignored his entreaties. After Emperor Huan's death, General-in-Chief Dou Wu hatched a plot to exterminate the eunuchs and recruited Liu Yu as a Palace Attendant. The plot failed, however, and Liu Yu was killed. "After the killing of Liu Yu, the eunuchs burnt all his memorials to the throne, branding them as unverifiable talk."[91]

Hou Sen, the younger brother of Regular Palace Attendant Hou Lan, "accumulated hundreds of millions through crooked means. There was a rich man, Zhang You of Zangke,[92] whom Hou Sen falsely accused of fabricating unverifiable talk. He killed the eight members of Zhang You's family and confiscated his house."[93] From these two cases, the fabrication of unverifiable talk was a crime punishable by the death of one's entire family, and the writings that were identified as unverifiable talk had to be destroyed.

As for disseminated talk, though it was often labeled as a "crime on par with Guan's and Cai's," and thus at a disadvantage in terms of political ethics because the legitimacy of its discourse had been deprived, it was not the same as unverifiable talk, which had a touch of strangeness and the macabre. The contents of disseminated talk were usually related to politics and political appointments. In our discussion on disseminated talk, though we mentioned that the crime of "misleading the masses with disseminated talk" was punishable by "the punishment of Guan and Cai," some rulers or members of the ruling class saw it as a kind of public discourse that allowed them to detect public opinion and observe political situations and trends, and served as a political warning sign.

89 Regular Attendants and Attendants within the Yellow Gate were senior positions for eunuchs at the time.

90 *History of the Later Han, juan* 57, "Biography of Liu Yu," pp.1855–1857.

91 *Ibid.*, p.1858.

92 Zangke was a commandery centered in the northwest of present-day Huangping County of Guizhou Province.

93 This account was cited in Li Xian's annotation of *History of Later Han, juan* 54, "Biography of Yang Bing," p.1774.

It should also be noted that while unverifiable talk was officially regarded as being the same punishable crime as portentous talk, wise men within the Han government did not in fact underestimate its psychological effects on the masses, nor did they disregard its function as a mirror of public opinion. In the Han system of government, the Inspectors were the representatives of the central government. They toured the regions and monitored local administrations and their efficiency. According to *Institutions, Posts and Rituals of the Han Official System*, "Inspectors were supposed to propagate rightful ways by touring the various commanderies and kingdoms to check on the state of their administration, to promote the competent or dismiss the incompetent, and to right any miscarriages of justice. There were six main duties of local administrators to be examined. Anything that was not on the list of six should not be checked." The third duty on that list was that the officials in the commanderies and kingdoms had to make sure they would not commit misdemeanors, such as having no sympathy for difficult or dubious legal cases, being cruel and committing murder, being capricious in meting out punishments and rewards, molesting and tyrannizing the people, and exploiting the populace. The standard of judgment regarding these misdemeanors was whether there were "natural disasters where mountains collapsed and the rocks split, and if there were macabre omens and unverifiable talk."[94]

That people during the early imperial period saw unverifiable talk as having the power equivalent to natural disasters to the extent of collapsing mountains and splitting rocks was not only because unverifiable talk and portentous talk could be used interchangeably; it was also because unverifiable talk was itself a disaster expressed in words, a special portent from Heaven. Wang Jia's belief that "Heaven had obfuscated their wills and they could not stop themselves" was a hint of this special feature. Such an understanding by the people of the early imperial period was based on theories of mysticism.

Xifu Gong had linked the unverifiable talk involving the passing of edict tokens of the Queen Mother of the West with the unusual astronomical movements of the planets Mars and Venus, and the Jiao Constellation. "There was fear that unusual changes were at hand," and so he even suggested to Emperor Ai that a "general-in-chief can be sent to the marshlands and armed defenses fortified, and a commandery administrator can be executed as a demonstration of power to cower the Four Barbarians. Abhorrence can be used to counter the unusual changes."[95] Li Xun called the Emperor's attention to the fact that "regarding precedents and examining changes in the past, unverifiable talk always came to pass." Unverifiable talk was almost equivalent

[94] *History of the Former Han, juan* 19 *shang*, "Table of Nobility Ranks and Government Offices": "Inspectors," annotated by Yan Shigu, p.742.

[95] *History of the Former Han, juan* 45, "Biography of Xifu Gong," p.2184.

to *chen* prophecy. Li Xun had acquired his knowledge from the "New Text" of the *Book of Documents* handed down by Xiahou Shichang and Xiahou Sheng. This school of thought was adept in elucidating the Great Plan Theory of the Five Agents and natural disasters, which had profound influence in Han-era politics. The "Treatises of the Five Agents" in the *History of the Former Han* were written based on the framework of the Great Plan Theory, gathering various scholarly views represented by Xiahou Shichang, Xiahou Sheng, and Xiahou Jian, as well as Liu Xiang and his son Liu Xin (?–23 CE).

The Great Plan Theory in the "Treatises of Five Agents" in *History of the Former Han* was based on a cosmology in which Heaven and Man had an organic and telepathic interaction. According to this cosmology, any unusual or strange phenomenon that occurred in the observable world could be a portent given by supernatural and mystical forces to punish the evildoings or reward the good actions of human beings, especially those of rulers. Different words were used to describe omens that punish evil, according to their varying levels of wickedness: portents (*yao*), signs (*nie*), calamities (*huo*), maladies (*ke*), and so on. "Those that are categorized as plants are referred to as portents. Portents are like embryos, meaning still being nourished."[96] Things that were called "out of the ordinary" or "portents and signs" might not necessarily carry negative connotations based on the theoretical framework of the Great Plan Theory of the Five Agents; they were determined by carefully examining the standpoint of the observer and interpreter. By punishing the evil deeds of rulers who had lost the people's allegiance, these omens were in fact in line with the people's will.[97] In the political and social context of the early imperial period, unverifiable talk was sometimes endowed with the symbolic meaning of a sign revealed by Heaven. The ability of some disseminated talk and unverifiable talk, which was widespread and enjoyed high levels of acceptance, to guide public opinion; the collective hope, demands, and consensus that were invested in it; and the people's belief in their mystical powers all could cause such talk to become auto-suggestive and self-fulfilling prophecies that had been given by Heaven. Sometimes, such talk even influenced the development of events and shaped the progression of history.

[96] *History of the Former Han, juan* 27 *zhong zhi shang*, "Treatise on the Five Agents, Part II," p.1353.

[97] The portentous talk as explained in the "Treatise on the Five Agents" in *History of the Former Han* and the *Yinyang* theory of the early imperial period will be specifically addressed in Chapter 4, under the section on prophetic rhymes.

2 Portentous Talk

"Portentous talk" (*yāoyán*), like disseminated talk and unverifiable talk, was a common speech tag in traditional Chinese political and social life. Compared with the latter two, portentous talk was especially loathed by rulers throughout the ages. In the course of more than 2,000 years, successive governments had done quite a good job of stigmatizing portentous talk. To most scholar-officials and the general public, portentous talk represented negative information that was grotesque, macabre, dangerous, and untrustworthy. In Modern Standard Chinese, disseminated talk and unverifiable talk are defined as falsities, fallacies, absurdities, and superstitions; hearsay that is not based on facts; information that is fabricated, which can be readily used by persons with ulterior motives to mislead and fool the people. Even as disseminated talk and unverifiable talk are seen as "rumors," portentous talk is defined as "heresy that baffles,"[1] "exceedingly strange heresy,"[2] "nonsense, lies," and "heresy, talk that confuses people's hearts."[3] Portentous talk is also a manifestation of rumor. This chapter attempts to acquire a fuller and deeper understanding of portentous talk during the early imperial period, as well as the political and social roles it played, by examining and interpreting the occurrences and contexts of portentous talk in historical texts.

The Semantic Meaning of the Word "Portentous" (*Yāo*) in Pre-Qin, Qin, and Han Texts

The word "portentous" (*yāo*) in Pre-Qin and the early imperial texts described things and phenomena that were abnormal, weird, and unusual. For example, it was written in "Discourse on Heaven" in *Xunzi*: "Accordingly, flood and drought cannot cause famine; cold and heat cannot cause sickness; and [portentous] and freak events (*yāoguài*) cannot cause misfortune."[4] In *Master Lü's Spring and Autumn Annals*, in the essay "What It Means to Be Worthy" under

[1] *Dictionary of Modern Chinese* (2005), p.1581. [2] *Cihai* (1999), p.2967.
[3] *Comprehensive Dictionary of Chinese Phrases* (1989), 4 *ce*, p.304.
[4] *Xun Zi: Collected Explications, juan* 11, p.307. English translation from Knoblock (1988), p.14.

"Discourse on the Opening of Spring," it was written that "when snow, frost, rain, and dew come in a timely manner, the myriad things flourish. When the people are cultivated, sickness, oddities, and ferocity (*yāolì*) will go away." According to Gao You's annotation: "*Yāo* means oddity; *lì* means ferocity."[5]

For people in the ancient world, certain strange phenomena were inevitably understood as involving the supernatural. For example, it was recorded in a third century BCE bamboo almanac, which was unearthed in a Qin-era tomb at Shuihudi,[6] that: "Birds and beasts with the ability to speak are portentous, but they cannot speak more than three words. If they speak more than three words, persons nearby will likely benefit, and they would stop."[7] In *Commentary of Zuo: The Fifteenth Year of Duke Xi*, the Lord of Qin was recorded as saying the following words: "That I am following the ruler [of Jin] westward is but a fulfillment of the portentous dream in the State of Jin." In the late Eastern Han Dynasty, a woman called Du Jiang lived in the Dongling District of Guangling Commandery.[8] She practiced the unorthodox arts and communicated with spirits. The county authorities believed her to be portentous and had her jailed, in fetters and handcuffs. Then, she changed her form, and no one knew where she went. The case was reported to the higher authorities. A shrine was erected at the location where it occurred, and she was given the title Holy Mother of Dongling.[9]

In the historical contexts of the Pre-Qin and early imperial periods, the abnormal, weird, and unusual were not necessarily equated with the negative and evil. For example, in *Commentary of Zuo: The Twenty-Sixth Year of Duke Zhao*, it was stated that "in the sixth year of the reign of King Ding [of the Eastern Zhou Dynasty], a portentous spirit (*yāo*) came in a séance to the people of Qin." It is explained in a Tang-period commentary that "Séance meant something from top down. At the time, there were portentous words circulating among the people in the State of Qin, as though the spirits were bearing down on them, from top down."[10] The "portentous" referred to here were the spirits that possessed the royal shamans, enabling them to make supernatural foretelling for the people of Qin. The abovementioned "portentous dream" in *Commentary of Zuo: The Fifteenth Year of Duke Xi* also referred to the spirits that possessed Hu Tu in his dream.

It was also for this reason that unusually beautiful individuals or things were often described by their contemporaries with the same word, *yāo*, which can be translated as "bewitching." For example, in *Rhapsody of the Goddess*, the late

[5] *Master Lü's Spring and Autumn Annals: New Expositions*, *juan* 21, p.1451.
[6] Located in present-day Yunmeng County, Hubei Province. [7] Wu Xiaoqiang (2000), p.129.
[8] Located in the present-day city of Yangzhou, Jiangsu Province.
[9] *History of the Later Han*, *zhi* 21, p.3461.
[10] *Commentary of Zuo on the Spring and Autumn Annals: Annotations*, p.1477.

Warring States Period poet Song Yu wrote: "Seen up close, she is bewitching; it is the same from afar."[11] In the literary works of the Han and Wei periods, "bewitching person (*yāorén*)"[12] and "bewitching woman (*yāonü*)"[13] referred to beautiful women, while *yāoyě*[14] and *yāogǔ*[15] were often synonymous with "pulchritude."

In the eyes of punctilious gentlemen, unusual beauty could of course be construed as suggestive of lewdness and impropriety. In the Preface to "Annals of Empresses" in the *History of the Later Han*, Consorts and Beautiful Ladies who found favor with Emperors because of their good looks were described as "finding favor with witchery (*yāoxìng*)"[16] In "Biography of Liang Ji" in *History of the Later Han*, Sun Shou (?–159), wife of Liang Ji (?–159), the powerful minister and affinal relative of several Eastern Han Emperors, was described as "beautiful in countenance and adept at striking bewitching poses (*yāotài*), such as fashioning her eyebrows to affect sadness."[17] This reflects the strong ideological overtones of the aesthetic preferences of historians at the time.

At a time when primitive beliefs and nature worship were prevalent, things and phenomena that were abnormal, weird, and unusual would often convey a sense of foreboding, giving rise to fear and vigilance. During the early imperial period, when people emphasized harmony between Heaven and Man, and believed in a telepathic interaction between the two, such phenomena were inferred as portents of Heaven's warnings. For this reason, a great deal of such

[11] *Selections of Refined Literature*, *juan* 19, p.268.

[12] Ying Yang (?–217), *Letter to Chong Huigong*: "Shine the brilliant light of the moon to illuminate the gentleness and grace of the bewitching person (*yāorén*)." (*Complete Writings of High Antiquity, the Three Eras, Qin, Han, the Three Kingdoms, and the Six Dynasties: Complete Writings of the Later Han*, *juan* 42, p.700)

[13] Cao Zhi (192–232), *Ballad of the Famous Capital*: "The famous capital has many bewitching women (*yāonü*); Luoyang has many youths." (*Commentaries and Annotations on the Collected Works of Cao Zijian*, p.61)

[14] Sima Xiangru's (*c.*179–117 BCE) *Rhapsody of the Supreme Forest*: "Beautiful ladies of dainty delicacy, like Blue Zither and Consort Fu, truly extraordinary, unmatched in the world, beguiling and bewitching (*yāoyě*), elegant and refined." (*History of the Former Han*, *juan* 27 *shang*, "Biography of Sima Xiangru, Part I," p.3039) English translation from Knechtges and Xiao, vol. II (2014), p.107. Lu Yun's *Poem to Gu Yanxian's Wife Written on Behalf of Her Husband*, second of two poems: "Among the aristocracy are many beguiling and bewitching ladies (*yāoyě*), beautiful women in their sumptuous attires." (*Selections of Refined Literature*, *juan* 25, p.354)

[15] Zhang Heng's (78–139 CE) *Rhapsody of the Western Capital*: "Their bewitching beauty (*yāogǔ*) was more seductive than that of Lady Xia; their beautiful voices were sweeter than that of Master Yu." (*Selections of Refined Literature*, *juan* 2, p.49) English translation from Knechtges and Xiao, vol. I (2014), p.237.

[16] "Finding favor with witchery (*yāoxìng*) is the mark of a government's destruction, and the sign that the Emperor's affinal relatives will bring chaos to the state. Detailed examples were recorded in histories of the past." (*History of the Later Han*, *juan* 10, p.399)

[17] *History of the Later Han*, *juan* 34, p.1180.

records is found in ancient texts dating back to the pre-Qin and early imperial periods, which were either handed down to us or recently excavated.

For example, in *Commentary of Zuo: The Fourteenth Year of Duke Zhuang* there is this: "Portents (*yāo*) arise because of Man. When Man is faultless, portents cannot emerge on their own; when Man abandons the right path, portents arise. This is the reason portents exist."[18]

"Section Six of the Jin" in *Discourses of the States* says: "Identify portents in folk rhymes."[19]

The essay "Music" under "Almanacs of the Third Month of Summer" in *Master Lü's Spring and Autumn Annals* says: "Evil (*yāo*) things are the portents of disasters, but if one does good deeds when one encounters portents (*yāo*), calamities will not befall one." "Heaven manifests portents to punish iniquitous men."[20]

The "Record on the Subject of Music" in *Book of Rites* says: "In ancient times, when Heaven and Earth adhered to their natures, the four seasons were what they should be. The people were virtuous and all the five grains were abundant. There were no fevers or diseases, and no portents (*yāo*) or prodigies. This was known as the period of great order."[21]

Silks with words written on them were discovered in Zidanku, Changsha, and they were identified as artefacts of the State of Chu from the Warring States Period. Among the fragmented text are the words: "portents (*yāo*) refer to phenomena such as celestial bodies moving disorderly ... and flowers and trees growing strangely."[22]

Among the collections of the Shanghai Museum are bound bamboo strips of the State of Chu from the Warring States Period. The essay "Master Rongcheng," written on these bamboo strips, records that: "There was a reign when no pestilence occurred, portentous signs (*yāoxiáng*) did not show themselves, and disasters disappeared. Fowl and beasts are plump and large; flowers and trees are luxuriant and tall. In the past, Heaven and Earth assisted Shun[23] and blessed the good people. This was the reign we mention here."[24]

It can be observed from historical writings of the time, such as *The Grand Scribe's Records* and *History of the Former Han*, that the word *yāo* did carry similar meanings in most contexts. Thus, inauspicious signs were referred to as "portentous" (*yāo*) or "portentous signs" (*yāoxiáng*); abnormal changes in

18 *Commentary of Zuo on the Spring and Autumn Annals: Annotations*, p.197.
19 *Discourses of the States*, *juan* 12, p.410.
20 *Master Lü's Spring and Autumn Annals: New Expositions*, *juan* 6, p.350.
21 *Annotations and Explanations of the Thirteen Classics: Book of Rites*, *juan* 39, p.1540.
22 Li Ling (1985), p. 50.
23 A mythical sage king in China's legendary age. He succeeded Yao, another mythical sage king, following the latter's abdication.
24 Ma Chengyuan (2002), pp.262–263.

natural or human phenomena were referred to as "portentous changes" (*yāo-biàn*); heavenly bodies that foretold disasters were called portentous stars (*yāoxīng*); armed rebels and rabble-rousers were called portentous bandits (*yāozéi*), and so on. An even more common phrase used was *yāoniè*, commonly understood as "evil and iniquitous."

Yet, for the people of Han-period China, *yāoniè* conveyed a more complex meaning than simply "evil and iniquitous" – it functioned as a warning on Heaven's behalf. There is a famous line in "Doctrine of the Mean" in *Book of Rites*: "It is a feature of supreme sincerity to be able to know things beforehand. When a state is about to flourish, there will be happy signs; when it is about to perish, there will be evil and iniquitous (*yāoniè*) omens."[25] *Yāoniè* here is often translated as "evil and iniquitous." This line was often cited by Confucian scholars during the early imperial period as the theoretical basis of the hypothesis that disasters were sent by Heaven. Why do the people of the early imperial period believe that *yāoniè* omens could make prophecies on political and human affairs?

In classical Chinese, the word *yāo* could also mean "tender and young." When Ban Gu complied "Treatise on the Five Agents" in *History of the Former Han*, he collated theories from various Western Han canonical schools, including Ouyang, Xiahou Sheng's and Xiahou Jian's studies on the "New Text" of *Book of Documents*; Jing Fang's (77–37 BCE) studies on *Book of Changes*; and the postulations of Liu Xiang and his son Liu Xin[26] to explain the Great Plan Theory of the Five Agents:

> Abnormalities that are found in plants are called *yāo*, which is in the bud, meaning that it is still insignificant and not manifested. Abnormalities that are found in insects and worms are called *niè*, which indicates the status of the germ. When abnormalities happen to domesticated beasts such as cows and goats, it is called "calamity" (*huò*), meaning that the abnormality is manifested. When abnormalities occur in human beings, they are called "malady" (*kē*), which is illness, meaning that it is serious. When the abnormality emerges on its own, it is called a "catastrophe" (*shěng*); when it comes from an external source, it is called a "sign" (*xiáng*).[27]

Distinctions were made between the meanings of *yāo, niè, huò* and *kē*, and so on, all of which described natural disasters. *Yāo* and *niè* were taken to mean "portentous," but the focus was their insignificant status; hence, they denoted the beginnings of disasters. It was precisely because they denoted the beginnings of disasters that they functioned as warnings and portents. *Divination of Portents Appended to Book of Changes*, written by Jing Fang, is one such

[25] *Annotations and Explanations of the Thirteen Classics: Book of Rites*, *juan* 53, p.1632.
[26] Refer to Wang Xianqian, *History of the Former Han: Additional Annotations*, citing Wang Mingsheng. (*Shang ce*, p.594)
[27] *History of the Former Han*, *juan* 27 *zhong zhi shang*, pp.1353–1354.

divination book that made prognostications on political and social changes based on abnormal portents that were manifested in the natural world. Therefore, *yāo* is translated as "portent" and "portentous" in this work.

According to "Treatise on the Five Agents" in *History of the Former Han*, "abnormalities that are found in plants are called portentous,"[28] echoing *Commentary of Zuo: The Fifteenth Year of Duke Xi*: "Abnormal things from the earth are portentous (*yāo*)." The word "portentous" was used to describe unusual phenomena related to plants. Therefore, when "rulers do not have good eyes so that they are deceived because of their fatuity, then they cannot tell good from evil. They only seek counsel from those whom they are intimate with and elevate their own kind. Those who achieve nothing are rewarded and the guilty are not put to death. All the officials are remiss in their duties and engage in improprieties." When these occurred, abnormal climate and phenophases might result, such as warm winters and intemperate springs and summers, which caused people to fall sick. Other phenomena included grass that was not withered by frost, mulberry and grain that grew on the same tree, plum trees that bore fruit in the twelfth month, withered trees that resurrected, and so on. All these were categorized as Portents of Plants.[29]

A close examination of "Treatise on the Five Agents" in *History of the Former Han*, however, shows that abnormalities in the skies and the stars and on earth among humans and beasts could all be referred to as portentous; it was not restricted to plants. For example, the phenomenon of identity misplacements in society, with strange and exotic clothing that expressed gender inversions and the blurring of man and beast, was identified as Clothing Portents. "Bizarre" morphological or behavioral phenomena that occurred in human beings – such as women changing into men, the growth of hair on the body or horns on the head, deformities or abnormalities in humans, dead people coming back to life, cannibalism, and the like – were considered Human Portents. Bizarre and abnormal morphologies or behaviors of domesticated animals – dogs, horses, and chickens growing horns, dogs mating with pigs, pigs living in houses, five-legged cows, roosters mutilating their own tails, hens changing into roosters, and so on – were considered Canine Portents, Porcine Portents, Bovine Portents, Equine Portents, and Galline Portents. Abnormalities pertaining to wild and mythical animals were referred to as Murine Portents, Lupine Portents, Avian Portents, Draconic Portents, Piscine Portents, and so on. Evil and iniquitous abnormalities of the climate and astronomy included Rain Portents, Crimson Night Portents, and Fallen Star Portents. In addition, geological upheavals and castle gates breaking down

28 *History of the Former Han*, *juan* 27 *zhong zhi xia*, p.1353.

29 "Treatise on the Five Agents, Part II" in *History of the Former Han*, *juan* 27 *zhong zhi xia*, pp.1405–1414.

on their own were all signs of portents. Fires that broke out in the palaces were seen as Portentous Fires.

What then should strange phenomena and abnormal speech expressed in language and writing be called?

The Semantic Meaning of "Portentous Talk" in Qin and Han Historical Discourse

According to "Disasters" in *Collected Discussions at the White Tiger Hall*: "What is portentous? It is when garments turn suddenly large or suddenly small; when speech is unusual."[30] Abnormal and strange speech was called "portentous talk."

In the historical discourse of the early imperial period, nonsensical talk and slander were sometimes referred to as portentous talk. The First Emperor of the Qin Dynasty had "someone investigate all the masters in Xianyang, to see if any of them has spread portentous words to confuse the masses."[31] During the reign of Emperor Wu of the Western Han Dynasty, the accusation against Liu An (179–122 BCE), King of Huainan, was "bewildering the people, betraying his ancestors, and recklessly creating portentous talk."[32] In other words, any kind of talk that was disrespectful and damaging to those in leadership positions could be labeled as "portentous talk."

Being disrespectful and damaging to those in leadership positions and engaging in nonsensical talk, slander, and inappropriate talk were listed together with portentous talk as serious criminal speech in the statutes of the Qin and Han dynasties. How were they different from one another? According to Zhang Renxi: "Any talk that expressed dissatisfaction with the dynasty could constitute slander." Nonsensical talk was "talk that incited against or advocated the overthrow of the dynasty's rule." As for the crime of inappropriate talk, it meant saying something that should not be said. However, there were no clear regulations in the law books as to what could or could not be said. Hence, definitions were very arbitrary.[33] To define the meaning of portentous talk, Zhang Renxi cited Yan Shigu's annotation of "Annals of Empress Lü, Empress of Emperor Gaozu" in *History of the Former Han*: "Erroneous talk is portentous talk."[34] But what is "erroneous talk"? "Given the context of the time, it was 'reciting inauspicious words' to confuse the masses."[35]

[30] *Collected Discussions at the White Tiger Hall: Explanations and Verifications*, *juan* 6, p.270.
[31] *The Grand Scribe's Records*, *juan* 6, p.258.
[32] *The Grand Scribe's Records*, *juan* 118, p.3094. [33] Zhang Renxi (2003), p.100.
[34] *History of the Former Han*, *juan* 3, p.96. [35] Zhang Renxi (2003), p.100.

Based on the above definitions and descriptions, the four types of criminal speech had a high level of homogeneity in terms of their content and form of expression – they were all crimes of disrespect that defied the will of leaders. The differences were that the crime of "slander" focused on punishing speech that used the past to denigrate the present, while "nonsensical talk" was usually seditious speech that incited against or advocated the overthrow of the dynasty's rule. The crime of "inappropriate talk" was like a catchall basket into which anything could be thrown. As for "portentous talk," there were two defining features: it was inauspicious and it bewildered the people.

Zhang Renxi's argument is quite solid, detailed, and accurate. Of course, if we look at historical records, in the actual political circumstances during the Qin and Han dynasties, it was at times difficult to differentiate the various discourses labeled as such based on their contents. For example, in the thirty-fifth year of the reign of the First Emperor of the Qin Dynasty (212 BCE), the scholars Hou and Lu criticized the First Emperor as an "obstinate and self-willed" person who "enjoys establishing his prestige through punishment and killing." They did not use the past to denigrate the present, but the First Emperor thought that "they had slandered me to substantiate my lack of virtue."[36] According to Han-era laws, "considering with resentment and criticizing" the politics of the day before the Emperor would constitute slander.[37]

Many speeches labeled as "nonsensical talk" did have incendiary and subversive features. For example, when the First Emperor toured Kuaiji,[38] both Xiang Yu (232–202 BCE) and his uncle Xiang Liang (?–208 BCE) were watching as he crossed the Zhe River. Xiang Yu said, "I could take that fellow's place." Xiang Liang covered his nephew's mouth with his hand and said, "Don't talk nonsense or all our clan will be executed!"[39] However, many speeches that were ruled to have violated the crime of making nonsensical talk were either ludicrous or wildly arrogant talk, or words that contradicted or were disrespectful to the Emperor. In Qin- and Han-era historical discourse, "nonsensical talk" and "portentous talk" were sometimes used interchangeably and therefore it is hard to differentiate between the two.

However, "inauspicious" and "deluding the people" could certainly be considered the characteristics of portentous talk. "Inauspicious words" referred to mystical talk that involved the *Yin* and *Yang* elements, natural disasters, good and bad fortune, spirits and deities, which matched the most common meanings of the word *yāo* during the early imperial period.

[36] *The Grand Scribe's Records*, *juan* 6, "Basic Annals of the First Emperor of Qin," p.258. English translation from Nienhauser, vol. 1 (1994), pp.149, 150.

[37] Tang Linghui (2000), p.113.

[38] Located northwest, west, and south of Lake Tai.

[39] *The Grand Scribe's Records*, *juan* 7, "Basic Annals of Xiang Yu," p.296. English translation from Nienhauser, vol. 1 (1994), p.180.

The first such exposition of portentous talk is recorded in "Treatise on Rhythm and the Calendar, Part I" in *History of the Former Han*. During the Yuanfeng reign period of Emperor Zhao of the Western Han Dynasty (80–75 BCE), the Prefect Grand Astrologer Zhang Shouwang requested the Taichu Calendar be changed. Zhang Shouwang "peddled the nonsensical talk that the Taichu Calendar was short of three-quarters of a day, and that the missing 705 *fen* was the cause of an imbalance in the *Yin* and *Yang*, giving rise to what was known as the chaotic times." He was impeached as "a Grandee of old, who wore the clothes of a Confucian scholar, saying inauspicious words and creating portentous talk to disturb the order of the state."[40] Although speech tags such as portentous talk, nonsensical talk, slander, and inappropriate talk were similar in nature in Han-era historical narratives, mystic elements like Heaven-sent disasters, deities and spirits, and good and bad fortune were mostly featured in speech labeled as "portentous talk."

The "Basic Annals of Emperor Gaozu" in *The Grand Scribe's Records* contains the famous story of Liu Bang (the founding Emperor of the Western Han Dynasty, reigned 202–195 BCE) slaying a white snake in a drunken stupor before he rose up in rebellion. This was the most important political myth pertaining to the legitimacy of the imperial clan of the Western Han Dynasty.[41] After Liu Bang cut the snake in two, some people "arrived at the site where the snake was killed and saw an old woman crying in the night. They asked her why she was crying. 'I am crying because someone killed my son,' the old woman said. 'Old lady, why was your son killed?' they asked. 'My son was the son of the White Emperor. He turned into a snake and was lying on the road,' she said. 'I am crying because he got killed by the son of the Red Emperor.' They thought that the old woman was not being honest and wanted to reproach her, but she suddenly vanished."[42] When Wang Chong (27–100 CE)[43] gave an account of this story in "Records of Portents" in *Critical Essays*, it changed from "They thought that the old woman was not being honest and wanted to reproach her" to "They thought that the old woman was speaking portentously and wanted to strike her."[44] This was an example of how the people of that era regarded stories about spirits and deities as portentous talk.

[40] *History of the Former Han, juan* 21 *shang*, p.978.
[41] Chapter 5 contains a more detailed discussion of this political myth.
[42] *The Grand Scribe's Records, juan* 8, p.347.
[43] A distinctive philosopher of the Eastern Han Dynasty. In his famous *Critical Essays*, Wang Chong raised many interesting questions from a critical perspective about early Chinese thought, history, literature, myth, religion, custom, and natural phenomena. See Loewe (1993), pp. 309–312.
[44] *Critical Essays: Expositions, juan* 22, p.924.

In the worsening social unrest of the Eastern Han Dynasty, many of the "bandits" who rose up in rebellion had backgrounds in wizardry or nascent Taoist religion. Their slogans and discourses that mobilized the masses often contained macabre and mystical elements and were often labeled "portentous talk" by the authorities. Those who created and propagated them were regarded as "portentous men" or "portentous bandits." When military strategists of later years spoke of maximizing the talents of their men, they proposed sending to the enemy those "who are adept at embellishing the stories of spirits and deities, and connecting them to the Mandate of Heaven," where they could disseminate "portentous talk and falsehoods," and "amplify the message to unnerve the enemy," thus bringing about the effects of psychological warfare.[45]

Portentous talk was orally propagated; when it was written down and collected into books, these were labeled as "portentous books" or "evil books." It is recorded in "Treatise on Astronomy, Part II" in *History of the Later Han* that on the thirteenth year of the Yongping reign period (70 CE) of Emperor Ming of the Eastern Han Dynasty (Liu Zhuang, reigned 57–75 CE), "Liu Ying, the King of Chu, Yan Zhong, and others made portentous books and plotted treason. When their plot was exposed, Liu Ying committed suicide, while Yan Zhong and others were executed."[46]

Gan Ji, a Taoist active in the last years of the Eastern Han Dynasty, claimed that he obtained a sacred text titled *Book of Great Peace with Green Headings*[47] from the spring waters in Quyang.[48] Given that the "discourse adheres to the School of the *Yinyang* and Five Agents, but contains many references to wizardry and witchcraft," officials memorialized the Emperor, calling the book "portentous and nonsensical ... improper to the point of absurdity."[49]

In the early years of the reign of Emperor Xian, the last Emperor of the Eastern Han Dynasty, armies from the east of the Pass rose against Dong Zhuo, who lorded over the imperial court that time. Frightened and wishing to move

[45] *The Tiger Military Treatise*, *juan* 1, "Using Men," p.3.

[46] *History of the Later Han*, *zhi* 11, p.3230.

[47] It is regarded as the precursor of *Scripture of Great Peace*, a canon of early Taoism.

[48] Located in the southeast of present-day Shuyang County, Jiangsu Province.

[49] *History of the Later Han*, *juan* 30 *xia*, "Biography of Xiang Kai": "In the beginning, during the reign of Emperor Shun [of the Eastern Han Dynasty], Gong Chong of Langya arrived at court to present a magical book containing 170 chapters, which his teacher Gan Ji had obtained from the spring waters in Quyang. The words of the book were written on raw white silk with red vertical lines, and the book title, *Book of Great Peace with Green Headings*, was written with red ink on a blue label. The discourse adheres to the School of the *Yin-yang* and Five Agents, but contains many references to wizardry and witchcraft. Officials memorialized the Emperor, calling the book presented by Gong Chong portentous and nonsensical, improper to the point of absurdity. And so, the book was put away. Later, Zhang Jiao possessed a portion of the book." (p.1084)

the imperial capital, Dong Zhuo convened a meeting with the nobles and officials, during which he said, "When Emperor Gaozu situated his capital within the Pass,[50] his dynasty lasted eleven generations. It has been ten generations since Emperor Guangwu located the capital at Luoyang. According to *Shi Bao Chen Prophecy*, it is appropriate to move the capital to Chang'an in accordance to the will of Heaven and the people." Grand Commandant Yang Biao (142–225) opposed the motion, saying: "*Shi Bao Shi Chen Prophecy* is an evil book; how can we trust it and do what it says?"[51] It seems that *Shi Bao Shi Chen Prophecy* was popular during the last years of the Eastern Han Dynasty, which was why Dong Zhuo cited it as argument of his motion in the court meeting. Yet, from the orthodox Confucian Yang Biao's perspective, the prophetic book should be called a "portentous and evil book."

The people of the Han era believed that the mystical features of portentous talk were not only expressed in content that was directly linked to the *Yin* and *Yang* elements, natural disasters, good and bad fortune, and spirits and deities. Sometimes, unusual choices of words and phrases, or the way they were expressed, or even words, phrases, and modes of expressions that appeared to be nothing out of the ordinary were seen to have mystical significance pertaining to evil and portents and could be regarded as portentous talk. This is what the *Collected Discussions at the White Tiger Hall* meant by "when speech is unusual."

For example, the "portentous talk" by Wu Zixu was adapted in *The Glory of Yue*, an unofficial local history of Yue and Wu areas written in the Eastern Han Dynasty, and retold in a more mythical style:

> Wishing to kill Wu Zixu, the King of Wu sent Feng Tong to summon him. When Wu Zixu saw Feng Tong, he knew Feng Tong had been sent by the King of Wu. "The King does not surround himself with ministers who help him but the words of hogs," Wu Zixu vented his spleen. "I will not live long. When I die, put my head on a high place so I will see the people of Yue entering the State of Wu, and my King captured! Throw my body into the deep river and that will be the end!" After Wu Zixu died, the King of Wu heard his words and believed them to be portentous talk. Bearing a deep grudge against Wu Zixu, he ordered his men to throw the latter's body into the Yangtze River estuary. When the soldiers picked up the body, it made a sound, billowing like a sprinting horse and causing all things to cower under its might. When his soul joined the sea, it seemed that sounds and signs lingered on. Later generations said Wu Zixu became a water immortal.[52]

[50] He meant that Emperor Gaozu had located the imperial capital in Chang'an.
[51] *History of the Later Han*, *juan* 54, pp.1786–1787.
[52] *The Glory of Yue: Expositions*, *juan* 14, p.326. Traditionally attributed to Yuan Kang and Wu Ping of the Eastern Han Dynasty, the authorship of *The Glory of Yue* is unknown.

The words of Wu Zixu, brimming over with passionate and righteous anger, were certainly not macabre and otherworldly; it was his extreme insolence that caused the King of Wu to decide that they were portentous talk. However, later generations of people (including the people who lived during the Eastern Han Dynasty) perceived the story of Wu Zixu as a legend. They believed that subsequent developments of the Wu-Yue conflict verified Wu Zixu's powers of divination. Thus, such speech phenomenon is classified as portentous speech.

The second characteristic of portentous talk was its ability to "delude the people." From the cases of portentous talk found in Qin- and Han-period historical records, not all of them had been propagated among the masses. Some of the portentous talk was limited in its reach and consequence, such as in memorials to the Emperor, private letters, making slanderous charges in private, and so on. But there was portentous talk that really possessed the power or potential to "delude the people." For example, the First Emperor of the Qin Dynasty accused the Confucian scholars of spreading "portentous talk to confuse the masses." Liu An, King of Huainan in the Western Han Dynasty, was accused of "bewildering the people, betraying his ancestors, and recklessly creating portentous talk." With the increasing social unrest and rise of nascent Taoist religion in the mid- and late Eastern Han Dynasty, a new phrase was coined: "portentous delusion" (*yāohuò*), referring to the use of portentous talk and evil arts to delude and agitate the people.[53]

Cases of Portentous Talk in the Qin and Han Dynasties

There were many cases related to portentous talk in the Qin and Han dynasties. Listing the typical and historically significant cases in chronological order, I will attempt to observe the political and cultural meanings of portentous talk, as well as official responses to them, according to their evolution in history.

The Case of Scholars Spreading "Portentous Talk to Confuse the Masses" in the Qin Dynasty

Many scholars have written about the burning of books in the thirty-fourth year of the First Emperor of the Qin Dynasty (213 BCE) and the killing of Confucian scholars in the thirty-fifth year, which were events that cannot be

[53] For example, *History of the Later Han*, *juan* 57, "Biography of Liu Tao": "It came to pass that Zhang Jiao of Julu deceptively used the Great Tao to deceive with masses with portentous delusion." (p.1849)

overlooked in Chinese political and cultural history. This section will only briefly discuss the connection between the killing of the Confucian scholars and "portentous talk."

The study of the history of Chinese thought and culture often juxtaposes the burning of books and the killing of "Confucian" scholars and emphasizes the profound connection between the two in terms of ideology and political interest, to present irrefutable proof of the First Emperor's obliteration of Confucianism. This view was questioned by Wang Chong in his *Critical Essays*:

> Everyone says: "The First Emperor of the Qin Dynasty burnt *Book of Odes* and *Book of Documents* and buried the Confucian scholars alive." They say that the First Emperor's purpose in burning *Book of Odes* and *Book of Documents* was to obliterate all the Five Classics, and his purpose in burying the Confucian scholars alive was to kill all those who collected and passed down the books. By burning the books and burying the scholars, *Book of Odes* and *Book of Documents* would be wiped out of existence. It is true to say that *Book of Odes* and *Book of Documents* were burnt and Confucian scholars were buried alive. But to say that he deliberately killed those people to obliterate *Book of Odes* and *Book of Documents* is false and an exaggeration.[54]

Wang argued that the burning of *Book of Odes* and *Book of Documents*, and other classical books was the result of a political debate between Li Si and Chunyu Yue in the Qin court on whether the empire should be governed according to ancient models and classical teachings. The First Emperor endorsed Li Si's proposal to burn classical writings and historical records other than the Qin's, in order to unify thought and guide public opinion. However, the killing of Confucian scholars was the result of the portentous talk attributed to them. "In the thirty-fifth year, many of these Confucian scholars spoke portentous words in Xianyang, and the First Emperor sent Grandee Secretaries to investigate and try them, during which, it is said, these scholars denounced one another. And so, the First Emperor decided to punish the 467 persons who violated the ban by burying all of them alive."[55] Wang Chong believed that there was no definite connection between the killing of Confucian scholars and the banning of Confucian texts. This version more or less corroborates the account recorded in "Basic Annals of the First Emperor of the Qin" in *The Grand Scribe's Records*. Wang Chong's differentiation of the cause and nature of the burning of the books, and the killing of the Confucian scholars, is justified.

In the "Basic Annals of the First Emperor of the Qin," the account of the killing of the scholars is preceded by that of the Scholars Hou's and Lu's sharp

[54] *Critical Essays: Expositions*, *juan* 7, p.354. [55] *Ibid.*, p.356.

criticism of the First Emperor and their escape, which enraged the Emperor.[56] In his fury, the First Emperor said:

> I have eliminated those books which I earlier confiscated from the world and judged useless, and recruited only the literary men and the *fangshi*[57] in great number, with the desire to bring about the great peace, and, with the *fangshi*, to seek wondrous drugs by means of alchemy.[58] Now I have heard that Han Zhong has never reported back after he left, and Xu Fu and his associates have spent cash countable only in myriads, but the elixir is yet to be found. I am only told every day that they accused each other of embezzlement. I respected and treated lavishly Scholar Lu and his like. Now they have slandered me to substantiate my lack of virtue.[59]

The main targets of his fury were the *fangshi*, including Han Zhong, Xu Fu, and Scholar Lu. However, Confucian scholars during the Qin and Western Han dynasties were often *fangshi* as well. Thus, the Emperor continued: "I will have someone investigate all the scholars in Xianyang, to see if any of them has spread portentous talk to confuse the masses." He subsequently sent Grandee Secretaries to round up the scholars for questioning. "The scholars accused and implicated one another to extricate themselves. Those who violated bans, more than 460 of them, he had trapped [and executed] at Xianyang, letting the world know it, in order to warn those [who might commit the same crime] later. He levied more exiles and sent them to the frontiers."[60]

The context of the narrative in "Basic Annals of the First Emperor of Qin" suggests that the scholars who were rounded up and interrogated had been closely linked to the *fangshi*. As to whether their "portentous talk" had involved the macabre, the historical texts are silent on this. After the scholars were buried alive or exiled, the First Emperor's eldest son Fu Su (?–210 BCE) remonstrated: "The world has just been pacified, and the masses in distant regions are yet to settle down. The scholars all recited and modeled themselves on Confucius. Now Your Majesty restrains them all by severe punitive laws. I am afraid that the people of the world are disturbed. May Your Majesty consider my words!"[61] Are the scholars and their "portentous talk" in fact reciting and modeling themselves on Confucius? Or did Fu Su mean that these scholars, apart from being *fangshi*, were also Confucian scholars, and thus worthy of his father's mercy?

56 The order of the narration seems to highlight the connection between the betrayal and "slander" of scholars Hou and Lu, and the killing of the Confucian scholars.

57 The original translation in Nienhauser's *The Grand Scribe's Records*, vol. 1, p.150, renders *fangshi* as "practitioners of [magic] methods." In this book, these practitioners of magic, alchemy, and so on will be referred to as *fangshi*.

58 The First Emperor was eager to seek the elixir for eternal life.

59 *The Grand Scribe's Records*, *juan* 6, "Basic Annals of the First Emperor of Qin," p.258. English translation based on Nienhauser, vol. 1 (1994), p.150.

60 *Ibid.* 61 *Ibid.*

The result of Fu Su's remonstrance was that he got himself exiled to a frontier commandery and failed to change the First Emperor's repressive attitude toward the Confucian scholars. We can, however, deduce that the "portentous talk" of those scholars was nothing more than them using the past to denigrate the present and "slanderous" words that contradicted the Emperor's will.

Events involving strange and macabre words did occur in the thirty-sixth year of the First Emperor of the Qin Dynasty (211 BCE), even if historical texts do not label them as "portentous words."

> A meteor fell in Dong Commandery. It hit the ground and became a stone. Some of the black-haired[62] inscribed the stone with these words: "After the First Emperor dies, his territory will be divided." Upon learning of this, the First Emperor sent down a Censor-in-Chief to interrogate people there one by one. None was willing to admit to it. He apprehended the residents near the stone, executed them all, and melted the stone.
>
> . . . In the fall, when a messenger from the east of the Pass was on the road near Pingshu of Huayin at night, a man with a jade disc in his hand stopped the messenger and said, "Give this to the Lord of Hao Pond for me." With this he said, "This year the primal dragon will die." The messenger asked him what the matter was, whereupon he suddenly disappeared, leaving his jade disc with the messenger. The messenger brought the jade disc back to report on it in detail. The First Emperor kept silent for a good while, then said: "All a mountain spirit can do is to foresee things one year ahead – but not beyond that!" Retiring from the court, he said: "The primal dragon was the primogenitor of human beings." He had the Imperial Storehouse examine the jade disc. It turned out to be the one which he dropped into the Yangtze as he was crossing it twenty-eight years before. After this, the First Emperor divined by hexagram, through which he obtained the advice: "Traveling and moving is auspicious."[63]

A falling meteor was considered by most to be an inauspicious omen during the early imperial period, and the inscription carved by the masses was even more so. "After the First Emperor dies, his territory will be divided" was not only a curse put on the Emperor by the people, it could also be seen as a warning from Heaven. As for "This year the primal dragon will die," not only was the wording mysterious, its appearance and propagation were downright macabre. The First Emperor could melt the stone and execute all who lived near it to vent his spleen. But, faced with the endless stream of macabre talk and the popular opinion they represented, he eventually had to keep silent for a good while before divining the spirits.[64]

62 Meaning the masses.

63 *The Grand Scribe's Records*, *juan* 6, "Basic Annals of the First Emperor of Qin," p.259. English translation based on Nienhauser, vol. 1 (1994), pp.150, 151.

64 In history, portentous talk often "spontaneously" emerged and spread widely to influence or agitate the masses, but its originators or masterminds were hardly ever found. Portentous talk was similar to the disseminated talk and unverifiable talk discussed earlier. Rulers hated such talk but were also powerless against it. Similar records are found as early as the *Commentary of Zuo*. In the twelfth month of the sixteenth year of Duke Xi of Lu (611 BCE), the rulers of the

The Case of Liu An, the King of Huainan, "Bewildering the People and Recklessly Creating Portentous Talk"

Those who are familiar with the history of the early imperial period will know about the failed attempt by Liu An, King of Huainan, (*c.*179–122 BCE) to rise up against Emperor Wu of the Western Han Dynasty (Liu Che, reigned 140–87 BCE). There are still disagreements over its origins, developments, and whether this incident, which occurred in the first year of the Yuanshou reign period (122 BCE), was indeed a rebellion or a miscarriage of justice. It is not my intention to provide a full review of the case here. What I wish to do is to sort out some of the details of this case, as recorded by *The Grand Scribe's Records* and *History of the Former Han*, where it involved portentous talk.

Liu An was the son of King of Huainan Liu Zhang (*c.*198–174 BCE), which made him a grandson of Emperor Gaozu of the Western Han Dynasty, and a paternal uncle of Emperor Wu. Liu Zhang was imperious and overstepped the boundaries of his rank, killing Shen Yiji, Marquess of Biyang, without any authorization, and plotting to overthrow Emperor Wen during his reign. Upon the discovery of his plot, Liu Zhang was stripped of his title and exiled to Shu Commandery. On his way to his place of exile, he refused food and died. He was posthumously given the title King Li.

According to *The Grand Scribe's Records* and *History of the Former Han*, Liu An "constantly resented the death of King Li" after he inherited the title of King of Huainan. He had great ambitions, and preferred reading books and playing music to hunting, dogs, and horses, which were the hobbies of most of the imperial princes of the time. He wanted to woo the people with surreptitious good deeds and spread his fame across the empire.[65] When the Revolt of the Seven Kingdoms occurred in the third year (154 BCE) of the

States of Lu, Qi, Song, Chen, Wei, Zheng, Xu, Xing, and Cao convened in the Huai region to discuss ways of protecting the state of Zeng from invasion by the Huai barbarians. They also talked about attacking the east. They were building city walls for the state of Zeng and the corvée laborers began to tire and fall ill. One night, someone went up to a hillock and shouted: "There is unrest in the State of Qi!" The various rulers hurried back to their home states before the wall was finished. Du Yu (222–285) annotated that "the corvée laborers came down with diseases and could not bear being stationed there for long, and so they made up portentous talk." (*Annotations and Explanations of the Thirteen Classics: Commentary of Zuo on the Spring and Autumn Annals*, *juan* 14, p.1809) The portentous words "after the First Emperor dies, his territory will be divided" were inscribed on a meteorite. Despite there being actual words and an exact location, and that "residents near the stone" were all killed, no one admitted to carving the words. The portentous words "this year the primal dragon will die" were even articulated through a supernatural being, and provided as physical evidence something that the First Emperor's had owned. Even a tyrant as brutal and overbearing as the First Emperor of the Qin Dynasty could do nothing about such portentous talk.

65 *The Grand Scribe's Records*, *juan* 118, "Memoirs of the Kings of Huainan and Hengshan," p.3082.

reign of Emperor Jing (Liu Qi, reigned 157–141 BCE), Liu An had wanted to throw in his lot with the rebel Kings. Eventually, he did not do so because of the opposition from his Chief Minister and the court's timely deployment of troops to Huainan.

It was written in "Memoirs of the Kings of Huainan and Hengshan" in *The Grand Scribe's Records* that in the second year of the Jianyuan reign period (139 BCE), shortly after Emperor Wu ascended the throne, Liu An went to the capital. Grand Commandant Tian Fen, Marquess of Wu'an, greeted Liu An at Bashang. Tian Fen said to Liu An: "His Majesty is still without an Heir-Apparent, while Your Highness is the grandson of Emperor Gaozu and your benevolence is known far and wide. In the event of His Majesty's passing, who would succeed to the throne but Your Highness?" Pleased with his words, Liu An presented Tian Fen with money and gifts.[66]

Similar stories can also be found in "Memoirs of the Marquesses of Weiqi and Wu'an" in *The Grand Scribe's Records*;[67] and "Biography of Liu Zhang, King Li of Huainan" and "Biography of Guan Fu" in *History of the Former Han*.[68] The narratives become questionable, however, on closer examination.

First, Emperor Wu fathered a son, Liu Ju, later the Heir-Apparent, when he was twenty-nine (in the first year of the Yuanshuo reign period, or 128 BCE). This was considered quite late in life at that time. Nevertheless, he had become Emperor at sixteen, and in the second year of the Jianyuan reign period, he was only eighteen years old, while Liu An was around forty. Although the Emperor was still without a son at the time, he was very young, and it was very unlikely that the question of succession would be a matter of any urgency for the court. Besides, Liu An was older than Emperor Wu by some twenty years. Even if the court needed to make early arrangements for Emperor Wu's succession, it was unlikely that Liu An would even be considered.

Second, Tian Fen found wealth and status as the younger brother of Empress Dowager Wang, Emperor Wu's birth mother. Tian Fen was made a Marquess and Grand Commandant. His life of tremendous wealth and prominent rank was by virtue of his status as an affinal relative of the imperial family: brother-in-law of Emperor Jing and maternal uncle of Emperor Wu. Later on, he would be dismissed from his positions because he offended Grand Empress Dowager Dou, and Emperor Wu would cease to look upon him with favor because of his high-handedness, but in the early years of Emperor Wu's reign, Tian Fen's star was at its brightest. Why then would he curse his sister's son to an early and heirless death, and incite a collateral uncle of the Emperor to revolt against the throne? Some have suggested that Grand Empress Dowager Dou's decision to take over the reins of government in the second year of the Jianyuan reign

66 *Ibid.* 67 *The Grand Scribe's* Records, *juan* 107, p.2855.
68 *History of the Former Han*, *juan* 44, p.2146; *juan* 52, p. 2393.

period was so that she could get rid of the Confucian officials appointed by Emperor Wu. It was essentially a bloodless palace coup that placed Emperor Wu in a precarious position. Tian Fen, having quietly switched sides against the Emperor, thus had that secret exchange with Liu An, King of Huainan. This theory is doubtful, given the paucity of solid supporting evidence. The supposedly secret conversation between Tian Fen and Liu An was never mentioned once in the sixteen years between the second year of the Jianyuan reign period and the first year of the Yuanshou reign period (122 BCE). It only started circulating, all the way up to the throne, nine years after Tian Fen's death and Liu An's suicide following the discovery of his planned revolt. It is possible that someone had fabricated the conversation after the failed rebellion. The Commandant of Justice in charge of the case at the time was Zhang Tang (?–115 BCE), a man who was well versed in the law, capable, and not given to venality. However, Zhang Tang was a devious person who bent and twisted the law to bring about convictions that pleased his superiors, whose desires he was adept at discerning. When Zhang Tang presided over the trials of the rebel Kings of Huainan, Hengshan, and Jiangdu, he "delved into the causes and rounded up all their accomplices, executing several tens of thousands of people." Ji An (?–112 BCE) commented on Zhang Tang that "he has sufficient cleverness to impede others from criticizing him and enough cunning to cover up his own blunders. He is adept at employing crafty words, flattery, sophistry, and cavils not to speak for the people of the realm, but only to please his master. He destroys whatever His Majesty does not desire, and praises everything that pleases His Majesty. He enjoys creating trouble from naught and displaying his expertise in the provisions of the law. In court, he harbors deceit to pander to His Majesty's will; outside the court, he holds rapacious officials in a bind to increase his power."[69] Zhang Tang had also been an official in Tian Fen's staff. It is not impossible that he exaggerated the details of the case to irrevocably condemn Liu An and Tian Fen in order to distance himself from Tian Fen and get into Emperor Wu's good graces. However, there is no conclusive evidence that he had done so.

In the sixth year of the Jianyuan reign period, a comet was seen. Based on the prevailing worldview of the time, most believed that it portended armed unrest. Liu An believed that as "His Majesty has no Heir-Apparent, the various Kings would fight for the throne if there is unrest in the empire." Thus, he bolstered his troops, and engaged several thousand peripatetic men of strange arts at great expense. Among the wordsmiths he employed, there were those who "recklessly created portentous talk and flattered the King."[70]

69 *The Grand Scribe's Records*, *juan* 122, pp.3138–3144; *juan* 30, p.1424; *juan* 120, p.3110.

70 *The Grand Scribe's Records*, *juan* 118, "Memoirs of the Kings of Huainan and Hengshan," p.3082.

The portentous words that were used to flatter Liu An would be similar to "His Majesty had no son and the Han Dynasty would not be at peace" and the like. Emperor Wu was twenty-one at the time and still had no son. Whether or not the abovementioned secret conversation between Tian Fen and Liu An in the second year of the Jianyuan reign period had really taken place, it would seem that Liu An had been watching Emperor Wu's situation very closely and harboring a psychological expectation for the latter's heirless state to continue.

In the fifth year of the Yuanshuo reign period (124 BCE), Liu Qian, the Heir-Apparent of the Kingdom of Huainan, broke the law and Liu An was implicated. As a punishment, Emperor Wu hived off two counties from Liu An's kingdom. "After the King of Huainan had part of his lands removed, his plotting of the rebellion became more intense. Various emissaries arrived from Chang'an and recklessly created portentous talk. The King of Huainan would be pleased with those who said that His Majesty had no son and the Han Dynasty would not be at peace; he would be angry at those who said that the Han Dynasty was at peace and that His Majesty had a son, averring that their words were ludicrous and false."[71] However, Emperor Wu already had his first son, who had been four at the time.[72] Although the young prince had yet to be made Heir-Apparent,[73] one should not say that the Emperor "had no son." Could it be that Liu An denied the fact that Emperor Wu had a son, or did not recognize Liu Ju as the Emperor's son and heir?[74] Could it be that there were certain rumors at court or among the general population? Or was Liu An so blinded by his preconceptions that he refused to believe what he did not want to believe, to the point of being delusional?[75]

71 *Ibid.*, p.3083.

72 Emperor Wu of the Western Han Dynasty had six sons. Besides the oldest son Liu Ju, he had a younger son Liu Fuling (the future Emperor Zhao, 94–74 BCE). His other sons were Liu Hong, King Huai of Qi (?–110 BCE); Liu Dan, King Ci of Yan (?–80 BCE); Liu Xu, King Li of Guangling (?–54 BCE); and Liu Bo, King Ai of Changyi (?–*c.*87 BCE). See *History of the Former Han*, *juan* 63, "Biographies of the Five Princes of Emperor Wu."

73 Liu Ju's investiture as Heir-Apparent occurred in the fourth month of the first year of the Yuanshou reign period, after the quelling of the King of Huainan Liu An's rebellion.

74 In the first year of the Yuanshou reign period, when Liu Ju was already seven years old, Liu An still had this to say to the two trusted members of his staff Wu Bei and Zuo Wu: "His Majesty does not have an Heir-Apparent. The moment he dies, the officials in court will make overtures to either King of Jiaodong or King of Changshan. With the various Kings and Marquesses fighting one another for the throne, how can I not be prepared? Besides, I am the grandson of Emperor Gaozu. I have conducted myself with benevolence and His Majesty has treated me with great kindness; I have been able to tolerate his reign. When His Majesty dies, how can I bow in subservience to a child!" (*The Grand Scribe's Records*, *juan* 118, p.3085) At the time, Liu Ju might still have been very young and had yet to be made Heir-Apparent, but it is rather interesting that Liu An was so obsessed with this issue.

75 Extant historical sources have not revealed any similar views held by Liu An's contemporaries or near-contemporaries after him. Coincidentally, when Emperor Wu eventually died and his young son Liu Fuling inherited the throne, his elder brother Liu Dan, King of Yan, rose up in

When the various Kings, Marquesses, and Chancellors convened to hear the accusations against Liu An, the King of Jiaodong Liu Duan said, "The King of Huainan Liu An flouts the laws, commits evil deeds, bears the intention to deceive, bewilders the people, betrays his ancestors, and recklessly creates portentous talk."[76] The many examples of "portentous talk" that circulated among the King and his subjects in the Kingdom of Huainan not only betrayed the ancestors of the imperial clan, they might have also deceived the people. This became one of the key accusations that convicted Liu An and determined his punishment. The actual contents of Liu An's "portentous talk," however, either existed in fragments or were mentioned in passing in Han-era historical writings, clouding the issues for those of us who wish to know the full facts of this major case from more than two millennia ago. We can no longer verify what it was that Liu An had been thinking and the basis of his thoughts, but we can speculate that the portentous talk might have involved palace secrets or scandals. It might have been discourse of an almost slanderous and absurd nature, with a touch of the macabre.

The Case of Zhang Shouwang "Saying Inauspicious Words and Creating Portentous Talk with the Intention to Disturb the Order of the State"

The early years of the reign of Emperor Zhao of the Western Han Dynasty were fraught with crises. Within the court, administration was in the hands of powerful ministers;[77] outside the capital, formidable kings were covetously eyeing the throne.[78] Natural disasters and other strange signs, such as floods, droughts, solar eclipses, snowless winters, fires at the city gates, fires in the

armed revolt against the new Emperor, claiming that "the young Emperor is not Emperor Wu's son." This echoed Liu An's "portentous talk."

[76] *The Grand Scribe's Records*, *juan* 118, "Memoirs of the Kings of Huainan and Hengshan," p.3094.

[77] Before he died, Emperor Wu decreed that Huo Guang, Jin Midi (134–86 BCE), and Shangguan Jie would assist his young son when the latter became Emperor. Jin Midi died in the second year of Emperor Zhao's reign, but Shangguan Jie fought with Huo Guang for control of the court. In the first year of the Yuanfeng reign period (80 BCE), Shangguan Jie was executed for taking part in King of Yan Liu Dan's failed rebellion. Thereafter, Huo Guang became the de facto military and political ruler of the empire in his capacity as Commander-in-Chief and General-in-Chief cum Intendant of the Masters of Writing.

[78] When Emperor Wu passed away, Liu Dan, King of Yan, was the oldest, and most talented and ambitious, of his brothers. When Emperor Zhao, the youngest son of Emperor Wu, ascended the throne, Liu Dan revolted with Liu Ze, grandson of King Xiao of Qi, and others, proclaiming to all kingdoms and commanderies that "the young Emperor is not Emperor Wu's son." Their armed rebellion was put down by Jun Buyi, Inspector of Qingzhou Region. In the first year of the Yuanfeng reign period, Liu Dan again plotted with Shangguan Jie, Shangguan Jie's son, Sang Hongyang, and others to overthrow the Emperor. The plot was discovered, and Liu Dan committed suicide. See *History of the Former Han*, *juan* 63, pp.2753–2759.

palaces, rats gamboling incessantly, crows and magpies fighting, tree branches in the shape of human heads, and so on were frequently reported all over the country.[79] The situation was interpreted to be the result of the imbalance of the *Yin* and *Yang* elements.

In the third year of the Yuanfeng reign period (78 BCE), the Prefect Grand Astrologer Zhang Shouwang submitted a memorial to the Emperor, which attributed the imbalance of the *Yin* and *Yang* elements to errors in the calendar, which had been created in the first year of the Taichu reign period (104 BCE) during Emperor Wu's time. Zhang Shouwang requested that the Yellow Emperor Calendar, which had been bequeathed to him, be used instead. The Emperor ordered Xianyu Wangren, the Commissioner of the Calendar, to gather a group of calendar experts, who would observe the waxing and waning of the sun and moon, and the twenty-four solar terms from the morning of the winter solstice of the third year of the Yuanfeng reign period, which fell on the first day of the eleventh month, to the twelfth month of the fifth year. They were to compare the eleven calendars that were popular at the time with their observations. Their conclusion was that Zhang Shouwang's Yellow Emperor Calendar showed the greatest deviance. A memorial that impeached Zhang Shouwang was submitted to the Emperor, accusing him of "disparaging the calendar system of the Han Dynasty and defying the natural order of the Heavens. By saying things he should not say, he has committed the offense of grave disrespect."[80]

Both defying the natural order of the Heavens and saying things one should not say constituted crimes of grave disrespect, but the court did not punish Zhang Shouwang at once. Instead, it requested that the calendar experts continue their observations for another year. The conclusion of that second round of observations was still not in Zhang's favor: the Taichu Calendar had the smallest deviation, while the Yellow Emperor Calendar showed the greatest inaccuracies. Zhang Shouwang was impeached again, for being an official with an 800-*dan* stipend and wearing Confucian robes, equivalent to those of an ancient grandee. He had also made the absurd assertion that the Taichu Calendar was erroneous three days out of four, thereby causing the imbalance of the *Yin* and *Yang* and chaos in the world. He was accused of "saying inauspicious words and creating portentous talk with the intention to disturb the order of the state – he is guilty of treason and heresy."[81] This was the origin of one of the Han-era definitions of "portentous talk": "saying inauspicious words." Although Emperor Zhao was willing to pardon him

79 See *History of the Former Han*, *juan* 27, "Treatise on the Five Agents."
80 *History of the Former Han*, *juan* 21 *shang*, "Treatise on Rhythm and the Calendar, Part I," p.978.
81 *Ibid.*

again, Zhang Shouwang stubbornly abided by his claims. He was handed over to be tried and he eventually died.

Although Zhang Shouwang was foolish and obstinate, he was only concerned with theoretical issues pertaining to the calendar. However, the calendar in the early imperial period symbolized the order of Heaven and was promulgated by the Emperor: it was the repository of the dynasty's legitimacy to rule. Although Zhang Shouwang's insistent criticism of the Taichu Calendar was both theoretically and politically sound, he was indeed saying things he should not have said. His assertion that the calendar caused "the imbalance of the *Yin* and *Yang* and chaos in the world" touched the political raw nerve of the ruling dynasty. It was quite justified to find him guilty of creating portentous talk. However, there was no obvious political goal in his "portentous talk," and its effects outside the calendar-making circle were limited. This might be the reason why he was repeatedly pardoned by Emperor Zhao, or rather the de facto ruler Huo Guang. Less fortunate was Sui Hong, who was also implicated in a case that involved portentous talk at around the same time.

The Cases of Chen *Prophecy–Style Portentous Talk Involving Sui Hong, Xiahou Sheng, and Others*

Sui Hong (?–78 BCE), also styled as Sui Meng, was a native of the Kingdom of Lu. He studied the *Commentary of Gongyang* (on the *Spring and Autumn Annals*) under Ying Gong, a student of Dong Zhongshu. He was appointed a Gentleman Consultant because of his knowledge of the Classics and rose to the position of Prefect of Insignia and Credentials.

In the first month of the third year of the Yuanfeng reign period (78 BCE) of Emperor Zhao of the Western Han Dynasty,

> A cacophony of several thousand people's voices was heard south of Laiwu Mountain, at Mount Tai. When the people went to the site, they saw a huge rock had stood up on its own. It was [three-and-a-half meters] high, with a circumference so big that forty-eight people could encircle it. About [two meters] of the rock was buried in the ground, with three other rocks nestled at its base in the manner of legs. After the huge rock had stood up on its own, several thousand white crows descended and gathered around it. At the same time, a tree that had withered and died in an Earth God shrine in Changyi came back to life, and a large willow tree that had broken into two in the Park of the Supreme Forest stood up on its own and was revived. Worms began to feed on the leaves of the tree and the nibbled leaves formed the words: "Bingyi, the grandson of a lord, rises."[82]

A huge rock standing up on its own, dead trees coming back to life, and words formed by worms nibbling on leaves – these strange signs in nature were

[82] *History of the Former Han, juan* 75, "Biography of Sui Hong," p.3153.

classic portents of disasters, according to the prevailing worldview of the early imperial period. Based on the Great Plan Theory of the Five Agents, they were manifestations of Portent of Plants, Portents of Metal and Rocks, and Insect Calamity. Based on Jing Fang's interpretation of the *Book of Changes* and the Dong Zhongshu School of the *Commentary of Gongyang*, rocks were of *Yin* in nature, while trees were of minor *Yang* or *Yin* in nature. Based on what he had learned in the Dong Zhongshu School of the *Commentary of Gongyang*, Sui Hong believed that

> Rocks and willow trees are of *Yin* in nature, symbolizing the commoners at the bottom rung of society. Mount Tai is the king of all mountains; it is where Emperors make offerings and give testimony to their achievements to Heaven following a dynastic change. That huge rocks are standing up on their own and withered willow trees are coming back to life is a sign that an ordinary man will become Emperor. A dead tree that comes back to life in an Earth God shrine is a sign that a disgraced noble ("grandson of a lord") clan will rise again.[83]

Therefore, the Liu imperial clan of the Han Dynasty was facing the prospect of being replaced by a scion of a former royal house who had been reduced to living among commoners. Such "extraordinary" discourse would naturally be construed by the Han Dynasty court as portentous talk!

But who was this scion of a disgraced noble clan? Scholars at the time had different explanations. According to Jing Fang: "The rock standing like a man implies that a commoner will become lord of all under Heaven. If the rock stands on a mountain, the new Emperor will bear the same family name; if it stands on the plains, he will bear a different surname. If it stands on water, he will be a sage; if it stands in the swamps, he will be a mean man."[84] As the rock was standing south of Laiwu Mountain, at Mount Tai, the commoner who would be Emperor should be a Liu. Sui Hong, however, subscribed to the Dong Zhongshu School. He averred that "the Han imperial clan is descended from the mythical Emperor Yao,[85] and abdicating the throne to another family is in its fate." Sui Hong said, "My late teacher Dong Zhongshu once said that even a ruler who had rightfully inherited his throne and who had followed the ways of the virtuous would not prevent a sage from inheriting the Mandate of Heaven." The Emperor of the Han Dynasty should follow the will of Heaven, scour the realm for a virtuous man, and abdicate the throne in his favor. Having given up his throne, the former Emperor should then retreat to a parcel of land

83 *Ibid.*, pp.3153–3154.

84 *History of the Former Han, juan* 27 *zhong zhi shang*, "Treatise on the Five Agents, Part II," p.1400.

85 A legendary Chinese sage king in the remote past. He abdicated his throne to a wise man of virtue from another clan instead of his own son. The imperial house of Western Han claimed to be descendants of Emperor Yao.

100 *li* in area, just like the descendants of the Yin and Zhou dynasties.[86] Sui Hong was obviously advocating that the Han imperial house should hand the empire over to a virtuous man bearing a different family name.

Absolutely convinced by this highly tabooed argument, Sui Hong asked his friend, the Chief of the Inner Palace Office, to submit a memorial to the throne. One can well imagine how those in power reacted to this. Emperor Zhao was already seventeen years old then, but political and military power remained in the hands of General-in-Chief Huo Guang, and the talk of abdication was deeply embarrassing to him. Huo Guang was incensed by Sui Hong's proposal and handed the case over to the Commandant of Justice for trial. In the end, Sui Hong was convicted and executed for the crime of "recklessly creating portentous talk to delude the people and being traitorous."[87] As he was said to have "deluded the people," Sui Hong's portentous argument might have spread within some circles and had had a degree of influence in society.

Subsequent developments became rather interesting. In the fourth month of the first year of the Yuanping reign period (74 BCE), four years after Sui Hong's execution, Emperor Zhao died of a sudden illness without an heir to the throne. Huo Guang and others invited Liu He (92–59 BCE), King of Changyi, a grandson of Emperor Wu and a nephew of Emperor Zhao, to succeed the late Emperor, which dovetailed with the portent of the withered tree in the Earth God shrine in Changyi coming back to life. Liu He ascended the throne on the Bingyin day in the sixth month, but by the Guisi day, twenty-seven days after the enthronement, Huo Guang and other senior officials had to request Empress Dowager Shangguan to depose him for his "licentiousness and depravity."[88] In the seventh month, Huo Guang and others decided to invite Liu Bingyi, a great-grandson of Emperor Wu, to ascend the throne. He would become Emperor Xuan.[89]

Liu Bingyi's grandfather Liu Ju, the Heir-Apparent who "rebelled," and father Liu Jin were both wrongly convicted and killed in the Witchcraft

86 *History of the Former Han, juan* 75, "Biography of Sui Hong," p.3154. 87 *Ibid.*

88 *History of the Former Han, juan* 8, "Annals of Emperor Xuan," p.238.

89 Emperor Xuan's original name was Bingyi. (*History of the Former Han, juan* 8, "Annals of Emperor Xuan") During the fall, in the seventh month, Huo Guang said: "According to our rites, people set great store by blood ties, which means they respect their ancestors. Those who respect their ancestors will respect their ancestors' achievements. Emperor Zhao had no heir, so we should choose a virtuous man from other branches of the imperial house. The great-grandson of Emperor Wu, named Bingyi, who has been under the care of the Lateral Court by imperial decree, is already eighteen years old. He studied the Classics such as *Book of Odes*, *The Analects* and *Book of Filial Piety* under teachers, conducts himself well, and is frugal and benevolent. He can become Emperor Zhao's heir, inherit his ancestors' great enterprise, and rule the people." The reason for changing his name to Liu Xun was given by Yan Shigu in his commentary: "The hardships in his early life resulted in him being sickly, hence he was named 'Bingyi' in the hope of driving his illnesses away before long. The name was later found to be coarse and was changed to 'Xun.'" (p.238)

Calamity of the second year of the Zhenghe reign period (91 BCE) of Emperor Wu. Liu Bingyi, who was only a baby at the time, was also thrown into prison. A subsequent amnesty freed him, and he was brought up by his grandmother's family, the Shi family, among the common people. On Emperor Wu's deathbed, he issued a decree to take Liu Bingyi in, raise him in the palace, and reinstate him in the imperial register, thus restoring his status as a member of the imperial clan. When Liu Bingyi reached eighteen, he was chosen by Huo Guang to become Emperor. His background fitted the description of "a disgraced noble ('grandson of a lord') clan." His meteoric rise from commoner to Emperor, his background, experience, and even his name perfectly dovetailed the worm-nibbled words: "Bingyi, the grandson of a lord, rises." To the people of the time, the various signs that occurred in the third year of the Yuanfeng reign period and Sui Hong's portentous talk – save the detail about abdicating the throne to a person bearing a different family name – had become a *chen* prophecy that came true. (*Chen* prophecy refers to unusual verbal or written discourse, or signs that revealed the Mandate of Heaven and prophesied the fate of individuals or regimes; see Chapter 4.) It would have had a considerable effect on justifying the legitimacy of Emperor Xuan's ascent to the throne. Thus, after he became Emperor, Emperor Xuan appointed Sui Hong's son as a Gentleman to acknowledge and thank Sui Hong.[90] Sui Hong had several hundred students, including famous ones such as Yan Pengzu, Yan Anle, and Gong Yu (124–44 BCE), who either became renowned masters of classical learning or rose to the top administrative rank of the Three Excellencies.

It was under the instruction of Huo Guang that the Commandant of Justice convicted Sui Hong for the crime of "recklessly creating portentous talk to delude the people." From the installation and then ousting of Liu He, to the ascent of Emperor Xuan, Huo Guang had been the kingmaker. In the early years of Emperor Xuan's reign, Huo Guang was still at the height of his power. Why then did he not stop Emperor Xuan from rehabilitating Sui Hong? The case that follows may help us understand Huo Guang's mental state at the time.

It is said that after Liu He, King of Changyi, was chosen by Huo Guang and other senior courtiers to become Emperor, he began acting strangely. He was said to be arrogant, extravagant, and licentious, and during his brief reign multiple natural disasters occurred.[91] Huo Guang began to hatch a plot to depose Liu He with his trusted subordinates the Grand Minister of Agriculture

[90] *History of the Former Han, juan* 75, "Biography of Sui Hong," p.3154.
[91] At least, this was how *History of the Former Han* described him. See *History of the Former Han, juan* 63: "Biographies of the Five Princes of Emperor Wu"; *juan* 38: "Biography of Huo Guang."

Tian Yannian (?–72 BCE) and General of Chariots and Calvary Zhang Anshi (?–62 BCE). It was a top-secret plan that no one else was privy to. Blissfully unaware of the plot against him, Liu He left the palace as usual to pursue his own amusements. The then Imperial Household Grandee Xiahou Sheng stopped the imperial retinue to give counsel to Liu He: "The sky has been dark for a long time without raining, which means subjects are plotting against their master. Why is Your Majesty leaving the palace at this point?"[92]

Xiahou Sheng was a member of the same clan as, and a student of, Xiahou Shichang, a famous scholar of the "New Text" of *Book of Documents* and the Qi School of *Book of Odes*. He also studied the *Book of Documents* and the Great Plan Theory under a number of masters and was good at expounding on natural disasters. He was frequently quoted in "Treatise on the Five Agents" in *History of the Former Han*. In the historical and cultural context of the early imperial period, and based on the theories of the Great Plan Theory, the sky being dark for a lengthy period of time without any rain falling, also known as "perpetual darkness," was Heaven's punishment for "an unrighteous Emperor who cannot establish his princely virtue." Such a ruler had "lost all the five faculties of speech, sight, hearing, thought, and compassion," and thus could not discern what he saw nor deal with matters appropriately. The result was that nothing could be accomplished. The top was weak, but the bottom was powerful, and there was a danger of a revolt from the bottom.[93] Apparently, Xiahou Sheng's advice to Liu He and his political prophecy was based on the Classical learning.

However, not only did Liu He not heed Xiahou Sheng's advice, he was furious and accused Xiahou Sheng of "making portentous talk." He ordered his men to tie Xiahou Sheng up and take him away. When the presiding official at Xiahou Sheng's trial reported the case Huo Guang, the latter became nervous, thinking that his co-conspirator Zhang Anshi had divulged the secret. Upon questioning him, however, Huo Guang ascertained that Zhang Anshi had not spoken to anyone about their plot. Feeling curious, Huo Guang summoned Xiahou Sheng for questioning and the latter replied: "It is written in the *Commentary on the Great Plan* that 'an unrighteous Emperor will be plagued by perpetual darkness, and a revolt from the bottom will occur. It is, however, taboo to speak of it so blatantly and thus, I had to say a minister was plotting against His Majesty.'"[94] Huo Guang and Zhang Anshi were shocked by what he said and, thereafter, dared not underestimate the predictive powers of men learned in the Classics. Not only was Xiahou Sheng not punished for his crime

92 *History of the Former Han, juan* 75, "Biography of Xiahou Sheng," p.3155.

93 *History of the Former Han, juan* 27 *xia zhi shang*, "Treatise on the Five Agents, Part IV," pp.1458–1459.

94 *History of the Former Han, juan* 75, "Biography of Xiahou Sheng," p.3155.

of "making portentous talk," he also was recommended to instruct the Empress Dowager on *Book of Documents* following the ouster of Liu He and installation of the Emperor Xuan. He was appointed Privy Treasurer of the Palace of Prolonged Trust and made the Marquess Within the Pass.[95]

After deposing Liu He and putting Emperor Xuan on the throne, and witnessing the veracity of Xiahou Sheng's interpretation of natural phenomena, Huo Guang would now have a different understanding of Sui Hong's "portentous talk" of a few years earlier. Sui Hong's rehabilitation might have been made possible under this political context.

Later on, Xiahou Sheng repeatedly remonstrated with the throne concerning natural disasters and omens, infuriating Emperor Xuan on numerous occasions. He was thrown into prison many times but was always pardoned. He died at a ripe old age of ninety as an official of the court. The mercy shown to Xiahou Sheng seemed to be the corollary of the Emperor's and Empress Dowager's personal trust in him; it did not represent Emperor Xuan's leniency on matters of portentous talk, as attested by the case of the Marquess of Wenshui Liu Anguo "submitting a memorial making portentous talk and having his fiefdom removed" in the second year of the Benshi reign period (72 BCE),[96] and the case of Yang Yun's "portentous talk," which implicated many important government officials, in the fourth year of the Wufeng reign period (54 BCE).

The Case of Yang Yun "Making Portentous Talk"

Yang Yun (?–54 BCE) was a native of Huayin. His father, Yang Chang (?–73 BCE), Marquess of Anping, a trusted subordinate of Huo Guang, successively served as Grand Minister of Agriculture, Censor-in-Chief, and Chancellor during the reign of Emperor Zhao of the Western Han Dynasty. Yang Yun's mother was the daughter of the great historian Sima Qian. As the younger son, Yang Yun could not inherit his father's noble title, but he found fame in court and rose to become Bureau Head of the Left through his own abilities and his aptitude in the study of history, a discipline that had been bequeathed to him through his family. For exposing the Huo family's plot to overthrow Emperor Xuan after Huo Guang's death, he was made Marquess of Pingtong and appointed Leader of Court Gentlemen and Chamberlain for Attendants.[97]

95 A noble title that enjoyed revenue from a certain amount of land and population without a fixed fiefdom in the early imperial period. It was ranked just below marquess with enfeoffment. See *History of the Former Han*, *juan* 75, "Biography of Xiahou Sheng," p.3155.

96 *History of the Former Han*, *juan* 15 *xia*, "Table of Sons of Nobles, Part II," p.484.

97 *History of the Former Han*, *juan* 66, "Biography of Yang Yun," pp.2889–2890.

Two events in Yang Yun's life immortalized him in Chinese history. After Sima Qian completed his compilation of *The Grand Scribe's Records*, the original manuscript was kept in the imperial archive, while a copy was kept at home. At first, the work was rarely shown to others. It was only after Yang Yun's mother handed him the copy of his maternal grandfather's monumental work, which he subsequently studied, that *The Grand Scribe's Records* began to be discussed and parts of it copied privately within a small circle.[98] This was the first event. In the fourth year of the Wufeng reign period (54 BCE), Yang Yun was convicted of treason for "making portentous talk." He was executed by being cut in two at the waist; his title was removed.[99] Yang Yun's case became the quintessential case study of being convicted for the crime of expressing one's opinion during the Western Han Dynasty. This was the second event. The case was much talked about at the time. *History of the Former Han* described it thus: The "senior ministers, Yang Yun, Ge Kuanrao [105–60 BCE], and others, had been sentenced for the crime of critical and derogatory speech, and were executed."[100] Liu Shi (75–33 BCE), the then Heir-Apparent who would later become Emperor Yuan, tactfully urged Emperor Xuan to reconsider: "Your Majesty is too severe in the application of the laws. It would be proper to employ Confucian scholars [in the government]." In response, Emperor Xuan made what would become a very famous argument in the history of Chinese political thought: "The Han Dynasty has its own way of balancing and measuring, which are alternatively taking the hegemonic way or the ideal kingly way. How could I put my sole trust in moral instruction and adopt the kind of government exercised by the Zhou Dynasty? The vulgar Confucians moreover do not understand what is appropriate to the time; they approve the ancient and disparage the present, causing people to be confused about names and facts, so that they do not know what principles they should adhere to. How could they be entrusted with responsibility?" He even declaimed: "The one who will bring chaos to my dynasty will be my Heir-Apparent!"[101] Liu Shi almost lost his chance of ascending the throne. Modern scholars may take the view that Yang Yun's execution marked the beginning of a long line of men who were ruined because of their poetry and writings.[102] In other words, the case was the first Literary Inquisition in Chinese history.

The case of Yang Yun "making portentous talk" was complex, and his punishment – from dismissal and exile to his fiefdom, to his execution and the

[98] *History of the Former Han*, *juan* 62, "Biography of Sima Qian," p.2737.

[99] *The Grand Scribe's Records*, *juan* 20, "Chronological Table of Marquesses since the Jianyuan Reign Period (with Table of Meritorious Ministers and Marquesses since the Reign of Emperor Zhao added by Chu Shaosun enclosed)," p.1066.

[100] *History of the Former Han*, *juan* 9, "Annals of Emperor Yuan," p.278. [101] *Ibid.*, p.277.

[102] Referring to Yang Yun's *Letter to Sun Huizong*, see Li Zhonghua (2003), p.26.

removal of his title – was a lengthy process. To say that he was "ruined because of his poetry and writings" or that it was a "Literary Inquisition" may be somewhat simplistic. According to *History of the Former Han*, Yang Yun was a man for whom the pursuit of righteousness was more important than money and gain. As an official, he was untainted by corruption, fair, able, and trusted by Emperor Xuan. He was on very friendly terms with the famous officials of the day, such as Wei Xuancheng (?–36 BCE), Zhang Chang (?–47 BCE), Ge Kuanrao, and Han Yanshou (?–57 BCE). However, he was a spiteful gadfly who found pleasure in exposing other people's secrets, thus making many enemies at court. The genesis of the case can be traced to the second year of the Wufeng reign period (56 BCE), when Yang Yun and Grand Coachman Dai Changle started attacking each other. Emperor Xuan had known Dai Changle since his commoner days; after he became Emperor, he promoted Dai to a position that allowed him to be at the Emperor's side. Dai Changle got carried away by his meteoric rise and revealed the details of Emperor Xuan's ascent to the throne to his subordinates. Someone then submitted a report accusing him of "making inappropriate talk" and his case was transferred to the Commandant of Justice.[103] Suspecting that Yang Yun was behind this, Dai Changle also submitted a report to denounce Yang Yun.

Dai Changle's denunciation consisted of two categories of alleged wrongdoings. The first category was the accusation that Yang Yun was full of complaints and showed disrespect to those above him, "slandering the court of the day and not observing the proprieties befitting a servant of the Emperor." For example, when Yang Yun submitted a memorial to plead the innocence of Han Yanshou, the Grand Administrator of Eastern Supporter Commandery, who had been found guilty of a crime and imprisoned, he had no confidence at all that Han Yanshou could be saved. "The righteous may not be able to keep himself safe. Even I cannot protect myself, just like what people say about a rat not being able to enter the rat hole because it was carrying in its mouth a head-pad bigger than the hole," Yang Yun said. When he went to see the historical portraits at the Western Pavilion, instead of commenting on the portraits of sage kings like Yao, Shun, Yu, and Tang, he deliberately pointed at those of licentious monarchs such as Jie and Zhou instead, saying to Wang Wu, Marquess of Lechang: "When His Majesty passes by, he should inquire more about the iniquities of these two. He would then learn something." Yang Yun also used the example of a fallen state in the past to elucidate present events. For example, when he heard that the Supreme Leader of the Xiongnu[104] had been killed, he said, "To think that there was

[103] *H istory of the Former Han*, *juan* 66, "Biography of Yang Yun," p.2891.
[104] A confederation of nomadic peoples inhabiting the eastern Asian steppes from the third century BCE to the late first century CE.

such an unwise ruler, who would not employ the strategies his senior courtiers had devised but instead sought his own demise!" He even went as far as to say: "People both in the past and present are all birds of a feather!"[105] If Yang Yun had indeed said these words, then he could be seen as being derisive of those above him. However, to say that he slandered the Emperor was to make a groundless accusation or sow discord between the Emperor and Yang Yun.

The second category involved the macabre and "inauspicious words." When the chariot of Dong Zhong, Marquess of Gaochang, crashed into the Lateral Gate of the North, Yang Yun said to Zhang Yanshou, Marquess of Fuping: "I hear how a speeding chariot had crashed into the palace gate in the past, breaking the latch of the gate and killing the horse. Emperor Zhao subsequently died. The same thing is happening again. It is not a human endeavor but Heaven's will."[106] It was mentioned above that Xiahou Sheng advised the King of Changyi: "The sky has been dark for a long time without raining, which means subjects are plotting against their master." In Dai Changle's denunciation, Yang Yun also said something similar to him in person: "The sky has been dark without any rain falling since the first month. Such a phenomenon is recorded in *Spring and Autumn Annals*, and Xiahou [Sheng] had spoken of it." It was therefore unlikely that Emperor Xuan would leave the palace and go to Hedong to make offerings to the Earth God. According to Dai Changle, these words indicated that Yang Yun was "making fun of His Majesty, being treacherous, and defying morals."[107]

The case fell into the hands of the Commandant of Justice Yu Dingguo (?–40 BCE), who decided that Yang Yun, despite enjoying the Emperor's trust, and serving as a minister and a bodyguard close to the Emperor, was disloyal and resentful, and had committed the crime of "spreading portentous talk and hateful words. He should be arrested and brought to trial."[108] Yang and Dai, however, were both trusted servants of the Emperor, and Dai Changle's accusations were mostly based on private conversations. Hard evidence would be difficult to come by, and a conviction would be construed as wrongful incrimination. Not wanting it to spiral out of control, Emperor

105 *History of the Former Han*, *juan* 66, "Biography of Yang Yun," p.2891.

106 According to historical records, there were quite a number of strange signs occurring in the Yuanfeng reign period of Emperor Zhao, such as a huge rock standing on its own and dead trees coming back to life. However, there was no parallel account of this particular occurrence in historical sources. It is uncertain where Yang Yun had heard about it.

107 *History of the Former Han*, *juan* 66, "Biography of Yang Yun," pp.2891–2892.

108 *History of the Former Han*, *juan* 66, "Biography of Yang Yun," p.2893. The punctuation in the Zhonghua edition of *History of the Former Han* places this phrase within Dai Changle's submitted report. This book goes by the punctuation in *Comprehensive Mirror in Aid of Governance*, and places this phrase within the judgment of the Commandant of Justice. (*juan* 24, p.872)

Xuan sought to let the matter rest by demoting both Yang Yun and Dai Changle to commoner status.

After losing his official post and title, Yang Yun went home where he engaged in business and built houses, using his money to amuse himself and living what seemed to be an agreeable life. More than a year later, however, he became once again a target of mean men. There was a solar eclipse and a stable hand submitted a report denouncing Yang Yun of being "arrogant and unrepentant, and the man who caused the solar eclipse to occur." The case was passed on to the Commandant of Justice, who found it to be quite serious. For example, when Yang Yun was chatting to his nephew Yang Tan, Marquess of Anping and Director of Dependent States, the latter said, "Du Yannian, Grand Administrator of Xihe Commandery, who was demoted for his crimes, is now reinstated as Censor-in-Chief. Your offense was a minor one and besides, you have made contributions to the state. You would be returned to an important position." Yang Yun replied: "What good are contributions? The Emperor is not worth my best effort." In response, Yang Tan actually said, "You are right about the Emperor. Both Ge the Metropolitan Commandant and Han the Grand Administrator of Eastern Supporter Commandery did their best and yet, they were executed for minor offenses."[109]

The investigation also uncovered a letter written by Yang Yun to his friend Sun Huizong. Sun Huizong, a native of Xihe, was then the Grand Administrator of Anding Commandery. Sun had written to Yang Yun, reminding him that a senior official who had been dismissed should tremble behind closed doors and put on a piteous mien instead of engaging in buying and selling, receiving guests, and earning the praise of others. Yang Yun's written reply, *Letter to Sun Huizong*, would go on to become a masterpiece of prose in Chinese literary history:

> It has been three years since I was convicted for my crimes. A farmer's life is hard. During the *Fu* and *La* seasonal breaks in summer and winter, I would reward myself by roasting a goat or grilling a lamb, and filling up a pitcher of wine. My hometown is in the Qin region and so I am good at playing music from there. My wife is a woman from the Zhao region and she plays the *se*[110] well. Among my maids are several who sing. After imbibing wine, my ears would turn red. I would look up at the sky, strike an earthen jar, and sing to the rhythm. And this is my song: "I plant my crops at the southern hill, where thorns and weeds are so plentiful I can't clear them. I planted beans covering an area of one *qing*,[111] but all I harvested were useless beanstalks. Man should find pleasure in life when he can! Who knows when wealth would come to him?" On days like these, I would be so happy that I wave my sleeves about and stamp my feet in a spontaneous dance. Indeed, I would be indulging in pleasure, but how is that wrong?

[109] *History of the Former Han*, *juan* 66, "Biography of Yang Yun," pp.2897–2898. Ge refers to Ge Kuanrao; Han refers to Han Yanshou.

[110] A Chinese plucked zither.

[111] A land area unit equivalent to 100 *mu*, or 11 acres.

I am fortunate that I have some savings from my official's stipend, which have allowed me to buy cheap and sell dear, acquiring for myself a ten per cent profit. Such is not a gentleman's vocation but a merchant's, and I have engaged in these degrading and shameful acts. Men of lowly status are the targets of slander, and I often tremble in fear. Even those who know me well would see which way the wind is blowing and mock me. Who is there to praise me? Did Dong Zhongshu not say: "Those who seek righteousness with urgency often worry they cannot ennoble the people with righteousness – this is what gentlemen-officials think about. Those who seek wealth with urgency often worry about being poor – this is what commoners do." People with different purposes have nothing much to say to each other. What right do you have to chastise me with the standards of gentlemen-officials?[112]

Ban Gu commented that Yang Yun wrote the letter because "Yang Yun, a son of a Chancellor who in his youth had shone at court, was dismissed for his ambiguous words, and is resentful of his current situation." Zhang Yan's interpretation was: "The southern hill symbolizes a ruler, while the thorns and weeds refer to the disarray at court. One *qing*, being equivalent to 100 *mu*, represents various officials. Beans, which are straight, being strewn in the wild means he has given up, while beanstalks, which are curved, denote the slander of court officials."[113] Such an interpretation is forced paralogizing, with which Emperor Xuan might not have agreed. However, it is easy to read the resentment and sarcasm between the lines. Slights and antipathies, both past and present, compelled Emperor Xuan not to let Yang Yun off lightly. The Commandant of Justice ruled that Yang Yun was guilty of high treason. The case of Yang Yun "making portentous talk" had become the typical case study of being convicted for the crime for expressing one's opinion during the Western Han Dynasty.

The Case of Gan Zhongke's "Renewal of Mandate"

During the reign of Emperor Cheng of the Western Han Dynasty, a native of the Qi region Gan Zhongke wrote *Calendar of the Heavenly Official* and *Scripture of Great Peace with the Embodiment of the Origin*, consisting of twelve chapters in total, which declared that "the Han Dynasty comes at the end of Heaven and Earth and it should renew its Mandate of Heaven. The Supreme Deity of Heaven sent the immortal Chijingzi to teach me this knowledge."[114]

The talk about the "Han Dynasty renewing its Mandate of Heaven" reminds one of Sui Hong's portentous talk that "the Han imperial clan is descended from the mythical Emperor Yao, and abdicating the throne to another family is

112 *History of the Former Han, juan* 66, "Biography of Yang Yun," pp.2895–2896.
113 *Ibid.*, pp.2894, 2896.
114 *History of the Former Han, juan* 75, "Biography of Li Xun," p.3192.

in its fate" during Emperor Zhao's reign. The difference was that Gan Zhongke stressed "renewing the mandate" instead of a dynastic change. Although *History of the Former Han* did not apply the label of "portentous talk" on Gan Zhongke's case, his arguments were definitely so. His two books would also be considered bona fide "portentous books" according to the standards of the early imperial period, and they came to have profound influence on the "portentous bandits" of the Eastern Han Dynasty. For this reason, this chapter includes Gan Zhongke's case as an example of portentous talk.

Gan Zhongke differed from Sui Hong in that he was not a government official. Therefore, his works were not submitted to the court, but propagated among the people through his disciples. His more well-known disciples included Xia Heliang, Ding Guangshi, and Guo Chang. Gan's theories would have had a certain level of influence in court and the wider society because the Colonel of the Capital Rampart Liu Xiang denounced him for "using demons and deities to deceive the Emperor and confuse the masses."[115] Gan Zhongke died in prison, and his disciples such as Xia Heliang were also implicated and accused of not respecting morals. However, this case seemed to have been quietly dropped and Xia and the others continued to spread Gan Zhongke's teachings among the people.

Shortly after Emperor Ai ascended to the throne, he was plagued with illnesses. There were multiple occurrences of natural disasters and his high-handed affinal relatives were dominating politics. Metropolitan Commandant Xie Guang and Chief Commandant of Cavalry Li Xun found favor with the Emperor because of their knowledge of the Great Plan Theory on interpreting natural disasters. On their recommendation, Xia Heliang and others gave a sermon to the Emperor on the teachings of Gan Zhongke:

> The fortune of Han Dynasty is in decline and the Mandate should be renewed. Emperor Cheng did not have any descendants because he ignored the Mandate of Heaven. That Your Majesty has been struck by a long illness and the realm plagued by frequent abnormities and disasters are warnings from Heaven. The reign period name must be changed at once for Your Majesty to enjoy longevity and beget offspring, then disasters will cease. Those who know the Way but not apply it, disaster will strike and death will come. Otherwise, there will be inundations and fires that will torment the people.[116]

This theory of "Mandate renewal" did not require dynastic change or political reforms; all it needed were changes and performances in rituals and symbols. Emperor Ai was desperate to find a cure of his illness, "Hoping that it would prove beneficial, he listened to the proposals of Xia Heliang and others." He changed the reign period name Jianping to Taichu Yuanjiang, a more "auspicious" one, in 5 BCE and styled himself the "Chen-Sage Liu

[115] *Ibid.* [116] *Ibid.*

Emperor of Great Peace"[117] Naturally, it resulted in "the Emperor's condition remaining unchanged" and the actions having "no favorable reactions, with prolonged drought." Finally, Emperor Ai dismissed and exiled Xie Guang and Li Xun. Xia Heliang and others were found guilty of "using evil arts to throw the court into confusion, subverting the state, deceiving His Majesty, and engaging in high treason." They were all executed for their crimes.[118]

The Case of the King of Chu Liu Ying Making Up Chen *Prophecies and Diagrams, and Being Accused of Portentous and Evil Conspiracy*

In the thirteenth year of the Yongping reign period (70 CE) of Emperor Ming of the Eastern Han Dynasty (Liu Zhuang, reigned 57–75 CE), a man named Yan Guang accused Liu Ying, King of Chu (?–71 CE), of producing *chen* prophecies and diagrams with Wang Ping, Yan Zhong, and others, with rebellious intent. The case was handed over to the relevant authorities for investigation.

Liu Ying was the son of Emperor Guangwu of the Eastern Han Dynasty Liu Xiu and Beautiful Lady Xu. As his mother was not favored by Emperor Guangwu, Liu Ying was enfeoffed the least bountiful and smallest kingdom. When Emperor Ming was the Heir-Apparent, he was especially close to his half-brother Liu Ying, and after he ascended the throne, he frequently bestowed rewards and honors on the latter.

As a young man, Liu Ying liked fraternizing with peripatetic men of chivalry and hosted many guests. As a King and nobleman, such behaviors would easily provoke suspicions. Later on, he became obsessed with Taoist teachings, and followed Buddhist practices such as fasting, making offerings, giving alms, and making atonements. He also "befriended many *fangshi*, and made a golden tortoise and jadeite crane, carving words to make auspicious symbols."[119] To Liu Ying, these might just be religious rituals carried out to seek longevity and luck. However, the apocryphal-prophetic discourse was of profound significance to the Eastern Han imperial house. As a belief and ideological system, it was held in the highest esteem, and it provided the strongest justification for imperial legitimacy. For this reason, Eastern Han Emperors were especially sensitive to their subjects manipulating the apocryphal-prophetic discourse and dabbling in the occult. What Liu Ying

117 Chen was the descendant of the sage king Shun, while Liu was the descendant of the sage king Yao. That Liu (Yao) succeeded Chen (Shun) was indicative of the Mandate of Heaven being legitimately passed on to the ruling Liu family of the Han Dynasty.

118 *History of the Former Han, juan* 75, "Biography of Li Xun," p.3193.

119 *History of the Later Han, juan* 42, "Biography of Liu Ying, King of Chu," pp.1428–1429.

did was a great taboo. The investigating authorities, eager to please the Emperor, reported that Liu Ying gathered cunning folk and made up *chen* prophecies and diagrams. He also usurped the prerogative of the Emperor in appointing ministers and officials on his own, providing his nobles and generals with a stipend of 2,000 *dan*. "He is guilty of high treason and we request his execution."[120] Emperor Ming, having considered his brotherhood with Liu Ying, demoted him to commoner status and exiled him to Danyang. However, Liu Ying understood the situation he was in and took his own life after reaching his place of exile.

What had this case of treason, which involved making *chen* prophecies and diagrams, got to do with portentous talk? As mentioned above, the relationship between portentous talk and *chen* prophecy was a very intricate one: portentous talk often occurred as quasi-prophecies. Although Liu Ying's crime was making up *chen* prophecies and diagrams, the "Treatise on Astronomy" in *History of the Later Han* referred to the case as "Liu Ying, King of Chu, making up portentous books and plotting treason with Yan Zhong and others."[121] Those implicated who were imprisoned and placed under house arrest were all guilty of "portentous and evil conspiracy."[122]

"Portentous Warlocks" and "Portentous Bandits" Who Confused the Masses with Portentous Talk

By the twelfth year of the Jianwu reign period (36 CE) of the Eastern Han Dynasty, Emperor Guangwu had basically pacified the major armed separatist forces that had emerged during the last years of Wang Mang's Xin Dynasty, and unified the empire. However, scattered across the land were local lords and important families, straggling armies, bands of armed men, and "bandits" who "rose up everywhere to raid government offices and kill officials. When troops from the commanderies and counties went to attack them, they would disperse; after the government troops left, they would congregate again. The situation was especially dire in the inspection regions of Qingzhou, Xuzhou, Youzhou, and Jizhou."[123] Such small-scale armed insurrections were a minor annoyance to the authorities; they were quickly pacified with incentivizing policies that encouraged local officials to take a proactive approach in putting them down.

However, in the seventeenth year of the Jianwu reign period, "the portentous warlock Li Guang and others rose up in insurrection and occupied the City of Wan." In the nineteenth year, "the portentous warlocks Shan Chen, Fu

[120] *Ibid.* [121] *History of the Later Han*, *zhi* 11, p.3230.
[122] *History of the Later Han*, *juan* 41, "Biography of Han Lang," p.1417.
[123] *History of the Later Han*, *juan* 1 *xia*, "Annals of Emperor Guangwu, Part II," p.67.

Zhen, and others rebelled and occupied Yuanwu."[124] These seemed to be major uprisings, for the court had to send troops led by Ma Yuan and Zang Gong, famous generals who helped found the Eastern Han Dynasty, to put them down. The reference to "portentous warlocks" was an indication that both insurrections involved religion (or a cult) and witchcraft, and that their leaders Li Guang, Shan Chen, and others engaged in macabre forms of speech or action. Did they fabricate and disseminate portentous talk for the purpose of instigating an uprising?

It was clearly written in "Biography of Zang Gong" in *History of the Later Han*: "In the nineteenth year, Shan Chen, Fu Zhen, and other disciples of the portentous warlock Wei Si gathered a band of men with their portentous talk and entered the city of Yuanwu, where they plundered its officials and people, and declared themselves Generals."[125] This was echoed in the "Biography of Ma Yuan" in *History of the Later Han*, which identified the teacher of Li Guang, Shan Chen, and others as Wei Si, a native of Juan. Earlier on, Wei Si had "used portentous talk to confuse the people, saying that he was a deity, and had several hundred followers. He was convicted and executed." Later, his disciple Li Guang and others proclaimed that Wei Si had become a god and would never die, in order to instigate the people. In the seventeenth year, Li Guang got a band of men together to attack the City of Wan. He killed Liu Min, Marquess of Wan, and declared himself the "Nanyue Master."[126]

"Multitudinous bandits" rose up in the mid- and late Eastern Han Dynasty because of the intense fighting among the imperial family, its affinal relatives, the eunuchs, and political cliques, and the frequent occurrences of natural disasters.[127] From the reigns of Emperor An and Emperor Shun (Liu Bao, reigned 125–144) to the reigns of Emperor Huan and Emperor Ling, popular armed resistance and rebellions in various regions and among various peoples, such as the "violent bandits," "sea bandits," "robbers," "thieves," and ethnic groups such as the Qiang peoples, the Southern Barbarians, and the Xianbei from northeast, gradually spread like contagion, with groups rising and falling in quick succession. Politically and socially, it was a stark and cruel time to live. Among these uprisings, quite a large number were led by "portentous bandits" with backgrounds in religion or witchcraft, who agitated their believers with portentous talk and the macabre arts.

In the first year of the Yangjia reign period (132) of Emperor Shun of the Eastern Han Dynasty, for example, "the portentous bandits Zhang He and

[124] *Ibid.*, pp.68, 70. [125] *History of the Later Han, juan* 18, p.694.
[126] *History of the Later Han, juan* 24, p.838.
[127] Bai Shouyi (1995), *shang ce*: "In the nineteen years of Emperor An's reign, there were as many as eleven floods, seven droughts, and seven locust infestations, affecting areas all over China." (p.430)

others in the six commanderies of Yangzhou attacked forty-nine counties, killing and injuring officials."[128] Following Emperor Shun's death, between the eleventh month of the first year of the Jiankang reign period (144) and the third month of the following year, Xu Feng, Ma Mian, and other natives of Yinling in Jiujiang "attacked the commandery and counties, killing and robbing officials and people. Xu Feng wore burgundy clothing and black ribbons, and styled himself 'the Supreme General.' Ma Mian donned a leather hat and yellow clothing, carried a jadeite seal, and called himself 'the Yellow Emperor.' They pitched their camp in Dangtu Mountain."[129] Hua Meng, the "bandit" of Liyang, also "declared himself 'the Black Emperor.' He attacked Jiujiang and killed the Commandery Administrator."[130] The so-called Supreme General, Yellow Emperor, yellow clothing, jadeite seal, and the later Black Emperor all revealed their close connections with nascent Taoist religion, and the view that the Five Agents rose and fell in succession in the apocryphal-prophetic discourse. The title of "Yellow Emperor" subscribed to the theory that each of the Five Agents generated the next. Thus, the Earth-Power (represented by the color yellow) would replace the Han Dynasty's Fire-Power by the force of generation. The other theory claimed that the succession of the Five Agents was a process of one surmounting the next. Thus, the Water-Power (black) would overcome the Fire-Power, which represented the Han Dynasty.

In the eleventh month of the first year of Emperor Huan's Jianhe reign period (147) and the second month of the first year of his Heping reign period (150), both "Li Jian, the bandit from Chenliu" and "Pei You, the portentous bandit from Fufeng" declared themselves "Emperor." "Emperor" refers to the "Yellow Emperor" frequently mentioned in the Taoist religion. In the tenth month of the second year of the Jianhe reign period, "Chen Jing from Changping styled himself 'Son of the Yellow Emperor' and appointed his own officials. Guan Bo from Nandun also called himself 'the Immortal' and plotted to rise up in rebellion."[131]

In the same eleventh month of the first year of the Jianhe reign period, "Liu Wen from Ganling conspired with Liu Wei, the portentous bandit from the Nan Commandery, and spread the unverifiable talk that the King of Qinghe should be Emperor. Both wanted to install Liu Suan as the Emperor."[132] Unverifiable talk here could also be understood as portentous talk. The same

[128] *History of the Later Han, juan* 6, "Annals of Emperor Shun," p.260.

[129] *History of the Later Han, juan* 6, "Annals of Emperor Chong," p.276; *juan* 38, "Biography of Teng Fu," p.1279.

[130] *History of the Later Han, juan* 38, "Biography of Teng Fu," pp.1279–1280.

[131] *History of the Later Han, juan* 7, "Annals of Emperor Huan," pp.291, 296.

[132] *History of the Later Han, juan* 55, "Biography of Liu Qing, King Xiao of Qinghe," p.1805. Liu Suan (?–147) was a great-great-grandson of Emperor Zhang. In the late Eastern Han Dynasty,

story was recounted in "Biography of Li Gu" in *History of the Later Han*: "Both Liu Wen from Ganling and Liu Wei from the Wei Commandery conspired to install Liu Suan as the Emperor. For this reason, Liang Ji falsely accused Li Gu of making portentous talk with Liu Wen and Liu Wei, and threw him into prison."[133] In the tenth month of the fourth year of the Yanxi reign period (161), "Huang Wu from Nanyang, with Hui De from the City of Xiang and Yue Ji from Kunyang, appointed each other to official positions using portentous words."[134] In the tenth month of the eighth year of the Yanxi reign period, "the portentous bandit Ge Deng from Bohai declared himself 'the Ultimate Supreme Emperor.'"[135] In the first month of the ninth year of the Yanxi reign period, "Dai Yi, from the Kingdom of Pei, acquired a golden seal with no inscriptions. He then made offerings at the well with Guangling native Long Shang and others, made talismanic writings, and declared himself 'the Ultimate Supreme Emperor.'"[136]

Emperor Ling's reign was especially plagued by many calamities. In his *Canonical Summaries*, Yu Huan summarized it thus: "In the middle of the Xiping reign period, many portentous bandits rose up in revolt, such as Luo Yao in the Three Metropolitan Areas. In the middle of the Guanghe reign period, there was Zhang Jiao in the east and Zhang Xiu in Hanzhong. Luo Yao taught his people how to be invisible, Zhang Jiao taught the Way of Great Peace, and Zhang Xiu the Way of the Five Pecks of Rice."[137]

In the eleventh month of the first year of the Xiping reign period (172), "the portentous bandit Xu Zhao from Kuaiji staged an uprising in Gouzhang, calling himself 'General-in-Chief' and installing his father as King of Yue. Tens of thousands of men breached the city walls and entered the city."[138] In the fourth year of the Xiping reign period, Feng Guang, the Gentleman of the Palace for All Purposes, and Chen Huang, an official who submitted an accounting of Kingdom of Pei to the throne, submitted a memorial to the Emperor, reporting that portentous rebels had recently been attacking Yizhou Region. They also said that the successive uprisings by bandits were a result of the incorrect use of the calendar that did not match the apocrypha. For example, "the calendar should set the Jiayin day, and not the Gengshen day, as the first day. In the apocrypha, the Gengshen day is never set as the first

several Emperors passed away without issue. Liu Suan was nominated twice for the throne by respected Confucian officials, yet rejected by eunuchs and imperial affinal families.

133 *History of the Later Han, juan* 63, p.2087.

134 *History of the Later Han, juan* 7, "Annals of Emperor Huan," p.309.

135 *Ibid.*, p.316.

136 *Ibid.*

137 *Records of the Three Kingdoms, juan* 8, "Book of Wei: Biography of Zhang Lu," cited in Pei Songzhi's annotation, p.264. *History of the Later Han, juan* 75, "Biography of Liu Yan," also cited in Li Xian's annotation. (p.2436)

138 *History of the Later Han, juan* 58, "Biography of Zang Hong," p.1884.

day."[139] They proposed that if changes were to be made in accordance to the apocrypha, peace would come to the realm. The Three Excellencies wanted to impeach Feng Guang and Chen Huang for disrespect to the throne, but the Emperor did not want to pursue the case.

Among the "portentous bandits" in the Eastern Han Dynasty, the most representative and influential was of course Zhang Jiao and his Way of Great Peace movement. Many historians have studied the various connections between the Way of Great Peace and the later Yellow Turban Uprising. I will attempt to explore the issue from the perspective of "portentous talk."

As we have discussed in "The Case of Gan Zhongke's 'Renewal of Mandate'" in this chapter, during the reign of Emperor Cheng of the Western Han Dynasty, Gan Zhongke wrote *Calendar of the Heavenly Official* and *Scripture of Great Peace with the Embodiment of the Origin*. During the reign of Emperor Shun of the Eastern Han Dynasty, "Gong Chong of Langya arrived at court to present a magical book containing 170 chapters, which his teacher Gan Ji had obtained from the spring waters in Quyang. The words of the book were written on raw white silk with red vertical lines, and the book title, *Book of Great Peace, with Green Headings*, was written with red ink on a blue label." The theoretical framework of the book was the Theory of the *Yinyang* and the Five Agents, and it contained many references to wizardry, witchcraft, and *chen* prophecy. "Officials memorialized the Emperor, calling the book presented by Gong Chong portentous and nonsensical, improper to the point of absurdity. And so, the book was put away."[140] The court of the day also considered the *Book of Great Peace, with Green Headings* a "portentous book."

Zhang Jiao founded the Way of Great Peace, with the *Book of Great Peace, with Green Headings* as the movement's manifesto. He also healed the sick with popular witchcraft such as using water mixed with paper talismans and making incantations. Over the course of ten years, he had amassed hundreds of thousands of followers. He reached out to the people in the commanderies and kingdoms, and there was no one in the eight inspection regions of Qingzhou, Xuzhou, Youzhou, Jizhou, Jingzhou, Yangzhou, Yanzhou, and Yuzhou who did not respond. He then appointed thirty-six divisions or *fang*, *fang* being the equivalent of a General. Large *fang* led over 10,000 men, while smaller *fang* had 6,000 to 7,000. Every *fang* had a Marshal.[141] Zhang Jiao launched a mass campaign and was good at using "unusual words" that sounded like slogans to get a head start in inciting the people. "The Blue Sky is dead; the Yellow Sky will stand. In the Jiazi year, great fortune comes to the land" was a very

[139] *History of the Later Han*, *zhi* 2, "Treatise on Rhythm and the Calendar, Part II," p.3037.
[140] *History of the Later Han*, *juan* 30 *xia*, "Biography of Xiang Kai," p.1084.
[141] *History of the Later Han*, *juan* 71, "Biography of Huangfu Song," p.2299.

successful "portentous" slogan. His followers wrote the word "*jiazi*" using white earth on gates of offices in the capital and government buildings in the inspection regions and commanderies, disseminating their slogan using shock and awe tactics.[142]

At the same time, there was other portentous talk spreading among the people that echoed the Yellow Sky discourse of the Way of Great Peace. Chapter 1 of this book said that in the second year of the Xiping reign period, "the people of Luoyang spread the unverifiable talk that a yellow man sporting a handsome beard and eyebrows was found in the middle of the eastern wall of the Office of the Rapid as Tigers [a contingent of palace guards]," and "tens of thousands went to watch it, and those served in the Forbidden City all came out, causing the roads to be blocked." By the first year of the Zhongping reign period (184), when Zhang Jiao and his brothers launched their armed uprising, calling themselves the Yellow Sky and donning yellow turbans, the people suddenly understood what had been obscured in the earlier unverifiable talk of the "yellow man."

On the Renwu day, in the fifth month of the first year of the Guanghe reign period (178), a man wearing white clothing tried breaking in through the Deyang Gate, declaring that "I am Liang Boxia and I am instructed [by Heaven] to go to the palace and be the Emperor." The Palace Attendants of the Yellow Gates and the Guards at the Gates were attempting to seize him when he suddenly vanished and could not be found. Cai Yong (133–192) thought that this macabre event was similar to one that had occurred during the reign of Emperor Cheng of the Western Han Dynasty, when a man in burgundy-colored clothing entered the palace and said, "The Supreme Deity of Heaven ordered me to reside here." The earlier event portended Wang Mang's usurpation, according to Cai Yong. "Comparing the past and present, there will be a presumptuous and cunning man who wants to do what Wang did, but he will not succeed." The occurrence at the Deyang Gate was then seen to be a portent of Zhang Jiao's uprising.[143] Although this occurrence was quite strange, early medieval historians such as Ying Shao, Yuan Hong, and Wei Zhao would rather believe that it had happened. They also saw its warning and symbolic functions as being quite important. However, they believed that Zhang Jiao's uprising was a momentary disturbance, insufficient to cause such a macabre occurrence. Ying Shao considered it a sign from Heaven of Dong Zhuo's subsequent tyranny and the massacre of the Palace Attendants of the Yellow Gates. Yuan Hong and Wei Zhao thought that it augured the Han Dynasty's demise in the hands of the Cao family.

142 *Ibid.* 143 *History of the Later Han, zhi* 17, "Treatise on the Five Agents," p.3347.

Thus, Zhang Jiao and his Way of Great Peace became representative of the "portentous bandits" in the final years of the Eastern Han Dynasty. His words, the events, the personalities, and the masses involved were all labeled "portentous" in contemporary and later historical accounts. For example, in Ying Shao's *Officials of the Han Dynasties*: "In possession of maleficence and falsehoods, Zhang Jiao caused chaos near and far, with eight inspection regions rising up in unison. Smoke and fires turned the sky a deep red, local officials died and lost their heads, and blood flowed like rivers."[144]

How the Qin and Han Authorities Responded to "Portentous Talk"

Draconian Laws and Punishments of the Qin and Western Han Dynasties

In his study of Qin and Han legal history, Zhang Renxi lists fifteen serious crimes in the early imperial period that would result in implicative punishment involving family members: robbery and theft, escaping convicts, possessing banned books, plotting a rebellion, witchcraft, cursing others, hiding criminals from the law, unjustly maligning someone, being chief instigators of crimes, failing to inform on criminals, slandering, lying, using inappropriate talk or portentous talk, and surrendering to the enemy. Not including cursing others, there were still four crimes related to expressing one's opinions: slander, lying, inappropriate talk, and portentous talk.[145] In the statutes of dynasties between the early imperial period and the Qing, there were often laws that targeted speech similar to "portentous talk" and the action of using "portentous talk" to delude the people. Such speech and actions were defined as high treason, punishable by execution and even the extermination of one's clan.

According to historical records, the criminalization of portentous talk started in the Qin Dynasty. Following his unification of China, the First Emperor of the Qin Dynasty was quite wary of centrifugal tendencies in public opinion and ideology. He was therefore very pleased with Chancellor Li Si's proposal. "Now these masters do not learn from the present but from the ancient, with which they criticize the present time and confuse the masses," Li said. To counter this subversion, "I would ask that you burn all the historical records in the Scribes' offices which are not Qin's. If not needed by the Office of the Erudits, all classics of *Odes* and *Documents*, and writings of the hundred schools, which anyone in the world has ventured to keep, should be brought

[144] *History of the Later Han*, *zhi* 28, "Treatise on Officials, Part V," cited in Li Xian's annotation, p.3622.

[145] Zhang Renxi (2003), pp.98–100.

to the governors and commandants to be thrown together and burned. Anyone who ventures to discuss (*ouyu*) the *Odes* and *Documents* will be executed in the marketplace. Those who use the ancient system to criticize the present, will be executed together with their families."[146] Immediately afterward, the First Emperor issued the order to burn the books. "*Ouyu*" was defined as "speaking with one another,"[147] requiring at least two persons. Anything more would constitute a crowd (*zhong*). In the context of the pre-Qin and early imperial periods, *zhong* meant more than three individuals.[148] It was written in the Qin statutes that "those who praise the enemy and frighten the people are to be disgraced. What does it mean to be disgraced? He is to be disgraced alive then decapitated."[149] This was in response to using words to confuse the masses. Because the masters "spread portentous words to confuse the masses," the First Emperor arrested more than 460 people and buried them alive. In the thirty-sixth year of his reign, as no one confessed to inscribing the words "After the First Emperor dies, his territory will be divided" on the meteorite, he executed all those who resided near the stone. These cases demonstrated the severity of the law and its enforcement against the crime of making and spreading portentous words. However, the actual wording of the law has been lost.

After Liu Bang took Xianyang in 206 BCE and stationed his troops at Bashang, he met the local elders and leaders of the various counties within the Pass. The elders complained that the Qin laws were so severe and punishments so harsh, that "those who slandered the government had their clans exterminated and those who gathered to discuss matters were executed at the marketplace." Then Liu Bang made his famous promise about reducing the "severe" Qin laws into three categories and abolishing the harsh laws which the local people griped about the most.[150] It was apparent that the criminalization of the expression of one's opinions had not been a popular policy. However, no mention was made of decriminalizing portentous talk in Liu Bang's promise.

It was recorded in the "Annals of Empress Lü, Empress of Emperor Gaozu" in *History of the Former Han* that in the first year of Empress Dowager Lü's rule (187 BCE), she issued a decree in spring, during the first month: "At a

146 *The Grand Scribe's Records*, *juan* 6, "Basic Annals of the First Emperor of Qin," p.255. English translation based on Nienhauser, vol. 1 (1994), p.147.

147 *The Grand Scribe's Records: Collected Explications*: "Ying Shao said: '[The First Emperor] prohibited the people from speaking with one another because he feared that they would slander him.'" *Standard Interpretations*: "*Ou* means a pair." (*The Grand Scribe's Records*, *juan* 6, "Basic Annals of the First Emperor of Qin," p.255)

148 *Discourses of the States*, *juan* 1, "Section One of the Zhou, Part I": "Three beasts form a *qun*, three men form a *zhong*, and three women form a *can*." (p.8)

149 Cited from the unearthed bamboo almanac at Shuihudi.

150 *The Grand Scribe's Records*, *juan* 8, "Basic Annals of Emperor Gaozu," p.362.

previous time, Emperor Hui [Liu Ying, reigned 195–188 BCE][151] said that he wanted to abolish the punishment of executing guilty persons together with three classes of their relatives, and the law against portentous talk. He had not completed his deliberations when he passed away. These will now be abolished."[152] Obviously, the law against portentous talk was still on the books at the time. Its punishment was more or less equivalent to that for slander, which was the execution of the perpetrator's clan or at least his own decapitation. In addition, his tongue would be removed before his execution.[153] For this reason, Yan Shigu, in his annotations, wrote: "The severity of the crime demanded the killing of the perpetrator's three classes of relatives. Erroneous speech was considered portentous talk and was given brutal punishments. All these would be abolished."[154]

In the second year of Emperor Wen's earlier reign period (178 BCE),[155] nine years after Empress Dowager Lü abolished the portentous talk ordinance, the court once again issued a decree abolishing the laws for slander and portentous talk. Emperor Wen's reason for abolishing the laws was this:

> The rulers of old had banners for the submission of advice to the court and wooden pillars that allowed criticisms to be written, which provided for the smooth running of the state and an avenue for remonstrance. The current laws have provisions against crimes of slander and portentous talk, which prevents ministers from speaking without inhibitions and the Emperor from hearing his own faults. How could this attract capable and good men from afar? These laws should be abolished. There are those among the people who curse the Emperor. They make a pact to keep it a secret but afterward they inform against one another. The officials think that they committed high treason. If there are any other kind of talk, the officials think it is slander. These are but the ignorance of ordinary people, and to impose capital punishments based on their ignorance is something that we do not agree with. Henceforth, persons who commit these acts will not be tried and convicted.[156]

This decree can be divided into two parts. The first part mentioned "crimes of slander and portentous talk." Emperor Wen believed that the blanket ban of offending criticisms that the ruler might not want to hear from his subjects would curtail advice to the throne and be detrimental to the ruler's awareness of the state of his realm. For this reason, he wanted the crimes of slander and portentous talk abolished. The second part describes how ordinary people complaining about or cursing the Emperor might inadvertently break the

151 Liu Ying, Heir-Apparent of Liu Bang and the second Emperor of the Western Han Dynasty.
152 *History of the Former Han*, *juan* 3, "Annals of Empress Lü, Empress of Emperor Gaozu," p.96.
153 *History of the Former Han*, *juan* 23, "Treatise on Punishment and Law," p.1104.
154 *History of the Former Han*, *juan* 5, "Annals of Emperor Jing," pp.145–146.
155 Liu Heng (reigned 180–157 BCE), a younger brother of Emperor Hui.
156 *The Grand Scribe's Records*, *juan* 10, "Basic Annals of Emperor Wen," pp.423–424.

law, making it easy for officials to convict them for "portentous talk" or "slander." Imposing capital punishments on ordinary people for their ignorance was not the right way to rule the people.

It should be noted that Yan Shigu, in his annotations of *History of the Former Han*, wrote: "The order abolishing the ordinance of portentous talk was issued in the first year of Empress Lü's rule, but now there was once again the crime of portentous talk. This law must have been reinstated in the interim."[157] There are no historical records of who reinstated it and when it was done. Emperor Wen's abolishment of the laws against slander and portentous talk was part of the legal reforms he implemented. He had had detailed discussions over these legal reforms with his chancellors Zhou Bo and Chen Ping, as well as senior ministers like the Grand Commandant and Commandant of Justice. He was advised "not to use corporal punishments and the death penalty, not to convict the wife of a criminal, not to criminalize slander, and abolish the law against minting coins."[158] Emperor Wen's legal reforms were highly commended by contemporary and later historians. Citing the "Basic Annals of Emperor Wen," Tang Linghui argues that after Emperor Wen decriminalized slander and portentous talk, more words of counsel could reach the throne with many officials daring to speak up. "Many spoke impassioned words," "but they were not punished."[159]

In the first year of the later reign period (163 BCE) of Emperor Wen, however, "the execution of the three classes of families"[160] was reinstated following the case of fraud committed by the *fangshi* Xin Yuanping. There are no records as to whether the law against portentous talk was concurrently reinstated. In the case of King of Huainan Liu An's rebellion during the reign of Emperor Wu, one of his more serious crimes was "recklessly creating portentous talk," proving that the law against portentous talk had been reinstated between the first year of the later reign period of Emperor Wen and the first year of the Yuanshou reign period of Emperor Wu. From the time Liu An's planned revolt was exposed, to his eventual suicide and the dismantling of his kingdom, his Queen, Heir-Apparent, and retainers who participated in the rebellion were executed with their families. "Several thousand marquesses, ministers, commandery officials, and local leaders" who were implicated "were all penalized according to the severity of their crimes."[161] The punishments were obviously severe.

157 *History of the Former Han, juan* 4, "Annals of Emperor Wen," p.118.

158 *History of the Former Han, juan* 49, "Biography of Chao Cuo," p.2296.

159 Tang Linghui (2000), p.112.

160 *History of the Former Han, juan* 23, "Treatise on Punishment and Law," p.1105. The incident is also recorded in "Basic Annals of Emperor Wen" in *The Grand Scribe's Records*.

161 *The Grand Scribe's Records, juan* 118, "Memoirs of the Kings of Huainan and Hengshan," p.3093.

Both Sui Hong and Zhang Shouwang received the death penalty during the reign of Emperor Zhao.

During the reign of Liu He, the emperor deposed later, Xiahou Sheng was accused of "making portentous talk," tied up, and taken away by Liu He's men. He was only pardoned because Huo Guang protected him.

In the second year of the Benshi reign period of Emperor Xuan, Marquess of Wenshui Liu Anguo submitted a memorial in which portentous talk was exposed. He had his fiefdom removed but was pardoned during an amnesty.

In the third year of the Wufeng reign period of Emperor Xuan, Yang Yun was demoted to commoner status for portentous talk and slander. A year later, he was denounced for not being repentant and being full of complaints. He was executed by being cut in half at the waist and his fiefdom was removed. His wife and son were implicated and banished to Jiuquan. Yang Tan was demoted to commoner status. Friends of Yang Yun, such as Commandant of the Stables of the Eternal Palace Wei Xuancheng, Governor of the Capital Zhang Chang, Sun Huizong, and others were all stripped of their positions.

During the reign of Emperor Cheng, Gan Zhongke was accused of making portentous talk and writing portentous books. He was sent to prison, where he died of an illness.

During the reign of Emperor Ai, Xia Heliang and others were accused of "using evil arts to throw the court into confusion, subverting the state, deceiving His Majesty, and engaging in high treason." They were all executed for their crimes.

The Western Han Dynasty was replete with cases of individuals being convicted for the crime of slander. Although people were no longer publicly executed for speaking with one another, deluding the people with portentous talk was still punishable by death.

The Recurring Cases of "Banishment for Portentousness and Evil" in the Eastern Han Dynasty and the Four Amnesties Given by the Authorities

The biggest case involving "portentous talk" in the early Eastern Han period was the case of Liu Ying, King of Chu, as discussed earlier in "The Case of the King of Chu Liu Ying . . . ." In the thirteenth year of the Yongping reign period of Emperor Ming, Liu Ying was accused of treason for making portentous and prophetic books; though he was convicted after investigations, many doubts remained. For example, did Liu Ying, Wang Ping, Yan Zhong, and others really make the *chen* prophecies and diagrams and plotted a rebellion? How many "accomplices" did they have? Emperor Ming's attitude was very clear: he wanted to hunt down every single one of them. "The King of Chu case dragged on for several years. Those implicated by their words, from relatives in the capital and nobles, to local leaders in the regions and commanderies and investigating officers, echoed one another's testimonies or denounced one another. There were about a thousand people who were put to death or exiled."[162] This case implicated many individuals, with several thousands of people thrown into prison. Many marquessates of the descendants of prominent men who had contributed to the dynasty were abolished, and numerous bureaucrats and scholar-officials were exiled, publicly executed, or banished for portentousness and evil.

Public opinion of the time had obvious reservations about the way the case was being dealt with. Indeed, several officials and scholars won widespread fame for fighting the just cause and saving innocent people in the King of Chu case. In the fourteenth year of the Yongping reign period, Yuan An (?–92 CE) accepted his commission as Grand Administrator of Chu Commandery at a most perilous time to try the King of Chu case. At the time, Emperor Ming was livid with rage, and investigating officials were hastening to settle the case. People confessed under torture and many were sentenced to death. When Yuan An arrived at the commandery, he "did not head for the Administrator's office in the first instance, but to the prisons. The names of prisoners who were incarcerated without clear evidence were submitted to the throne requesting to be set free. His Assistants and Division Heads kowtowed before Yuan An in an attempt to stop him, saying that those who sided with Liu Ying were guilty of the same crime. Yuan An disagreed and said, 'If it breaches the law, I will take full responsibility and you will not be implicated.' He then submitted the list of names to the throne." "Over 400 families were freed."[163]

The Acting Attending Censor Han Lang (26–109 CE) and the staff of the Three Excellencies were trying the main suspects of the King of Chu case, Yan Zhong, Wang Ping, and others, in the capital. Their testimonies implicated the Marquess of Suixiang Geng Jian, the Marquess of Langling Zang Xin, the Marquess of Huze Deng Li, the Marquess of Qucheng Liu Jian, and so on. However, Geng Jian and others insisted that they had never before met Yan Zhong and Wang Ping. The investigating officials at the time were second-guessing the Emperor's intentions and everyone was looking out for himself. They would rather wrongly convict some people than let any of those who were guilty escape punishment. After determining that Geng Jian and others had not been involved in the King of Chu case, Han Lang boldly reported to Emperor Ming:

> Your servant sees that the officials investigating the prisoners say they are portentous and evil, and that all of Your Majesty's servants should hate them. The officials would

[162] *History of the Later Han, juan* 42, "Biography of Liu Ying, King of Chu," p.1430.
[163] *History of the Later Han, juan* 45, "Biography of Yuan An," p.1518.

rather criminalize all than decriminalize even one so that they do not have to be accountable later. Therefore, questioning one prisoner would implicate ten others and questioning ten prisoners would implicate a hundred others. When the excellencies and ministers have an audience with Your Majesty at court and Your Majesty asks them about the case, they would kneel to say: "In the old days, heinous crimes would result in the execution of the nine classes of relatives of the criminal, but Your Majesty is merciful and punishes only the criminal. All your subjects under Heaven are fortunate." However, when the officials return to their homes, they may not say anything but they would look up and sigh. Everyone knows many people were wronged, but no one dared to defy Your Majesty.[164]

Two days later, Emperor Ming went in person to the prisons in Luoyang to question the prisoners. Over a thousand innocent people were freed.

Jiao Kuang, Grand Administrator of Hedong, was arrested for being implicated in the King of Chu case, and died of an illness on the way to prison. His wife and children were jailed and tortured for a long period of time. Jiao Kuang's students and friends, afraid of being implicated, changed their names to escape persecution. Only a student from the same commandery, Zheng Hong, "shaved his head and in shackles, went to court to submit a memorial to clear Jiao Kuang's name. Emperor Ming realized that Jiao Kuang had been wronged and pardoned his family. Prostrating himself, Zheng Hong brought Jiao Kuang's body, and his wife and children, back to their hometown. Zheng Hong became famous because of what he did.[165]

By the fifteenth year of the Yongping reign period, the prisoners of the King of Chu case, which had gone on for many years, had exposed one another, and many people were implicated and imprisoned. Empress Ma, concerned about the excessive use of criminal punishment, spoke to the Emperor at an opportune time. The Emperor, moved by her words, "woke up at night and thought about Empress Ma's advice, and many prisoners were eventually freed." It was then that the case finally came to a close.[166]

The extent of the harm that the King of Chu case had done to society and the internal rifts it had caused to the ruling class might have prompted Emperor Zhang (Liu Da, reigned 75–88 CE) to declare an amnesty in the twelfth month of the first year of the Yuanhe reign period (84 CE):

The *Book of Documents* says: "If the father is not kind, the son will not be dutiful; if the older brother is not affable, the younger brother will not be respectful – they have nothing to do with one another."[167] The cases of portentous talk of the past had

[164] *History of the Later Han, juan* 41, "Biography of Han Lang," pp.1417–1418.
[165] *History of the Later Han, juan* 33, "Biography of Zheng Hong," p.1155.
[166] *History of the Later Han, juan* 10 *shang*, "Annals of Empress Ma, the Empress Mingde," p.410.
[167] A paragraph from "Announcement to Kang" in *Book of Documents*, which was rephrased in *Commentary of Zuo: The Thirty-Third Year of Duke Xi*.

implicated many people. The punishment for a person who had committed the crime extended to the families of his father, his mother, and his wife. They were prohibited from becoming officials and serving the dynasty. Even those who were virtuous and talented could not serve to the end of their days. We are full of pity for them for they were prevented from starting their lives afresh. From this day on, all who have been banished for portentousness and evil will no longer be so. They will be allowed to walk the road of atonement, but they cannot be palace guards on night duty.[168]

It can be surmised from this decree that for the cases of portentous talk in the Eastern Han Dynasty not only were the main culprits severely punished, the number of people implicated was also large. The "banishment for portentousness and evil" extended to the families of the offender's father, mother, and wife.[169] The Yuanhe decree only provided amnesty for light offenders implicated in prior cases. The main culprits and their families were not pardoned, and laws related to portentous talk were not abolished.

Due to their uncle Zuo Sheng's "execution for portentous talk and his family members becoming the property of the state," Emperor An's biological mother, Lady Zuo, whose full name was Zuo Xiao'e, and her older sister, Zuo Da'e, "entered the Lateral Court when they were a few years old. When they grew up, they were talented and beautiful. Zuo Xiao'e was well-read in history and liked poetry. When Emperor He gave palace maids to the various kings, the sisters ended up in the palace of the King of Qinghe. Having heard that Zuo Xiao'e was beautiful, [the King of Qinghe] Liu Qing bribed the lady in charge of palace maids. After he acquired her, he bestowed far more love and favor on her than on his other consorts."[170] Emperor An was born ten years after the amnesty of the first year of the Yuanhe reign period. Zuo

168 *History of the Later Han*, *juan* 3, "Annals of Emperor Zhang," pp.147–148.

169 *History of the Later Han*, *juan* 33, "Biography of Zhu Fu." In his annotation, Li Xian cited *Officials and Rituals of the Han Dynasties*: "The Erudit was an official post first created in the Qin dynasty. In the early years of Emperor Wu's reign, he created the post of Erudit of the Five Classics. The number was later increased to fourteen positions. The Grand Master of Ceremonies would choose an intelligent and well-respected man to be the Libationer to lead them. The nomination criteria reads: "One who loves and respects his parents when they are alive, and observes all the funerary rites at their passing. He must know the *Book of Changes*, *Book of Documents*, *Book of Filial Piety*, and *The Analects* well, have a comprehensive knowledge of a wide range of books, track down the smallest details, and be able to expound on profundities. He is to live like a recluse, find delight in the righteous path, and not seek fame. He must not have knife wounds or be suffering from chronic illness. Families of his thirty-six relations must not cavort with portentousness and evil, and receive no rewards from kings and nobles. He is judged to be well-behaved based on the Four Codes of Conducts and be erudite in the Classics." Below is to be written "Nominated by such-and-such an official or such-and-such a garrison." (p.1145) In other words, if the "families of his thirty-six relations" were implicated by offenders of cases of "portentousness and evil," the person could not be appointed an Erudit. It can be seen that banishment for portentousness and evil could implicate a great number of people and affect their careers in government.

170 *History of the Later Han*, *juan* 55, "Biography of Liu Qing, King Xiao of Qinghe," p.1803. There were other versions of the story. Sima Biao's (243–306) *Sequel to the History of the*

Sheng's execution and Zuo Xiao'e's entering the palace might have occurred before the first year of the Yuanhe reign period. It would seem that the Zuo sisters and the people implicated by this case had not been pardoned. After the Yuanhe amnesty, there were still occasional cases of portentous talk, with culprits' family members being implicated and punished. People were still punished for their involvement with "portentousness and evil."

The post of Regional Inspector was first created in the fifth year of the Yuanfeng reign period (106 BCE) during the reign of Emperor Wu of the Western Han Dynasty to oversee the commanderies and kingdoms under his purview by conducting inspection tours. The Eastern Han Dynasty continued the system of having Inspectors. Although the Inspector's responsibilities, powers, and regions under his jurisdiction differed from time to time, all Inspectors in both Han dynasties were "in charge of six tasks" and had to supervise and inspect the regions under them. The third among the six tasks was to ascertain if officials in the commanderies and kingdoms had properly discharged their duties with regard to crime and punishment, and to monitor natural disasters and omens such as "collapsing mountains and fissuring rocks; portentous signs and unverifiable talk."[171] In other words, "portentous talk" in the regions was important information that the Inspector had to take note of, collect, and investigate. During the Yongyuan reign period (89–105 CE) of Emperor He (Liu Zhao, reigned 88–105 CE), Wang Huan, Inspector of Yanzhou Region, "maintained law and order in Yanzhou's commanderies, and morality became prevalent and the dynasty's prestige increased. He was later found guilty of untruthfulness during his investigation of a case involving portentous talk. A few years later, the court reinstated him and appointed him as Attending Censor."[172] In the twelfth year of the Yongyuan reign period, "reports from Dongping and Qinghe submitted to the court accused Qing Zhongliao and others of making portentous talk, implicating almost a thousand people." The Director of Imperial Secretariat Huang Xiang "reported the truth to the Emperor and saved the lives of many."[173] It is obvious that even after Emperor Zhang's Yuanhe amnesty, monitoring and investigating portentous talk were still key responsibilities of Regional Inspectors and local officials.

Former Han declared that Zuo Sheng was an elder brother of Zuo Xiao'e. Another account in *Annals of the Later Han* claimed that "her father was found guilty." With three records giving three different accounts, the version in *Book of the Later Han* is probably the correct one. See Zhou Tianyou, *Collections and Annotations of the Eight Versions of the History of the Later Han*, p.319.

171 *History of the Later Han*, *zhi* 28, "Treatise on Officials, Part V," with Li Xian citing Cai Zhi's *Rituals of the Han Dynasties* in his annotation, pp.3617–3618.

172 *History of the Later Han*, *juan* 76, "Biographies of Upright Officials: Wang Huan," p.2468.

173 *History of the Later Han*, *juan* 80 *shang*, "Biographies of Writers: Huang Xiang," p.2615.

A case involving portentous talk in a couple of commanderies or kingdoms could implicate up to a thousand people.

Emperor He died in the first year of the Yuanxing reign period (105) and Empress Dowager Deng ruled as Regent. She granted the Eastern Han Dynasty's second amnesty for persons implicated in cases of portentous talk. Empress Dowager Deng ordered that all those who had been convicted of crimes of portentousness and evil since the Jianwu reign period be pardoned and resume their status as commoners.[174] It is apparent that the Yuanhe amnesty had not been able to bring relief for those prohibited from becoming officials due to previous crimes of portentousness and evil.

In the second month of the fourth year of the Yongchu reign period (110), Emperor An "decreed that those who had been exiled to the borders because of portentous talk and other crimes since the Jianchu reign period were allowed to return to their home commanderies, while those who had become slaves and maids in the palace were to be released from their bondage and become commoners."[175] This was the third amnesty in the Eastern Han Dynasty and it targeted those who had been implicated, mostly family members of the main culprits. Emperor An was seventeen years old at the time, having gone through the ceremony that marked him as an adult in the previous year. However, Empress Dowager Deng was still ruling as Regent and, therefore, the Yongchu amnesty could be considered an addition to and a continuation of the Yuanxing amnesty. It was mentioned above that Emperor An's biological mother Zuo Xiao'e had become a maid in the palace because of her uncle's guilt in a case involving portentous talk. The amnesty in the fourth year of the Yongchu reign period might have provided a chance for women who were in a similar situation as that of Zuo Xiao'e to be free again.

Shortly after Emperor Huan succeeded to the throne, a major case involving "portentous talk" occurred. In the first year of the Jianhe reign period, Liu Wen, a native of Ganling, and Liu Wei, a native of the Nan Commandery, spread the portentous talk that Liu Suan, King of Qinghe, would become Emperor. Although the uprising led by Liu Wen and Liu Wei failed soon afterward and Liu Suan had not played any part in it, he was impeached and demoted to a marquess. He committed suicide and his kingdom was dissolved. Li Gu, Grand Commandant and leader of the scholar-officials, had previously supported the succession of the older Liu Suan at the deaths of Emperor Chong and Emperor Zhi. Liang Ji took advantage of the situation and slandered Li Gu, accusing him of being an accomplice of Liu Wen and Liu Wei in spreading portentous talk. Li Gu was imprisoned.

[174] *History of the Later Han*, *juan* 10 *shang*, "Annals of Empress Deng, the Empress Hexi," p.422.

[175] *History of the Later Han*, *juan* 5, "Annals of Emperor An," p.215.

On the Yihai day of the fifth month, in the third year of the Jianhe reign period, Emperor Huan issued the decree:

> Because the late Emperor Zhang had compassion for people who had been imprisoned or exiled for crimes of previous generations, he bestowed his favor on them by ordering in the first year of the Jianchu reign period that the exiled be allowed to return to their homelands and the enslaved be freed as commoners. Should we not emulate the benevolent policies of the late Emperor? We hereby decree that for cases of portentousness and evil that occurred between the first year of the Yongjian reign period and the present, distant relations of the main culprits who were found guilty by implication, as well as officials and commoners who had their death penalties reduced to exile, are to return to their home commanderies. This order is not applicable only to family members who became the property of the state.[176]

This was the fourth amnesty in the Eastern Han Dynasty for people implicated by cases of portentous talk. Emperor Zhang had granted the amnesty in the first year of the Yuanhe reign period, but in Emperor Huan's decree, "the late Emperor Zhang had compassion for people who had been imprisoned or exiled for crimes of previous generations, [and] he bestowed his favor on them by ordering in the first year of the Jianchu reign period that the exiled be allowed to return to their homelands and the enslaved be freed as commoners." This should be referring to Emperor Zhang's decree to encourage farming, issued in the first month of the first year of the Jianchu reign period. It was to encourage uprooted people to return to their original homes and had nothing to do with people who had been implicated in cases of portentousness and evil.[177] The amnesty of the third year of the Jianhe reign period focused on exiled persons implicated in cases of portentousness and evil since the reign of Emperor Shun. Family members who had become property of the state or the palace were not included in the amnesty. After this order was issued, however, there was fierce infighting among the imperial affinal relatives, the eunuchs, and members of different political cliques. There were also successive occurrences of natural disasters and droughts, and frequent portents. Conflicts in society became intense and cases of portentous talk often occurred, which implicated many people. In the first year of the Yongshou reign period (155), in a memorial to Emperor Huan listing the social ills of the time, Academy Student Liu Tao wrote: "The high-born families are killed and the wealthy are found guilty of portentous talk and rebellion."[178] It can be surmised that being found guilty of the crime of portentous talk and being implicated in cases of portentousness and evil had already become serious social problems. Even the high-born and wealthy were not spared.

[176] *History of the Later Han, juan* 7, "Annals of Emperor Huan," p.293.
[177] *History of the Later Han, juan* 3, "Annals of Emperor Zhang," p.132.
[178] *History of the Later Han, juan* 57, "Biography of Liu Tao," p.1843.

The "crimes" of people often labeled in historical texts as "portentous traitors," "portentous warlocks," and "portentous bandits," such as Li Guang, Shan Chen, Zhang He, Liu Wen, Liu Wei, Xu Zhao, and Zhang Jue, were not confined only at the speech level. They used portentous talk to delude the people into rising up in armed rebellion. Naturally, the authorities would use force to wipe out these armed rebels. Although some "portentous persons" did not plot an uprising but merely practiced the Taoist arts together, the authorities were still apprehensive and accused them of deluding the masses with portentous talk, and pinned the crime of portentousness and falsehood on them. For example, Wei Si merely "spread the portentous talk that he was a god, gathering several hundred disciples," but the authorities saw them as dangerous foes and "executed all of them." The subsequent armed rebellion of Li Guang and Shan Chen, Wei Si's disciples who had escaped arrest, might well have been compelled by the authorities' prior brutal suppression. Then there was Liu Gen, a native of Yingchuan, who was a recluse in Mount Song. It was only because "meddlesome people came from afar to learn Taoism from Liu Gen"[179] that Grand Administrator Shi Qi seized him for peddling portentousness and falsehoods.

Based on the above cases involving portentous talk and the authorities' response, we may make the following observations:

First, the response of the authorities in the Qin and Han dynasties to "portentous talk" was mainly suppression with oppressive laws and severe punishments. In the 440 years of the Qin, Western Han, and Eastern Han dynasties – apart from two short periods when the laws were relaxed (in the first year of Empress Dowager Lü's rule and the second year of Emperor Wen's reign)[180] – the authorities had always considered the making and dissemination of "portentous talk" as a serious speech crime that had to be punished by laws pertaining to portentous talk. Although four amnesties were granted in the Eastern Han Dynasty, they mainly covered persons or family members who had been implicated. The main culprits were never pardoned. It is interesting that on the two occasions when the laws were relaxed in the Western Han Dynasty, historians made much of them in their writings, with reams written praising the benevolent policies of the rulers. When the laws were tightened shortly afterward, however, they seemed to have developed "aphasia."

[179] *History of the Later Han, juan* 82 *xia*, "Biographies of Alchemists: Liu Gen," p.2746.

[180] The first period was less than eight years. The second period could be as short as fifteen years, but it would not have exceeded fifty-six years. It was recorded in *History of the Former Han, juan* 11, "Annals of Emperor Ai" that shortly after Emperor Ai ascended the throne (7 BCE), he decreed the "abolishment of the Renzi law and laws against slander." (p.336) However, no mention was made of laws against portentous talk.

Second, the actual clauses of the "portentous talk laws" of the Qin and Han dynasties, for example, the detailed definition of "portentous talk," have yet to be found in extant historical texts and unearthed bamboo almanacs.[181] Previously, we examined the characteristics of talk labeled as "portentous" in Qin and Han texts, and we found that they mostly involved saying inauspicious words and deluding the people. "Inauspicious words" referred to speech containing supernatural elements such as the macabre, spirits and deities, the *Yin* and *Yang* elements, the Five Agents, and so on. It also included absurd heresies.[182] These features basically match the cases examined in the previous two sections. However, we have also noted that some of the incriminating speech labeled as "portentous talk" were no more than complaints, words that those in power found objectionable, or disseminated talk and unverifiable talk circulated in private among the people.

Third, given that the actual clauses of "portentous talk laws" are not available, the sentencing guidelines of the crime of "portentous talk" during the early imperial period and the related details cannot be accurately described at this point in time. Based on available historical sources, the natures of the crime of "portentous talk" were "high treason" and "grave disrespect." During the Qin and early Western Han periods, the punishments were execution of the culprit, extermination of his family and relatives, and even cutting off the tongue before execution. These were severe punishments indeed. After Emperor Wen's legal reforms that abolished cruel corporal punishments, kings and nobles found guilty of the crime of "portentous talk" were demoted to commoner status and took their own lives as a result. Their fiefdoms were abolished, and their relations and retainers were punished as well. In other cases, culprits were executed or "cut into two at the waist." Exterminations of families and relatives were uncommon, but there were many cases of relations becoming property of the state or being exiled. In the Eastern Han Dynasty, cases involving "portentous talk" and "portentousness and evil" often implicated many people, who would be barred from serving in government. These

[181] The crime of and laws pertaining to portentous talk were still in existence during the Three Kingdoms Period, the Western and Eastern Jin dynasties, and the Northern and Southern dynasties. The extant *Laws of the Tang* and the laws of subsequent dynasties contain clearer clauses regarding portentous talk. For example, in *Laws of the Tang: Explanations and Definitions*, *juan* 18, "Making Portentous Books and Portentous Talk": "Those who make portentous books and portentous talk are to be strangled to death." (p.345) According to *Laws of the Tang*, the three conditions for establishing guilt were creating the portentous talk on one's own, the detrimental effects it had on society, and deluding the masses. It is interesting that the laws and their annotations did not mention whether the people thus deluded were guilty of any crime.

[182] They were, of course, determined from the perspective of the authorities, e.g. strange words such as the rock inscription: "After the First Emperor dies, his territory will be divided," King of Huainan Liu An's nonsensical talk about Emperor Wu having "no sons," Yang Yun's "the Emperor is not worth my best effort," and so on.

included relations, subordinates, and friends. The main targets of "portentous talk laws" were those who the people in power felt had undesirable political intentions or political influence. As for calendar experts questioning the current calendar system from a theoretical standpoint (e.g. the Zhang Shouwang case), officials attacking each other for injudicious words (e.g. the Yang Yun case), or when the contents of the portentous talk benefited the ruler (e.g. the Xiahou Sheng case), the authorities were sometimes forgiving even if some of the words might have been macabre to the extreme. As for "portentous talk" that became *chen* prophecy after coming true (often to the authorities' advantage), culprits who had been imprisoned or killed often got rehabilitated, even rewarded (e.g. Sui Hong and Xiahou Sheng).

Fourth, the one feature of portentous talk that rulers in the Qin, Han, and later periods detested most was its potential and ability to delude the masses. Macabre words that were not disseminated and confined within the scope of memorials to the Emperor or private conversations were sometimes tolerated. But the moment the portentous talk reached out to the masses and entered non-official or non-mainstream propagation channels, deluding and inciting the people with macabre words, it might develop into public opinion that was detrimental to the rulers, and seriously harm and threaten the political order. Therefore, the authorities in the Qin and Han dynasties employed severe laws and punishments to nip portentous talk in the bud.[183] The portentous talk that

[183] Strict discipline and uniformed discourse are of key importance in military organizations, which is why military leaders in all periods had been most alert to the ability of portentous talk to incite. Military laws also contained the most severe punishments for disseminating portentous talk. In "Dragon Strategy: Military Campaigns" in *Six Secret Teachings*, King Wu of the Western Zhou Dynasty asked Jiang Taigong how one could know the enemy's strength or weakness before the fighting began, and how one could discern the signs for victory or defeat. Jiang Taigong said: "The sign of victory or defeat is indicated first and foremost in the spirit of the enemy troops. An astute commander can discern it but whether one can use it to his advantage depends on the commander himself. One should have detailed intelligence about the enemy's attacks and retreats, movements, the portentous signs that are said, and the things the soldiers talk about among themselves. When the whole army is happy, the soldiers fear the commands, and respect the orders of their commanders; when they feel happy about defeating the enemy, feel honored about being courageous, and commend one another for being fierce in battle – these are the signs of strength. When the whole army is nervous, when the troops are sloppy and untidy, frightening one another with the enemy's power, spreading news about their weak position, and whispering to one another; when the portentous talk cannot stop and the troops are speaking falsehoods to one another; when they do not fear orders nor respect their commanders – these are the signs of weakness." (p.463) In *The Tiger Military Treatise*, *juan* 2, "Military Orders": "Using portentous talk and macabre words, making up spirits and gods, interpreting dreams, using disseminated talk and evil words to delude and frighten the troops – these are portentous soldiers and they are to be executed." (p.12) The portentous talk and disseminated talk targeted by military laws might not involve macabre or evil elements, but they were certainly talk that damaged the morale of one's own troops. Uniformed discourse was imperative in the army; otherwise, morale would be shaken. At the same time, military theorists also realized the value of portentous talk in psychological warfare, and advocated using portentous talk to delude and vanquish the enemy. *Military Classic: Precis, Volume I*,

reached out to the masses and entered non-official or non-mainstream propagation channels, taking shape in the process of dissemination, with the ability to "delude the masses" is the kind of talk to take note of in the study of rumors.

The Discourse Strategies of Intellectuals during the Early imperial Period in Deconstructing the Stigma of "Portentous Talk"

The Subversion Discourse Strategy

Some of the discourse labeled as "portentous talk" in the early imperial period was similar to "nonsensical talk." Such talk was not totally absurd or macabre, but used words that offended those in power. Stopping all portentous talk with severe laws and punishments might, within a certain scope and to a certain extent, suppress public opinion against the ruler and maintain a period of social stability, but it obstructed proper and effective communications between the court and the people, and between various levels and factions within the governing class. It actually adversely affected political and social stability in the long run. In a letter to a friend, Liu Tui of the Tang Dynasty made this criticism: "When portentous talk [was criminalized] during the Qin Dynasty and the people [implicated in portentous talk cases] were prohibited from becoming officials in the Eastern Han, it resulted in public fear and people could only look at each other in silence and die in the wilderness."[184] Hu Yin (1098–1156) of the Song periods wrote: "The portentous talk laws came about because [the authorities] assumed that there were people with intentions to sway and delude the masses, and those who wanted to revolt from within and without. The shortcoming of these laws was that tyrants and domineering officials made use of them to strike fear in people's hearts both in and outside government, and blocked the avenues of remonstrance."[185]

In fact, discerning political thinkers in the early imperial period were already aware that the label of "portentous talk" was often abused by tyrants to reject advice and clamp down on criticisms. When Emperor Wen abolished the crimes of slander and portentous talk in the second year of his reign, the reason given was: "The current laws have provisions against crimes of slander and portentous talk, which prevents ministers from speaking without inhibitions and the Emperor from hearing his own faults. How could this attract

juan 4, "Reconnoitering Enemy Positions": "The warhorses gallop in fright, the soldiers terrified, deluding one another with portentous talk and whispering into one another's ear – these are the signs of an army's collapse." (p.162)

184 *Collected Works of Liu Tui*, *juan* 6, p.30.

185 *Zhitang's Humble Opinions on History*, *juan* 1, p.425.

capable and good men from afar?" In his famous *Essay on Governing and Security* submitted to the throne, Jia Yi (200–168 BCE), a political theorist of the early Han, wrote a brilliant, oft-cited section on "portentous talk":

It was not so by the Qin Dynasty. Their social milieu was not one that prized humility, but one that valued exposing the secrets of others. They had never prized civility and righteousness, but placed high value on punishment. When Zhao Gao assisted Hu Hai [the Second Emperor of the Qin Dynasty], he taught him the various punishments: when they were not executing people or cutting off their noses, they were exterminating three branches of a person's family. This was why Hu Hai started killing people the day after he ascended the throne. He treated earnest remonstrance as slander and considered well-thought-out deliberations as portentous talk. To him, killing people was like cutting grass. Was it because Hu Hai had an evil nature? It was because what he had been taught was unreasonable.[186]

Using his critique of the politics of the Qin Dynasty, Jia Yi was reminding the Western Han rulers that the existence of laws against slander and portentous talk not only prevented people from speaking out and alienated virtuous and good men, but they also blurred the differences between good and evil, right and wrong, and suppressed all advice given by subjects loyal to the Emperor and the state. From a theoretical standpoint, Jia Yi subverted the authorities' stigmatization of portentous talk.

Lu Wenshu, a renowned minister during the reign of Emperor Xuan of the Western Han Dynasty, was a specialist in trying cases based on the *Spring and Autumn Annals*. He was also an expert on calendars, mathematics, and foretelling disasters. Shortly after Emperor Xuan ascended the throne, Lu Wenshu, who was then Acting Clerk for the Commandant of Justice, submitted a memorial proposing the advocacy of virtue and leniency in punishments:

The Qin Dynasty was a time when books and learning were despised while martial strength and courage were championed, when benevolent and virtuous men were scorned while judiciaries and jailers were respected. Righteous remonstrance was seen as slander and criticisms of wrongs were considered portentous talk. For this reason, the court did not favor moral men, who hid their loyalty and earnest words in their hearts. Instead, the court filled its ears with fawning flattery, and false adulations delighted its heart. It failed to see the dangers right before their eyes. This was the reason why the Qin Dynasty lost the empire.

... I hear that phoenixes would only gather at places where crows and owls were not harmed. Only when people are not executed for slander would good advice be forthcoming.

[186] *History of the Former Han*, *juan* 48, "Biography of Jia Yi," p.2251. "Teachers of Heirs-Apparent" in *New Writings* contains a similar record. Hu Yin's argument was derived from Jia Yi's.

. . . If Your Majesty could abolish the crime of slander, there would be honest advice, people will offer wise remonstrance, and the mistakes that caused the Qin Dynasty to fall would be swept away.[187]

Lu Wenshu requested the abolishment of the crimes of slander (and portentous talk) to stop the stigmatization of upright speech. He was obviously using Jia Yi's argument that speech labeled as "portentous talk" by the authorities was often good advice that offended the rulers. The suppression of such speech with harsh punishment was proof of a nation's demise.

The Historical Narrative Discourse Strategy

Jia Yi and Lu Wenshu unequivocally criticized rulers who stigmatized conscientious advice, which benefited society and the state but offended the rulers' sensibilities, by labeling them as "portentous talk." However, some political theorists and historians used historical narratives to build up a typical connection between foolish tyrants and the stigmatization of loyal remonstrance.

In *Exoteric Traditions of the Han Version of the Odes*, *juan* 2, King Jie of the Xia Dynasty rejected the advice of his loyal subjects and "indulged in drinking and debauchery." Yi Yin went to see Jie and said, "When a ruler does not listen to his subjects, he will lose his mandate. His demise will be at hand!" Jie clapped his hands and said, "You are making portentous talk again! I am the King of the realm, just as the sun is in the sky. Does the sun die? I die when the sun dies."[188] The author of the *Exoteric Traditions of the Han Version of the Odes* painted a vivid picture of the reckless arrogance of a foolish tyrant. His use of the word "again" was ingenious, for it highlights the fact that King Jie's labeling of loyal remonstrance as "portentous talk" had become the norm.

It is recorded in "The Hereditary Houses of Chen and Qi" in *The Grand Scribe's Records* that Duke Ling of Chen and the Grandees Kong Ning and Yi Xingfu were having illicit sexual relations with Lady Xia, and were openly fornicating in court. Dismayed by the situation, the Grandee Xie Ye tried to persuade the Duke to stop: "When the ruler and his subjects are debauched, who will the people look up to?"[189] In the narrative recorded in *Commentary of Guliang: The Ninth Year of Duke Xuan*, Xie Ye's advice was somewhat different: "It is still acceptable for the people of the state to hear this, but it is not acceptable for righteous people to hear this."[190] In Liu Xiang's *Garden of*

187 *History of the Former Han*, *juan* 51, "Biography of Lu Wenshu," pp.2369–2371.

188 *Exoteric Traditions of the Han Version of the Odes: Collected Expositions*, *juan* 2, *di* 22 *zhang*, pp.57–59. A similar account is recorded in Liu Xiang, "Ridiculing Excess" in *New Order*.

189 *The Grand Scribe's Records*, *juan* 36, p.1579.

190 *Annotations and Explanations of the Thirteen Classics: Commentary of Guliang on the Spring and Autumn Annals*, *juan* 12, p.2414.

Tales, Xie Ye's advice became much more detailed: "The State of Chen will come to an end! I urgently advise Your Highness, but Your Highness does not heed my advice and loses your dignity." "The poem in the *Book of Odes* 'Be watchful of what you say; be reverently cautious of your outward demeanor; in all things be mild and proper' refers to this. Your Highness is not watchful and is recklessly indulgent. You will either die or be killed." Duke Ling's response was also very typical: "He killed Xie Ye for making portentous talk."[191]

Similar narrative strategies are seen in the typical stories of the collapse of the Xia and Shang dynasties recorded in Liu Xiang's *Biographies of Exemplary Women, juan* 7. The first story, similar to the one in *Exoteric Traditions of the Han Version of the Odes*, describes King Jie of the Xia Dynasty's depravity and extravagance, and his being besotted with Mo Xi's beauty. However, the person who advised him was changed to Guan Longfeng. The second story describes the debauched and cruel King Zhou of the Shang Dynasty favoring Da Ji, and creating ponds of wine and forests of meat.[192]

Books such as the *Exoteric Traditions of the Han Version of the Odes*, *Garden of Tales*, *Biographies of Exemplary Women*, and the above-mentioned *The Glory of Yuen* narrated historical tales and legends; they are not, strictly speaking, historical and factual. However, be it the political arguments of Jia Yi and Lu Wenshu or the novelizations of history in *Exoteric Traditions of the Han Version of the Odes* and *Garden of Tales*, we can see that in their historical narratives, historians and political theorists during the early imperial period intentionally or otherwise employed the narrative strategy of highlighting the proclivity of tyrants to label loyal advice as "portentous talk," thus deconstructing the authorities' stigmatization of "portentous talk" to a certain extent.

The Mysticism Discourse Strategy

In a milieu where ideas of *Yinyang* and the Five Agents, and the connection between Heaven and Man were prevalent, where offending but good advice, complaints and sarcastic remarks, and ideological heterodoxy and heresy were stigmatized by the authorities as "portentous talk" and ruthlessly suppressed, certain speech or forms of expression that were genuinely macabre might not, in fact, be seen as totally negative. Sometimes, they were even considered to hold clues to revelations or warnings from Heaven. In the discourse of Han politicians, thinkers, and classical scholars, who were experts in the theories of *Yinyang* and interpreting disasters, such speech was not stigmatized despite its "portentous" label. For example, Jing Fang, an expert on the "New Text" of

[191] *Garden of Tales: Collations and Verifications, juan* 1, p.4

[192] *Biographies of Exemplary Women: Additional Annotations*, pp.729–730.

Book of Changes during the Western Han Dynasty, predicted political and social changes based on the "portents" manifested in natural phenomena, and described the connections between strange signs in nature and human affairs on the one hand, and politics and society on the other. The title of his book is *Divination of Portents Appended to Book of Changes*. Also known as *Divination of Portentous Changes Appended to Book of Changes*, the divinations in the book were referred to as "portentous words."[193] They did not have negative connotations, however, and senior officials of the early imperial period often cited them in their memorials to the Emperor. One of these – "Portentous talk may delude the masses. This is what is known as having no integrity. [As a result,] there will be dead people on the roads, and Majors will die" – was used by historians of the early imperial period to explain the unverifiable talk regarding the major flood inundating the capital in the tenth month of the third year of the Jianshi reign period of Emperor Cheng, as well as the incident of the Sishang girl Chen Chigong trespassing in the palace, as signs that the Wang clan, the Emperor's affinal relatives, was about to usurp the throne.[194]

Besides Jing Fang, there were other Western Han intellectuals who were experts in connecting natural phenomena and portents with the political situation. Those who could postulate a more or less complete theoretical framework included Meng Xi, Liangqiu He, Ge Kuanrao, and Gu Yong of the School of *Book of Changes*; Xiahou Shichang, Yi Feng, and Kuang Heng of the Qi School of *Book of Odes*; Xiahou Shichang, Ou Yang, Ni Kuan, Xiahou Sheng, Xiahou Jian, and Li Xun of the "New Text" School of *Book of Documents*; Dong Zhongshu, Humu Sheng, Sui Hong, and Yan Pengzu of the Gongyang School of *Spring and Autumn Annals*; and Liu Xiang and Zhai Fangjin (?–7 BCE) of the Guliang School of *Spring and Autumn Annals*.

The Gongyang School of *Spring and Autumn Annals* after Dong Zhongshu employed a method of discourse that compared natural phenomena and signs with historical events and changes, which had a profound influence on politics and society in the early imperial period.[195] In this regard, the Guliang School was deficient. Although Liu Xiang was a famed expert of the Guliang School,

193 Gu Yong (?–*c.*8 BCE), a Confucian official serving under Emperor Cheng of the Western Han Dynasty and an expert on the Great Plan Theory, cited a line of Jing Fang's "portentous words" in his memorial to the throne: "When door latches are loose and locks vanish, rulers are lacking in virtue and ministers engage in misconduct; there will be risks of insubordinate ministers usurping the throne." (*History of the Former Han, juan* 85, p.3470) This line was also quoted in "Treatise on the Five Agents" in *History of the Former Han, juan* 27. (p.1401) Jing Fang's book was still extant in the Sui and Tang dynasties.

194 *History of the Former Han, juan* 27 *xia zhi shang*, "Treatise on the Five Agents, Part IV," p.1474.

195 *History of the Former Han, juan* 27 *shang*, "Treatise on the Five Agents, Part I": "Dong Zhongshu studied *Commentary of Gongyang on the Spring and Autumn Annals* and started to explore the theory of *Yin-yang*. He was commended by Confucian scholars." (p.1317)

he learned Taoist arts as a child before studying *Book of Changes*. He was a learned man with many talents, and was not restricted by the different schools. As a member of the imperial clan, Liu Xiang was concerned about the domineering power of the Wang family, the Emperor's affinal relatives, and he hoped to construct a historical narrative based on signs and portents to warn the Emperor. To this end, he "collated the records of auguries and natural disasters from antiquity, the Spring and Autumn Period, and the Warring States Period, to the Qin and Han Dynasties, and studied and organized the events. He explained what the signs meant and wrote down how they had come true, and classified them under categories. The book *Commentary and Discussion on the Five Agents in the Great Plan*, with eleven chapters, was submitted to the Emperor."[196] He "classified" the various disasters and signs according to their symbolic meanings based on the theoretical framework of the Great Plan Theory of the Xiahou School, which he had come across when he was organizing the palace's cache of hidden books. He "studied and organized the events" chronologically, classifying them into different categories of natural disasters, and incorporated them into the Great Plan Theory of the Five Elements.

The *Commentary and Discussion on the Five Agents in the Great Plan* amalgamated the Great Plan Theory of the "New Text" School of the *Book of Documents* and the Guliang School of *Spring and Autumn Annals*, establishing a new school of thought outside the Gongyang School of interpreting natural disasters and signs. Liu Xiang's son Liu Xin had spent much time learning and studying and found another way. He studied the Old Texts such as *Commentary of Zuo* and argued for a slightly different approach toward the Great Plan Theory. When he wrote "Treatise on the Five Agents" in *History of the Former Han*, Ban Gu followed Liu Xiang's approach and used the categorization of portents in Xiahou Shichang's Great Plan Theory as his basic framework, and identified parallels in the historical events from the Spring and Autumn Period to the time of Wang Mang. In his interpretation, Ban Gu took from the above-mentioned representative scholars from the School of *Book of Changes*, the "New Text" School of *Book of Documents*, the Gongyang and Guliang Schools, as well as the interpretations of Liu Xiang and his son Liu Xin, to create an opus of portents-based historiography of the early imperial period.

The "Treatise on the Five Agents" explained the various signs and portents occurring in nature and human society, and their symbolic meanings within the theoretical framework of the Great Plan. Of the five matters of Appearance, Speech, Sight, Hearing, and Thought, the second one on Speech ("defiant speech") referred to signs related to the contents of speech and the way they

196 *History of the Former Han, juan* 36, "Biography of Liu Xiang," p.1950.

were expressed. "Defiant speech" mainly referred to the ruler's mentality and values expressed through his speech, as well as his wrong words, tone, and attitude, which did not win the people's hearts. Examples included insulting words, exaggerated and absurd speech, giving inauspicious names, being thick-skinned and avaricious, being tyrannical and extravagant, following old ways and being ineffective, lacking political wisdom, saying inappropriate words, being impolite in speech, and so on.

You are what you say. Chinese popular wisdom has always held that by observing a person's speech and his appearance, one can predict the person's fortune or misfortune. From this perspective, "defiant speech" was a way to predict the future by observing a person's true nature through events and occurrences. However, the explanations of people in the early imperial period were much more mystical. According to "Treatise on the Five Agents," the occurrence of these portentous signs in speech "refers to instability,"[197] reflecting abnormality and dysfunction in the state's governance. As Confucius says: "The superior man lives in his house and sends forth his words. If they are evil, they will be opposed at a distance of over a thousand *li*; how much more in the nearer circle!"[198] When the ruler's orders and speech ran counter to public opinion, or when they were full of bluff, muddled, and confusing, it would naturally result in ineffective governance. The nature of such mistakes was interpreted as "excessive wrongdoing" and "overstepping of authority," and it was expressed as being excessively unpleasant and undignified in speech, and meting out punishments recklessly. With all the *Yin* element being unyielding, it would result in an overabundance of *Yang* energy. Heaven's punishment would be perpetual *Yang*, that is, prolonged drought without rain. Prolonged droughts affected crops, which had severe effects on the state's income and people's lives. "Banditry" in the form of armed revolts would be frequent, resulting in "fear and worry among the ruler and the ruled," even "extreme fear." The entire society would be plunged into extreme anxiety. Based on the logic of this discourse, portentous talk, which contained abnormal speech characteristics, would be seen as a warning signal from Heaven. When portentous talk was expressed in verse (e.g. poems and children's songs), it would become "portentous poetry."[199]

[197] *History of the Former Han*, *juan* 27 *zhong zhi shang*, "Treatise on the Five Agents, Part II," p.1376.

[198] "The Great Treatise, Part I" in *Book of Changes* in *Annotations and Explanations of the Thirteen Classics: Book of Changes*, *juan* 7, p.79.

[199] See the section on prophetic rhyme in Chapter 4.

3 Popular Songs and Rhymes

In the writings of the pre-Qin and early imperial periods, the character *yáo* in the Chinese word for rumors (*yáoyán*) originally referred to songs and rhymes that circulated among the common people.[1]

"Verses accompanied by musical instruments were called songs (*gē*); those that were unaccompanied were called rhymes (*yáo*)."[2] Both songs and rhymes in pre-Qin times could be sung, but songs were accompanied by musical instruments,[3] while rhymes were "sung without musical instruments, with the singers' voices free and unfettered."[4] In the early imperial period, songs sung in the ancestral temple of the imperial family and the imperial palace, and songs sung at religious ceremonies, hunts, banquets, and excursions were mostly accompanied by musical instruments.[5] As for the songs extemporaneously sung by the common people in their daily lives, they were also referred to as "songs" (*gē*), but these were often sung without musical accompaniment. For example, when Lady Qi (?–194 BCE), Emperor Gaozu's favorite consort, was imprisoned by Empress Lü, she "pounded grains and sang the song."[6] When Zhu Maichen (?–115 BCE) walked in solitude with firewood strapped on his back, he sang loudly as he walked.[7] In these two instances, it is hard to

[1] *Comprehensive Dictionary of Chinese Phrases*, (1993), 11 *ce*, p.382.

[2] *Annotations and Explanations of the Thirteen Classics: The Mao Commentary, juan* 5, "Odes of Wei: Of the Peach Trees in the Garden," p.357.

[3] They were also called "stringed songs" because they were often accompanied with stringed instruments such as the *qin* and *se*. They were also said to be accompanied with "silk and bamboo," or stringed and woodwind musical instruments.

[4] *Annotations and Explanations of the Thirteen Classics: Commentary of Zuo on the Spring and Autumn Annals, juan* 12, "The Fifth Year of Duke Xi," p.1796.

[5] For example, when Emperor Wu and Emperor Xuan of the Western Han Dynasty wanted to win the support of the intelligentsia, they commissioned many songs that extolled the achievements and virtues of rulers for educational and propaganda purposes. Songs like these were also noteworthy as social and cultural phenomena, which are outside the scope of this book.

[6] *History of the Former Han, juan* 97 *shang*, "Biographies of Imperial Affines: Biography of Empress Lü, Empress of Emperor Gaozu," p.3937.

[7] *History of the Former Han, juan* 64 *shang*, "Biography of Zhu Maichen": "Zhu Maichen, alias Zhu Wengzi, was a native of Wu. His family was poor but he liked to study. Not knowing how to make a living, he often cut and sold firewood, using the proceeds to feed his family. He would carry bundles of firewood and chant lines from books as he walked, while his wife, also carrying

imagine that their singing was accompanied by musical instruments. From their forms of expression, the songs "The Ying River Is Clear," "One *Chi* of Cloth," and "There Is No Happiness in Giving Birth to a Boy," recorded in *The Grand Scribe's Records* and *History of the Former Han*, and songs like "Dong Zhuo Escapes," recorded in *History of the Later Han*, were in fact folk ballads or children's songs. Having rhyming lyrics meant that ballads could be easily picked up and disseminated orally. It would seem that ballads had wider circulation among people who were illiterate or had little education, such as commoners and children, and their lyrics were more vernacular and easily remembered.

The melodies and tunes of songs and rhymes that circulated among the people had long been lost and we do not know what they sounded like. However, the lyrics of some ballads are preserved in the records of historians and men of letters, and they can be considered as a form of popular or non-official discourse.[8] Historical texts written after *History of the Later Han* often referred to the words of these ballads as *yáoyán*, or rhymes. This writer believes that these popular rhymes should be considered as a manifestation of rumors in Chinese history, in the same category as forms of expressions such as disseminated talk, unverifiable talk, and portentous talk. Given its rhyming form, it spread more easily and had a bigger impact than other rumor forms.

With the rise of "New History" in the twentieth century, which focuses on the daily lives and thoughts of ordinary people, and their effects on political and social issues, popular rhymes have since come to acquire greater historical value.[9] For modern and contemporary scholars, folk rhymes were not only

firewood behind him, would repeatedly advise him not to sing when they were on the road. In response, Zhu Maichen raised his voice and chanted even louder. Embarrassed by her husband, Zhu Maichen's wife demanded a divorce. Zhu Maichen laughed and said: 'I will become rich and honored at fifty and now I am already forty. You have suffered with me for a long time, but when I am rich and honored, I will reward you.' His wife retorted angrily: 'People like you will die in the gutter! There is no way you will be rich and honored.' Zhu Maichen could not persuade his wife to stay and she left him. Later on, Zhu Maichen was walking alone and singing, when he passed the cemetery carrying firewood on his back. His former wife and her husband were visiting the cemetery, and when they saw how hungry and cold Zhu Maichen was, they gave him food and water." (p.2791) A decade later, Zhu Maichen was appointed to high office by Emperor Wu.

8 In Chinese historiographical tradition, there are frequent examples of rhymes being recorded. The biggest collection of rhymes is found in treatises of the Five Agents in various standard histories. Many other rhymes were also sourced from non-official histories and journals by individuals and recorded in their works, such as Guo Maoqian's (1041–1099) *Collection of Music Bureau Poems*, Yang Shen's (1488–1559) *Odes and Rhymes of the Past and Present*, Du Wenlan's (1815–1881) *Ancient Rhymes and Adages*, and others.

9 In fact, when British historian Thomas Babington Macaulay (1800–1859) wrote his famous five-volume *The History of England from the Accession of James II* in the early nineteenth century,

popular literature created extemporaneously and freely by the people,[10] but were also valuable sources of social and political history, with a strong capacity for social critique and political forecast.[11] There are also a number of scholars of public opinion and communications who view popular songs as expressions of public opinion in ancient times. In his 1936 English-language work *A History of the Press and Public Opinion in China*, Lin Yutang argues that the folk ballad was a form of political criticism voiced by the public in ancient China. Compared with people in the West, the Chinese were more severe critics of their rulers, and no absolutist monarch had been able to halt the flow of anti-government criticisms propagated in the form of whispers and rhymes.[12] In modern and contemporary works on historiography, folk ballads are often defined as "revelations of the people's inner thoughts"[13] and "expressions of the people's collective will."[14] Many scholars of Qin and Han history have pointed out that popular rhymes were a special form of expression used by the people of Han-period China when they participated in and criticized the

he made use of a substantial number of popular ballads, rumors, and satirical tracts to reveal popular sentiments in different political and social contexts. He believed that it was only in the coarse and sharp language of popular ballads that the people's emotions, happiness, and pain could find expression. If one ignores popular ballads, one will not know the history of the people. See Palmer (1988), p.6. It was only after it was initiated by Liang Qichao and J. H. Robinson in the early twentieth century, and its subsequent promotion by the French Annales School, that studying the everyday lives, thoughts, and beliefs of ordinary people gradually became an academic endeavor recognized by the international community of historians. See Zhao Shiyu (2002), pp.166–167.

10 Works that study rhymes from the perspectives of folk literature and folkloristics include Zhou Zuoren, *A Short Disquisition on Children's Literature* (2002); Zhong Jingwen, *Collected Essays on Songs and Rhymes* (1989); Zhu Ziqing, *Chinese Songs and Rhymes* (1965); Tian Ying, *Essays on Ancient Songs and Rhymes in China* (1959); Zhu Jiefan, *Disquisitions on Chinese Songs and Rhymes* (1974), *I Sing Songs and Rhymes* (1974), and *Collected Essays on Chinese Ballads and Customs* (1984); Zhang Zichen, *A Short History of Songs and Rhymes* (1981); Lü Xiaohuan, *A Study of Ancient Folk Ballads in China* (2006); and so on.

11 Traditional political thought in China viewed children's rhymes as prophetic rhymes (*chēnyáo*) that expressed Heaven's will. Therefore, children's rhymes recorded in old histories were usually loaded with political critique and *chen* prophecies. Works such as Oyanagi Shigeta, "Children's Songs and Rhymes, *Chen* Diagrams, and Religious Bandits" (1934); Ying-hsiung Chou, *The Wooden-Tongued Bell: The Uses of Literature and Poetry-Collecting in Han China* (1977); Kushida Hisaharu, *Ancient "Rhymes" and "Prophecies" in China* (1999); and Xie Gui'an, *A Study of the Culture of Chen and Rhymes of China* (1998), etc. focus on the *chen* prophecy characteristics of rhymes in the early imperial period, even calling them prophetic rhymes. Then there are a number of researchers who subscribe to the "spirit of science," who feel that the interpretation of rhymes as prophecies is really quite "superstitious." Could prophetic rhymes really tell the political future? Or did they come true only in hindsight? If they really did possess "prophetic powers," what was the source of these powers? Please refer to Chapter 4 of this book for a more thorough discussion.

12 Lin Yutang (1936), p.20. This argument has had a profound influence on scholars of press and public opinion history. For example, Zhu Chuanyu (1974) had this to say about rhymes and adages: "In terms of their function and influence, they are as good as the newspapers of today." (p.103) Yan Xinheng (1984) had a similar view.

13 Wang Zijin (2006), p.377.

14 Tian Ying (1959), p.87.

politics of the day. Popular rhymes, as public opinion, played a supervisory role in society, and had a positive effect on improving contemporary governance and politics.[15]

Popular Songs and Rhymes Are an Important Component of Social and Political Life in the Han Periods

"My heart is grieved, and I sing songs and rhymes."[16] The ancient Chinese were adept at singing and often expressed their inner thoughts through songs, as described in "Canon of Shun" in *Book of Documents*: "Poetry is the expression of will; singing is the prolonged manifestation of that expression."[17] Thus, Confucius says: "If you do not study *Book of Odes*, we have nothing to talk about."[18] "When noblemen and grandees were in negotiations with neighboring states, they conversed with subtle words. At diplomatic meetings between hosts and guests, they would express their wishes by quoting lines from *Book of Odes*."[19]

Most of the lines that noblemen and grandees in pre-Qin China recited at social functions were from poems that were well documented and familiar. For grandees of the various states who had received similar instruction in poetry, the words and metaphors of these poems had already formed a set of tacit and effective communication symbols that allowed them to express their thoughts and feelings directly or tactfully, subtly, and even implicitly. However, the spontaneous singing and reciting that expressing intense personal feelings, at a specific time and place by individuals who had been moved to do so, was a common occurrence as well. For example, when Ji Zi, the uncle of the deceased King Zhou of the recently overthrown Yin Dynasty, went to pay obeisance to the ruling King of the newly founded Zhou Dynasty, "he traveled past the ruined capital of the former Yin dynasty. Saddened by the rubble of the palaces and houses ... he wanted to cry but he could not ... and so he composed and sang a poem as a dirge to his fallen state."[20] Boyi and Shuqi, the brothers who considered themselves the loyal subjects of the Yin dynasty,

[15] See Tong Xigang, "Rhymes and Rhymes Reporting of the Han Period" (1999); Ma Xin, "Rhymes and Adages Commenting on Current Politics and the Concept of Participation of People during the Han Dynasties" (2001); Xie Gui'an, "Ancient Political Folk Ballads and Their Functions in Society and Public Opinion" (2002); Hu Shouwei, "'Rhymes Reporting' and Administration of the Eastern Han" (2004); etc.

[16] *Annotations and Explanations of the Thirteen Classics: the Mao Commentary, juan* 5, "Odes of Wei: Of the Peach Trees in the Garden," p.357.

[17] *Annotations and Explanations of the Thirteen Classics: Book of Documents, juan* 3, "Book of Yu: Canon of Shun," p.131.

[18] *Annotations and Explanations of the Thirteen Classics: The Analects, juan* 3, "Jishi," p.2522.

[19] *History of the Former Han, juan* 30, "Treatise on Literature," pp.1755–1756.

[20] *The Grand Scribe's Records, juan* 38, "The Hereditary House of Song Wei Zi," p.1621.

refused to eat any edibles from the land of Zhou and hid themselves in Mount Shouyang. Just before dying from hunger, they composed a song to express their stand.[21] After Ji Huanzi (?–492 BCE) accepted the gift of dancing girls from the State of Qi, Confucius (551–479 BCE) decided to leave the State of Lu because he realized that politically, there was nothing he could achieve there. When he was on the road, he sang: "The mouths of those women can drive out ministers and trustworthy men,/and being in proximity with those women causes ruin and death./How carefree I am now,/to spend the rest of my days in peace!"[22]

Ordinary people often sang to express their feelings too. Many of the over 300 poems collected in *Book of Odes* were adapted from the unstudied rhymes of ordinary people during the Zhou period. In the rural areas, "men and women who had not done what they were supposed to do would disparage one another by singing songs."[23] There were singing in the cities too. For example, *The Grand Scribe's Records* depicted Jing Ke (?–27 BCE), the famous assassin, as "drinking every day in the market of the State of Yan with dog butchers and Gao Jianli. Gao Jianli would play the *zhu* and Jing Ke would sing in the market in time with the music." The song that Jing Ke sang before he set off to assassinate the King of Qin had become legendary: "The wind howls fiercely and the Yi River is cold;/the hero goes, never to return."[24]

By the early imperial period, the custom of spontaneous singing was still prevalent among all classes of people in the whole empire. "Singing was extemporaneous and the dancing spontaneous."[25] Besieged at Gaixia, Xiang Yu sang a dirge: "My strength uplifted a mountain,/my vigor shadowed the world./But the times do not favor me,/and Piebald cannot gallop fast enough."[26] Liu Bang, Emperor Gaozu of the Western Han Dynasty, often sang to express his feelings. After he defeated Xiang Yu and returned to his hometown in triumph and glory, "he gathered the friends from his past, elders and young men of the town to drink to their hearts' content. He selected 120 children of Pei to teach them songs." At the height of the revelry, Emperor

[21] *The Grand Scribe's Records, juan* 61, "Memoirs of Boyi," p.2123.

[22] *The Grand Scribe's Records, juan* 47, "The Hereditary House of Confucius," p.1918.

[23] *History of the Former Han, juan* 24, "Treatise on Food on Money, Part I," p.1121. He Xiu also wrote: "Men and women nursing grudges would follow and sing to each other. The hungry would sing about food; those who were laboring would sing about their work." (*Annotations and Explanations of the Thirteen Classics: Commentary of Gongyang on the Spring and Autumn Annals, juan* 16, "The Fifteenth Year of Duke Xuan," p.2287) The descriptions here were vignettes of life in pre-Qin rural society as remembered and understood by people of the early imperial period.

[24] *The Grand Scribe's Records, juan* 86, "Memoirs of Assassins," p.2534.

[25] Lin Jianming, et al. (1985), p.367.

[26] *The Grand Scribe's Records, juan* 7, "Basic Annals of Xiang Yu," p.333. English translation from Nienhauser, vol. 1 (1994), p.205.

Gaozu played the *zhu* and composed a song, which he sang: "A great wind blows and the clouds rise up high!/I've conquered the realm and now I'm home!/How do I get brave men to protect the land?"[27] In the Jia and Yi copies of the Qin-period bamboo almanac unearthed in Shuihudi, songs and music are listed, together with food, drink, and religious offerings, as the basic elements of everyday life at that time.

Cao San (?–190 BCE) was Chancellor of State during the reign of Emperor Hui of the Western Han Dynasty (Liu Ying, reigned 195–188 BCE). The back garden of Cao San's residence was near the quarters of officials, where a great deal of drinking and singing went on every day. Members of Cao San's staff could not bear the noise, but they were powerless to do anything about it. So, one day they invited Cao San to visit the back garden in the hope that the Chancellor would hear the drunken songs and cacophony and mete out an appropriate punishment. Unexpectedly, Cao San "got his men to set up a table and began drinking himself, singing and shouting loudly in tandem with those officials."[28] The famous event of "Passing Edict Tokens of the Queen Mother of the West" occurred in the early months of the fourth year of the Jianping reign period of Emperor Ai, and "the people from the commanderies and kingdoms gathered in the imperial capital's streets and alleys in their thousands. They set up gaming facilities and worshipped the Queen Mother of the West with song and dance."[29] The scale of the event would have been quite substantial.

There should be quite a large number of popular songs and rhymes in the early imperial period. The "Treatise on Literature" in *History of the Former Han* recorded and collected the following regional songs and rhymes: fifteen songs and rhymes from the Wu, Chu, and Ru'nan regions; nine songs and rhymes from the Yan and Dai regions singing about Yanmen, Yunzhong, and Longxi; four songs and rhymes from Handan and Hejian; four songs and rhymes from the Qi and Zheng regions; four songs and rhymes from Huainan; three Qin songs and rhymes from the area administered by the Grand Administrator of Eastern Supporter Commandery; five Qin songs and rhymes from the area administered by the Governor of the Capital; one rhyme from Puban of Hedong; four songs and rhymes from Luoyang; seven Zhou songs and rhymes with musical scores from He'nan; seventy-five Zhou songs and rhymes with musical scores; two Zhou songs and rhymes; and five songs and rhymes from the Nan Commandery.[30] Those that are thematically organized include

[27] *The Grand Scribe's Records*, *juan* 8, "Basic Annals of Emperor Gaozu," p.389.

[28] *The Grand Scribe's Records*, *juan* 54, "The Hereditary House of Chancellor of State Cao," p.2030.

[29] *History of the Former Han*, *juan* 27 *xia zhi shang*, "Treatise on the Five Agents, Part IV," p.1476.

[30] *History of the Former Han*, *juan* 30, "Treatise on Literature," pp.1753–1755.

fourteen songs and rhymes about Han triumphs and conquests. It is estimated that these songs and rhymes, which had been collected and written down, were but a small portion of the total number of popular songs and rhymes at the time.[31]

It was precisely because popular songs and rhymes were such an important component of society at the time, with a rich content that covered many aspects of social and cultural life, that Sima Qian, when he was compiling *The Grand Scribe's Records* and "narrating the histories of the Yellow Emperor in the beginning and the Warring States Period in the middle, he acquired his sources either from famous mountains and derelict ruins, or from old customs and folk rhymes."[32] The treatises and monographs in *The Grand Scribe's Records* and *History of the Former Han* that described the geography, customs, and people's lives in various chapters such as "Memoirs of Profiteers" and "Treatise on Geography" also saw "popular rhymes and customs" as valuable information that reflected the folkways, character, values, and social lives of individual regions.[33] The personalities of historical figures and their thought processes scattered in the "Annals," "Memoirs" or "Biographies," and "Hereditary Houses" in these historical texts become more alive through these songs and rhymes. However, given the limitations of traditional historiography and discourse frameworks, the songs and rhymes that were preferred and

[31] *The Grand Scribe's Records* and *History of the Former Han* contain many tragic songs of consorts vying for the Emperor's favor in Emperor Gaozu's final years, as well as the tragic songs of Lady Qi, King of Zhao Liu Ruyi, and other members of the imperial house when they were persecuted by Empress Lü after Emperor Gaozu's death. The many similarly themed emotive "tragic songs" that narrated the persecution in these texts was an indication of the strong condemnation of Empress Lü by the compilers of *The Grand Scribe's Records* and *History of the Former Han*, as well as their clear endorsement of the legality of the Liu imperial house's subsequent extermination of the Lü family. Other songs, such as "The King of Yan's Song" and "The King of Guangling's Song" of the Western Han Dynasty, and "The King of Hongnong's Song" of the Eastern Han Dynasty, revealed the brutal political struggles and treacherous court life of the early imperial period. Scholar-officials, when inebriated, sang songs to assuage their indignation, such as "Dongfang Shuo's Song" and "Li Ling's Song." These tragic songs, spontaneously composed by individuals, also contained a rich source of historical and cultural information, but they were not the same as the popular rhymes discussed in this book.

[32] *The Grand Scribe's Records: Afterword of the Grand Scribe's Records: Commentaries*, p.9.

[33] According to *History of the Former Han*, *juan* 69, "Biographies of Zhao Chongguo and Xin Qingji: Comments," the commanderies of Tianshui, Longxi, Anding, and Beidi neighbored the Qiang peoples, and the prevalent martial customs in those commanderies meant that their people were warlike and liked horse riding and archery. "Their manners and customs have been so since ancient times. Their songs and rhymes are rousing and impassioned to the ear, recalling the styles of the past." (p.2999) Yan Shigu's annotation of *History of the Former Han*, *juan* 76, "Biography of Han Yanshou" reads: "Popular and rhymes and customs here referred to songs in the streets that educated the people about good and evil." (p.3211)

recorded by historians for posterity tended to be related to political life and events.[34] These songs and rhymes often featured barbed lyrics that criticized injustices and social ills of the day.

The promotion and ennoblement of General-in-Chief Wei Qing (?–106 BCE), brother-in-law of Emperor Wu of the Western Han Dynasty, was justified by his many military successes. However, when even his three infant sons were made marquesses, the people felt it was unfair, even as they admired Wei Qing's achievements. Inevitably, they attributed the Wei family's exalted position to low-born Empress Wei Zifu (?–91 BCE), and sang this song: "Don't be too happy if you give birth to a boy,/and don't be too unhappy if you give birth to a girl!/Don't you see how Wei Zifu has conquered the world?"[35]

During the reigns of Emperor Yuan and Emperor Cheng, the government was in shambles given the intense and frequent political conflicts between eunuchs, the Emperors' affinal relatives, and officials. Many of the songs and rhymes critical of contemporary politics collected in *History of the Former Han* were of this period, including a popular song criticizing the eunuch Shi Xian (?–33 BCE) and Wulu Chongzong for colluding in taking over the reins of government: "Oh, Lao [Liang] and Shi [Xian],/the frequent guests of Wulu [Chongzong]!/Their seals are so numerous and the ribbons on them so long!";[36] a "Chang'an rhyme" mocking their downfall: "Yi [Jia] demoted to Yan[men],/[Wu]lu demoted to [Xuan]tu,/Lao [Liang] and Chen [Shun] can look forward to nothing.";[37] a rhyme in which "the people" rebuked the Emperor's affinal relatives, the Wang family, for arrogantly usurping the Emperor's powers and their superciliousness: "When the Five Marquesses first came into prominence,/the Marquess of Quyang [Wang Gen, ?–2 BCE] was the most domineering among them./He burst the Gaodu River,/bringing the water to the capital,/and extended his mansion to Waidu, beyond the city wall./He built his terrace so high by the water that it resembled the Emperor's White Tiger Palace."[38] These songs, which mentioned specific names and targeted specific politicians and political factions, might have reflected widespread public opinion or might have been the creations of hostile political cliques.

[34] Tian Ying (1959), p.73.

[35] *The Grand Scribe's Records, juan* 49, "The Hereditary Houses of the Imperial Affines," cited by Chu Shaosun, p.1983.

[36] *History of the Former Han, juan* 93, "Biographies of Flatterers: Biography of Shi Xian," p.3727. Lao Liang, Shi Xian, Yi Jia, and Wulu Chongzong formed a clique. "Seals" referred to official posts that were manipulated by this clique.

[37] *Ibid.*, p.3730.

[38] *History of the Former Han, juan* 98, "Biography of Empress Wang Zhengjun, Empress of Emperor Yuan," p.4024.

During the Yongshi (16–13 BCE) and Yuanyan (12–9 BCE) reign periods of Emperor Cheng, the dominance of the Emperor's affinal relatives and the defiance of powerful clans at the local level resulted in weak governance. In the capital city of Chang'an, youths formed gangs that assassinated officials in return for payment and robbed ordinary people, resulting in many being killed or maimed in the city. Ranked top among candidates in the capital area, Yin Shang was appointed Prefect of Chang'an and given special discretionary powers to maintain law and order. He ordered security officials at the grass-roots level and local elders to report "frivolous and ill-disciplined youths, traders and artisans who were not registered residents, and people donning suspicious clothing and armor and carrying weapons" in the city of Chang'an. Several hundred names were collected. "One morning, Yin Shang gathered the officials of Chang'an and in several hundred chariots, they went around arresting those whom they believed were robbers who caused social unrest." All those arrested were buried alive. "A hundred days later, the families of those who had died were ordered to dig up the corpses. There was much wailing by the families and sighing in the streets." Immediately afterward, criminals began to leave the capital, and the people of Chang'an started to sing this song: "Where do I go to find my child's dead body?/At the young people's burial place east of the official pillar./You are not prudent in life./Where can I bury your bones in death?"[39] The lyrics, which were mournful and full of longing, seemed to reflect the point of view of the dead youths' families. The song did not celebrate the return of law and order, nor did it curse the law enforcers for their cruelty. However, the line "You are not prudent in life" subtly expressed the sorrow of an unjust and needless death, the collateral damage of heavy-handed and swift justice.

Then there were certain songs and rhymes with barbed and harsh lyrics that condemned specific politicians or sociopolitical phenomena. For example, there used to be a Hongxi Reservoir in Ru'nan, which created wealth for the whole commandery. During the reign of Emperor Cheng, there were heavy rains in the east of the Pass, which caused the reservoir waters to overflow and flood the surrounding areas. Believing that draining all the water from the reservoir would save the expenses of shoring up its banks and solve the

[39] *History of the Former Han*, *juan* 90, "Biographies of Cruel Officials: Biography of Yin Shang," pp.3673–3674. Just before he died, Yin Shang advised his sons: "A great man who is an official should not be afraid of being dismissed for his cruelty. He will be reinstated once the efficiency and effectiveness of his service are being recalled. However, if he loses his post because of weakness and incompetence, then he will never be reinstated for the rest of his life. The humiliation will be greater than being found guilty for corruption. Be careful not to be weak and incompetent!" Yin Shang's words reflected the values typically subscribed to by "cruel officials" whose pragmatism was informed by the attitude that it was better to be cruel than to indulge.

problem of flooding, then Chancellor Zhai Fangjin (?–7 BCE), alias Zhai Ziwei and a Ru'nan native, got the Emperor's approval to decommission the reservoir. During the time of Wang Mang's regency, frequent droughts resulted in repeated famines. The people of Ru'nan began to put the blame on Zhai Fangjin, accusing him of wanting to decommission the reservoir because he had wanted but failed to seize the fertile lands below the reservoir. A children's rhyme started making the rounds in the commandery: "Who destroyed the reservoir?/Zhai Ziwei of course./What we have now for staple are beans,/what we have now for soup are taro roots./The world is ever-changing and the reservoir will be repaired./Who said that?/Two yellow swans."[40] Yellow swans were metaphors for heavenly messengers. A story went around that after the reservoir had been decommissioned, Emperor Cheng had a dream in which he ascended to heaven, where a furious Supreme Deity of Heaven rebuked him: "Why did you destroy my Jumping Dragon Pool?"[41]

Zhai Fangjin had drained the reservoir to mitigate the problem of flooding but it resulted in water shortage during droughts. It is understandable that the people of Ru'nan blamed him for his lack of foresight. However, the accusation that he had destroyed the livelihood of his home commandery because of a private grudge only came after his family's extermination following his son Zhai Yi's failed armed revolt against Wang Mang. It is not very convincing to argue that politics had nothing to do with the emergence of the rhyme. Kushida Hisaharu speculated that the "yellow swans" in the children's rhyme was an oblique reference to Wang Mang, indicating the hopes the people of Ru'nan placed on Wang Mang to repair the Hongxi Reservoir. In the drought of the second year of the Yuanshi reign period, Wang Mang did implement a series of relief measures.[42] The actual restoration of the Hongxi Reservoir, however, was only placed on the government's agenda by Grand Administrator Deng Chen (?–49 CE) during the Jianwu reign period in the Eastern Han Dynasty. Director of Waters Xu Yang, who was in charge of repairing the reservoir, said to Deng Chen: "In the past, the Great Yu broke the banks of the Yangtze and redirected the Yellow River to benefit the world; today Your Excellency is restarting what has been neglected to enrich the state and bring peace to the

40 *History of the Former Han, juan* 84, "Biography of Zhai Yi," p.3440. This rhyme is cited in *History of the Later Han, juan* 82, "Biographies of Alchemists, Part I: Biography of Xu Yang" with slightly different wording: "Zhai Ziwei, the destroyer of my reservoir. He makes us eat beans and consume taro roots. The world is ever-changing and the reservoir will be repaired." (p.2710)

41 *History of the Later Han, juan* 82, "Biographies of Alchemists, Part I: Biography of Xu Yang," p.2710.

42 Kushida Hisaharu (1999), p.119.

people. The words in the children's rhyme will be fulfilled here."[43] Obviously, rhymes that had been popular in the Ru'nan region during Wang Mang's Xin Dynasty were still deeply lodged in the collective memories of local officials and people in the early years of the Eastern Han Dynasty.

In the third year of the Dihuang reign period (22 CE) of Wang Mang's Xin Dynasty, Wang Mang sent Grand Master Wang Kuang (?–23 CE) and General of a New Beginning Lian Dan (?–22 CE) to Shandong to put down the Chimei Rebels. "Wreaking havoc wherever they went," the government troops prompted strong resentment among the people. Subsequently, there emerged "Words of the East" that condemned Wang Kuang and Lian Dan: "It would be better to meet the Chimei/than to meet the Grand Master./The Grand Master can still [be tolerated],/but the [General of a] New Beginning would kill me."[44]

The key officials of the Gengshi regime, Li Yi, Zhu Wei, Wang Kuang, and Zhang Ang, were abusing their powers and putting on airs in the east of the Pass and the Three Metropolitan Areas by appointing "officials who were mean men, merchants, cooks, and kitchen hands." The people of Chang'an mocked these Gengshi parvenus with this rhyme: "The boy who was dragged up in the kitchen/becomes Leader of Palace Gentleman;/the putrid goat's stomach/becomes Chief Commandant of Cavalry;/and the rotten goat's head/becomes the Marquess Within the Pass."[45] There was a rhyme that ridiculed the excesses of the nomination system in the late Eastern Han Dynasty: "A Flourishing Talent is nominated/yet he does not know the classics./A Filially Pious and Incorrupt is nominated/yet he lives not with his father./A poor man enjoying the fame of the unsullied is filthy like mud,/but high-ranked generals are cowardly like hens."[46] These were excellent rhymes that were on the lips of many. Another example was "The people's hair is like leeks that grow back after they are cut. Their heads are like a chicken that still crows after its head is cut off. Officials are not to be feared and the peopled are

[43] *History of the Later Han, juan* 82, "Biographies of Alchemists, Part I: Biography of Xu Yang," p.2710.

[44] *History of the Former Han, juan* 99, "Biography of Wang Mang, Part III," p.4175.

[45] *History of the Later Han, juan* 11, "Biography of Liu Xuan," p.471.

[46] *Collection of Music Bureau Poems, juan* 87, "Lyrics of Miscellaneous Songs and Rhymes, Part V" added in *History of the Later Han*: "A Flourishing Talent is nominated yet he does not know the books. A Filially Pious and Incorrupt is nominated yet he lives not with his father." (p.1224) Based on *The Master Who Embraces Simplicity*, the *Ancient Rhymes and Adages, juan* 6, added: "The poor and unsullied are filthy like mud, top scholars and good generals are cowardly like hens." It also pointed out that in *Imperial Reader of the Taiping Era, juan* 496, "hens" is replaced by "houseflies." (p.95) *Poems of the Pre-Qin, Han, Wei, Jin, and the Northern and Southern Dynasties: Poems of the Han, juan* 8: "The quote in *History of Jin*: 'Flourishing Talents are nominated. Filthy like mud. Good generals are nominated. Cowardly like hens.' is different from this one." (p.242)

not to be taken lightly. But all they want is peace."[47] This rhyme revealed the fierce antagonism between officials and the people with its incisive and vivid language, as well as its moving and engaging imagery.

These popular songs and rhymes demonstrated the people's intense criticism of political power, the concern for current affairs, and the swift response to them. The intellectual and ruling classes of the early imperial period paid a great deal of attention to such non-official discourse because of their ability to unite the people, express the people's will, and influence public opinion. These popular songs and rhymes enjoyed a unique position in the political discourse of the time.

The Unique Position of Popular Songs and Rhymes in Intellectual Discourse during the Han Periods

Compared with the vilification and suppression of disseminated talk, unverifiable talk, and portentous talk by the authorities, popular songs or rhymes, which belonged in the same category of rumor-like popular or non-official expressions, were treated very differently in official political discourse and actual social and political life during the early imperial period.

In traditional Chinese political thought and discourse, popular songs and rhymes had always performed very important political functions. The first of these functions was education. *Book of Documents* contains the Great Yu's counsel on good governance: "Caution them with gentle words, correct them with the might of the law, persuade them with the songs on the nine subjects."[48] This was because "emotions are formed inside one and expressed in speech. When speech is not sufficient to express the emotions, one sighs. When sighing is still insufficient, one sings songs."[49] Given that singing was a natural expression of genuine emotions, songs possessed an enormous power to convince and influence in the process of education. In Confucian political thought and discourse, however, songs and rhymes composed and sung by ordinary people had another important function: they could reveal and express the people's will. Therefore, they had the symbolic significance of demonstrating the legitimacy and the level of acceptance of a monarch's rule.

Such discourse on people's songs or expressions was closely related to the idea that the people were the foundation of the state, an idea that had been

[47] *Poems of the Pre-Qin, Han, Wei, Jin, and the Northern and Southern Dynasties: Poems of the Han, juan* 8, citing Cui Shi, *Disquisitions on Government*, p.241.

[48] *Annotations and Explanations of the Thirteen Classics: Book of Documents, juan* 4, "Book of Yu: Counsels of Great Yu" (Kong Anguo's commentary), p.135.

[49] *Annotations and Explanations of the Thirteen Classics: the Mao Commentary, juan* 1, "Odes of Zhou and South: Guan Ju" (Mao's commentary), p.270.

popular since the Western Zhou Dynasty.[50] Pre-Qin philosophers believed that the people should be the foundation of the government of a ruler, who should "love what the people love, and hate what the people hate."[51] "The reason why policies can be implemented is because they are in line with the people's will; the reason why policies are ineffective is because they are against the people's will."[52] Mencius (372–289 BCE) even advocated using the people's support or opposition as the final arbiter of regime and policy changes, claiming that he who had the people's support would be the Son of Heaven, and he who lost the people's support would lose his realm.[53] It was in these songs and rhymes of ordinary people that the voice of the masses was reflected.

The response of popular songs and rhymes to contemporary politics could be quite sensitive and direct. For example, Zi Chan (?–522 BCE) took over the reins of the State of Zheng and reformed the state's land distribution system, which affected the interests of those who occupied more land than permissible. Within one year of his administration, the coach drivers chanted: "He takes my clothes and hat and puts them away;/he takes my land and redistributes it./Who wants to kill Zi Chan?/I will join you!" The loathing expressed in the rhyme was reminiscent of "When will you, the Sun, expire? We will all perish with you."[54] Three years later, however, the coach drivers chanted differently: "I have children and Zi Chan educates them;/I have land and Zi Chan makes it productive./If Zi Chan dies,/who can succeed him?"[55] Such is the capriciousness of public opinion!

Mencius believed that the opinions of the people were more worthy of attention than a ruler's ministers:

> When all those about you say, "This is a man of talents and worth," you may not therefore believe it. When your great officers all say, "This is a man of talents and virtue," neither may you for that believe it. When all the people say, "This is a man of talents and virtue," then examine into the case, and when you find that the man is such, employ him. When all those about you say, "This man won't do," don't listen to them.

50 The idea that the people were the foundation of the state was by no means unique to ancient China. Most rulers who subscribed to the notion of universal kingship in the ancient world would consider the improvement of the people's welfare as part of their duties. See Schwartz (1985), p.48.

51 *Annotations and Explanations of the Thirteen Classics: Book of Rites*, *juan* 42, "Great Learning," p.1675.

52 *Guan Zi: Annotations and Interpretations*, *shang ce*, "Shepherding the People, Part I," p.1. In the Sibu Beiyao Edition, it reads: "The reason why policies flourish." The annotator made the correction based on Guo Moruo's *Collected Annotations of Guan Zi*.

53 Hsiao Kung-Ch'üan (1982), p.95. Similar arguments are found in *Discourses of the States* and *Commentary of Zuo*. Refer to Liu Zehua (1992) and Zheng Changgan (1995).

54 *Annotations and Explanations of the Thirteen Classics: Book of Documents*, *juan* 8, "Book of Shang: Speech of Tang" (Kong Anguo's commentary), p.160.

55 *Annotations and Explanations of the Thirteen Classics: Commentary of Zuo on the Spring and Autumn Annals*, *juan* 40, "The Thirtieth Year of Duke Xiang," p.2014.

When all your great officers say, "This man won't do," don't listen to them. When the people all say, "This man won't do," then examine into the case, and when you find that the man won't do, send him away. When all those about you say, "This man deserves death," don't listen to them. When all your great officers say, "This man deserves death," don't listen to them. When the people all say, "This man deserves death," then inquire into the case, and when you see that the man deserves death, put him to death. In accordance with this we have the saying, "The people killed him."[56]

He even gave such expressions of people's voices as popular songs and rhymes, the symbolic significance of demonstrating a regime's legitimacy and the level of its acceptance:

Shun assisted Yao in the government for twenty and eight years – this was more than man could have done, and was from Heaven. After the death of Yao, when the three years' mourning was completed, Shun withdrew from the son of Yao to the south of South River. The princes of the kingdom, however, repairing to court, went not to the son of Yao, but they went to Shun. Litigants went not to the son of Yao, but they went to Shun. Singers sang not of the son of Yao, but they sang of Shun. Therefore I said, "Heaven gave him the throne." It was after these things that he went to the Middle Kingdom, and occupied the seat of the Son of Heaven. If he had, before these things, taken up his residence in the palace of Yao, and had applied pressure to the son of Yao, it would have been an act of usurpation, and not the gift of Heaven. This sentiment is expressed in the words of "The Great Declaration":[57] "Heaven sees according as my people see; Heaven hears according as my people hear."[58]

From Mencius's point of view, popular songs and rhymes were an important cypher that demonstrated how much a sovereign's rule was accepted by his people. Why did Yao not bequeath his throne to Yao's son Danzhu but abdicated in favor of Shun instead? It was because it was the people's will. What was the sign of the people's will? When the various lords repaired to court, they went not to the son of Yao, but to Shun. Litigants went not to the son of Yao, but to Shun. Singers sang not of the son of Yao, but of Shun. Songs thus became a symbol of the people's voice.

In the chapter "Zhongni" in *Lie Zi*, an early medieval Taoist text:

Yao ruled the state for fifty years. He did not know if the realm was well administered or not. He did not know if the people were willing to support him or not. He turned and asked the men around him, and the men around him had no answer. He asked the ministers at court, and the ministers at court had no answer. He asked those who were not serving the government, and they too had no answer. And so, Yao put on

56 *Mencius: Standard Interpretation*, *juan* 5, "King Hui of Liang, Part II," p.144. English translation based on James Legge's translation found at ctext.org/mengzi/liang-hui-wang-ii.

57 A missing chapter of *Book of Documents*.

58 *Mencius: Standard Interpretation*, *juan* 19, "Wan Zhang, Part I," pp.644–645. English translation based on James Legge's translation found at ctext.org/mengzi/wan-zhang-i. "Basic Annals of Emperor Wu" in *The Grand Scribe's Records* contains a similar narrative.

commoners' clothes and walked along the main thoroughfares, where he heard a children's rhyme that went: "You have nurtured us, the people, and everything was according to your standards. No one knows anything, but to obey the laws of the ruler." Delighted, Yao asked the child, "Who taught you this rhyme?" The child answered, "I heard it from the Grandees." Yao asked the Grandees and they answered, "This is an ancient poem." Upon returning to the palace, Yao summoned Shun to his presence and abdicated his throne, transferring to Shun the right to rule the state. Shun accepted it without demur.[59]

This story of Yao was used to again validate the classical Confucian understanding of children's rhymes: that they were not simply random words chanted by children, but the true voices of the people, reflecting their support or opposition to the regime. Children's rhymes were extremely important indicators of a ruler's legitimacy.

The Confucian definition of popular songs and rhymes was widely accepted in the classicist and historical discourse of the early imperial period. Starting from the early imperial period, laudatory songs and rhymes sung by "the people" became an indispensable sign that demonstrated the legitimacy of a sovereign's rule. In the descriptions of Jia Yi and *Masters of Huainan* of the virtues of Kings Wen and Wu of the Zhou period, "the people of the Nine Regions and the Kingdoms of the Four Wild Domains sang songs and rhymes about the righteousness of Kings Wen and Wu" and "all under Heaven sang songs and rhymes and made music about them."[60] In the narrative of *The Grand Scribe's Records*, when Gugong Danfu again cultivated the legacy of Hou Ji and Gong Liu, the ancestors of the Zhou Dynasty, accumulated virtue, and carried out justice, "the people put all this to song and music in order to praise his virtue."[61]

In the historical discourse of the early imperial period, songs and rhymes sung among the people also became important indicators of popular assessments of the achievements of political figures and the effectiveness of local governance. In the early years of the Western Han Dynasty, during the successive chancellorships of Xiao He (257–193 BCE) and Cao San, the people were rested, the administration was kept simple, and the policies were stable. The history books recorded "the people's songs" in praise of Xiao He and Cao San: "Laws laid down by Xiao He/were clear-cut and uniformed./ When Cao San replaced Xiao He,/he adhered to Xiao's laws/and did not

[59] *Lie Zi: Collected Expositions, juan* 4, pp.143–144.

[60] *New Writings, juan* 10, "Talks on Rites and Appearance, Part II," p.379. *The Great and Bright of Huainan: Collected Expositions, juan* 12, "Responses of Tao," p.412.

[61] *The Grand Scribe's Records, juan* 4, "Basic Annals of the Zhou," p.114. English translation from Nienhauser, vol. 1 (1994), p.57.

change anything./Cao's policy of non-action resulted in peaceful lives for the people."[62]

In the second year of the Taishi reign period (95 BCE) of Emperor Wu of the Western Han Dynasty, Bai Gong, Palace Grandee of the Kingdom of Zhao, constructed the Bai Canal, which directed water from Jing River into the Wei River and irrigated more than 4,500 *qing* of farmland. Benefiting from the canal, the people sang: "Where are the fields?/At Chiyang and Gukou./The Kingdom of Zheng Canal was built before, then the Bai Canal follows./The lifted shovels are like clouds;/the opened canals are like rain./One *shi* of water from Jing River contains several *dou* of soil./Watering and fertilizing the field,/ my crops are growing./They supply millions of people in the capital with food and clothing."[63]

When Zhao Guanghan (?–65 BCE) was Commandery Administrator and Governor of the Capital, he was honest and meticulous, and he went after the local strongmen. "Officials and commoners were full of praise for him. The elders said there had been no Governor of the Capital like him since the founding of the Han Dynasty." Later on, he was found guilty of wrongful enforcement of the law and insulting senior ministers and was executed. "Several tens of thousands of officials and people wept outside the palace," or said they wanted to die in his stead. "The people have sung songs in memory of him to this day."[64]

The brothers Feng Yewang and Feng Li were successive Commandery Administrators of the Shang Commandery and other commanderies. Their administrations were clean and competent, and the people of the commanderies sang: "The older Feng/and the younger Feng:/both brothers took office one after the other./They were intelligent, wise, and love the people./Their administrations spread virtue to the people/as it had been done in the Kingdoms of Lu and Wei./These two gentlemen were like the Duke of Zhou and Kang Shu."[65]

[62] *The Grand Scribe's Records*, *juan* 54, "The Hereditary House of Chancellor of State Cao," p.2031. In *History of the Former Han*, *juan* 39, "Biography of Cao San," the lyrics are similar with slight changes. (p.2021) The song was also mentioned in *History of the Former Han*, *juan* 89, "Biographies of Upright Officials: Comments": "In the early years of the Han, the shortcomings of the Qin were reversed: the people were given rest, things were kept simple, and laws were relaxed. The Chancellors Xiao He and Cao San led the state with benevolence and non-action, and the people composed the "Clear-Cut and Uniformed Song." (p.3623)

[63] *History of the Former Han*, *juan* 29, "Treatise on Rivers and Canals," p.1685.

[64] *History of the Former Han*, *juan* 76, "Biography of Zhao Guanghan," p.3206.

[65] *History of the Former Han*, *juan* 79, "Biography of Feng Li," p.3305. The lyrics of this rhyme are too literary and polished.

In tracing the genealogy of the Ban family, the composer of *History of the Former Han* praised his own forebear Ban Ziru for "being valiant and having songs sung about him by people in the regions and commanderies."[66]

It was precisely within such a social and political context and cultural and psychological milieu that Wang Mang, who was planning to usurp the throne, found it necessary to fabricate many auspicious signs, including several tens of thousands of songs and rhymes, to create the illusion that he had the support of public opinion. Those opposed to Wang Mang's Xin Dynasty, however, claimed that "the officials and people have long sung about their pining for the Han,"[67] to prove that the people wanted the return of the Han Dynasty and that the Xin Dynasty was doomed to fail. When Cao Pi's men persuaded him to replace the Han Dynasty, they put forth arguments to support the legitimacy of the Wei Dynasty receiving the Mandate of Heaven and replacing the Han. Apart from references to *chen* prophecies and auguries, they also had to "use the songs and rhymes of the people" to prove that "the Han Dynasty has declined and its Agent has ceased." The Wei Dynasty should therefore take over the Mandate.[68]

Eulogizing songs and rhymes sung by the people were "proof" of a ruler's "good governance."[69] Employing the same logic, a ruler's bad governance would attract songs and rhymes with sarcastic and angry lyrics that reflected negative public opinion. According to the *Mao Commentary on Book of Odes*, an original function of songs was to "ridicule those who are above": "Those who are above used songs to educate those below; those who are below used songs to ridicule those above. The criticisms were disguised in the words: those who said them were blameless; those who heard them should take heed."[70] The *Mao Commentary* also argued that "Sang Rou" was a poem that criticized King Li of the Western Zhou Dynasty. Because King Li refused to admit to the wickedness of his rule, Rui Liangfu said, "I know what you have really done, and have composed songs about your deeds and errors. You should hear them and change."[71]

A rebellion broke out in Zhuya in the first year of the Chuyuan reign period (48 BCE) of Emperor Yuan of the Western Han Dynasty, and Jia Juanzhi (?–43 BCE) opposed sending troops down south to suppress it.

66 *History of the Former Han, juan* 100, "Afterword and Family History, Part I," p.4198.
67 *History of the Later Han, juan* 21, "Biography of Pi Tong," p.758.
68 *Records of the Three Kingdoms, juan* 2, "Book of Wei: Annals of Emperor Wen," annotations by Pei Songzhi (1982), p.75.
69 *Annotations and Explanations of the Thirteen Classics: Book of Documents, juan* 4, "Book of Yu: Counsels of Great Yu," Kong Yingda's standard interpretation, p.135.
70 *Annotations and Explanations of the Thirteen Classics: the Mao Commentary, juan* 1, "Odes of Zhou and South: Guan Ju" (Mao's commentary), p.271.
71 *Annotations and Explanations of the Thirteen Classics: The Mao Commentary, juan* 18, "Greater Odes of the Kingdoms: Sang Rou" (Mao's commentary), p.561.

Drawing lessons from history, he argued that the Qin Dynasty had "raised armies to attack faraway places, craved external expansion, and wanted a large territory." As a result, "the state collapsed and the dynasty ended at the end of the Second Emperor's reign." "'The Song of the Great Wall' is still being sung today."[72]

It was precisely because they were certain that popular songs and rhymes reflected public opinion that most political thinkers during the early imperial period believed rulers had to listen to popular songs and rhymes carefully when they ruled. They should pay particular attention to the sarcasm and anger contained in the lyrics. For example, Wang Fu believed that the quick demise of the Qin Dynasty was because the rulers "did not take the advice of officials and did not hear the rhymes of the people." "Its decline was due to its detachment from the people."[73] During the Yongshou reign period of Emperor Huan of the Eastern Han Dynasty, when Liang Ji dominated the government, there were many occurrences of droughts and other natural disasters. Academy Student Liu Tao (?–185) submitted a memorial to the throne, expressing the wish that Emperor Huan would "listen to the rhymes chanted among the people and ask elderly men on the roads what their worries are."[74] In the eighth year of the Yanxi reign period (165), Grand Commandant Yang Bing's nominee for the Capable and Good, Sincere and Upright was a member of the imperial clan Liu Yu. After his arrival at the capital, Liu Yu, "having heard songs and rhymes when [he] was in the local areas," submitted a memorial to Emperor Huan to expose various "incidents of arrogant officials terrorizing the people with their tyranny, and voices from near and far that cry out in sorrow."[75]

Local officials also often make inquiries about popular songs and rhymes and customs in the areas they governed to familiarize themselves with the local conditions and public mood and improve their administrations. For example, when Han Yanshou (?–57 BCE) was appointed Grand Administrator of Yingchuan, he gathered the respected elders of the commandery and "asked all of them about local customs and popular rhymes, and the hardships the people were facing." Based on the requests of the commandery's residents,

[72] *History of the Former Han, juan* 64, "Biography of Jia Juanzhi," p.2831. The contents of "The Song of the Great Wall" is unknown, but it would have been a song sung by the people of the Qin Dynasty criticizing the court for grand engineering works that exhausted the people.

[73] *Disquisitions of the Hidden Scholar: Annotations, juan* 2, "Light and Darkness, Part VI," p.59.

[74] *History of the Later Han, juan* 57, "Biography of Liu Tao," p.1846.

[75] *History of the Later Han, juan* 57, "Biography of Liu Yu," p.1855. Zhu Chuanyu (1974) believed that the "Emperors [of the Eastern Han Dynasty] did not necessarily heed the words of their ministers, but they did believe in popular rhymes and adages. Therefore, ministers and officials often cited rhymes and adages in their memorials to reinforce their arguments because it showed that they were reflecting public opinion and presenting the views of the majority." (p.108)

he revised the rites and regulations.[76] When Yang Xu (142–189) was appointed Grand Administrator of Nanyang, he visited the commandery in civilian clothing beforehand. "He surveyed the counties and towns, and asked about local customs and rhymes, before he took up his post. He knew very well which county officials were corrupt and which were not, and who among the officers and people were good and who were mischievous. All within the commandery were petrified and in awe."[77]

Although popular songs and rhymes were a kind of non-official discourse that was sometimes labeled as "talking portentously" (*yányāo*) and "portentous rhymes" (*yáoyāo*), they were not stigmatized or even criminalized like disseminated talk, unverifiable talk, and portentous talk in the mainstream political discourse of the early imperial period. Instead, popular songs and rhymes were seen as a true reflection of the people's will.

The Influence and Function of Popular Songs and Rhymes as Public Opinion in Political Practice

An empire could be won on the battlefield, "but could an empire be governed from the saddle of a warhorse?"[78] Military power and tyranny alone are not sufficient to permanently suppress resentment and discontent and maintain long-term political authority. The hearts and minds of the people have a direct effect on the legitimacy and acceptability of the regime and its governance, and in turn on social harmony and political stability. And public opinion is the barometer of the people's will.

David B. Truman argues that:

> A primary concern of all organized political interest groups ... is the character of the opinions existing in the community. Group leaders, whatever else they may neglect, cannot afford to be ignorant of widely held attitudes bearing upon the standing and objectives of their organizations. Estimating the direction and incidence of public opinions, moreover, goes hand in hand with more or less continuing efforts to guide and control them.[79]

Truman's argument about political figures' due recognition of public opinion is made in the social and political context of modern America, a context that is of course completely different from China during the early imperial period. However, following centuries of sustained and comprehensive discourse by political thinkers and historians, as well as a wealth of practical experience, political leaders in the early imperial period seemed to have acquired some

76 *History of the Former Han, juan* 76, "Biography of Han Yanshou," p.3210.
77 *History of the Later Han, juan* 31, "Biography of Yang Xu," p.1110.
78 *The Grand Scribe's Records, juan* 97, "Memoirs of Scholar Li and Lu Jia," p.2699.
79 Truman (1981), p.213.

understanding of the social and political influence, and function, of popular songs and rhymes.

Listening to Songs and Rhymes and Conforming to the People's Will

"Singing of Songs That Expressed the Desire to Return to the East"

After Xiang Liang's death, Xiang Yu followed Song Yi to the north to combat the main forces of the Qin army and render aid to the State of Zhao. Liu Bang was ordered to enter the Hangu Pass to the west, and a pact was made that "whoever enters the Pass first will be its King." As the Qin army was held up by Xiang Yu, Liu Bang entered the Pass effortlessly and took Xianyang, the Qin capital, first. Based on the pact, Liu Bang should have been made the King Within the Pass, ruling the central area of Qin.

However, Xiang Yu soon entered the Pass with his powerful army, took Xianyang from Liu Bang, and made himself King Ba of Western Chu. Suspicious of Liu Bang's power and political ambitions, he reneged on his pact and made him King of Han, so that Liu would be shunted to the peripheral regions of Hanzhong, Ba, and Shu. Leading 30,000 of his staff and soldiers, as well as several tens of thousands of followers of the State of Chu and the various lords, Liu Bang headed to Hanzhong to take up his fiefdom. Given that most of Liu Bang's soldiers were natives of the lands east of Mount Xiao and Hangu Pass, however, there was "singing of songs that expressed the desire to return to the east" along the way and many soldiers deserted. One of Liu Bang's followers, Han Xin (?–196 BCE),[80] suggested that since "the staff and soldiers of the army are easterners, and are yearning day and night to go home, using the intensity of their desire could result in a great success." What he was suggesting was to exploit and manipulate the feeling of homesickness expressed in their songs by transforming the sadness into high morale, turn eastward, and become a contender for the whole empire.[81] Liu Bang's ambition was to be Emperor and Han Xin's words were a perfect match for his intentions. In line with the wishes of his men, Liu Bang turned and headed back toward the area

[80] This was an offspring of the late King Xiang of the State of Han of the Warring States Period, also known as Xin the King of Han. There was another Han Xin (?–196 BCE) who was among the deserted soldiers but later became famous as a gifted military commander on Liu Bang's side.

[81] *The Grand Scribe's Records*, *juan* 8, "Basic Annals of Emperor Gaozu," p.367. Chen Zhi (1979) speculated that the song sung by Liu Bang's troops was "Mount Wu Is High" in *Eighteen Military Songs of the Han*. (p.30) *Collection of Music Bureau Poems*, *juan* 16, contains the song "Mount Wu Is High": "Mount Wu is high and immense;/River Huai is deep and hard to cross./I wish to go home back east,/but why can't I?/The mountain is high and the river waters swift./I watch the distance from the riverbank/and my tears drench the front of my clothes./A sojourner far away misses his home,/but what can he do?" (p.228)

within the Pass, setting the scene for the confrontation between Xiang Yu and himself.

The "Song of Pingcheng" In the seventh year after the founding of the Western Han Dynasty (200 BCE), Emperor Gaozu personally led his army into battle and defeated Xin the King of Han. Riding on his victory, he pursued the Xiongnu, the warlike nomads in the north who had formed an alliance with Xin the King of Han, to Pingcheng, where he found himself surrounded at Mount Baideng by 320,000 elite Xiongnu troops. In the midst of this crisis, a song was heard among the Han soldiers: "How truly terrible it was at Pingcheng!/Seven days of not being able to eat/or to fire a crossbow!" Using a stratagem devised by Chen Ping (?–178 BCE), Emperor Gaozu eventually managed to escape.[82] Later, Emperor Gaozu implemented the Appeasement through Marriage Policy, and there was a temporary ceasefire between Han Dynasty China and the Xiongnu. It is hard to determine how much influence the war-weary sentiments expressed by the "Song of Pingcheng" had on this policy, but the hardships suffered during the war with the Xiongnu as expressed by this song obviously left an indelible impression on the collective memory of the people of the Western Han Dynasty.

In the third year of Emperor Hui's reign (192 BCE), Chanyu Modu (?–174 BCE) of the Xiongnu sent a rudely worded missive to Empress Dowager Lü,

[82] *History of the Former Han, juan* 84, "Biography of the Xiongnu, Part I," p.3755. Historical records are vague as to what the stratagem was and how it was carried out. According to *The Grand Scribe's Records, juan* 56, "The Hereditary House of Chancellor Chen," "Emperor Gaozu used Chen Ping's clever stratagem on the Chanyu's [the title of Xiongnu's Supreme Leader] Queen and broke out of the siege." (p.2057) *The Grand Scribe's Records, juan* 93, "Memoirs of Han Xin and Lu Wan": "The Emperor sent someone to present lavish gifts to the Queen, who urged her husband Modu: 'Even if you conquer the lands of the Han, you cannot reside in them. Let the lords of the two lands not fight each other.'" (p.2633) *The Grand Scribe's Records, juan* 110, "Memoirs of the Xiongnu": "Emperor Gaozu sent a secret emissary bearing many gifts to the Queen, who then advised Chanyu Modu: 'The rulers of both sides cannot lay siege to each other. If you conquer the lands of the Han, you can never reside there. Besides, the gods are helping the Han ruler. I hope the Chanyu would consider it with great care.' Modu had arranged to meet with Wang Huang and Zhao Li, generals of Xin the King of Han, but they did not turn up. Suspecting that they were in cahoots with the Han Dynasty, Modu listened to the Queen's advice and opened up a gap in the siege." (p.2894) It seemed that Emperor Gaozu of the Han Dynasty had sent someone to bribe the Xiongnu Queen, so that she would persuade her husband to call off the siege. However, Lü Simian believed that "this was not what actually happened"; the truth might have been quite unpalatable. Refer to Lü Simian (1983), p.64. See "The Hereditary House of Chancellor Chen" in *The Grand Scribe's Records*: "After Emperor Gaozu escaped, Chen Ping's stratagem was kept a secret. No one in the world knew what it was." (p. 2057) *History of the Former Han, juan* 94, "Biography of the Xiongnu, Part II" recorded that Yang Xiong submitted a memorial in the fourth year of the Jianping reign period of Emperor Ai of the Western Han Dynasty: "At the time [Emperor Gaozu] had many clever advisers and capable men, but even then he only escaped through a plan that no one wanted to talk about." (p.3813) It would seem that the stratagem was quite secretive.

and the incensed Empress Dowager summoned the ministers for an audience. Fan Kuai (?–189 BCE), General Superior and the brother-in-law of Empress Dowager Lü, was in favor of war, but he was immediately chastised by Leader of Court Gentlemen Ji Bu, who informed the Empress Dowager that the song sung by the troops in Pingcheng was still being sung; "the injured and traumatized are just beginning to get back on their feet, but Fan Kuai wants to agitate for war."[83] It was quite likely that public opinion influenced the Dowager Empress into eventually taking Ji Bu's advice and continuing the Appeasement through Marriage Policy. Even by the time of Emperor Wu's reign, when the Emperor and his ministers were discussing whether to wage war against the Xiongnu or make peace with them, Censor-in-Chief Han Anguo (?–127 BCE) was still revisiting the hoary chestnut: "The hunger at Pingcheng, where there was no food for seven days, is sung about by all under Heaven."[84] He recommended that the Appeasement through Marriage Policy be continued. However, times were different and the relative strengths between the two empires had changed. With Emperor Wu aggressively preparing for war, this old song could only evoke shameful memories and the desire for vengeance.

The "One Chi *of Cloth Song"* During the reign of Emperor Wen of the Western Han Dynasty, there was a popular song called the "One *Chi* of Cloth Song." According to *The Grand Scribe's Records* and *History of the Former Han*, this is the story behind the song:

> Liu Zhang, King of Huainan, was the youngest son of Emperor Gaozu. After Emperor Wen ascended to the throne, Liu Zhang, believing himself to be the favorite brother of Emperor Wen, who often turned a blind eye to his misdemeanors, became imperious and overstepped the boundaries of his rank. He killed Shen Yiji, Marquess of Biyang, without any authorization, and "plotted to become Emperor of the East."[85] In the sixth year of Emperor Wen's reign (174 BCE), Liu Zhang plotted to overthrow the Emperor but the attempt failed. By law, he should have been beheaded, but out of brotherly love and not wanting to be accused of fratricide, Emperor Wen stripped him of his kingly rank and exiled him to the Shu region. Liu Zhang died on the way to his exile after refusing food, and was buried at Yong with honors accorded to the rank of a marquess. In the eighth year of his reign, Emperor Wen felt pity for the King of Huainan and made the latter's four sons marquesses.

In the twelfth year of Emperor Wen's reign, there was a popular song among the people that went: "One *chi* of cloth could still be sewn./One *dou* of millet

83 *History of the Former Han*, *juan* 94, "Biography of the Xiongnu, Part I," p.3755.
84 *History of the Former Han*, *juan* 52, "Biography of Han Anguo," pp.2399–2400.
85 From Jia Yi, *Essay on Governing and Security*. See *History of the Former Han*, *juan* 48, "Biography of Jia Yi," p.2232.

could still be pounded./But two brothers could not co-exist with each other." When Emperor Wen heard about this song, he believed it was a song that ridiculed his inability to co-exist with his youngest brother. "When Yao and Shun exiled their family members, and when the Duke of Zhou killed [his brothers] Guan Shu and Cai Shu, all under Heaven praised them for their sagacity," the Emperor signed. "Why? Because they did not allow their personal feelings to get in the way of the greater good. Do the people actually think that I covet the King of Huainan's lands?"[86] To prove that his banishment of Liu Zhang had nothing to do with personal gain, he changed the King of Chengyang's title to King of Huainan, conferring on the new King all the lands of the former King of Huainan. Emperor Wen also gave Liu Zhang the posthumous title King Li.

The above narrative brings up several points and questions. One, what this popular song was describing was actually a common social phenomenon. It was not so much a spontaneous song that criticized current political events as a sung adage that encapsulated human wisdom. Why did Emperor Wen take it personally? Two, if the popular song was indeed a criticism of Emperor Wen for his role in Liu Zhang's death, then why was it not heard immediately after the event (the sixth year of Emperor Wen's reign)? Why did it emerge in the twelfth year of Emperor Wen's reign, when the dust had settled? Three, after Liu Zhang's death, the Kingdom of Huainan was not abolished – only the title of the King of Huainan had been left vacant. Why would Emperor Wen think that the people suspected him of coveting the King of Huainan's lands? Four, during Liu Zhang's journey to his place of exile, Yuan Ang advised Emperor Wen: "The King of Huainan has fallen to his present state because Your Majesty had always indulged him and did not appoint a strict Tutor and Chancellor of State to guide him. Besides, the King of Huainan has an unyielding temperament. Now that he is being treated so harshly, I am worried

[86] *The Grand Scribe's Records*, *juan* 118, "Memoirs of the Kings of Huainan and Hengshan," p.3080. *History of the Former Han*, *juan* 44, "Biography of King Li of Huainan," p.2144, gave a similar account, except the last line reads: "But two brothers do not co-exist with each other." It is recorded in Gao You, *Preface and Table of Content of The Great and Bright of Huainan: Collected Expositions* that: "A song of the time went: One *chi* of silk is so good. One *sheng* of millet is so full. But two brothers could not co-exist with each other." (*The Great and Bright of Huainan: Collected Expositions*, p.1) In his *Literary Talks Outside the Door*, Lu Xun cited Xun Yue's *Annals of the Former Han*: "One *chi* of cloth is so warm. One *dou* of millet is so full. But two brothers do not co-exist with each other." (*Complete Works of Lu Xun*, *juan* 6, "Miscellaneous Writings at Qiejie Pavilion," p.91) Lu Xun believed a comparison of *History of the Former Han* and *Annals of the Former Han* showed that "the latter seems to be the original version," but "Chinese men of letters tend to have the habit of changing other people's writings." In ancient times, what was spoken and what was written down were usually different. These versions probably show the gist of a vernacular song that had been rendered into a literary form. However, Lu Xun's citation is not found in *Annals of the Former Han* and his source is unknown.

that he would suddenly die from exposure to the elements in his journey. Your Majesty would then be faulted for killing your younger brother. What can we do!" Emperor Wen answered: "This is exactly what I worry about."[87] Therefore, there are scholars who speculate that *The Grand Scribe's Records* was hinting between the lines that Emperor Wen was responsible for Liu Zhang's death, and that this song was Sima Qian's subtle criticism of Emperor Wen.[88]

It might have been the awareness of these questions that enjoined Sima Guang to bring forward the "One *Chi* of Cloth Song" to the seventh year of Emperor Wen's reign in his *Comprehensive Mirror in Aid of Governance*. A reassessment of the historical event based on this time sequence may shine a clearer light on what actually happened.

In the tenth month of the sixth year of Emperor Wen's reign, Liu Zhang was stripped of his kingly rank and exiled to the Shu region. He subsequently took his own life. In the same year, Jia Yi, then Grand Tutor of the King of Changsha, believed that the rebellions of King of Jibei and then King of Huainan were grave indications that the growing strength of the various kings of the Liu clan was already posing a serious threat to imperial authority and the state. For this reason, Jia Yi submitted *Essay on Governing and Security*, which proposed "the enfeoffment of many kings to diminish the actual powers of the kings."[89] Emperor Wen agreed with Jia Yi and appointed him as Grand Tutor to one of his favorite sons, King Huai of Liang.

In the seventh year of Emperor Wen's reign, a popular song went: "One *chi* of cloth could still be sewn./One *dou* of millet could still be pounded./But two brothers could not co-exist with each other." "The Emperor heard it and fell ill."[90] The phenomenon described in the song should have been quite a common occurrence among the common folk, and the song might have been around for a long time. That Emperor Wen heard it then and took it personally might be an indication that the song resonated with his inner guilt. And so, in

87 *The Grand Scribe's Records*, *juan* 118, "Memoirs of the Kings of Huainan and Hengshan," p.3079.

88 Kushida Hisaharu (1999), p.47. If being responsible means indulging the King of Huainan, then Yuan Ang's statement was very clear. There are also those who suspect that Emperor Wen's indulgence was merely a façade. His true intention was entrapment, enticing his younger brother to transgress to the point of no return and eventual death. However, this view smacks of conspiracy theory and lacks hard evidence.

89 *Comprehensive Mirror in Aid of Governance*, *juan* 14, p.471. However, *The Grand Scribe's Records*, *juan* 84, "Memoirs of Qu Yuan and Scholar Jia" states that Jia Yi was the Grand Tutor of King of Changsha who composed *Rhapsody of the Owl* in "the year of Chanyan." (p.2497) The "year of Chanyan" refers to a Mao year, which corresponded to the sixth year of Emperor Wen's reign (the Dingmao year). More than a year later, Emperor Wen summoned him, and they had their meeting at Xuanshi Hall. Emperor Wen appointed Jia Yi as Grand Tutor of King Huai of Liang and then Jia Yi submitted the *Essay on Governing and Security*. Hence, it might have been the seventh year of Emperor Wen's reign.

90 *Comprehensive Mirror in Aid of Governance*, *juan* 14, p.480.

the summer of the eighth year of his reign, Emperor Wen made the four sons of King of Huainan marquesses.

In the eleventh year of Emperor Wen's reign, King Huai of Liang died without an heir. The Emperor followed Jia Yi's advice of reducing the powers of the various kings[91] and re-enfeoffed his third son, Liu Wu, from King of Huaiyang to King of Liang, which bordered Mount Tai in the north and Gaoyang in the west. Liu Wu was thus granted large counties including more than forty walled cities. In the following year, the Kingdom of Huainan was reinstated, and Liu Xi, King of Chengyang, was appointed King of Huainan and moved there.[92] Liu Zhang, the former King of Huainan, was posthumously conferred the title King Li of Huainan and entombed according to kingly honors. In the sixteenth year, Liu Xi, King of Huainan, was reinstated as King of Chengyang. The Kingdom of Qi was divided into six kingdoms and conferred to each of King Daohui of Qi's six sons, while the Kingdom of Huainan was divided into three and given to each of King Li of Huainan's three sons.

By taking these political steps, Emperor Wen was progressively implementing Jia Yi's proposal of "the enfeoffments of various kings to diminish the actual powers of the kings" after Liu Zhang's death. In the course of implementation, Emperor Wen played it safe and was very mindful of the reaction from the public. As much as possible, he tried to reduce the political fallout and the animosity from the kings and their kin. Therefore, whether or not the "One *Chi* of Cloth Song" was really the direct result of the Liu Zhang incident, Emperor Wen would still consider it as the people's criticism. In response, he adjusted the process and pace of reducing the kings' powers and conferred some favors to Liu Zhang's descendants without affecting his ultimate political goal. He thus neutralized the people's criticism and lessened the obstruction against reducing the powers of the kings.

"When the Capital Fancies Bouffant Hair, Hair Rises by One Chi *Elsewhere"* The Emperors and Empresses of the Western and Eastern Han dynasties often ordered the reduction of palace expenditure. "However, the extravagance continued until the state weakened and chaos ensued." More

[91] Jia Yi proposed culling lands from Huainan in favor of Huaiyang to strengthen the power of the kingdoms of Huaiyang and Liang (fiefdoms of Emperor Wen's close brother and son), so that they would curb and contain the kingdoms of Qi, Zhao, Wu, and Chu. "Those among the major kings who harbored disloyal intentions would be petrified and would not dare engage in conspiracies." (*History of the Former Han, juan* 48, "Biography of Jia Yi," p. 2261.

[92] Liu Xi was the son of Liu Zhang (not the same person as the rebellious King of Huainan). The latter was rewarded by Emperor Wen for his meritorious service in killing members of the Lü clan. Both father and son had Emperor Wen's trust.

often than not, "mere moments passed following the policy's implementation" before it became a dead letter. It was difficult to carry out the austerity measures through to the end. The reason could be that "while officials might not have carried out the orders, the capital was slow to implement them in the first place."[93] During the reign of Emperor Zhang of the Eastern Han Dynasty, Empress Dowager Ma lived a frugal life and advocated thrift. However, this rhyme was heard in the streets of Chang'an: "When the capital fancies bouffant hair,/hair rises by one *chi* elsewhere;/when the capital fancies thick eyebrows,/women elsewhere drew their eyebrows to cover half their forehead;/ when the capital fancies large sleeves,/women elsewhere made their sleeves with a whole bolt of cloth."[94] It sounded like a humorous rhyme, but it referred to an actual fact. When she was young, Empress Dowager Ma was famous for her height and beautiful hair. She wore her hair "in four big chignons, winding the remaining hair around the chignons three times. She did not paint her eyebrows but the end of her left eyebrow had a small imperfection, which she touched up in the shape of a millet."[95] Given that Empress Dowager Ma's clothes and hairstyle might have set fashion trends in the capital at the time, her frugality drive would naturally invite the people's scorn. Her older brother Ma Liao, "concerned that her great work would not be completed," advised her by telling her about the rhyme. Empress Dowager Ma eventually took her brother's advice to cut palace expenses.[96]

Making the Most of Songs and Rhymes to Manipulate the Popular Will

According to studies of public opinion, public opinion often arises from external information stimuli, such as revolutions, social changes, emergencies, and so on. Some of these emergencies are not critical in themselves, but because they involve important social issues that cause public distress, or they happen to be in conflict with beliefs held by certain groups of people, or they match their psychological expectations, these emergencies may then become information stimuli that are a fuse to something else. When this information collides with the value systems, historical memories, material interests, and psychological factors of these groups of people, a variety of discussions or emotional responses will arise, whose interactions will cause them to gradually

93 *History of the Later Han, juan* 24, "Biography of Ma Liao," p.853.

94 *Ibid.*

95 *History of the Later Han, juan* 10 *shang*, "Annals of Empresses, Part I: Annals of Empress Ma, the Empress Mingde," annotated and quoted in Li Xian, *Eastern Library's Records of Han*, p.408.

96 *History of the Later Han, juan* 24, "Biography of Ma Liao," p.853.

converge into popular will and public opinion. During this process, the leaders of these groups of people play quite an important role in shaping and directing public opinion.[97] As seen in the history of the early imperial period, not only did leaders passively defer to the popular will as revealed by popular songs and rhymes, at times they also exploited methods such as information stimuli to attempt to steer the direction of public opinion.

It is recorded in the Basic Annals of Xiang Yu and Emperor Gao in *The Grand Scribe's Records* that in the fifth year of the King of Han (202 BCE), the Chu army was surrounded at Gaixia with several rings of Han troops and the various lords allied with Han. After dark, Chu troops heard the Han army on all four sides singing songs that were popular in the Chu regions. The commanders and soldiers of the Chu army "thought Han had taken all the Chu territories" and there was great disquiet among the Chu troops. Xiang Yu was alarmed and said, "Has Han already secured all regions of Chu? Why is it that there are so many men of Chu out there?" He could not sleep and drank in his tent. With tears in his eyes, he sang: "My strength uplifted a mountain,/my vigor shadowed the world./But the times do no favor me,/and Piebald cannot gallop fast enough./Piebald cannot gallop fast enough,/and what can I do about it?/Oh Yu, oh Yu!/What can I do about you?" The Beautiful Lady Yu, who kept him company, sang with him.[98] "His attendants all wept; no one could lift up his head." Xiang Yu then mounted his horse and, accompanied by some 800 horsemen, broke out of the siege under the cover of night. He finally cut his own throat and died at Wu River, after which the Chu army fell to pieces.

Both Liu Bang and Xiang Yu were from Chu, and there were many Chu natives in the Han army. That there were people in the Han army who could sing Chu songs should come as no surprise for the Chu army.[99] A careful reading of the historical accounts in *The Grand Scribe's Records* and *History of the Former Han* reveals that the traumatizing effects of "Chu songs on all four sides" on Xiang Yu and the Chu troops might have been due to the following reasons.

[97] Chen Lidan (1999), pp.51–57.

[98] Sima Qian's account of the siege at Gaixia was based on Lu Jia's *Spring and Autumn Annals of the Chu and Han*, a book that had been lost by the time of the Song periods. In Zhang Shoujie's *Standard Interpretations*, he quoted Beautiful Lady Yu's sung response from *Spring and Autumn Annals of the Chu and Han*: "The Han troops have occupied the lands, and Chu songs are sung on all four sides. The Great King's will is spent, how could your lady live on?" (*The Grand Scribe's Records, juan* 7, "Basic Annals of Xiang Yu," p.334) English translations based on Nienhauser, vol. 1 (1994), p.205.

[99] Liu Bang was from Chu and the "Song of Great Wind" he composed was in Chu style. His favorite consort, Lady Qi, was also a Chu native. After he became Emperor Gaozu of the Western Han Dynasty, Liu Bang ordered Lady Qi to choreograph a Chu dance, while he composed a Chu song. See *The Grand Scribe's Records, juan* 55, "The Hereditary House of Marquess of Liu," p.2047.

First, "why is it that there are so many men of Chu out there?" The thunderous sounds of loud singing on all four sides meant that the sheer number of people who could sing Chu songs far exceeded the psychological expectations of Xiang Yu and the Chu troops. Naturally, it had a devastating psychological impact on them.

Second, with so many Chu natives in the Han army, did it imply that Liu Bang and his allies had gained control of the vast territory of Chu, and even Western Chu, which was Xiang Yu's base? Since the time of the Warring States Period, the territory of Chu had covered an extensive area, with a complex array of ethnic groups and languages. Chu songs would have included the many dialects and melodies of different regions.[100] Common sense tells us that the singing of Chu songs on all four sides was probably not a choral performance under a single conductor. The Chu army probably heard snatches of different regional songs sung all around them. It was for this reason that Xiang Yu and the Chu troops shared a common anxiety: "Has Han already secured all regions of Chu?" The Chu troops were so demoralized that even their heroic commander whose "strength uplifted a mountain" and "vigor shadowed the world" chose to abandon his command and break out of the siege with a small number of men.

This was an exciting example of psychological warfare. Psychological warfare can only be employed as a supplement to weapons to weaken the enemy's will to resist; it cannot replace military might. Chu and Han had been in confrontation for five years and by the time of the siege at Gaixia, the Han army had turned around from a position of weakness to a position of strength. The Chu army, on the other hand, "had tired soldiers and exhausted its food supply." That the Han army, in alliance with Han Xin, Peng Yue, and Ying Bu, had surrounded the Chu army with their superior forces was the main reason for their victory. However, the skills of Liu Bang and his strategists in manipulating and channeling popular songs and opinions broke the enemy's morale, lowered the cost of victory, and reduced the number of casualties on their side. Were the "Chu Songs" a psychological war deliberately planned and waged by Liu Bang and his strategists? Historical records did not explicitly say so and some scholars may not think so. However, when people read this passage in Sima Qian's "Basic Annals of Xiang Yu," be they ancient men or contemporary individuals, how many would not smile and even slap their

[100] *The Grand Scribe's Records: Collected Explications*, citing Ying Shao and Yan Shigu, averred that the Chu song that the Han troops were singing was the "Rooster Crowing Song." (*The Grand Scribe's Records*, *juan* 7, "Basic Annals of Xiang Yu," p.333) There are various theories as to which region the song originated from. Was the "Rooster Crowing Song" the only song that was sung at the time? The records do not say.

thighs, and consider this a quintessential example of psychological warfare that employed public opinion? If we insist on interpreting this incident as unplanned and fortuitous, then we could only say that it was God's master stroke of genius. Xiang Yu's lamentation on the banks of River Wu that "it is Heaven that destroys me, not any fault of mine in battle" would then be true.

Public opinion may not be a clear-headed and highly uniformed consciousness. At times, it is a fuzzy blob of social opinions or points of view that is full of contradictions and quick to change.[101] Public opinion may not be founded on real information or truth. It comes from the head, the heart, feelings, emotions, and it often contains a mixture of rational and irrational elements.[102] In certain specific times and spaces, characterized by higher population densities and rates of interaction, more openness of space, and more power to exert influence within that space, a public opinion space may be formed. With innumerable personal opinions at work within that "space," and after multiple interactions, coordination, synthesis, and discarding, public opinion would be formed at a quicker pace than in ordinary environments, with a greater propensity for quick dissemination.[103] Such a public opinion space appeared in the encampment of the Chu troops on a sleepless night at Gaixia. The snatches of popular songs from home acquired a symbolic imagery like that of pictures, music, poetry, and so on that magically conjured up images in their memories and intensified their collective anxiety. The final result was the collective view that they had no hope of winning and resistance was futile.[104]

Another method of conducting public opinion wars in the early imperial period was to cherry-pick popular rhymes to create an illusion of or superficial public opinion that was detrimental to one's political foes. Tian Fen had become an enemy of Dou Ying and Guan Fu. Now, Guan Fu was a man of heroic deeds, whose friends were men of great valor and cunning. His family's wealth amounted to tens of millions, and his house hosted almost a hundred retainers a day. He owned many ponds and much farmland, and members of his clan and his retainers tyrannized Yingchuan. A popular local song went: "When the waters of the Ying River are clear,/the Guan clan is at peace;/when the waters of the Ying River are murky,/the Guan clan will be exterminated."[105] Tian Fen picked this song as proof to support his indictment against Guan Fu, accusing him of "consorting with evil and cunning men, and oppressing commoners. With his millions in wealth, he tyrannizes the whole of Yingchuan, demeans members of the imperial clan, and torments his own

101 Wang Xiong (2002), p.8. 102 Chen Lidan (1999), p.11. 103 *Ibid.*, p.48.
104 See Lippmann (1922), p.163.
105 *The Grand Scribe's Records*, *juan* 107, "Memoirs of the Marquesses of Wei Qi and Wu'an," p.2847.

flesh and blood."[106] The fact is, as an affinal relative of the Emperor, Tian Fen had been appointed Grand Commandant and then Chancellor. According to *The Grand Scribe's Records*, "the house that he built surpassed all others. His farmlands and orchards were most fecund, and the many people he sent to various commanderies and counties for purchases thronged the roads. A bell and drum were installed at the front of his hall, and a flag hoisted on a curved pole. Beautiful women in the inner sanctum of his house numbered in the hundreds. The gold, jewels, dogs, horses, and baubles given to him by various lords were so numerous that they could not be counted."[107] His arrogance, extravagance, and tyranny over the common folks were as appalling as Guan Fu's, if not more so. Surely, there would have been talk circulating that was damaging to him. Tian Fen was trusted by Emperor Wu of the Western Han Dynasty and protected by Empress Dowager Wang, however, and "transferred the Emperor's powers into his own hands." He threw Guan Fu into prison and hunted down members of the Guan clan. By clamping down on dissent, he made sure that public opinion against himself could not reach the throne. Guan Fu and his family members were eventually executed in the marketplace.

The will of the people can be quelled with power and it can also be exploited by those who wish to do so, but it can never be suppressed for long, nor can it be permanently misled. Justice, after all, resides in the people's hearts. Going by the way the narrative was presented in "Memoirs of the Marquesses of Weiqi and Wu'an" in *The Grand Scribe's Records*, while Sima Qian criticized Guan Fu for "lacking in learning and humility," and not being popular with the people of Yingchuan, he had greater scorn for Tian Fen, censuring him for "engaging in political trickery on account of his exalted status, and framed two upright men for his resentment over a cup of wine. How tragic! By displacing his anger on others, he had abbreviated his life!"[108] Whenever Tian Fen is mentioned in *The Grand Scribe's Records*, the tone is often sarcastic. Although Sima Qian did not criticize Emperor Wu and Empress Dowager Wang, readers of a later age would have a tacit understanding of the unspoken reproach in these passages.

To make up popular rhymes and pass them off as public opinion, and "maximize the prestige elements in [one's] message as well as reduce the likelihood that competing symbols will be perceived by [one's] audience"[109] were also ploys taken by certain Han-era politicians to manipulate public opinion. In the spring of the fourth year of the Yuanshi reign period of Emperor Ping of the Western Han Dynasty, Wang Mang sent eight special emissaries, including Director of Uprightness under Grand Minister over the Masses Chen Chong, Grand Coachman Wang Yun, Messengers Clad in

[106] *Ibid.*, p.2851. [107] *Ibid.*, p.2844. [108] *Ibid.*, p.2856. [109] Truman (1981), p.242.

Embroidered Garments Qiao Xuan and Ban Zhi, and others, "to travel across the empire separately, to examine and observe the people's customs." Besides "investigating the people's customs, and propagating the imperial virtue and culture," the eight special emissaries also bore the important responsibilities of propagating Wang Mang's merits and auspicious portents auguring his mandate to rule ("announcing the court's meritorious policies"), suppressing dissident voices ("killing the evil and rewarding the good"), and unifying public opinion (by collecting laudatory popular songs and rhymes).[110] Qiao Xuan, one of the emissaries, refused to go along with Wang Mang. He "discarded his emissary's carriage, changed his name, and secretly returned home to hide himself from the world."[111] Another emissary Ban Zhi, who did not wish to "extol auspicious auguries and songs of praise,"[112] resigned from his official post to save himself from peril. The following year, when Wang Mang appointed himself Regent, he did not mention anything about the noncompliance of certain emissaries. Instead, he declared outright that all eight special emissaries had returned to court "and had said that the customs of the empire have been unified." The emissaries returned to court had falsely invented accompanied and unaccompanied songs and rhymes from the commanderies and kingdoms to praise Wang Mang's achievements and virtuous conduct, totaling "30,000 words."[113] It is interesting that these officially fabricated songs and rhymes were obviously not accepted or disseminated by the people. None of these songs and rhymes has survived.

The Political Influence and Limitations of Popular Songs and Rhymes

Chinese scholars of public opinion give multiple definitions of what public opinion is, the more popular of which is "the collective name for broadly similar opinions, emotions, and behavioral tendencies held by majority members of a society toward public affairs or phenomena that concern them."[114] As for the people's will, it is defined as "the collective name for the people's consciousness, motivations, and aspirations; it is the force amassed by the common pursuit of the whole population, which reflects the overall will of the whole society."[115] A common scholarly view of popular songs and rhymes of the early imperial period was that they were a form of public opinion expressed in a special way within an authoritarian political framework. They contained "witty comments that praised or criticized the

[110] *History of the Former Han, juan* 12, "Annals of Emperor Ping," pp.357, 359; *History of the Later Han, juan* 81, "Biographies of Loners: Biography of Qiao Xuan," p.2667.
[111] *History of the Later Han, juan* 81, "Biographies of Loners: Biography of Qiao Xuan," p.2667.
[112] *History of the Former Han, juan* 100, "Afterword and Family History, Part I," p.4204.
[113] *History of the Former Han, juan* 99 *shang*, "Biography of Wang Mang, Part I," p.4076.
[114] Yu Guoming (2001), p.9. [115] Wang Xiong (2002), p.4.

politics of the time,"[116] often reflecting unofficial and non-mainstream voices. Can we then say that popular songs and rhymes circulated among the people were the collective expression of the consciousness, motivations, and aspirations of the majority of the people, representing their voice?

Popular songs and rhymes that were handed down to subsequent periods had undergone selection, editing, and enhancement by ancient historians; it is therefore inevitable that they would be informed by the historical views, knowledge, and bias of these historians. Still, songs and rhymes that had been selected probably had made some social and political impact in their time. Of course, we cannot determine whether they represented the will of the majority by using quantitative methods such as opinion polls or the ballot box.[117] Having said that, analyses of popular songs and rhymes of the early imperial period and their historical contexts using the actual texts yield the following points:

First, a small number of songs and rhymes – for example, the "Song of Pingcheng" during the reign of Western Han Dynasty's Emperor Gaozu, the "One *Chi* of Cloth Song" during the reign of Emperor Wen, and the "Wheat Is Blue Song" during the reign of Eastern Han Dynasty's Emperor Huan – might have attracted widespread interest because they commented on sensitive social issues, or caused popular concern and even resonated with the people because they commented on or ridiculed significant political incidents and important people. The phrase "all under heaven sing the song(s)" often appears in historical records, indicating that the geographic spread of these songs and rhymes might have been quite extensive and the number of people who agreed with their observations quite large. Having said that, the majority of songs and rhymes were mainly comments on local issues and local personalities (including local government officials). The interested parties and scope of dissemination were often limited to specific locales, as suggested by phrases such as "the song is sung in Chang'an," "children at the capital sing it," "the song is sung in the alleys and on the roads," "the song is sung in the neighborhoods,"

116 Lin Jianming et al. (1985), p.368. The writers of this book believed that references in classical texts, such as "all under heaven sing about it," "children sing about it," "songs were composed by the people," "songs about it were sung in Chang'an," "the people sing about it," "those on the alleys and roads sing about it," "neighborhoods sing about it," "songs about it were sung in Liangzhou," etc., represented the voice of the people. Among extant *Yuefu* poems of the Han periods, there are many "popular songs and rhymes of the streets and lanes," which are also evidence of the people composing songs.

117 Even in modern democratic systems of government, it is technically very difficult to determine whether the majority of society possess more or less identical opinions, emotions, and behavioral tendencies on a particular matter or phenomenon through questionnaire design and interpretation of election results or opinion polls. There are also multiple human factors that interfere and limit these processes. See Glynn (1999), p.19.

"the song is sung in Liangzhou," "it is being spoken of in Nanyang," and "it is being sung about in the two Commanderies of Ru'nan and Nanyang."

There were also some songs and rhymes with narrower areas of concern. For instance, issues and gossip that revolved around individuals might become a shared opinion within a small circle, but they were not necessarily public opinion on a larger scale.[118] During the Yongping reign period of Emperor Ming of the Eastern Han Dynasty, there was an eminent Confucian scholar and Grand Master of Ceremonies, Zhou Ze, who had such lofty standards of self-discipline that it bordered on the ridiculous. One time, he fell ill and stayed in the Palace of Abstinence. His wife, concerned about his illness at his age, surreptitiously went to inquire about her husband's condition. Zhou Ze was livid that his wife had breached the rules of abstinence. He had her arrested and thrown into prison as an act of penitence. The people of their time sang a song about his unreasonable behavior: "To be born at the wrong time/and be the wife of the Grand Master of Ceremonies./Out of 360 days in a year,/359 days are spent in abstinence."[119] It was likely that songs of this nature would only be disseminated among people who knew about Zhou Ze and his family.

Traveling by road was an arduous undertaking in ancient times. Those who had to traverse the precipitous terrains of the northwest and southwest dreaded these regions. "The Long Mountains stretch for 180 *li* from east to west. When one reaches the peak and looks east toward the Qinchuan region, which extends for 400 to 500 *li*, it disappears into the horizon. When people from east of the mountains climb up the peak and see all that is below them, none would be spared the sadness that rise up within. It is for reason that this song is written: 'From its source in the Long Mountains,/water flows down in four streams./Remember that I am traveling,/drifting in the wilderness./From a height I look afar,/my tears fall in two streams.'"[120] Although the lyrics of this song had obviously undergone embellishment, after more than 2,000 years, modern-day readers can still feel awe and helplessness in the face of such lofty majesty . At that time, however, unless one had a first-hand experience on site, how many people could actually be genuinely touched by the song?

"The songs in the streets and alleys described things that did not go beyond a village or a neighborhood. The naiveté of the words, the veracity of the things described, and the brevity of the songs: these were the primary sources for local chronicles."[121] The real and credible voices of the people amassed

118 Chen Lidan (1999), p.28.

119 *History of the Later Han, juan* 79, "Biographies of Confucian Scholars, Part II: Biography of Zhou Ze," p.2579.

120 *History of the Later Han, zhi* 23, "Treatise on Commanderies and Kingdoms, Part V," p.3518. Annotation by Li Xian, citing Guo Zhongchan's *Records of Qinzhou.*

121 Shen Changzhi, cited in Xu Hualong (1990), p.6.

within a small range could at times be considered public opinion despite their narrow themes and limited propagation.

In the final years of the Eastern Han Dynasty, there were more than 30,000 Academy Students in the capital. Among them were many excitable men who were banished from government for their involvement in the struggle between political cliques, but there were also a number of elderly students steeped in the Classics, who remained in the capital in the futile hope that they would gain some kind of employment in the government. In the first year of the Chuping reign period of Emperor Xian (190), more than forty scholars took an examination. Those who scored top grades were conferred the post of Gentlemen-of-the-Palace, and those who obtained middling grades were given the post of Member of the Suite of the Heir-Apparent. Those who got bottom grades would have been dismissed, but the Emperor issued a decree: "Confucius lamented about 'not speaking of what one has learned.' If one does not speak of what one has learned, the knowledge acquired would be forgotten as days go by. At present, the elderly scholars over sixty years of age left their homes to earn their livelihoods and cannot engage in any specific occupations. They entered schools as children with their first topknots, yet return home empty handed and grey haired. They languish in villages and fields for protracted periods of time and forever relinquish any hopes of glory and honor. We are filled with pity for them. Those who have been dismissed based on their examination grades shall be accepted as Members of the Suite of the Heir-Apparent." In other words, scholars over sixty years old who got bottom grades in the examination were still appointed as Members of the Suite of the Heir-Apparent. Naturally, they were so grateful that they composed a rhyme, which was disseminated: "My hair was a pristine white;/I didn't have enough to eat./I packed my clothes/to go back home./But my Sage-Lord pitied me/and I learned of my appointment as Gentleman./I discarded my commoner's clothes/and put on silk."[122] Although the number of failed scholars given government appointments was small, the court's caring policy gave great consolation to the scholars and was popular within a subscribed circle of opinion.

In his study of the relationship between political interests and public opinion in the United States, Truman argues that it is incorrect to say public opinion is the opinion of the majority. For one thing, the minority are also a part of the public; for another, it is almost impossible for the "public" in the United States to include all adults. There is no opinion of the majority.[123] In theory, we can assume that a country or society has an abstract, sustainable, and stable

[122] *History of the Later Han*, *juan* 9, "Annals of Emperor Xian," and Li Xian's annotation, which cited Liu Ai's *Annals of Emperor Xian*, p.374.

[123] Truman (1981), pp. 219–220.

fundamental interest, as well as a corresponding "people's will." In reality, as long as actual issues, advantages, interests, or policies are involved, no abstract, sustainable, stable majority or public, whose interests and opinions are always in synchrony, will exist in any country or society. The people's will and public opinion will change in tandem with time, space, context, political and social conditions, and so on. The aforementioned song composed by the coach drivers of the State of Zheng in response to Zi Chan's land policies is an example. These opinion makers would have been people with land and slaves, whose interests were at stake. Their voices could not represent the "majority" of the State of Zheng at the time. In the process of formulating policy and governing, if there is overemphasis on public opinion as collective will, where only similar or shared opinion of the majority is considered public opinion, then there is the possibility of neglecting the reasonable demands of a segment of the population and ignoring real and credible opinions of the people. Of course, we should not simplistically magnify popular voices that center on a specific issue within a specific section of people as "voices of the majority."

Second, while the popular songs and rhymes of the early imperial period might have been a form of "non-official" and "non-mainstream" discourse, they did not necessarily reflect the voices of ordinary people and commoners. The civil service recruitment system of the Han periods provided the intelligentsia, especially Confucian scholars, with the opportunity to get involved in politics as a group. In the recruitment process, focus was given to the candidates' reputations, which also expanded the influence of the opinions of the intellectuals.[124] It was very popular among the learned elites of the two Han dynasties (especially the Eastern Han Dynasty) to compose songs and rhymes to praise one another and disseminate their opinions of their peers.[125] These songs were mostly circulated among the middle and upper classes such as government officials and the literati, and were very different from demotic popular songs and rhymes in language, styles, and themes.

As the rulers of the two Han dynasties were partial to Confucianism, the commendations the intellectual elites gave one another were focused on achievements in classical learning. Examples in the Western Han Dynasty included the following: "The five deer[126] are magnificent,/but Zhu Yun will break their antlers";[127] "Do not teach *Book of Odes* in Kuang Ding's[128] presence;/when he teaches *Odes*,/his expositions pleases many";[129] and

[124] Yan Buke (1997), p.327. [125] Bai Shouyi (1995), pp.423, 425.
[126] Referring to Wulu Chongzong, whose surname "Wulu" is literally "five deer."
[127] *History of the Former Han*, *juan* 67, "Biography of Zhu Yun," p.2913.
[128] Referring to Kuang Heng.
[129] *History of the Former Han*, *juan* 81, "Biography of Kuang Heng," p.3331.

"To know *The Analects*,/read Zhang's[130] writings."[131] Examples in the Eastern Han Dynasty included the folloiwng: "The one who asks incessantly is Jia the Long Head";[132] "The ethical and refined is Feng Zhongwen";[133] "The Confucius at the west of the Pass is Yang Boqi";[134] "Knowing the Five Classics inside out – Zhou Xuanguang";[135] "Expounding on the classics volubly – Yang Zixing";[136] "Explaining the classics without end – Palace Attendant Dai";[137] "No parallel in the Five Classics – Xu Shuzhong";[138] "Myriad theories of the Five Classics – Jing Dachun";[139] and many other rhymes.

The annual assessment of officials and bureaucrats in the two Han dynasties did not only list their ranking and placement; comments were also often appended to their names. Having said that, very few were actually comments on exemplary achievements and morals or dire incompetence. Most of them gradually became clichés that were simplified into four-character or eight-character remarks.[140] Among the Eastern Han literati, it was popular to place four-character phrases before their names in their rhyming commendations and assessments of one another. They were obviously influenced by the practice in the bureaucratic assessment, with which they were so familiar. These seven-character rhymes (the three-character personal names added to the four-character phrases) had narrow themes and formulaic and conceptual language. While they did not easily resonate with the common people, they had an effect of disseminating popular opinions among the ruling and intellectual class.

Third, the political effect of public opinion is seldom linked to the size of the public.[141] The impact of public opinion on politics is not necessarily directly proportionate to the size of the interest groups and stakeholders it represents. A smaller number of people can often lead public opinion to a certain extent, and gain society's interest and acceptance, if they have a clear goal, resolute course of action, accurate focus, and synchronized coordination, and if they

130 Referring to Zhang Yu.

131 *History of the Former Han*, *juan* 81, "Biography of Zhang Yu," p.3352.

132 Referring to Jia Kui. *History of the Later Han*, *juan* 36, "Biography of Jia Kui," p.1235.

133 Referring to Feng Bao. *History of the Later Han*, *juan* 28, "Biography of Feng Bao," p.1004.

134 Referring to Yang Zhen. *History of the Later Han*, *juan* 54, "Biography of Yang Zhen," p.1759.

135 Referring to Zhou Ju. *History of the Later Han*, *juan* 61, "Biography of Zhou Ju," p.2023.

136 Referring to Yang Zheng. *History of the Later Han*, *juan* 79 *shang*, "Biographies of Confucian Scholars, Part I: Biography of Yang Zhen," pp.2551–2552.

137 Referring to Dai Ping. *History of the Later Han*, *juan* 79 *shang*, "Biographies of Confucian Scholars, Part I: Biography of Dai Ping," pp.2554.

138 Referring to Xu Shen. *History of the Later Han*, *juan* 79 *xia*, "Biographies of Confucian Scholars, Part II: Biography of Xu Shen," pp.2588.

139 Referring to Jing Dan. *History of the Later Han*, *juan* 83, "Biographies of Hermits: Biography of Jing Dan," p.2764.

140 Liu Pak-yuen (2003), pp.150–153.

141 Truman (1981), p.220.

can successfully articulate the legitimacy of their issue and disseminate their arguments in a convincing manner. During the reigns of Emperors Huan and Ling of the Eastern Han Dynasty, the political conflicts between the bureaucrats, literati, and eunuchs, as well as their supporters and followers, were especially intense. In almost twenty years of successive clashes, the bureaucrats and literati were always weaker in terms of power and numbers. Twice, their clique suffered banishment, with many of their ranks falling victim to the persecution. At the same time, however, they set the agenda for the conflicts, gained widespread sympathy, and expanded the impact of public opinion.[142] Their successful strategy of leading public opinion included advocating "just comment" (*qingyi*), with the result that "all below the Excellencies and Ministers were afraid of their censure, and all came to their gates,"[143] and using songs and rhymes to disseminate their values and political ideologies.

After Liang Ji murdered Emperor Zhi using poison, he backed Liu Zhi, Marquess of Liwu and his younger sister's husband, as the claimant of the throne. Li Gu, Du Qiao (?–147), and others, who were in opposition to Liang Ji, supported Liu Suan (?–147), King of Qinghe. Although he was framed and put to death, Li Gu was hailed as the spiritual leader by the intelligentsia such as the bureaucrats and literati. After Liu Zhi (Emperor Huan of the Eastern Han Dynasty) ascended the throne, he immediately promoted his teacher Zhou Fu, a native of Ganling, as Master of Writing. Fang Zhi, who was from the same commandery (Qinghe) as Zhou Fu, was then Governor of He'nan. He was close to Li Gu, Du Qiao, etc., and enjoyed a good reputation. A rhyme mocking Zhou Fu began to emerge from Qinghe Commandery: "Fang Bowu (Fang Zhi) sets the standard for the empire;/Zhou Zhongjin (Zhou Fu) receives his official seal because he was the teacher."[144] Lü Simian averred: "This was done by officious paid retainers, and had nothing to do with the whole situation."[145] Placed within the political context of the time, however, the rhyme, which mocked Zhou Fu on the surface, was actually critical of Zhou Fu's backers Emperor Huan and Liang Ji. The rhyme praised Fang Zhi in name, but the praise was also extended to Li Gu, Du Qiao, Chen Fan, and so on, who were on the same side as Fang Zhi politically. The event that triggered this rhyme was trivial, and Fang Zhi, Zhou Fu, and their paid retainers were not major players in the conflicts between the cliques. But as one side highlighted the values and morality of a member of its clique, the legitimacy

142 That readers have gotten this impression from historical texts is of course due to the fact that historical narratives and interpretations had always been in the hands of intellectuals such as these bureaucrats and literati. Still, a careful reading of these historical narratives reveals that the bureaucrats and literati did have the upper hand in public opinion during this period of fierce political struggle.

143 *History of the Later Han*, *juan* 67, "Biographies of Partisan Prohibitions," p.2186.

144 *Ibid.* 145 Lü Simian (1983), p.325.

of the issue was established, which influenced the direction of subsequent public opinion. When *History of the Later Han* described this rhyme in the very beginning of "Biographies of Partisan Prohibitions," it was not without reason that the compiler wrote: "The issue of cliques thus began."[146]

In the old recruiting system of the Chamberlain for Attendants nominating Cultivated Talents, "sons of powerful and wealthy families received nominations mostly through connections, while poor virtuous men were left out because of their poverty." Such a system, in which the upright were denied the opportunity for advancement, was roundly criticized by the literati. After Emperor Huan had Liang Ji killed, he appointed Chen Fan as Chamberlain for Attendants. Working together with General of the Gentlemen-of-the-Household for All Purposes Huang Wan, Chen Fan proposed the reform of the nomination system, based on the popular rhyme circulating in the imperial capital that "wanting to recruit the incompetent – go to Chamberlain for Attendants [nominating] Cultivated Talents," and took the opportunity to promote large numbers of "gentlemen with ambition."[147] Famous members of political cliques Fan Pang and Cen Zhi gained the trust of Zong Zi, Grand Administrator of Ru'nan, and Cheng Jin, Grand Administrator of Nanyang, respectively, and were appointed to their Bureaus of Merit, where they ran the day-to-day affairs of the commanderies. In the two commanderies, this rhyme was sung: "The actual Grand Administrator of Ru'nan is Fan Mengbo [referring to Fan Pang];/Zong Zi, the native of Nanyang, just signs his name./ The actual Grand Administrator of Nanyang is Cen Gongxiao [referring to Cen Zhi];/Cheng Jin, the native of Hongnong, just practices throat singing," which highlighted the political clique members' talent, virtue, and popularity, as well as boosted the morale of likeminded peers. When Academy Students sang: "Li Yuanli [Li Ying] is the model for all in the empire,/Chen Zhongju [Chen Fan] is not afraid of the powerful,/and Wang Shumao [Wang Chang] is the finest in the land,"[148] not only were they clearly stating their support for the leadership of senior officials Li Ying, Chen Fan, and Wang Chang in the fight against the eunuchs by consolidating their alliance and coordinating their strength, they were also emphasizing their moral and political superiority. According to Lin Yutang, the Eastern Han's Academy Students Movement produced extraordinary stories of heroism, especially in the effective expression of people's opinions.[149] Making judicious use of songs and rhymes was an important strategy of the clique members in creating heroes and guiding people's opinions.

146 *History of the Later Han, juan* 67, "Biographies of Partisan Prohibitions," p.2186.
147 *History of the Later Han, juan* 61, "Biography of Sun Wan," p.2040.
148 *History of the Later Han, juan* 67, "Biographies of Partisan Prohibitions," p.2186.
149 Lin Yutang (1936), p.28.

Public Opinion among Commoners and the Supervision of Public Opinion in the Western and Eastern Han

Popular songs and rhymes performed the role of unofficial public opinion in social and political life in the early imperial period, a role that was recognized and respected to a certain extent by the authorities. They were co-opted by the central government to monitor local administrations.

The Supervision Mechanism Employed by the Central Government to Monitor Local Administrations during the Han Periods

The Western and Eastern Han dynasties were the periods when dynastic despotism was developed and consolidated in China. They were also the periods when the system used by the centralized government to oversee local administration was cemented. The bedrock of local administration in the early imperial period was the commandery–county system, with a strong focus on the commandery system. "The Commandery Administrator ruled the commandery, with comprehensive civil, judicial, fiscal, and military authority. He was in essence a typical head-of-state-like local governor, and the control he exercised over his functionaries and subordinate counties was a clear indication of the absoluteness of his powers."[150] Power has the quality of infinite expansion, and power that is not restrained or supervised will be abused. The abuse of power naturally results in political venality, depletion of political legitimacy, and wastage of social resources.[151] For this reason, the central governments of the Western and Eastern Han dynasties put quite a lot of work into monitoring and controlling the powers of local governments. Apart from setting the criteria for manpower selection and appointment, imposing ethical constraints in the form of the moral effects of their administrations, and regulatory and legal supervision, the central government also designed a control mechanism that featured multichannel and multilevel administrative assessments and oversight.

First, the central government's vertical assessments of officials and bureaucrats in the commanderies and kingdoms were conducted by the Office of the Chancellor (or Grand Minister over the Masses) during the Western Han Dynasty and the Three Excellencies during the Eastern Han Dynasty – the Grand Commandant oversaw military matters, the Minister over the Masses oversaw civil administration, and the Minister of Works oversaw works. The main task fell to the office of the Minister over the Masses. (However, actual power gradually shifted to the Imperial Secretariat.) Based on the account

[150] Yen Keng-Wang (1990), p.3. [151] Ye Changlin and Li Ruihua (2006), p.15.

books submitted by the commanderies and kingdoms, there would be a minor audit every year and a major one once every three years[152] to evaluate the work performance and gauge the achievements of the administrators of the commanderies and kingdoms, as well as their officials, in their administrative, legal, financial, and defense duties.

Second, in his supervision of the local administration, the Chancellor of the Western Han Dynasty, as the direct superior of the Administrators and Chancellors of State of the kingdoms and commanderies, did not limit himself to a passive auditor's role. Sometimes, he would intervene in the local administration and monitor local officials by dispatching Divisional Heads of the Bureau of the East to check on specific matters,[153] or "send people to inspect the various regions"[154] at irregular intervals. In the fifth year of the Yuanshou reign period (118 BCE) of the Western Han Dynasty's Emperor Wu, the position of Director of Uprightness was created in the Chancellery not only to specifically monitor senior officials in the central government, but also to "help in monitoring the affairs of the various regions." "The Director of Uprightness could investigate the veracity of the reports made by the regions and commanderies."[155] It is recorded in the "Biography of Bao Xuan" of *History of the Former Han* that just over a year after Bao Xuan was transferred to and appointed Governor of Yuzhou Region, the Director of Uprightness of the Chancellery Guo Qin reported that Bao Xuan's administration was cumbersome and harsh. He heard that Bao Xuan appointed commandery functionaries and tried cases, which should have been the Commandery

152 Yen Keng-Wang (1990), p.259.

153 Yen Keng-Wang (1990), p.271. *Comprehensive Canon, juan* 32: "In the thirteenth year of Emperor Wen's reign [169 BCE], the Censors breached the law and failed in their duties. For this reason, the Chancellor sent his Divisional Heads to monitor and investigate the Censors." (p.382) *History of the Former Han, juan* 29, "Treatise on Rivers and Canals": "In that year, the river waters in Bohai, Qinghe, and Xindu overflowed their banks and inundated thirty-one counties and towns, destroying over 40,000 government buildings and private residences. Chief Commandant of the River Banks Xu Shang and the Chancellor's Divisional Head Sun Jin were sent to gauge the situation together and devise solutions." (p.1690) *History of the Former Han, juan* 77, "Biography of Sun Bao": "At that time, the Emperor's [Emperor Cheng] maternal uncle the Marquess of Hongyang [Wang] Li sent his messenger to seize and cultivate several hundred *qing* of land with the help of Li Shang, Grand Administrator of the Nan Commandery. Many of these lands were hill slopes and bodies of water belonging to the Privy Treasurer, which had been leased by farmers and farmed on. Wang Li memorialized the throne proposing that he would sell the lands to the state, and the Emperor ordered the commandery government to compensate Wang Li according to the normal land price, which came up to more than 100 million in cash. When [the Director of Uprightness of the Chancellery Sun] Bao heard about this, he sent a Divisional Head of the Chancellor to investigate. The Divisional Head exposed their deceit and Sun Bao indicted Wang Li and Li Shang, accusing them of deceiving the Emperor, and being cunning and dishonest." (pp.3258–3259)

154 *History of the Later Han, juan* 28, "Treatise on Officials, Part V," p.3617.

155 *History of the Later Han, juan* 24, "Biography of Ma Yan"; and Li Xian's annotation of *Sequel to the History of the Former Han*, pp.860–861.

Administrator's responsibility. It meant that Bao Xuan's inspection went beyond what was permitted by imperial order. When he made his rounds of inspection, his carriage did not adhere to the proper protocol. He rode on a single horse and spent nights in rural government buildings, which caused many to criticize him. For this reason, Bao Xuan was relieved of his duties.[156] When Emperor Ai showered favors on Dong Xian, Bao Xuan advised the Emperor in a memorial, saying, "when Gong Sheng was Director of Uprightness, all the commanderies and kingdoms were serious about nominating people into government. The Three Metropolitan Areas did not dare to resort to any trickery when they appointed and transferred officials."[157] Chen Zun was the Grand Administrator of He'nan and his younger brother Chen Ji the Governor of Jingzhou Region. "On their way to their posts, they passed by the house of a rich man in Chang'an, surnamed Zuo, who was an in-law of the late King of Huaiyang. The brothers drank and made merry at his house." When Director of Uprightness Chen Chong heard about this, he reported the Chen brothers, accusing them of "not conducting themselves properly or with caution" and "disrupted the proper separation of the sexes." The brothers were relieved of their positions.[158] It is obvious that apart from supervising the Three Metropolitan Areas of the imperial capital, the Director of Uprightness of the Chancellor's Office also oversaw the regions and commanderies.

During the reign of Emperor Wu, due to the erratic dispatches of Censors and Divisional Heads (from different agencies), the powers were unfocused and the scope of supervision undefined, which resulted in unexceptional results. In the first year of the Yuanfeng reign period (110 BCE), the post of Censors Monitoring the Commanderies was abolished. In the fifth year, thirteen Regional Inspectors were appointed as permanent censors who went on regular inspection tours of commanderies and kingdoms. (In the late Western Han and Eastern Han dynasties, the positions were re-designated as Regional Governors and they became the highest-ranking executive officials at the local level.) As the position of Inspector had evolved from the Divisional Heads "sent [by the Chancellor] to inspect the various regions," Inspectors were placed under the Office of the Chancellor in the beginning.[159]

Third, the Western Han Dynasty, in its early years, continued the institutions and systems of the Qin Dynasty: the Secretariat and the Office of the Chancellor were set up in parallel, with the former functioning as a check on the latter and appointing Censors Monitoring the Commanderies in the various commanderies. The position of Censors Monitoring the Commanderies was

156 *History of the Former Han*, juan 72, "Biography of Bao Xuan," p.3086. 157 *Ibid.*, p. 3090.

158 *History of the Former Han*, juan 92, "Biography of Youxia: Biography of Chen Zun," pp.3711–3712.

159 Yen Keng-Wang (1990), p.271.

abolished during the Yuanfeng reign period of Emperor Wu of the Western Han Dynasty, after which Inspectors under the supervision of the Chancellor's Office were sent to the regions. However, "it would seem that the Secretariat still had direct supervision over the Inspectors, with the Palace Aide to the Censor-in-Chief performing the role."[160] In addition, the Director of Uprightness of the Chancellor's Office supervised the Censors and Regional (Governors) Inspectors. During the Eastern Han Dynasty, the Regional Inspectors often intervened in the local military administration on top of their supervisory roles, and gradually became the highest-ranking executive official at the local level.

Fourth, the Emperors of the Western and Eastern Han sent special emissaries on tours of commanderies and kingdoms at irregular intervals to monitor the local administration. The duties of these emissaries, who were all appointed by the Emperor, included pacifying the people (showing concern for the people, disaster relief), education (propaganda), nominating talent (nominating those with virtue and ability), auditing the performance of officials, making judicial reviews, and observing local customs. Those who served as special emissaries during the Western and Eastern Han included Internuncios, Erudits, Grandees Remonstrant, Grand Palace Grandees, Imperial Household Grandees, Division Heads of the Chancellor's Office, Division Heads of the Secretariat, and so on. Their numbers were not fixed. The original duties of Internuncios were attending to the Emperor, acting as intermediaries between the inner and outer courts, serving as aides for guests, and guarding the palace. Erudits were the Emperor's consultants who participated in policy discussions, instituting rituals and ceremonies, and keeping files and documents. Their official grades were low, but their positions were exalted. As for the Grandees Remonstrant, Grand Palace Grandees, Imperial Household Grandees, and so on, they were constantly in the Emperor's presence to advice, remonstrate, and deliberate. They were the Emperor's senior consultants who often took part in and laid down important policies and laws. Most of these special emissaries were trusted by the Emperor, who would directly report to him the information

[160] *Ibid.*, p.272. It is unknown when this came about. *History of the Former Han, juan* 66, "Biography of Chen Xian": "Emperor Yuan promoted [Chen] Xian to Palace Aide to the Censor-in-Chief, who had general purview over the reports from the regions and commanderies and assessed the administrative performance of the Inspectors. At court, he applied the statutes, and all officials below the rank of the Excellencies and Ministers were afraid of him." (p.2900) *History of the Former Han, juan* 83, "Biography of Xue Xuan": "Shortly after Emperor Cheng ascended the throne, [Xue] Xuan was the Palace Aide to the Censor-in-Chief, who applied the statutes at court and supervised the Inspectors outside the central government." (p.3386) By the reigns of Emperors Yuan and Cheng, the functions of the Palace Aide to the Censor-in-Chief in having general purview over the reports from the provinces and commanderies and supervising the Inspectors had become fixed.

that they had gathered. They had a significant impact on the performance appraisals of local officials.[161]

Although the mechanisms for the central government's supervision of local administrative powers were designed to be rigorous and thorough during the Western and Eastern Han dynasties, they were all power-versus-power checks. Using power to constrain power means creating a monitoring or mutual-monitoring dynamic between higher and lower powers, as well as between parallel powers.[162] Such constraints, where the monitoring was conducted internally within the political framework, were based on the premise that all parties of the internal monitoring system in the power structure monitored and constrained one another in strict accordance to the law, that is, the monitors did not disregard the law by giving or receiving favors. In real life, however, the recurrence of officials scratching each other's back and instances of mass corruption had proved that it was hard to uphold this premise. There might have been mutual demands for interests between the monitoring departments and the departments being monitored, they might reach some kind of compromise to cover up each other's abuses of power, or they might forge some kind of working relationship to obtain even more unlawful benefits.[163]

To take the example of the Han periods, the Administrators and Chancellors of the commanderies and kingdoms "had six basic but extremely important powers. (1) They had absolute powers of control over their own officials and functionaries. (2) They had absolute powers of control over the county administrations under their jurisdiction. (3) They had special powers to nominate officials and commoners within their borders for career positions in the central government. (4) They had almost absolute powers to make decisions over judiciary matters. (5) They had almost absolute powers over the allocation of local finances. (6) They had considerable powers to deploy local troops."[164] "The chief executive and his subordinate functionaries built up a personal co-dependency relationship." "Each level of administrative organization had a single power center, and it only accepted supervision from its superiors. There were no horizontal restraints on its power from equally-ranked peers, nor monitoring from subordinates below, not to mention checks on its powers from the people."[165] Therefore, by the reign of Emperor Xuan of the Western

[161] For instance, in the fourth year of Emperor Xuan's Yuankang reign period, Grand Palace Grandee Ge Kuanrao "was sent to investigate the customs of various localities, where he commended, nominated, demoted, and dismissed many." (*History of the Former Han, juan* 77, "Biography of Ge Kuanrao," p.3244) During the reign of Emperor Yuan, Erudit Zheng Kuanzhong was sent to investigate the customs of various localities. He reported on the administrative performance of Wang Zun, Inspector of Yizhou Region, who was promoted to Chancellor of Dongping. (*History of the Former Han, juan* 76, "Biography of Wang Zun," p.3229)

[162] Hou Jian (2001), p.100. [163] Guan Yanchun (2003), p.37.

[164] Yen Keng-Wang (1990), p.76. [165] Meng Xiangcai (1996), p.261.

Han Dynasty, it was already observed that the administrators and chancellors of the commanderies and kingdoms "submitted account books to the court that deviated from actual facts, in order to deceive the throne and avoid punishments." Their superiors and supervisors, the Chancellor's Office and Secretariat, "did not mind," however.[166] Gong Yu (127–44 BCE) submitted a memorial during the reign of Emperor Yuan, averring that since the time of Emperor Wu, "various commanderies and kingdoms have been afraid that disaster would befall them, and have therefore tended to appoint those who are well-versed in history and records-keeping, and who are adept in deceiving superior levels of government, to high office."[167] Given the geographic vastness of the Han Empire, and the limitations in transport and communications, if local officials intentionally deceived the central government, and if their subordinates served them as they would their sovereign, then the central government and the relevant bodies, even if they were serious about monitoring and auditing local administrations, would still find it very difficult to discover and handle information pertaining to the dereliction of duty, desuetude of discipline, breaking the law, and crimes committed by local officials in a timely, comprehensive, and accurate manner. Besides, managerial departments in the central government and dedicated supervisory bodies were often intentionally neglectful of, or even had their interests entwined with, the very organizations they were supposed to monitor.

The Emperors of the Western and Eastern Han dynasties were at times aware of such abuses of power in the local administrations. Apart from limiting their authority, social forces and public opinion among commoners were also gradually employed to place checks on local governments.

In the Western Han Dynasty, Chancellors "Asked about Hardships," Inspectors Collected "Unverifiable Talk," and Special Emissaries "Observed Customs"

In contemporary political science theory, public opinion supervision is categorized under rights-versus-power checks. Using rights to constrain power means "using universal civil rights as a social force to restrict and balance political power, in order to prevent the perversion and abuse of political power, and to protect the legal rights and interests of citizens, and the overall interests of society." Public opinion is the most basic form of expression of citizens' diverse rights. The sharing and limitation of state power by the citizenry are realized through public opinion supervision.[168]

166 *History of the Former Han, juan* 8, "Annals of Emperor Xuan," p.273.
167 *History of the Former Han, juan* 72, "Biography of Gong Yu," p.3077.
168 Ye Changlin and Li Ruihua (2006), p.16; Guan Yanchun (2003), p.37.

Public opinion supervision and rights-vs-power checks are a power restriction mechanism unique to modern democratic societies.[169] The "public opinion supervision" within the political framework of the Western and Eastern Han dynasties was of course not identical to the public opinion supervision outlined in contemporary political science discourse. Their scales and efficacies were also different. However, the concern over people's opinions in the Han governments' supervision of local administrations did introduce into the political system's internal monitoring mechanism an external supervisory power that reflected to a certain extent the wishes and interests of the ruled population. This external force effected a soft supervision of local administrations and their chief executives, which was comprehensive, flexible, timely, and open. It enabled the Emperor, the court, and the relevant supervisory organs to obtain what information they needed at a very low cost, thereby raising the efficiency and competency of the supervision and restriction of local administrative institutions.

As mentioned in the section "The Unique Position of Popular Songs and Rhymes in Intellectual Discourse during the Han Periods" earlier in this chapter, the people-oriented Confucian political thought, which had been popular since the Western Zhou Dynasty, bestowed on songs and rhymes a special status, treating them as popular will that was expressed or public opinion of the commoners. Since the reign of Emperor Wu of the Western Han Dynasty, Confucian discourse had become increasingly popular in the political arena. As the central government assessed local administrations based on the people-oriented Confucian thought, it was a given that public opinion of the commoners was one of the reference indicators in the supervision and assessment of local officials.

The Officials in Charge of Accounts who compiled annual account books submitted to the central government by commanderies and kingdoms during the Western Han Dynasty were mostly senior aides such as Commandery Aides and Chief Clerks of Kingdoms.[170] Both Commandery Aides and Chief Clerks of Kingdoms were appointed by the central government; they were not the subordinates of the Administrators or Chancellors in the commanderies and kingdoms. Therefore, they became important channels for the central government to scrutinize the local administration and probe the people's will. For example, in the third year of Emperor Xuan's Dijie reign period (67 BCE), Wang Cheng, the Chancellor of the Kingdom of Jiaodong, was commended for "extraordinary work in administration" and rewarded with the title of Marquess within the Pass, with a stipend of 2,000 *shi*. Later on, the Emperor "ordered the Chancellor's Office and Secretariat to ask Commandery Aides

[169] Hou Jian (2001), p.102. [170] Yen Keng-Wang (1990), p.262.

and Chief Clerks of Kingdoms who were in charge of accounts about the strengths and weaknesses of the administrations of the commanderies and kingdoms they came from." The Official in Charge of Accounts in the Kingdom of Jiaodong revealed to the Chancellor's Office and Secretariat that "the former Chancellor of Jiaodong [Wang] Cheng had exaggerated his achievements in order to gain commendation by false means."[171] Citing "Old Rituals of the Han Dynasties," Yen Keng-Wang described this process: "After the Commandery Aides and Chief Clerks of Kingdoms submitted their annual reports, the Chancellor would sit at court, and personally asked about the hardships of the people."[172] Given that the Administrators and Chancellors of the commanderies and kingdoms in the Wester Han "had absolute powers of control over their own officials and functionaries," the Commandery Aides and Chief Clerks of Kingdoms appointed by the central government were not trusted by the Administrators and Chancellors. As they feared their superior officials, the Aides and Chief Clerks might not have been able to speak freely. Besides, Administrators and Chancellors might intentionally deceive, and so "appointed those who are well-versed in history and records-keeping, and who are adept in deceiving superior levels of government, to high office." This avenue of discerning the people's will was often congested.

The second channel of gathering public opinion from among the people was through the Regional Inspectors, who regularly toured the commanderies and kingdoms. In the discussion on unverifiable talk in Chapter 1, it is mentioned that the statutory scope of the duties of the Western and Eastern Han Inspectors involved examining six tasks of local administrators. The third task on the list was whether the officials in the commanderies and kingdoms were hated by the people because they did not concern themselves with difficult or dubious cases, were cruel and committed murder, were capricious in meting out punishments and rewards, molested and tyrannized the masses, and exploited the people. The standard of judgment regarding these misdemeanors was whether the "mountains collapsed and the rocks split, and if there were

[171] *History of the Former Han, juan* 89, "Biographies of Upright Officials: Biography of Wang Cheng," p.3627.

[172] Yen Keng-Wang (1990), citing *Sequel to the History of the Former Han: Additional Annotations*, p.265. It was recorded in "Old Rituals of the Han Dynasties" in *Six Works about Han Officials*: "After Commandery Aides and Chief Clerks of Kingdoms submitted their annual reports, the Chancellor would be sent to sit at court, and the Emperor would personally ask about the hardships of the people." (p.38) There are differences in the wording and punctuation of the two quotations. According to Yan's edition and punctuation, the Chancellor would receive the officials in charge of account and ask them about the administration and situation in their localities. According to the punctuation in *Six Works about Han Officials*, the Emperor, accompanied by the Chancellor, personally received the Officials in Charge of Accounts to ask them about the administration and situation in their localities.

macabre omens and unverifiable talk."[173] In the context of the Han periods, unverifiable talk was actually an expression of public opinion among the people.[174] In the written sources of the Han periods, unverifiable talk and rhymes were sometimes used interchangeably, which meant that gathering people's songs and rhymes (i.e. public opinion) was also part of the Inspectors' duties. While the actual process remains unknown, this was obviously a reference to supervision by public opinion.

The third channel of compiling public opinion was through the special emissaries sent by the court at irregular intervals to collect information on local customs. The sending of these custom emissaries was first recorded during the reign of Emperor Wu of the Western Han Dynasty. In Jia Yi's *Essay on Governing and Security*, his bitter criticism of the early Han's social ills included "six matters that would elicit deep signs," one of which involved "a fraudster who paid several hundred thousand *shi* of millet and over 60,000 copper coins in taxes to travel around the commanderies and kingdoms in a government carriage." According to Ru Chun's annotations: "This referred to a wealthy man who paid money and grain in exchange for a high rank, or the position of an emissary, to ride a government carriage around the commanderies and kingdoms for his own glory." According to Yan Shigu's annotations: "Ru's theory is untrue. This referred to a fraudster who used a counterfeited imperial order to collect a large amount of taxes, and who also rode a government carriage on false pretenses on a tour of the commanderies and kingdoms."[175] Whoever was right, it would seem that special emissaries touring the commanderies and kingdoms were already a common sight in the early years of the Western Han Dynasty.

According to *The Grand Scribe's Records* and *History of the Former Han*, groups of special emissaries were sent to various commanderies and kingdoms at irregular intervals during the reigns of Emperors Wu, Xuan, Yuan, Cheng, Ai, and Ping, and during Wang Mang's Xin Dynasty. As for historically verifiable special emissaries who collected information on local customs, three groups were sent during the reign of Emperor Wu, three during the reign of Emperor Xuan, two during the reign of Emperor Yuan, four during the reign of Emperor Cheng, one during the reign of Emperor Ai (the time when Wang Mang ordered his men to fabricate popular songs and rhymes), and three during the Xin Dynasty. One of the missions of these special emissaries was

[173] *History of the Later Han*, *juan* 28, "Treatise on Officials, Part V," Li Xian's annotation citing Cai Zhi, *Rituals of the Han Dynasties*, pp.3617–3618.

[174] See Lu Zongli (2003).

[175] *History of the Former Han*, *juan* 48, "Biography of Jia Yi," pp. 2244, 2246.

to "observe customs," an important aspect of which was gathering public opinion such as popular songs and rhymes.[176]

Eastern Han's "Rhymes Reporting"

Regional Inspectors who "examined the six tasks" were originally dedicated monitors who represented the central government (subordinate to the Chancellor's Office initially and subsequently the Palace Aide to the Censor-in-Chief) in monitoring local executive officials in situ. By the late Western Han Dynasty, however, they had already become local executive officials in their own right and were sometimes called Regional Governors. They were de facto the highest-ranking local executive officials. In the early Eastern Han Dynasty, the name of the position reverted back to Inspector, but the post became even more localized (in the late Eastern Han, the name was changed to Regional Governor). For example, Inspectors during the Western Han had to go to the imperial capital to make assessments reports at the end of the year. In the Eastern Han, this task was merged into the annual reports prepared by Officials in Charge of Accounts from the commanderies and kingdoms.[177] Its independent monitoring functions gradually diminished.

The special emissaries who toured the commanderies and kingdoms during the Eastern Han Dynasty were few in number and their duties were simpler. During the reigns of Emperors An and Ling, Regular Attendants, Palace Internuncio, Imperial Household Grandees, and so on were tasked to deliver medicines to areas devastated by the plague. Only the special emissaries during the reign of Emperor Shun had any important monitoring functions. In the first year of the Han'an reign period (142), eight emissaries were sent by imperial

176 Also, in the nomination and selection of scholar-officials in the regions and commanderies during the Western and Eastern Han, a key factor for consideration was the candidates' reputation in their villages and neighborhoods. By the Eastern Han Dynasty, it had even developed into the custom of the "Monthly Assessment." Gu Yanwu's *Records of Daily Recognitions: Collected Expositions*, *juan* 13, "Just Comments": "The wise kings of ancient times ensured the uprightness of his barons in the following way: apart from institutionalizing penalty to alert those who were serving in their posts, they also appointed neighborhood masters and set up village schools so that just comments could be heard in the localities, to compensate for the inadequacies of punitive measures. That rites existed in the countryside was recorded in *Classic of Rites*; and marking off separate hamlets for undesirables was mentioned in 'Charge to the Duke of Bi.' Since the times of the two Han dynasties, this system has been adhered to. The primary consideration for nominees from the localities had to be their personal histories. A single blot on the commentaries about them and they would be held in contempt for the rest of their lives. The gentleman fears punishment, and the mean man possesses shame. When education on virtue finds success below, severity above is unnecessary; when standards are set in the countryside, the people will not transgress." This was also a form of monitoring of public opinion, but it was mainly used in the process of the nomination and selection of officials, and will not be further elaborated here.

177 *History of the Later Han*, *juan* 4, "Annals of Emperor Shang," annotations by Li Xian, p.198.

decree to make a tour of the empire to investigate local customs. The eight emissaries chosen were "all renowned Confucian scholars of great learning who occupied exalted positions," such as Palace Attendants Zhou Ju (?–149) and Du Qiao, Acting Imperial Household Grandee Zhou Xu, former Inspector of Qingzhou Region Feng Xian, Master of Writing Luan Ba (?–168), Attending Censor Zhang Gang (108–143), Inspector of Yanzhou Region Guo Zun, and Grand Commandant's Chief Clerk and Acting Imperial Household Grandee Liu Ban. Visiting various locations in the empire, they were authorized by the court "to make a report to the throne from their relay horses for serious cases involving Regional Inspectors and officials whose stipends amounted to 2,000 *shi* (Grand Administrators); and to make immediate arrests for serious cases involving County Prefects and below. As for honest and upright officials who achieved a great deal in office and had the people's support, they should be commended to the court."[178]

In the course of performing their duties, Du Qiao commended Li Gu, Grand Administrator of Mount Tai, as the top-performing official in the whole empire; while Zhou Ju reported corrupt and crafty officials but extolled those who were honest. Zhang Gang, who was the lowest ranking among the eight, as well as the youngest and most hotheaded, "buried his chariot wheels at a post stop in Luoyang" and said, "With jackals and wolves roaming the roads, why would I go after foxes!" Not wishing to catch the flies in the commanderies and kingdoms, Zhang Gang preferred to go after the tigers in the imperial capital. He submitted a memorial to impeach General-in-Chief Liang Ji and Governor of He'nan Liang Buyi for corruption, excesses, and framing loyal and good people. He also exposed "fifteen things that showed their total disregard for the Emperor."[179] Emperor Shun could not act according to Zhang's advice. The other special emissaries visited various places, and most of their impeachments involved "the relatives and cronies of Liang Ji and the eunuchs." However, the Emperor's affinal relatives and eunuchs "made supplications for one another and the matters were laid to rest."[180] Then, there was Lei Yi, who "was Probationary Internuncio. He went on a tour of the commanderies and kingdoms to investigate the local customs, and indicted seventy grand administrators, prefects, and chiefs."[181] However, there was no permanent arrangement for special emissaries to tour the regions, and their effectiveness as monitors varied according to individuals and time.

178 *History of the Later Han*, *juan* 61, "Biography of Zhou Ju," p.2029; *juan* 56, "Biography of Zhang Gang," p.1817.
179 *History of the Later Han*, *juan* 56, "Biography of Zhang Gang," p.1817.
180 *Comprehensive Mirror in Aid of Governance*, *juan* 52, p.1693.
181 *History of the Later Han*, *juan* 81, "Biographies of Loners: Biography of Lei Yi," p.2688.

The timely and sustained transmission of public opinion from the people to the throne was difficult.

Another avenue through which the people's opinions were collected during the Eastern Han Dynasty was the annual submission of accounts by the commanderies. Nominally, it was officiated by the Office of the Three Excellencies (in particular, the Office of the Minister over the Masses), but in practice the Imperial Secretariat oversaw the whole exercise. At times, the Emperor himself would receive and question the local officials in person.[182] The Accounts Clerks during the Eastern Han who "submitted account books to the central government were never Commandery Aides or Chief Clerks of Kingdoms, but there were records of occasions when the more senior Division Heads were sent." "According to written records, all Accounts Clerks sent to the central government were natives of the commanderies."[183]

Senior functionaries who were natives of the commanderies and who had the opportunity to directly communicate with the Emperor could have been an effective avenue of public opinion for the central government. However, the Administrators and Chancellors of commanderies and kingdoms during the Eastern Han Dynasty had absolute control over their subordinate functionaries and the power to nominate persons within their commanderies and kingdoms to the central government for official appointments. Besides, they also controlled massive political and economic resources within their jurisdictions. "When Administrators and Chancellors of commanderies and kingdoms had been in office for a long time in the same locality, they tended to collude with powerful local interests through the appointments and nominations of officials and functionaries, forming a kind of common entity bound by shared interests."[184] Most of the senior functionaries who were Accounts Clerks hailed from prominent families and clans in the commanderies and kingdoms that had close ties to the Administrators and Chancellors. It was very unlikely for them to genuinely reflect the people's opinion.

"[Emperor] Guangwu had originally lived among the people for a long period of time. He could discern the truths and falsities of the world, and had witnessed farmers' struggles and the people's afflictions. Therefore, when the empire was pacified, he strived not to disrupt the people's lives by dismantling the onerous regulations of Wang Mang and restoring the lenient laws of the Han era." To this end, he "made extensive inquiries about the people's hardships and collected popular rhymes."[185] Drawing on his personal

[182] *History of the Later Han, juan* 31, "Biography of Zhang Kan": "The Emperor [Guangwu] often summoned to his presence Accounts Clerks from the commanderies to inquire about local customs and circumstances, as well as the abilities or lack thereof demonstrated by the former and current Commandery Administrators and County Prefects." (p.1100)

[183] Yen Keng-Wang (1990), pp.262, 263.

[184] Zhou Changshan (2006), p.106.

[185] *History of the Later Han, juan* 76, "Preface to the Biographies of Upright Officials," p.2457.

experience of growing up among the grassroots, Emperor Guangwu of the Eastern Han Dynasty set up a system for monitoring public opinion regarding the work performance of local officials called "Rhymes Reporting." This was an innovation in the monitoring of governance in ancient China.

Rhymes here meant popular songs and rhymes circulated among the people, which is discussed in this chapter. In the political and historical discourse of the Western Han Dynasty, popular songs and rhymes were already an important indicator of how people judged the performance of political figures and the effectiveness of local governance. The central government of the Eastern Han Dynasty institutionalized the collection of popular songs and rhymes. Not only could policy makers refer to the public opinion reflected in these songs and rhymes, they could directly use them as information resources to monitor and evaluate the administration and governance of the regions and commanderies. The actual procedure was as follows: The functionaries of the Office of the Three Excellencies, which assessed the performance of local officials, collected popular songs and rhymes from different localities every year. After they arranged and categorized the songs and rhymes, they would list the critiques made of local officials by the people, as well as the people's worries and complaints. The Three Excellencies would then convene a conference with their functionaries, and the conclusions were written up as an assessment report. The report would then be vetted by the Imperial Secretariat before submission to the Emperor.[186]

This measure prompted the appearance in the early Eastern Han (especially during the reigns of Emperors Guangwu and Ming) of a group of famous officials whose concern for the people, personal honesty, and outstanding achievements were lauded in the popular songs and rhymes. Fan Ye described it in glowing terms:

> No one was indolent within and outside the court, and the people were given rest. Local officials vied with one another to work hard. For example, Du Shi, the Grand Administrator of Nanyang, who was called "Mother Du," and Ren Yan and Xi Guang, who transformed local customs in the borderlands, were among the officials with the most outstanding achievements. Individuals like Diwu Lun and Song Jun were also worthy of praise.[187]

Zhang Kan, who governed the Shu Commandery, was meticulous and did not seek personal gain, which greatly pleased the people of Shu. When he

[186] *History of the Later Han*, *juan* 60 *xia*, "Biography of Cai Yong," annotation by Li Xian, quoting *Officials and Rituals of the Han Dynasties*: "The Three Excellencies heard the assessments of the officials and the people's afflictions, before drawing up a list and submitting them to the throne. This was what it meant by Rhymes Reporting." (p.1996)

[187] *History of the Later Han*, *juan* 76, "Preface to the Biographies of Upright Officials," p.2457.

governed Yuyang, he was fair in meting out both rewards and punishments. He opened up over 8,000 *qing* of rice fields and encouraged the people to farm, thus enriching them. The people sang about him in a song: "The branches of the mulberry tree are not forked/and the ears of the wheat sport two branches./ With Honorable Zhang in office,/we are beside ourselves with joy."[188]

When Chen Jun was Grand Administrator of Langya, he "gave succor to the poor and the weak, and commended the righteous. He restrained his military subordinates, forbidding them from interfering in the matters of the commandery and the counties. The people sang songs in praise of him."[189]

When Zhao Xi (4 BCE – 80 CE) was Grand Administrator of Pingyuan, he improved law and order within the commandery, "raised up the righteous and eliminated the wicked. It came to pass that Qingzhou Region was devastated by a plague of locusts, but they immediately died when they flew into the borders of Pingyuan. There were many bountiful years in Pingyuan and the people sang songs about it."[190]

When Dong Xuan was enforcing the law as Prefect of Luoyang, he did not make any exceptions for the rich and powerful. He was known in the imperial capital by the nickname "Crouching Tiger," and he was lauded in a popular song: "The drums alerting people of crimes are silent because of Dong Shaoping [referring to Dong Xuan]."[191]

When Song Jun (?–76 CE) was Chief of Chenyang, he founded schools, banned immoral religious rituals, introduced civilized manners, and transformed the local customs. All the people led peaceful lives. When he was moved to Shangcai, where he served as Prefect, he refused to implement the unreasonable punishments meted out by his superiors. When he was Grand Administrator of Jiujiang, he forbade the people from hunting tigers. The tiger menace stopped and locusts did not invade the commandery. When he was appointed Grand Administrator of He'nei, "there were major initiatives in policies and education." Song Jun was Chancellor of the Kingdom of Donghai for five years before he was implicated in a wrongdoing and dismissed. "In memory of [Song] Jun's kindness and the reforms he undertook, the officials and people of Donghai composed a song in his honor. Several thousand people went to the court and begged for his return."[192]

Lian Fan served as Grand Administrator in the commanderies of Wuwei and Wudu, where he "educated the people and provided them with guidance in

188 *History of the Later Han, juan* 31, "Biography of Zhang Kan," p.1100.
189 *History of the Later Han, juan* 18, "Biography of Chen Jun," p.691.
190 *History of the Later Han, juan* 26, "Biography of Zhao Xi," p.914.
191 *History of the Later Han, juan* 77, "Biographies of Cruel Officials: Biography of Dong Xuan," p.2490.
192 *History of the Later Han, juan* 41, "Biography of Song Jun," p.1413.

accordance with their circumstances and customs, and he administered both places well." In Shu Commandery, where he was Grand Administrator, Chengdu was a place where the people were rich and the resources plentiful, but the houses, being narrow and very close to each other, were fire hazards. The former Grand Administrator had banned people from working at night to reduce the use of naked flames as illumination, but they did so surreptitiously, and the conflagrations continued. Lian Fan lifted the ban, but imposed strict rules requiring residents to store a greater amount of water to better prepare themselves during fires. The people sang a song about him: "Lian Shudu [referring to Lian Fan],/why he arrives so late?/He does not ban the flames/ and the people work in peace./I'd never had a short coat before but now I have five pairs of trouser legs."[193]

There were unique advantages to using public opinion and social forces to supplement legal and administrative checks for the purpose of restricting local political power, including comprehensiveness, flexibility, timeliness, openness, and low costs. The "Rhymes Reporting" system that Emperor Guangwu instituted has been positively viewed by modern scholars of public opinion and historians, especially those with an interest in the history of checks and balances on institutions. Having said that, a number of problems did arise in the implementation of this system. Fan Ye wrote:

> During the Jianwu (25–56 CE) and Yongping (58–75 CE) reign periods, officials were subjected to overly harsh treatment; local officials were replaced based only on rhymes and one-sided indictments. For this reason, Zhu Fu[194] repeatedly made submissions to the throne to mitigate the severity, and individuals such as Zhongli Yi also made frequent counsel. They spoke as elders but their advice was not taken. Therefore, there were deficiencies in the renaissance of the Han Dynasty.[195]

While there was a "continuous stream" of excellent officials who performed well after the reigns of Emperors Zhang and He, there was "a lack of" renowned officials who could educate the people and enjoyed their adulations.[196]

Based on the two remonstrances written by Zhu Fu recorded in the "Biography of Zhu Fu" in *History of the Later Han* and other related accounts, the "Rhymes Reporting" system in early Eastern Han Dynasty faced the following problems during its execution:

193 *History of the Later Han*, *juan* 31, "Biography of Lian Fan," p.1103.

194 A native of Xiao County in the Kingdom of Pei. As an earlier follower of Emperor Guangwu in founding the Eastern Han Dynasty, he was granted the title Marquess of Wuyang, and served the empire in many important positions. However, he was aggressive and dominated his colleagues, and was ordered to take his own life Emperor Ming.

195 *History of the Later Han*, *juan* 76, "Preface to the Biographies of Upright Officials," p.2457.

196 *Ibid.*, p.2458.

One. "Due to the reason that many officials earning 2,000 *shi* were inadequate in their duties, the Emperor would admonish and dismiss those with minor misdemeanors."[197]

Emperor Guangwu did not trust his regional and commandery officials, and would therefore pick on their smallest mistakes and summarily dismiss them. With the punishments incommensurate with the errors made, the foundation of the legal system was destroyed. This problem was corroborated in "Biography of Shentu Gang" in *History of the Later Han*: "At the time, many officials within and outside the court were personally selected by the Emperor. Given the strict regulations governing them, the excessive burden of their work, and [the severe punishments where] even Masters of Writing and Members of the Imperial Coterie were dragged before the throne and flogged, officials did not dare speak their minds."[198]

Two. "The frequent personnel changes disrupted the people's lives."[199]

The original intent of imposing exacting standards for senior regional and commandery officials would be to ensure that the people could live and work in peace. However, the constant and sudden personnel changes achieved the opposite: the people's lives were disrupted.

Three. "I believe that momentous achievements cannot be hurried; grueling enterprises require many days to succeed. Recently, however, Administrators and Chancellors have seen constant changes, with the newly appointed hastening along the roads in exhaustion. They have little experience in their new appointments and before they could achieve anything in office, they are severely reprimanded and dismissed. Unable to protect themselves, they watch one another with unease." "An object that grows in sudden spurts will expire before its time; anyone who is impatient to succeed will fail. To rush to succeed in an enduring enterprise will not benefit Your Majesty. One does not use the world for an instant; success in the empire does not come in a day."[200]

Zhu Fu believed that the assessment of a local official's governance required long-term observation of his consistent performance and the enduring effects of his administration. If an official who cared for the people was in office for just a short time and his official position was precarious, he would not have the assurance of security and stability to do his job well. The only result would be the "rush to succeed in an enduring enterprise."

Four. "Since [Your Majesty's] ascension to the throne, the old systems have been abandoned. Censors and supervisors are trusted, but the Office of the Three Excellencies is idle. As long as someone impeaches a senior official with

[197] *History of the Later Han, juan* 33, "Biography of Zhu Fu," p.1141.
[198] *History of the Later Han, juan* 24, p.1017.
[199] *History of the Later Han, juan* 33, "Biography of Zhu Fu," p.1141. [200] *Ibid.*, p.1142.

a 2,000-*shi* stipend, the latter would be dismissed. The case does not go through the Three Excellencies for reviewing and the charges are not properly investigated. Your Majesty considers the emissaries your close advisers and the emissaries employ attendant clerks to act as their eyes and ears. The matters should be handled by Masters of Writing, but now are in the hands of functionaries with 100-*shi* stipends. This has resulted in all your servants being harsh in showing off their competence."[201]

The "Biography of Zhu Fu" pointed out that "according to the old system, Regional Governors who made a report of maladministration against an official with a 2,000-*shi* stipend had to submit it to the Three Excellencies in the first instance. The Three Excellencies would dispatch Division Heads to investigate and verify the accusation before demoting or dismissing the accused."[202] Liu Pak-yuen's research also proved that according to official procedures, assessments of officials submitted to the Eastern Han court had to first go through the Three Excellencies, who would then submit the results of their assessment to the Emperor. As the court's secretaries, the Masters of Writing were only required to audit the assessment report submitted by the Three Excellencies, before passing it to the Emperor.[203] Emperor Guangwu disregarded the normal procedures, however. With his own men as his eyes and ears, he demanded that the Inspectors and special emissaries bypass the Office of the Three Excellencies and, through the Imperial Secretariat, directly report the public opinions and other information they had collected to the throne. He allowed the Masters of Writing and minor functionaries with a 100-*shi* stipends to usurp the authority of the Three Excellencies to make assessments of officials. When the Emperor received the reports, he did not subject the cases to the related investigations, but made his own decisions to promote, move, demote, or dismiss the officials. Such a careless, pared down, and hasty assessment process lacked procedural justice and checks and balances.

Five. Zhu Fu reminded Emperor Guangwu "to heed official appointments 1,000 *li* away and cautiously review reports that are prejudiced,"[204] because those who monitored senior local officials at the time were periodically incautious when collecting evidence against the latter, often replacing them based on "rhymes and one-side comments" alone. Popular songs and rhymes sung by the people were a unique form of public opinion. They might reflect the all-encompassing will of the people, or the opinion of a minority. With different interest groups having different demands, there would be different desires and opinions expressed. "The will of the people is like flowing water." Each desire and opinion has its superficialities, limitations, and context. Superficial public opinion could only reflect partial truths. Choosing to hear and believe these

[201] *Ibid.*, p.1143. [202] *Ibid.* [203] Liu Pak-yuen (2003), p.145.
[204] *History of the Later Han*, *juan* 33, "Biography of Zhu Fu," p.1144.

partial truths would result in the twisting and misconstruction of the people's will. What was worse was that "some officials may settle scores with their enemies over a small grudge, or randomly collect faults and wrongdoings in the attempt to align themselves with the Emperor's will."[205] They took the opportunity to either settle private grudges by framing their adversaries, or conduct slapdash investigations to meet their performance targets. They would rather frame the innocent than let any guilty person go free, and good and upright officials were harmed in the process.

Six. Under these circumstances, "all of them vied with one another to perform empty deeds for immediate benefit. The guilty ones are not subdued in their hearts and the innocent are indicted by empty reports."[206] "Pressurized by possible impeachments and fearful of the Inspectors' criticisms, officials with 2,000-*shi* stipends and senior officials engage in deception to obtain false honors."[207] There were, of course, many excellent officials whose real achievements were sung about in popular songs and rhymes, but there were also many who bought the people's goodwill and acquired fame with short-term policies. There were even those who fraudulently created songs and rhymes.

For example, the "people" of Jingzhou Region praised Inspector Guo He in this song: "Guo Qiaoqing [referring to Guo He] is the benevolent and wise man who advances virtue;/he is loyal and upright before the court, and all are at peace under his administration."[208] Grand Administrator Cen Xi was lauded in this song by the "coach drivers" of Wei Commandery: "I have the thorns of the trifoliate orange,/and Honorable Cen cuts them;/I have thieving pests, and Honorable Cen stops them./I fear not the barking of dogs/so that fur grows beneath my feet./With food in my mouth, I pat my full belly./What do I know of calamities and disasters?/I am happy that I was born,/right at this moment./ How good Honorable Cen is!/How great he is!"[209] The "functionaries and people" in Shunyang County praised County Prefect Liu Tao with this song: "We are unhappy/because we miss our Honorable Liu./When will he return to appease the people?"[210] In Jizhou Region, "the people" extolled Huangfu Song in this song: "In this chaotic world, marketplaces are ruined,/mothers cannot protect their sons, and wives lose their husbands./It is Huangfu who restores peace to our abodes."[211] These "popular songs" were either bereft of real content or too literary; some were so difficult to enunciate that they were almost tongue twisters. It is hard to imagine that they would be popular among

205 *Ibid.*, p.1142. 206 *Ibid.*, p.1143. 207 *Ibid.*, p.1142.
208 *History of the Later Han*, *juan* 26, "Biography of Guo He," p.908.
209 *History of the Later Han*, *juan* 17, "Biography of Cen Xi," p.663.
210 *History of the Later Han*, *juan* 57, "Biography of Liu Tao," p.1848.
211 *History of the Later Han*, *juan* 71, "Biography of Huangfu Song," p.2302.

illiterate people or people with little education such as commoners and children.[212] The administration and governance at regional, commandery, and county levels during the Eastern Han Dynasty might not have been better than the Western Han's, but the number of officials popularly lauded in songs far exceeded the latter. The reason for this is obvious.

The third, fourth, and fifth points of Zhu Fu's remonstrance directly touched upon systemic issues.

According to Zhou Changshan's research on the term lengths of office for Administrators and Chancellors in the commanderies and kingdoms during the Han periods, senior local officials tended to serve longer periods during the Western Han Dynasty, many of whom stayed in office for ten years and longer.[213] It might have been because the supreme rulers of the Western Han treated the Administrators and Chancellors in the commanderies and kingdoms with a certain level of leniency. Besides, the systems for official appointments and monitoring had yet to be set up or finalized in the early years of the fledgling dynasty. During his reign, Emperor Wu of the Western Han Dynasty greatly increased the centralization of power and the monitoring and control of senior local officials. "Officials such as the Excellencies and Ministers, and below, were replaced at a rapid rate, with many changes in policies. Metropolitan Commandants and Regional Inspectors who detected any wrongdoings among the officials would impeach them and publicize their private matters. Some officials resigned after being in office for only a few months. The old ones leaving and the new ones coming to replace them pass one another on the roads."[214] There were very few who remained in office for a long time, and by the reign of Emperor Xuan of the Western Han Dynasty, the term length of office had been stabilized to three years.

During his reign, Emperor Xuan knew the deficiencies of government at the time because he had had a humble background and sought the truth. He would receive in person Inspectors, Administrators, and Chancellors to examine their speech and actions, meting out rewards and punishments accordingly.

212 Of course, we cannot rule out that it was the result of embellishments by official scribes, and editors and writers of history texts.

213 *History of the Former Han*, *juan* 86, "Biography of Wang Jia": "During the reign of Emperor Wen, occupiers of official positions or their eldest sons and grandsons took the name of their positions as their family names. The Cang and Ku families were the descendants of officers working in the granaries (*cang*) and warehouses (*ku*). Senior officials with 2,000-*shi* stipends were also happy and stable in their official positions." (p.3490) *History of the Former Han*, *juan* 23, "Treatise on Punishment and Law": By the time Emperor Wen ascended the throne, "officials had stability of jobs and the people were happy with their vocations." (p.1097) *History of the Later Han*, *juan* 33, "Biography of Zhu Fu": "The prosperity of the Great Han was the result of the accumulation of effective policies. All officials remained at their posts for long periods of time until their retirement. They gave the names of their official positions to their descendants as family names." (p.1142)

214 *History of the Former Han*, *juan* 86, "Biography of Wang Jia," p.3490.

Emperor Xuan said with some emotion: "It is because of good policies and good officials that the people are living in peace and not resentful. Those who have worked with me to achieve this are these excellent 2,000-*shi* officials!" He believed that constant changes and replacements of officials would result in restlessness among those below them. When a competent official remained in his post for a long time, the people would be educated and civilized. He personally wrote letters to encourage officials who performed well, promoting them and rewarding them with gold. Some were conferred the title of Marquess Within the Pass and would be appointed to fill vacancies among ranks of the Excellencies and Ministers. Therefore, "all officials did their job well and the people lived and worked in peace. This was a time in the Han period with the greatest number of good officials. This was also why there was the auspicious augury of phoenixes and the achievements of the Han's renaissance."[215]

Among the twenty-four Grand Administrators in the thirty-two years of the Eastern Han's Jianwu reign period whose term lengths of office are known, fifteen served more than six years, with the rest serving over three years.[216] This would have been the result of Zhu Fu's remonstrance obtaining the support from most of the court officials and Emperor Guangwu's endorsement. The replacement of senior regional and commandery officials became less frequent.[217] Among the fifteen Grand Administrators and Chancellors during the reigns of Emperors Ming and Zhang whose term lengths of office can be confirmed, eleven served lengthy terms. However, in the century that saw the reigns of Emperors He, An, Shun, Huan, and Ling, there were only eight who served lengthy terms in office. It was perhaps because "the power of the empire was declining, with the Emperor's authority shunted aside. Real power was successively held by the Emperor's affinal relatives and the eunuchs in turn, and positions were seized to uphold one's interests." "During the reign of Emperor Xian, term lengths of local officials rebounded to become lengthy again. Ten out of eleven individuals served lengthy terms of over nine years. Behind all this, however, was the growing power of local warlords and their separatist regimes."[218]

215 *History of the Later Han, juan* 61, "Biography of Zuo Xiong," p.2016.

216 Zhou Changshan (2006), pp.96–106.

217 *Ibid. History of the Later Han, juan* 33, "Biography of Zhu Fu": "The Emperor opened the matter for discussion and most officials agreed with [Zhu] Fu. From then on, there were fewer replacements of Regional Governors and Commandery Administrators." (p.1142)

218 Zhou Changshan (2006), pp.107, 108. *History of the Later Han, juan* 61, "Biography of Zuo Xiong": "Be it Inspectors or County Prefects, they were replaced too often. Everyone had their own ideas and did not make long-term considerations." (p.2016) "It was not adopted because the eunuchs usurped the Emperor's authority. Henceforth, nominations and replacements occurred in succession. County Prefects were changed monthly; the leaving of the old and arrival of the new became an endless hassle. Some departments and offices were vacant.

There were pros and cons to senior officials in commanderies and kingdoms serving lengthy terms. If senior officials were competent and had the people's interests at heart, having lengthy terms of office would mean they could placate the people, understand the people's conditions, prevent their subordinate functionaries from thieving, and save money on supervising incoming officials. It would be good for governance.[219] "However, the friendships formed over a long time, the various relationship networks, and the formation of private forces could not be avoided."[220] Insidious common interest groups comprising powerful local people and senior local officials would be formed. If senior officials were corrupt, cruel, and incompetent, lengthy terms of office would hurt the people and the administration. Still, it was necessary that senior officials had relatively stable term lengths of office. The precipitous replacement of officials based on isolated and one-off opinions was not conducive to good and effective governance at the local level.

Zhu Fu criticized Emperor Guangwu for dismantling normal procedures by allowing Inspectors and special emissaries to bypass the Office of the Three Excellencies and directly submit information on public opinion that they collected to the Emperor. The Emperor allowed junior officials with 100-*shi* stipends to usurp the Three Excellencies' authority to review. Charges that were received did not undergo any investigation by the relevant departments, and decisions on promotions, transfers, demotions, and dismissals were summarily made. However, how effective was the monitoring of public opinion during the Eastern Han when it had gone through the proper channels?

According to Ying Shao's description, when the Three Excellencies conducted the "Rhymes Reporting" exercise in accordance to normal procedures, their staff would arrange all the "rhymes" collected[221] and collate them into annual reports assessing the performance of senior local officials. The Three Excellencies would then give their collective critiques and "dismiss or promote them based on how the people's songs and rhymes judged them." In actual practice, however, everyone would heap effusive praises on the official assessed when the report had something good to say, but everyone would

Whenever work became overwhelming, some officials even ran off." (p.2019) *History of the Later Han, juan* 64, "Biography of Lu Zhi": "These days, Commandery Administrators and Inspectors are transferred several times a month. [The court] should promote the good and dismiss the bad based on their achievements to separate the capable from the incapable. If the assessment of nine years of performance is impossible, three years will also do." (p.2117)

219 *History of the Former Han, juan* 89, "Biography of Huang Ba": "The frequent replacements of senior officials resulted in money spent on handing over, and wicked functionaries destroying records and stealing things, thus incurring quite a lot of public and private costs, all of which came from the people. Besides, the new official might not be good, or even worse than the old one. It only looked beneficial but was actually not." (p.3631)

220 Zhou Changshan (2006), p.102.

221 The methods and channels through which they were collected are unknown.

remain silent and be noncommittal when the comments were bad. Of course, if the senior official assessed had neither fame nor influence and was unfortunately embroiled in a private grudge against one of the assessors present, or if the latter for some reason did not like him, then he could be made an example of as a sacrificial lamb. Sometimes, the real reasons behind an official's promotion, transfer, demotion, or dismissal were quite vague and ambiguous. On occasions when one of the Three Excellencies conducting the assessment was overly cautious (such as Zhu Tian, Minister over the Masses during Emperor Huan's reign), he would "forget the virtue of outspokenness, fear the mockery of those above and below him, huddle up with his back to the sky, and be unable to make clear conclusions." The assessment would be totally devoid of principles, very much inferior to the deeds of famous ministers in the Western Han, where "Shentu [Jia] reprimanded Deng Tong, and Wang Jia returned the imperial edict still under seal."[222]

In the second year of the Yanxi reign period (159), Emperor Huan ordered the Division Heads of the Office of the Three Excellencies to report rhymes.[223] Fan Pang, a famous member of the literati, was then a Division Head of the Grand Commandant, and he reported more than twenty Regional Inspectors and senior officials with 2,000-*shi* stipends who attached themselves to the "powerful." However, "the Master of Writing reprimanded Fan Pang for impeaching too many people, suspecting that he had personal scores to settle." Fan Pang "knew that his ideals would not be fulfilled, submitted a self-impeachment, and left his post."[224]

It was written in the sealed memorial to Emperor Ling submitted by Cai Yong in the sixth year of the Xiping reign period (177) that most of the Regional Inspectors did not perform their duties as monitors; some were even colluding with the people they were supposed to oversee. The Office of the Three Excellencies and the Imperial Secretariat, which were responsible for assessing the senior local officials based on rhymes and public opinion, were procrastinating and not doing anything. An imperial edict was issued in the fifth year of the Xiping reign period, which suggested sending eight emissaries to observe local customs and having the Three Excellencies report rhymes to the throne. "At the time, those who followed the rules were happy that their wishes were met, while the evil and crooked men lived in fear."[225] Some court

[222] *History of the Later Han*, *juan* 24, "Treatise on Officials, Part I," annotation by Li Xian citing *Officials and Rituals of the Han Dynasties*, p.3560.

[223] The Office of the Three Excellencies conducted "Rhymes Reporting" annually. The Emperor's promulgation of this order to report rhymes was probably a special occasion unrelated to the annual reporting.

[224] *History of the Later Han*, *juan* 67, "Biographies of Partisan Prohibitions: Biography of Fan Pang," p.2204.

[225] *History of the Later Han*, *juan* 60 *xia*, "Biography of Cai Yong," p.1996.

officials then had hopes for more public opinion monitoring and cleaning up the administration, but the suggestion was like stone skimming over the water surface – moments later, the surface was again calm and ripple-free.

In the fifth year of the Guanghe reign period (182), an imperial edict was issued requiring the Excellencies and Ministers to make use of popular rhymes to report Inspectors and 2,000-*shi* officials who put the people in danger.[226] The Grand Commandant Xu Yu and the Minister of Works Zhang Ji were in charge, but they "were diffident to the eunuchs and received their bribes." They "did not dare investigate" the eunuchs' family members and retainers who were senior local officials, "even though they were corrupt and degenerate." In contrast, twenty-six officials in small, remote commanderies who "had clean administrations that benefited the people" were framed. Therefore, the officials from these commanderies approached the court to state their case. Minister over the Masses Chen Dan and Gentleman Consultant Cao Cao (155–220) raised the matter to the throne and excoriated the officials in charge: "The reports that the Excellencies and Ministers made were informed by the personal wishes of their clique. It is as though they are freeing the owls but incarcerating the phoenixes." When the matter blew up, Emperor Ling reprimanded Xu Yu and Zhang Ji, and "appointed as Gentlemen Consultants all those who had been punished based on the rhymes."[227]

For this reason, Chen Dan offended the eunuchs, who framed him and threw him in prison, where he eventually died. "Henceforth, government and morals grew increasingly corrupt, and the powerful and cunning grew in strength." "The Three Excellencies sided with the wicked and were seldom summoned by the throne. Bribery was rife. The strong caused resentment but were not reported; the weak adhered to the proper way but most were framed and destroyed." Cao Cao "knew that the situation would not be righted, and never

226 *History of the Later Han, juan* 57, "Biography of Liu Tao." *Records of the Three Kingdoms, juan* 1, "Book of Wei: Annals of Emperor Wu," Pei Songzhi's annotation of "Book of Wei": "The imperial edict issued this order to the Office of the Three Excellencies: report ineffective administrations in the regions and counties, and dismiss those about whom the people make [negative] rhymes." (p.3)

227 *History of the Later Han, juan* 57, "Biography of Liu Tao," p.1851. The use of "Rhymes Reporting" to assess senior local officials during the Eastern Han Dynasty was sometimes taken very seriously. Inspector of Yizhou Region Chi Jian was dismissed because "his administration was troubled and rhymes were heard from afar." The court replaced him with Liu Yan as Governor of Yizhou Region. (*History of the Later Han, juan* 75, "Biography of Liu Yan," p.2431) Another case was recorded in *Records of the Three Kingdoms, juan* 8, "Book of Wei: Biography of Gongsun Du": Gongsun Du was a junior functionary but "after having been nominated for Possessing the Tao, he was appointed Gentleman of the Imperial Secretariat. Shortly after, he was promoted to Inspector of Jizhou Region. He was dismissed because of rhymes." (p.252)

offered advice again."[228] By then, the system for monitoring public opinion based on popular songs and rhymes sung by the people ceased to exist except in name.

It is interesting that the "Rhymes Reporting" style of monitoring public opinion evolved into "reporting matters heard in the wind" during the Western and Eastern Jin dynasties. Monitoring officials could report matters based on hearsay without ascertaining the truth or revealing the names and identities of the persons who had made the report.[229] Rhymes could refer to popular songs or other forms of hearsay or rumor. In ancient China, songs and rhymes, a unique form of rumor, were very intimately linked to public opinion and the monitoring of public opinion.

[228] *Records of the Three Kingdoms*, *juan* 1, "Book of Wei: Annals of Emperor Wu," Pei Song's annotation of "Book of Wei," p.3

[229] See Qiu Yongming (1992), p.125.

4 *Chen* Prophecies and Prophetic Rhymes

Chen Prophecy

What Is Chen *Prophecy?*

What is *chen*? During the early imperial period, philologists usually interpreted the word *chen* as "to be fulfilled,"[1] "subtle,"[2] and "secret writing."[3] *Chen* were words that seemed trivial and insignificant, but were in fact laden with meaning, mystery, and mysticism. They were words that prophesied future events that eventually came true. "The words were said beforehand, and the evidence came afterward."[4] *Chen* prophecy refers to unusual verbal or written discourse, or signs that revealed the Mandate of Heaven and prophesied the fate of individuals or regimes. These words and signs contained cryptic messages, and made their revelations and prophecies in a metaphorical and obscure manner.

1 "Radical Yan" in *An Explication of Written Characters*: "*Chen*. It means to be fulfilled." (Xu Guyi Congshu Edition, *juan* 3 *shang*, p.3a; Pingjinguan Congshu Fu Song Edition, *juan* 3 *shang*, p.69) Duan Yucai, *An Explication of Written Characters: Annotations*, *juan* 3 *shang*: "*Chen*. It means to be fulfilled. Writings that are verified. The books that emerged from the Yellow and Luo Rivers [in ancient legends] were known as *chen*." (p.90 *xia*) Duan claimed that the words "Writings that are verified. The books that emerged from the Yellow and Luo Rivers were known as *chen*." were based on *Selections of Refined Literature* and Li Shan's annotations of the two *fu* rhapsodies *Rhapsody of the Owl* and *Rhapsody of the Wei Capital*. However, according to Xu Chengqing, *An Explication of Written Characters: Emendations*: "These ... words were professed by Li Shan and not the words of *An Explication of Written Characters*, which explains the differences in the complexities of the writing." (citing a quotation in *An Explication of Written Characters: Elucidations*, p.2911) It is verified in *The Grand Scribe's Records*, *juan* 84, "Memoirs of Qu Yuan and Scholar Jia" (Sima Zhen: *The Grand Scribe's Records*: *Commentaries*), citing *An Explication of Written Characters* that "*Chen*. It means words that are fulfilled." (p.2497) Xu Chengqing's argument that Duan Yucai's annotations were not the original text of *An Explication of Written Characters* could stand.

2 *Explanation of Names*, *juan* 6, "Explaining Literature and Arts," *di* 20: "The words are thin and insignificant, but they come to pass."

3 *Book of Cangjie*, *juan shang*: "It means secret writing, which emerged from the Yellow and Luo Rivers." (p.7)

4 *History of the Later Han*, *juan* 59, "Biography of Zhang Heng," p.1912.

Readers would naturally associate the phrase "unusual discourse" with unverifiable talk and portentous talk in Chapters 1 and 2, respectively. The unverifiable talk, portentous talk, and *chen* prophecy of the early imperial period were all blanketed in a kind of mystic miasma. Not only were unverifiable talk and portentous talk sometimes used interchangeably in historical texts, some unverifiable talk and portentous talk were given the function of making prophecies and issuing warnings on Heaven's behalf – in fact, almost equivalent to *chen* prophecy. As Li Xun suggested, "It is not impossible for unverifiable talk to have prophetic qualities." We could actually put it this way: unverifiable talk and portentous talk were *chen* prophecies that had yet to come true; *chen* prophecies were unverifiable talk and portentous talk that had come true. The curse that said, "After the First Emperor dies, his territory will be divided"; the portentous talk of people like Sui Hong and Xiahou Sheng; the Earth-Power unverifiable talk that emerged during the years of the Western Han-to-Xin and Eastern Han-to-Wei dynastic changes; and slogans like "The Blue Sky is dead; the Yellow Sky will stand. In the Jiazi year, great fortune comes to the land" – all of these were later verified as *chen* prophecies that came true.

There were also certain widely circulated and widely accepted disseminated talk, unverifiable talk, and portentous talk, which, as repositories of people's hopes, prayers, and consensus, and in whose mysterious powers the people of the time believed, became auto-suggestive and self-fulfilling *chen* prophecies. At times, they could even influence developments and change the course of history.

The belief in prophecy was very common in the social and political life of pre-Qin China. There are copious records of it in extant historical writings, as well as in almanacs excavated from ancient tombs. Many enigmatic prophecies regarding the political development of states, the fates of rulers, and high-level personnel changes are found in the *Commentary of Zuo*, *Discourses of the States*, and *The Grand Scribe's Records*. Early purveyors of prophecies were often diviners in the service of the state, such as Grand Scribes and Royal Secretaries. Their prophecies were often closely linked to divination arts, such as divinations using yarrow, stars, dreams, and physiognomies. Their prognostications would come to pass and were often very accurate. Then, there were "strange, coded prophecies that foretold good or ill fortune,"[5] which were expressed as spoken or written words and had great symbolic power. While they had yet to acquire the name "*chen*," they could be considered the

[5] *Catalog of the Complete Library in Four Sections*, *juan* 6, "Classics: Book of Changes," 6 *fulu*, "The Magical Chart of *Kun* Changes," annotations by academy staff, p.47.

forerunners of *chen* prophecies. Chao Fulin appropriately referred to such prophecies as "*chen* prophetic expressions."[6]

According to Chao, "the rise of *chen prophetic* expressions began in the Western Zhou, grew in the Spring and Autumn and Warring States Periods, and finally flourished in the Qin and Han."[7] The word "*chen*" first appeared in the term "Qin *chen*" in a Han-period text: "The Hereditary House of Zhao" in *The Grand Scribe's Records*. Related to "Qin *chen*" was "Zhao *chen*," a prophetic expression that had yet to be labeled as "*chen*." These two "*chen* prophetic expressions" occurred on three occasions in *The Grand Scribe's Records*: the accounts in "The Hereditary House of Zhao" and "Memoirs of Bian Que and the Duke of Cang" were very detailed and were identical in general, while "Treatise on Feng and Shan Offerings" gave a pared-down narrative.

According to "The Hereditary House of Zhao," Zhao Jianzi (Zhao Yang, ?–476 BCE) was seriously ill and fell into a coma for five days. After Bian Que (Qin Yueren, a legendary physician at the time) examined him, he told Zhao Jianzi's trusted retainer Dong Anyu that his lord's illness was rather peculiar:

> In the past, Duke Mu of Qin [reigned 659–621 BCE] had the same condition; he woke after seven days. On the day he woke up, he told Gongsun Zhi and Ziyu: "I went to the Supreme Deity's residence where I was very happy. That I stayed for a long time was because I was receiving instructions. The Supreme Deity said to me: 'The State of Jin will soon descend into chaos, and the disorder will last five generations. Their descendant will proclaim himself Hegemon, but will die before he grows old. The son of the Hegemon will cause the men and women in the State of Jin to become indistinguishable from each other.'" Gongsun Zhi put these words down in writing and kept it. It was then that the Qin *chen* began to spread. The chaos during the time of Duke Xian [of Jin], the hegemony of Duke Wen, and the debauchery of Duke Xiang after his return from his defeat of the Qin army at Mount Xiao – all these are well-known to you. Your lord's current ailment is the same as Duke Mu's, and it will improve within three days. After it improves, words will be spoken.[8]

"Qin *chen*" referred to the *chen* prophecy that the Supreme Deity revealed to Duke Mu of Qin when the latter was in a coma, which revealed the fortunes of the State of Jin.

But the story did not end there. Just as Bian Que had predicted, Zhao Jianzi woke up two-and-a-half days later, and he told his Grandees that he had in fact gone to the residence of the Supreme Deity, who revealed to him the fortunes of the states of Jin, Qin, and Zhao. The Supreme Deity said, "The State of Jin will decline and eventually fall after seven generations. People bearing the

[6] Chao Fulin (1993), p.21. [7] *Ibid.*

[8] *The Grand Scribe's Records*, *juan* 43, "The Hereditary House of Zhao," pp.1786–1787. In *juan* 105, "Memoirs of Bian Que and the Duke of Cang," the word "*chen*" was replaced by "*ce*." (p.2787)

family name Ying [referring to the royal house of Qin] will deal a crushing defeat to the people of Zhou west of Fankui, but they will not occupy that land. I now recall the meritorious deeds of Shun. The time will come when I shall make Meng Yao, a female descendant of Shun, the wife of your seventh-generation male descendant." Zhao Jianzi also saw his son standing in attendance at the Supreme Deity's side. The Supreme Deity gave Zhao Jianzi a dog of the north, saying: "Give this to your son when he grows up."

Soon afterward, Zhao Jianzi went on a journey and met a divine being. He asked the divine being why the Supreme Deity would want him to pass the dog of the north, which the Supreme Deity had given to him, on to his son. The divine being explained, "The child is my lord's son; the dog of the north is the ancestor of the State of Dai. My lord's son shall one day occupy Dai. Your descendant will implement political reforms and put on barbarian clothing. He will conquer two states in the land of the Di [in the north]."[9] This was the "Zhao *chen*."

The Qin *chen* and Zhao *chen* were divine edicts received by Duke Mu of Qin and Zhao Jianzi, respectively, in their sleep, and had similarities to the divination of dreams. For example, the image of the dog of the north in the Zhao *chen* could only be understood after its meaning was revealed by a divine being (equivalent to a shaman or diviner who foretold the future by interpreting dreams). The way the language and images were expressed, however, was very similar to the *chen* prophecies that came later.

In *The Grand Scribe's Records*, a line in Jia Yi's (200–168 BCE) *fu* rhapsody, *Rhapsody of the Owl*, read: "I opened up the book to divine the sign and see what *ce* measures."[10] In *History of the Former Han*, the same line reads: "I opened up the book to divine the sign and see what *chen* measures."[11] The word quoted in *The Grand Scribe's Records*, "*ce*," was used in yarrow divination. In earlier times, *chen prophetic* expressions and the divinatory words of yarrow divination were very similar in origin. For this reason, the people in the early Western Han Dynasty might have grouped *chen prophetic* expressions and divinatory words together as one. Therefore, the divination book that Jia Yi used was also called a "*chen* prophetic book." Another possibility was that people in the Eastern Han Dynasty grouped divination books and *chen* prophetic books in the same category, which was why Ban Gu (32–92 CE) replaced "*ce*" with "*chen*."[12]

[9] *The Grand Scribe's Records, juan* 43, "The Hereditary House of Zhao," p.1788.

[10] *The Grand Scribe's Records, juan* 84, "Memoirs of Qu Yuan and Scholar Jia," p.2497.

[11] *History of the Former Han, juan* 48, "Biography of Jia Yi," p.2226.

[12] *The Grand Scribe's Records, juan* 123, "Memoirs of Dayuan": "The Son of Heaven [Emperor Wu of the Western Han Dynasty] opened up the *Book of Changes* for divination, and the book read: 'The divine horse will come from the northwest.' After acquiring a good horse from Wusun, he named that horse 'Heavenly Horse.' After obtaining the Sweat-Blood Horse from

The Forms That Chen *Prophecies Take*

Spoken Form Like unverifiable talk, disseminated talk, portentous talk, and rhymes, much of the *chen* prophecies during the early imperial period were in spoken form, and took definite shape in the course of their propagation.

In the first year of the reign of the Qin Dynasty's Second Emperor (209 BCE), 900 border guards, including Chen Sheng (?–208 BCE) and Wu Guang (?–208 BCE), were dispatched in the seventh month to defend the marchlands at Yuyang. They were delayed by rains and, according to the law, soldiers who arrived at their posts late would be executed. Discussing this with Wu Guang, Chen Sheng said, "We would die if we run; we would also die if we revolt. Since we would die in both cases, why don't we die founding a state?" Hence, they decided to launch an armed rebellion. To "raise their prestige among the guards," they wrote the characters "Chen Sheng will rule" in red on a piece of white silk and stuffed it into a fish that someone else had caught. A border guard purchased the fish for his table and was amazed to find the piece of cloth inside the fish. Hiding himself in a temple near the army encampment, Wu Guang mimicked the howl of a fox as he cried out: "The Great Chu will rise up, and Chen Sheng will rule!" The soldiers were frightened by these cries in the night. The following morning, they talked among themselves and pointed Chen Sheng out to one another.[13]

The "vulpine cry" of "the Great Chu will rise up, and Chen Sheng will rule!" spread among the 900 border guards as disseminated talk. Subsequently, in tandem with the expansion of Chen Sheng's rebel forces, it circulated among many more people in a much larger area, adding fuel to the fire of anti-Qin

Dayuan, which grew stronger, the Son of Heaven renamed the Wusun horse 'Paramount Horse of the West' and named the Dayuan horse 'Heavenly Horse.'" (p.3170) The account recorded in *History of the Former Han, juan* 61, "Biography of Zhang Qian" was somewhat similar. (pp.2693–2694) The phrase "opened up the *Book of Changes* for divination" means to make prognostications with yarrow divination books such as the *Book of Changes*. Xun Yue (148–209), *Annals of the Former Han, juan* 14, "Annals of Emperor Xiaowu, Part V": "At the beginning of the fourth year of the Taichu reign period [101 BCE], His Majesty [Emperor Wu] opened up the *chen* prophetic book, which read: 'The divine horse will come from the northwest.' Later on, he acquired a good horse from Wusun and named it the Heavenly Horse. He then obtained the Dayuan horse, which sweated blood, and it was said that its ancestor had been the son of the Heavenly Horse. Therefore, it was named Heavenly Horse and the Wusun horse was renamed the Paramount Horse of the Northwest." This was proof that the people of the Eastern Han Dynasty considered yarrow divination books as *chen* prophetic books. The apocryphal-prophetic books that became popular from the mid- and late Western Han Dynasty usually eschewed the format of yarrow divination books. Interestingly, however, the new anthologies of *chen* prophecies that appeared after the Southern Song Dynasty, such as *Back-Pushing Drawing* and *Divination before the Horse*, and fortune-telling poems in Buddhist and Taoist temples, reverted to the formats of the yarrow divination books.

13 *The Grand Scribe's Records, juan* 48, "The Hereditary House of Chen She," p.1950.

sentiments of the time and becoming a public opinion herald for Chen Sheng's founding of the Kingdom of Zhangchu.

There was a kind of divination by weather, popular throughout the Warring States and early imperial period, called "watching air currents," where diviners observed clouds and air currents in the sky to make prognostications about the future.[14] During the reign of the First Emperor of the Qin Dynasty, sorcerers who observed air currents foresaw that "a Son of Heaven air current will be present in the southeast." The First Emperor made five tours of his empire following his unification of China. Apart from his first tour to Longxi in the west, the other four were taken in the southeast – in the former states of Qi, Yan, Chu, and so on (covering the present-day provinces of Shandong, Jiangsu, Hunan, Hubei, Anhui, and Zhejiang). There were, of course, political, military, and economic objectives to the First Emperor's multiple tours, but it was recorded in *The Grand Scribe's Records* that "the First Emperor of Qin Dynasty often said: 'A Son of Heaven air current will be present in the southeast.' For this reason, he traveled to the east to suppress it."[15] Therefore, it was possible that the First Emperor traveled to the southeast to quash any potential threat that could endanger his dynasty. Alas, what man proposes, God disposes. The main rebel leaders who eventually overthrew the Qin Dynasty, Chen Sheng, Wu Guang, and Xiang Yu,

[14] "The Sacrifice against the Coming of the Enemy" in *Mo Zi*: "In watching air currents, there are categories such as air currents of major generals, air currents of minor generals, air currents of leaving, air currents of coming, and air currents of defeat. Those who comprehend these know the successes, failures, and good and ill fortunes of the future." (*Mo Zi: Annotations*, *juan* 15, p.574) Among the texts written on silk discovered in a Western Han tomb at Mawangdui was one *Miscellaneous Astrological and Meteorological Divinations*. During the early imperial period, there were Observers of Air Currents and Assistant Observers of Air Currents installed at court who were solely responsible for observing clouds, air currents, and stars. Famous ones included Xin Yuanping during the reign of Emperor Wen, and Wang Shuo during the reign of Emperor Wu. *The Grand Scribe's Records* and *History of the Former Han* contain quite a number of records of air currents divination in the early Han. For example, it was recorded in *History of the Former Han*, *juan* 8, "Annals of Emperor Xuan" that "in the second year of his later reign, Emperor Wu fell ill and was going back and forth between the Changyang and Wuzuo Palaces. Diviners who watched the air currents said a Son of Heaven air current was present in the prisons of Chang'an. The Emperor sent his emissaries to re-examine those who had been imprisoned [for witchcraft] in various bureaus in the imperial capital, and had them all killed, regardless of the severity of their crimes." (p.236) *History of the Former Han*, *juan* 97 *shang*, "Biographies of Imperial Affines": "Emperor Wu's Lady Gouyi, the Favorite Beauty Zhao, was Emperor Zhao's mother. Her hometown was in Hejian. Emperor Wu was passing by Hejian on a hunting expedition when an Observer of Air Currents said that an extraordinary woman was in the area. The Emperor sent his men to bring her before him. When the lady arrived, her hands were balled into fists. The Emperor himself proceeded to peel open her fingers and she opened up her hands at once. For this reason, she found favor with the Emperor and was referred to as 'Lady Fists.'" (p.3956)

[15] *The Grand Scribe's Records*, *juan* 8, "Basic Annals of Emperor Gaozu," p.348.

and the man who went on to found the Western Han Dynasty, Liu Bang, were all from the southeast.

In the twelfth year of the reign of Emperor Gaozu (195 BCE) of the Western Han Dynasty, the Emperor made his older brother's son Liu Bi (216–154 BCE) the King of Wu. Having formally conferred the title, Emperor Gaozu summoned Liu Bi before him. Upon reading his physiognomy, the Emperor told Liu Bi that he had the face of a rebel. He began to regret his decision to make his nephew the King of Wu, but the title had already been conferred. Emperor Gaozu could only pat Liu Bi on the back and warn him that "a rebellion would break out in the southeast fifty years after the founding of the Han Dynasty," and that Liu Bi had better not be that rebel, for after all, they belonged to the same Liu family.[16] During the time of Emperor Jing's reign, the court adopted the proposal of Chao Cuo (200–154 BCE), the Censor-in-Chief, to confiscate the lands of the kingdoms. In response, Liu Bi led Wu, Chu, and five other kingdoms in rebellion in the third year of Emperor Jing's earlier reign period (154 BCE) under the clarion call of putting Chao Cuo to death and ridding the Emperor of evil counsel. The rebellion was subsequently put down by Zhou Yafu (?–143 BCE) and Liu Bi was killed.

Citing Xu Guang, Pei Yin wrote in *The Grand Scribe's Records: Collected Explications* that fifty-three years separated the year of the Han Dynasty's founding and the third year of Emperor Jing's reign, the year when Liu Bi revolted.[17] He also identified Emperor Gaozu's words – "a rebellion would break out in the southeast fifty years after the founding of the Han Dynasty" – as a *chen* prophecy. He quoted Ying Shao: "Diviners have a knowledge of the fifty-year period. This might have been the case when the First Emperor of the Qin Dynasty toured the east to suppress the [Son of Heaven] air current, and subsequently Liu [Bang] and Xiang [Yu] emerged in the southeast." Sima Zhen explained in *The Grand Scribe's Records: Commentaries* that Ying Shao had meant that the rebellion in the southeast fifty years hence was a prognostication by air current diviners, and having heard this, Emperor Gaozu was worried that the second catastrophe would occur before the first one had run its course. It was for this reason that he issued his warning to his nephew Liu Bi.[18]

Sima Zhen was of the opinion that Emperor Gaozu's warning words to Liu Bi were derived from the Qin period prophecy: "a Son of Heaven air current will be present in the south and the east." During the reign of Emperor Wu of the Western Han Dynasty, Liu An, King of Huainan, summoned his advisor Wu Bei (?–122 BCE) to have a discussion about an uprising against the court. Wu Bei believed that the earlier rebellion of the Kingdoms of Wu and Chu had "opposed Heaven and Man" and had not been in agreement with the times. If

[16] *The Grand Scribe's Records*, *juan* 106, "Memoir of Liu Bi, King of Wu," p.2821.
[17] *Ibid.*, p.2822. [18] *Ibid.*

they were to plot a rebellion now, he could see no joy, only grief. Liu An disagreed: "Chen Sheng and Wu Guang had the smallest of territories with a hundred men. Rising up at Daze Township, they raised their arms and all under heaven responded to their battle cry. They proceeded westward until they reached Xi with an army of 1,200,000 men. My kingdom may be small, but I have 200,000 battle-ready soldiers. Why do you say that my revolt would bring no joy but grief?" Wu Bei explained:

> [In the final days of the Qin Dynasty,] fathers could not protect their sons and older brothers could not look after their younger brothers. The laws were harsh and the punishments brutal. The people craned their necks to see and strained their ears to hear. They looked up to Heaven and lamented; they beat their breasts and hated their rulers. Eight out of ten households wished to revolt. It was then that someone said to [Liu Bang, the future] Emperor Gao[zu], "The time has come." But the [future] Emperor said: "Wait a little. A sage will rise up in the southeast." Within a year, Chen [Sheng] and Wu [Guang] raised their cry and Liu [Bang] and Xiang [Yu] responded, together with the rest of the realm. This was taking advantage of an opportunity and striking when the Qin was on the verge of collapse. The people supported it with much fervor, as though they had seen rain after a prolonged drought. For this reason, [Liu Bang] could rise from the troops and embark on a heroic enterprise to become Emperor. Your Highness can only see the ease with which Emperor Gaozu conquered the empire, but can Your Highness not see the recent failures of the rebellion by [the Kingdoms of] Wu and Chu?[19]

From "a Son of Heaven air current will be present in the southeast" and "a rebellion would break out in the southeast fifty years after the founding of the Han Dynasty," to "a sage will rise up in the southeast," it is apparent that this particular *chen* prophecy had been widely disseminated by word of mouth, had undergone several changes, and had repeatedly appeared in the decades that saw the end of the Qin and the founding of the Han.

In addition, there were quite a number of *chen* prophecies that were expressed in folk songs and rhymes. These "prophetic rhymes" will be discussed in the subsequent section.

Chen *Prophecy in Writing* The belief in the sacred symbolism of written words is an ancient one in China. The long-standing monopoly on the written word exercised by the elite fed the fire of this belief, resulting in people having absolute faith in the mysterious powers of written words. In addition, the unique methods in which Chinese characters were formed (e.g. the "form imitation" of pictograms, "indication" of ideograms, "joined meaning" of compound ideographs)[20] offered the possibility of multiple interpretations

19 *History of the Former Han*, *juan* 45, "Biography of Wu Bei," p.2171–2172.

20 Other classifications include phono-semantic compounds, phonetic loan characters, and "derivative cognates."

through the dismantling and reconstruction of the characters. When *chen* prophecies were written in Chinese characters, the cryptic and metaphoric nature of these "strange, coded prophecies that foretold good or ill fortune" could be better expressed, resulting in their enhanced conformation to the popular imagination of "prophecies from Heaven," their greater tenacity to survive over time, and expanded space for their propagation.[21]

In the case of the piece of cloth with the characters "Chen Sheng will rule" stuffed inside a fish prior to Chen Sheng and Wu Guang's armed revolt, the written form was used as a medium for the information, which was then propagated through the spoken words of the border guard who had bought and cooked the fish. The collections of *chen* prophecies in written form were called *chen* prophetic books. In the thirty-second year of his reign (215 BCE), the First Emperor of the Qin dynasty sent Scholar Lu, a *fangshi* from the Yan region, to look for immortals across the seas. Scholar Lu returned and presented the emperor with a copy of *Collection of Transcribed Diagrams and Scripts*, which featured a sentence that read: "The one who will destroy Qin is *Hu*."[22] This line was a typical coded *chen* prophecy, and the book, *Collection of Transcribed Diagrams and Scripts*, might have been an early anthology of *chen* prophecies, featuring both words and illustrations.[23]

The early *chen* prophetic books might have been collections of divinatory words compiled and edited by *fangshi*, such as the one mentioned by Jia Yi in *Rhapsody of the Owl*: "I opened up the book to divine the sign and see what *chen* measures." After the middle of the Western Han Dynasty, *chen* prophetic books written by *fangshi* began to appear. Containing many references to contemporary issues, the *chen* prophecies in these books were clearly political and made bold demands. For example, the *Calendar of the Heavenly Official* and *Classic of Great Peace with the Embodiment of the Origin*, written by the *fangshi* Gan Zhongke of the Qi region during the reign of Emperor Cheng of the Western Han Dynasty, proclaimed that "the Han Dynasty coincides with the end of Heaven and Earth, and should renew its mandate from Heaven. The

21 The fact that we can read spoken *chen* prophecies and folk songs and rhymes of the early imperial period today is because they were selected, documented, edited, transformed into written words, and finally recorded in historical texts by historians.

22 *The Grand Scribe's Records*, *juan* 6, "Basic Annals of the First Emperor of Qin," pp.252–253. *Hu* was commonly understood at the time as barbarians, such as the Xiongnu. The First Emperor of Qin thus made an immediate response by sending large contingent to the north to fight the *Hu* barbarians. Ironically the name of the Second Emperor of Qin, who was responsible for the Qin Dynasty's quick collapse, was Hu Hai.

23 Zhang Heng, *Pondering the Abstruse*: "Ying [Zheng, the First Emperor of the Qin dynasty] interpreted the *chen* and guarded against the barbarians, but even as he was alert to external threats, his empire collapsed from within." (*History of the Later Han*, *juan* 59, "Biography of Zhang Heng," p.1924) This line from Zhang Heng's *fu* rhapsody shows that the people of the Eastern Han Dynasty considered *Collection of Transcribed Diagrams and Scripts* a *chen* prophetic book.

Heavenly Deity has sent Chijingzi, the immortal, to teach me the Way."[24] Gan Zhongke had many disciples to whom he taught his books, and they in turn imparted his teachings to their many disciples. Classified by the Western Han court as portentous books, *Calendar of the Heavenly Official* and *Classic of Great Peace with the Embodiment of the Origin* contained a great deal of expositions on apocryphal-prophetic discourses, including the "Chijingzi *chen* prophecy," which was very popular during the late Western Han. For these reasons, they should be categorized as *chen* prophetic books.

In the final days of the Xin Dynasty, armed uprisings and banditry were endemic, and there were frequent border incursions from non-Han peoples. The people resented Wang Mang's regime and were nostalgic for the good old days of the Han Dynasty. In such a milieu, there would have been quite a number of self-authored *chen* prophetic books circulating among the people. Among those that were recorded in history was the 100,000-word *chen* prophetic book written by the diviner Wang Kuang for Li Yan, Governor of Weicheng. According to this book,

> Emperor Wen is incensed and trains his troops in the underworld, informing the Xiongnu in the north and the Yue peoples in the south. Liu Xin in Jiangzhong will wreak vengeance on his enemies.[25] To restore and inherit the enterprise of his ancestors, he will launch a military campaign in the fourth year. There will come a great bandit in the rivers and lakes who will call himself King of Fan.[26] His family name will be Liu and he will lead tens of thousands of men. He will not accept the court's amnesty but will endeavor to strike the Qin region and Luoyang. The attack will occur in the eleventh year, when Venus will shine bright and Jupiter will enter the east of the Well Constellation. His orders will be implemented.[27]

The book revealed the fates of Wang Mang's senior ministers, all of which were dated. It also prophesied in no uncertain terms that the Jingchu region would rise up, assisted by a person bearing the surname Li. Li Yan ordered his functionaries to make copies of the book for dissemination.

The period between the late Western Han and the Xin saw the appearance of a large number of apocryphal-prophetic texts that incorporated yarrow divination words, *chen* prophecies, *Yinyang* and the Five Agents, myths, and interpretations of "New Texts" of the pre-Qin classics. Books such as *Diagram*

[24] *History of the Former Han, juan* 75, "Biography of Li Xun," p.3192.

[25] Liu Xin, Marquess of Yanxiang, was a distant member of the Liu imperial house. He took part in Zhai Yi's revolt against Wang Mang in 7 CE and was crowned by Zhai Yi as Emperor.

[26] In the fifth year of the Tianfeng reign period (18 CE), Fan Chong (?–27 CE), a native of Langya Commandery, led a peasants' revolt against the Xin Dynasty. Within a few years, his troops numbered in the tens of thousands and his influence encompassed eastern China and the Central Plains. He was later made a marquess by an "Emperor" crowned by another rebellion force at Luoyang. He then conquered Chang'an, the center of the Qin region, and crowned a distant member of the Liu imperial house as his own "Emperor."

[27] *History of the Former Han, juan* 99 *xia*, "Biography of Wang Mang, Part III," pp.4166–4167.

of the Yellow River, Script of the Luo River,[28] *Diagram of the Purple Pavilion,* and *The Token of Red Secret Appended to the Diagram of the Yellow River* were in open circulation. After the fall of Wang Mang's Xin Dynasty, Gongsun Shu (?–36 CE), the former Grand Administrator of Daojiang (the commandery of Shu), "was partial to matters pertaining to talismans, deities, and omens, and made absurd references to *chen* prophetic records." The *chen* prophetic records he referred to included apocryphal books such as *Examining Divine Luminaries Appended to the Book of Documents, Records of Models of Dynastic Changes Appended to Diagram of the Yellow River, Images of Surveying the Earth Appended to Diagram of the Yellow River*, and *The Talisman of Quoting the Spirits Appended to the Spring and Autumn Annals.*[29]

During the Eastern Han Dynasty, apocryphal-prophetic books were seen as supplementary to Confucian classics. Emperor Guangwu ordered the scholars in his service to collect the various apocryphal-prophetic texts that were circulating among the people. These texts were then edited, published, and promulgated by imperial order.

Pictorial Symbols A unique feature that set *chen* prophecy apart from unverifiable talk, disseminated talk, portentous talk, and rhymes was its frequent expression as pictorial symbols, in addition to its spoken and written forms. For example, the earliest versions of *Diagram of the Yellow River* and *Script of the Luo River*, considered the forerunners of apocryphal-prophetic discourses, were said to feature both words and illustrations. The *chen* prophetic books during the early imperial period were very likely the same. For this reason, apocryphal-prophetic discourses were often referred to as "diagram books," "*chen* prophecy and diagrams," and "apocrypha and diagrams" during the early imperial period. At times, diagrammatic *chen* prophecies originated in nature, which compelled people to believe that they were truly a sign from Heaven. Unusual human physical characteristics, such as lines on the palm or

[28] *History of the Former Han, juan* 99 *zhong*, "Biography of Wang Mang, Part II": "On the Wuchen day of that month, the west bank of the Jing River at Changping Hall collapsed, congesting the Jing River, which broke its embankments and flowed northward. Wang Yi, Grand Minister of Works, was sent to inspect the damage and he returned to give his report, whereupon the ministers congratulated the Emperor. They believed that it was the fulfilling of the prophecy in *Diagram of the Yellow River* that said, 'Overpowering the water with earth,' which was the auspicious sign of the Xiongnu's fall." (p.4144) *History of the Former Han, juan* 84, "Biography of Zhai Yi": "After the Grand Empress Dowager took over the reins of government, there were auspicious signs of turtles, dragons, unicorns, and phoenixes, and blessed auspices of the Five Powers, in succession and complete. The *Diagram of the Yellow River* and *Script of the Luo River* originated in faraway Kunlun, from the wild lands. The ancient *chen* prophecies that was written down have been confirmed in the present day." (p.3432)

[29] *History of the Later Han, juan* 13, "Biography of Gongsun Shu," p.538.

marks on the skin, were often seen as divine revelations. Such revelations had already appeared in pre-Qin texts, as seen in the following stories.

Song Zhongzi, daughter of Duke Wu of Song (reigned 765–748 BCE), married Duke Hui of Lu (reigned 766–723 BCE). It was recorded in *Commentary of Zuo* that "when Zhongzi was born, the lines of her palm formed the words "to be Lady of Lu." Therefore, Zhongzi belonged to our state."[30] Kong Yingda's explanation was that "the natural lines on her hand formed words, as though it was Heaven's will that she would be the Lady of the State of Lu. Therefore, she was given in marriage to the State of Lu."[31]

Song Zhongzi was the mother of Duke Huan of Lu (reigned 711–694 BCE). The fourth son of Duke Huan, named You (?–644 BCE) and given the posthumous epithet Cheng, was known in history by various names such as Gongzi You and Cheng Jiyou. He was the de facto ruler of the State of Lu for sixteen years during the reign of Duke Xi of Lu, and was the progenitor of the Jisun clan, the most powerful noble family in the State of Lu from the eighth to sixth centuries BCE. When his mother Wen Jiang was pregnant with him, his father Duke Huan ordered a diviner[32] to perform a divination. The diviner foretold: "It is a boy and his name shall be 'You.' He will be the Duke's right-hand man, handling the affairs of state and assisting the Duke's family." "When he was born, the lines of his palm formed the word 'You,' and he was subsequently named You."[33]

In the seventeenth year of his reign (541 BCE), Duke Ping of Jin fell ill. Zi Chan,[34] representing the State of Zheng, visited the State of Jin to see how Duke Ping was faring. As they were discussing Duke Ping's illness, Zi Chan and Shu Xiang, the Grandee of Jin, spoke about the legend of how Tang Shuyu, the founding ruler of the State of Jin, was named. Tang Shuyu was a

30 *Commentary of Zuo: The First Year of Duke Yin.* Yang Bojun wrote in *Commentary of Zuo on the Spring and Autumn Annals: Annotations* that "marks mean words," and that he suspected "the original text in *Commentary of Zuo* was [just] 'Lady of Lu.'" (pp.3–4)

31 *Annotations and Explanations of the Thirteen Classics: Commentary of Zuo on the Spring and Autumn Annals, juan* 2, p.1713.

32 His name is unknown. What we know is that his son Chu Qiu served the Lu court as Grandee Diviner.

33 *Commentary of Zuo: The Second Year of Duke Min. Commentary of Zuo on the Spring and Autumn Annals: Annotations*, pp.263–264. A record of this event is also found in *Commentary of Zuo: The Thirty-second Year of Duke Zhao*: "Cheng Jiyou was the youngest son of Duke Huan and Wen Jiang's beloved son. During her early pregnancy, a divination was performed and the diviner reported: 'He will be of good repute on the day he is born. His name shall be "You" and he will help the Duke's family.' When he was born, it was exactly as the diviner had said. The lines of his palm formed the word 'You' and he was subsequently named You. Later on, he rendered services of great merit to the State of Lu, and he was conferred the land of Fei and made Senior Minister." (*Commentary of Zuo on the Spring and Autumn Annals: Annotations*, p.1520)

34 Also known as Gongsun Qiao (?–522 BCE), he was a well-known statesman and reformer of the State of Zheng during the Spring and Autumn Period.

son of King Wu of the Western Zhou Dynasty, and the younger brother of King Cheng. Both he and King Cheng were born of the same mother. Tang Shuyu's given name was Yu and the land of Tang was enfeoffed to him. According to the legend, when his mother Yi Jiang was pregnant with him, she "dreamed that the Supreme Deity of Heaven spoke to her, saying: 'I shall name your son "Yu," and confer him the land of Tang. He belongs to the Shen Constellation and his descendants will be many.'" When he was born, the lines of his palm formed the word "Yu" and he was named thus. When King Cheng vanquished the land of Tang, his younger brother Yu was enfeoffed this piece of land.[35]

In pre-Qin texts, these unusual, natural born lines on the palms of individuals were seen as written symbols that conveyed Heaven's will, which prophesied their future destinies or political achievements.

In the apocryphal-prophetic texts that were popular during the early imperial period, unusual or even bizarre physical appearances, and their special symbolic meanings, were often singled out for praise. Examples included the dragon-like forehead of the Yellow Emperor, the four eyes of Cangjie, the bovine head of Fu Xi, the serpentine body of Nü Wa, Yao having eight-colored eyebrows, the avian beak of Gao Yao, the double irises of Shun, the triple earholes of Yu, Tang having three elbows, King Wen of the Western Zhou Dynasty having four nipples, King Wu having double rows of teeth, and the Duke of Zhou sporting a hunchback. As for Confucius, he had "a mouth like the sea and a head with a dented crown. He had a square face, with a frontal bone on the right side of the forehead and a sun-like nose. He had long eyes and the forehead of a dragon. His lips were like the Dou Constellation and his countenance brilliant; his cheeks were even and his throat was supported by two spokes. He had double rows of teeth. He had the body of a dragon, the back of a turtle, and the paws of a tiger. His ribs are fused and his arms long. His chest was like the Shen Constellation and the crown of his head was depressed."[36] All these physical abnormalities were seen as signs that their bearers were sages and kings who had been conferred the Mandate of Heaven. The murals and carvings in the tombs at Wuliang and Yi'nan depicted many deities and ancient kings with bizarre physical features. According to historical records, many emperors of the Eastern Han Dynasty and their consorts liked to boast about their "noble countenances" and "unusual appearances," which was the fashionable thing to do at the time. It was recorded in *History of the Later Han* that "born with a deviated chin and broken nose bridge, Zhou Xie was

[35] *Commentary of Zuo*: *The First Year of Duke Zhao*. *Commentary of Zuo on the Spring and Autumn Annals: Annotations*, pp.1217–1218.

[36] *Spring and Autumn: Diagram Depicting Confucius*. *Compendium of Apocryphal Books*, *juan zhong*, pp.574, 576.

frightfully ugly. His mother wanted to abandon him, but his father refused, saying: 'I have heard that many sages were unusual of appearance. This will be the son who will prosper my clan.'"[37] It came to a point where the Emperor had to issue a decree to order "the families of the Emperor's meritorious servants not to make additions when listing their meritorious services in their genealogies or biographies to give false facts, or give descriptions of their physical appearance that would be detrimental to the truth, such as saying that their mouths and teeth had grown an extra *cun*, or that they had dragon miens and mouths of a tiger, or they sported peculiar hairs and unique bones. These extremely strange physical traits would not be recognized in the imperial decrees."[38]

However, the interpretation of unusual physical traits and appearances depended on the people involved, the time and place, and the social and political contexts. Zhen Xun (?–10 CE), son of Zhen Feng,[39] was flippant by nature and had a predilection for carnal pleasures. It was said that his arm had a mark that formed the two characters *tianzi* ("Son of Heaven"), which should have been an auspicious sign. He resorted to forging talismanic writings (similar to *chen* prophecies) to obtain an enfeoffment for his father and when that succeeded, he created another talismanic writing saying that Princess Huanghuang, the widow of Emperor Ping of the Western Han Dynasty and daughter of Wang Mang, should marry him (Zhen Xun). Incensed, Wang Mang said, "Princess Huanghuang is the Mother of the Realm. What nonsense is this!"[40] Zhen Feng had to take his own life as a result, and Zhen Xun was arrested and executed. Given the rumors about the characters *tianzi* on Zhen Xun's arm, Wang Mang examined it in person and gave his own analysis of the markings by taking "*tianzi*" apart to form new words with new meanings: "The words are '*yi da zi*' ('one-big-son') or '*yi liu zi*' ('one-six-son'). *Liu* is pronounced the same way as *lu* ('to kill'). It is obvious that Zhen Xun and his father are meant to be killed."[41]

Gongsun Shu of the late Xin Dynasty was partial to citing auspicious signs and *chen* prophetic records to reinforce the legitimacy of his independent regime in the Shu region. He claimed that the lines on his palm formed characters that read "Emperor Gongsun," which he considered an auspicious

37 *History of the Later Han*, "Biography of Zhou Xie," *juan* 53, p.1742.

38 *Eastern Library's Records of Han*, *juan* 22, citing *Imperial Reader of the Taiping Era*, *juan* 363, p.922.

39 Zhen Feng (?–10 CE), a senior official in the late Western Han Dynasty, was, together with Liu Xin and Wang Shun, a trusted right-hand man of Wang Mang. He was one of the advocates of Wang Mang's regency during Emperor Ping's reign. After Wang Mang replaced the Western Han Dynasty with his own Xin Dynasty, the distance between Wang Mang and Zhen Feng grew because of the latter's strong personality.

40 *History of the Former Han*, *juan* 99 *zhong*, "Biography of Wang Mang, Part II," p.4123.

41 *Ibid.*

sign. However, *History of the Later Han* accused him of "inscribing his own palm" to create unusual palm lines.[42]

In the third year of Emperor Zhao's Yuanfeng reign period, a worm-nibbled leaf formed the words "Bingyi, the grandson of a lord, rises." This was also an example of a pictorial *chen* prophecy formed in nature.

Sometimes, the markings on stones and rocks resembled words or pictures, and these natural patterns were seen by people in ancient times as signs from Heaven. During the period when the Western Han Dynasty was being gradually replaced by the Xin, local officials reported many such "heavenly revelations" in the form of stone markings or written words on metal, but many of them were in fact man-made forgeries. For example, in the same month that Emperor Ping died of illness in the twelfth month of the fifth year of the Yuanshi reign period, Meng Tong, Magistrate of Wugong County, claimed that a round white stone with a square base was found when someone was digging a well. On it were words written in red that read, "Inform Wang Mang, Duke of Anhan, that he should be Emperor." This stone was submitted to the court by Wang Mang's trusted official Xie Xiao, Commandery Administrator of southern Chang'an,[43] becoming an important ideological basis for Wang Mang's regency as "Acting Emperor."

By the third year of the Jushe reign period (8 CE), the anti–Wang Mang uprisings at various locations had been suppressed and Wang Mang's rule was more or less stabilized. The building up of public opinion for Wang Mang to rise from a de facto to a de jure Emperor began in earnest, with reports of talismanic writings across the empire. The Ba Commandery presented a stone cow, while Fufeng presented a stone marking discovered in Yong, which arrived at the imperial capital on the ninth and fifteenth days of the eleventh month, respectively. The actual words on these stones are no longer extant. It was said that when Wang Mang received them at the hall in front of the Stables of the Eternal Palace, there was a sudden gust of wind in the sky, which was darkened by the rising dust. When the wind stopped, a bronze talisman and a piece of silk on which a diagram had been drawn were seen in front of them, which read: "Heaven's instructions to the Emperor: the person who presented these is to be made a marquess. Receive the Heavenly order and carry out the divine command."[44]

On seeing the considerable political rewards obtained by most of the forgers of such talismans, Ai Zhang, who was studying in Chang'an, decided to fashion a bronze chest with two pieces of paper stuck on it, on which were written "Diagram on a Golden Chest with the Seal of the Supreme Deity of

[42] *History of the Later Han, juan* 13, "Biography of Gongsun Shu," p.535.

[43] *History of the Former Han, juan* 99 *shang*, "Biography of Wang Mang, Part I," pp.4078–4079.

[44] *Ibid*., pp.4093–4094.

Heaven" and "The Red Heavenly Emperor's Seal: the Golden Decree of Appointment Given by Mou to the Yellow Heavenly Emperor" ("Mou" refers to the personal name of Emperor Gaozu of the Western Han Dynasty). On the Golden Decree of Appointment was written: "Wang Mang is the true Son of Heaven; the Empress Dowager is to submit to the Mandate of Heaven." Both the Diagram on the Golden Chest and the Golden Decree of Appointment mentioned Wang Mang's eight senior officials, Ai Zhang's own name, as well as two fictitious names, Wang Xing and Wang Sheng, all of whom were to be appointed officials or have titles conferred on them, and become Wang Mang's right-hand men.[45] When Wang Mang got wind of this, he was ecstatic. He went to Emperor Gaozu's temple in person to "receive in obeisance the golden chest and the sacred abdication." He proclaimed that he had received the talismanic writings from Heaven and Emperor Gaozu's conferment of the empire. In the eleventh month of the same year, he ascended the throne as Emperor and founded the Xin Dynasty.

To replace the old with the new, Wang Mang wanted to abolish the Han Dynasty title of his aunt Wang Zhengjun, the Grand Empress Dowager. Subsequently, a person called Zhang Yong informed the Emperor that there was writing on a bronze flat that read: "The Grand Empress Dowager shall be Grand Empress Dowager, the Gracious Mother of the House of Xin." It was exactly what Wang Mang needed. He immediately issued a decree to change Wang Zhengjun's title to "Grand Empress Dowager, the Gracious Mother of the House of Xin" based on the writing on the bronze flat. He also announced that the unverifiable talk regarding Passing Edict Tokens of the Queen Mother of the West during the reign of Emperor Ai had in fact been the auspicious portent of Wang Zhengjun's future status as the Mother of the Xin Dynasty. Wang Mang even told his ministers at court, inadvertently revealing more than what he wanted to hide, that the senior officials had examined the bronze flat, and all of them said that the words had not been inscribed nor written but were natural.[46]

In the fifth year of the Shijianguo reign period (13 CE) of the Xin Dynasty, the residents of Chang'an refused to refurbish their houses because they heard that Wang Mang wished to move the capital to Luoyang. Again, Wang Mang cited the writing on a piece of stone: "The writing on the Black Dragon Stone says: 'To consolidate the Emperor's power, the capital must be at Luoyang.' The talisman is clearly written. Who dares disobey it!"[47]

[45] *Ibid.*, p.4095.

[46] *History of the Former Han*, *juan* 98, "Biography of Empress Wang Zhengjun, Empress of Emperor Yuan," p.4033.

[47] *History of the Former Han*, *juan* 99 *zhong*, "Biography of Wang Mang, Part II," p.4132. The origin of the Black Dragon Stone is unknown. It was recorded in "Biography of Wang Mang, Part II" that in the fall of the first year of the Shijianguo reign period, Wang Mang sent the Five

Origins of Chen *Prophecies*

It stands to reason that *chen* prophecies, which revealed the Mandate of Heaven and prophesied the fate of individuals or regimes using cryptic messages, and metaphoric and obscure revelations and prophecies, would have mysterious origins. This was the reason why Gan Zhongke, who created the Chijingzi *chen* prophecy, had to say, "The Supreme Deity of Heaven has sent Chijingzi, the immortal" to teach him the Way. The apocryphal-prophetic texts that had the imprimatur of the Eastern Han court were allegedly written by Confucius to "create institutions for the Han Dynasty," which was of course false.

By discarding the mysticism and enigma associated with *chen* prophecies and scrutinizing their details and the events surrounding them in historical texts, we can discern several origins of *chen* prophecies during the early imperial period.

Curses Wu Zixu (?–484 BCE) was a nobleman of the State of Chu in the Spring and Autumn Period whose father and elder brother were killed by King Ping of Chu in a court political struggle. Wu Zixu, promising revenge, fled to the State of Wu. As a trusted political advisor and capable military commander, he served several Kings of Wu and defeated the mighty army of Chu and took its capital, where he exhumed King Ping's corpse and gave it three hundred lashes to exact vengeance. During the reign of King Fuchai of Wu (reigned 495–473 BCE), the State of Wu defeated its neighboring state Yue. The King of Yue sued for peace. Wu Zixu advised King Fuchai to follow up his victory by conquering the State of Yue. King Fuchai, however, agreed to settle for peace with Yue and ordered Wu Zixu to commit suicide. Before his death, Wu Zixu asked that "his head be placed on a high place so that he could see the soldiers of Yue march into Wu." This curse later came true. Ten years after Wu Zixu's death, King Goujian of Yue conquered the State of Wu, just as Wu Zixu had foreseen.

During the Qin Dynasty, the people in the Dong Commandery inscribed these words on the stone: "After the First Emperor dies, his territory will be divided." This was also a curse that came to pass later.

In the final days of the Qin Dynasty, many in the former pre-Qin kingdoms took up arms against the central government in response to Chen Sheng's

Awesome General Wang Qi and eleven others to promulgate the forty-two chapters of *Talismanic Writings* all over the empire to garner public support for the Xin Dynasty's replacement of the Han. The forty-two chapters included five virtuous and auspicious matters, twenty-five talismanic writings, and twelve auspicious portents. The Black Dragon Stone was the ninth of the twelve auspicious portents. (pp.4112–4113)

rebellion. Fan Zeng (277–204 BCE) tried to persuade Xiang Liang (?–208 BCE), a rebel leader in the former State of Chu, to install Xiong Xin, the grandson of the late King Huai of Chu, as King. Fan Zeng said, "It is certainly fitting that Chen Sheng suffer defeat. When Qin exterminated the six states, Chu had committed the least offense. Ever since King Huai of Chu went to Qin and failed to return, the people of Chu have never ceased to mourn him. This is why Master Nan of Chu said: 'Even if Chu has but three households left, it will be Chu that destroys Qin.'"[48]

A native of Chu, Master Nan lived during the Warring States Period and wrote *Master Nan*, a book with thirty-one chapters.[49] Later commentators of *The Grand Scribe's Records* suggested that Master Nan "was a native of Chu who was adept in talking about *Yinyang*."[50] It was also said that "Master Nan was a Taoist scholar who had the knowledge of foretelling failings and successes and who knew that it had to be Chu that would destroy Qin."[51] The writings of Master Nan are no longer extant, but given his knowledge background – he was both "adept in talking about *Yinyang*" and "had the knowledge of foretelling failings and successes" – the *chen* prophecy that Fan Zeng invoked might have been written by him. What then were the "three households"? According to the interpretation of some commentators, "the people of Chu hated Qin so much that even if there were three households left among them, they would destroy Qin." An alternative interpretation suggested that "the three households were the three influential clans of Chu: the Zhao, Qu, and Jing clans."[52] Either way, it would have been a cursing *chen* prophecy that vented the anger and resentment of the people of Chu.[53]

The intention of curses was to vent one's emotions and not to make *chen* prophecies. When a curse came true, however, it would turn into a *chen* prophecy.

"Divine Revelation" It was reasonable to consider *chen* prophecies, which spoke on behalf of Heaven, as divine revelations. For example, it is

[48] *The Grand Scribe's Records*, *juan* 7, "Basic Annals of Xiang Yu," p.300. English translation from Nienhauser, vol. 1 (1994), p.183.
[49] *History of the Former Han*, *juan* 30, "Treatise on Literature," p.1733.
[50] *The Grand Scribe's Records*, *juan* 7, "Basic Annals of Xiang Yu," p.300. [51] *Ibid.*
[52] *Ibid.*, p.301.
[53] The third theory by Sima Zhen and Zhang Shoujie, argued in their commentaries on *The Grand Scribe's Records*, was that the "three households (*sanhu*)" referred to place names (Sanhuting and Sanhujin). "Master Nan knew about *Yinyang* and had the knowledge of foretelling failings and successes. He said those words because he was aware that Sanhu would be the cause of Qin's fall. Later on, Xiang Yu did cross Sanhujin and decimated Zhang Han's army, forcing the latter to surrender, which led to Qin's demise. Master Nan was good at making *chen* prophecies." (*Ibid.*) Based on their arguments, this was a coded *chen* prophecy. However, the interpretation is a little farfetched. I would concur with the earlier explanations.

mentioned in Chapter 2 that in the fall of the thirty-sixth year of the First Emperor's reign, a person stopped a messenger of the Qin court to ask him to pass a jade disc to the "Lord of Hao Pond," and then prophesied that "this year the primal dragon [referring to the First Emperor of the Qin Dynasty] will die." This was considered portentous talk at the time. However, the First Emperor did die the following year at Shaqiu (northwest of present-day Guangzong, Hebei Province) after falling ill in the middle of his tour of the empire. The portentous talk that came to pass became a *chen* prophecy. Sima Zhen, writing in *The Grand Scribe's Records: Commentaries*, explained: "The River Deity gave the piece of jade to the Deity of the Hao Pond to tell him of the First Emperor's impending demise. As the Qin was ruling by the Water-Power, the water deities informed each other in advance before the Qin ruler's imminent death."[54] According to Sima Zhen's explanation, this was a divine revelation-type *chen* prophecy that had originated from a water deity.

After Liu Bang slayed a white snake in a drunken stupor, an old woman was seen crying in the night. When passers-by asked her why she was crying, she said, "My son was the son of the White Emperor. He turned into a snake and was lying on the road. I am crying because he got killed by the son of the Red Emperor." The passers-by "thought that the old woman was speaking portentously and wanted to strike her." Again, this portentous talk came true and became a *chen* prophecy after Liu Bang founded the Western Han Dynasty. As the old woman was the mother of a deity (the son of the White Emperor, one of the five Heavenly Emperors), it was therefore also a divine revelation.

In the third year of the Jushe reign period (8 CE) of Wang Mang's regency, senior ministers began reporting and submitting talismanic writings to the court to persuade Wang Mang to ascend the throne. Liu Jing, Marquess of Guangrao and a member of the Han imperial clan, submitted a memorial, which claimed: "In the middle of the seventh month, Xin Dang, Chief of the Changxin Commune, located in Linzi County of the Qi Commandery, had several dreams one night [in which a person appeared and] said: 'I am the messenger of the Lord of Heaven. The Lord of Heaven ordered me to tell the Commune Chief this: "The Acting Emperor should become the real Emperor. If you do not believe me, there is a new well in this commune."' When the Commune Chief woke up in the morning and went in search around his commune, there was indeed a new well a hundred *chi* deep."[55] The messenger was sent by "the Lord of Heaven," which was in fact the Supreme Deity of Heaven.

After Wang Mang became Emperor, he launched a propaganda exercise across the empire, publicizing the various talismanic writings and good omens

[54] *The Grand Scribe's Records*, *juan* 6, "Basic Annals of The First Emperor of Qin," p.260.
[55] *History of the Former Han*, *juan* 99 *shang*, "Biography of Wang Mang, Part I," p.4093.

that had been encountered. One of these involved Gentleman-in-Attendance Wang Xu, who came across a man wearing a white unlined garment with a crimson-patterned square collar and a small hat, standing in front of Wanglu Hall at the Stables of the Eternal Palace. The man said to him: "The sun and the sky are of the same color today because Heaven is entrusting the land and the people all under Heaven to the Emperor." A moment later, the man in the white garment suddenly vanished into thin air.[56] This man in white was naturally a divine being, and what he said would be divine revelation.

It is quite apparent that these "divine revelations" had dubious origins and were subjected to obvious human manipulation.

The people of the Eastern Han Dynasty also believed that Confucius was an author of apocryphal-prophetic writings. They referred to him as the Achromatic King, son of the Black Emperor, who "created institutions for the Han Dynasty." This theory also suggested that the *chen* prophecies were divine revelations.[57]

Forgeries Apart from "divine revelations," talismanic writings of Zhen Xun, the red words written on the white stone, and Ai Zhang's Golden Decree of Appointment, historical records also contained examples of unequivocally forged *chen* prophecies, such as the prophecy that "the Great Chu will rise up, and Chen Sheng will rule!" and the *chen* prophetic books written by Wang Kuang.

The period from the final years of the Xin Dynasty to the Gengshi reign period was a time of internecine strife when warlords battled one another for the Chinese empire. According to "Biography of Geng Chun" in *History of the Later Han*, the King of Zhending Liu Yang, plotting a rebellion, forged a *chen* prophetic book in the early years of the Jianwu reign period, which read: "After the Crimson Nine,[58] the Goitrous Yang will be lord."[59] Given that Liu

56 *History of the Former Han*, *juan* 99 *zhong*, "Biography of Wang Mang, Part II," p.4113.

57 *Critical Essays: Expositions*, *juan* 26, "The Knowledge of Truth" described such a belief: "Confucians consider as sages those who knew a thousand years into the past and ten thousand generations into the future." "When Confucius was about to die, he left behind *chen* prophetic books." (p.1069)

58 "Crimson" symbolized the Fire-Power of the Western Han Dynasty. "Nine," however, was ambiguous in various contexts. Some argued that it should refer to Emperor Cheng, the ninth Emperor of the Western Han, an argument that was first proposed in Gan Zhongke's Chijingzi *chen* prophecy. Another theory suggested that Emperor Gengshi, Liu Xuan, was the ninth-generation descendent of Liu Bang, while Liu Yang was the tenth-generation descendent. On his part, Liu Xiu, the founding Emperor of the Eastern Han Dynasty, claimed that he was also a ninth-generation descendent of Liu Bang.

59 Commanding an army of more than 100,000 men, Liu Yang was the most powerful of the three Kings north of the Yellow River at the end of the Xin Dynasty. When Liu Xiu and Wang Lang were vying for supremacy in the region north of the Yellow River, Liu Xiu forged a marital

Yang was afflicted with goiter, "the Goitrous Yang" in the prophecy was tailor made for him.[60]

In the early years of the Eastern Han Dynasty, officials were often appointed or dismissed by Emperor Guangwu in accordance with *chen* prophecies. Wishing to standardize numerous apocryphal-prophetic texts, Emperor Guangwu ordered Yin Min, who had erudite knowledge of the classics and books, to check and edit the *chen* prophecies and diagrams. The Emperor hoped to make use of this exercise to expunge all the *chen* prophecies recorded during the Xin Dynasty that could be advantageous to Wang Mang and his Xin regime. Debunking such apocryphal-prophetic discourse, Yin Min said to Emperor Guangwu: "*Chen* prophetic books were not written by the sages, and they contain much coarse language and many erroneous words. They resemble the words of the common folk and I fear that they may mislead young people." Emperor Guangwu did not take his advice. And so, when Yin Min was editing the apocryphal-prophetic texts, he inserted the line "The gentleman without a mouth will assist the Han," suggesting that a person with the surname Yin could be made a senior official.[61] Emperor Guangwu was perusing the edited texts when he detected this, and he summoned Yin Min for an explanation. "Your servant sees that people in the past had made additions and omissions to the diagrams and books," Yin Min answered, "and so I boldly overstate my abilities for the chance to advance myself." Emperor Guangwu was very displeased. Although Yin Min was not punished, his career stalled because of what he had done.[62] In fact, there were many at the time who made their own changes to *chen* prophecies and even created their own.

Even after Emperor Guangwu promulgated the standard version of the apocryphal-prophetic texts across the empire in the thirty-second year of the Jianwu reign period (56 CE) and banned the forgery of *chen* prophecies and auguries, the forging of *chen* prophecies and diagrams continued unabated during the Eastern Han Dynasty. Examples included several Kings (Liu Ying, King of Chu, and Liu Yan, King of Fuling) who forged *chen* prophecies and diagrams during the Yongping reign period of Emperor Ming, and the case of Su Lang, a native of Fufeng, who "forged *chen* prophecies and diagrams, and died in prison."[63]

alliance with Liu Yang, marrying the latter's niece Guo Shengtong, who later became the Empress of Emperor Guangwu.

60 *History of the Later Han, juan* 21, "Biography of Geng Chun," p.763.

61 "The gentleman without a mouth" was a riddle that was a visual play on words. The character for "gentleman" (君) bereft of its "mouth" (口) would yield the character "Yin" (尹).

62 *History of the Later Han, juan* 79 *shang*, "Biographies of Confucian Scholars, Part I: Biography of Yin Min," p.2558.

63 *History of the Later Han, juan* 40 *shang*, "Biography of Ban Gu," p.1334.

It should be noted that among the forged *chen* prophecies, some came true while others did not. The reasons for this will be discussed below.

Coded Chen *Prophecies* Many of the *chen* prophecies in Chinese history were fake. A popular non-mystical explanation for *chen* prophecies that had come true was that they "might be spuriously recorded by persons who wrote after the events to prove their veracity."[64] Sun Jiazhou's "Examples and Explanations for Han-era *Chen* Prophecies that 'Came True,'" however, provides a brilliant discussion of *chen* prophecies that came to pass during the early imperial period.[65]

The cases of *chen* prophecies that Sun Jiazhou discussed in his essay included "Bingyi, the grandson of a lord, rises" and "Depose Emperor Chang and install the grandson of a lord"; "Liu Xiu is to be Son of Heaven," *The Token of Red Secret*, and "The Liu Family will be revived, and the Li Family will assist them"; and "The one who replaces the Han will be Dangtu Gao." These three *chen* prophecies all came true and were not "spuriously recorded by persons who wrote after the events."

The words "Bingyi, the grandson of a lord, rises" appeared on insect-nibbled leaves in the third year of the Yuanfeng reign period (78 BCE) of Emperor Zhao of the Western Han Dynasty. The prophecy was miraculously fulfilled four years later in the person of Emperor Xuan. In the first year of the Jianwu reign period (25 CE) of the Eastern Han Dynasty, Gongsun Shu in the Shu region in the west declared himself Emperor of the Great Cheng Dynasty and proclaimed the start of the new Longxing reign period.[66] He "promulgated notices all over the Middle Kingdom and cited apocrypha and diagrams to delude the people," in an attempt to vie with Emperor Guangwu for political legitimacy. In the narrative of *History of the Later Han*,

> [Gongsun Shu] falsely cited *chen* prophetic books. He believed that Confucius, by narrating twelve generations of lords [of the State of Lu] in *Spring and Autumn Annals*, constituted the ruling pattern for the dynasty whose color was red. This proved that the Han Dynasty, after the reigns of twelve Emperors from Emperor Gaozu to Emperor Ping, was at the end of its allotted life. The same family could no longer be conferred the Mandate of Heaven. He also cited [apocryphal writings such as] *Records of Models of Dynastic Changes*: "Depose Emperor Chang and install the grandson of a lord"; *Images of Surveying the Earth*: "The Mandate conferred to the Yellow Emperor is held by the Gongsun family"; and *The Talisman of Quoting the Spirits*: "The Grand Administrator in the west will vanquish the Liu." He claimed that Grand Administrator in the west would thoroughly subjugate the Liu family. According to the rotation of the

64 *Critical Essays: Expositions*, *juan* 26, "The Knowledge of Truth," p.1070.
65 Sun Jiazhou (1997).
66 *Record of States South of Mount Hua: A Collated, Illustrated, and Annotated Edition*, *juan* 5, "Records of Gongsun Shu and the Two Liu Regional Governors," pp.330–331.

Five Powers, the Red would be followed by the Yellow, which would in turn be followed by the White. The Metal-Power, symbolized by the color white, resided in the west. It was therefore right and proper that he, Gongsun Shu, replaced the Wang family.[67]

Gongsun Shu meant that in accordance with the rotation of the Five Powers and apocryphal-prophetic discourse, it was only with the expiration of the Western Han Dynasty's Fire-Power after the reigns of twelve Emperors that Wang Mang's Xin Dynasty could succeed to the empire with its Earth-Power. With the fall of Wang Mang, it stood to reason that Metal-Power should take over. Metal-Power, symbolized by the color white, was dominant in the west. Gongsun Shu, who was the warlord ruling the region of Shu in western China, was a perfect fit according to this line of reasoning. The *chen* prophecy "Depose Emperor Chang and install the grandson of a lord" meant that after Emperor Chang, a man named Gongsun (literally "grandson of a lord") would legitimately succeed to the throne. He, Gongsun Shu, was the legitimate Son of Heaven; Liu Xiu was nothing. The *chen* prophecy "Depose Emperor Chang and install the grandson of a lord" originated from the insect-nibbled *chen* prophecy "Bingyi, the grandson of a lord, rises" during the reign of Emperor Zhao. Emperor Guangwu rebutted Gongsun Shu by writing in his letter that "the *chen* prophetic words 'grandson of a lord'" had already been fulfilled in the person of Emperor Xuan; it had absolutely nothing to do with Gongsun Shu.[68]

We know that "Bingyi, the grandson of a lord, rises" was a diagrammatic *chen* prophecy that was formed in nature, and that it was subsequently included in the apocryphal-prophetic texts in the late Western Han Dynasty. However, words were added to these texts in tandem with the changing circumstances. For example, "Depose Emperor Chang and install the grandson of a lord" in *Records of Models of Dynastic Changes Appended to Diagram of the Yellow River* in fact referred to the story of the return to the throne of a descendent of the King of Changyi, who had succeeded to the throne following the death of Emperor Zhao and who was then deposed. In this case, the words were actually presented as a prophecy. What was interesting was that Gongsun Shu, who occupied the Shu region after the collapse of the Xin Dynasty, took "grandson of a lord" to mean his surname Gongsun and claimed he was the fulfilment of the *chen* prophecy.

"Liu Xiu is to be Son of Heaven,"[69] *The Token of Red Secret*, and "The Liu Family will be revived, and the Li Family will assist them"[70] were a set of *chen*

[67] *History of the Later Han*, *juan* 13, "Biography of Gongsun Shu," p.537. [68] *Ibid.*, p.538.

[69] *History of the Later Han*, *juan* 1 *xia*, "Annals of Emperor Guangwu, Part II," p.86; *juan* 15, "Biography of Deng Chen," p.582; *juan* 23, "Biography of Dou Rong," p.798.

[70] *History of the Later Han*, *juan* 15, "Biography of Li Tong," p.573; *juan* 15, "Biography of Wang Chang," p.579.

prophecies that saw wide circulation between the late Western Han and early Eastern Han dynasties. *The Token of Red Secret* was part of the *Diagram of the Yellow River* series of *chen* prophetic books. Its most famous *chen* prophecy was "Liu Xiu raises an army to seize the immoral; the four barbarians gather and dragons joust in the wild; when four and seven meet, the fire will be lord."[71] Some have theorized that the "Liu Xiu is to be Son of Heaven" *chen* prophecy and *The Token of Red Secret* were of the same origin. During the reign of Emperor Zhao, Sui Hong prophesied that the Han Dynasty would decline and that the Emperor should abdicate in favor of a virtuous man. During Emperor Cheng's reign, Gan Zhongke proposed that the Han "should renew its Mandate of Heaven." By the time of Emperor Ai, anti-Han sentiments were already widespread across the empire. Emperor Ai did consider giving up his throne to Dong Xian. Although it was a farcical attempt, it suggested that he was subconsciously fearful of his family's uncertain hold on the Mandate of Heaven and anxious for their future, and thus seeking a solution. While Wang Mang's subsequent regency and overthrowing of the Han Dynasty was the result of careful deliberation and planning, it could also be considered a natural outcome of the people's loss of faith in the Han Dynasty.

The "Liu Xiu is to be Son of Heaven" *chen* prophecy might have first appeared on the first year of the Jianping reign period (6 BCE) of Emperor Ai. It was said that Liu Xin changed his name to Liu Xiu in the hope of fulfilling this prophecy. According to Sun Jiazhou, however, "Liu Xiu" in the *chen* prophecy might not be referring to a person called Liu Xiu at all. With Gan Zhongke's suggestion that the Han "should renew its Mandate of Heaven" regaining popularity at the time, some people might have harbored the hope that an outstanding person (*xiu*) of the Liu imperial clan would replace Emperor Ai and revive the Han Dynasty. This theory is quite sound.[72] Records in *History of the Former Han* and *History of the Later Han* indicate that the "Liu Xiu is to be Son of Heaven" *chen* prophecy was widely known during the late Western Han, the Xin, and the Eastern Han dynasties. When Wang Mang's regime began to implode and the empire was rocked by massive unrests, the people began to feel "nostalgia for the Han." It was against this milieu that *The Token of Red Secret* and the *chen* prophecy "The Liu Family will be revived, and the Li Family will assist them" were widely circulated, providing strong public opinion and theoretical backing for Liu Xiu's

[71] *History of the Later Han*, *juan* 1 *shang*, "Annals of Emperor Guangwu, Part I," pp.21–22; *juan* 23, "Biography of Dou Rong," p.798; *History of the Former Han*, *juan* 36, "Biography of Liu Xin," citing Ying Shao, p.1972. An alternative for the second line "the four barbarians gather and dragons joust in the wild" was "Liu cultivates virtue and become Son of Heaven."

[72] Sun Jiazhou (1997), p.84.

ascension to the throne. Many historical records have also proved that these two *chen* prophecies had been widely circulated long before Liu Xiu, Emperor Guangwu, declared himself Emperor.

The *chen* prophecy "The one who replaces the Han will be Dangtu Gao" first appeared in the debate between Liu Xiu, who was reigning as Emperor Guangwu, and Gongsun Shu over who had the Mandate of Heaven, in which the former asked: "The one who replaces the Han will be Dangtu Gao. How could you be the personification of Gao?" In his annotation, Li Xian cited *Eastern Library's Records of Han* and wrote, "The Yellow will inherit from the Red. His family name will be Dangtu and his given name Gao."[73] Emperor Guangwu's letter to Gongsun Shu was cited in *Record of States South of Mount Hua*: "The Han imperial family will last 920 years until it falls in the hands of a descendant, after which it will be handed over to a Chancellor named Dangtu Gao. How could Gao be personified in you?"[74]

It is now almost impossible to trace the origins of this *chen* prophecy and identify who Dangtu Gao was, and few people after Gongsun Shu's time bothered to do so. However, this prophecy and Dangtu Gao resurfaced in the final years of the Eastern Han Dynasty to stir up the ambitions of contesting warlords. For example, Yuan Shu (?–199), a scion of the Ru'nan Yuan clan that produced "three Excellencies in four generations," claimed that his name "Shu" and his courtesy name "Gonglu" were both similar in meaning to the word "tu" in "Dangtu." "He averred that his names fulfilled the prophecy. He also claimed that because the Yuan family had been descended from the Chen family, which in turn were descendants of Shun, the legendary sage king of Earth-Power who succeeded the throne from sage king Yao of Fire-Power who abdicated, thus the Yellow would replace the Red according to Rotational Changes of the Five Powers. Accordingly, he began his intention to stage a revolt."[75]

Zhou Shu, a native of Langzhong in the western part of Ba Commandery, was in his youth a student of Yang Hou (72–153 CE), a native of Guanghan and a master of apocryphal-prophetic learning. His fellow students included Dong Fu and Ren An (124–202 CE). Zhou Shu, who never served in government, was an erudite student of astrology, as well as *chen* prophecies and diagrams. His explanation for "Dangtu Gao" was that "Dangtu Gao referred to Wei."[76] In the days leading to the forced abdication of the last Eastern Han Emperor in favor of Cao Pi, the first Wei Dynasty Emperor, ministers loyal to

[73] *History of the Later Han, juan* 13, "Biography of Gongsun Shu," p.538.

[74] *Record of States South of Mount Hua: A Collated, Illustrated, and Annotated Edition, juan* 5, "Records of Gongsun Shu and the Two Liu Regional Governors," p.331.

[75] *History of the Later Han, juan* 75, "Biography of Yuan Shu," p.2439.

[76] *Records of the Three Kingdoms, juan* 42, "Book of Shu: Biography of Zhou Qun," p.1020.

the Wei such as Assistant Grand Astrologer Xu Zhi cited Zhou Shu's interpretation, using it as one of the arguments for Cao Pi's ascension to the throne.[77]

A common thread in these few *chen* prophecies that had come true was that they were coded *chen* prophecies or riddle-type *chen* prophecies. Taking advantage of the polysemic feature of Chinese words and phrases, they best exemplified *chen* prophecies as "strange, coded prophecies that foretold good or ill fortune," allowing decoders of *chen* prophecies a much wider scope for interpretation.

Another example of coded *chen* prophecy was the one contained in *Collection of Transcribed Diagrams and Scripts*, a *chen* prophetic book brought back by Scholar Lu, who had been sent by the First Emperor of the Qin Dynasty in the thirty-second year of his reign to look for immortals across the seas. It was written in the book: "The one who will destroy Qin is *Hu*." Thinking that "*Hu*" referred to barbarians, more specifically the Xiongnu people, who were a major threat in the north at the time, the First Emperor "sent General Meng Tian to attack the *Hu* in the north with 300,000 men and capture the land south of the Yellow River."[78] The traditional historical view has been that the Qin Dynasty's fall was not because of any Xiongnu invasion, but the inept and tyrannical rule of Hu Hai, the Second Emperor. Pei Yin's *Collected Explications* cited Zheng Xuan's commentary: "'Hu' referred to Hu Hai, the name of the Second Emperor. When [the First Emperor of] the Qin Dynasty saw this in the book of diagrams, he did not know that it was a person's name. Instead, he prepared for an attack against the northern barbarians."[79]

In the first year of the Jianwu reign period, Liu Xiu, occupying the area north of the Yellow River, declared himself Emperor. Gongsun Shu dreamt that someone said to him, "*Ba si zi xi* for a period of twelve." The four characters "*ba si zi xi*" combine to form the two characters "Gongsun,"[80] and Gongsun Shu believed it was a *chen* prophecy that prophesied that he would be Emperor for twelve years. After he woke up, he told his wife about his dream. She said, "One could hear the Tao in the morning and die in the evening, let alone twelve years!" And so, Gongsun Shu proclaimed himself the Emperor of the Great Cheng Dynasty.[81] In the twelfth year of the Jianwu reign period, military commanders of the Eastern Han Dynasty – Wu Han, Liu Shang, Zang Gong, and others – broke through the defenses of Chengdu and

[77] Sun Jiazhou (1997), pp.87–88. [78] Northwestern part of present-day Inner Mongolia.

[79] *The Grand Scribe's Records*, *juan* 6, "Basic Annals of The First Emperor of Qin," pp.252–253. Given its title, *Collection of Transcribed Diagrams and Scripts* might be a collection of *chen* prophecies accompanied by diagrams.

[80] The four characters "八厶子系" (*ba si zi xi*) combine to form "公孫" (*gongsun*).

[81] *Record of States South of Mount Hua: A Collated, Illustrated, and Annotated Edition*, *juan* 5, "Records of Gongsun Shu and the Two Liu Regional Governors," pp.330–331.

massacred the entire Gongsun clan. The Great Cheng Dynasty lasted for a period of twelve years.

Where did coded *chen* prophecies come from? Who created them? Under what contexts were they created? What did they mean originally? The answers to these questions are not important because the language and words used in coded *chen* prophecies were ambiguous or polysemic. In different contexts, areas, and times, in the hands of various decoders, and presented to varying audiences, they could transmit different meanings and information. A first-level, literal interpretation of the words themselves would often lead to an erroneous understanding because the will of Heaven could not be so easily divulged. It would always allow for multiple decoding, but "genuine" divine revelation would only be revealed after the fact. The answer would be found beyond the words of the prophecy, even as it could be found within them. The prophecies could have a second, third, or even multiple lives, disseminating different prophetic revelations in a different time and area, such as "Bingyi, the grandson of a lord, rises"; "The Liu Family will be revived, and the Li Family will assist them"; and "The one who replaces the Han will be Dangtu Gao." Seen in this light, the probability of these *chen* prophecies coming true was really quite high.

Apocryphal-Prophetic Discourse in Dynastic Change and the Transfer of the Mandate of Heaven

The nascent form of the Theory of the Rise and Fall of the Five Powers, which demonstrated the necessity and legitimacy of regular dynastic changes based on the subjugation of each of the Five Agents over the other, was propounded by Zou Yan during the Warring States Period, but it only saw actual political application at the time of the First Emperor of the Qin Dynasty. After repeated practical study and modifications by the political theorists of the Western Han Dynasty, it was finally transformed by Liu Xiang and Liu Xin into the more systematic Theory of the Rotational Changes of the Five Powers, which was based on the waxing and waning of each of the Five Powers as they engaged in an eternal cycle of mutual subjugation and re-generation. Both Wang Mang and Liu Xiu employed this theory to demonstrate the legitimacy of founding new dynasties to replace the old.

According to the Theory of the Rotational Changes of the Five Powers, the occasion of a Son of Heaven receiving the Mandate of Heaven had to be evidenced by talismanic portents (or talismanic writings). In the Western Han Dynasty, talismanic portents cited were mostly good omens occurring in nature that portended auspiciousness. Wang Mang declared that when "Emperors receive the Mandate of Heaven, there will be auguries of virtue and auspiciousness that attest to the rotation of the Five Powers."

He promulgated the forty-two chapters of *Talismanic Writings*, which included five virtuous and auspicious matters and twelve auspicious portents, which were good omens; and twenty-five talismanic writings, "the stone in the well, and the golden chest," which were considered *chen* prophecies.[82] When Liu Xiu proclaimed himself the Son of Heaven, the main talismanic writing he used as proof of his legitimacy was the *chen* prophetic book *The Token of Red Secret*. Talismanic writings were taken as letters of appointment conferred by the Supreme Deity of Heaven to the Son of Heaven, and diagram books (*chen* prophecies and diagrams) and auguries were the physical manifestations of these letters of appointment.

"The Deity in Heaven Bestows the Augury That Reveals the Talisman of Red Words on the Stone" – Apocryphal-Prophetic Discourse in Wang Mang's Receiving the Mandate of Heaven In the twelfth month of the fifth year of the Yuanshi reign period (5 CE), Emperor Ping of the Western Han Dynasty died a sudden death. In the three short years that followed, Wang Mang completed the entire process of his own elevation from "Acting Emperor" to the actual Son of Heaven on the throne, and replacing the Western Han Dynasty with his own Xin Dynasty. In those three years, reports of good omens and talismanic writings from various localities deluged the capital Chang'an, providing an all-out talismanic offensive to induce the birth of the Xin Dynasty. It could be said that Wang Mang's was the most dramatic exploitation of talismanic writings among all dynastic changes in Chinese history.

The first salvo of this talismanic offensive was fired on behalf of Wang Mang's biggest political backer: his aunt Wang Zhengjun, Empress of Emperor Yuan of the Western Han Dynasty and biological mother of Emperor Cheng, who at the time presided over the affairs of state in her capacity as Grand Empress Dowager.

> [She] was given succor by [the legend of] Shalu in Yuancheng in the beginning. The brilliance and auspiciousness of the Female Lord of the *Yin* Essence merged with [Emperor] Yuan to beget [Emperor] Cheng, creating a felicitous augury for all under Heaven. Her rise was portended by the Queen Mother of the West and endorsed by the deities to bless our imperial clan and safeguard our rightful heir, so as to multiply our descendants and continue our achievements in the Han Dynasty.
>
> . . .
>
> After the Grand Empress Dowager presided over the affairs of state, there were portents of tortoises, dragons, *qilin*, and phoenixes. The good omens of the Five Powers have regenerated one another in complete circles. *Diagram of the Yellow River* hailed from

82 *History of the Former Han*, *juan* 99 *zhong*, "Biography of Wang Mang, Part II," p.4112.

faraway Kunlun; *Script of the Luo River* came from Chongye. The *chen* prophecies of old have come to pass in the present. These are the indications that the Supreme Deity of Heaven desires to safeguard our imperial clan and wants us to attain heroic achievements.[83]

According to "Biography of Empress Wang Zhengjun, Empress of Emperor Yuan" in *History of the Former Han*, during the reigns of Emperors Wen and Jing of the Western Han Dynasty, Wang He, the ancestor of Wang Zhengjun's and Wang Mang's family, moved to the Weisu Ward in Yuancheng, which was located in the Wei Commandery. To the east of Yuancheng was Wulu, where the ruins of Mount Shalu from the Spring and Autumn Period were located. The local elders made this prophecy:

When Shalu collapsed in the past, during the Spring and Autumn Period, the Grand Astrologer of the State of Jin conducted a divination. He said: "The *Yin* element overpowered the *Yang* element, and the Earth and Fire Agents were in conflict. It was for this reason that Shalu collapsed. A wise woman will rise 645 years from now." It will probably be like the Tian family of the State of Qi! Now Wang Wengru has moved here, and the time corresponds to the words of the divination. East of Yuancheng lies the ruins of Wulu, which was where Shalu used to stand. Eighty years from now, an exalted woman from the Wang family will rise up in the empire.[84]

This wise or exalted woman was of course Wang Zhengjun. "The brilliance and auspiciousness of the Female Lord of the *Yin* Essence" referred to the time when Madam Li, Wang Zhengjun's mother, was pregnant with her, she "dreamed that the moon fell into her embrace."[85] Even the event of the Passing Edict Tokens of the Queen Mother of the West during Emperor Ai's reign, which had been triggered by unverifiable talk, was interpreted as an augury that foreshadowed Wang Zhengjun's elevation to Mother of the Realm. More importantly, "ancient *chen* prophecies" such as *Diagram of the Yellow River* and *Script of the Luo River* had prophesied the Grand Empress Dowager's achievements in bringing peace and stability to the imperial clan, a prophecy that had actually come true. Thus, all the symbols for the Mandate of Heaven were there: the legends surrounding her birth, the auguries, and talismanic writings. The greatness of the Wang clan and the regency of Wang Mang had all been due to the Grand Empress Dowager, a woman favored by Heaven. Naturally, this was the first layer of discourse to justify the legitimacy of Wang Mang's replacement of the Western Han with his Xin Dynasty.

"Whenever an Emperor or a King is conferred the Mandate, there will be virtuous and auspicious auguries."[86] "The Deity in Heaven bestows the augury

[83] *History of the Former Han, juan* 84, "Biography of Zhai Yi," p.3432.
[84] *History of the Former Han, juan* 98, p.4014. [85] *Ibid.*, p.4015.
[86] *History of the Former Han, juan* 99 *zhong*, "Biography of Wang Mang, Part II," p.4112.

that reveals the talisman of red words on the stone."[87] The second layer of discourse for Wang Mang's rise to the throne contained the enormous quantities of good omens and "talismanic writings" that were supportive of his goal. The "talismanic writings," all of which pronounced that Wang Mang ought to be Emperor, were either "divine revelations," "naturally formed" markings on stones, or words inscribed on bronze round flat by person or persons unknown. To put to rest any doubt others might have had about the authenticity of these "talismanic writings," Wang Mang claimed that they had all been examined and verified by himself and the court ministers. For instance, he and Wang Shun, the Grand Guardian and Marquess of Anyang, as well as others, examined the stone cow from Ba Commandery and the words on the stone from Yong. After examining the bronze round flat with the talismanic writing "The Grand Empress Dowager shall be Grand Empress Dowager, the Gracious Mother of the House of Xin," the ministers at court unanimously declared that the "words were neither inscribed nor drawn; they were natural," and thus they had not been forged by human hands.

During the Han periods, when apocryphal-prophetic discourse was very popular, many people were quite sensitive to the mystical nature of Chinese characters and firmly believed in their prophetic powers. In the sixth month of the second year of the Jianping reign period, Xia Heliang, a disciple of Gan Zhongke, and others invoked the Chijingzi *chen* prophecy and suggested that Emperor Ai of the Western Han Dynasty change his reign period title, in order to regain the Mandate of Heaven. To this effect, Emperor Ai issued a decree that ordered the change of the name of the reign period to "the first year of the Taichu Yuanjiang reign period." However, this reign period title was abolished in the eighth month of the same year. Demonstrating his creativity, Wang Mang offered this interpretation of the event: "The words 'the first year of the Yuanjiang reign period' meant that reign period was changed to indicate a senior military commander [*jiang*] becoming regent."[88] In other words, what had been a reign period title to symbolize the Han imperial clan's regaining of the Mandate of Heaven, became a *chen* prophecy that foretold the changing of a reign period title to commemorate a "senior military commander" (Wang Mang had been Commander-in-Chief) becoming regent. And it had come true! Using reign period titles as *chen* prophecies was common during the early medieval empires such as the Wei, Jin, and Northern and Southern dynasties. These were highly fortuitous and random *chen* prophecies that revealed the will of Heaven and even came true, and they were more believable than "divine revelations" or "writing on stones." Wang Mang demonstrated his great foresight by interpreting Emperor Ai's reign period title as a *chen*

[87] *History of the Former Han*, *juan* 99 *shang*, "Biography of Wang Mang, Part I," p.4091.
[88] *Ibid.*, p.4094.

prophecy that benefited him, which could also be seen as the third layer of discourse to justify his founding of a new dynasty.

Wang Mang was very sensitive to the symbolic meanings of Chinese characters, and had considerable associative abilities in his decoding of these symbols. For example, he deconstructed the words *tianzi* ("Son of Heaven") on Zhen Xun's arm into the words "*yi da zi*" ("one-big-son") or "*yi liu zi*" ("one-six-son"), where *liu* ("six") meant *lu* ("to kill"). After he ascended the throne as Emperor, he declared:

> All the people now say that the Supreme Deity of Heaven has abolished the Han Dynasty and founded the Xin; abandoned the Liu family and raised up the Wang. The character *liu* is made up of the three characters *mao*, *jin*, and *dao*.[89] For this reason, the *gangmao* ornament worn during the first month of the year will be prohibited and the knife-coins (*jindao*) will cease circulation. We consulted with many ministers and officials, who all said that the interaction between Heaven and Man made it immediately apparent. All should remove their *gangmao* from their clothing, and the knife-coins are to be taken out of circulation. Heaven's will is thus obeyed and the people gratified.[90]

Worried that the people might associate the knife-coins they used or the *gangmao* (a good-luck charm popular during the Han periods) they wore with the Liu family, Wang Mang decided to abolish the knife-coins and ban the *gangmao* altogether. This could be considered a form of suppression using the magic of the written word.

The fourth layer of discourse was that the Wang family was the descendants of Shun,[91] and (in Sui Hong's words) "the Han imperial clan is descended from the mythical Emperor Yao, and abdicating the throne to another family is in its fate." Celebrated by Confucians as the epitome of virtuous acts, the legend of Yao giving up his throne for Shun became the historical precedent for the Western Han Dynasty making way for the Xin.

The fifth layer of discourse concerned the Five Powers: Yao and the Han Dynasty were of the Fire-Power, while Shun and the Xin Dynasty were of the Earth-Power. According to the apocryphal-prophetic discourse of the rotational changes of the Five Powers, Fire gave rise to Earth, and Earth followed Fire. "The white stone with crimson words appeared in Wugong County in the

89 The traditional form of the character *liu* (劉) can be broken up into three components: *mao* (卯), *jin* (金), and *dao* (刂 or 刀).

90 *History of the Former Han*, *juan* 99 *zhong*, "Biography of Wang Mang, Part II," p.4110.

91 *History of the Former Han*, *juan* 98, "Biography of Empress Wang Zhengjun, Empress of Emperor Yuan": "Wang Mang claimed to be a descendant of the Yellow Emperor. In *Root of Self*, his self-penned genealogy, he wrote: 'The Yellow Emperor's family name was Yao, and Yu Shun was his eighth-generation descendant.'" (p.4014) *History of the Former Han*, *juan* 99 *shang*, "Biography of Wang Mang, Part I": "I am lacking in virtue but I am fortunate in being a progeny of the Yellow Emperor and a descendant of the Emperor Yu [Shun]." (p.4095)

last years of the reign of Emperor Ping of the Han, indicating that the Fire-Power was diminishing, to be replaced by the Earth-Power. The Supreme Deity of Heaven showed overwhelming concern by abandoning the Han and raising the Xin."[92] It was also for this reason that Wang Mang specifically chose the Dingmao day for the abdication ceremony at Emperor Gaozu's temple, because "*ding* meant fire, which was the Power of the Han, while *mao* referred to the surname Liu of the Han imperial clan. This indicated that the Fire-Power of the Han Dynasty and the Liu family had diminished and [the mandate] had been passed on to the Xin Dynasty."[93]

Wang Mang was not the only one playing the *chen* prophecy game. Anti–Wang Mang forces also frequently employed apocryphal-prophetic discourse to challenge or question Wang Mang's claim that he received the Mandate of Heaven.

Zhi Yun was a native of Xiping in the Ru'nan Commandery, and was an expert in *The Han Version of the Odes*, *The Yan School of Commentary of Gongyang on the Spring and Autumn Annals*, and astronomy. In the final years of the Xin Dynasty, there was massive social unrest and "banditry was rife." Observing the stars, Zhi Yun averred that the planets Saturn, Jupiter, and Mars were grouped in the region of the Yi and Zhen constellations. They left and appeared again, indicating that the Han Dynasty would regain its Mandate of Heaven, and blessings would be returned to the virtuous. The one whose plans were in accordance with Heaven's would find great success according to a pre-Qin astrological theory that linked the movements of heavenly bodies with the fortunes of geographic regions. Thus, he declined an appointment offered to him by the local official and went west to Chang'an, where he submitted a memorial to Wang Mang, warning him that the apocryphal-prophetic texts had already foretold that "the Han's history will be long and Confucius constituted the institutions for the dynasty whose color was red." "The Liu family enjoys the longevity of Heaven," and there was a chance that the Han Dynasty could regain the Mandate of Heaven. Although he, Zhi Yun, might be a subject of Wang Mang, Heaven was Wang Mang's father, and he should obey his father's orders and follow his will. "The imperial regalia belongs to he who possesses the Mandate of Heaven; it is not to be taken in vain." Zhi Yun advised Wang Mang to "return to Heaven what had been taken from Heaven" and restore the imperial regalia to the Liu family of the Han Dynasty. If he did so, he would be seen as "understanding the Mandate." Otherwise, he would be tarnished with the charge of "usurpation."[94]

Naturally, Wang Mang was furious. He had Zhi Yun arrested at once for high treason and threw him in prison. However, Zhi Yun had invoked

[92] *History of the Former Han, juan* 99 *zhong*, "Biography of Wang Mang, Part II," p.4113.
[93] *Ibid.* [94] *History of the Later Han, juan* 29, "Biography of Zhi Yun," p.1025.

apocryphal-prophetic discourse, which was precisely the ideological bedrock of Wang Mang's own discourse on receiving the Mandate of Heaven. Zhi Yun could not be found guilty based on this. And so, Wang Mang ordered the Attendants within the Yellow Gate and Members of the Imperial Coterie to threaten Zhi Yun and make him confess to being "mentally insane and incoherent." In response, Zhi Yun "glared at them and gave them a stern rebuke: 'What I said were Heaven's words and will, which could not be fabricated by a mad man!'"[95] Wang Mang could not do anything to him. Eventually, Zhi Yun was released during an amnesty and fled south to Cangwu.

In the final years of the Xin Dynasty, Wei Xiao (?–33), a member of a prominent family in Tianshui, launched an armed revolt against Wang Mang. He took the advice of his Military Counsellor Fang Wang and built a temple to honor Emperor Gaozu, Emperor Wen, and Emperor Wu of the Western Han Dynasty to demonstrate his loyalty to the Han imperial clan. He also promulgated anti–Wang Mang notices in all the commanderies and kingdoms:

> Wang Mang, formerly the Marquess of Xindu, has insulted and slighted Heaven and Earth. Violating the Way and defying reason, he murdered the late Emperor Ping with poison and usurped his throne. Feigning possession of the Mandate of Heaven, he forged talismanic writings, which inveigled the people and incurred the wrath of the Supreme Deity of Heaven. He claimed abnormal decorations and writings to be good omens, and made sport of the gods by lauding disasters. All the bamboo in the lands of Chu and Yue are not enough to record his sins, which are known to all under Heaven, and seen and heard by all.[96]

The phrases "forged talismanic writings" and "made sport of the gods" Wei Xiao used in the notices referred to Wang Mang forging talismanic writings and divine revelations to lie to the people. Like Zhi Yun, Wei Xiao openly challenged the legitimacy of Wang Mang's discourse on "being conferred the Mandate of Heaven." There were also others within and outside the government who cited apocryphal-prophetic texts to question Wang Mang's claims. For example, the Taoist priest Ximen Junhui, a paid retainer of General of the Guards Wang She and one who "had an interest in astrology and *chen* prophetic books," said to Wang She: "A brilliant star swept into the imperial palace. A member of the Liu family will rise, and he goes by the name of the Preceptor of State."[97] Encouraged by this, Wang She communicated with Commander-in-Chief Dong Zhong and Preceptor of State Liu Xiu (i.e. Liu Xin). He planned to kidnap Wang Mang and surrender to the rebels in order to safe and preserve the Wang clan. However, the plot failed, and he took his own life.

95 *Ibid.* 96 *History of the Later Han, juan* 13, "Biography of Wei Xiao," pp.514–515.
97 *History of the Former Han, juan* 99 *xia*, "Biography of Wang Mang, Part III," p.4184.

"Liu Xiu Raises an Army to Seize the Immoral" – Apocryphal-Prophetic Discourse in Emperor Guangwu's Receiving the Mandate of Heaven

Even as Wang Mang's Xin Dynasty was in its death throes, regional warlords were contesting one another for the grand prize of the imperial throne. Nostalgia for the Han Dynasty was the prevalent sentiment, and multiple military factions were hailed as their leaders' members – both genuine and bogus – of the Han Dynasty's Liu imperial clan. In addition to these, there were regional powers that raised the banner of "aiding the Han" to justify their military adventures. However, buffeted by the belief that had been current in the mid- and late Western Han, that "the Han imperial clan . . . abdicating the throne to another family is in its fate" and "the destiny of the Han will decline midway," and assailed by Wang Mang's propaganda that "the Fire-Power was diminishing, to be replaced by the Earth-Power," the very legitimacy of the Liu family's imperial authority was being challenged.

For example, Wei Xiao, the warlord in Longxi, was loath to subordinate himself under Liu Xiu after the latter proclaimed himself Emperor. Although he adopted Liu Xiu's reign period title Jianwu, he sent the orator Zhang Xuan to Dou Rong (16 BCE – 62 CE), the commander of the five commanderies west of the Yellow River, to persuade the latter to join forces. "The present contest of heroic men has yet to yield its victors and its vanquished. If the various territories join forces with Longxi and Shu, one could be as grand as the King of the Six States or at worst, be like the Commandant [of Nanhai] Zhao Tuo." Zhang Xuan proposed that the regional warlords maintain control over their own territories. He even began by saying: "The Gengshi regime collapsed shortly after it came into being, which was the fulfillment of the prophecy that a single family could never rise again."[98] Derived from such prognostications as "the destiny of the Han will decline midway" and "the Fire-Power was diminishing," what Zhang Xuan said was an attempt to fundamentally subvert the belief that the Han Dynasty's Liu family would regain the Mandate of Heaven.

To the southwest in Western Shu, the self-proclaimed Emperor Gongsun Shu also challenged Liu Xiu's legitimacy by using apocryphal-prophetic discourse: "According to the rotation of the Five Powers, the Red would be followed by the Yellow, which would in turn be followed by the White. The Metal-Power, symbolized by the color white, resided in the west. It was therefore right and proper that he, Gongsun Shu, replaced the Wang family."[99]

Liu Xiu was born in Jiyang County on the Jiazi day of the twelfth month of the first year of Emperor Ai's Jianping reign period. Although the *chen* prophecy that "Liu Xiu is to be Son of Heaven" was becoming widespread

[98] *History of the Later Han, juan* 23, "Biography of Dou Rong," p.798.
[99] *History of the Later Han, juan* 13, "Biography of Gongsun Shu," p.538.

at the time, Liu Xiu was so named not for the fulfillment of the prophecy, but to commemorate the appearance in the county of an unusually excellent crop with nine ears of grain that year.[100] On one occasion in Wancheng in the final years of the Xin Dynasty, before Liu Xiu and his brother launched their armed rebellion, Liu Xiu, his older brother Liu Yin, and his older sister's husband Deng Chen were drinking and talking with several people, one of whom was Cai Shaogong, who was a native of Rang County. Shaogong, who was quite knowledgeable about *chen* prophecies and diagrams, mentioned that "Liu Xiu is to be Son of Heaven." Someone in the party asked, "Does it refer to the Preceptor of State Liu Xiu?" To which Liu Xiu answered half in jest, "How do you know it is not referring to me?" Everyone present laughed in merriment.[101] From this narrative, it can be surmised that neither Liu Xiu himself nor the people present at the party (with the exception of Deng Chen) had seriously considered that Liu Xiu's name was the fulfillment of the *chen* prophecy. Even Cai Shaogong, who was quite knowledgeable about *chen* prophecies and diagrams, did not see the connection between the two.

Eventually, Liu Yin was killed and Emperor Gengshi lost the support of his men. Liu Xiu, then the King of Xiao, controlled the area north of the Yellow River, "traversing regions and occupying lands with a million armored soldiers." It was then that the *chen* prophecy "Liu Xiu raises an army to seize the immoral" in *The Token of Red Secret* once again caught the attention of the world. After Emperor Gengshi was killed by the Chimei Rebels, Liu Xiu's subordinate commanders urged him to take the throne. When Liu Xiu and his army arrived at Haocheng, Qiang Hua, a classmate of Liu Xiu's when he was a young student in Chang'an, came from Within the Pass to offer him *The Token of Red Secret*, in which was written "Liu Xiu raises an army to seize the immoral; the four barbarians gather and dragons joust in the wild; when four and seven meet, the fire will be lord."[102] Liu Xiu finally gave in to his men's persuasion and proclaimed himself Emperor in the sixth month of the same year. At the ceremony to make offerings to the deities, the invocation read:

> The Supreme Deity of Heaven and the Gods of the Earth so love the people that they bestow on us their Mandate and entrust the people to me, Liu Xiu. As father and mother to my people, I, Liu Xiu, do not deserve the honor. However, my subordinate men all said in one accord: "After Wang Mang usurped the throne, an indignant Liu Xiu rose up in arms. He vanquished Wang Xun and Wang Yi at Kunyang; destroyed Wang Lang and the Bronze Horse Army north of the Yellow River. Liu Xiu has pacified all under Heaven and all within the Seas are blessed. He carries the will of Heaven and Earth, and receives the support from the people." It is written in the *chen* prophetic books: "Liu

[100] *History of the Later Han, juan* 1 *xia*, "Annals of Emperor Guangwu, Part II," p.86.
[101] *History of the Later Han, juan* 15, "Biography of Deng Chen," p.582.
[102] *History of the Later Han, juan* 1 *shang*, "Annals of Emperor Guangwu, Part I," pp.21.

Xiu raises an army to seize the immoral; the *mao* and *jin*[103] cultivates virtue to be the Son of Heaven." I resolutely refused to take their advice but they were persistent. I had to reject them thrice. All my subordinates said: "The Mandate of the Supreme Deity of Heaven must not be delayed." How then could I not submit before it?[104]

Obviously, the *chen* prophecy in *The Token of the Red Secret* played a vital role in the discourse of Liu Xiu receiving the Mandate of Heaven. Dou Rong convened a meeting with the powerful men and commandery administrators of the area west of the Yellow River, after which they rejected Wei Xiao's proposal to "join forces with Longxi and Shu." Instead, "the decision was made to turn to the east" and submit to Emperor Guangwu. The decision was informed by three important considerations. One, "the Han was the inheritor of Yao's destiny and it was long-lived. The present Emperor's name [Liu Xiu] is seen in diagram books." Thus, as seen in *The Token of the Red Secret*, Liu Xiu receiving the Mandate of Heaven had been prognosticated. Two, "the erudite men of times past who were adapt in the Way and the Arts such as Gu Yong and Xia Heliang had established that the Han would regain the Mandate of Heaven. This has been spoken of for many a year." It was not, as Zhang Xuan said, "that a single family could never rise again." Three, "in the realm of human affairs, among the few people who have declared themselves Emperor, [the one in] Luoyang has the vastest land, the strongest army, and the strictest discipline. Observing the talismanic writings and the current state of the world, a person with another surname would probably not be able to carry [the Mandate]."[105] Whether it was the appeal to the supernatural for the sovereign's legitimate mandate to rule or the realpolitik in the analysis of rival political powers, the discourse was most precise and appropriate.

"The One Wins the Throne Not by Deceit" Discourses such as "A commoner shall acquire all under Heaven" and "Are kings, nobles, commanders, and counsellors high-born by nature?" were popular in the sociopolitical context of the late Qin and early Han. Emperor Gaozu of the Western Han Dynasty "rose up in rebellion as an ordinary man and was exalted as Emperor after fighting many men ... many among his followers were desperados and reprobates."[106] However, with the encroachment and dissection of political, economic, and cultural resources by members of the imperial clan, affinal relatives of Emperors, powerful local clans, and families whose members served as government officials for generations, the political compact that

[103] *Mao* (卯) and *jin* (金), the constituents of Liu Xiu's surname Liu (劉).
[104] *History of the Later Han*, *juan* 1 *shang*, "Annals of Emperor Guangwu, Part I," pp.22.
[105] *History of the Later Han*, *juan* 23, "Biography of Dou Rong," p.798.
[106] *Collected Notes on the Twenty-Two Histories: Collations and Verifications*, *juan* 2, "The Circumstances of Commoners, Commanders, and Officials in the Early Han," p.36.

governed the relationship between the ruler and the ruled gradually diminished. The connection of one's family lineage and prestige with the Mandate of Heaven and talismanic portents became an essential factor in the discussion of the legitimacy of the imperial clan and nobility preserving their prerogatives during the Han periods. According to Ban Biao (3–54 CE), a historian who wrote during the Eastern Han Dynasty, first, "the reign of an Emperor must be marked by actions that are enlightened, wise, and virtuous; and an enterprise that is abundant and profitable, and one that will accumulate for generations. . . . A man without solid foundation, whose achievements and virtues were not recorded, could never rise up to become the most exalted in the realm."[107] Second, "the Han is the inheritor of Yao, as evidenced by talismanic portents and writings; the one wins the throne not by deceit."[108] For this reason, Wang Mang had had to put in a tremendous amount of work to construct the discourse of his receiving the Heavenly Mandate. The Eastern Han Dynasty, on its part, established that "the Liu family were the inheritors of Yao's polity, whose virtue was bequeathed across generations. There were omens of snakes and dragons, substantiated by the colored clouds in the sky. The five stars congregated in the heavens, signifying the concord between Heaven and Man." In other words, talismanic portents had prognosticated that the Mandate of Heaven would be conferred on the Liu family.[109]

Fan Ye's conclusion in "Biography of Yuan Shu" in *History of the Later Han* was as follows:

> The fulfillment of portents concerning the Mandate of Heaven could be seen but not articulated. Those who received this great blessing probably possessed faithfulness and complied with the Way! If one's actions did not comply with the Way, he could never receive the Mandate despite his great power and many stratagems. Attempts to acquire the unattainable would result in the gradual loss of loyalty and faith, and the occurrence of arrogations of power and treachery. By forging ahead with impropriety and abandon, did he think he could deceive Heaven? Although he used talismans and portents to fraudulently proclaim himself Emperor, no one would stand for it![110]

It was believed that conceited and crafty men who insisted on fighting for the imperial throne despite not having received the Mandate of Heaven could never succeed by sheer luck. They would only bring calamity to themselves and others; they would die in ignominy and their extended families would be executed.

However, at a time when the dust had yet to settle on the internecine battle for the empire, how did one identify the person on whom the Mandate of

107 *History of the Former Han*, *juan* 100 *shang*, "Afterword and Family History, Part I," p.4208.
108 *History of the Later Han*, *juan* 40 *shang*, "Biography of Ban Biao, Part I," p.1324.
109 *History of the Wei*, *juan* 2, "Annals of Emperor Taizu, Part II," p.37.
110 *History of the Later Han*, *juan* 75, p.2444

Heaven was bestowed? Apocryphal-prophetic discourse and the Theory of the Rotational Changes of the Five Powers had laid down a preset process to prove the legitimacy of dynastic change. Support from *chen* prophecies, or the lack thereof, became part of the body of evidence to determine whether a ruler had legitimately received the Heavenly Mandate.

The Belief in Chen *Prophecies and the Social Psychology of the Han Periods*

Utilitarian Strategic Considerations The mysterious and unfathomable divinatory power of *chen* prophecies, which made them supernatural symbols that conveyed divine revelation, were supposed to be the reasons why people believed in them. However, given that they became entwined with politics and acquired an inestimable influence in power struggles, *chen* prophecies inevitably entangled themselves with various interest groups. On encountering *chen* prophecies, many of the politically powerful inexorably paid heed to strategic considerations that were somewhat utilitarian.

Wang Mang's very first stepping-stone in his portents-strewn path to the imperial throne was the white stone found in Wugong County.

> Xie Xiao, Commandery Administrator of southern Chang'an, reported to the throne that Meng Tong, Magistrate of Wugong County, found a round white stone with a square base when someone was digging a well. On it were words written in red that read, "Inform Wang Mang, Duke of Anhan, that he should be Emperor." This marked the beginning of the talismanic writings. Wang Mang ordered the court dignitaries to report to the [Grand] Empress Dowager, who said: "This deceives all under Heaven; it must not proceed!" Grand Guardian Wang Shun said to the [Grand] Empress Dowager: "Matters have come to this, and there is no other way. We are powerless to stop it even if we want to. Besides, Wang Mang does not dare harbor any treacherous thoughts; he merely wants the title of Regent to augment his power in order to make all under Heaven accept his rule." On hearing this, the [Grand] Empress Dowager acquiesced.[111]

Although Grand Empress Dowager Wang Zhengjun placed Wang Mang in important positions in government, as Empress of Emperor Yuan of the Western Han Dynasty and mother to Emperor Cheng, she remained loyal to the Liu imperial clan and had no intention of replacing the Western Han with another. In fact, it was not in her interest to abrogate the Liu family's right to rule. When the white stone with the red words appeared, she realized at once that such spuriousness could not possibly deceive the people. However, Wang Mang had laid the groundwork in and outside the government for years and his time had come. "Matters have come to this" and it was "powerless to stop it." Besides, Wang Mang did not dare "harbor any treacherous thoughts" and

[111] *History of the Former Han*, *juan* 99 *shang*, "Biography of Wang Mang, Part I," p.4079.

merely wanted "the title of Regent." Grand Empress Dowager Wang had no choice but to acquiesce to Wang Mang's regency. After this levee was breached, Wang Mang continued to press on; there was no stopping the Western Han Dynasty's demise.

The accounts in historical texts give a clear indication that all knew full well that most of Wang Mang's "talismanic portents" were forgeries. However, the Grand Dowager Empress chose to turn a blind eye to what was going on, the "court dignitaries" lent their support, and local officials and commoners inundated the court with talismanic writings in exchange for monetary reward and career advancement.[112] "Many erudite scholars obtained official positions and noble ranks by hailing [Wang Mang's] achievements and virtues with talismanic writings."[113] "Many at the time strived to earn the rank of marquess by submitting talismanic writings. Those who did not do so said to one another in jest: 'Is it only you who have not received the Supreme Deity of Heaven's writings?'"[114] It came to a point where Wang Mang's trusted right-hand man Grand Censor Chen Chong felt he had to say something, and he told Wang Mang, "This has opened the path for wicked ministers to pursue their own gain, and it perverts the Mandate of Heaven. Its source should be cut off."[115]

As mentioned above, the Longxi warlord Wei Xiao built a temple to honor Emperors Gaozu, Wen, and Wu of the Western Han Dynasty near the end of the Xin Dynasty to demonstrate his loyalty to the Liu imperial family. Wei Xiao did this on the advice from his Military Counsellor Fang Wang:

> You, sir, wish to yield to the Mandate of Heaven and accede to the will of the people, and take up arms in aid of the Han. At present, [Emperor Gengshi] is in Nanyang and Wang Mang still occupies Chang'an. Although you wish to fight in the name of the Han, the truth is the Han has not given you any mandate to act. How then do you make the people believe you? You should build a temple to Emperor Gaozu at once, and pay obeisance and make offerings to him. As it is said: "In accordance to the Divine Way, lay down one's instructions." You should seek help from men and gods.[116]

By paying obeisance to the Han imperial clan, Wei Xiao attempted to gain the people's trust and show his pro-Han and anti–Wang Mang stand. This expedient measure of "laying down one's instructions in accordance with the Divine

112 For offering the Golden Chest talismanic writing to the court, Ai Zhang was appointed as one of the Four Supports, the highest official post in the Xin Dynasty, and was conferred the rank of Superior Duke. The former Foreman Clerk of the City Gates Wang Xing and pastry seller Wang Sheng were appointed among the ranks of the Four Generals simply because their names were mentioned in the talismanic writings. Liu Gong and Liu Jia, members of the Han imperial clan, were made marquesses for submitting talismanic writings to the court.

113 *History of the Former Han*, *juan* 87 *xia*, "Biography of Yang Xiong, Part II," p.3583.

114 *History of the Former Han*, *juan* 99 *zhong*, "Biography of Wang Mang, Part II," p.4122.

115 *Ibid.* 116 *History of the Later Han*, *juan* 13, "Biography of Wei Xiao," pp.514–515.

Way" was actually quite similar to Wang Mang's discourse on receiving the Mandate of Heaven using forged talismanic writings.

Before his ascent to the throne, Emperor Guangwu of the Eastern Han Dynasty won public support with the help of *chen* prophecies. As Emperor, he "appointed Sun Xian, General of the Pacification of the Di Barbarians, as Acting Commander-in-Chief" because a *chen* prophecy had mentioned that "Sun Xian would conquer the Di Barbarians." The appointment resulted in "unhappiness among all."[117] Also, because *The Token of Red Secret* contained the line "Wang Liang governs the region of Wei and performs the role as Black Tortoise,"[118] Wang Liang, Prefect of Yewang, landed a big promotion and became Grand Minister of Works.[119] The Eastern Han Dynasty's esteem for and promotion of apocryphal-prophetic discourse resulted not only in career officials trying their luck – even intellectuals became enthused. "Those who kept up with the times would run to the Emperor's side to fabricate implausible stories and vie with one another to speak."[120] "For this reason, the people of later times strived to study apocrypha and diagrams to right the world and acquire gains."[121] Yin Min, who had erudite knowledge of the classics and books, debunked such apocryphal-prophetic discourse, but Emperor Guangwu was not convinced. And so, Yin Min took advantage of his position as editor of the apocryphal-prophetic texts to insert the line: "The gentleman without a mouth will assist the Han,"[122] hoping to inveigle a promotion from the Emperor.

An Analysis of the Psychology of the Belief in Chen *Prophecies*

A survey of the emergence, dissemination, and application of *chen* prophecies in Han society would yield a surfeit of strategic deliberations, realpolitik considerations, traces of manipulation, and incredibly absurd superstition. There was in fact no shortage of rational criticism and skepticism of *chen* prophecies among intellectuals at the time.[123] It would be an

[117] *History of the Later Han, juan* 22, "Biography of Jing Dan," p.773.

[118] The Black Tortoise (*Xuanwu*) was the god of water based in the north.

[119] Yewang, present day Qinyang Countym Henan Province. And Grand Minister of Works was in charge of civil and irrigation works. *History of the Later Han, juan* 1 *shang*, "Annals of Emperor Guangwu, Part I," p.23; "Biography of Wang Liang," p.774

[120] *History of the Later Han, juan* 82 *shang*, "Biographies of Alchemists, Part I," p.2705.

[121] Hua Jiao, *History of the Later Han, juan* 2, "Biography of Lang Yi," p.23. (*Eight Versions of the History of the Later Han*, p.535)

[122] "The gentleman (*jun* 君) without a mouth (*kou* 口)" implied Yin Min's surname Yin (尹).

[123] For example, Yin Min told Emperor Guangwu: "*Chen* prophetic books were not written by the sages, and they contain much coarse language and many erroneous words. They resemble the words of the common folk and I fear that they may mislead young people." (*History of Later Han, juan* 79 *shang*, "Biographies of Confucian Scholars, Part I: Biography of Yin Min," p.2558) Huan Tan (23 BCE – 50 CE) told Emperor Guangwu: "Your servant does not study *chen* prophecies." "The Emperor asked him for the reason why and Huan Tan replied by

oversimplification, however, to analyze the psychology of the belief in *chen* prophecies during the Han periods solely from the perspectives of political utilitarianism and superstition. Even if many of the *chen* prophecies were fabrications, the need to fabricate and the actual function of *chen* prophecies in political struggles at the time had already demonstrated their unique value in the battle for the people's minds. In other words, the belief in *chen* prophecies was a real and widespread phenomenon in society at the time.

Even forgers or people who were just trying their luck might have believed in *chen* prophecies or regarded their powers with reverence. For example, Wang Mang's discourse of his receiving the Mandate of Heaven was a result of the manipulation of "talismanic writings" by many individuals. Wang Mang himself knew what Grand Empress Dowager meant when she said, "This deceives all under Heaven." However, he renamed the knife-coin the Huoquan coin because the original name (*jin dao*) suggested the surname Liu.[124] He also banned the wearing of *gangmao* for the same reason.[125] "Wang Kuang's *chen* prophecy averred that the Jingchu region would rise up, assisted by a person bearing the surname Li. To suppress it, [Wang Mang] appointed Li Chen, Palace Attendant and Grandee Herdsman, as General-in-Chief and Governor of Yangzhou Region, conferred on him the name 'Sheng' [literally "sage"], and ordered him to lead a military offensive."[126] These actions demonstrated Wang Mang's genuine fear of the mysterious symbolic power of Chinese characters and *chen* prophecies. In the sixth month of the fourth year of the Dihuang reign period (23 CE), the army of the Xin Dynasty suffered a major defeat in Kunyang. "Wang Mang's troops were defeated outside the capital

remonstrating that *chen* prophecies were not canonical." (*History of Later Han*, *juan* 28 *shang*, "Biography of Huan Tan," p.961) Zheng Xing told Emperor Guangwu: "Your servant does not deal with *chen* prophecies." (*History of Later Han*, *juan* 36, "Biography of Zheng Xing," p.1223) Zhang Heng (78–139 CE) submitted a memorial to Emperor Shun of the Eastern Han Dynasty, stating that *chen* prophecies and diagrams were forgeries. "*Chen* prophecies and diagrams should be collected and prohibited." (*History of Later Han*, *juan* 59, "Biography of Zhang Heng," p.1912) When Dong Zhuo was planning to move the imperial capital to Chang'an in accordance with the *Shi Bao Shi Chen Prophecy*, Minister over the Masses Yang Biao (142–225 CE) argued: "How could *Shi Bao Shi Chen Prophecy*, which is a portentous and evil book, be trusted?" (*Records of the Three Kingdoms*, *juan* 6, "Book of Wei: Biography of Dong Zhuo," annotations by Pei Songzhi, citing Hua Jiao, *History of the Later Han*, p.177) These critiques, which have been widely cited in academic writing will not be further elaborated in this book.

124 *History of the Later Han*, *juan* 1 *xia*, "Annals of Emperor Guangwu, Part II," p.86. The traditional form of character Liu (劉) can be broken down into three components: *mao* 卯, *jin* 金, and *dao* 刂.

125 The *gangmao* was an ornament in the shape of a rectangular cube. It was fashionable in court and among scholars of the Western Han Dynasty because people believed that it could ward off evil spirits.

126 *History of the Former Han*, *juan* 99 *xia*, "Biography of Wang Mang, Part III," p.4168. Annotation by Yan Shigu: "Changing his old name to 'Li Sheng' in order to fulfill the *chen* prophecy."

and his senior ministers were plotting treason within; there was no one around him whom he could trust."[127] Wang Mang, "realizing that he had been defeated, led his ministers to the southern suburbs, where he recounted to them, right from the beginning, the entire process of him receiving the talismanic signs and the Mandate of Heaven. Lifting his eyes to Heaven, he said, 'Since the Supreme Deity of Heaven conferred His Mandate upon Wang Mang, why does He not destroy these multitudinous bandits? If I have erred, please strike me dead with Your lightning!' He then beat his breast and wept. When he could weep no more, he prostrated himself and struck his forehead upon the ground."[128] When the Chimei Rebels breached the defenses of Chang'an in the tenth month, Wang Mang, with the help of his ministers, sought refuge at the in the Stable of the Eternal Palace. Even moments before his death, Wang Mang "was still clutching the talismanic writings and *weidou*."[129] Ironically, the "talismanic writings" that Wang Mang himself had fabricated eventually became symbols that he fervently believed in and totally depended on.

Chen prophecies also played an important part in the discourse of Liu Xiu receiving the Mandate of Heaven. Not only did Emperor Guangwu employ *chen* prophecies to win popular opinion over to his side, boost confidence among his own men, and convince the people, he also relied on them to resolve conflicts and make decisions on unresolved matters,[130] including the appointments of senior officials based on such prophecies.

"It is said that men skilled in the Taoist arts such as Ximen Junhui and Li Shou had cited the *chen* prophecy that 'Liu Xiu is to be Son of Heaven.' There had been several such prophecies since the time when Emperor Guangwu was a commoner. In time, he became the Son of Heaven, which made him a firm believer in these writings."[131] According to historical accounts, Emperor Guangwu genuinely believed in *chen* prophecies and was extremely serious in his study of *chen* prophetic texts. A solar eclipse occurred on a gloomy Yiwei day in the second month of the seventeenth year of the Jianwu reign period. "The Emperor avoided the Audience Hall because of the solar eclipse, and studied a great number of *chen* prophecies and diagrams. Seated in the corridor, he was exposed to the elements for a while. He caught a chill, fell sick, and suffered greatly from dizzy spells. His attendants informed the Clerk

[127] *Ibid.*, p.4186. [128] *Ibid.*, pp.4187–4188.

[129] *Ibid.*, p.4191. The *weidou* was a sacred object shaped like an iron for pressing clothes. Wang Mang never went anywhere without it, believing that it could subjugate his enemies.

[130] "At the time Emperor [Guangwu] believed in *chen* prophecies and often used them to decide on doubtful matters." (*History of the Later Han, juan* 28 *shang*, "Biography of Huan Tan," p.959)

[131] Hua Jiao, *History of the Later Han, juan* 2, "Biography of Lang Yi." (*Eight Versions of the History of the Later Han*, p.535)

of the Commander-in-Chief that the Emperor was so sick that he could not move."[132] Not only did Emperor Guangwu study *chen* prophetic books in earnest, he also discussed them with his trusted ministers.[133]

In the first year of the Zhongyuan reign period, Emperor Guangwu "issued [standard texts of] *chen* prophecies and diagrams across the empire," an act that has been cited as proof that the Emperors of the Eastern Han Dynasty promoted apocryphal-prophetic discourse. However, texts of *chen* prophecies and diagrams had always been widely disseminated in society between the late Western Han and early Eastern Han. Why was it necessary for them to be "issued" before promoting them across the empire? In fact, after Emperor Guangwu ascended to the throne, he ordered people such as Xue Han and Yin Min to "edit and standardize the *chen* prophecies and diagrams" by removing all the talismanic writings and *chen* prophecies edited and recorded for Wang Mang by Chief Commandant of Cavalry Cui Fa and others during the Xin Dynasty.[134] They also deleted and revised any content that could be detrimental to the Eastern Han Dynasty's imperial family. It took thirty years for the content to be revised and "issued across the empire." The Emperor's aim was to standardize apocryphal-prophetic discourse and put an end to the threat posed by the forging of *chen* prophetic writings for traitorous outcomes. The nervous attention paid to this thirty-year exercise also demonstrated Emperor Guangwu's firm belief in and his fear of *chen* prophecies.

According to "Biography of Zhang Heng" in *History of the Later Han*: "In the beginning, Emperor Guangwu was well-versed in *chen* prophecies. Emperors Xianzong [Ming] and Suzong [Zhang] inherited their father's and grandfather's theories."[135] However, historical records show that Emperors Ming's and Zhang's aptitude for *chen* discourse was not only the result of them inheriting "their father's and grandfather's theories."

According to "Annals of Emperor Ming" in *Eastern Library's Records of Han*:

Emperor Xiaoming [referring to Emperor Ming] was especially partial to the study of the Classics. Following his ascension to the throne, he revised, drafted, and edited the canonical commentaries in accordance with *chen* prophecies and diagrams. He made his teacher Grand Master of Ceremonies Huan Rong Marquess Within the Pass, and personally wrote syntactic and semantic analyses on the Five Agents. At the end of

132 *History of the Later Han, juan* 1 *xia*, "Annals of Emperor Guangwu, Part II," annotations by Li Xian, citing *Eastern Library's Records of Han*, p.68.

133 "Your servant [Zhu] Fu has been fortunate to discuss *chen* prophecies and diagrams with Your Majesty, which is why I am bold enough to speak above my station." (*History of the Later Han, juan* 33, "Biography of Zhu Fu," p.1145)

134 *History of Later Han, juan* 79 *shang*, "Biographies of Confucian Scholars, Part I: Biography of Yin Min," p.2558.

135 *History of Later Han, juan* 59, p.1911.

every Drinking and Archery Ceremony, the Emperor would sit and give a lecture to the Confucian scholars, and all would be pleased. There were innumerable learned men at the time, and the members of the official class and the gentry who gathered and observed at the ceremonial site were innumerable.[136]

The edicts of Emperors Ming and Zhang, recorded in *History of the Later Han*, also cited apocryphal-prophetic texts very often to support their discourse on politics and rituals.

The affinity for apocryphal-prophetic discourse continued after the reigns of Emperors Ming and Zhang. Deng Sui (81–121 CE), who became Empress Dowager after the death of Emperor He (reigned 88–105 CE), was the de facto ruler for the next sixteen years in her capacity as regent. "After she entered the palace, she read widely in the Five Classics and the relevant commentaries, *chen* prophecies and diagrams, esoteric writings, weather divination, *Laozi*, *Mencius*, 'Proceedings of Government in the Different Months' in *Book of Rites*, and *Model Sayings*. She did not read frivolous works and legalist writings such as those by Shen Buhai and Han Feizi."[137] In the third year of Emperor An's Yongchu reign period (109 CE), the planet Venus entered the Dou Constellation and Luoyang was inundated. Empress Dowager Deng sent a Regular Palace Attendant to consult with Yang Hou, a famous master of apocryphal-prophetic discourse. Yang Hou made this suggestion: "With many princes of the blood in the capital, there may be upheavals. They should be sent back to their own kingdoms." The Empress Dowager took his advice, and soon Venus disappeared and the flooding in Luoyang subsided. It was as Yang Hou had predicted.[138] In the sixth year of the Yongchu reign period (112 CE), Empress Dowager Deng issued an edict in Emperor An's name: "The twenty-eight generals who helped found the dynasty in the Jianwu reign period were courageous servants who were named in *chen* prophetic books." As ancestral offerings to some of them might have ceased, Empress Dowager Deng ordered that "those among the descendants of the twenty-eight generals who had lost their fiefdoms would be given back their lands."[139]

Gongsun Shu, who fought with Liu Xiu for the empire at the end of the Xin Dynasty, and Yuan Shu, one of the many warlords at the end of the Eastern Han Dynasty, were both firm believers of *chen* prophecies. When coded *chen* prophecies such as "Depose Emperor Chang and install the grandson of a lord"

[136] *Eastern Library's Records of Han: Collations and Annotations*, *juan* 2, p.58.

[137] Sima Biao, "Empresses and Consorts: Biography of Empress Deng, the Empress Hexi" in *Sequel to the History of the Former Han*. (*Eight Versions of the History of the Later Han*, p.318)

[138] *History of the Later Han*, *juan* 30 *shang*, "Biography of Yang Hou," p.1048.

[139] *History of the Later Han*, *juan* 17, "Biography of Feng Yi," p.652. Actually, Deng Yu (2–58 CE), Empress Dowager Deng's grandfather was ranked top among the twenty-eight founding heroes.

and "The one who replaces the Han will be Dangtu Gao" were decoded, both of them believed that they were the ones to fulfill the prophecies. In the early years of the Eastern Han Dynasty, there was a "mountain bandit," Zhang Man, at Xincheng who "made offerings to Heaven and Earth and proclaimed himself King." In the spring of the third year of the Jianwu reign period, General of the Conquering of the Lu Barbarians Zhai Zun (?–33 CE) took Xincheng and captured Zhang Man. Zhang Man said with profound regret, "The *chen* prophecy has misled me!"[140] The contents of the *chen* prophecy is unknown. Since Zhang Man's uprising ended in failure, the *chen* prophecy did not come true and could only be considered portentous talk, or Zhang Man had misread the *chen* prophecy. Whatever it was, Zhang Man's belief in the *chen* prophecy was genuine.

The belief in *chen* prophecies was not only popular among the denizens of high-level power struggles but was also prevalent in the wider society. In the final years of the Xin Dynasty, there was a native of Beihai called Feng Meng who was from a poor family. He was a Commune Chief but later went to Luoyang to study the *Spring and Autumn Annals*. Well-versed in the *Yin* and the *Yang*, Feng Meng knew that Wang Mang would soon be defeated. And so, he put a clay basin over his head and cried in the marketplace, "Xin! Xin!"[141] In the late Eastern Han Dynasty, General-in-Chief He Jin (?–189 CE) invited Dong Zhuo and his army to Luoyang to support the administration. After he entered the capital, Dong Zhuo replaced the Emperor and placed another one on the throne and took total control of the government and the army. Minister over the Masses Wang Yun hatched a secret plot with Dong Zhuo's lieutenant Lü Bu and Supervisor Shisun Rui to assassinate Dong Zhuo. Someone wrote the character *lü* on a piece of cloth and carried it in the marketplace, singing, "Bu!" (The word "*bu*" means "cloth.") This was reported to Dong Zhuo but he did not understand.[142] Similar rumors would often emerge in times of social upheaval, especially as a kind of "explanation" after a major event. It should be noted that historians during the Han and Wei dynasties saw them as coded *chen* prophecies and included them in their narratives.

In the early years of the Jianwu reign period of the Eastern Han Dynasty, the Xiongnu made incessant southward incursions into the Chinese empire. Emperor Guangwu ordered "the construction of war chariots that were pulled by several cows. These chariots, which had watchtowers, were stationed at the border to guard against the Xiongnu." When the people saw this, they talked

[140] *History of the Later Han*, *juan* 20, "Biography of Zhai Zun," p.739.

[141] *History of the Later Han*, *juan* 83, "Biographies of Hermits: Biography of Feng Meng," p.2760.

[142] *History of the Later Han*, *juan* 72, "Biography of Dong Zhuo," p.2331. Annotations by Li Xian, citing *Records of Heroes*: "A Taoist priest wrote on a piece of cloth the character '*lü*' and showed it to Dong Zhuo, but Dong Zhuo did not know it referred to Lü Bu."

among themselves, saying, "The *chen* prophecy says that the Di Barbarians of the north will retreat a thousand *li* during the time of the ninth-generation Han ruler. Could it be referring to this?" In the twenty-fourth year of the Jianwu reign period, the Xiongnu state was divided into Northern and Southern Xiongnu. The Supreme Leader of Southern Xiongnu made friendly overtures to the Eastern Han court, expressing his wish to always be the barrier between Han China and "the northern barbarians." In the following year, Southern Xiongnu scored a major victory over Northern Xiongnu, and "the Supreme Leader of the Northern Xiongnu retreated a thousand *li* in great fear."[143] After that, the people believed that the *chen* prophecy "the Di Barbarians of the north will retreat a thousand *li* during the time of the ninth generation Han ruler" had come to pass.

Shan Yang, a native of Shanyang, was well versed in astrology and arithmetic. His official appointments included Prefect Grand Astrologer, Palace Attendant, and Grand Administrator of Hanzhong. He was eventually promoted to Master of Writing and died in office. At the end of Emperor Ling's Xiping reign period (172–178 CE), a yellow dragon was seen at Qiao.[144]

> The Imperial Household Grandee Qiao Xuan [109–183 CE] asked Shan Yang, "What omen is this?" Shan Yang said: "A King will rise in the state. In less than fifty years, the dragon will reappear and it will be the fulfillment of this." Yin Deng, a native of Wei Commandery, secretly put this in writing. By the spring of the twenty-fifth year of the Jian'an reign period, a yellow dragon was seen again in Qiao. In the winter of that year, the Han abdicated power to the Wei.[145]

In the twenty-fifth year of the Jian'an reign period (220), Cao Cao died and Emperor Xian of the Eastern Han Dynasty abdicated in favor of Cao Pi. A little over forty years separated the late Xiping reign period and the twenty-fifth year of the Jian'an reign period.

Dong Fu was a master in the study of apocryphal-prophetic discourse who lived in the Shu region in the late Eastern Han Dynasty. He studied under Yang Hou, who was also from his commandery. Dong Fu returned home to teach his students, some of whom had traveled great distances to learn from him. The court thought highly of him and attempted to recruit him as Palace Attendant during the reign of Emperor Ling. In a private conversation with Liu Yan (?–194), a member of the Han imperial clan and Grand Master of Ceremonies,

[143] *History of the Later Han*, *juan* 89, "Biographies of the Southern Xiongnu," p.2943.

[144] Qiao Commandery in the Kingdom of Pei (present-day Bozhou, Anhui Province). Cao Cao was a native of Qiao. Chapter 1 of this book discusses the myriad good omens, strange occurrences, signs, and legends regarding red (Fire) and yellow (Earth) replacing each other at the cusps of the Western Han-Xin and Eastern Han-Wei dynastic changes. The sighting of "yellow dragons" was the most common sign.

[145] *History of the Later Han*, *juan* 82 *xia*, "Biographies of Alchemists, Part II: Biography of Shan Yang," p.2733.

he said, "The capital will descend into chaos, but a Son of Heaven air current appears in the constellation that corresponds to the Yizhou Region."[146] Believing in Dong Fu's prognostication, Liu Yan made a request to the court to send him to the Yizhou Region as Governor. Emperor Ling died the following year, triggering convulsive waves across the empire. Alas, the "Son of Heaven air current" did not eventually find its match in Liu Yan, but rather in the person of Liu Bei.

These *chen* prophecies had been circulated among the common people or in private for years, and people believed in them.

The "Treatise on the Five Agents" in *History of the Later Han*, which recorded strange happenings and portentous changes that occurred in the Eastern Han Dynasty, often linked *chen* prophecies with political events to explain the reasons for strange occurrences. It also saw these strange occurrences as the verifications of various *chen* prophecies. For example:

> On the Xinyou day in winter, in the tenth month of the first year of Emperor An's Yongchu reign period, water gushed out from the mountains in Xincheng in He'nan, and destroyed the people's farmlands. The groundwater was three *zhang* deep. At the time, Minister of Works Zhou Zhang and others plotted a coup because Empress Dowager Deng installed the son of King of Qinghe instead of the Heir-Apparent Liu Sheng as Emperor. The plot was discovered in the eleventh month, and Zhou Zhang and the other plotters were executed. In the same year, there were forty-one inundations in the commanderies and kingdoms that drowned many people. According to a *chen* prophecy: "Water is the quintessence of pure *Yin*. When the *Yin* element is powerful and brims over, mean men become despotic and arrogate powers to themselves. They are jealous of the virtuous and use their official positions to settle personal scores. Gentlemen are encroached upon and taken advantage of; while mean men ride on the wave of victory. The loss and fulfillment of ambitions cause the flooding waters."[147]

Another example occurred on the Bingchen day in the sixth month of the fourth year of Emperor He's Yongyuan reign period:

> Thirteen earthquakes occurred in the commanderies and kingdoms. According to the apocrypha *Spring and Autumn the Progeny of Han*: "When a female ruler is powerful and servants of the Emperor arrogate powers to themselves, the ground will quake and split apart; the borders of the fields will be thrown up and the mountains will collapse." At the time, Empress Dowager Dou was regent and her older brother Dou Xian dominated the court. They were the reason for the natural disasters. Five days later, the Emperor ordered Dou Xian to return his seals. The Dou brothers were sent back to their fiefdom where they were forced to take their own lives.[148]

146 *History of the Later Han, juan* 82 *xia*, "Biographies of Alchemists, Part II: Biography of Dong Fu," p.2734.
147 *History of the Later Han, zhi* 15, "Treatise on the Five Agents, Part III," p.3309.
148 *History of the Later Han, zhi* 16, "Treatise on the Five Agents, Part IV," p.3328.

Fan Ye did not finish writing the treatises in *History of Later Han*. The treatises in the extant version of *History of Later Han* were added to by Liu Zhao of the Southern Liang Dynasty using materials from *Sequel to the History of the Former Han*, written by Sima Biao (243–306 CE) of the Western Jin Dynasty. The "Treatise of the Five Agent" in *History of the Later Han* was an amalgamated product incorporating the writings of Ying Shao, Dong Ba, and Qiao Zhou, who collected "the records of strange occurrences since the Jianwu reign period."[149] Therefore, the above discussions reflected the knowledge of scholars of history and apocryphal-prophetic texts in the late Eastern Han regarding *chen* prophecies and their connection with society and politics, as well as their acknowledgment of the cautioning and symbolic powers of *chen* prophecies.

Zheng Xuan, another eminent scholar of the Classics and the Apocrypha in the late Eastern Han Dynasty, had a dream in the spring of the fifth year of Emperor Xian's Jian'an reign period (200 CE). In his dream, Confucius said to him, "Arise! Arise! This year is the Chen year; next year is the Si year." "After he woke up and matched his dream to apocryphal-prophetic texts, he knew that he would die soon. He fell ill shortly after."[150] This shows that the belief in *chen* prophecies was deeply entrenched in the everyday lives of people, in addition to their social and political lives.

Dou Rong, the warlord occupying the region west of the Yellow River during the final years of the Xin Dynasty, gave up his land of his own accord and submitted to the authority of Emperor Guangwu of the Eastern Han Dynasty. Highly favored by Emperor Guangwu, the exalted Dou clan boasted "one duke, two marquesses, three princesses (as daughters-in-low), and four officials ranking 2,000 *shi*." Despite Emperor Guangwu's belief in and focus on *chen* prophecy, he did not want the descendants of noblemen and officials to master it. Having figured out the Emperor's mindset, Dou Rong found even more favor with Emperor Guangwu and deflected suspicion by telling the Emperor that he did not allow his sons to "observe the stars and peruse *chen* prophetic books, but wanted them to be deferential and cautious, following the Way with great care. He did not wish them any talent or ability."[151] As a result, Emperor Guangwu did not reproach Dou Rong the way he reproached Yin Min and Zheng Xing. Given the capricious nature of kings and emperors, Dou Rong's perspicacious caution was understandable.[152]

Zhou Qun, a scholar of apocryphal-prophetic discourse from the Shu region, who was mentioned above as the first person to decode the *chen* prophecy,

[149] See Chen Yexin (2002), p.44.
[150] *History of the Later Han*, *juan* 35, "Biography of Zheng Xuan," p.1211.
[151] *History of the Later Han*, *juan* 23, "Biography of Dou Rong," p.807.
[152] See Lu Zongli (1984), p.82.

"The one who replaces the Han will be Dangtu Gao," learned apocryphal-prophetic discourse and divination using stars from his father, Zhou Shu (a student of Yang Hou's). "He was dedicated to his vocation and built a small tower in his garden. Possessing many slaves because of his family's wealth, he often ordered his slaves to observe strange occurrences in the sky from the tower. Whenever they saw an air current they would inform him at once, and he would climb the tower and observe it himself, regardless of whether it was day or night. Zhou Qun saw every air current and weather abnormality, which was why most of his prognostications came to pass."[153]

Like Zhou Qun, Chengdu native Du Qiong was a student of a student of Yang Hou's. Du Qiong's teacher was Ren An, the eminent scholar of the Apocrypha, and he became an expert in Ren An's teachings. However, "despite his erudite learning he did not observe the stars at first." He also "did not teach any of his sons, thus no one could inherit and pass on his knowledge apocryphal-prophetic learning." He once spoke of the difficulties to Qiao Zhou, another up-and-coming scholar of the Apocrypha: "This art is hard to grasp ... one must work hard day and night before one could know it well. However, one fears of revealing Heaven's secrets, so it is better not to know it."[154]

We can see that that people's attitudes toward *chen* prophecies during the Eastern Han were a mixture of belief and fear. Learning and decoding the prognosticative information contained in *chen* prophecies was a serious, difficult, and politically risky endeavor.

The concept of the Mandate of Heaven, which had developed during the Western Zhou Dynasty, was linked to both national and personal destinies. The Mandate of Heaven that determined the nation's political future developed a set of highly institutionalized political symbols, following its enrichment by Confucian scholars in the Han periods and elucidation by apocryphal-prophetic masters. This set of symbols provided a standardized ritual for the legitimate transition of the most powerful office in ancient China, which helped focus and consolidate various social forces, and minimized the inevitable social upheavals that accompanied dynastic change. However, the meaning and sanctity of these symbols were given by men. When the meanings of these symbols were withdrawn by men, the whole ritual would become a farcical performance. *Chen* prophecies, good omens, and so on could be fabricated, and in many instances they were indeed fabricated. Many scholars thus emphasize the deceptive function of apocryphal-prophetic discourse as a political weapon at the time. If everything was forged for utilitarian purposes

153 *Records of the Three Kingdoms*, *juan* 42, "Book of Shu: Biography of Zhou Qun," p.1020.

154 *Records of the Three Kingdoms*, *juan* 42, "Book of Shu: Biography of Du Qiong," p.1021. See Lu Zongli (1984), p.85.

and devoid of belief, then *chen* prophecy would become a joke bereft of any sanctity. Where was its symbolic meaning? How could it have any effect on political struggles?

Many of the *chen* prophecies recorded in historical texts were made up after the events had occurred. Although the people at the time knew very well that this was going on, it did not diminish their interest and belief in *chen* prophecies. The reason was this: the more unstable the situation, the less confidence the people had, and the more they wished to know the future. While many *chen* prophecies were indeed fake, there were predictions that actually came true. What was interesting was the more popular the *chen* prophecy was, the more believers it had, and the greater possibility it had of coming true. The difference between *chen* prophecy and the divination practiced by ancient royal families to seek divine revelation was this: divination was an opaque procedure where only a select few were allowed to make interpretations; whereas a *chen* prophecy, whoever its author might have been, had to undergo a baptism of fire in the course of its dissemination. *Chen* prophecies that nobody wished to believe in would be disregarded, but *chen* prophecies that everyone wished to believe in would become popular very quickly, thus affecting the balance of political power. *Chen* prophecies had an irreplaceable and indispensable function in the social and political contexts of the time. For this reason, most people – both within and outside the government, from the most exalted to the most humble – believed in *chen* prophecies with all their heart.

Prophetic Rhyme

Prophetic rhyme was a form in which *chen* prophecies were expressed, and it usually presented itself as children's songs. Compared with the popular songs and rhymes discussed in Chapter 3, prophetic rhymes were more like children's songs that were high in entertainment value. Be that as it may, they were often considered coded *chen* prophecies with strange words and hidden meanings that could foretell the future. For this reason, they were collected in the "Treatises of the Five Agents" in both *History of the Former Han* and *History of the Later Han* and were referred to as portentous rhymes and portentous poetry.[155]

[155] Wu Chengxue (1996): "Prophetic rhymes used the form of songs and rhymes to forecast Heaven's future arrangements for the nation, politics, and even individuals." (p.104) Xie Gui'an (1998): "Prophetic rhymes were mysterious and prophetic songs that combined the mystical and predictive nature of *chen* with the popularity of colloquial songs and rhymes. They were a symbol that expressed mystery in a demotic form, prognosticating the rise and fall of individual careers, and the success and failure of political endeavors; or a political tool that made use of prophetic narratives." (p.5)

Prophetic Rhymes during the Reigns of Emperors Yuan and Cheng

Prophecies in the form of children's songs had been recorded in early historical texts such as *Commentary of Zuo*, *Discourses of the States*, "Basic Annals of the Zhou" and "The Hereditary House of Jin" in *The Grand Scribe's Records*, and so on, "unequivocally reflecting the pre-Qin notion that regarded rhymes as *chen*."[156] These prophecies in the form of children's songs were classified under portentous poetry in "Treatise on the Five Agents" in *History of the Former Han*.

Only three prophetic rhymes were recorded in "Treatise on the Five Agents" in *History of the Former Han*, all of which appeared during the reigns of Emperors Yuan and Cheng.

The first rhyme went:

> Water brims over the well./It puts out the smoke from the stove;/floods the Jade Hall;/ and flows out the Golden Gate.[157]

This prophetic rhyme was supposed to have been popular during the reign of Emperor Yuan of the Western Han Dynasty. Water brimming over the well and putting out the smoke from the stove was a possible and frequent occurrence in daily life, and so the narrative of this rhyme might not have had a specific political reference.[158] However, some scholars aver that this rhyme expressed the rage of the people directed against the extreme political venality during Emperor Yuan's reign, when real power was in the hands of the eunuch Shi Xian – an irrepressible rage that could topple the polity of the ruling elite.

According to the *Yinyang* and Five Agents discourse popular throughout the early imperial period, water from wells was of the *Yin* element and smoke from stoves was of the *Yang* element. Therefore, water brimming over the well and putting out the smoke from the stove was a sign of a dominant *Yin* and a weak *Yang*, which, in the political and cultural contexts of the time, signified the arrogation of political power by female rulers, affinal families of Emperors, and eunuchs, or the insubordination of powerful ministers toward weak Emperors.

There had been an earlier example of well water appearing in an omen. When Emperor Xuan of the Western Han Dynasty was still a penurious scion of the imperial clan eking out a living among the common folk, he was already aware of the "long-standing distinction and power of the Huo family, and his heart could not be still."[159] After he ascended to the throne, Emperor Xuan

156 Wu Chengxue (1996), p.104.

157 *History of the Former Han*, *juan* 27 *zhong zhi shang*, "Treatise on the Five Agents, Part II," p.1395.

158 Liu Kaiyang (1983), p.89.

159 *History of the Former Han*, *juan* 68, "Biography of Huo Guang," p.2951.

pretended to respect and trust Huo Guang, but he was in fact wary of him. When they were riding in the same carriage, Emperor Xuan felt as if "there was a thorn in his back."[160] After Huo Guang died, the relationship between the Huo family and Emperor Xuan became increasingly tense. The court removed Huo Guang's sons from positions of power, and Huo Guang's widow Huo Xian dreamed of disasters befalling the Huo family's mansion: "Water overflowed from the well and flooded the courtyard, and the stove was hung from a tree."[161] Soon afterward, the Huo family's plot to depose the Emperor was exposed and the whole clan was exterminated.

On the Wuzi day of the third month in the second year of Emperor Cheng's Jianshi reign period (31 BCE), the line in the prophetic rhyme, "Water brims over the well," came true when a well in the Northern Palace brimmed over slightly and water flowed southward. According to "Treatise on the Five Agents" in *History of the Former Han*, "Jade Hall and Golden Gate [referred to] the residence of the most exalted." Water brimming out of the well, flooding the Jade Hall, and flowing out of the Golden Gate obviously symbolized a dominant *Yin* element putting out the *Yang* and would be "fulfilled in the palace."[162] Emperor Cheng of the Western Han Dynasty had placed the family of Empress Dowager Wang in important positions in government, and within the Inner Palace, he favored Zhao Feiyan and her sister exclusively. The Emperor was excessively decadent and liked to venture out of the palace incognito. It would be perfectly reasonable to say that the prophecy of a dominant *Yin* element putting out the *Yang* came to pass during the reign of Emperor Cheng.[163] However, "Treatise on the Five Agents" in *History of the Former Han* placed the fulfillment of the prophetic rhyme several decades later when Wang Mang overthrew the Western Han.

The second rhyme went:

Lustrous tails of the swifts/encountered at the time/of Young Master Zhang./The wooden door with a jade door ring./The swift flies hither;/pecks at the Emperor's grandson./The Emperor's grandson dies,/the swift pecks at arrows.[164]

[160] *Ibid.*, p.2958. [161] *Ibid.*, p.2955.

[162] *History of the Former Han, juan* 27 *zhong zhi shang*, "Treatise on the Five Agents, Part II," p.1395.

[163] In the spring of the second year of Emperor Cheng's Suihe reign period (7 BCE), Li Xun submitted a memorial that mentioned strange occurrences: "The unverifiable talk and rhymes of the people pinpoint events and name names. All three things have come to pass, which brings a chill to one's heart." The annotation by Ru Chun reads: "'Pinpoint events' meant the overflowing water of the well. It was said that a well would brim over, and brimmed over it eventually did. 'Name names' referred to the 'Lustrous Tails of the Swifts' [rhyme]." (*History of the Former Han, juan* 84, "Biography of Zhai Fangjin," pp.3421–3422) This indicates that there were people who believed that the "Water Brims over the Well" rhyme prognosticated the events of Emperor Cheng's reign and that the "Lustrous Tail of the Swift" referred to Zhao Feiyan.

[164] *History of the Former Han, juan* 27 *zhong zhi shang*, "Treatise on the Five Agents, Part II," p.1395.

When Emperor Cheng was on the throne, he would often venture out of the palace in the company of Zhang Fang, the Marquess of Fuping.[165] When they traveled incognito, the Emperor would disguise himself as a servant of the Marquess. He indulged in various pleasures such as cockfighting and horse racing. There was an occasion when Emperor Cheng was at a party hosted by Princess Yang'e where he "saw the dancer Zhao Feiyan and laid with her." Soon afterward, Emperor Cheng took Zhao Feiyan into his harem and made her Empress. Zhao Feiyan's younger twin sister, Zhao Hede, was also brought into the palace and made a Brilliant Companion. Both the Zhao sisters were barren, and they made sure the other consorts of the Emperor were childless by poisoning those who were pregnant and killing the Emperor's sons, resulting in the Emperor becoming heirless. Therefore, the "Lustrous Tails of the Swifts" rhyme might have been a narrative children's song, "using the life of a swift[166] to allude to the story of Zhao Feiyan's rise from poverty to riches, and her subsequent fall and demise"[167] in sarcastic language. The "Treatise on the Five Agents" in *History of the Former Han* placed the appearance of this rhyme before Emperor Cheng met Zhao Feiyan, which made it a prophetic children's song.

The third rhyme went:

> Crooked paths spoil the fertile fields;/slanderous talk hurts good men./The sweet osmanthus tree flowers but bears no fruit;/the yellow bird nests atop its crown./It was envied in the past,/but now it is pitied.[168]

The first line of this children's song decried the objectionable behavior of taking "crooked paths" and engaging in "slanderous talk." Then, using the allegory of the flowering but fruitless sweet osmanthus tree and the yellow bird that nested on its crown, the song reminded those who did bad things that while they might have the upper hand at the moment, they would come to an ignominious end. The writer of "Treatise on the Five Agents" believed that the song contained a coded message: "The sweet osmanthus is red, symbolizing

165 Zhang Fang was the great-great-grandson of Zhang Tang, a "cruel official" during the reign of Emperor Wu of the Western Han Dynasty, and the great-grandson of Zhang Anshi, Commander-in-Chief during Emperor Xuan's reign. His father was Zhang Lin and his mother Princess Jingwu. Zhang Fang held several posts in succession: Palace Attendant, Leader of Court Gentlemen, Imperial Household Grandee, and Inspector of the Pingle Garrison. "He slept and woke up together with the Emperor, who showered him with exceptional favor. He often accompanied the Emperor in the latter's incognito travels, from Ganquan Palace in the north to the Changyang and Wuzuo Palaces in the south. In Chang'an, they indulged in cockfighting and horse racing for several years." (*History of the Former Han*, *juan* 59, "Biography of Zhang Fang," pp.2654–2655)

166 Zhao Feiyan's given name "Feiyan" literally means "flying swift."

167 Lei Qunming and Wang Longdi (1988), p.29.

168 *History of the Former Han*, *juan* 27 *zhong zhi shang*, "Treatise on the Five Agents, Part II," p.1396.

the color of the Han Dynasty. That it flowered but bore no fruit referred to the Han imperial clan not having heirs to continue the dynasty. Wang Mang claimed the color yellow represented him, and the yellow bird did nest on the crown of the tree."[169] In other words, the song prophesied that the Earth-Power would replace the Fire-Power. There are those who speculate that it was a case of "some person or persons in the know who sensed the political ambitions of a certain powerful minister, and then created the coded prophecy to make people notice."[170] In other words, this was a prophetic rhyme that had been manipulated by a human agency. However, this writer is of the opinion that what the rhyme described and criticized were common occurrences in everyday lives; it might not have any specific political reference. The manner in which "Treatise on the Five Agents" decoded the rhyme was politically motivated.

Prophetic Rhymes between the Two Han Dynasties

Going out the Wu Gate/and gazing at Tiqun,/I see a cripple,/who says he wants to go up to Heaven./If he could make it to Heaven,/then there would be no one left on earth![171]

This children's song, which was popular in the Tianshui region during the final years of Wang Mang's Xin Dynasty, seemed to be poking fun at "an arrogant person who over-estimated his own abilities."[172] The Wu Gate was the name of a city gate of Ji County (present-day Gangu County in Tianshui, Gansu Province) and Tiqun was the name of a mountain in Gansu. According to "Treatise on the Five Agents" in *History of the Later Han*, Wei Xiao had then just raised an army in Tianshui. He grew ambitious, desiring to be Emperor, but was eventually defeated. Wei Xiao had become crippled in his youth, and this children's song was seen as a prophetic rhyme that mocked Wei Xiao's failed attempt to become Emperor.

Harmony or disharmony:/it's in the Chimei./Gain or loss:/it's north of the River.[173]

This children's song began circulating in Nanyang during the Gengshi period. According to "Treatise on the Five Agents" in *History of the Later Han*, "Emperor Gengshi [Liu Xuan] was in Chang'an at the time, while Emperor Shizu [Liu Xiu], then Commander-in-Chief, had pacified the region north of the Yellow River. The senior ministers of Emperor Gengshi arrogated the throne's authority, and thus the portentous rhyme was created. Later, Emperor Gengshi was killed by the Chimei Rebels and so, Emperor Gengshi and the

169 *Ibid.* 170 Xie Gui'an (1998), p.167.
171 *History of the Later Han*, *zhi* 13, "Treatise on the Five Agents, Part I," p.3281.
172 Lei Qunming and Wang Longdi (1988), p.36.
173 *History of the Later Han*, *zhi* 13, "Treatise on the Five Agents, Part I," p.3280.

Chimei were not in harmony. Emperor Shizu (Guangwu), on the other hand, prospered in the region north of the Yellow River."[174] This would be a rhyme that commented on current affairs, offering an accurate prediction of the political situation. It later became a prophetic rhyme that came true.

Yellow cow and white belly;/the five-*zhu* coins will come back.[175]

This children's song was popular in the Shu region around 30 CE. Gongsun Shu had founded the Great Cheng Dynasty in that region and proclaimed himself Emperor. The words of this rhyme were entertaining, catchy, and easily understood. The use of "yellow cow" and "white belly" as the opening might be reflective of the Shu people's nostalgia for the Han Dynasty, and their wish for the return of the five-*zhu* coin, the currency of the Western Han Dynasty that had been abolished and replaced by the Huoquan coin during Wang Mang's Xin Dynasty. Gongsun Shu's regime abolished copper coins and set up the Office of Iron to mint coins, causing disruptions to the local economy. It was explained in "Treatise on the Five Agents" in *History of the Later Han* that "people at the time whispered that Gongsun Shu, wishing to succeed Wang Mang who had claimed the color Yellow, claimed the color white for himself. The five-*zhu* coin was the currency of the Han Dynasty and would come back. Eventually, Gongsun Shu was defeated."[176] The yellow cow was analogous to Wang Mang because he claimed to possess Earth-Power, whose color was yellow. The white belly was analogous to Gongsun Shu because he claimed possession of Metal-Power, whose color was white.

Prophetic Rhymes during the Reigns of Emperors Huan and Ling

The wheat is green, the barley wilted./Who are the harvesters? The wives and mothers-in-law./Where are the husbands and fathers-in-law? They're fighting the barbarians in the west./Even officials are buying horses/and gentlemen are preparing carriages./Please whisper among yourselves for the men.[177]

This was a children's song that protested against war and its heavy toll on the people.[178] In the later part of Emperor Huan's reign, Han China and the Qiang peoples were engaged in constant warfare, resulting in "large numbers of men being conscripted for war, leaving the women to harvest the crops."[179] "Treatise on the Five Agents" in *History of the Later Han* dated the song as appearing in the early part of Emperor Huan's reign, with the obvious intent to highlight its prophetic qualities. However, the song's unforgiving criticism of society imbued it with "predictive properties" in any war-torn period.

174 *Ibid.*, pp.3280–3281. 175 *Ibid.*, p.3281. 176 *Ibid.* 177 *Ibid.*
178 Lei Qunming and Wang Longdi (1988), p.52. 179 Liu Kaiyang (1983), p.90.

Crow on the city wall;/ its tail completely bare./Father is an officer;/son a soldier./ A man dies;/a hundred carriages continue forward.

The rumbling carriages/enter Hejian./The beauty of Hejian counts her coins./Coins fill her room; gold fills her hall./The millstone is wanting; the millet is pounded./ A drum hangs from the beam./I wish to strike it but the officials were angry.[180]

This was also a children's song with a strong social message. The first stanza spoke of a ruler whose only preoccupation was to amass riches. In times of war, both fathers and sons had to be conscripted. When soldiers died on the front, reinforcements continued to be sent from the rear. The second stanza described the extravagance and avarice of a mother and her son in Hejian (referring to Emperor Ling and his mother Empress Dowager Dong). The final stanza depicted the people's rage: a person wanted to strike the drum of remonstrance but his actions provoked the loathing of the authorities.[181] "Treatise on the Five Agents" in *History of the Later Han* dated the song in "the beginning of Emperor Huan['s reign]" to underscore its prophetic qualities because the principal targets of its second stanza were Emperor Ling and his mother:

The entire song spoke of political avarice. "Crow on the city wall; its tail completely bare" meant a person who was ensconced up high, feeding on his own, and not sharing with those below him. It referred to a lord of men who amassed wealth by seizing the people's riches and levying heavy taxes. "Father is an officer; son a soldier": when the barbarian generals revolted, a father became a military officer while his son became a soldier, and both went to fight the rebels. "A man dies; a hundred carriages continue forward": after one man died fighting the barbarians, one hundred carriages were sent to the front. "The rumbling carriages enter Hejian" referred to the imminent passing of the Emperor, with carriages rumbling into Hejian to hail [the future] Emperor Ling. "The beauty of Hejian counts her coins. Coins fill her room; gold fills her hall." This line referred to Emperor Ling's mother, Empress Dowager Yongle, who liked to collect gold to fill her halls after her son's enthronement. "The millstone is wanting; the millet is pounded" referred to Empress Dowager Yongle, despite amassing gold and money, always complaining that she did not have enough, and ordering her subjects to pound millet for her to eat. "A drum hangs from the beam. I wish to strike it but the officials were angry." This referred to Empress Dowager Yongle teaching Emperor Ling to peddle official posts for cash, giving government positions to the wrong people. The loyal and honest men in the empire were infuriated and wished to strike the drum to see the Emperor. The officials in charge of the drum, however, flattering the Emperor and aligning themselves with the imperial will, stopped the petitioner in anger.[182]

180 *History of the Later Han, zhi* 13, "Treatise on the Five Agents, Part I," pp.3281–3282. In *Ancient Rhymes and Adages, juan* 6, p.99, the line "Births nine chicks a year" was added after "Crow on the city wall; its tail completely bare," based on *Bai's Encyclopedia, juan* 94; and *Imperial Reader of the Taiping Era, juan* 920.

181 See Liu Kaiyang (1983), p.90.

182 *History of the Later Han, zhi* 13, "Treatise on the Five Agents, Part I," p.3282.

Seen as a prophetic rhyme, the line "A man dies" might have referred to Emperor Huan because "the Emperor promoted eunuchs to high positions, where they could take part in politics. Surrounded by punished men [referring to castrated eunuchs], the Emperor was like the overseer of prisoners."[183] "A hundred carriages" referred to Emperor Ling.[184] "The rumbling carriages enter Hejian" described the court sending "men to welcome Emperor Ling, who trooped into Hejian in batches" after Emperor Huan's death.[185] This prophetic rhyme might have been adapted by person or persons from an existing children's song in Emperor Ling's time.

Youping sells seals fairly;/famous people and big clans aren't appointed.[186]

At the end of the Yanxi reign period (158–167 CE), Emperor Huan appointed Dou Wu (?–168 CE, courtesy name, Youping), father of Empress Dou, as Colonel of the City Gates. During the reign of Emperor Ling, Empress Dowager Dou ruled in her son's stead and appointed Dou Wu as General-in-Chief. Dou Wu worked with Grand Tutor Chen Fan, and placed members of their clique, such as Li Ying, Du Mi, and Liu Meng, in important positions. They got rid of the eunuchs, which won them the support from literati-officials and bureaucrats. It was recorded in the history books that they "made appointments based on virtue, and all the right people were appointed. All the famous people and big clans gave up hope."[187] This rhyme, a compliment to Dou Wu and his clique, might have been composed by a member of the same clique. "Treatise on the Five Agents" in *History of the Later Han* dated this rhyme at "the beginning of Emperor Huan['s reign]," making the "Youping Sells Seals" rhyme a prophecy.

In the middle of a one-*qing* field of reeds there is a well./The graceful and thin grass on its four sides cannot be put in order./Come, have another drink!/It's all right this year but it will be raucous the year after next.[188]

This simple, easy-to-understand children's song describes a farmer's life. However, it was interpreted by "Treatise on the Five Agents" in *History of the Later Han* as an abstruse prophetic rhyme written in code. Reeds symbolized virtuous men, while a well denoted proper norms and standards. "In the middle of a one-*qing* field of reeds there is a well" meant that there were many virtuous men who upheld propriety. "The graceful and thin grass on its four

183 The same word, *tu* (徒), was used for "man" and "prisoner."
184 *History of the Later Han*, *zhi* 13, "Treatise on the Five Agents, Part I," annotation by Liu Zhao, p.3282.
185 *History of the Later Han*, *zhi* 13, "Treatise on the Five Agents, Part I," annotation by Liu Zhao citing Ying Shao, p.3282.
186 *History of the Later Han*, *zhi* 13, "Treatise on the Five Agents, Part I," p.3282.
187 *Ibid.*, p.3283. 188 *Ibid.*

sides cannot be put in order" suggested that evil men were in control; they had become very powerful and the situation was beyond hope. "Come, have another drink" meant that "depraved meat-eaters did not care about good governance and simply indulged in banquets and songs." "It's all right this year" meant that despite being banished this year, members of the clique had yet to see the worst. "Raucous the year after next" referred to the execution of Chen Fan and Dou Wu, following which "the empire would descend into anarchy."[189]

Chen Fan and Dou Wu were executed in the first year of Emperor Ling's Jianning reign period (168 CE). This rhyme was dated at "the end of Emperor Huan['s reign]," which made it a prophetic rhyme.

So many small carriages with white canopies./Harmony comes to Hejian!/Harmony comes to Hejian![190]

Emperor Huan died on the twenty-eighth day of the twelfth month, in the first year of the Yongkang reign period (168 CE). He died without a son to succeed him, and Empress Dowager Dou immediately took over the reins of government. Within the palace, she and her father, Colonel of the City Gates Dou Wu, made the decision to install Liu Hong – the Commune Marquess of Jiedu (in Hejian Commandery's Raoyang County) and great-grandson of Liu Kai, King Xiao of Hejian – as Emperor. He would be known in history as Emperor Ling. According to "Annals of Emperor Ling" in *History of the Later Han*, the court sent Acting Imperial Household Grandee Liu Shu with the token of authority to Hejian with the Left and Right Guards of the Feathered Forest to welcome Liu Hong to the capital. Dou Wu, also carrying a token of authority, greeted the retinue at Xiamenting, and escorted Liu Hong into the palace on a King's carriage, which featured a green canopy.[191]

In accordance with the protocol for dress and traveling in the Eastern Han Dynasty, a carriage with a white canopy would either be used in a simple funeral or as a multipurpose carriage for traveling short distances, "carrying riders who were in pursuit of criminals, investigating cases, or carrying imperial orders."[192] It was recorded in "Treatise on the Five Agents" in *History of the Later Han* that "both the emissary and the Marquess of Jiedu arrived from Hejian in white-canopied carriages." Some scholars averred that "it was the time of Emperor Huan's funeral, which explained why the carriages had white canopies";[193] or that the small white-canopied carriage was a funeral carriage, where the white canopy symbolized death, foretelling Emperor

[189] *Ibid.* [190] *Ibid.*
[191] *History of the Later Han*, *juan* 8, "Annals of Emperor Ling," pp.327–328.
[192] *History of the Later Han*, *juan* 29, "Treatise on Travel and Dress, Part I," p.3651.
[193] Gao Dianshi (1990), p.29.

Ling's demise. Both explanations do not stand up to logic or the protocol of the time.[194]

A more logical explanation is that this children's song depicted a scene in everyday life; it had nothing to do with the retinue of carriages ferrying Liu Hong from Hejian to the capital. "Treatise on the Five Agents" in *History of the Later Han* dated this rhyme at the end of Emperor Huan's reign, once again tortuously "decoding" it as a coded prophetic rhyme that provided an explanation for the legitimacy of Liu Hong's enthronement as Emperor.

Prophetic Rhymes during the Reigns of Emperors Ling and Xian

A marquess who is not a marquess,/and a king who is not a king,/go up to Beimang with a thousand carriages and ten thousand horses.[195]

Emperor Ling died in the third month of the sixth year of the Zhongping reign period (189 CE). In the eighth month of the same year, General-in-Chief He Jin and Metropolitan Commandant Yuan Shao (?–202 CE) conspired to kill the eunuchs. Their plot was discovered, however, resulting in He Jin's murder at the hands of Regular Palace Attendants Zhang Rang, Duan Gui, and others. Yuan Shu, the General of the Gentlemen-of-the-Household Rapid as Tigers who was also He Jin's co-conspirator, set fire to the Eastern and Western Palaces, and attacked the eunuchs. Holding Liu Bian (176–190 CE), who was the reigning Emperor Shao of the Eastern Han Dynasty, and Liu Xie (181–234 CE), the King of Chenliu, as their hostages, the eunuchs fled to Mount Beimang with the nobility and officials of the court, with Dong Zhuo and others in pursuit with their troops. Eventually, the eunuchs were killed or took their own lives by drowning. The nobility and officials, together with Dong Zhuo, greeted Emperor Shao and the King of Chenliu at the foot of Mount Beimang. Several months later, Dong Zhuo deposed Emperor Shao and installed Liu Xie as Emperor, who became known in history as Emperor Xian of the Eastern Han Dynasty. The "A Marquess who is not a Marquess" rhyme would be a narration of that event in the lives of Emperors Shao and Xian. "Treatise on the Five Agents" in *History of the Later Han* placed it during the "end of Emperor Ling['s reign]," indicating that the rhyme had already foretold, even before Emperor Ling's death, the palace coup and the ascension of Emperor Xian to the throne.

Enjoying a happy life,/Dong Zhuo escapes./Wandering around the city's four walls,/ Dong Zhuo escapes./Receiving the Son of Heaven's grace,/Dong Zhuo escapes./Putting on gold and purple,/Dong Zhuo escapes./Leaving the Emperor's grace,/Dong Zhuo

[194] Kushida Hisaharu (1999), p.180.

[195] *History of the Later Han*, *zhi* 13, "Treatise on the Five Agents, Part I," p.3284.

escapes./Putting carriages and horses in order,/Dong Zhuo escapes./Rearing to go,/ Dong Zhuo escapes./Bidding farewell to the city,/Dong Zhuo escapes./Going out from the Western Gate,/Dong Zhuo escapes./Looking back at the palace, Dong Zhuo escapes. Gazing at the capital,/Dong Zhuo escapes./Enduring hunger day and night,/ Dong Zhuo escapes./Feeling sad and distressed,/Dong Zhuo escapes.[196]

This children's song contained thirteen lines of five characters each, which was quite a rare format. According to Cui Bao's *Annotations Past and Present*: "The 'Dong Zhuo Escapes' song was composed by street children in the Later Han."[197] This children's rhyme might have already been popular in the streets of Luoyang before Dong Zhuo arrived at the capital. The refrain "Dong Zhuo escapes" (*dong tao*) might have functioned as an auxiliary word or onomatopoeic suffix tagged to the last syllable of every line,[198] and had nothing to do with Dong Zhuo's name. However, "Dong Zhuo believed that the "Dong Zhuo Escapes" song had already revealed his main motive, and so he placed a strict prohibition on it, resulting in several thousand deaths."[199] He also ordered the refrain "Dong Zhuo escapes" (*dong tao*) to be changed to "Dong Zhuo at peace" (*dong an*).[200] "Treatise on the Five Agents" in *History of the Later Han* interpreted the "*dong*" in "*dong tao*" as referring to Dong Zhuo, and the song indicated that "while Dong Zhuo might have been domineering and brutal, he still ended up fleeing and having his clan exterminated."[201] Whether or not the "Dong Zhuo Escapes" song really foretold Dong Zhuo's eventual escape, Dong Zhuo's sensitive or hypersensitive response to it actually helped the song's dissemination and aroused the people's fervent wish for his imminent demise.

A thousand *li* of grass;/why is it green?/Ten days of divination;/it shall not grow.[202]

This was a prophetic rhyme that carried a curse as well as a coded riddle. The characters for "a thousand *li* of grass" and "ten days of divination" formed the words "Dong" and "Zhuo," respectively.[203] "Treatise on the Five Agents" in

196 *Ibid.*

197 *Collection of Music Bureau Poems*, *juan* 34, preface of "Lyrics of Xianghe Songs, Part IX," p.504.

198 We shall leave this question for the linguists to answer. Lei Qunming and Wang Longdi (1988): "This might have been a song for a children's game: one person would sing, 'Enjoying a happy life' and so on, and the rest would sing the refrain 'Dong Zhuo escapes' together. It might not have referred to anything specific." (p.60)

199 *History of the Later Han*, *zhi* 13, "Treatise on the Five Agents, Part I," annotations by Liu Zhao, citing Ying Shao's *Comprehensive Meaning of Customs and Habits*, p.3284.

200 *History of the Later Han*, *zhi* 13, "Treatise on the Five Agents, Part I," annotations by Liu Zhao, citing Yang Fu's *Biography of Dong Zhuo*, p.3284.

201 *History of the Later Han*, *zhi* 13, "Treatise on the Five Agents, Part I," p.3284.

202 *Ibid.*, p.3285.

203 The characters *qian li cao*, (千里草, "A thousand *li* of grass") combine to form the word *dong* (董); the characters *shi ri bu* (十日卜, "ten days of divination") combine to form the word *zhuo* (卓).

History of the Later Han dated this song as appearing "shortly after Emperor Xian's enthronement," which was the period when Dong Zhuo usurped the power of the throne and dominated the court. It could be that someone created this song and taught the children to sing it, or that it was a spontaneous popular composition. Some scholars argue that children's songs that contained specific names of people and dates of their rise and fall could not have been produced before the fact. Children's rhymes with word games and puns would have been created after the fact.[204] In the case of Dong Zhuo, the extent of his misrule was such that after his assassination, "soldiers shouted 'long live the Emperor,' and the people sang and danced on the streets. The gentlewomen of Chang'an sold their jewelry and clothes to buy wine and meat for the people who were celebrating in the packed streets."[205] It was therefore eminently possible that cursing rhymes such as the "A Thousand *Li* of Grass" song could have been circulating before Dong Zhuo's death.

Southern reaches of Yan/and northern edges of Zhao;/the center doesn't close and it's big as a whetstone./Only here can one be safe in the world.[206]

This children's song was supposed to have been popular in the early years of Emperor Xian's reign. At the time, "there was agitation in all directions and bandits were instigating one another. There was chaos everywhere."[207] Where could one go in search of a land where peace prevailed? There would have been quite a number of rhymes like the "Southern Reaches of Yan" song, which spoke of the people's dream to live in a peaceful and happy place, in different locations. In the early years of Emperor Xian's reign, Gongsun Zan (?–199 CE), the Marquess of Yi, controlled the Youzhou Region. He and Yuan Shao, who controlled the Jizhou Region, were bitter enemies and they fought each other for many years. When Gongsun Zan heard this children's song, he reckoned that the region of Yi (an ancient settlement dating back to the Warring States Period and designated as Yi County during the early imperial period)[208] was the safe location that the song foretold. And so, he constructed his Yi Capital, "repairing the city walls and storing grain in anticipation of momentous changes in the empire."[209] In the third year of the Jian'an reign

204 Tian Ying (1959), p.75.

205 *History of the Later Han, juan* 72, "Biography of Dong Zhuo," pp.2331–2332.

206 *History of the Later Han, zhi* 13, "Treatise on the Five Agents, Part I," annotations and citations by Liu Zhao, p.3285.

207 *History of the Later Han, juan* 74 *xia*, "Biography of Liu Biao," p.2421.

208 In the northwestern part of present-day Xiong County, Hebei Province.

209 *History of the Later Han, zhi* 13, "Treatise on the Five Agents, Part I," annotations and citations by Liu Zhao, p.3285; *Records of the Three Kingdoms, juan* 8, "Book of Wei: Biography of Gongsun Zan," annotations by Pei Songzhi, citing *Records of Heroes*, p.245.

period (198 CE), Yuan Shao attacked Gongsun Zan and laid siege to Yi Capital. The following year, Yi Capital fell and Gongsun Zan died.

According to Liu Zhao's annotations and commentaries on Gongsun Zan in "Treatise on the Five Agents" in *History of the Later Han*, "Gongsun Zan defeated the Yellow Turbans in the beginning and killed Liu Yu. Riding on his victories, he advanced south and occupied the region of Qi. Despite his military prowess, he could not expand his territories nor did he harbor great ambitions. He wanted to fortify his city and wait and see; to watch the fighting and killing from the sides. And so, he died in the region of Yi."[210] When Gongsun Zan began his career in the final years of Emperor Ling's reign as the Chief Clerk of the Liaodong Kingdom, he was responsible for the quashing of the Wuhuan people, earning for himself the epithet "the Chief Clerk on a White Horse." Later on, he defeated the Yellow Turban Rebels in the Qingzhou Region and at one time controlled what is today parts of Liaoning, Hebei, Shandong, Henan, and Jiangsu provinces. He made himself Inspector of three regions and became one of the most powerful warlords in the north. He then killed his superior Liu Yu, the Regional Governor of Youzhou, and took over the entire Youzhou Region. After he constructed the Yi Capital, however, "he could not expand his territories nor did he harbor great ambitions. He wanted to fortify his city and wait and see; to watch the fighting and killing from the sides." His passivity eventually led to his defeat. Did his belief in the predictive power of the "Southern Reaches of Yan" rhyme affect his choice of political and military strategies in the latter part of his career?

Even more interesting were Pei Songzhi's comments in *Records of the Three Kingdoms*: "Your Majesty's servant Songzhi believes that the words in all children's songs would come to pass. This particular one, however, seemed not to have done so. It caused [Gongsun] Zan to have no greater ambition than to safeguard Yi. In fact, [Gongsun] Zan's defeat of the Yellow Turbans had imbued him with grand aspirations: he had made himself Inspector of three regions and attempted to destroy Yuan [Shao]. [His belief in the song] resulted in his defeat."[211] Pei Songzhi was of the opinion that the prognostications of prophetic rhymes usually came true, but this "Southern Reaches of Yan" rhyme was actually a trap that lulled Gongsun Zan into a passive defense of Yi Capital and killed his ambitions. This explanation seemed to suggest that Heaven was playing a trick on Gongsun Zan, but this writer believes that it was Gongsun Zan himself who misread the true meaning of the "Southern Reaches of Yan" rhyme.

210 *History of the Later Han*, *zhi* 13, "Treatise on the Five Agents, Part I," annotations by Liu Zhao, p.3285.

211 *Records of the Three Kingdoms*, *juan* 8, "Book of Wei: Biography of Gongsun Zan," annotations by Pei Songzhi, p.245.

The eighth or ninth year is the beginning of the end./There's no one left in the thirteenth year.[212]

Liu Biao (142–208 CE), a member of the Han imperial clan, was one of the famous "Eight Ethical Leaders" in the Eastern Han Dynasty. He was appointed Inspector of Jingzhou Region in the first year of Emperor Xian's Chuping reign period (190 CE). By the third year of the Chuping reign period, he was appointed General of the Southern Defense and Governor of Jingzhou Region. In the first year of the Jian'an reign period, Liu Biao "expanded his lands until they reached the Nanling Mountains in the south and Hanchuan in the north. His territory extended for several thousand *li* and his army numbered over one hundred thousand men."[213] During his eighteen-year rule of the Jingzhou Region, "peace prevailed over ten thousand *li* and everyone, young and old, obeyed him." He "loved the people, cultivated the literati, and was serene and self-sufficient."[214] He had "ten thousand *li* of fertile land and his officials and people were wealthy."[215] After Liu Biao died, his two sons and subordinate commanders fought among themselves. The Jingzhou Region was eventually conquered and taken over by Cao Cao.

This children's song was supposed to have been circulated in the Jingzhou Region in the early years of the Jian'an reign period. It foretold that the eighth or ninth year of the Jian'an reign period would mark the end of the good times in the Jingzhou Region. By the thirteenth year, there would be no one left there. According to "Treatise on the Five Agents" in *History of the Later Han*, "'The beginning of the end' referred to the death of Liu Biao's wife, resulting in the reduction in the number of his military commanders. 'There's no one left in the thirteenth year' referred to Liu Biao's own death in the thirteenth year [of the Jian'an reign period], resulting in the movement of his people to the Jizhou Region."[216] There was no historical record of the year of the death of Liu Biao's first wife, or when Liu Biao married his second wife, Madam Cai. However, Liu Biao's death in the thirteenth year of the Jian'an reign period was a historical fact. If this rhyme had really been circulating in the early years of the Jian'an reign period, then its *chen* prophecy was very accurate indeed. However, the rhyme was more likely the creation of the Jingzhou people after Liu Biao's death to narrate past events and express their sadness.

212 *History of the Later Han*, *zhi* 13, "Treatise on the Five Agents, Part I," p.3285.
213 *History of the Later Han*, *juan* 74 *xia*, "Biography of Liu Biao," p.2421. 214 *Ibid.*
215 *Records of the Three Kingdoms*, *juan* 54, "Book of Wu: Biography of Lu Su," p.1269.
216 *History of the Later Han*, *zhi* 13, "Treatise on the Five Agents, Part I," p.3285.

Origins of Prophetic Rhymes

What we know about prophetic rhymes of the early imperial period comes from the records in *History of the Former Han* and *History of the Later Han*. Most of them "appeared" and "circulated" in the final years of the Western Han Dynasty, during the transition between the two Han periods, and near the end of the Eastern Han Dynasty. However, rumors (including those that were expressed in the forms of folk and children's rhymes) should be ubiquitous at all times. The children's songs that had been included in the "Treatises on the Five Agents" in both *History of the Former Han* and *History of the Later Han* would have been selected and edited by the writers of these books, and they represented only a tiny portion of all the rhymes in existence. The reasons for their selection by historians were (1) their connection with major historical events and figures, and (2) the "accuracy" of their "prophecies." Children's rhymes that did not come true were only unverifiable talk and portentous talk; they were not considered prophetic rhymes. The years spanning the end of the Western Han Dynasty and the beginning of the Eastern Han, as well as the final years of the latter, witnessed the most tumultuous political upheavals and social instability during the early imperial period. It was a time when the people had the most urgent need for *chen* prophecies. For this reason, it was also a time when *chen* prophecies were at their most active and their socio-political effects at their most powerful. We can therefore see why historians of the Han and Jin periods had chosen to put these *chen* prophecies on record.

Combing through the narratives and interpretations of the prophetic rhymes that were selected by the writers of the "Treatises on the Five Agents" in both *History of the Former Han* and *History of the Later Han*, this writer classifies the origins of prophetic rhymes into the following categories:

Prophetic Rhymes That Cursed and Criticized These children's songs often contained curses, sarcastic language, and strong social criticism. Examples included the rhymes "Going Out the Wu Gate," "The Wheat Is Green," "Crow on the City Wall," and "A Thousand *Li* of Grass."

Cursing is a form of psychological venting. Mass curses (e.g. the stone inscription produced by the masses in Dong Commandery) or curses that were in line with mass psychology (e.g. the dying words of Wu Zixu and the words of Master Nan) expressed the rage of the people. "The adage in the streets go: 'When a thousand people point at one, one would die without falling ill.'"[217] Such instances of collective rage might affect the hearts and minds of the people, as well as public opinion.

[217] *History of the Former Han*, *juan* 86, "Biography of Wang Jia," p.3498.

There is also a connection between curses and the notion of linguistic taboo. "Linguistic taboo was founded on the belief in the mystic and magical power of language; it is an ancient sorcery embedded in custom and culture. When a writer of poetry intentionally composed *chen* poems, the words would be endowed with a mystical and supernatural power to inflict harm on his enemy and achieve his goals. Poetry formed a connection with ancient sorcery to become a subduing spell, a curse."[218] And so, "when a thousand people point at one, one's fall is at hand."[219]

Prophetic Rhymes That Commented on Current Affairs These children's songs commented on current affairs, social phenomena, and social trends, and narrated the people's version of historical events from the perspectives of the people or a specific group of people. Examples included the rhymes "Lustrous Tails of the Swifts," "Harmony or Disharmony," "A Marquess Who Is Not a Marquess," "Yellow Cow and White Belly," "The Eighth or Ninth Year Is the Beginning of the End," and "Youping Sells Seals Fairly." They were the direct reflection of the views and historical perspectives of the people or a specific group of people. Also, they often made prognostications and expressed wishes.

Some of the prophetic rhymes that cursed and commented on current affairs were able to reflect the people's feelings and voices. "Contained within them was an irresistible social power, and the reflection of a historical trend. It was possible and inevitable that they would come true, and therefore their prophecies were often fulfilled."[220]

Prophetic Rhymes That Were Divine Revelations These refer to spontaneous creations, entertaining folk ballads and children's songs that did not have any political motives. Examples included the rhymes "Water Brims over the Well," "Crooked Paths Spoil the Fertile Fields," "In the Middle of a One-*Qing* Field of Reeds There Is a Well," "So Many Carriages with White Canopies," "Dong Zhuo Escapes," and "Southern Reaches of Yan."[221]

218 Wu Chengxue (1996), p.108.

219 Zhang Taiyan, "Proposal for a Nominal Government under Provincial Autonomy" in Zhang Taiyan (2001), p.229.

220 Xie Gui'an (1998), pp.54–61.

221 There is a story in *The Labyrinthine Chamber*, a Song-period novel: "In the ninth year of [Emperor Yang of the Sui Dynasty's] Daye reign period, the Emperor graced Jiangdu with his presence again. A maid of the Labyrinthine Chamber sang in a loud voice in the night: 'The poplars and willows south of the river are wilting; the plum flowers north of the river are blooming. Where do the poplar flowers land at the end of their flight? The plum flowers bear fruit as they always do.' When the Emperor heard the singing, he dressed and got up to listen to the song. He summoned the maid and asked her: 'Who told you to sing this song? Did you sing this of your own accord?' The maid said: 'Your servant has a younger brother among the

They were believed to inadvertently reveal Heaven's secrets by hinting at or foretelling historical events that would occur in the future. Such prophetic rhymes were characterized by the naturalness of their expression. At first glance, they did not resemble "*chen* prophecies" or "portentous talk"; they were just ordinary folk ballads and children's songs. These prophetic rhymes were in fact coded *chen* prophecies. The divine secrets they contained were often "realized" or "deciphered" by people after the occurrence of the events.

Prophetic Rhymes That Were Pre-Dated Both pre-event prognostication and retrospective narration and critique had their uses, but in essence, they were totally different. A prophetic rhyme should reveal a prophecy before an event, with the situation developing to fulfill that prophecy. However, children's songs that cursed or commented on current affairs normally appeared after the event. Having said that, these criticisms and comments met the psychological expectations people had for the event or provided the explanations they needed. And so, the timings of these songs were consciously or subconsciously moved forward by people (or by later historians), which made them prophetic rhymes. This was exactly how the compilation and writing of the "Treatises on the Five Agents" in *History of the Former Han* and *History of the Later Han* were done.

Discourses on the Belief in Prophetic Rhymes

How could children's rhymes foretell Heaven's will? Why did the prognostications of children's songs come true? For Pei Songzhi, these were unnecessary questions: "Your Majesty's servant Songzhi believes that the words in all children's songs would come to pass." Faith does not need a reason. For this writer studying the prophetic rhymes of the Han periods, however, the following questions must be asked: How did the ancient Chinese come by this belief? How was this belief discussed in the context of the Han periods?

The Sounds of Nature Theory Eminent scholars had written in the past, averring that "all rhymes and adages were the sounds that nature made on its own to articulate its will. For example, ripples form naturally when the wind moves across the water. The finite words with infinite meanings could

commoners who got hold of this song. He said: 'Many children on the streets sing this song.' After a prolonged silence, the Emperor said: 'This is a divine revelation! This is a divine revelation!'" In this song, "poplar (*yang*, 杨)" is homophonic to the surname of the Sui imperial house, while "plum (*li*, 李)" stands for the imperial house of Tang, which eventually replaced the Sui. This story vividly demonstrates the awareness of divine revelation types of prophetic rhymes in traditional Chinese political culture. (*Collection of Tales and Short Stories*, *juan* 32, 6 *ce*, p.14)

communicate the people's circumstances and propagate the rulers' virtue."[222] "Rhymes and adages were voices of the people and sounds of nature before the advent of the written word, learned in alleys and neighborhoods, circulated among women and children. They were spontaneous, original, and entertaining. Everybody danced to them and sang them often."[223] These descriptions were particularly true for children's rhymes.

It was written in "Li Lou, Part I" in *Mencius*: "'There was a boy singing: 'When the water of the Canglang is clear,/it washes the strings of my cap;/ when the water of the Canglang is muddy,/it washes my feet.' Confucius said: 'Hear what he sings, my children. When clear, then he will wash his cap-strings; and when muddy, he will wash his feet with it. This different application is brought by the water on itself.'"[224] The boy was singing a children's song, whose lyrics were ingenuous and candid, seemingly bereft of any deeper meaning. However, Confucius used the song to instruct his students on ethics, that a "clear" person was exalted and a "muddy" person debased.

In "Qi Section VI" of *Strategies of the Warring States*, Tian Dan wanted to attack the Di barbarians of the north, and consulted with Lu Zhonglian beforehand. Lu Zhonglian told him: "If you attack the Di barbarians, you will not defeat them." Unconvinced and angry, Tian Dan retorted: "Holding a five-*li* inner city and a seven-*li* outer city, I managed to defeat over ten thousand soldiers and destroy ten thousand carriages of the Yan, and recovered the ruins of Qi. How could I not defeat the Di?" He left Lu Zhonglian in anger. Tian Dan went ahead with his attack but the Di "did not fall after three months."[225] A children's song began circulating in the State of Qi: "Big hat that looks like a basket;/sword that comes up to the chin./Cannot defeat the Di;/piled up in a mound."[226] On hearing this song, "Tian Dan became frightened." He asked Lu Zhonglian for advice again, and this time he defeated the Di barbarians.[227] Tian Dan had ignored the counsel of the wise, but a children's song that mocked gave him a fright.

In *The Psychology of Chinese Songs and Rhymes*, Xu Hualong cited Western scholars' discourse on folk rhymes: "Folksongs are spontaneous and ingenuous. The people only sing when they are directly and immediately moved by passionate feelings." "The Brothers Grimm could confidently say that they did not find a single lie in folksongs; Victor Hugo could declare that

222 Liu Yusong, Preface, in Du Wenlan (2000), p.1 223 Tian Beihu (1904), pp.4–5.

224 *Annotations and Explanations of the Thirteen Classics: Mencius*, *juan* 7 *shang*, p.2719. The English translation is based on James Legge's translation.

225 *Strategies of the Warring States: Collected Annotations and Authentications*, *juan* 13, p.690.

226 *Comprehensive Mirror in Aid of Governance*, *juan* 4, citing "Children's Rhymes of Qi": "Big hat that looks like a basket; sword that comes up to the chin. Cannot defeat the Di; bones piled up in a mound." (p.144)

227 *Strategies of the Warring States: Collected Annotations and Authentications*, *juan* 13, p.690.

not a single falsehood could be found in the *Iliad*. It is their authenticity and reliability that imbue folksongs with a historical value that can never be found in written works."[228] Similar discourses were found in ancient China.

In his annotations of the prophetic rhymes in *Commentary of Zuo: The Fifth Year of Duke Xi*, Du Yu (222–285) explained:

> That very young children with nary a thought could create playful words suggested that they might have been possessed [by spirits]. Whether or not they come true, erudite gentlemen and introspective men would collect and record them as a warning, just in case they are fulfilled in the future. It will profit the instruction of the world.

Kong Yingda elaborated it further:

> That very young children with nary a thought and unskilled in writing, could gather and create playful words, meaningful words that rhyme, suggested that they might have been possessed by spirits. Whether or not they come true, they should not be given to common use. Erudite gentlemen and introspective men would collect and record them as a warning, just in case they are fulfilled in the future. It will profit the instruction of the world. These were some that were recorded in classical writings.[229]

While very young children might not have learned how to read and write, they had "a partiality for songs and rhymes because when they were in the crib, they heard the children's songs sung to them by their mother and grandmothers." "Their minds were filled with fantastical ideas about the real world and at the same time, they loved to imitate."[230] When they played together, they might sing songs that rhymed, and were fun and easy to understand. Their thoughts were simple and unadulterated by the cares and cunning calculations of the world. If one were to carefully analyze the songs that they sang, one might find that they carried profound meanings. The words of some of these songs became *chen* prophecies, and they actually came true later on. If erudite men with profound knowledge and men who were introspective recorded these prophetic rhymes and their historical contexts in their writings, they could be used later on as a historical reference and guide, as well as a tool to make predictions of developments in the world. It would indeed profit the instruction of the world.

The Divine Possession/Planet Mars Theory In the above annotations and explanations, Du Yu and Kong Yingda attributed the likely fulfilment of prophecies in children's rhymes to possible possession by spirits. According to *Critical Essays*: "When children sing songs, we do not know where they got

228 Xu Hualong (1990), p.33.

229 *Annotations and Explanations of the Thirteen Classics: Commentary of Zuo*, *juan* 12, pp.1795–1796.

230 Xu Hualong (1990), pp.101–102.

the songs from; the songs simply issue forth from their mouths. When they issue forth from their mouths, the words form, which may be the work of spirits."[231] Therefore, Zhou Zuoren averred: "In China, children's rhymes were not seen as songs of the innocents but as the vehicles of ghosts and deities, like the words of possessed mediums."[232] In other words, the divine secrets that were revealed, deliberately or otherwise, in children's rhymes were actually the revelations of Heaven, ghosts, or deities, using children as their vehicles. Such a discourse that appealed to mysticism was found in written texts of the Eastern Han Dynasty at the latest. It was written in "Discussion on Ghosts" in *Critical Essays*: "What the world calls children's rhymes are guided by the planet Mars, which was what he [Wang Chong] had said."[233] In "Records of Portents" in the same book: "When stars fall, the planet Mars reveals itself portentously. Therefore, when the people next to the rock were inscribing words on it, they might have been possessed. The words: 'The First Emperor dies' might have been instructed by Mars."[234]

In ancient China's pantheon of stellar and planetary gods, the planet Mars was a law enforcement deity that oversaw crime and punishment, as well as disasters and strange occurrences.[235] Whenever empires were at the edge of collapse, Heaven would issue a stern warning, ordering the planet Mars to possess the body of children, or instruct children to disseminate *chen* prophecies in the form of children's rhymes. This was a very convincing discourse during the Han periods. By the Wei, Jin, and the Northern and Southern dynasties, it had even evolved into the legend of Mars transforming itself into a child to propagate children's rhymes.

> Whenever the five heavenly bodies (Jupiter, Mars, Saturn, Venus, and Mercury) waxed and waned, and shifted their positions, their spirits would descend upon earth as humans. Jupiter descends as an exalted official; Mars descends as a child, singing rhymes and playing; Saturn descends as an elderly person or a woman; Venus descends as an adult man in the forest or the foot of a mountain; and Mercury descends as a woman. Whether there would be good fortune or bad, it was up to them to reveal.[236]

231 *Critical Essays: Expositions, juan* 22, "Records of Portents," p.930.

232 Zhou Zuoren, "A Study of Children's Songs," in *Shaoxing County Education Society Monthly* 4 (January 1914). Cited in Kushida Hisaharu (1999), p.5.

233 *Critical Essays: Expositions, juan* 22, p.941. 234 *Ibid.*, p.923.

235 *The Grand Scribe's Records, juan* 27, "Treatise on Astronomy" (Zhang Shoujie's *Standard Interpretations*, citing *Divinations of the Heavenly Official*): "Mars is the law enforcement star whose movements are irregular. Its abode determines the fate of the state, whether it be wrecked by vicious bandits, pestilence, deaths, hunger, or wars. It revolves with an unstable aura. It moves back and forth, suddenly forward, suddenly back. Its calamities are catastrophic. Mars oversees death; it mirrors the Grand Herald. Mars oversees the military; it is like the Commander-in-Chief. It watches the arrogant and rebellious; it is a law-enforcing official. Its spirit may be in the form of the Wind Deity, who induces children to sing songs and play." (p.1318)

236 *History of Jin, juan* 12, p.320.

According to "Treatise on the Five Agents" in *History of Jin*:

> In the second year of Sun Xiu's Yong'an reign period, the sons of frontier generals, who were hostages at the capital, were playing together, when a strange little boy suddenly appeared and said: "The Three Excellencies are uprooted. Sima Ru." He also said: "I am not human; I am the planet Mars." After he spoke, he rose up to the sky. They looked up and saw a bolt of white silk swaying. It disappeared after a little while.[237]

The Portentous Poetry Theory "Portentous poetry" referred to strange and unusual talk that appeared in the form of rhyming text.[238] The term "portentous poetry" (*shīyāo*) first appeared in "Treatise on the Five Agents" in *History of the Former Han*, citing *The Five Agents in the Great Plan.* In this context, it was a portent that the orders from the top were in contradiction to the people's will, resulting in cacophony, chaos, and the inability to rule the empire. When punishments for crimes were meted out wrongly and not in accordance to laws, there would be many wronged spirits of the dead, resulting in an unstable *Yin* element and an overabundance of the *Yang* element. With an overabundance of the *Yang* element, there would be more hot and sunny days than cloudy ones, resulting in damaged crops, leading to rebellion and banditry, and causing much anxiety in court and among the people. All in all, a terrible prospect. Rulers became irascible and the officials, fearful of punishment, kept their peace. The anger collective in the realm was then channeled into children's rhymes; thus, portentous poetry arose.[239]

In the "New Text" of the *Book of Documents* and "Treatise on the Five Agents" in *History of the Former Han*, children's rhymes, portentous talk, and unverifiable talk were all categorized as portentous poetry. A ruler issued orders that defied the people's will, but instead of self-reflection, he amped up the punishments and oppressed those beneath him. From the perspective of the Great Plan Theory of the Five Agents, there would be an overabundance of the *Yang* element, which would cause drought and an agricultural disaster. Those in service of the ruler, being afraid of punishment, did not dare articulate their objection to his orders. The wrath of the people would then be vented in the form of children's rhymes.[240]

[237] *History of Jin*, *juan* 28, p.843.

[238] Here, the word *yāo* (妖) does not mean "evil." Please see Chapter 2 for an analysis of the meaning of *yāo* in the context of the early imperial period.

[239] *History of the Former Han*, *juan* 27 *zhong zhi shang*, pp.1376–1377.

[240] *History of Southern Qi*, *juan* 19, "Treatise on the Five Agents" put it in more detail: "Those below were sad and bitter over the actions of those above, but did not dare remonstrate for fear of severe punishments. Their emotions would first be channeled into songs and rhymes. Songs and rhymes are matters of the mouth. When the currents of the mouth were in counterflow, bad words or strange rhymes emerged." (p.381) For a more complete discussion of the genesis and

As to why the overabundance of the *Yang* element would give rise to portentous poetry and children's songs, *Critical Essays* gave this explanation: "The children's songs of the world are not composed by children; they are guided by the *qi*."[241] "*Qi*" here refers to the *Yang* element, which *Critical Essays* also refers to as the Ultimate *Yang* Element.

The element in the universe that becomes portentous is the Ultimate *Yang* Element. Portentousness and toxicity are the same. When an element injures a person, it is toxicity; when an element changes, it is portentousness. The world says that children's rhymes are guided by the planet Mars. They say what they witness. Mars is the planet of fire, and fire has a toxic glimmer. Thus, when Mars is observed to be stationary in a constellation, disaster will befall the state. When the fire element is unsteady, the portentous form may live or die. . . . In the Great Plan Theory of the Five Agents, the second agent is fire and the second matter is spoken words. Speech and fire are of the same element, and so children's rhymes and songs are portentous talk. What is spoken will be written as text, thus strange texts exist in the world. The world says that children are of the *Yang* element, thus portentous talk originates from little children.[242]

While the "Ultimate *Yang* Element" included physical concepts such as sunlight and heat radiated from the sun, it referred more to the symbolic meaning of "*Yang* element" and "Extreme *Yang* Element" as expounded by the *Yinyang* and the Five Agents theory.

How were the *Yang* element and portentous talk connected? Wang Chong agreed with the Great Plan Theory of the Five Agents that "speech and fire are of the same element." He even accepted the popular legend of Mars descending to earth and teaching children to compose songs and rhymes.[243] He believed that "children are of the *Yang* element." Mars, the planet of fire, was also of the *Yang* element, and given that speech and fire were "of the same element," "portentous talk originates from little children" and "children's rhymes and songs are portentous talk." When the portentous element (the Ultimate *Yang* Element) exuded its "toxicity," at times "it will not use its toxicity when its form is seen." Sometimes, "its sound is heard but no words are formed, and at other times, "it reveals its words but its sound is not known." "Portentous poems, children's rhymes, and words on rocks" belonged to the last category.[244]

development of "portentous poetry," see Wu Chengxue, "Studies on *Chen* Rhymes and *Chen* Poetry" (1996), pp.105–107.

241 *Critical Essays: Expositions*, *juan* 22, "Records of Portents," p.923.

242 *Critical Essays: Expositions*, *juan* 22, "Discussion of Ghosts," pp.941–944.

243 This legend was not recorded in the "Treatise on the Five Agents" in both *History of the Former Han* and *History of the Later Han*. However, it was recorded in Pei Songzhi's annotations of *Records of the Three Kingdoms*, and the "Treatises on the Five Agents" in *History of Song* and *History of Jin*.

244 *Critical Essays: Expositions*, *juan* 22, "Discussion of Ghosts," p.945.

"Words on rocks" refers to the words "After the First Emperor dies, his territory will be divided" that were inscribed on a fallen meteorite in the thirty-sixth year the First Emperor of the Qin Dynasty. According to *The Grand Scribe's Records*, "the planet Mars was observed to be stationary in the Xin Constellation. A star fell in the Dong Commandery, which turned into a rock upon landing." The account in *Critical Essays* reads:

> When the star fell, the planet Mars became portentous, which was why the people near the rock engraved words on it. It might have carved the words "the First Emperor dies" itself, or it might have taught the people to do so. This was like children's rhymes, which are not composed by children but guided by the elements.[245]
>
> Nature is simply what it is, thus elements form naturally. It is the same with children's rhymes that issue forth from the mouth. If children's rhymes are not taught, then they issue forth from the mouth. Sounds that issue forth from the mouth become words. It may be so.[246]

According to these accounts, children who sang songs and the people who inscribed words on the rock were like sleepwalkers or possessed mediums who had no control over what they sang or carved. They were merely the vehicles or mouthpieces of Mars and the *Yang* element.

Chen Prophecies and Prophetic Rhymes Were Also Rumors

Calamities in the form of war, famine, pestilence, earthquake, drought, inundation, and so on have been the constant bane of human life. When these calamities became too much for human beings to cope with, they would be attributed to fate or supernatural retribution. Only then could these disasters become bearable.

Given that disasters originated in the supernatural, the attempt to communicate with the supernatural to know the future became a common human desire across all cultures. The belief in prophecies could be found among all major ancient civilizations. Prophecy differs from prediction in that the latter makes deductions about the future based on facts, experience, reason, and knowledge. Prophecy, however, refers to spoken or written information on future (or historical) events and processes that has been revealed to human beings by a supernatural source. For example, it is said that the prophetic poems in the Bible were closely linked with the destinies and histories of the Near Eastern empires of Assyria, Babylon, and Persia and the states of Israel and Judah in the ancient world.[247]

[245] *Critical Essays: Expositions*, *juan* 22, "Records of Portents," p.923. [246] *Ibid.*, p.930.
[247] Aberbach (1993), p.1.

Prophecies emerged and were communicated in myriad ways, which could be presented as interesting and colorful cultural expressions in different civilizations and historical periods. In the ancient Mediterranean world, divination and oracles played important roles in the daily lives and politics of Greece and Rome.[248] In China during the Shang and Zhou dynasties, divination using tortoise shells, yarrow, stars, dreams, and so on were very popular among both the political elite and ordinary people.[249] Divination using tortoise shells and yarrow was often in response to questions that had been prepared beforehand. The diviner would initiate the divining process, the result of which would be randomly presented as symbols such as signs and numbers, for example, cracks on burnt tortoise shells, the arrangement of the yarrow and sequence of hexagrams, and so on. Divination using cosmic boards such as the Five Agents, selection of auspicious days, and so on relied on specific tools to make complex calculations and deductions. Divination using stars and dreams, however, was passive divination. Diviners made use of traditional divination books and their own training to interpret the prophetic significance of strange phenomena in the natural and human worlds that had already occurred. The answers obtained through divination were signs (such as cracks on tortoise shells and images of hexagrams) that were highly symbolic, which required the interpretation and explanation of diviners with specialized knowledge, before they could become prophecies intelligible to the people. In oracles, special individuals in the service of the gods would use special techniques to enter into a trance-like state (during which they were possessed by spirits) to ask the gods questions or to speak on their behalf.[250]

The belief in prophecy stems from faith in the supernatural. Most ancient Chinese believed that their own activities and destinies were controlled by supernatural beings. In politics as well as in their everyday lives, people used a variety of divination methods to seek supernatural revelation in order to get a glimpse of the intentions of the gods, or to provide psychological support or legitimacy for their choices and decisions. From the early imperial period onward, however, divination using tortoise shells and yarrow gradually disappeared from political rituals and activities; it became more prevalent in

[248] In the ancient Greek and Roman belief systems, divination was the art and science of interpreting symbolic information from the gods. These symbols were often unpredictable and even minuscule – so insignificant that they escaped notice. Oracles were divine information expressed in human language and were often expressed as answers to questions. See Aune (1983), p.23.

[249] Li Ling (2006) classified ancient Chinese divination into three major categories: divination related to astronomy and calendrical systems, such as divination using stars, calendars, and cosmic boards; divination related to the worship of animal or plant spirits, such as divination using tortoise shells and yarrow; and divination related to human physiology, psychology, illness, ghosts, etc., such as divination using dreams. (p.67)

[250] For example, the trances of shamans and Taoist mediums.

everyday life, where it tended to people's queries and anxieties. Divination arts using astronomy, calendrical systems, and cosmic boards were incorporated into the mystical theories of Confucianism, Taoism, the *Yinyang* School, and other schools of thought, giving rise to a worldview in which there was telepathic interaction between Heaven and Man and the discourse of punitive disasters sent from Heaven. The Confucian elite made judicious use of this discourse, explaining various natural or supernatural phenomena as signs of Heaven's will, to influence political decisions. By the late Western Han Dynasty, all sectors of society were inundated with political prophesies that claimed to speak on Heaven's behalf and prognosticated the rise and fall of the dynasty and individual destinies. Some of these political prophecies were referred to as *chen* prophecies, which amalgamated with Confucian mysticism to produce numerous volumes of apocryphal books (also known as apocryphal-prophetic texts). These books and texts were to become the mainstream discourse framework for Chinese politics, society, and religion in the next few centuries.

The *chen* prophecies popular during the early imperial period were a type of "non-divination" political prophecy that used the spoken or written word. *Chen* prophecies did not require special rituals or techniques, nor any individuals with specialized knowledge or skills to decode their meanings. Oracles and divinatory words were prophecies that were obtained when people made use of various esoteric arts to know Heaven's will. *Chen* prophecies, however, often emerged serendipitously and naturally. Many *chen* prophecies either featured profound and abstruse texts, or seemingly straightforward words that contained ambiguous meanings. There would be much uncertainty and vagueness when decoding them, but usually one would suddenly see the truth when the prophecies came to pass.[251] The ancient Chinese believed that *chen* prophecies could tell the future only through cosmic inspiration and inadvertent revelation from Heaven.

Such prophecies cannot be compared with the prophecies propagated by prophets in the Hebrew and early Christian traditions.[252] One of the main differences between the two is that the Hebrew and early Christian prophecies had a strong component of moral judgment, highlighting their religious and

251 *Chen* prophecies of the Han and later periods were often presented as riddles and folk rhymes.

252 According to Paul Boyer (1992), the majority of Christians in the West firmly believed that the Bible had prophesied the progress of history, as well as the order of events that would herald the Armageddon. Even in contemporary times, belief in prophecies occupies a far more important position in American thought than intellectual and cultural historians would admit. Since the Second World War, the proselytizers of dispensational premillennialism have always played an important role in building and shaping public opinions and standpoints in a range of issues from the Soviet Union, the European Union, and the Middle East, to computers and environmental crisis. (p.ix)

moral aspirations. The *chen* prophecies of the Han periods, however, focused on the political struggles, political players, and shifting powers of the secular world, which underlined their political aspirations.[253] Of course, *chen* prophecies and Hebrew and early Christian prophecies shared many commonalities, such as their concerns with important social issues, the appeal to mystical and supernatural powers, their claims to speaking on behalf of Heaven, the use of words, their criticism of and challenge against contemporary political authority and order, the prophesying of future developments in politics and society, and so on. Another important difference is that in the Hebrew and early Christian traditions, the prophet was an indispensable medium between God and the people. God had to make his intentions known to the prophet before the latter could propagate the prophecy. Therefore, the influence and vitality of a prophecy in the Hebrew and early Christian traditions largely depended on the personal relationship between the prophet and God, as well as his reputation and qualifications. *Chen* prophecies of the Han periods, however, were usually created or propagated by anonymous individuals, or fraudulently attributed to famous persons such as Yao, Laozi, Confucius, and Liu Xiang. Often, *chen* prophecies were the result of collective creation.[254] Anonymity and fraudulent attribution were necessary not only because of safety concerns. The influence and vitality of *chen* prophecies in China depended not on the reputation and reliability of their creators or propagators, but on their level of acceptance by the people.

Given that popular folk songs occupied a unique position in the discourse on governance in ancient China, being seen as voices that could be heard by Heaven as well as voices that transmitted Heaven's will, certain children's rhymes that carried prophetic messages were considered expressions of *chen* prophecies, that is, prophetic rhymes.

The *chen* prophecies and prophetic rhymes of the early imperial period shared many similarities with the disseminated talk, unverifiable talk, and portentous talk that were demonized by the authorities. Certain spoken information, curses, satire, criticisms, and commentaries on current affairs and politics that circulated among the people through unofficial channels were usually labeled as disseminated talk, unverifiable talk, portentous talk, or rumors. At times, however, their ideas and inferences were in concert with the developments of the world. When that happened, they became *chen*

253 In this regard, *chen* prophecies differed greatly from the prophecies of the Old Testament prophets. However, they had similarities with the prophecies of Nostradamus (1503–1566) and Dr. John Dee (1527–1608), which were popular in Europe in the Middle Ages.

254 Famous collected works of *chen* prophecies after the Tang Dynasty had fraudulently attributed authors. *Back-Pushing Drawing* was attributed to Li Chunfeng and Yuan Tiangang; *Ten-Thousand-Year Song for the Universe* to Jiang Taigong; *Divination before the Horse* to Zhuge Liang; *Plum Blossom Poetry* to Shao Yong; and *The Pancake Song* to Liu Ji.

prophecies and prophetic rhymes. In fact, prophetic rhymes were defined as "portentous rhymes" and "portentous poetry" within the discourse framework of the "Treatises of the Five Agents" in both *History of the Former Han* and *History of the Later Han*. Sometimes, only a fine line separated talk and prophecy. Whether it was disseminated talk, unverifiable talk, portentous talk, *chen* prophecies, or prophetic rhymes, many contained words "whose sources were not seen and whose ends were not known; words that came and went like the wind."[255] Needless to say, much of the information therein had been manipulated and forged by human agencies. *Chen* prophecies and prophetic rhymes were unique because they made use of the distinctive qualities of Chinese words, employing rhymes, joining and partitioning, ambiguity, and so on to enhance the vagueness and abstraction of language. This allowed decoders ample space for imagination to interpret the Heaven-sent information that they so anticipated.[256]

Like disseminated talk, unverifiable talk, and portentous talk that got people's attention, successful *chen* prophecies and prophetic rhymes focused on important issues that people were concerned about. In a context marked by ambiguity, chaos, and uncertainty, they propagated among the masses certain information that was not easily verified in official channels using language that was sarcastic or vague, at the same time as they expressed collective opinions or wishes. In other words, what *chen* prophecies and prophetic rhymes conveyed was not so much prophecies revealed by Heaven, but the people's hopes for the future – just like disseminated talk, unverifiable talk, and portentous talk, whose propagators and audience dealt with opinions, not facts. In this respect, *chen* prophecies and prophetic rhymes, despite their air of mystery and mysticism, were in fact one of the ways in which rumors were expressed.

[255] Xie Gui'an (1998), p.5.

[256] Refer to Wu Chengxue (1996), p.105; Xie Gui'an (1998), pp.7–8.

5 Political Myths and Popular Legends

Political Myths

A type of "civilizational myth," political myths were fictitious stories that featured a pantheon of gods, which were created by people with specific political tendencies for certain political objectives. The stories made use of the religious ideologies, as well as myths and legends, of that society's culture and traditions.[1] Political myths were also the strategic manifestations of a dynasty's founding and administration, and the suitable use of religious resources and power.[2] They were one of the fundamental political symbols of imperial legitimacy in Chinese history.

Myths about Founding Rulers

Sun Kuang-Teh made a brilliant study on myths about founding rulers in Chinese history in his essay "Political Myths in China's Official Histories." According to him, there were myths about twenty-three founding rulers (including Cao Pi, Wang Mang, Liu Bei, and Sun Quan) since the Han periods, accounting for 92 percent of the total number. This is an indication that myths about founding rulers did not come about by chance; there had to be a reason for their emergence.[3]

Political myths recorded in history included mystical stories, *chen* prophetic expressions, visions, dreams, air currents observed, songs and rhymes, and so on that were related to political figures. They also included the mystical exploits of their ancestors. The contents of the myths should contain evidence of human tampering, but they might not all have been deliberate forgeries. Founders of dynasties and their supporters might intentionally create myths because myths made founding and maintaining their regimes a little easier. As for ordinary people, they might have unintentionally participated in the creation of myths because they wanted to seek a reasonable explanation for the

[1] Leng Dexi (1996), p.40. [2] Huang Zhenyun (2010), p.98.
[3] Sun Kuang-Teh (1986), pp.65–66.

founding ruler's success, as well as to rationalize and justify their submission to the new ruler.[4]

Most myths about founding rulers occurred before they had established their regimes because that was the time when they were needed most. According to Francis Delaisi, a leader of any kind of organization would see his authority increase tenfold immediately after he takes possession of a magical object. In the scramble for control of an empire, myths were very useful in defeating one's rivals and obtaining political power. Having a myth differentiated one from one's rivals; it seemed to identify one as the recipient of Heaven's Mandate. On the one hand, the myth could intimidate one's rivals and weaken their morale; on the other hand, it could attract the submission of heroic men and the support of ordinary people.[5]

Of course, the occurrence of a myth before the founding of a regime or during the birth of a ruler was simply what historical records tell us; it might not have happened at those times. It was possible that the myth was created by people after the person became Emperor or even after his death.[6] However, the earlier the myth was put together and disseminated (preferably before the ruler founded his regime), the more credible and convincing it would be.

The abundant and colorful myths surrounding Liu Bang, the Founding Emperor of the Western Han Dynasty, will be discussed as case studies later in this section. Before he took to the throne, Wang Mang, the founder of the Xin Dynasty, created a series of myths, including the divine exploits of his ancestor, who was allegedly the legendary Yu Shun, and various talismanic writings, *chen* prophetic expressions, visions, dreams, songs, and rhymes. Even the myths about his aunt Wang Zhengjun, the Grand Empress Dowager of the Western Han Dynasty who enabled him to rise to the pinnacle of power, were appropriated by him as myths of the Xin Dynasty.[7] However, Wang Mang carried his mythmaking too far. Between the middle of the third year of the Jushe reign period and his own enthronement, too many myths were created in quick succession, beyond what their intended audience could bear. And besides, the brevity of the Xin Dynasty shredded the credibility of these myths to pieces.

When Liu Xiu, the Founding Emperor of the Eastern Han Dynasty, was fighting for the control of the empire, he benefited greatly from the *chen* prophecies of *The Token of the Red Secret*. Apart from *chen* prophecies, there was also a myth surrounding his birth recorded in "Annals of Emperor Guangwu, Commentary" in *History of the Later Han*:

[4] *Ibid.*, pp.112–113. [5] *Ibid.*, p.67. [6] *Ibid.*, p.69.

[7] Such as the prognostications of diviners regarding "wise woman," "exalted woman," and "exalted beyond words." The details of these myths are given in the section "*Chen* Prophecy" in Chapter 4.

Lord Nandun, the father of Emperor Guangwu, was Prefect of Jiyang. On the Jiazi day of the twelfth month in the first year of the Jianping reign period, Emperor Guangwu was born at night in Lord Nandun's residence in the county. A red light was shining in the room. (Annotation by Li Xian, citing *Eastern Library's Records of Han*: "The light shining in the room made it as bright as daytime.") Finding it strange, Liu Qin [Lord Nandun] asked the diviner Wang Chang to divine the sign. Wang Chang dismissed his attendants and said to Liu Qin, "This sign is auspicious beyond words." In that year, a beautiful crop seedling, with nine ears on a single stalk, was found growing in the county. And so, Liu Qin named his son Liu Xiu.[8] The following year, a *fangshi* by the name of Xia Heliang submitted a memorial to Emperor Ai, averring that the Han Dynasty was in decline and the Mandate of Heaven should be renewed. As a result, the reign period name was changed to the first year of the Taichu reign period and Emperor Ai gave himself the title Chen-Sage Liu Emperor of Great Peace in the hope of suppressing the ill fortune. After Wang Mang usurped the throne, he was wary of the Liu family. As knife-coins suggested the character "Liu," he changed the currency to Huoquan coins. Some said that the word "*huoquan*" resembled "the Immortal of White Water." Later, an Observer of Air Currents, Su Bo'a, was sent by Wang Mang as his emissary to Nanyang, where he saw the castle walls of Chongling in the distance. He exclaimed with surprise, "What beautiful currents, lush and verdant!" Shortly after Emperor Guangwu raised his army in rebellion, he returned to Chongling. From afar, he looked at the area south of his residence and saw flames shooting up to the sky, which disappeared after a while. In the past, Taoist priests such as Ximen Junhui and Li Shou had said that a man named Liu Xiu would definitely become the Son of Heaven. Perhaps when kings receive the Mandate of Heaven, there would really be auspicious signs. Otherwise, how could he have ridden the dragon and pacified Heaven?[9]

A red light shining in the room during one's birth, a stalk of grain with nine ears, "beautiful currents" around one's residence, and flames shooting up in the sky were symbols featured in myths of great men that were often found in historical records.

Myths about Successor Rulers

Founding rulers of dynasties were not the only ones who had myths created about them; some of the successor rulers of the early imperial period had them too.

Lady Bo, mother of Emperor Wen of the Western Han Dynasty (Liu Heng, reigned 180–157 BCE), was originally a Palace Maid of Wei Bao, one of the warlords in the period between the final years of the Qin and the early years of the Western Han. Xu Fu, a well-known diviner of physiognomy at the time, predicted that Lady Bo would give birth to an Emperor. Following Wei Bao's capture by the Han army, Lady Bo was transferred into the palace of the King

[8] *Xiu* (秀) literally means "earring of grains."

[9] *History of the Later Han*, *juan* 1 *xia*, "Annals of Emperor Guangwu, Part II," p.86.

of Han, where she was not summoned into the King's presence for more than a year. Taking pity on her, Liu Bang summoned her one day into his chambers. A delighted Lady Bo said to Liu Bang: "I dreamt last night that a dragon crouched on my chest." Liu Bang replied: "This is a sign of greatness; let me make it come true for you."[10] After that occasion, Lady Bo saw very little of Liu Bang. However, she became pregnant and gave birth to the Emperor's son Liu Heng, who was made King of Dai when he was eight. After Emperor Gaozu died, most of his favorite consorts suffered persecution at the hands of Empress Dowager Lü. As she had rarely shared a bed with the late Emperor, Lady Bo escaped the wrath of Empress Dowager Lü and was allowed to follow her son to the Kingdom of Dai, where she lived for many years. After Empress Dowager Lü died, the senior ministers at court removed members of the Lü family from power. To prevent the emergence of a powerful Empress Dowager and her relatives, the senior court officials chose the King of Dai as Emperor because Lady Bo was weak and the Bo family was a small one. The prediction that Lady Bo would give birth to an Emperor came true.

Wang Zhi, mother of Emperor Wu of the Western Han Dynasty, was originally the wife of Jin Wangsun, a commoner. Her mother, Zang Er, went to a diviner of yarrow, who predicted that "her two daughters would rise to greatness." Zang Er forced Wang Zhi to leave the Jin family and then presented her to Liu Qi, the Imperial Heir-Apparent. Wang Zhi bore Liu Qi three daughters and a son. "When her son [Liu Che] was still in her womb, Lady Wang dreamt that the sun was in her bosom and told the Heir-Apparent her dream. The Heir-Apparent said, 'This is a sign of greatness.'"[11] Shortly afterward, Emperor Wen died and the Imperial Heir-Apparent ascended the throne, who became known in history as Emperor Jing. His wife Empress Bo had no sons, but he had fourteen sons by his other consorts, many of whom were older than Liu Che. In the fourth year of Emperor Jing's reign (154 BCE), Emperor Jing had Liu Rong, his eldest son by his favorite consort Lady Li, invested as Imperial Heir-Apparent. Liu Che was made the King of Jiaodong. However, animosity rose between Lady Li and Liu Piao, who was Senior Princess Guantao and Emperor Jing's elder sister. In the conflict that ensued, Lady Li lost and Emperor Jing removed Liu Rong's title of Imperial Heir-Apparent. With the support of Senior Princess Guantao, Wang Zhi was made Empress and the seven-year-old Liu Che became the Imperial Heir-Apparent and eventually, Emperor Wu of the Western Han Dynasty.

Favorite Beauty Zhao, mother of Emperor Zhao of the Western Han Dynasty, was a native of Hejian. "Emperor Wu was passing by Hejian on a hunting expedition when an Observer of Air Currents said that an extraordinary woman

[10] *History of the Former Han*, *juan* 97 *shang*, "Biographies of Imperial Affines, Part I," p.3941.
[11] *Ibid.*, p.3946.

was in the area. The Emperor sent his men to bring her before him. When the lady arrived, her hands were balled into fists. The Emperor himself proceeded to peel open her fingers and she opened up her hands at once. For this reason, she found favor with the Emperor and was referred to as 'Lady Fists.'" Favorite Beauty Zhao was especially favored by Emperor Wu, and she resided in the Gouyi Palace. "In the third year of the Taishi reign period, she gave birth to Emperor Zhao, who was called Son of Gouyi, after being pregnant for fourteen months. The Emperor said: 'I hear that Yao was born after fourteen months in his mother's womb. It is the same with [the Son of] Gouyi now.' He thus ordered that the gate of the palace where the boy was born be named the Gate of Yao's Mother."[12] An unusually long pregnancy was also a feature of birthing myths during the early imperial period. It was even said that in high antiquity, Fu Bao had been pregnant for twenty-five months before giving birth to the Yellow Emperor.[13]

Emperor Wu had six sons, two of whom died early. In the second year of the Zhenghe reign period (91 BCE), the Imperial Heir-Apparent Liu Ju (128–91 BCE, Emperor Wu's eldest son by his Empress) was framed in the Witchcraft Calamity, forcing him into armed rebellion. Liu Ju eventually took his own life. His wives and children were all killed, and his mother, Empress Wei Zifu, killed herself. Emperor Wu's two other adult sons Liu Dan, the King of Yan, and Liu Xu, the King of Guangling, "made many mistakes" and he did not appoint any Heirs-Apparent for the rest of his reign. Emperor Wu died in the second year of the Houyuan reign period (87 BCE). In his will, he instructed Huo Guang, Jin Midi, and Shangguan Jie to help and support his youngest son Liu Fuling (who was eight years old at the time) to succeed to the throne, who became known in history as Emperor Zhao.

Liu Xun (also known as Liu Bingyi), who led the revival of the Western Han Dynasty during his reign as Emperor Xuan, had an extraordinary background. His grandparents (the late Imperial Heir-Apparent Liu Ju and his wife) and parents were all killed during the Witchcraft Calamity. Liu Bingyi, then several months old, "was imprisoned in the jail located at a commandery's liaison office even though he was still in his swaddling cloths."[14] Fortunately for him, Inspector for Commandant of Justice Bing Ji, who took pity on him, was in charge of the jail and protected him in secret. A year later, Emperor Wu realized that Liu Ju had been framed and exterminated the families of all those officials who had caused Liu Ju harm. However, the Witchcraft Calamity implicated a great many people, and the cases remained unresolved several years later. "In the second year of the Houyuan reign period, Emperor Wu fell ill and spent his time in the Changyang and Wuzuo Palaces. An Observer of

[12] *Ibid.*, p.3956. [13] *Compendium of Apocryphal Books*, *juan xia*, p.1179.
[14] *History of the Former Han*, *juan* 8, "Annals of Emperor Xuan," p.235.

Air Currents said that there was a Son of Heaven air current in the jails of Chang'an. The Emperor sent his emissaries to the jails in the capital to kill all the inmates, regardless whether they had been imprisoned for heavy or light crimes. Guo Rang, Prefect of the Palace Internuncios, went to the jail at night but Bing Ji refused to open the gates. The emissary could not enter, and the Emperor's great-grandson was saved because of Bing Ji."[15] Liu Bingyi was released when he was five years old, and was brought up in the Shi family, his paternal grandmother's family. A *chen* prophecy was going around during the reign of Emperor Zhao that "Bingyi, the grandson of a lord, rises." When Emperor Zhao died without an heir, Huo Guang and other senior ministers invited Liu He, the King of Changyi, to succeed to the throne. Shortly afterward, they forcibly removed Liu He from the throne and decided to make Liu Bingyi the Emperor.

The parents of Liu Hu, Emperor An of the Eastern Han Dynasty, were Liu Qing, King Xiao of Qinghe, and Lady Zuo. All of Emperor Zhang's eight sons were born of consorts; Empress Dou was childless. The mother of Emperor Zhang's fourth son, Liu Zhao, was Honorable Lady Liang, who died due to Empress Dou's bullying. Empress Dou then raised Liu Zhao as her own son. Liu Zhao became Imperial Heir-Apparent and ascended to the throne at the age of ten. He was Emperor He of the Eastern Han Dynasty. When Emperor He died, Empress Dowager Deng and her elder brother Deng Zhi installed the three-month-old Liu Long as Emperor, known in history as Emperor Shang. When Emperor Shang died eight months later, Empress Dowager Deng and Deng Zhi decided to place Emperor Shang's cousin Liu Hu on the throne. When Emperor An was still living in the palace of the King of Qinghe, "there was divine light shining in the house on several occasions, and a red snake was found coiled on the bed."[16]

Empress He, the wife of Emperor Ling of the Eastern Han Dynasty, was a strong-willed and jealous woman. Beautiful Lady Wang, one of Emperor Ling's consorts, became pregnant. Fearful of Empress He's persecution, Beautiful Lady Wang "took medication to abort the child, but the fetus remained unscathed and she dreamed several times that she was walking while carrying the sun."[17] Eventually, she gave birth to Liu Xie. When Empress He found out, she killed Beautiful Lady Wang with poison. Liu Xie was raised by Empress Dowager Dong. After Emperor Ling died, Liu Bian, Empress He's eldest son, succeeded his father. Shortly after Liu Bian ascended the throne, however, fighting broke out among the imperial affines, headed by He Jin, the officials and bureaucrats, and the eunuchs, led by the Ten Regular Attendants. Liu Bian was taken out of the palace as the eunuchs' hostage. After he returned

[15] *Ibid.* [16] *History of the Later Han, juan* 5, "Annals of Emperor An," p.203.
[17] *History of the Later Han, juan* 10 *xia*, "Annals of Empresses, Part II," p.449.

to the palace, he was controlled by the warlord Dong Zhuo, who had entered the capital to "aid the Emperor." Liu Bian, Emperor Shao of the Eastern Han Dynasty, was on the throne for five months before being deposed by Dong Zhuo and replaced by his younger half-brother Liu Xie, known in history as Emperor Xian of the Eastern Han Dynasty.

None of these successor Emperors who had myths created about them – Emperors Wen, Xuan, An, and Xian – was the designated Imperial Heir-Apparent nor (according to tradition and custom) officially the first in line to the throne. They were also in positions of weakness vis-à-vis the other qualified sons and grandsons of their predecessors.[18] Their ascension to the throne was often the result of the wrangling and compromise between different powers in specific political contexts. There was a considerable degree of luck involved. Although Emperors Wu and Zhao were heirs designated by their predecessors, they were not (according to the principle of primogeniture) officially the first in line to the throne. Their succession was also a result of luck. Compared with dynastic founders, who fought heroically in bloody battles in times of great upheaval, the struggles of succession were mainly played out within the imperial family, the palace, and the court. While many details remain unknown and unknowable, the intrigues and power plays also had their fair share of bloodshed. Successor Emperors who fortuitously rose to the very top really needed myths to consolidate and fortify their positions, as well as boost their self-confidence. The myths surrounding Emperors Wen, Wu, An, and Xian, whether they had occurred before or after their births, were "one-sided stories" told by their mothers or family members. It was very possible that they were fabricated after their ascension to the throne, or even before. The mothers of these Emperors were lowly ranked palace women who did not always feel secure. In order to win the Emperor's favor, enhance their own status, and ensure their and their children's safety, they certainly had the motivation to grasp any opportunity to remind the Emperor the existence and the extraordinary nature of the "dragon seed" in their wombs.

Founding Myths of the Western Han Dynasty

The sheer amount of details in the myths surrounding Liu Bang, Emperor Gaozu or Emperor Gao, founder of the Western Han Dynasty, might have something to do with the fact that he was a commoner without any of the advantages of a powerful and wealthy family background. That production is driven by needs is perhaps also an applicable theory in political and social behavior.

[18] In terms of bloodlines, family backgrounds, and the status of their biological mothers.

"Basic Annals of Emperor Gaozu" in *The Grand Scribe's Records* began by narrating several mythical stories involving Liu Bang before the founding of the Han.[19] As Takigawa Kametaro wrote: "The events in 'Basic Annals of Emperor Gaozu,' from the divine encounter at the banks of the swamp to the clouds and air currents observed in Mount Mang and Mount Dang, were all records of auguries before Emperor Gaozu rose to prominence."[20] These included Mother Liu dreaming of an encounter with a deity (a dragon) as she slept on the banks of a swamp and conceiving Liu Bang as a result; Liu Bang having unusual physical traits, such as "a high-bridged nose, the countenance of a dragon, a beautiful beard, and seventy-two black moles on his left thigh," and often being marveled at by experts in physiognomy;[21] dragons often appearing above him when he was inebriated, and the wine shops that he frequented enjoying exceptionally good business; killing a large snake when he was drunk at a swamp in Fengxi, giving rise to the contemporary legend of the Son of the Red Emperor slaying the Son of the White Emperor. At the time, there was widespread talk of "a Son of Heaven air current in the southeast," the attempted suppression of which was the reason why the First Emperor of the Qin Dynasty paid several inspection visits to the southeast. Liu Bang thought that he was the target of these visits and thus hid among the swamps and rocks of Mount Mang and Mount Dang, but his wife always managed to locate his hiding place because there were allegedly "clouds and air currents above where he stayed."

Many historians of subsequent periods questioned these politically charged stories, believing them to be deliberate fabrications, or spurious attributions of divinity and mysticism where there had been none. According to Liang Yusheng (1745–1819), "*Records of the Sayings of Master Zhu* argued that the story of Emperor Gaozu being the Son of the Red Emperor was

19 Traditional annotations of historical texts (e.g. *The Grand Scribe's Records: Commentaries*) pointed out that in "Annals of Emperor Gao" in *History of the Former Han*, Emperor Gaozu had "the given name Bang and the courtesy name Ji," but "Basic Annals of Emperor Gaozu" in *The Grand Scribe's Records* "provided only the courtesy name, which cast some doubts." It was possible that before Emperor Gaozu became noble, his older brothers were named Liu Bo and Liu Zhong, and he was Liu Ji. The prosaic names of the three brothers simply indicated their birth order, i.e. "first son" (Bo), "second son" (Zhong), and "third son" (Ji). It was only after he became Emperor that Liu Ji changed his name to Liu Bang. The name of Liu Bang's father was not recorded in the history books; neither was his mother's maiden name. However, people in the early imperial period went on to mythologize them, and apocryphal books claimed that Liu Bang's father was named Liu Zhijia and his mother Wang Hanshi.

20 *The Grand Scribe's Records: Collected Annotations and Verifications, with Additional Annotations, juan* 8, p.232.

21 It was because of Liu Bang's extraordinary appearance that Master Lü gave him his daughter, the future Empress Lü, in marriage. When Liu Bang was still a Commune Chief, his wife and children were weeding in a field one day when an elderly expert in physiognomy foretold that Madam Lü and her children would be exalted, but when he saw Liu Bang, he said: "Sir, your appearance shows that you will be noble beyond description."

false.[22] *Sequel to Verifications Past and Present* averred that the killing of the snake was contrived mysticism. The Grand Scribe recorded it because he had a predilection for curious things."[23]

Why would *The Grand Scribe's Records*, a great historical work that has been lauded as "the true words of its time with no deviance, and therefore trustworthy for its time and famous for all ages,"[24] would include "ridiculous" fabrications or "contrived mysticism" in its "Basic Annals of Emperor Gaozu"? One explanation was that Sima Qian "was partial to strange things," "did not check [their veracities]," and "was unable to glean the meaning from them," resulting in "fantastic and farfetched" stories being included in his historical work.[25] Another explanation was that these mythical stories were not originally written by the Grand Scribe, but were added in later by others.[26]

The Grand Scribe's Records was completed in the second year of the Zhenghe reign period (91 BCE), during the reign of Emperor Wu of the Western Han Dynasty. It began to be circulated some twenty years later in 73 BCE, during Emperor Xuan's Benshi reign period. Due to various political and ideological hindrances, *The Grand Scribe's Records* saw limited circulation during the early imperial period, with very few copies extant. Manuscripts

[22] A similar doubt was expressed in Shao Taiqu, "Annals of Emperor Gao" in *Questions about The Grand Scribe's Records*: "The falsehood regarding the White and Red Emperors was but similar to the lies of the white fish and red bird [in the Western Zhou Dynasty]." Cited in Yang Yanqi et al. (1986), p.358.

[23] *Records of Questions about The Grand Scribe's Records, juan* 6, p.215.

[24] *Generality of Historiography: General Expositions, juan* 5, "Selection and Writing," p.115. Qian Zhongshu praised *The Grand Scribe's Records* for "not being partial to curiosities nor readily believing anything" (citing Li Yindu), for not recording fantastic events, and for "its equable and meticulous language." The only flaw in an otherwise perfect work was that "*The Grand Scribe's Records* was not able to completely remove the 'strange happenings' and 'trivial hearsay' consistently. Occasionally, one encounters stories such as Mother Liu encountering a dragon and the Marquess of Wu'an thanking a ghost." (*Limited Views*, 1 *ce*, pp.482, 483.)

[25] Xu Jing, *Collected Works of Yagetang, juan* 4, "On Basic Annals of Emperor Gao," cited in Yang Yanqi et al. (1986), p.358. Citing Shen Qinhan, Wang Xianqian also supported this explanation in his *History of the Former Han: Additional Annotations, juan* 1 *shang*, "Annals of Emperor Gao," p.27.

[26] Cui Shi: "The story of the Son of the Red Emperor slaying the Son of the White Emperor in the various editions was added in from 'Treatise on Sacrifices' [in *History of the Former Han*]." (*Finding the Sources of The Grand Scribe's Records, juan* 3, p.61) Gu Jiegang (1982): "However, these stories (slaying of the snake, clouds and air currents) could not have exited during Sima Qian's time; they must have been fabricated later." (p.493) Lü Simian (1983): "The story about the Son of the Red Emperor might have been concocted because the flags and colors of Emperor Gaozu, when he was Duke of Pei, were all red. It might not have anything to do with the sequential order of the Five Elements. The 'Basic Annals' in *The Grand Scribe's Records* said that all the flags were red. Therefore, the identification of the slayed snake as the Son of the White Emperor and the slayer as the Son of the Red Emperor was probably an addition and fabrication by people in later periods, and not the original writings of Sima Tan and Sima Qian." (p.817)

were lost or repaired, and passages were erroneously copied or even changed. By the time of the Eastern Han Dynasty, Sima Qian's original version had become hard to find. Since its completion 2,000 years ago, *The Grand Scribe's Records* had been copied countless times in the first millennium of its existence, and had undergone multiple printings in its second millennium. There would have been copious typographical errors introduced. For this reason, the veracity of popular editions of *The Grand Scribe's Records* or some of its sections, as well as the identities of their "writers," are issues that scholars of *The Grand Scribe's Records* and history of the early imperial period have to grapple with.

In his review of Liu Bang's achievements in founding the Han Dynasty, Jia Yi averred that Liu Bang "started out as a commoner and conquered the empire, making servants of noblemen everywhere and becoming the empire's ruler. He advanced beneficial policies and removed those that were harmful to the people. Under him, all the armies of the empire were at rest. In him was the pinnacle of virtue of the entire world."[27] He made no mention at all of myths and auguries. According to "Basic Annals of Emperor Gaozu" in *The Grand Scribe's Records*, noblemen, military commander, and civil ministers "requested in one accord the King of Han to become Emperor."[28] Their reasoning was that "Your Highness is of humble birth, but you have crushed tyranny and pacified the empire. Those who made contributions have been given lands and made kings and marquesses. If Your Highness does not claim the exalted title, all of us will doubt our own titles."[29] After Liu Bang became Emperor, he threw a banquet at the Southern Palace in Luoyang, where he had a discussion with his generals. "What was the reason that enabled me to conquer the empire? What was the reason that made Xiang Yu lose the empire?" he asked. Gao Qi and Wang Ling (?–181 BCE) answered: "When Your Majesty sent a person to attack a city or land, the person would be conferred the city or land if the latter surrendered. The benefits were shared among everyone. Xiang Yu was jealous of the virtuous and the able. He harmed those who made contributions and doubted those who had virtue. When he conquered land, he would not share its benefits. This was the reason why he lost the empire." Liu Bang's own conclusion for his success was this:

27 *New Writings: Annotations*, *juan* 10, "Significance of the Investiture of the Imperial Heir," p.409.

28 According to "Annals of Emperor Gao, Part II" in *History of the Former Han*, the noblemen who made the request included Han Xin (the King of Chu), Han Xin (the King of Han), Ying Bu (the King of Huainan), Peng Yue (the King of Liang), Wu Rui (the original King of Hengshan), Zhang Ao (the King of Zhao), Zang Tu (the King of Yan), etc.

29 *The Grand Scribe's Records*, *juan* 8, "Basic Annals of Emperor Gaozu," p.379.

In terms of laying down strategies and plans in camp, and winning victories a thousand *li* away, I am no match for [Zhang Liang]. In terms of safeguarding the state, pacifying the people, supplying the army, and keeping supply lines open, I am no match for Xiao He. In terms of commanding a million troops, scoring victory in every battle, and vanquishing the foe in every attack, I am no match for Han Xin. These three are the elite among men. That I could employ their talents was the reason why I could conquer the empire. Xiang Yu had Fan Zeng but did not use him. That was the reason why he was captured by me.[30]

Following his enthronement, Liu Bang wanted to make his father Honorary Emperor. According to "Annals of Emperor Gao" in *History of the Former Han*, Liu Bang's justification was this: "We put on armor and brandished weapons to lead the troops in attack and, pacify revolts, and put noblemen in charge of lands. We gave the troops rest and brought great peace to the empire. All these came to pass because of the teachings of [our father]."[31] A careful reading of *History of the Former Han* and the relationship between Liu Bang and his father would reveal that what Liu Bang said about "teachings" and so on was not totally sincere. Regardless, the discourses of Jia Yi, the various noblemen, generals, ministers, and even Liu Bang himself regarding the success of Liu Bang in founding the dynasty all referred to human agents. There was no mention of the mystical or supernatural. At the end of "Basic Annals of Emperor Gaozu," Sima Qian made these comments to explain the legitimacy of Liu Bang's enterprise: "The ways of the three dynasties of Xia, Shang, and Zhou went in cycles, ending and then beginning. By the period between the Zhou and the Qin, the shortcomings had become palpable. Instead of changing them, Ying Zheng [the First Emperor] of the Qin Dynasty imposed cruel laws. Was it not most ridiculous? This was why the Han Dynasty could flourish. It reformed the failings that it had inherited, giving rest to the people and receiving the Mandate of Heaven."[32] Summarizing Liu Bang's achievements, Sima Qian wrote in "Autobiography Afterword of the Grand Scribe": "[Xiang] Yu was brutal and tyrannical, while [the King of] Han was benevolent and virtuous. He built up his strength in the Shu and Han regions, then returned north to pacify the Three Qin. He then vanquished Xiang Yu and became Emperor. When the empire was at peace, he enacted institutional reforms and changed people's customs."[33]

It could be surmised from these accounts that even if the myths surrounding Liu Bang were not works of fiction created in a later period, at least they had not become part of the mainstream political and historiographical discourse in the early Western Han Dynasty. Based on currently available historical

[30] *Ibid.*, p.381. [31] *History of the Former Han*, *juan* 1 *xia*, p.62.
[32] *The Grand Scribe's Records*, *juan* 8, pp.393–394.
[33] *The Grand Scribe's Records*, *juan* 130, p.3302.

sources, however, it is also impossible to determine if the myths contained in "Basic Annals of Emperor Gaozu" were indeed creations or additions of a later period.

Certain chapters in *The Grand Scribe's Records*, such as "Basic Annals of The First Emperor of Qin," "The Hereditary House of Chen She," and others, also contain enigmatic prophecies and political myths, but historians of later periods had not cast doubts on whether they were authentic or originally written by Sima Qian.[34] The early Western Han political theorist Lu Jia recorded in his *New Words* that

> The General Fan Kuai asked Lu Jia: "Since ancient times, rulers have talked about receiving the Mandate of Heaven and auspicious omens. Are there really such things?" Lu Jia answered: "Yes. When one's eyelid twitches one receives food and wine; when the lamp wick flares one received money. When the magpie screeches someone comes; when spiders gather there will be myriad happy occurrences. Since there are signs for small things, there are also signs for major events. When our eyelid twitches, we say an incantation. When the lamp wick flares, we bow before it. When the magpie screeches, we feed it. When the spiders gather, we leave them alone. With a great treasure like the throne, how could one receive it without the Mandate of Heaven? Auspiciousness is a treasure and a sign. Heaven uses the treasures as signs in response to mankind's virtue, thus they are called auspicious omens. Without the Mandate of Heaven or treasured signs, one's efforts would be in vain."[35]

Yu Jiaxi believes that "based on the meaning of the words of Lu Jia recorded here, it could be surmised that they were contained in Lu Jia's twenty-three chapters. Based on citations in *Critical Essays*, one also knows that Lu Jia had a penchant for expounding on destiny and the supernatural. The elucidation on auspicious omens in this passage matches the objective and contents of the book."[36]

In his *Spring and Autumn Annals of the Chu and Han*, Lu Jia also recorded the story of how Fan Zeng (277–204 BCE) suggested that Xiang Yu kill Liu Bang as soon as possible because Liu Bang's "currents" resembled dragons, serpents, clouds, and tigers, and would therefore never be a servant to

[34] Since the Qing Dynasty, antiquity-doubting scholars who have questioned the authenticity and originality of the myths in *The Grand Scribe's Records* have mainly focused on "Basic Annals of Emperor Gaozu" because the myths surrounding Liu Bang and his founding of the Western Han Dynasty seemed to suggest a hint of the Theory of the Rise and Fall of the Five Powers, a theory that would only flourish at the end of the Western Han. However, recent scholarship has argued that the story about the Red Emperor and the White Emperor might not be connected to the Theory of the Five Powers. Instead, it might have something to do with the belief in the Emperors of the Five Directions, which had been popular before the founding of the Qin Dynasty. That such myths appeared at the end of the Qin and early Han was entirely possible.

[35] This paragraph is a lost passage from *New Words*, collected by Wang Liqi from *Miscellaneous Records of the Western Capital. Extensive Records of the Taiping Era, juan* 135, cited this passage from *Novels of Yinyun*. (*New Words: Collations and Annotations*, pp.180–181)

[36] Yu Jiaxi (1980), p.526.

anyone.[37] Discourses on Liu Bang's leadership as "conferred by Heaven" and not the result of human effort also frequently appeared in *The Grand Scribe's Records*.[38] Following his defeat at Gaixia, Xiang Yu sought to deflect blame from himself. "It is Heaven that destroys me. It is not any fault of mine in battle," he said. Later, he said again: "Since Heaven wants me to perish, why bother to cross the river?"[39] When Liu Bang was attacking Ying Bu, he was wounded by a stray arrow. When his injury worsened, he refused treatment and said: "As a commoner, I brandished the three-*chi*-long sword to conquer the empire. Was it not the Mandate of Heaven? My life is in the hands of Heaven."[40] These accounts suggest that in the period from the Chu-Han conflict to the early Western Han Dynasty, notions of auguries and the Mandate of Heaven, as well as founding myths of dynasties, had had a good opportunity for incubation, survival, and propagation in the then sociopolitical context and historical discourse. Therefore, the myths about Liu Bang in *The Grand Scribe's Records* might not have been just unsubstantiated gossip.

Xu Jing wrote: "Since ancient times, whenever Kings and Emperors received the mandate and rose up, they would invoke auguries to highlight supernatural occurrences."[41] Yu Yue (1821–1907) also wrote:

> "Basic Annals of the Five Emperors" made exceptionally good selections, and so the annals of Tang and Yu were all from *Book of Documents*. For those before Gaoxin, the absurd details were not included. Featuring strange creatures and objects, *Basic Annals of Yu* and *Classic of Mountains and Seas* were not included as histories. However, "Basic Annals of Emperor Gaozu" contains the stories of Mother Liu dreaming of a deity and the White Emperor transforming into a snake. This was because at the time, they were believed to be signs of the Mandate of Heaven being received and could not be expunged. The criticism of later generations that the Grand Scribe had a predilection for curiosities is overly harsh.[42]

In other words, the inclusion of myths of the dynasty's founding Emperor in "Basic Annals of Emperor Gaozu" was a natural and obligatory methodology

37 Also a lost passage that Wang Liqi recorded in "Annotations on the Wei River" in *Water Classic* in *Extensive Records of the Taiping Era*, *juan* 15, 87, and 872. See *New Words: Collations and Annotations*, *juan* 184. There is a similar account in "Basic Annals of Xiang Yu" in *The Grand Scribe's Records*.

38 See *The Grand Scribe's Records*, *juan* 10, "Basic Annals of Emperor Wen"; *juan* 55, "The Hereditary House of Marquess of Liu"; *juan* 92, "Biography of the Marquess of Huaiyin."

39 *The Grand Scribe's Records*, *juan* 7, "Basic Annals of Xiang Yu," pp.334, 336. English translation from Nienhauser, vol. 1 (1994), pp.206–207.

40 *The Grand Scribe's Records*, *juan* 8, "Basic Annals of Emperor Gaozu," pp.391.

41 Xu Jing, *Collected Works of Yagetang*, *juan* 4, "On Basic Annals of Emperor Gao," cited in Yang Yanqi et al. (1986), p.358. Wang Xianqian, "Annals of Emperor Gaozu, Part I" in *History of the Former Han: Additional Annotations* cited Shen Qinhan, who also held this view. (*juan* 1 *shang*, p.27)

42 *The Grand Scribe's Records: Collected Annotations and Verifications, with Additional Annotations*, *juan* 8, p.232, citations.

of history writing in the social, political, and cultural contexts of the time, reflecting the "historical truths" of that particular time and space. Sima Qian should not be faulted for being "partial to strange things" and not checking the veracities of the stories.

The most dramatic myths surrounding Liu Bang were his mother dreaming of the deity, the slaying of the snake at Fengxi, and the clouds and air currents at Mount Mang and Mount Dang. The story of Mother Liu's dream was a version of the conception myths of clan ancestors and cultural heroes in pre-Qin and early Han sources. I have written on this elsewhere and will not elaborate here.[43] Past discussions of the snake-slaying myth mostly focused on the killing of the Son of the White Emperor by the Son of the Red Emperor, and the argument over its link with the Theory of the Rotational Changes of the Five Powers prevalent during the early imperial period. However, Liang Yusheng noticed a similarity between this snake-slaying myth and another earlier popular myth that also featured a snake. "During the time of the rise of Duke Wen of Jin [of the Spring and Autumn Period], a snake was blocking his way. He dreamed that Heaven killed the snake, saying: 'Why did you obstruct the way of the sage ruler?' And the snake died. When Emperor Gaozu of the Western Han Dynasty was on the rise, a snake also blocked his path. He slayed the snake and an old woman wept in the night."[44] The story about Duke Wen of Jin was recorded by Jia Yi in "Spring and Autumn" in *New Writings*:

> Duke Wen of the State of Jin was on a hunting expedition when the vanguard returned and said: "A snake as high as a dike is blocking the way in front." Duke Wen said: "Let us return on our carriages." His carriage driver said: "Your servant hears that one should welcome an auspicious sign but intercept a portentous one. There is now an evil portentous one before us, please allow me to strike it." Duke Wen said: "No. I hear that when the Son of Heaven dreams of evil, he will put right the Way; when the various Lords dream of evil, they will put right their administration; when Grandees dream of evil, they will put right their official duties; and when commoners dream of evil, they will put right their conduct. If these are done, harm will not befall them. I have been remiss in my conduct and Heaven is showing me a portentous sign. If I attack it, it will be against the will of Heaven." ... [Duke Wen] returned and put right the administration of his land. After three months, he dreamed of Heaven slaying a large snake, saying: "How dare you block the way of an enlightened ruler!" When Duke Wen woke up, he sent his men to take a look. The snake had already putrefied. Duke Wen was delighted. He adhered to his policies and continued to implement them without interruption, eventually establishing his hegemonic enterprise. Therefore, it is said: welcoming the portentous with virtue will turn the portent into a blessing.[45]

[43] Lu Zongli (2001), pp.415–434.
[44] *Records of Questions about The Grand Scribe's Records*, *juan* 6, p.215.
[45] *New Writings: Annotations*, *juan* 6, pp.248–249.

In "Miscellaneous Matters, Part II" in *New Order*, Liu Xiang gave a similar account, but with a different ending. "Within five days, the official guarding the snake dreamed that the Supreme Deity of Heaven killed the snake, saying: 'Why did you obstruct the way of the sage ruler? You must die for your transgression.' When he woke up, he looked at the snake and saw that it had decomposed."[46] However, this story was not recorded in *Commentary of Zuo* or "The Hereditary House of Jin" in *The Grand Scribe's Records*. It was probably only during the early imperial period that it became popular. Liu Bang's encounter with the snake that was the avatar of the Son of the White Emperor and the gigantic snake that Duke Wen of Jin came across on his hunting trip were both portentous signs that involved the obstruction of one's way.[47] However, they were very different in their responses: Liu Bang went forward and slayed the snake, while Duke Wen of Jin retreated and reformed his administration. In the latter response, the snake was still ultimately killed by Heaven. Jia Yi's and Liu Xiang's accounts invite speculation on whether the authors were being subtly sarcastic.

Liang Yusheng made another discovery: "It was written in *History of Song* that 'When Emperor Wu [Liu Yu] was rising up, a large snake was seen at an islet. When it was shot at, [children in] blue clothing were seen pounding medicinal herbs.' Why were the first and second incidents similar?"[48] The extant copy of *History of Song* does not contain the story, but it was recorded in "Annals of Song, Part I" in *History of the Southern Dynasties* that:

> The Emperor had always been poor and none among his contemporaries could understand him, except Wang Mi of Langya who had great respect for him. There was one time when the Emperor owed Diao Kui thirty thousand coins taken from a community fund. He could not repay the debt after a period of time and was incarcerated by Diao Kui. Wang Mi repaid the debt with his own money without telling the Emperor, and the latter was freed. Subsequently, when the Emperor was chopping reeds at a new islet, he saw a snake several *zhang* long. He shot it with an arrow and injured it. He returned to the islet the following day and heard the sound of pounding. He went to take a look and saw several children in blue clothing pounding medicinal herbs in the thicket. He asked them why they were doing this and they answered: "Our king was shot by Liu Jinu [referring to Liu Yu]. We are preparing a poultice to apply to the wound." The Emperor asked: "Why did your divine king not kill him?" They said: "Liu Jinu is an immortal

[46] *New Order*, *juan* 2, p.10.

[47] Although pre-Qin writings contained stories where snake dreams were signs of giving birth to daughters, both *Commentary of Zuo: The Fourteenth Year of Duke Zhuang* and "The Hereditary House of Zheng" in *The Grand Scribe's Records* depicted the inner snake fighting the outer snake and being killed. In *Commentary of Zuo: The Sixteenth Year of Duke Wen*, the snake was described as originating in the Palace of the Brooks. All these stories considered snakes to be portentous signs.

[48] *Records of Questions about The Grand Scribe's Records*, *juan* 8, p.215.

king; he cannot be killed." The Emperor roared at them and they dispersed. He took the medicine back with him.[49]

It would seem that by the time the Qin Dynasty was giving way to the Han, and the Jin to the Song, the slaying of large snakes had become the motif of myths surrounding genuine Sons of Heaven who removed obstacles and founded their dynasties.

Examining these myths from a secular and realist perspective, one could easily reach the same conclusion as Ao Ying of the Ming Dynasty: "There is nothing strange in seeing a snake and killing it. However, the story about the nocturnal weeping of the divine mother was mystifying the incident to boost the morale for his advance to the west. The descent of Heavenly beings when Tian Dan was defending Jimo and the message in the fish's belly when Chen Sheng was rising up in rebellion were similar examples."[50] Yang Xunji wrote: "The Duke of Pei mystified the killing of the snake to inveigle the foolish men and women of the empire. Bursts of colors in the sky, appearance of green and red dragons, birds that spew fire, fish that jump over boats: all these were signs auguring the rise of Emperors. The ruse of the killing of the snake was devised for this reason."[51]

In other words, seeing a snake on one's way and killing it is a perfectly reasonable situation that can occur in real life. However, the nocturnal cries of the divine mother and identifying oneself as divine might have been absurd inventions designed to inveigle. In fact, the narration in *The Grand Scribe's Records* contained subtle deconstructive hints. In a show of objectivity, Liu Bang learned of the weeping at night from a passer-by (instead of one of his followers), after which he was "secretly pleased and thought highly of himself." The psychology described here was not so much the genuine emotions of a Son of Heaven receiving the Heavenly Mandate, but a demonstration of the cunning use of mass psychology and the ambiguous inner world of an ambitious politician with an eye on the main prize. That "his followers increasingly feared and respected him" showed the political effect of the myth in real life.

The myth of clouds and air currents over Mount Mang and Mount Dang unfolded this way:

The First Emperor of the Qin Dynasty often said: "There is a Son of Heaven air current in the southeast." Therefore, he visited the east to suppress it. Emperor Gaozu, supposing that he was the reason for the air current and the object of the First Emperor's reaction, hid among the swamps and rocks of Mount Mang and Mount Dang. However,

49 *History of the Southern Dynasties*, *juan* 1, pp.1–2.

50 Cited in Ling Zhilong, *History of the Former Han: A Forest of Commentaries*, from *Records of Questions about The Grand Scribe's Records*, *juan* 8, p.215.

51 *The Grand Scribe's Records: Collected Annotations and Verifications, with Additional Annotations*, *juan* 8, p.234.

Empress Lü and others who sought him often found him. Finding it strange, Emperor Gaozu asked why they could locate him. Empress Lü said: "There are often clouds and air currents above where you are, which is why I can often find you." Emperor Gaozu was pleased. The young men in Pei heard about this and many wanted to follow him.[52]

The "Son of Heaven air current" that the First Emperor of the Qin Dynasty was so worried about originated with diviners who specialized in observing air currents. As discussed in Chapter 4, the prophecy of the "Son of Heaven air current in the southeast" had already been widely propagated at the end of the Qin Dynasty; it was not a fabrication by historians or a post-event *chen* "prophecy" that was tailor-made for Liu Bang. Interestingly, *The Grand Scribe's Records* tells its readers that after Liu Bang learned about this prophecy, he supposed that he was the reason for the air current and the object of the First Emperor's reactions, and hid among the swamps and rocks of Mount Mang and Mount Dang.[53] This meant that Liu Bang understood the prophecy to be referring to himself and believed that "the Son of Heaven air current" was upon him, revealing a strong psychological tendency toward "self-fulfilling prophecies."

When Liu Bang was hiding among the swamps and rocks of Mount Mang and Mount Dang, he did not have a fixed abode, but his wife Lü Zhi could always locate him. This was supposedly because she often "discovered" clouds and air currents floating above her husband's location. When Fan Zeng advised Xiang Yu to kill Liu Bang before it was too late, his reason was that "I have had a man observe his aeromantic signs, and they are always in the form of dragons or tigers appearing in all five colors. This is the aeromantic sign of the Son of Heaven. Set upon him quick. Do not miss the chance."[54] If the accounts in *The Grand Scribe's Records* and *Spring and Autumn Annals of the Chu and Han* were reliable, then this myth would have been quite widely propagated at the time and had many believers. According to *The Grand Scribe's Records: Standard Interpretation*, citing Jing Fang's *Climatic Divination: Attached to Book of Changes*: "How does one know that a virtuous person is hiding somewhere? The Master said: 'There are often big clouds of five colors around the location, but there will be no rain. One will find a hidden virtuous person

52 *The Grand Scribe's Records*, *juan* 8, "Basic Annals of Emperor Gaozu," p.348.

53 *The Grand Scribe's Records: Collected Annotations and Verifications, with Additional Annotations*, *juan* 8, citing Zhao Yi: "'Supposing [himself]': that Emperor Gaozu as a commoner would suppose himself to be the Son of Heaven demonstrated how ambitious he was. *History of the Former Han* deleted the words." (p.234)

54 *The Grand Scribe's Records*, *juan* 7, "Basic Annals of Xiang Yu," p.311. English translation from Nienhauser, vol. 1 (1994), p.190. A similar account was written by Lu Jia in *Spring and Autumn Annals of the Chu and Han*, cited in *New Words: Collations and Annotations*, p.184: "I have had a man observe the Duke of Pei. His air currents shoot up into the sky, with the five colors intertwined. They looked like dragons, snakes, tigers, clouds, or men. These were not the air currents of a servant of man. Why not kill him?"

below them.'" Given the popularity of divination by observing air currents and weather during the early imperial period, Empress Lü's ability to locate where Liu Bang was using air currents would be perfectly reasonable to the people of the Han periods.

It was written in *The Grand Scribe's Records* that Liu Bang was "secretly pleased and thought highly of himself" after he slayed the snake, and following that, "his followers increasingly feared and respected him." When he learned that there were "often clouds and air currents above" where he was, he was "pleased" and the "young men in Pei heard about this and many wanted to follow him." Although the accounts of the myths about the slaying of the snake and the clouds and air currents were brief, the structure, propagation, and the psychological impact they had on Liu Bang himself and the young men of Pei were vividly recorded. Liu Bang's self-satisfaction and the myths' political power revealed between the lines also resulted in subsequent doubts about the framework of the myths. Xu Fuyuan of the Ming Dynasty questioned the clouds and air current myth based on ordinary human behavior: "Would Emperor Gaozu not have secretly told Empress Lü where he was hiding? One was hiding, the other was seeking, and in the process of seeking, strange occurrences came to pass; they were used to move the masses."[55] Xu Jing also suspected that Liu Bang and Lü Zhi were in cahoots in fabricating a miracle to "agitate the young men of Pei."[56] Just like the killing of the snake at Fengxi, secret communications between Lü Zhi and her itinerant husband, who was in hiding, on where and when to meet were quite possible in real life. Claiming that there were clouds and air currents above Liu Bang's location was a way to protect her and her husband, as well as a ruse to trick their followers with stories of the supernatural.

Emperor Wen of the Western Han Dynasty "asked not about the real world but asked about the supernatural," so interested was he in the latter that he leaned forward in his chambers late at night. Emperor Wu of the Western Han Dynasty was "especially reverential in the sacrifices to the spirits and deities,"[57] anxiously asking "if there were signs that the Three Dynasties [of Xia, Shang, and Zhou] had received the Mandate of Heaven."[58] During the reign of Emperor Zhao, there was a warning about dynastic change and a commoner becoming Emperor. By the reigns of the Emperors Yuan, Cheng, Ai, and Ping, the political climate of the Western Han Dynasty was already saturated by talks about divine retribution and collective anxiety. Emperor Ai

[55] *The Grand Scribe's Records: Collected Annotations and Verifications, with Additional Annotations*, *juan* 8, p.234, citation.

[56] *Collected Works of Yagetang*, *juan* 4, "On Basic Annals of Emperor Gao," cited in Yang Yanqi, et al. (1986), p.358.

[57] *History of the Former Han*, *juan* 25 *shang*, "Treatises on Sacrifices, Part I," p.1215.

[58] *History of the Former Han*, *juan* 56, "Biography of Dong Zhongshu," p.2496.

even believed in Xia Heliang's Chijingzi *chen* prophecy that the Han Dynasty was in decline and should renew its Mandate of Heaven,[59] and changed his reign period name and his own title. In the middle-to-late period of the Western Han Dynasty, generals and ministers from commoner backgrounds were no longer natural features of the political landscape, and the imperial family itself no longer possessed the heroism and valor of its forebears, challenging the established social hierarchy. Thus, the founding myths of the dynasty were not simply the collective memory of a glorious past; they also addressed the legitimacy and self-confidence of the ruling house.[60] In the final years of the Xin Dynasty, the people were full of nostalgia for the Han Dynasty, and the different rebellion armies backed members of the Liu imperial clan as their leaders. *Chen* prophetic books such as *The Token of the Red Secret* appeared, further enriching and mystifying the myths about Liu Bang and his founding of the Han Dynasty. Taking shape in the late Western Han Dynasty and settling into their final forms in the Eastern Han, these elaborated versions of the dynastic founding myths were contained in the apocryphal books, which were lost in the Sui and Tang dynasties, but fragments could still be found as citations in other writings:

1. The elaboration of Mother Liu's dream and conception (please refer to my paper, "On the Myth of Miraculous Birth and the Legitimation of Han Imperial Power");
2. The elaboration of Liu Bang's unusual physical appearance ("a high-bridged nose, the countenance of a dragon, a beautiful beard, and seventy-two black moles on his left thigh");
3. The elaboration of the snake-slaying story at the swamp in Fengxi; and
4. The elaboration of the stories about "the Son of Heaven air current in the southeast" and "air currents above Mount Mang and Mount Dang."

In addition, new political prophecies and myths appeared that spoke of:

1. "Liu Ji [referring to Liu Bang] becoming the Son of Heaven";
2. The family name encoded in the characters *mao*, *jin*, and *dao* (forming a logograph suggesting the name "Liu"); and

59 *History of the Former Han*, *juan* 11, "Annals of Emperor Ai," p.340.

60 Sima Xiangru's *Essay on the Feng and Shan Sacrifices* heaped praise on the virtue of the Great Han Dynasty by citing various auguries: "The coiled yellow dragon rose up because of its virtue . . . saying that it was riding on the Mandate of Heaven." (*Selections of Refined Literature*, *juan* 48, p.678) Yang Xiong's *Condemning the Qin and Lauding the Xin*: "Meeting the ancestor of the Han, dragons cavorted at Feng[xi] and Pei." (*Selections of Refined Literature*, *juan* 48, p.680) These reflected the political and cultural milieu after the middle of the Western Han where it was popular to recount the miracles associated with Emperor Gaozu's founding of the dynasty.

3. The fate of the Liu ruling family after Liu Bang's founding of the Han Dynasty.[61]

In *History of the Former Han*, Ban Biao wrote that:

> Therefore, the Liu family inherited the blessing from Yao and their progenies found fame in history books. Tang Yao possessed Fire-Power and the Han succeeded to that as well. It all began at a swamp in Pei, where the Divine Mother wept in the night, highlighting the augury of the Red Emperor. . . . The world saw that Emperor Gaozu had risen up as a mere commoner, but they knew not the reason. They thought that in turbulent times, one could simply rise up with a sword in hand. Itinerant strategists even compared the battle for the empire with chasing a deer: he who is lucky and fast shall seize it. Little do they know that it is the Mandate of Heaven that confers one with the imperial regalia; one does not obtain them by one's wit or might. . . . As for Emperor Gaozu, there were five reasons for his ascendance: 1. He was the descendant of Yao; 2. He had an extraordinary appearance; 3. He was majestic and auguries indicated that he would prevail; 4. He was benevolent, virtuous, and forgiving; and 5. He was good at identifying talent and placing the right people in the right positions. . . . In the beginning, when Mother Liu dreamed of an encounter with a divine being and became pregnant with Emperor Gaozu, the sky churned with lightning, thunder, and dark clouds, and creatures like dragons and serpents appeared. When he grew up, he was special and was different from most people. Mother Wang and Wu Fu saw a creature resting on him when he was drunk and decided to waive all his drinking debts. Seeing his unusual appearance, Master Lü betrothed his daughter to him. It was to suppress the Son of Heaven air current in the east that the First Emperor of the Qin Dynasty toured that area of his empire, and it was the clouds and air currents Empress Lü saw in the sky that led her to Emperor Gaozu's location. Emperor Gaozu first received the Mandate of Heaven when he slayed the white snake. When he advanced into the area within the Hangu Pass, the Five Stars gathered together. Therefore, both the Marquess of Huaiyin and the Marquess of Liu said that Emperor Gaozu had been conferred the Mandate of Heaven; it could not be achieved through human endeavor.[62]

In their accounts of the founding of the Han, both Ban Gu ("Annals of Emperor Gao" in *History of the Former Han*) and Xun Yue (*Annals of Han*) replicated almost all the stories in "Basic Annals of Emperor Gaozu" in *The Grand Scribe's Records*. Both spoke of slaying the snake, auguries, the color red and Fire-Power, and receiving the Mandate of Heaven.[63]

Disagreeing with Emperor Guangwu's decision to locate the Eastern Han capital at Luoyang, Du Du submitted *Rhapsody on Discussions of Capitals* to extol the splendor and majesty of Chang'an. He began by proclaiming: "At the

[61] These myths and legends were recorded in works such as *Apocryphal Poetry*, *Diagram of the Yellow River*, *Spring and Autumn*, and *Book of Documents* collected in *Compendium of Apocryphal Books*.

[62] *History of the Former Han*, *juan* 100, "Afterword and Family History," pp.4208–4212.

[63] See *History of the Former Han*, *juan* 1 *xia*, "Annals of Emperor Gao," p.82 and *Annals of the Two Han Dynasties*, *juan* 1, "Annals of Emperor Gaozu," pp.1–2.

founding of the Great Han, Emperor Gaozu had great merit. The white snake was slayed, black clouds gathered, and the Five Stars congregated east of the Well Constellation."[64] In various parts of his *Critical Essays*, Wang Chong discussed the mythical stories about Mother Liu's dream, the slaying of the snake, clouds and air currents above Mount Mang and Mount Dang, Liu Bang's dragon countenance and the moles on his thigh. He praised Liu Bang as being exalted by Heaven and that auspicious signs foretelling the rise of the Han Dynasty had been abundant during the Western Zhou Dynasty. However, he dismissed the accounts of draconic conception and darkening of the skies as absurd, and argued that the snake that was slayed in Fengxi was not the Son of the White Emperor but a malevolent creature.[65] When Kong Rong and Cao Cao were discussing the merits of wine, Kong Rong said: "If Emperor Gaozu was not inebriated when he killed the white snake, he would not have been able to release its spirit."[66]

Obviously, the founding myths recorded in "Basic Annals of Emperor Gaozu" in *The Grand Scribe's Records* were, by the Xin and Eastern Han dynasties, common historical knowledge and part of the people's collective memory; they had become the essential discourse on the legitimacy of the Han Dynasty to rule. Even the "sword"[67] used by Liu Bang to kill the snake was exalted as a state regalia and became, together with the legendary imperial jade seal inherited from the Qin Dynasty, "Treasures of the Imperial Carriage."[68] "When the sacred retinue commenced, an erudite person would carry the imperial seal, while another would brandish the snake-slaying sword. Both would accompany the Emperor. The rest of the retinue would be on horseback behind the carriage."[69] "On the Gengyin day in the leap month of the fifth year

[64] *History of the Later Han*, *juan* 80 *shang*, "Biographies of Writers: Du Du," p.2598.

[65] See the following sections in *Critical Essays*: "Auspicious Signs," "On Anthroposcopy," "Heaven's Original Gift," "Miracles," "Exaggerations," "Interaction among Similar Kinds," "Extoling the Han," and "Records of Portents."

[66] Annotations of "Biography of Kong Rong" in *History of the Later Han*, citing *Collected Works of Kong Rong*. *History of the Later Han*, *juan* 70, p.2273.

[67] In the commentaries of "Basic Annals of Emperor Gaozu" in *The Grand Scribe's Records*, it was written that "according to the *Old Rituals of the Han Dynasties*: "The sword that slayed the snake was seven *chi* long." However, Emperor Gaozu said: "I, a commoner, conquered the empire with a three-*chi*-long sword." The two records differed. Cui Bao wrote in *Annotations Past and Present* that "When Emperor Gaozu was a Commune Chief, he should be carrying a three-*chi*-long sword, but after he rose in status, he would be carrying a seven-*chi*-long precious sword." It was for this reason that *Old Rituals* referred to the sword measuring seven *chi*. It was further annotated in the standard interpretation that "the snake was big and it was reasonable that he sought another sword to kill it. Three-*chi*-long swords were swords that one carried on normal occasions." It would seem that the people of Han, Jin, and Tang dynasties were quite serious in their discussions of the appearance of this legendary "precious sword." (*The Grand Scribe's Records*, *juan* 8, "Basic Annals of Emperor Gaozu")

[68] *History of Song*, *juan* 18, "Treatise on Rites, Part V," p.506.

[69] *History of Song*, *juan* 29, "Treatise on Officials, Part I," p.1239.

of the Yuankang reign period [295] of Emperor Hui of the Western Jin Dynasty, the armory caught fire. Principal Imperial Consultant Zhang Hua (232–300), suspecting that a revolt might occur, secured the place in the first instance before putting out the fire. Therefore, treasures that had been accumulated over generations, such as the head of Wang Mang, the shoes of Confucius, the sword used by Emperor Gaozu of the Han Dynasty to slay the white snake, as well as weapons and equipment for two million soldiers, were totally destroyed in an instant."[70] The material and ceremonial repositories of the snake-slaying myth, as well as all the spiritual symbols and sustenance of myths relating to Liu Bang and the founding of the Han Dynasty, were lost in that conflagration.

We refer to the stories about Mother Liu's dream, Liu Bang's unusual appearance, killing the snake in Fengxi, clouds and air currents, and so on, as "myths" simply because we think that these stories were surreal and supernatural, and could not occur in real life. These myths had been created based on the customs and beliefs that had been current in a specific social, political, and cultural context of the time. However, this is not to say that all the stories were fabricated afterward. Certain elements in the stories might have been based on facts. For example, Liu Bang's physiognomy might have been unusual, his slaying of the snake was not an impossible occurrence in real life, and he and his wife might have had a secret way of communication when he was hiding in the mountains, but for the sake of safety they had to provide a supernatural explanation.

"Naturally, a founding emperor who was able to found a dynasty and rule the entire known world would not be an ordinary person. He would have traits that were different from ordinary people."[71] His exceptional charisma and abilities might cause the people around him to feel a special attraction for him, and hope that something extraordinary would happen to him. The social and political turbulence at the end of the Qin Dynasty, the numerous myths of divine birth from antiquity, the arts of physiognomy and air current observation popular since the Warring States Period, and the psychological desire of the masses for a bona fide Son of Heaven – all these factors created a rich milieu for the making of political myths. At the same time, the Liu Bang that was depicted in *The Grand Scribe's Records* had a strong tendency for "self-fulfilling prophecy" and genuinely believed that he was the chosen one. Under suitable circumstances, he was able to make use of his supreme self-confidence, acute political sensitivity, rich life experience, and adroit interpersonal communication skills to convey strong psychological hints to his

[70] *History of Song*, *juan* 33, "Treatise on the Five Agents, Part III," p.933.
[71] Sun Kuang-Teh (1986), pp.65–66.

followers, and even to the people, in order to influence their actions and elevate their esteem for him.

"The stories in myths are probably fiction, but the existence of myths is a fact. There must be a reason and a purpose for the occurrence of these facts."[72] In the course of the battle for the empire and the accompanying psychological impact, a series of mythical stories was created and propagated. These surreal and supernatural stories were allowed to survive in the real world, fulfill their actual purpose in the social and political lives of the times, and participate in the creation of human history. In this sense, the mythical stories of the founding emperor recorded in "Basic Annals of Emperor Gaozu" in *The Grand Scribe's Records* reflected, albeit indirectly, historical truth.

Folk Legends

The section on unverifiable talk in Chapter 1 mentions a story recorded in "Treatise on the Five Agents" in *History of the Later Han*. In the eighth month of the first year of the Yongkang reign period, officials in the Ba Commandery reported an auspicious sign to Emperor Huan of the Eastern Han Dynasty: a yellow dragon had been seen! What was actually going on? It turns out that the weather was hot and some people wanted to bathe in the pond. Seeing that the pond was muddy, "they joked to one another that 'there is a yellow dragon in the pond.' The story eventually spread among the people."[73]

Jokes were also a form of unverifiable talk. Some jokes were spread by word of mouth and eventually turned into popular legends, which was one of the typical ways that folk beliefs came about. Using the accounts recorded by Eastern Han scholar Ying Shao in his *Comprehensive Meaning of Customs and Habits*, this section attempts to explore the process by which certain folk beliefs of the early imperial period emerged.

Legends of Deities and Lords

Various magical practices and beliefs with strong elements of primitive religion had been popular among the common people since the Warring States Period, such as the belief in immortals, witchcraft, mediums, the selection of auspicious days for life events, taboos, observing air currents, physiognomy, divination using chicken bones, divination using stars, talismanic portents, miscellaneous worship, and unauthorized worship. These remained popular in the early imperial period across all sections of society, details of which are recorded in extant primary sources. For example, during the reigns of

72 *Ibid.*, pp.52.
73 *History of the Later Han, juan* 17, "Treatise on the Five Agents, Part V," p.3344.

Emperors Zhao and Xuan of the Western Han Dynasty, "when praying and offering sacrifices to famous mountains and rivers, the wealthy struck cows to kill them, played drums, staged plays with actors and marionettes. Those in the middle erected south-facing stages on thoroughfares and platforms on water. They slaughtered goats and dogs, and played music on the *se* and *sheng*. The poor used five types of chicken and pork to pray for divine protection, and distributed cured meats. During their sacrifices, the community areas would be packed with carriages and people." "They were negligent in their behavior but supplicated to spirits; they were slothful with proper conduct but attentive to offering sacrifices." "They were necromancers in the alleys and streets, and mediums in the neighborhoods."[74] In the final years of Emperor Ping's reign, Wang Mang turned a blind eye to and even encouraged the worship of deities and spirits that had not been sanctioned by the state. "From the Six Gods including Heaven and Earth, to the various minor deities and spirits, there were 1,700 places of worship using over 3,000 kinds of animal and bird offerings, including cows, goats, and pigs, for sacrifices."[75] Although these numbers included some of the "unauthorized deities," there would have been numerous private devotions to minor deities that were not listed in the official registers. The situation was more or less the same in the Eastern Han Dynasty. "Weird Deities" in *Comprehensive Meaning of Customs and Habits* described how some of these minor deities came to be worshipped by the common people during the Eastern Han.

The Lord of the Dried Fish In the wetlands of Tongyang, Ru'nan (present-day Xincai, Henan Province), someone had set a trap, which ensnared a musk deer. Before the trapper arrived to collect the animal, a merchant went past in his caravan and took the musk deer. Feeling bad for taking away the deer, he left behind a dried fish as a form of compensation. The trapper eventually appeared and saw the dried fish. Feeling shocked because it was a remote swamp that usually saw no passers-by, he believed the dried fish to be a divine object. Word got around and people began to come and pray to the dried fish, asking to be healed of illnesses and for blessings. Many of their prayers were answered, and devotees built a temple in its honor. Dozens of necromancers attached themselves to the temple, which attracted people from several hundred *li* away to worship the Lord of the Dried Fish.[76] A few years later, the merchant who had left the dried fish passed by and witnessed the strange phenomenon. He told the people: "This is my fish. It is not a god!" He took the

[74] *Discourses on Salt and Iron: Annotations, juan* 6, "Short of Supply," pp.351–352.
[75] *History of the Former Han, juan* 25 *xia*, "Treatise on Sacrifices, Part II," p.1270.
[76] Deities were already referred to as "Lords" (*jun*) during the Warring States Period.

dried fish from the altar, and the temple dedicated to the Lord of the Dried Fish was abandoned.[77]

The Lord of the Plum There was a Zhang Zhu who lived in Nandun, Ru'nan (present-day Xiangcheng, Henan Province), who saw a plum pit when he was planting crops. He wanted to remove it, but then he saw there was a hole in the trunk of a mulberry tree. He decided to plant the plum pit there and watered it with the slop left over from his field. Later on, some people saw that the mulberry tree kept bearing plums, and told other people. Someone who had an eye ailment rested beneath the shade of that tree. He later said that the Lord of the Plum had healed his eyes and offered a pig to the deity. People with pain in the eyes and minor illnesses also went to the tree and were healed of their ailments. Like barking dogs, the people spread the news, saying the blind had regained their sight, which resulted in visitors from near and far. Often, there would be thousands of carriages and horses, with an overabundance of wine and meat. About a year later, Zhang Zhu returned from afar and saw what was happening. He said with shock: "This is not a god. I planted this!" As a result, it was discontinued.[78]

The fact that there were thousands of carriages and copious supplies of wine and meat indicated that devotees of the Lord of the Plum were composed not only of nearby villagers but also rich and powerful people. However, the cult of the Lord of the Plum collapsed immediately after Zhang Zhu's revelation.

The Virtuous Stone Gentleman Deity A stone statue of a man stood at the Peng Family Cemetery in Ruyang, Ru'nan (present-day Shangshui, Henan Province). One hot day, an elderly farmer's wife, who had bought several wheat cakes at the market, rested for a while next to the stone man and placed the wheat cakes on the head of the stone man. When she got up and went on her way, she did not realize that she had left behind a wheat cake on the stone man. A passer-by walked past and thought it strange that a wheat cake should be there, whereupon another passer-by joked and said: "The stone man heals illnesses. This is a thanksgiving offering from one who was healed." And so, it began to spread among people that touching the stone man's head would heal headaches and touching his abdomen would cure stomachaches. Even those who got well by themselves also believed that the stone man had healed them. People began to refer to the stone man as the Virtuous Stone Gentleman or

77 *Comprehensive Meaning of Customs and Habits: Annotations, juan* 9, p.403. The same story is found in *The Master Who Embraces Simplicity* and a similar story in Liu Jingshu's *Strange Garden*, which involved a sturgeon in a withered tree. Many minor deities worshipped by the common people in ancient China came about in similar fashion.

78 *Comprehensive Meaning of Customs and Habits: Annotations, juan* 9, p.405.

Virtuous Stone Lord. Before long, carriages and horses congregated around the stone man, with countless tents erected and music that could be heard several *li* away. So busy was it that the commandery's Regimental Chief Commandant often had to come and maintain public order. Several years later, when the elderly woman who had left behind the wheat cake heard what had gone on, she told the village elders what really happened. The worship of the Virtuous Stone Lord stopped at once.[79]

The geneses of these three cults were quite similar: misunderstandings or jokes were propagated by word of mouth, giving rise to gods and deities that were worshipped not only by ordinary people but also by local officials and society's elites. Ying Shao's rationalist accounts demonstrated a typical case of the Eastern Han's success in suppressing rumors. The moment the truth was revealed, mysticism and superstition were swept away, and "deities" that had been dried fish, plum pits, and stone men were pulled down from their pedestals. Having said that, many deities that had emerged from misunderstandings and jokes have been worshipped among the people from the early imperial period up to the present day.[80] The Lords of the Dried Fish, the Lord of the Plum, and the Virtuous Stone Lord might have been discredited, but more of their kind persisted and thrived. Actually, beliefs or "superstitions" do not require scientific proof, nor do devotees care about the truth of their gods' origins. What believers are really concerned about is their gods' efficacy in answering their prayers (based on their personal experience as well as those of the believers around them), and their ability to provide spiritual succor.

"Folk Stories" and "Folk Sayings"

"Correcting Errors" in *Comprehensive Meanings of Customs and Habits* sought to correct the errors of "folk stories" and "folk sayings" that were popular at the time, criticizing certain folk beliefs that had come about through repeated propagation of untruths.[81] The following contain a few examples.

Shrine of the Prefect of Ye It was said that during the reign of Emperor Ming of the Eastern Han Dynasty, Wang Qiao, a native of Hedong and a Gentleman of the Imperial Secretariat, was appointed the Prefect of Ye. Wang Qiao, who possessed magical powers, often arrived at court on the first of

[79] *Comprehensive Meaning of Customs and Habits: Annotations, juan* 9, pp.406–407. Similar versions of the story are found in *Feng's Records of Things Heard and Seen*, *The Master Who Embraces Simplicity*, and *Imperial Reader*.

[80] See Lu Zongli and Luan Baoqun, *Chinese Folk Deities* (2000).

[81] There are quite a number of references to "folk stories" and "folk sayings" in the primary sources of the early imperial period, such as Wang Chong's *Critical Essays*. This section will cite only a few cases from *Comprehensive Meaning of Customs and Habits*.

every month for an audience with the Emperor. Given the frequency of Wang Qiao's visits to the capital, the Emperor wondered why he was never accompanied by horses and carriages. He secretly ordered the Grand Astrologer to observe Wang Qiao. The Grand Astrologer subsequently reported that whenever Wang Qiao arrived at court, two wild ducks would often fly in from the southeast. Crouching at a hidden place, the Grand Astrologer trapped the birds; when they opened the traps, they saw only a pair of shoes, which the Imperial Manufactories identified as shoes presented to officials of the Imperial Secretariat in the middle of the fourth year of the Yongping reign period. Whenever Wang Qiao was at court, the drum at the gate of Ye would sound on its own, and it was so loud that it could be heard in the capital. It came to pass that Heaven sent a jadeite coffin before the hall of Wang Qiao's office. He ordered his functionaries to carry it into the office, but it would not budge. Wang Qiao then said: "The Supreme Deity of Heaven wishes to call me to His presence." He bathed, changed his clothes, and lay inside the sarcophagus. After the lid was placed over him, he was buried east of the city. The site became a grave mound on its own, and the cows in the county sweated with lolling tongues. No one knew how it became a grave mound, and the people erected a shrine, calling it the Shrine of the Lord of Ye. Governors, Grand Administrators, and other officials all paid their respects at the shrine when they first assumed their duties in the area. The prayers of the officials and people were all answered. If they transgressed, they immediately met with misfortune. Emperor Ming had the drum sent to him and placed it in a commune in the capital, but it did not emit any sound. The Grand Astrologer observed it, and then climbed up the Western Gate to watch the stars and air currents. He declared that this Prefect of Ye was the immortal Wang Qiao.[82]

Wang Qiao was included in "Biographies of Alchemists" in *History of the Later Han*,[83] which had a similar account of his life as *Comprehensive Meaning of Customs and Habits*. The former might have even lifted the story from the latter. During the Han periods, there was a Shrine of the Lord of Ye in Ye County (present-day Ye County, Henan Province) dedicated to the worship of Wang Qiao. Both officials and the people prayed and offered sacrifices at the shrine. However, Ying Shao averred that the shrine had been erected

82 *Comprehensive Meaning of Customs and Habits: Annotations*, *juan* 2, pp.81–82.

83 *History of the Later Han*, *juan* 82 *shang*, p.2712. Wang Qiao, or Wang Ziqiao, was an immortal frequently seen in the texts of Taoism and the Taoist religion. There were many stories regarding his origins, and the name Wang Qiao could have been referring to different persons at different times. The name was found in a silk scroll *The Art of Nurturing Health*, uncovered in the No. 3 Han Tomb in Mawangdui, which recorded that Wang Ziqiao's father asked the immortal Peng Zu about acquiring health and well-being. In "Lessons to Prosper the Clan" in *Masters of Huainan*, Wang Qiao and Chi Song were juxtaposed. The Wang Qiao in "Biographies of Alchemists" in *History of the Later Han* was just one of several Wang Qiaos, but he was often confused with the immortals Wang Qiao and Wang Ziqiao in folk beliefs.

during the Spring and Autumn Period, and its principal deity should in fact be the Duke of Ye, a Grandee of the State of Chu.[84] The Duke of Ye was a descendant of King Zhuang of Chu. His family name was Shen and his given name was Zhuliang. He also had a courtesy name: Zigao. He served the state with merit and was enfeoffed at Ye. Given the centuries that had passed since the Spring and Autumn Period, however, the common people of the Eastern Han Dynasty did not know the origins of this Shrine of the Duke of Ye, and folk stories began to circulate, attributing the temple to Wang Qiao, the Prefect of Ye, who supposedly possessed magical abilities. Such cases of mistaken identity were actually quite common in Chinese folk religions.[85]

Emperor Wen of the Western Han Dynasty Emperor Cheng of the Western Han Dynasty was well versed in *Book of Odes* and *Book of Documents*, and read many books of the past and present. In his spare moments, he learned about court rituals and was especially adept at standards and precedents of the Han imperial house. He often summoned Colonel of the Capital Rampart Liu Xiang before him. One day, he asked Liu Xiang about the popular story of Emperor Wen of the Western Han Dynasty. According to the story, Emperor Wen was born in a military camp. When he grew up and became educated, he did not know where his father was. It was his habit to offer sacrifices outside the Eastern Gate of Dai in the morning. It was during this time that Emperor Gaozu kept having dreams about his son offering sacrifices to him, and he sent an emissary to Dai to make inquiries. He finally found the young man and made him King of Dai. Later, when the court welcomed the King of Dai to the throne, he arrived late and therefore might not be enthroned. The sun then appeared in the middle of the sky again so that he could ascend the throne. As the Son of Heaven, Emperor Wen was so frugal that he had the portiere of the Front Hall made by sewing together fabric file envelopes. He often held court at Mingguang Palace. He mourned for Empress Dowager Bo for three years, living in a hut and sleeping on an earthen pillow according to the rites. When he fell seriously ill, he knew his sons could not observe the three-year mourning period and changed it to thirty-six days. During his reign, the empire was peaceful and prosperous. Only three hundred criminal cases were heard, and millet was priced at one *qian* per *sheng*.

[84] "Annotations on the Ru River" in *Water Classic*, cited by Wang Liqi: "East of the Li River, straight up to the north of the Shrine of the Duke of Ye. In front of the shrine was a stele that gave an account of the Duke of Ye, whose name was Zhuliang and whose courtesy name was Zigao. During Qin and Han times, the shrine had two towers and altars, but it was destroyed during the Yellow Turban Uprising and left in ruins."

[85] See Lu Zongli and Luan Baoqun, *Chinese Folk Deities* (2000).

Emperor Cheng asked Liu Xiang if the story was true. Liu Xiang replied that none of it was true.[86]

Liu Heng, Emperor Wen of the Western Han Dynasty, was the son of Emperor Gaozu and one of his consorts. His mother, Lady Bo, was of humble birth, and both mother and son lived in Dai for years, in the peripheries far away from the power center and court intrigues. It was sheer luck that he became Emperor after the death of Empress Dowager Lü, something that we discussed in the "Myths about Successor Rulers" section earlier in this chapter. Emperor Wen was a cautious man. His administration was marked by benevolence, a laissez faire approach, and fiscal frugality. He levied low taxes and implemented legal reforms during his reign. He and his son Emperor Jing presided over the period of peace and prosperity known in history as the Good Governances of Emperors Wen and Jing. It was natural that the people would be curious about the childhood, ascendance, and personal character of such an Emperor, and that they would make up stories among themselves and spread these stories. Apparently, these stories made it to the palace, which prompted the conversation between Emperor Cheng and Liu Xiang.

According to Ying Shao, Liu Heng was born in the palace and spent his whole life either in the imperial palace or the palace in his kingdom. There was no question of him being born in a military camp, not knowing where his father was, and the story about his offering sacrifices outside the Eastern Gate of Dai and how his father subsequently found him.

The story about the sun appearing in the sky again because of his late arrival at the enthronement ceremony was another fabrication. According to historical records, Liu Heng was enthroned in the evening.

Although Emperor Wen was famous for being frugal, the Front Hall of the Stables of the Eternal Palace was extravagantly luxurious, with carvings, paintings, and gold ornaments. It could not be, as the popular stories described, that the portiere of the Front Hall was sewn together using the fabric file envelopes of memorials submitted by officials.

Finally, Emperor Wen died before Empress Dowager Bo. So there was no question of him observing three years of mourning for his mother. "These and a dozen other details were falsehoods spread by ordinary people, who exaggerated and drew the wrong conclusions."[87]

Dongfang Shuo It was said that Dongfang Shuo was the spirit of Venus. He was the legendary Feng Hou during the time of the Yellow Emperor and Wuchengzi during the reign of Yao. During the Zhou Dynasty, he was Lao Dan (i.e. Laozi), as well as Fan Li in the State of Yue, who later went by the

[86] *Comprehensive Meaning of Customs and Habits: Annotations*, *juan* 2, pp.93–94.
[87] *Ibid.*, p.99.

name Chiyizi Pi in the State of Qi. His sage words could cause kings and hegemons to prosper. He was ever changing and ephemeral.[88]

Appointed Gentleman during the reign of Emperor Wu of the Western Han Dynasty, Dongfang Shuo subsequently held the post of Grand Palace Grandee, among others. He was erudite and witty, and had a sense of humor. He often observed the Emperor's moods and offered frank admonitions to the throne. Although Emperor Wu often heeded his words, the Emperor regarded him as an entertaining jester and did not appoint him to important positions. Dongfang Shuo "liked to talk with ordinary people, hence many stories about him were popular among people of later generations." "These frivolous stories were spread and made much of among commoners, children, and shepherd boys. A great many meddlers in subsequent periods began to attribute strange tales to him."[89] Dongfang Shuo had been a popular legendary figure among the common people since the Western Han, with many strange tales created about him. The folk belief that he was a spirit of Venus was naturally a folk legend that could not be rationally verified.

Liu An, King of Huainan It was said that Liu An, King of Huainan, gathered several thousand paid retainers and *fangshi* around him, and wrote the books *Great Treasure*, *The Garden's Secret*, and *Inside the Pillow*. They succeeded in creating gold and silver and ascended to Heaven in broad daylight.[90]

During the reign of Emperor Wu of the Western Han Dynasty, Liu An had to take his own life, and his kingdom was rescinded because he "flouts the laws, commits evil deeds, bears the intention to deceive, bewilders the people, betrays his ancestors, and recklessly creates portentous talk." Several thousand others were implicated, including his queen, eldest son, paid retainers, and their families. Chapter 2 contains more details of his demise. However, many ordinary people believed that Liu An and his retainers were experts in alchemy, and had risen to Heaven as a result. In strong language, Ying Shao dismissed these tales: "Was Liu An an immortal because of his abilities? Some of his retainers might have escaped and made up these falsehoods because they were ashamed of what they had done. The people of later generations parroted the falsehoods and they became widespread."[91] If what he said was true, then the stories about Liu An echoed the emergence and propagation of the rumors regarding the Qing Dynasty's Yongzheng Emperor stealing the throne from his brother.

88 *Ibid.*, p.108.
89 *History of the Former Han*, *juan* 65, "Biography of Dongfang Shuo," pp.2860, 2873–2874.
90 *Comprehensive Meaning of Customs and Habits: Annotations*, *juan* 2, p.115.
91 *Ibid.*, p.116.

Myths, Legends, and Rumors

The "folk sayings" and "folk stories" of the Han Periods that Ying Shao criticized were typical of rumors. Political myths and legends of folk deities were also closely linked to rumors.

The majority of rumors are very time specific and disappear within a short space of time. This is because rumors are "explanations" of certain ambiguous situations or vague occurrences in a specific time and place. With changing circumstances or increased clarity, the rumors will lose their *raison d'être*. Nevertheless, there are certain rumors that will stand the test of time. Passed from one generation to the next, they become folklore or historical myths. These include origin myths (such as myths about common ancestors and cultural heroes) whose purpose is to cement ethnic cohesiveness and transmit cultural heritage, and political myths that defend the legitimacy of the ruling family and maintain social stability. These myths might have been subsequently historicized and textualized to become part of official and orthodox historical narratives. The explanations of important events offered by some rumors meet certain psychological expectations of the people and provide sufficient room for imagination. After long periods of accumulative telling and re-telling, they become folklore and conspiracy theories that refuse to die, such as Liu An rising up to Heaven as an immortal in the Han Periods, Emperor Taizong of the Northern Song Dynasty murdering his older brother Emperor Taizu, and the Yongzheng Emperor stealing the throne from the rightful heir in the Qing Dynasty.

In recent years, there is a new sub-branch in the study of rumors: the urban legend. Urban legends are not necessarily urban; they actually refer to modern or contemporary folk legends. Given increasing urbanization in contemporary society, people's lifestyle and mentality, whether they live in urban or rural areas, are very different from those of a traditional agricultural society. It is for this reason that the term "urban legend" was coined. Traditional political myths, folklore, and urban legends possess the general characteristics of rumors: they emerge spontaneously and it is difficult to pinpoint their origins; they are not firsthand knowledge but information that one hears from "friends" or "reliable sources"; the information resembles or claims to be the truth, but it is impossible to verify or it has yet to be verified; the information often contains a cautionary element; apart from officially sanctioned origin and political myths, folk legends are usually propagated by the people or via non-official channels through verbal or textual forms; the form and content of political myths and folk legends will undergo various additions, omissions, augmentation, and re-creation in the course of their transmission. Political myths and folklore are different from rumors in the normal sense in that (1) they are usually in the form of stories with more or less complete plot structures, and (2) they often have a longer period of relevance, with similar themes and plots reappearing in renewed or rejuvenated forms.

6 Observations and Thoughts

The disseminated talk, unverifiable talk, portentous talk, rhymes, *chen* prophecies, prophetic rhymes, political myths, and popular legends during the early imperia period in China were all rumors or rumor-like expressions (hereafter referred to as rumor-type expressions). The origins of rumor-type expressions of the early imperial period were usually hard-to-trace information sources such as hearsay, legends, and folk stories. They were spread primarily through unofficial and non-mainstream interpersonal networks, with oral transmission as the main mode of circulation, supplemented by the written word. Their contents often involved curses, commentary, speculation, the weird and absurd, and strange portents. While the information they carried might not have been approved or verified by authoritative channels, they were not necessarily fabrications and falsehoods. In terms of linguistic expression, they were unclear, ambiguous, and amenable to multiple definitions and interpretations. Rumor-type expressions played an important role in politics and society during the early imperial period.

The Value of Rumors as Historical Sources and How They Can Enlighten Us

Historians have in recent years paid more attention to the daily lives, beliefs, mental states, and thinking of ordinary people in the past, so as to offer more diverse and multidimensional historical perspectives. Perhaps because of lingering doubts as to the reliability or even historical veracity of the sources, rumor-type expressions have yet to be accorded adequate attention or sufficiently made use of in historical research. There are even contemporary historians who believe that traditional historical texts included such rumor-type expressions for the purpose of "propagating mysticism."[1] "In order to propagate the notions of karmic retribution, the Mandate of Heaven, and the

[1] Bai Shouyi (1994), pp.952–953.

divine right to rule, [traditional historical texts] included copious supernatural and strange legends."[2]

The format of these traditional historical texts reflected the general overview and investigative angles of historians when they were constructing their historical narratives, and the individual weightage they gave to the people, culture, society, and natural phenomena they wrote about, as well as the interactions between them (what Sima Qian referred to as "changes from the past to the present" and "the relationship between Heaven and Man"). Since Sima Qian and Ban Gu, the complete formats of biographic-type histories not only featured narratives of people and events, as well as chronological lists of events, in annals, biographies, tables, and histories of hereditary houses, they also included treatises of different categories that recorded the developments of various institutions (such as rituals and political institutions), literature, and branches of knowledge (such as astronomy, the Five Agents, calendars, economic activities, and human geography). Not only did they have the quality of monographic histories, they were also important tools for historians to "understand the changes from the past to the present" and "study the relationship between Heaven and Man." The format of the ten treatises in *History of the Former Han* was especially lauded by future historians and became the model on which subsequent official histories were based. In *History of the Former Han*, the "Treatise on the Five Agents" contained copious rumor-type expressions such as talismanic writings, *chen* prophecies and apocrypha, unverifiable talk, portentous talk, prophetic rhymes, and the like. Many of the historical sources cited in this book are found in "Treatise on the Five Agents." However, the scholarship, ideologies, and historical value of "Treatise on the Five Agents" have long been criticized and questioned by commentators and historians of historiography.

In an expressly written chapter in his *Generality of Historiography*, Liu Zhiji (661–721), a traditional commentator of history, criticized "Treatise on the Five Agents" in *History of the Former Han* for being "disorganized and cumbersome" and "bizarre in its reasoning."[3] When he was writing *Comprehensive Institutions*, Du You (735–812) "removed the contents that contained the Five Agents theory, believing that 'things that did not fall under state rituals, laws, and institutions should not be recorded and be discarded as useless' (Li Han's preface to *Comprehensive Institutions*)."[4] When Zheng Qiao (1104–1162) was writing "Short Treatise on Disasters and Signs" in his *Comprehensive History*, he "only recorded actual events, removing the theory

[2] Song Yanshen (1992), p.113.
[3] *Generality of Historiography: General Expositions*, *juan* 19, p.533.
[4] Zou Xianjun (1989), p.309.

of the Five Agents and events corresponding to them, in order to put an end to its evil."[5]

Contemporary historians criticized the three treatises on astronomy, auguries, and the Five Agents in Shen Yue's *History of Song* for using twelve *juan* of texts to "collect a comprehensive mystic record of physiognomy, astrology, aeromancy, the *Yin* and the *Yang*, strange occurrences, talismanic writings, *chen* prophecies and apocrypha, Buddhist prophecies, and so on, whose overall aim was merely an attempt to prove the divine right of emperors and their inevitable destiny in receiving the Mandate of Heaven."[6]

Other criticisms of traditional historical texts recording rumor-type expressions include their "fabrications and falsehoods," their "propensity to collect strange, false, and trivial events to propagate strange hearsay," and the "irrational" narrative style of "mixing up historical record with strange hearsay and trivialities."[7] In this regard, Liu Zhiji, writing in *Generality of Historiography*, was scathing in his criticism. He believed that while historians should "solicit alternative views and seek myriad discourses," they had to make careful selection of historical sources instead of including all kinds of strange and fantastic occurrences into their histories.[8] Examples of "hearsay" such as "Yu's son Qi being born from rock, Yi Yin's conception at Kongsang, people taking rafts up to the Milky Way, Heng'e stealing medicine and fleeing to the moon," "Yao having eight eyebrows, Kui having one leg; a crow's head turning white and a horse sprouting horns, saving Prince Dan of the State of Yan from harm; barking dogs and clucking chickens following Liu An's ascent to the sky" ... all these were "unverifiable talk that were farfetched and highly dubious rumors." "By not discerning the proper from the improper, there was a profusion of weeds." As for "Ji Kang's *Biographies of Exalted Gentlemen*, which collected fables from the seven states; Xuan Yan's *Annals of Emperors*, which collected *chen* prophecies and apocrypha attached to the Six Classics"; Fan Ye's *History of the Later Han*, which recorded "Wang Qiao's shoes turning into wild ducks, originally from *Comprehensive Meaning of Customs and Habits*, and the talking goats in the story of Zuo Ci, originally collected in *The Master Who Embraces Simplicity*" ... these were "errors made in citations from texts."[9]

Liu Zhiji's criticisms of the "irrational" narrative tendencies in historical texts were expressed as historians not being rigorous in their collection and selection of historical sources, as well as their mystical interpretations of the

[5] *Comprehensive History: Twenty Treatises*, "Preface to Short Treatise on Disasters and Signs," p.1905.
[6] Bai Shouyi (1994), p.952. [7] *Ibid.*, pp.965–967. [8] Chen Guangchong (1984), p.40.
[9] *Generality of Historiography: General Expositions*, *juan* 5, "Selection and Writing," pp.115–118.

narratives. If Liu Zhiji's criteria for collection and selection were to be strictly adhered to, rumor-like expressions would be completely erased from historical narratives, and this book would not have been possible.

In his study of the Bible and the language of myth and literature, Canadian scholar Northrop Frye identified four major language modes in verbal communication: descriptive, dialectical (conceptual), rhetorical (figurative), and poetic or imaginative. Each mode has its function, strength, and limits. It seemed to be that descriptive language was the most appropriate, basic, and objective language type in transmitting historical information and preserving historical truths; while vague, ambiguous, metaphoric, or imaginative forms of expression would damage the reliability, veracity, and clarity of the information.

Frye argued that first, metaphoric and imaginative forms of linguistic expression were in fact the predecessors of all forms of expressions (including descriptive, rhetoric, etc.). In the earliest times, "real" historical information was expressed and transmitted through metaphoric and mythical language.

Second, the line between literary and historical narratives was not clear cut for people during the Middle Ages and earlier. Neither were the lines between myths, legends, and history.

Third, what does "historical truth" actually mean? All texts have their own specific contexts. In all literary or historical writing, their writers' knowledge of "history" would be influenced by the historical conditions specific to space and time (including society, politics, ideology, official versions of events, the people's versions, etc.). Historical truth cannot be divorced from historical context. To understand the historical context, one must understand the popular attitudes, beliefs, and thinking in both the official and people's versions of the historical context. Myths and legends are often important historical materials for the understanding of popular attitudes. In this respect, myths and legends can be considered reliable and truthful historical records.

Fourth, historical materials like myths and legends often contain erroneous or misleading information, such as dates, names, events, and other historical details. However, the details are not as important as the worldviews, beliefs, values, and the focus of attention these historical materials reveal. Myths and legends did not set out to falsify history, but to provide interpretations using essentially true symbols that were appropriate to the context of their time.[10]

If we replace the abovementioned "myths" and "legends" with "rumor-type expressions," and link them up with the context of the *Yinyang* and Five Agents theories that were prevalent in the early imperial period, we would then be able to understand the unique historical value inherent in these types of expressions and information. For example, an important historiographical

[10] Frye (1990), pp.5–6, 33, 98, 119.

category in the period between the late Eastern Han Dynasty and the Northern and Southern dynasties was "archaic history." In the thirteen categories of historical texts listed in "Treatises on Books" in *History of Sui*, archaic history was second only to official history. Famous books on archaic history included Qiao Zhou's *Verifications of Archaic History*, Xu Zheng's *Historical Records of the Three Sovereigns and the Five Emperors*, and Huangfu Mi's (215–282) *Genealogical Annals of the Emperors and Kings*.[11] According to Liu Jie, "Qiao Zhou's *Verifications of Archaic History* was based on old writings to rectify what Sima Qian had left out. Actually, what Sima Qian had left out were things that 'noble and learned gentlemen found hard to speak of.'"[12] What "noble and learned gentlemen found hard to speak of" referred to ancient myths and legends that had been around since pre-Qin times, which were later absorbed by apocryphal-prophetic discourse and incorporated into narratives of archaic history.

Historical Records of the Three Sovereigns and the Five Emperors began with Pangu's creation of Heaven and Earth, while *Genealogical Annals of the Emperors and Kings* provided lineages of emperors and kings, dates, and events, covering the period between the Three Sovereigns and the Han and Wei dynasties. Both books pushed back the period covered by archaic history by a great many years. The stories of the creation of the universe, the Three (Heavenly, Earthly, and Human) Sovereign Divinities, the nine-headed Human Sovereign Divinity, the names, lives, and miracles of ancient emperors and kings, and so on originated from the myths of archaic history in apocryphal writings. In fact, there are almost no written records of the history before the Xia, Shang, and Zhou dynasties, apart from archaeological artifacts. Even works such as *Commentary of Zuo* and *The Grand Scribe's Records*, considered rigorous by "noble and learned gentlemen," contained records of archaic history that were vague and unverifiable. What was more significant was that after centuries of reverence and instruction by official academic organizations and famous classicists, this mythologized archaic history had become indisputable "common knowledge" among classicists and historians of the time; they were considered "real history." From a modern-day perspective, the "archaic history" narrated by these two books could hardly be considered historical, but they contain many ancient myths and legends. "Myths and legends often contain a shadow of historical truth, which reflects

[11] Song Yanshen (1992), p.88. These three books are no longer extant, with fragments cited in other books. The compilation of fragments of *Genealogical Annals of the Emperors and Kings* is quite extensive, but most of the contents of the other two books are lost. The lengthy "ancient history" written according to the Theory of the Rise and Fall of the Five Powers in "Treatise on Auguries" in *History of Song* is quite similar to the compilation of fragments of *Genealogical Annals of the Emperors and Kings*.

[12] Liu Jie (1982), pp.71–72.

an outline and fragment of history." They have unique historical value by serving as corroborative sources in the study of prehistoric society.[13]

Written records gradually proliferated after the Xia, Shang, and Zhou dynasties, but naturally, it was impossible to record everything. The acquisition, selection, and verification of historical sources are essential features of a historian's work. The standard for selection and verification is subjective; it also involves the historian's own talent, knowledge, and insight, as well as the historical styles and outlooks of the period. If one believes that historical narratives must be rooted in realism and rationalism, and be secular and tangible – what Zheng Qiao referred to as "the record of actual occurrences" – then strange hearsay, gods and spirits, talismans and prophecies, unverifiable and portentous talk should form no part of history. However, if one believes that historical narratives should "highlight political or ethical meaning" and "articulate great virtues and reveal the obscure to enlighten princes," then even the likes of Liu Zhiji, who vilified historical styles that were based on "fabrications and falsehoods," would not "totally object to including *chen* prophecies and apocrypha, and how they were borne out by real events, in historical texts."[14] Talismans and prophecies, in an oblique way, still had to bear the moral responsibility, which Han-era Confucian scholars had imposed on them, of explaining contemporary politics with punitive disasters sent from Heaven. Besides, what is considered supernatural and bizarre observations and records in the present day might have been thought of as historical truths and important by traditional historians, thus deserving a place in the history books.[15] Therefore, when Chang Qu wrote *Record of States South of Mount Hua*, he often cited apocryphal books in his account of the past and present of the Ba-Shu region.[16] Likewise, when Li Daoyuan annotated *Water Classic*, he "cited over four hundred ancient books, as well as various gravestone inscriptions and ancient legends," and "recorded popular songs and rhymes, adages, local dialects, and legends, making it an excellent source for the study of society of the time. It also preserved many lost books and histories of antiquity."[17] Apart from recording events and institutions, the "absurd fabrication" and mystical stories contained in these historical narratives also describe the attitudes, beliefs, thoughts, and lifestyles of individuals within a particular historical context, as well as the social and cultural milieu at the time. These records reveal a kind of alternative "historical truths" for present-day cultural, social, intellectual, and religious historians.

13 Song Yanshen (1992), pp.88–89.
14 Peng Ya-Ling (1993), pp.186–188.
15 Lu Yao-Tung (1998), p.56.
16 *Record of States South of Mount Hua: A Collated, Illustrated, and Annotated Edition*, pp.1–2, 113.
17 Song Yanshen (1992), pp.91–92.

Another reservation historians have about rumor-type expressions is that most of them had been transmitted by word of mouth and had constantly evolved before they were finally recorded, edited, and rendered as written texts by official historians. By then, they might have changed so much that they were totally different from their original form. For example, popular songs and rhymes were originally transmitted orally, but today we can only encounter them through extant texts. What should have been rich and colorful songs that covered multiple aspects of social and cultural life were selected, edited, and embellished by historians through the ages, becoming verses that were related to political life and events, or interpreted as related to certain political figures, events, or sociopolitical phenomena. Can these songs and rhymes that exist as written texts truly reflect the real voices of the people? Can they truly reflect actual historical truths? According to Tian Ying, "in and of themselves, children's songs emphasize fun and rhyme, which are often more important than meaning. Therefore, future generations would find it difficult to understand them. For the same reason, they also lend themselves to forced and spurious interpretations."[18] He meant that the politicizing of songs and rhymes by historians had distorted their original meanings and intentions. Zhou Zuoren averred that ancient children's songs belonged to the same school as treatises on the Five Agents. They were "originally written by adults" to "tie in with related historical facts, and therefore their relevance to historical events enabled their transmission to the present day."[19] Kushida Hisaharu believed that songs and rhymes from the Han Periods were written by intellectuals who falsely attributed their works to commoners and children. The contents of the songs expressed the political views of members of the Han intellectual elite.[20]

Extant popular songs and rhymes that were recorded had indeed been edited and their language embellished by historians and the literati through the ages. Works that historical texts identified as popular rhymes and children's songs might have been created by commoners, children, or even literati-officials. Naturally, it is difficult for us in the present day to confirm the identities of the original creators of these songs and rhymes. It is impossible to recreate the original milieu within which these songs existed. When we consider the level of acceptance and comprehension of most people, however, we can tell whether a song was popular among the masses or the intellectual elite, whether it represented the people's voice or the non-mainstream views of the literati, by

[18] Tian Ying (1959), p.73. At the same time, however, he also believed that ancient songs and rhymes were "the voice of the people." (p.81)

[19] Zhou Zuoren, "A Study of Children's Songs," cited in Kushida Hisaharu (1999), p.5

[20] In the Introduction to his famous *The Crowd: A Study of the Popular Mind*, Gustave Le Bon wrote: "The creators and leaders of civilizations have historically been the small minority of intellectual aristocrats, not the masses. The masses have only been a powerful destructive force." (p.5) Kushida Hisaharu's argument echoes Gustave Le Bon's.

examining its linguistic style and theme. Songs that were popular among ordinary people relied on oral transmission by commoners and children. Their words had to be simple and catchy and their themes closely tied to the everyday lives of the people. Even if they had been embellished by historians, the styles of these songs can still be discerned. Some of the extant songs and rhymes from the early imperial period have lively lyrics, vivid imagery, and real emotions. No matter who had written them, it would have been the ordinary folks who enjoyed and disseminated them. As for the songs written in literary language and in an affected style, even if historians had identified them as popular songs and rhymes, they could never have been liked or transmitted by ordinary folk. In the study of disseminated talk, unverifiable talk, portentous talk, rhymes, *chen* prophecies, prophetic rhymes, myths, and legends, we should assiduously examine and verify the historical sources.

The Origins of Rumors: Floating and Rootless, Flowing without Pause

Apart from certain portentous talk with specific names whose originators could be identified with certainty, most rumor-type expressions of the early imperial period, like modern-day rumors, were like rivers without sources, trees without roots: it was impossible to pinpoint their beginnings. Their creators were often anonymous, and in the process of their verbal transmission, their wordings could end up completely different from the original.[21]

"Conduct of the Scholar" in *Book of Rites* commended the scholar for his inimitable character, for having no occasion to regret what he had done in the past, nor making preparations for what might come to him in the future, for not repeating any error of speech, nor pursuing the source of any disseminated talk against him. One did not pursue the source of disseminated talk because it was like ripples on water, the origin of which was hard to locate. Why was it hard to locate? Because it was talk disseminated by the people. In his *Collected Commentaries on the Book of Odes*, Zhu Xi defined the word *liuyan* ("disseminated talk") in "Dang" in the Greater Odes of the Kingdoms section as "floating and rootless information." The First Emperor of the Qin Dynasty was relentlessly trying to locate the author of the portentous talk: "after the First Emperor dies, his territory will be divided"; Wang Mang made multiple arrests to find out who had started the unverifiable talk of a yellow dragon

[21] Xu Hualong (1990), citing George Lyman Kittredge in Francis James Child's *The English and Scottish Popular Ballads*: it is very seldom, or even impossible, that a definite date could be pinned on the creation of a folk ballad. After the song had been created by its originator, it was immediately passed on to the people, who transmitted it verbally. By then, it was no longer controlled by its originator. (pp.31–32) The creation process of other rumor-type expressions was similar to that of folk ballads.

falling and dying. Both failed. Early Confucians were therefore wise in advising one not to pursue the source of any disseminated talk.

Another characteristic of rumor-like expressions was their volatility and openness to change. The original meaning of the *liu* in *liuyan* was the flow and spread of water, while the *e* in *eyan* (unverifiable talk) also meant movement and change. It was not without reason that the ancient Chinese chose the words *liu* and *e* to describe these verbally transmitted rumor-like expressions that had not been verified. Rumor-like expressions in the early imperial period did have a volatile nature, characterized by movement, change, and their ability to spread.[22] In the course of their "long-distance journey" of verbal transmission, they underwent creation and embellishment by the people who disseminated them. In this sense, whether or not these rumors had specific names, their creators could not be any specific entity or group. It was impossible – and unnecessary – to trace their sources.

Jean-Noël Kapferer wrote that the origin of rumors was unimportant. Even if a person did start a rumor, the foundation of the rumor is still other people: those who heard and then spread the rumor. Trying to locate the origin of a rumor is to simplify the phenomenon of rumors to an issue that is purely personal, totally disconnected from the group, and morbid.[23] His views are in agreement with our observations of rumor-like expressions in the early imperial period.

Why Did Rumors Start and Thrive?

It is neither necessary nor possible to trace the source of rumor-type expressions. It is necessary, however, when one studies the social and political history of the early Chinese imperial period, to ask the following questions: Why did rumors start? Why did they thrive?

We can surmise that countless rumor-type expressions emerged in the several centuries of the early imperial period, and what we encounter today are but a tiny portion of that number, the few that happened to be selected and recorded by historians of that era and subsequently preserved for posterity. Most of the extant disseminated talk, unverifiable talk, portentous talk, rhymes, *chen* prophecies, and so on occurred and spread during the following periods: the reigns of Emperors Cheng, Ai, and Ping of the Western Han Dynasty; the reigns of Emperors Huan and Ling of the Eastern Han Dynasty; the period between the two Han dynasties; and the transition from the Eastern Han to Wei Dynasty. Perhaps these chaotic times were conducive to the occurrence and

[22] According to studies in modern psychology and sociology, rumors also have the same features and volatility.

[23] Kapferer (1991), p.25.

spread of rumor-type expressions. Or perhaps historians deliberately recorded more of such rumor-type expressions to bolster their negative judgments of the politics of these periods. Whatever it was, from a general psychological and sociological perspective, these historical circumstances were fertile ground for the proliferation of rumors.

For instance, whenever there were serious imbalances in the Western Han Dynasty's power structure,[24] or when the political conflicts in the late Eastern Han Dynasty became intense, criticisms and disseminated talk would suddenly proliferate both at court and among the people. Strange occurrences in nature and social crises were also conducive to the emergence of unverifiable talk. During the transition from the reign of Emperor Yuan to Emperor Cheng of the Western Han Dynasty, the eunuchs, affinal relatives of Emperors, and court officials fought one another. There was constant talk of Imperial Heirs-Apparent being replaced, floods and droughts afflicted various parts of the empire, and the people's lives were severely disrupted. Unverifiable talk was rife during that period. When social and political order was impaired, portentous talk that was subversive and mutinous readily surfaced. Most critical folk rhymes targeted policy blunders and government corruption, and the transitions from the reign of Emperor Yuan to Emperor Cheng, from Western Han to Eastern Han, and the final years of the Eastern Han were peak periods of folk rhymes' propagation. *Chen* prophecies, prophetic rhymes, and political myths often appeared during times of political instability and dynastic change.

Modern research finds that whenever conflicts, contradictions, unrest, or crises appear in society, the rumor mill would be especially active.[25] Times like these bring about feelings of insecurity, anxiety, fear, helplessness, and anger, which people desperately need to express and rationalize. In such a milieu, people "discover" explanations for the current state of affairs that are "rational," and prophecies that could satisfy "mass expectations" and "rational imaginations." Information provided by official channels is often regarded as incomplete, unclear, even deliberately obfuscating the truth, and thus unable to satisfy the people's psychological needs.[26] And so, rumor-type expressions emerge and spread far and wide. This is a universal human response, demonstrable among people of all nationalities throughout history.

24 For example, when Huo Guang, Wang Feng, and Wang Mang arrogated political power to themselves; when Dong Xian was excessively rewarded with imperial favor; when the positions of imperial heirs were threatened.

25 Allport and Postman (1965), pp.36–37; Knopf (1975), p.12.

26 Shibutani (1966), pp.36, 46, 49, 56.

Forms of Expression, Propagation, and Structure of Rumors

Forms of Expression of Rumors

Rumor-type expressions in the early imperial period included disseminated talk, unverifiable talk, portentous talk, folk rhymes, *chen* prophecies, prophetic rhymes, political myths, folk legends, and so on.[27]

In the early imperial period, disseminated talk referred to speech that was widely disseminated among the people, even though its origins were hard to trace and its veracity impossible to prove. Such talk criticized and commented on contemporaneous political and other issues that concerned the public, or provided unofficial or non-mainstream explanations for them. As for whether the disseminated information was true, whether the criticism was justified, whether it should be deemed slander, public criticism, or public opinion, one has to consider the actual historical context and the standpoint and interests of the people involved.

Speech that was described as "unverifiable talk" in Han-era historical texts often resembled disseminated talk. The difference was that disseminated talk referred to speech that was spread both at court and among the people, whereas unverifiable talk usually described speech, which at times had a hint of the macabre, that was propagated among the common people. Both disseminated talk and unverifiable talk were suited for spreading "things heard through the grapevine," exchanging doubts and dissatisfaction over uncertain situations, and providing explanations for current events that differed from official versions.

In the legal discourse of the early imperial period, portentous talk included heresies that were criminal because they were seditious and posed a threat to rulers.[28] In political discourse, portentous talk was inauspicious and had the capacity to delude the masses. It was inauspicious because it might have had something to do with supernatural or mysterious phenomena, but most often it was considered inauspicious because it was seen as "abnormal speech" or even "nonsensical talk." It often contained viewpoints that the authorities abhorred and sought to eradicate. As for the capacity to delude the masses, it was not exclusive to portentous talk; all rumor-type expressions had this ability.

Rhymes were different from other rumor-type expressions in that they were catchy and easy to remember, thus facilitating their spread among less

[27] If rumors were defined according to the veracity of their content or the motive of their propagation, then slander and lies could also be counted as rumor-type expressions. However, this book defines rumors based on the scope of propagation and their effect on the public. Talk that was slanders and lies should be explored elsewhere.

[28] Actually, disseminated talk, unverifiable talk, rhymes, *chen* prophecies, etc. often featured this characteristic as well.

educated groups such as commoners and children. Another difference was that they were not denigrated in mainstream political thought during the early imperial period; in fact, they were considered natural expressions of the people's will and could be openly cited in respectable situations. The words used in rhymes were vivid, full of imagery, and sharp. In addition to transmitting information and commenting on politics, rhymes facilitated the expression of strong emotions such as sarcasm and anger, and they were better for cursing and ranting.

Speech information like disseminated talk, unverifiable talk, portentous talk, and rhymes usually had shorter periods of validity. If they survived for longer periods of time, and the desires they expressed came true,[29] or if their vague and abstract words provided sufficient space for their recipients' imagination to "decipher" the information from Heaven that they had been awaiting, then such speech would be considered *chen* prophecies and prophetic rhymes.

Rumor-type expressions that survived for even longer periods of time, and that had additional details added in retellings, might eventually develop into officially sanctioned political myths or popular legends.

The Spread and Structure of Rumors

Rumor-type expressions spread mainly through non-official channels. The disseminated talk, unverifiable talk, and portentous talk of the early imperial period, for example, were spread mostly among individuals in their private conversations. As Du Yannian was recorded as saying: "The masses will holler and the commoners will whisper, and *liuyan* will be disseminated in all directions."[30] Many rumormongers claimed that they had received their information as "disseminated talk they had heard on the roads." They could have been speaking the truth, or they might have wanted to conceal their sources.

When the rumors were of great public interest or attracted much attention among the people, non-official channels of information would emerge from the shadows with much fanfare. For example, the non-official dissemination of information during the episode of Passing Edict Tokens of the Queen Mother of the West, which occurred during the reign of Emperor Ai of the Western Han Dynasty, was vividly described "Treatise on the Five Agents" in *History of the Former Han*. When news related to the tokens was received, it radiated out from multiple points, gathering more and more disseminators as it spread. "These people let their hair down and went barefoot, broke through passes in the night, scaled walls to enter buildings. Some dashed about in carriages, or

[29] Some *chen* prophecies could survive for as long as years, decades, or even centuries, reappearing at different times and locations in history.

[30] *History of the Former Han, juan* 60, "Biography of Du Yannian," p.2663.

made use of the stage service along postal routes." They spread the news as they hurried along. "They met and congregated on the roads, swelling their numbers to several thousands."[31] Of course, most disseminated talk and unverifiable talk were not spread in such a dramatic fashion. However, given the communications technology of the time, the ways through which rumors circulated were quite diverse, and the speed with which they spread was phenomenal. In his annotations of "Book of Wei: Biography of Guanqiu Jian" in *Records of the Three Kingdoms*, Pei Songzhi cited the letter from Wen Qin to Guo Huai: "Our troops were garrisoned at Xiang. As commander of a partial army, your subordinate was leading a quick march straight to the capital on the sixteenth day of the leap month. However, rumors of our attack arrived even before we did. Guanqiu [Jian] was not aware of it and even blames your subordinate for the failure of this military action. Our armies were subsequently decimated."[32] This incident shows us that rumors traveled faster than a fast-approaching army. The speed of oral transmissions and their destructive capabilities were quite apparent.

The high efficiency of information transmission via unofficial channels might have something to do with the collective anxiety of a population living in a surfeit of strange occurrences or sociopolitical crises. Within such a context, the people's sense of insecurity and fear would be magnified multiple times. Their demand for rumor-type information would greatly increase, as would their notion of group dependence. There were several examples of this: "When the residents of the imperial capital spoke fearful words to one another for no reason, and said that a great flood was imminent, the people ran and trampled on one another. The old and the weak cried out";[33] "at the time there was unverifiable talk in the capital that rebels were approaching from the east. The people were fleeing and frightening one another by spreading the news";[34] "there was unverifiable talk among the people that all natives of Liangzhou would be executed, which spread and caused fear and disturbance."[35] Speaking "fearful words to one another," "fleeing and frightening one another by spreading the news," and "spread[ing] and caus[ing] fear and disturbance" vividly depicted the interactive processes of people informing, stimulating, and comforting one another in the course of transmitting rumors.

Although disseminated talk, unverifiable talk, and portentous talk were mainly transmitted orally, their dissemination in written form had already appeared in the Western Han Dynasty, when "lowly persons" caused

31 *History of the Former Han, juan* 27 *xia zhi shang*, "Treatise on the Five Agents, Part IV," p.1476.
32 *Records of the Three Kingdoms, juan* 28, p.766.
33 *History of the Former Han, juan* 82, "Biography of Wang Shang," p.3370.
34 *History of the Later Han, juan* 24, "Biography of Ma Yan," p.861.
35 *History of the Later Han, juan* 66, "Biography of Wang Yun," p.2176.

"disseminated talk to be propagated and written words to fly, which results in much clamoring among the people."[36] In the Eastern Han Dynasty, Zhang Jiao and others spread the unverifiable talk that "the Blue Sky is dead; the Yellow Sky will stand. In the Jiazi year, great fortune comes to the land." His followers wrote the word "*jiazi*" with white earth on gates of offices in the capital and government buildings in the inspection regions and commanderies.[37] There were also cases when high-level political conflicts broke out into the open, official channels like "distributing written notices in the commanderies and kingdoms" were employed to spread rumors and attack political foes.[38]

The spontaneous singing of songs was a part of life for people in the early imperial period. From famous individuals like Xiang Yu and Liu Bang, to ordinary people at the grassroots level, the spontaneous singing and dancing were quite common. During the episode of Passing Edict Tokens of the Queen Mother of the West, people gathered in "streets and alleys in their thousands. They set up gaming facilities and worshipped the Queen Mother of the West with song and dance" in the capital, as well as in the commanderies and kingdoms. The scenes of the massive crowds in the streets were incredible.[39] For this reason, songs and rhymes and prophetic rhymes were often able to spread across larger areas. The "Song of Pingcheng," which came about when Han troops were trapped in Pingcheng by the Xiongnu in the early years of Emperor Gaozu's reign, was first sung by soldiers, but "all under Heaven sang it" later on. The song continued to evoke emotions among the people even by the reign of Emperor Wu. Songs and rhymes that reflected the feelings of the people were sung by children and the people on the streets and roads, in their neighborhoods, and in Chang'an.

Similar to unverifiable talk, disseminated talk, portentous talk, and rhymes, the early spread of *chen* prophecies was oral in form, with the prophecies taking definite shape in the course of their interpersonal transmissions. It was recorded in "The Hereditary House of Chen She" in *The Grand Scribe's Records* that Chen Sheng ordered one of his men to mimic the howl of a fox, crying out the words: "The Great Chu will rise up, and Chen Sheng will

36 *History of the Former Han, juan* 36, "Biography of Liu Xiang," p.1945.

37 *History of the Later Han, juan* 71, "Biography of Huangfu Song," p.2299.

38 *History of the Former Han, juan* 84, "Biography of Zhai Yi," p.3426. When Emperor Wu of the Western Han Dynasty passed away, his youngest son, Liu Fuling, was proclaimed the new Emperor. The latter's elder brother, Liu Dan, the King of Yan, refused to acknowledge the fact and "claimed that the young Emperor was not Emperor Wu's son, and that not all the senior officials at court supported him. Thus, all under Heaven should unite together to attack him. Liu Dan sent his men to distribute these writings to the various commanderies and kingdoms in order to unsettle the people." (*History of the Former Han, juan* 63, "Biography of Liu Dan, King Ci of Yan," p.2753) This method was similar to Zhai Yi's.

39 *History of the Former Han, juan* 27 *xia zhi shang*, "Treatise on the Five Agents, Part IV," p.1476.

rule!" The border guards who were traveling with him became "frightened by these cries in the night. The following morning, they talked among themselves and pointed Chen Sheng out to one another."[40] The brief record vividly describes the transmission of this *chen* prophecy and the way it had taken shape. Another example was the *chen* prophecy "A Son of Heaven air current will be present in the south and the east" that originated with aeromancers. In the decades straddling the Qin and Western Han dynasties, this particular *chen* prophecy spread within the government and among the people, and its language and content underwent multiple changes in the course of its dissemination to fit in with different historical contexts.

After the middle of the Western Han Dynasty, collections of written *chen* prophecies became important conduits of their propagation. Gan Zhongke recruited large numbers of students and taught them the *chen* prophecies collected in *Calendar of the Heavenly Official* and *Scripture of Great Peace with the Embodiment of the Origin*; Governor of Weicheng Li Yan ordered his clerks to copy the 100,000-character *chen* prophecy book compiled by the diviner Wang Kuang for distribution. In the late Western Han Dynasty and the early Eastern Han, there was a large number of popular apocryphal-prophetic texts. Liu Xiu's former fellow student Qiang Hua traveled from within the Hangu Pass to present Liu Xiu with a copy of *The Token of Red Secret* and urged him to proclaim himself Emperor. *The Token of the Red Secret* was an anthology of written *chen* prophecies.

Some *chen* prophecies were presented as images and symbols formed in nature, for example, unusual physical characteristics on a person (such as the lines on their palms or marks on their skin), insect-nibbled leaves that resembled words, and pictorial patterns on rocks. Like coded *chen* prophecies that were transmitted in written form, these mysterious images in nature had to be "decoded" before or after events. Different stances, perspectives, and hopes would produce different interpretations. In the course of their widespread propagation, these decoded versions also had to compete with one another and gain support. Only after multiple rounds of attrition would an eventual winner emerge.

Another way *chen* prophecies were spread was through esoteric transmission between individuals. Examples include the Xin Dynasty Taoist priest Ximen Junhui privately telling General of the Guards Wang She that the name of Preceptor of State Liu Xiu (Liu Xin) fulfilled the *chen* prophecy and would become Emperor; the Eastern Han *fangshi* Shan Yang telling Imperial Household Grandee Qiao Xuan that the Kingdom of Wei would rise, and "Yin Deng, a person from the Wei Commandery, recorded these words in

[40] *The Grand Scribe's Records*, *juan* 48, p.1950.

secret";[41] and Master of apocryphal-prophecies Dong Fu telling Liu Yan in private that "the capital shall be in chaos, and there is a Son of Heaven air current in the constellation that corresponds to the Yizhou Region."[42] Du Qiong, a master of apocryphal-prophecies in the Shu Region, refused to teach his sons apocryphal-prophetic learning because "one must work hard day and night before one could know it well. However, one fears of revealing Heaven's secrets, so it is better not to know it."[43] This was because the content of *chen* prophecies often involved the legitimacy of imperial authority, dynastic change, and the rise and fall of important figures, which meant they were politically sensitive. Their open propagation would have serious political consequences and endanger one's life.

The political myths that were popular during the early imperial period were either post-event fabrications or had begun as rumors. They were usually started by the people involved, their family members, or persons of interest, before being spread and constructed through unofficial channels. These stories had become rich and complete in detail in the process of formation, and what they eventually became depended on the fortunes of their characters. Winners of power struggles had their stories officially and popularly endorsed, entering dynastic lore and history books and becoming political myths. Losers sometimes had their stories recorded in history books and disseminated among the people, but they were dismissed as portentous talk or stories that embarrassed their protagonists.

In the late Eastern Han Dynasty, the auspicious sign of the yellow dragon in Ba Commandery originated on a hot day when some people wanted to bathe in a pond. Seeing that the pond was muddy, "they joked to one another that 'there is a yellow dragon in the pond.' The story eventually spread among the people."[44] A joke made by ordinary people reached the commandery office and eventually found its way to the imperial court. It became a fully formed piece of unverifiable talk. The genesis of many cults and beliefs of the early imperial period were misunderstandings, misinformation, and jokes. After word spread that prayers for health and happiness were answered, folk beliefs and cults emerged, for example, the Lord of the Plum and the Lord of the Dried. Unlike disseminated talk, unverifiable talk, portentous talk, and *chen* prophecies, popular jokes, folk sayings, or misunderstandings might not be related to current affairs and politics but were simply aspects of everyday

[41] *History of the Later Han, juan* 82 *xia*, "Biographies of Alchemists, Part II: Biography of Shan Yang," p.2733.
[42] *Ibid.*, p.2734.
[43] *Records of the Three Kingdoms, juan* 42, "Book of Shu: Biography of Du Qiong," p.1022.
[44] *History of the Later Han, juan* 17, "Treatise on the Five Agents, Part V," p.3344.

life. However, their transmission and structure were exactly the same as those of rumor-type expressions.

"Misleading the Masses": Consensus-Building during the Spread of Rumors

Rumor-type expressions such as disseminated talk, unverifiable talk, portentous talk, rhymes, *chen* prophecies, and prophetic rhymes that made an impact all had one thing in common: they "misled the masses." This was the key reason why Chinese rulers throughout history worked so hard at clamping down on rumor-type expressions in the political and social life of the state.

Based on the cases recorded in the historical texts of the Qin and Han dynasties, not all rumor-type expressions had gained widespread dissemination among the masses. Some portentous talk was only evident in situations where their impact was minimal, such as memorials to the throne, private letters, and incidents of slander between individuals. Some *chen* prophecies were only privately transmitted in small circles. However, most rumor-type expressions did spread far and wide and had their ability to "mislead the masses" put to the test. The First Emperor of the Qin Dynasty accused scholars of spreading "portentous words to confuse the masses."[45] One of the accusations of treason against Liu An, King of Huainan, was "bewildering the people, betraying his ancestors, and recklessly creating portentous talk."[46] Wang Yu, the son of Wang Mang, was accused of propagating "disseminated talk to agitate the public, which is an offence similar to that of Guan and of Cai."[47] In the late Western Han Dynasty, Zhai Yi and other rebels in Dong Commandery propagated disseminated talk, while bandits in the west misled the people.[48] In the final years of the Xin Dynasty, the Lulin Rebels "falsely disseminated groundless talk to mislead the people."[49] By the middle and late Eastern Han Dynasty, with increased chaos in society and the rise of the nascent Taoist religion, there were many such incidents. The phrase "portentous delusion" was coined to describe the inciting and misleading of the masses with portentous words and portentous arts.[50]

45 *The Grand Scribe's Records, juan* 6, "Basic Annals of The First Emperor of Qin," p.258.
46 *The Grand Scribe's Records, juan* 118, "Memoirs of the Kings of Huainan and Hengshan," p.3094.
47 *History of the Former Han, juan* 99 *shang*, "Biography of Wang Mang, Part I," p.4065.
48 *Ibid.*, p.4089.
49 *History of the Former Han, juan* 99 *xia*, "Biography of Wang Mang, Part III," p.4181.
50 For example, *History of the Later Han, juan* 57, "Biography of Liu Tao": "It came to pass that Zhang Jiao of Julu deceptively used the Great Tao to deceive with masses with portentous delusion." (p.1849)

Rumors that had the power to "mislead the masses," that is, influence their intentions and desires, were those that spread more extensively and were accepted by a greater number of people. Classic examples include the incident of the Passing Edict Tokens of the Queen Mother of the West during the reign of Emperor Ai of the Western Han Dynasty, which saw tens of thousands of people flood the streets; and the rapid spread of the slogan "The Blue Sky is dead; the Yellow Sky will stand" across the entire empire during the late Eastern Han Dynasty. In the second year of the Tianfeng reign period of Wang Mang's Xin Dynasty, unverifiable talk about a yellow dragon that had fallen down and died in the Huangshan Palace spread, attracting tens of thousands who rushed there to see it.[51] During the Eastern Han Dynasty, in the second year of the Xiping reign period, the people of Luoyang "spread the unverifiable rumor that a yellow man sporting a handsome beard and eyebrows was found in the middle of the eastern wall of the Office of the Rapid as Tigers. Tens of thousands went to watch it, and those who served in the Forbidden City all came out, causing the roads to be blocked."[52] Although these two pieces of unverifiable talk were patently false information, they were able to attract and mobilize tens of thousands of people within a short space of time, palpable evidence of their ability to mislead the masses.

According to the classic discourse on the study of rumors, the moment a rumor-type expression is accepted by the public and enters non-official channels of transmission and propagation, its originator (if indeed there is one) will no longer be able to control its growth and transformation. The transmission process is not unidirectional but multidirectional, not passive but active, not closed but open. Every transmitter participates in the creation of its content. Consensus is formed during the transmission process, through interaction, addition, deletion, and embellishment. The political, social, or religious motives in the final form of the rumor, as well as its appeals, expectations, object of criticism, and even form of expression, are collective and do not belong to any individual. The collective responses when Huo Guang attacked his political foes (when the masses hollered, the commoners whispered, and *liuyan* were disseminated in all directions) and during the incident of the Passing Edict Tokens of the Queen Mother of the West were examples of this. The reason why rumors are able to "mislead the masses" is because they are often the true reflections and expressions of the emotions, moods, and expectations of a specific group of people in a specific time and space. One could say that under certain conditions and to a certain extent, rumors reflect public opinion.

The ability of strangely worded unverifiable talk, portentous talk, and *chen* prophecies of the early imperial period to "mislead the masses" had even more

[51] *History of the Former Han*, *juan* 99 *zhong*, "Biography of Wang Mang, Part II," p.4139.

[52] *History of the Later Han*, *zhi* 17, "Treatise on the Five Agents, Part V," p.3346.

to do with their specific historical and cultural contexts. People at that time believed that any abnormal events or strange portents that occurred in the natural and human world were likely to be signs of the intentions of supernatural entities to reward or punish humankind, especially rulers, for their deeds. *Commentary of Zuo: The Fifteenth Year of Duke Xuan* puts it succinctly: "Abnormalities in weather are disasters, phenological anomalies are portents, and improper morals among the people breed chaos. When there is chaos, portents and disasters arise."[53] Therefore, portentous talk was backed up by Heaven's will and supernatural powers. In a society where people firmly believed in *Yinyang* and the Five Agents and that punitive disasters were sent from Heaven, the strange and portentous features of such rumors were in fact the actual proof of their acceptance by the people.

The study of *Yinyang* and the Five Agents during the Han periods promoted the notion of warnings from Heaven, even as it emphasized that portents originated in humankind – when humankind did no wrong, there would be no portents.[54] According to "Treatise on Literature" in *History of the Former Han*, scholars of *Spring and Autumn Annals* defined portents thus: "Portents arise because of Man. When Man loses propriety, portents arise. When Man is faultless, portents cannot emerge on their own." Thus, virtue could triumph over inauspiciousness, and righteousness could overcome hindrances. If rulers shunned the appearance of portents instead of examining themselves, then they were putting the cart before the horse, and naturally, they would be distressed for not being able to defeat the portents.[55]

"Treatise on the Five Agents" in *History of the Former Han* recorded Liu Xiang as saying that the snake that had emerged from the Palace of the Brooks in the summer of the sixteenth year of Duke Wen, as documented in *Commentary of Zuo*, was a Serpentine Portent, which foretold that the state would be afflicted by troubles pertaining to women, and that Duke Wen's mother would die. The fall came and Duke Wen's mother did die. Incensed, the Duke tore down the Terrace of the Brooks. However, "portents appear because of people's deeds; their appearances are not harmful in themselves." Instead of righting his ways and treating the snake's punishment with respect, he committed acts of impropriety. The result was the compounding of his sins, resulting in even more disasters.[56]

[53] *Commentary of Zuo on the Spring and Autumn Annals: Annotations*, p.763.

[54] *Commentary of Zuo: The Fourteenth Year of Duke Zhuang*: "Portents arise because of Man. When Man is faultless, portents cannot emerge on their own; when Man abandons the right path, portents arise. This is the reason portents exist." (*Commentary of Zuo on the Spring and Autumn Annals: Annotations*, p.197)

[55] *History of the Former Han, juan* 30, p.1773.

[56] *History of the Former Han, juan* 27 *xia zhi shang*, "Treatise on the Five Agents, Part IV," p.1468.

In the twelfth month of the second year of the Yanguang reign period (123) of Emperor An of the Eastern Han Dynasty, the capital, as well as various commanderies and kingdoms, was hit by earthquakes. Grand Commandant Yang Zhen took the opportunity to present a memorial to the throne, attacking the eunuchs: "Your Majesty's servant heard it from my teacher that 'the Earth is the essence of the *Yin* element; it should uphold the *Yang* element smoothly and steadily.' It quakes now because of an overabundance of *Yin* element." He added: "This is the sign of the seizing and arrogating of power by palace servants." "*Book of Documents* says: 'Usurpation is symbolized by constant sunshine. There should be no such thing as a minister conferring dignities or rewards, displaying the terrors of majesty, or receiving the revenues.' May Your Majesty strive toward the virtue of strength and abandon the arrogant ministers so as to stem the flow of portentous talk."[57] In other words, if humankind did no wrong and the rulers repented, portentous talk would cease to have the chance of misleading the masses.

Concepts in traditional Chinese political thought included "what the people desire, Heaven will comply with";[58] "Heaven sees as my people see; Heaven hears as my people hear";[59] and "the reason why policies can be implemented is because they are in line with the people's will; the reason why policies are ineffective is because they are against the people's will."[60] The Han-period scholars were merely interpreting, within the framework of the Great Plan Theory of the Five Agents, the theoretical basis of rumor-type expressions such as portentous talk reflecting the people's will: when the ruler's orders went against the people's will, when he was harsh and cruel, and his ministers held their peace for fear of punishment, the pent up resentment would be released in the form of songs and rhymes, becoming portentous poetry. When the political situation and society were in the midst of crises or disasters, there would be an intense psychological need for such rumors. This was the reason for the copious quantities and widespread dissemination of unverifiable talk, portentous talk, and *chen* prophecies in the periods of transition from the Western Han to the Eastern Han, and in the mid- and late Eastern Han. This was the reason for successive large-scale armed rebellions led by "portentous bandits" and "portentous warlocks" who used portentous talk as their rallying cry.

According to a theory of communications studies, "communications cannot directly produce social benefit; it must first act on the psychology of the

[57] *History of the Later Han, juan* 54, "Biography of Yang Zhen," p.1765.

[58] *Annotations and Explanations of the Thirteen Classics: Book of Documents, juan* 11, "Great Declaration, Part I," p.181.

[59] *Annotations and Explanations of the Thirteen Classics: Book of Documents, juan* 11, "Great Declaration, Part II," p.181.

[60] *Guan Zi: Annotations and Interpretations, shang ce*, "Shepherding the People, Part I," p.1.

receiver, using the receiver's psychology as a medium to transform, before demonstrating its social function."[61] This view agrees with observations and studies in social psychology. From this standpoint, it follows that a rumor on its own cannot incite people and disrupt society. "Misleading the masses" only occurs when receivers of a rumor psychologically agree with the views and emotions the rumor expresses, or when the rumor appears at the right time to facilitate the reflection and expression of the moods and expectations of certain people in a specific context. There would have been hundreds of thousands of rumors that were propagated in the early imperial period, but most are lost to antiquity. Only those rumors that represented the people's will and public opinion in specific historical contexts, and had an impact on society and politics, would have a chance to be selected by historians and written in annals and biographies, or recorded in treatises of the Five Agents, allowing us to recreate, through these slightly distorted mirrors, more accurate historical vignettes and the general mood of society in certain specific times and spaces.

Rumors and Public Opinion

Rumors Are a Form of Presentation of Public Opinion in Society

Public opinion is opinion expressed by the public. The more mainstream view in scholastic fields such as political science, sociology, and communications studies avers that the emergence of civil society and the consequent formation of public opinion are only possible in democratic systems and societies. This was already addressed by Hyunyi Cho's "Public Opinion as Personal Cultivation: A Normative Notion and a Source of Social Control in Traditional China," which argues that public opinion is not exclusive to democratic systems and civil society, and that civil society is not a prerequisite of public opinion. In any form of society, interactive communications exist between its classes and members. These communications give rise to public opinion, which differs in forms of presentation and methods of expression according to different social, political, and ideological conditions.[62]

Some scholars of public opinion are of the view that references to the "people's hearts" (*minxin*) and "people's will" (*minyi*) in the political discourse of ancient China are equivalent to the public opinion of modern times.[63] Others

[61] Sun Xupei (1997), p.75. [62] Cho (2000), p.301.

[63] Yu Guoming (2001), p.9. *Yulun*, the Chinese word that is used today to denote "public opinion," first appeared in *Records of the Three Kingdoms*, *juan* 13, "Book of Wei: Biography of Wang Lang" (p.412), referring to the talk (*lun*) of the masses (*yuren*), a pre-Qin reference to chariot makers, low-ranking officials, or ordinary people. Although there are similarities between modern-day public opinion and the *yulun* mentioned in *Records of the Three Kingdoms*, there are many differences as well.

have pointed out that the people's will and public opinion are not identical concepts. The former are unexpressed views that exist within the minds of the people, which can be considered latent public opinion;[64] the latter are social viewpoints that must be openly expressed.[65] The people's will is the foundation of public opinion, but it does not follow that the people's will is expressed as public opinion. Public opinion draws support mainly from the voice of ordinary people; many non-mainstream ideas and views are often expressed in the form of public opinion.[66] Based on the above definitions in public opinion studies, the rumor-type expressions of the early imperial period, as unofficial and non-mainstream views that were expressed publicly or privately, should also be considered a form of uniquely expressed public opinion under an authoritarian political system. This is especially true of popular songs and rhymes. Due to their high moral standing in traditional Confucian discourse, and their symbolic status as conduits of Heaven's and the people's will, they were held in high regard not only by ancient politicians and philosophers, but also by contemporary Chinese scholars, who identify popular songs and rhymes as "expressions of the people's collective will."[67]

The Impact of Rumors on the Public and Their Limitations: From the Perspective of Songs and Rhymes

A popular definition of public opinion among scholars is that it is "the collective name for broadly similar opinions, emotions, and behavioral tendencies held by majority members of a society towards public affairs or phenomena that concern them."[68] As for the people's will, it is "the collective name for the people's consciousness, motivations, and aspirations; it is the force amassed by the common pursuit of the whole population, which reflects the overall will of the whole society."[69] Given that rumors in the early imperial period were a form of expression of public opinion, can we therefore say that rumors were the collective embodiment of the consciousness, motivations, and aspirations of the majority, and that they represented the voice of the majority?

Popular songs have lyrics that rhyme; they are simple and easy to memorize. In ancient China, where literacy levels were low, songs and rhymes would gain

64 Ideas that are not openly expressed; public emotions that are felt but not easily pinned down.
65 The expressions and exchanges of views could be whisperings at street corners, or raucous cries that provoke a huge response.
66 Chen Lidan (1999), p.27.
67 Tian Ying (1959), p.87. He also wrote: "Ancient China had a simple but correct point of view: popular songs and rhymes are seen as the people's voice." (p.81) Zhu Chuanyu (1974): "The Han periods had a kind of written text that was most able to express the people's will, and these were rhymes and adages." (p.102)
68 Yu Guoming (2001), p.9. 69 Wang Xiong (2002), p.4.

widespread popularity very quickly. They were the most common form of expression of public opinion in ancient China. Using songs and rhymes as an example, we shall examine to what extent rumor-type expressions in the early imperial period represented the people's will.

Under a totalitarian political system, ancient China's "unitary political structure with its dynasty-state isomorphism determined the unitary configuration of its system of communications." "The Emperor not only dictated political power, he was also both the ultimate originator and receiver of all of society's information."[70] The people, and even members of the ruling class, often needed special ways of expressing non-mainstream and unofficial views. Songs and rhymes, "whether they were deliberately composed by individuals or inadvertently drummed up by the masses, became ordinary ditties after their dissemination. It was practically impossible to trace their source or to ban them."[71] Naturally, they became an important way to express one's views.

Although songs and rhymes could, to a certain extent, reflect the people's voice in history, it is actually a fallacy to simplistically define them as "the true voice of the masses," and the collective embodiment of the consciousness, motivations, and aspirations of the majority.

Public opinion scholar Liu Jianming classifies public opinion into three categories: the will of the people, the will of the masses, and the opinion of the group. He believes that the people's will is quantifiable. Only when over 70 percent of the people agree on a particular opinion can it be called "the will of the people" (or public opinion). "There was no such thing as a 'public' in feudal society. Due to closed regional interactions and the lack of public responses, as well as the absence of entities that gave expression to democratic principles and activities, it was very difficult for shared opinions in society to take shape." Public opinion could only exist within very narrow spaces in society. Therefore, it was impossible for the people's will and public opinion in the modern sense to take shape in ancient China.[72] The same scholar, however, saw folk rhymes and adages as unique, averring that "the changes in folk rhymes were in fact the changes in the people's heart." Folk rhymes indicated the direction in which the people's will was turning and forecasted the results of political conflicts. "The views expressed by folk adages were often erroneous, and their conclusions were at times absurd, but they were the true reflection of the general mood of a society."[73] Here, Liu Jianming actually defines songs and rhymes as being representative of the people's will. Such discourses emphasize the Chinese characteristics of songs and rhymes, and their special place in public opinion. Although they contravene certain theories in modern public opinion studies, they descend from a long line of discourses

[70] Sun Xupei (1997), p.34. [71] Yan Xinheng (1984), p.43.
[72] Liu Jianming (2001), pp.43, 92, 102. [73] *Ibid.*, pp.128, 135.

on folk songs and rhymes that had been informed by traditional Chinese political thought. Therefore, they remain quite popular among historians of folk songs and rhymes in China.

Even in modern-day America, according to American political scientists, the existence of a "public" that consists of all adults is virtually impossible. It is wrong to speak of "the public" in any continuing and general sense; the public comes into being in response to a specific situation or issue.[74] The public in "a continuing and general sense" has never existed, whether in China or anywhere else, whether in the past or in the present, nor has public opinion in "a continuing and general sense." Every public opinion has its own preset agenda and specific demand. Individuals from different social classes, occupations, families; individuals with different identities; those from different entities, regions, at different times and under different conditions would achieve their own consensus and form different public opinion groups based on their different concerns and consideration of their different interests. As examined in Chapter 3 of this book, there were very few songs and rhymes in the Han periods that addressed sensitive topics of wide concern, or they commented on and ridiculed political events of state importance and the politically powerful that could have gained widespread attention and even sympathetic response.[75] Most songs and rhymes were directed at particular political and social issues that were the concern of specific regions, social classes, and groups. There were therefore limitations in their agendas and how representative of the people's will they were. It is obviously not accurate to equate folk songs and rhymes with the general will of the people. Of course, both non-mainstream and mainstream opinions (or what are known as group opinion and will of the masses) might have been legitimate and reasonable in their political and social criticisms and were worthy of the authorities' attention. It was precisely in this regard that the people's expressions of views, such as songs and rhymes, could articulate and guide the people's moods, give off warning signs, and function as both watchtower and safety net, thus becoming a buffer that allowed society to self-regulate.[76]

[74] Truman (1981), p.219.

[75] Of course, it is impossible for us to conduct questionnaire surveys or public polls to gauge the historical circumstances more than 2,000 years ago when these songs and rhymes were sung. We can, however, scrutinize the writings of early imperial period politicians and philosophers, and study historical texts in detail, to analyze the causes, spread, scope, and communication techniques of songs and rhymes in specific historical contexts. We can also examine the attitudes of the authorities toward songs and rhymes, as well as their responses and assessments. It is therefore possible for us to give appropriate interpretations of the social and political impact of specific songs and rhymes. See Glynn (1999), p.31.

[76] See Yang Mingpin (2001), pp.36–39.

Guiding Public Opinion from the Perspective of Folk Songs and Rhymes

Although folk songs and rhymes could not be generally defined as "the true voice of the people," the deliberate lionization and sophisticated discourse of political thinkers since pre-Qin times had given them the symbolic function of demonstrating the legitimacy and acceptance of a monarch's rule, as well as the role to check on totalitarian power in their capacity as an expression of the people's will.

With their wealth of practical experience, those individuals who held power and the intelligent political leaders during the early imperial period were vigilant toward the sharp criticisms contained in folk songs and rhymes, as well as their keen attention and rapid response to current politics. At the same time, these people understood the ability of folk songs and rhymes to bring people's emotions together, express the people's will, and influence public opinion. And so, both intellectuals and rulers of the time paid a great deal of attention to this non-official and non-mainstream form of expression, which became a form of public opinion that could be spontaneously and openly articulated within a totalitarian political framework.

It is necessary to point out that historical records depicting the attention paid to the people's will, as reflected by folk songs and rhymes,[77] on the part of rulers during the Han periods, were just isolated cases. Rulers basically used their discretion to decide whether to make adjustments to policies or decisions in response to "the people's will." It is hard for us to prove or confirm if there had been an unequivocal cause-and-effect relationship between a particular song and a policy's formulation or adjustment. We also do not find an institutionalized framework that referred to public opinion for policy formulation or adjustment.[78] Instead, we find that political leaders were unwilling to be always made to hear songs and rhymes and comply with the people's will. They were much more interested in making use of songs and rhymes to guide

[77] Such as the "Song of Pingcheng" during the time of Emperor Gaozu of the Western Han Dynasty and Empress Lü, and the "One *Chi* of Cloth Song" during the reign of Emperor Wen.

[78] Wang Meifang (2005): State-level supervision, such as the legislative oversight of the National People's Congress, the administrative oversight of the government, and the judicial oversight of the judiciary, is hard supervision backed up by legal and administrative force. "Public opinion oversight, however, is soft supervision that consists of views freely expressed by the public, and a formless but powerful movement of opinion that exists. It is not backed up by any legal or administrative force, but exerts the pressure that is formed by public opinion." (p.38) Public discussions of politics using songs and rhymes during the early imperial period would have been a kind of soft supervision; it articulated the psychological pressure of society but had no mandatory effect. It was up to the rulers whether or not they would respond. The Eastern Han Dynasty's public opinion monitoring system, which used folk songs and rhymes as the main assessment of the competence of its bureaucrats, was an exception and will be discussed in the next section.

public opinion and manipulate the people's will. Non-mainstream political groups that were suppressed might fabricate their own "folk rhymes" to attempt to set the public opinion agenda. Folk rhymes that spread within a specific area reflecting the demands of specific groups might also be misconstrued as possessing a broad public opinion base.

As defined by public opinion studies, a prerequisite of public opinion is the free and voluntary expression of demands. Views that are not freely or voluntarily expressed cannot be considered the opinion of the public, but opinion that is forced on the public.[79] The main voice of public opinion is the voice of the ordinary people; many ideas that find themselves outside the mainstream are often articulated in the form of public opinion.[80] Folk rhymes of the early imperial period were highly critical. They paid keen attention and responded rapidly to current politics. At the same time, they had the ability to bring people's emotions together, express the people's will, and influence public opinion. Using folk songs and rhymes to "guide" public opinion and manipulate the people's will in the midst of political struggles was irresistibly attractive to political leaders (including the ones in power and those who opposed them) of that time. However, history proves that bowing to the people's will and adapting to the prevailing circumstances were the right paths in guiding public opinion. Wang Mang's fabrication of multiple "folk rhymes" in various localities to create a veneer of public approval was a fool's errand. During the reigns of Emperors Huan and Ling of the Eastern Han Dynasty, the political conflict between bureaucrats, literati-officials, and eunuchs (and their supporters and followers) was especially intense. In the two decades of continuous fighting, the bureaucrats and literati-officials were at the losing end in terms of numbers and political power and suffered "Partisan Prohibitions" twice, losing many of their comrades to persecution. However, they controlled the agenda of the struggle, successfully demonstrated the legitimacy of their agenda, and propagated their ideas in a convincing manner. They garnered much sympathy for their cause and caught the public's attention, thus expanding the influence of public opinion.

Rumors and Supervision by Public Opinion

Seen as a weapon against totalitarianism and corruption of power,[81] supervision by public opinion has been a popular topic in public opinion studies, political science, sociology, and history in recent years in contemporary China.

[79] Wang Xiong (2002), pp.4–7. [80] Chen Lidan (1999), p.27.

[81] In his discussion on supervision by modern-day news and public opinion, Yang Mingpin (2001) pointed out that supervision by public opinion in society is "a check on state power

In its superintendence of local administration, the government of the Han periods made use of grassroots public opinion, such as unverifiable talk and folk rhymes, to introduce into its internal audit system an external supervisory element that reflected, to a certain extent, the wishes and interests of those who were ruled. This provided the Emperor, the court, and relevant control bodies the intelligence they needed, at low cost, to effectively improve the supervision of the local governments' efficiency and competence. The Eastern Han Dynasty's "Rhymes Reporting" system was an important attempt at supervision by public opinion in Chinese history. According to Qiu Yongming, "it was rather brilliant if one considers its intention of focusing more attention on public opinion in society. It removed the limitations of understanding the bureaucracy through official channels and expanded the source of information. While the picture obtained of what was happening might be superficial, it was nevertheless true."[82]

According to my observation, the more systematic methods with which the central governments of the early imperial period collected public opinion from the grassroots included the interview and inquiry of Accounts Clerks from the commanderies and kingdoms, the Regional Inspectors' inspection of "unverifiable talk" and folk rhymes collected in the commanderies and kingdoms during their tour of duty, the observations of "customs" by special emissaries sent at irregular intervals, and the Eastern Han Dynasty's "Rhymes Reporting."

Given that there were personal attachments between Accounts Clerks and heads of the commanderies and kingdoms, and that the families of Accounts Clerks in the Eastern Han often had symbiotic relationships with these local leaders, Accounts Clerks might not be completely truthful to the central government nor fully reflect the people's will. Regional Inspectors represented the central government in their dedicated capacities as monitors of local administrations. Their interests were less entangled with those whom they were monitoring. While they were not high-ranking officials, they wielded enormous powers. Supported by the court, they became "spirited and enthusiastic, and assiduous in their investigations, resulting in many demotions and dismissals."[83] Through the collection, organization, and reporting of "unverifiable talk" and folk rhymes by these Regional Inspectors, the supervision by public opinion role of rumor-type expressions might be better performed. However, Regional Inspectors during the Han periods were often harsh and

organizations, [and] an important rectification mechanism of political functions in society." (pp.36–37) Liu Jianming (2001) wrote that "supervision by public opinion is society's preservative." (p.276) Glynn (1999) observed that even within totalitarian political systems with their many restrictions, public opinion remained one of the few methods that could limit totalitarian power. (p.6)

[82] Qiu Yongming (1992), p.125. [83] Yen Keng-Wang (1990), p.293.

exacting in their investigations, which might have resulted in them twisting or abusing the people's will. The main job of Regional Inspectors was to uphold the central government. They did so by investigating whether local leaders, powerful families, and Kings encroached upon the Emperor's political and economic interests. The focus of their investigations was the administrative "capabilities" of local leaders and whether justice had been served in the commanderies and kingdoms; public opinion at the grassroots level was only one indicator of local governance. As for custom emissaries, they were ad hoc appointments and could not become a sustained and effective channel.

The most effective supervision by public opinion in the early imperial period was of course the "Rhymes Reporting" system established by Emperor Guangwu of the Eastern Han Dynasty. The local governance and administrative competence during the reigns of Emperor Guangwu and Emperor Ming suggested that this system had achieved certain positive outcomes, but profound lessons were learned. Similar to other methods of collecting public opinion in the early imperial period, the intention of "Rhymes Reporting" was not the total supervision of public authority by public opinion. Its purpose was to ensure that the Emperor had complete control over local political power. The collection, arrangement, filtering, and submission of songs and rhymes were done by either the bureaucrats in the Office of the Three Excellencies or agents commissioned by the Emperor. Without a separate and independent channel of communication, the process lacked openness and transparency. The songs and rhymes were anonymously submitted, and their verification and evaluation not only lacked proper procedures, they were sometimes even deliberately overlooked. This allowed those involved to do as they pleased with the information collected.

Any group opinion that is voluntarily and freely generated could have a certain level of rationality and legitimacy, but it may also contain irrational and unreasonable elements. It will definitely be one sided, and it will have its limitations. One-sided public opinions can only reflect partial truths. Of course, public opinions that are partially true may reveal the correct facts and express the correct views. However, when there was no legal and administrative oversight, no procedural justice, no checks and balances, then partial information might become what Emperors choose to hear or believe, and become their excuse for their despotic actions and behavior. Institutional justice and administrative order would then break down. By the late Eastern Han, officials in charge of public opinion supervision were eager to please and became careless. They could not perform their duty, and even used their positions for personal gain. Throw in the interference and damaging effects of various political interest groups, and this well-intentioned system eventually degenerated into an institutional cancer that peddled deliberate falsehoods, silenced dissent, and settled personal scores.

The Mentality of Those Who Believe in and Spread Rumors: An Analysis

"Heaven Had Obfuscated Their Wills and They Could Not Stop Themselves"?

The fourth year of Emperor Ai's Jianping reign period in the Western Han Dynasty saw the occurrence of the mass panic incident of the Passing Edict Tokens of the Queen Mother of the West. Ignited by unverifiable talk, it went on to spread fear and panic across the empire for the greater part of the year.[84] The whole country was shocked by the scale of the mass incident, the fanaticism of its participants, and the area it affected. A year later, Chancellor Wang Jia, who was still disturbed by the incident, could not find a rational explanation for the people's irrational behavior. He could only attribute it to Heaven relieving them of their senses: "The unverifiable talk among the people led to panic over the tokens. They walked with their hair down and feet unshod, and those on horses dashed forth in great speed. Heaven had obfuscated their wills and they could not stop themselves."[85] Do people really believe in and spread rumors because Heaven has obfuscated their wills and they cannot help themselves?

In an ancient society where information was hard to come by through channels that were not fully open, it was not possible that all speech information could quickly attract the people's attention, be disseminated far and wide, and become widespread rumors. Every piece of "successfully" spread rumor occupies a specific time and space, and its "success" is due to a set of highly complex internal and external factors. There are, however, a few basic factors that are essential.

The Importance of the Theme of Speech Information to the Receiving Group Every human group is defined by its own population, class, social stratum, society, region, and ideology, but the most basic factor is where their common interest lies. While class, social stratum, society, region, and ideology may exert a profound influence on defining what the common interest is, constant changes in social and political backdrops mean that the components of the interest group are also dynamic and not confined to the original class, region, ideology, and so on. In general, the more a theme involves material and political advantages that are important to the group, or the more it engages with social, political, and religious issues that are of concern to the group, the easier it attracts interest and attention. The disseminated talk and

84 See Chapter 1 of this book.

85 *History of the Former Han*, *juan* 86, "Biography of Wang Jia," p.3496.

unverifiable talk of the early imperial period involved social and political issues that appeared "absurd" at times, for example, the Edict Tokens of the Queen Mother of the West, "the Yellow Sky will stand," and the capital's imminent inundation, but they were probably important to the people who believed and spread them, and closely linked to their immediate interest.

The Level of Acceptance of the Demands Contained in the Speech Information and the Way It Is Expressed In "Literary Exaggerations" in *Critical Essays: Expositions*, Wang Chong offered an explanation for the mentality of those who added to, subtracted from, and embellished information during its dissemination process:

> The affliction of the world is the affliction of exaggeration when speaking and hyperbole when writing. The good is overstated; the bad is amplified. Why is this so? It is because people like novelty. Words that are not novel are ignored. Therefore, if one is not effusive with one's praise, those who are listening will be less than pleased; if one is not vociferous in one's condemnation, those who are listening will be dissatisfied. When one hears a single thing, he must exaggerate it tenfold; when one sees a hundred things, he must increase them to a thousand ... baseless rumors that are spread by the people, that proceed from the mouths of mean men, that circulate in the streets and alleys – they are like that. The writings of various schools of thought, and the various explications, were written by virtuous men. Given that these are the quintessence of profound and clever thoughts, they should speak the truth. But even they contain exaggerations. Perhaps the classical texts of Confucianism speak the truth? No one is more circumspect in their words than the sages, and Confucian classics will remain unchanged for ten thousand generations. But even they contain exaggerations.[86]

Based on Wang Chong's observation, addition, subtraction, and embellishment occurred not only in inconsequential writings and rumors, myths and legends. Even revered texts like the classics and histories were similarly afflicted.

What is interesting is that while widespread rumors experience multiple changes and embellishments, their main intentions, demands, expectations, and the targets of their criticism remain clear cut and consistent, unlike the parlor game of Chinese whispers, where what is said at the end deviates greatly from the beginning. Wang Chong's explanation that "people like novelty" does not quite support this observable fact.

Studies in the psychology of mass communications indicate that people do not store into or transfer out of their brains information that they have read, heard, or acquired by other means without sieving it through some kind of filter. People always embellish information according to their own beliefs and circumstances to dovetail it with their expectations and needs.[87] People only

[86] *Critical Essays: Expositions*, *juan* 8, p.381. [87] See Harris (1989), p.33.

believe what they want to believe, what they hope will happen, and what is believable, giving rise to what psychologists call selective cognitive process.[88] The scholar of rumors Gordon W. Allport also pointed out that the spread of any rumor had its limitations. Due to selective cognition, the rumor would only be transmitted within like-minded people, mainly affecting those who are "easily influenced."[89] The coming together of this group of people thus constitutes a group with a shared interest in a specific time and place.

The greater the sociopolitical significance and interest of the issue associated with a rumor, the more influential the rumor is and the bigger the interest group affected by it. It is precisely because this group of people is very clear and consistent in what they need, what they believe in, and what they expect, that the transmitted, altered, and embellished version of the rumor that is spread, while possibly different from the original version, will not dilute, weaken, or distort the group's common goals, demands, and articulation. In fact, it will help make the information more acceptable. Therefore, talks of rumors "misleading the masses," while they might be effective in terms of propaganda, could not reveal the true nature of the rumors' effects on the people. According to Wang Jia, people believed in the unverifiable talk about the Queen Mother of the West and the tokens because "Heaven had obfuscated their wills and they could not stop themselves." Perhaps it was not so much Heaven's obfuscation as it was self-delusion. The ready acceptance and extensive spread of disseminated talk or unverifiable talk was often the result of people on the transmission chain choosing to believe and spread the rumor; it was not due to the manipulation of a small number of people with ulterior motives.

This also demonstrates that the level of acceptance of rumor-type expressions is not predicated on the credibility of the facts. Therefore, the accepted wisdom that "facts will stop rumors" needs to be reassessed.

"Facts Shall Stop Rumors"

Under normal circumstances, free flow of information stops public panic and facts released by agencies of authority stop rumors. This is assuming, of course, that the agency of authority enjoys impeccable credibility among the people who are willing to accept the facts that it provides.

In the early imperial period, rumors usually began spreading when the authorities gave vague, uncertain, or even false explanations of certain issues. For example, following Dong Zhuo's assassination in the late Eastern Han

[88] This selectiveness is not only personal but social as well. Specific social, cultural, and religious backgrounds, as well as the social and political situations of that particular place and time, will influence the selection process. See Overholt (1986), p.18.

[89] Allport and Postman (1965), p.35, 180.

Dynasty, "there was unverifiable talk among the people that all natives of Liangzhou would be executed, which spread and caused fear and disturbance. [Liangzhou military] leaders within the Pass were all on high alert and readied their troops to defend their territories."[90] This rumor did not emerge out of nowhere. After the assassination of Dong Zhuo, Wang Yun and other senior officials were undecided on what to do with Dong Zhuo's Liangzhou Army, which had followed him to Chang'an. The military men were not killed, not rewarded, not pardoned. They were not trusted but neither were they decommissioned and disbanded. This uncertainty gave rise to unverifiable talk, leaving the officers and soldiers of the Liangzhou Army on tenterhooks.

> Li Jue [one of the Liangzhou Army commanders] and others became even more afraid and knew not what to do. Jia Xu, a native of Wuwei who was then in Li Jue's camp, urged them thus: "I hear it discussed in Chang'an that all Liangzhou natives are to be killed. If you abandon your troops and flee on your own, even a Commune Chief could bind you. It is far better to lead your armies westward and attack Chang'an, to avenge Lord Dong. If you succeed, you could serve the state and set all under Heaven to rights; if you fail, you could still escape." Li Jue and others agreed and said to one another: "The capital does not pardon us; we shall fight to the death. If we take down Chang'an, we shall gain the empire; if we cannot take it down, we shall plunder the Three Metropolitan Areas for their women and chattels and return to the west. At least we can still live a bit longer." Everyone thought it was right and swore pledges with one another. Leading thousands of troops, they advanced westward [toward Chang'an] in the night.[91]

It had reached the boiling point, and the situation could not be reversed even if the authorities clarified the situation and dispelled the rumors.

Successful rumors often contain a kernel of truth. For example, the unverifiable talk about the inundation during the reign of Emperor Cheng of the Western Han Dynasty originated from the fact that "the commanderies and kingdoms have suffered from floods, which have swept away and killed many thousands of people."[92] Some rumors were even confirmed to be true afterward, like the "disseminated talk of Guan and Cai" that was circulated throughout the country during Wang Mang's regency, as well as *chen* prophecies and prophetic rhymes that were fulfilled.

Rumors that were named and whose origins were certain can also be found in historical writings. They were usually created and released by individuals or groups with specific political or ideological demands. The intent of such rumors was the dissemination of false information for their creators' private gain. Even false speech information might produce the social effects of

[90] *History of the Later Han, juan* 66, "Biography of Wang Yun," p.2176.
[91] *History of the Later Han, juan* 72, "Biography of Dong Zhuo," p.2333.
[92] *History of the Former Han, juan* 10, "Annals of Emperor Cheng," p.306.

consoling the masses or giving vent to their anger. For example, "Wang Mang had committed regicide by poisoning and killing Emperor Ping" was a rumor that had no basis in fact and one that was impossible to verify. After Wang Mang became Regent, however, he fabricated a large number of talismanic writings, gradually forcing the Han imperial family toward a certain demise. This naturally resulted in the rumor resonating with a good many people, and it became a "reasonable" explanation for the political situation of that time.

It was recorded in *Eastern Library's Records of Han* that:

> Gongsun Shu was fearful following Wei Xiao's defeat and he wanted to pacify his people. Outside the walls of Chengdu was a granary from the Qin period, renamed the White Emperor Granary, which had been empty since Wang Mang's rise to power. Gongsun Shu ordered his men to falsely claim that the White Emperor Granary was pouring out mountains of grain. The markets and streets of the city were emptied of people, who had gone in large numbers to see the phenomenon. Then, Gongsun Shu convened with his ministers, asking them, "Is the White Emperor Granary producing grain?" "No," they replied. Gongsun Shu then said: "One must not believe in unverifiable talk; it is the same with the talk about King Wei's defeat!"[93]

As the supreme ruler of the region, Gongsun Shu ordered his men to spread false information about the long disused White Emperor Granary "pouring out mountains of grain," which attracted large crowds of senior officials and ordinary people to see it, only to leave disappointed.[94] Gongsun Shu believed that his strategy of fighting falsehoods with falsehood would numb the local officials and people to other "unverifiable talk,"[95] so that the news of Wei Xiao's defeat would not demoralize the people and the army.

Gongsun Shu seized and occupied the Shu region during the transitional period from the Xin to Eastern Han Dynasty, but he had little ambition, preferring to indulge in *chen* prophecies and apocrypha and talismanic writings. He had a "severe and exacting personality, and scrutinized the most minute trifles. He did not flinch from killing, but he lacked a greater vision." His actions "grieved the hearts of his warriors,"[96] and his "rule was strict and harsh."[97] That the people of Shu were restive was evident in the earlier appearance of the children's rhyme: "Yellow cow and white belly; the five-*zhu* coins will come back." When the authorities promulgated a lie that became an unverifiable rumor, the officials and people responded with great speed and

93 *Eastern Library's Records of Han: Collations and Annotations*, *juan* 21, p.912. A similar account is found in "Biography of Gongsun Shu" in *History of the Later Han*.
94 *Record of States South of Mount Hua: A Collated, Illustrated, and Annotated Edition*, *juan* 5, "Records of Gongsun Shu and the Two Liu Regional Governors," p.331.
95 This is the same psychological affect depicted in the famous "The Boy Who Cried Wolf" story.
96 *Eastern Library's Records of Han: Collations and Annotations*, *juan* 21, p.912.
97 *Record of States South of Mount Hua: A Collated, Illustrated, and Annotated Edition*, *juan* 5, "Records of Gongsun Shu and the Two Liu Regional Governors," p.330.

helped spread it to large numbers of people. As a result, "the markets and streets of the city were emptied of people, who had gone in large numbers to see the phenomenon." Although this could be attributed to the curiosity and herd mentality of the officials and people, the main reason for this was the restiveness of the people in the Shu region. Not only did Gongsun Shu not reflect on this and find out about the people's concerns, he actually thought that he could henceforth manipulate public opinion with impunity. He believed that he could issue "true lies" ("it is the same with the talk about King Wei's defeat") in line with his personal interest and insult the people's intelligence. His lies quickly came to naught, and the unverifiable talk that he had fabricated became one of the last few straws that broke the camel's back of his political credibility. With such political naïveté, it is little wonder that failure came so quickly for this warlord.

"The Blue Sky is dead; the Yellow Sky will stand. In the Jiazi year, great fortune comes to the land."[98] This slogan in the final years of the Eastern Han Dynasty, composed by Zhang Jiao and his brothers, was also a rumor created by a few individuals, but it was a masterpiece in meticulous planning and calculation. The rhyming slogan drew attention to the wildly popular Earth-Power symbols that came about because of the people's antipathy to the Han regime, even as it summed up and received the rich political and religious resources that came with it. By combining elaborate organization, extensive groundwork, and secularized religious belief, an unverifiable rumor in that crisis-filled world became a most unifying political slogan and an enormously attractive mythical vision.

In the words of Jean-Noël Kapferer:

> Regardless of the efforts made by informative sources and of their prestige, if the information they convey does not satisfy a desire, answer to a latent preoccupation, or provide an outlet for a psychological conflict, no rumor will arise from it. Harmless words and innocent confidentialities may, on the contrary, be snapped up and turned into rumors because there is interest in their consumption.
>
> One could go so far as to say that rumors do not convince or persuade people: rather they seduce them. . . . quite simply, rumors express and justify out loud what we think to ourselves or do not dare to hope. Thus a rumor, unlike any other message, enjoys a unique characteristic: it justifies public opinion while revealing it, i.e. it rationalizes at the same time as it satisfies.[99]

Therefore, whether a popular rumor was factual, credible, or provable was not the main factor that determined whether it could be accepted by a specific group of people. This is because the main function of rumors was not to provide the public with accurate news and information during times of

[98] *History of the Later Han, juan* 71, "Biography of Huangfu Song," p.2299.
[99] Kapferer (1990), p.82.

uncertainty and restiveness; their raison d'être was to fittingly reflect and satisfy the collective moods, hopes, and imaginations of a group of people in a specific time and place. Rumors reflect the inner emotions, thoughts, and secrets of a specific group of people within a specific historical context. Those who are in power can make use of this medium to understand the people's mentality. In this sense, disseminated talk and unverifiable talk, despite the fabricated and deceptive information that they conveyed, could reveal a facet of truth within a specific historical context. The group mentality, as well as the social and cultural milieus, in specific historical contexts that were reflected by widely accepted and propagated disseminated talk and unverifiable talk were therefore real.

"Rumors Stop When They Reach the Wise"

It is written in "The Great Compendium" in *Xun Zi*: "It is said that 'a rolling ball stops when it reaches a crater, and rumors stop when they reach the wise.' This is the reason why those preconceived and evil philosophers hate Confucians. An uncertainty should be measured against things in the distant past and verified with the new and recent. Consider them with a balanced mind, and the rumor shall stop and the evil words shall cease."[100]

From the phrase "it is said," we can infer that the notion "rumors stop when they reach the wise" was already quite popular in the Warring States Period. How should the wise respond when they hear rumors? They should do so by measuring them against things in the distant past and verifying them with the new and recent, and then considering them with a balanced attitude. This meant if one evaluates a rumor calmly using one's historical knowledge and personal experience, the spread of the unreliable information would stop at one and go no further. Kong Yingda explained the line in "Conduct of the Scholar" in *Book of Rites*, "hear disseminated talk but not investigate their source," as the scholar not tracing the origin of a rumor because having "profound knowledge and consideration of things, they would demolish it when they heard it."[101] His explanation was practically identical to the notion that "rumors stop when they reach the wise."

Traditional wisdom posits that rumors stop when they reach the wise. This is predicated upon such talk being full of false, embellished, absurd, and unreasonable information, and therefore, any person with wisdom, using his or her general knowledge and thinking deeply, would be able to deduce and expose the falsity of the rumors. The discussion on hearsay recorded in "Investigating Hearsay" under "Discourse on Being Cautious in One's Conduct" in *Master*

[100] *Xun Zi: Collected Explications*, *juan* 19, p.516.
[101] *Annotations and Explanations of the Thirteen Classics: Book of Rites*, *juan* 59, p.1669.

Lü's Spring and Autumn Annals is a classic discourse in ancient Chinese political thought on countering rumors with intelligence, knowledge, and rationality:

When one hears something, one must investigate. After multiple telling, white would turn into black, and black into white. A dog resembles a *jue*[102] and a *jue* resembles a female ape. A female ape resembles a human being, but a human being is far from resembling a dog. This is the reason why the foolish make such serious errors. Investigating something on hearing it shall bring forth goodness; if one does not investigate, one might as well not hear it.

. . .

When one hears something, one must consider it thoroughly. For a hearsay regarding a person, one must verify it using reason. Duke Ai of Lu asked Confucius: "It is said that the Music Master Kui had one leg. Is it true?" Confucius said: "A long time ago, Shun wanted to propagate his teachings to all under Heaven using music, so he ordered Zhong Li to select Kui from among the commoners and promote him. Shun appointed Kui as Music Master. Kui went on to rectify the six pitch-standards and harmoniously tuned the five tones, circulating the eight winds and causing all under Heaven to submit to Shun. Zhong Li wanted to seek more men, but Shun said: 'Music is the essence of Heaven and Earth, the key to success and loss. Only a sage is capable of creating harmony, which is the principle of all music. Kui can make harmonious music and thus bring peace to the world. There is only one like Kui and that is enough.' What Shun actually meant was 'There is only one like Kui and that is enough,' not 'Kui has one leg.'"[103]

A man surnamed Ding in the State of Song did not have a well at home. Having to obtain water from elsewhere, he had a man stationed away from his house. When a well was finally dug at his house, Ding told others: "I dug a well and acquired a man." Someone heard it and told someone else: "Ding dug a well and found a man." The people in the capital began to talk about this and it reached the ears of the Song ruler, who sent his men to ask Ding. Ding said: "What I meant was acquiring an extra man to do my work, not finding a man in the well." If one seeks talented men in such a manner, one might as well not hear about them.

. . .

There are many words that seem wrong but are right, and many that seem right but are wrong. One must differentiate what is right and what is wrong. This is something that even sages must be careful of. How then can one be careful? By examining what one has heard by using reason that is natural to things and man, one shall acquire the truth.[104]

Citing famous cases such as "Kui having one leg" and "Ding digging a well and finding a man," the above discourse emphasizes using common sense,

102 A mythical creature that resembled a monkey.

103 The confusion had arisen from the phrase *yizu* (一足), which can mean "one is enough" or "one leg."

104 *Master Lü's Spring and Autumn Annals: New Expositions*, *juan* 22, pp.1536–1537.

common knowledge, reason, and careful deduction to dissect information obtained from hearsay, in order to expose the untruths in rumors that have been compounded through repeated telling. Traditional wisdoms such as these were beacons of rationalism, and they are still considered effective antidotes against rumors. Much nonsensical talk and absurd hearsay is demolished when common sense, common knowledge, reason, and careful deduction are employed.

Sometimes, however, the powers that be would use the argument that "rumors stop when they reach the wise" to seize the intellectual high ground in their battle against rumors, from which they would look down on and dismiss rumor-type expressions, as well as the individuals who believe and spread them. They do this in the hope that believers and propagators of rumors would be regarded as self-evidently foolish. No one wants to appear foolish. When the Emperor swaggered into court wearing "new clothes" that only "the wise" could see, you had to follow other "wise men" in heaping praises on the Emperor's new clothes, even if all you saw was a naked body on the throne.

The problem is that rumors are not always false, embellished, absurd, and unreasonable. They may also contain some elements of truth and reflect real opinions and reasonable wishes. Modern social psychology also tells us that models of propagation that cause untruths to be compounded through repeated telling, such as the cases of white becoming black and vice versa or dogs resembling human beings, are only applicable in the passive propagation of insignificant information, or in controlled experiments. In real life, widespread rumors are often deliberately chosen by their propagators, and the additions, subtractions, and embellishments in the process of their propagation often do not distort or change their inherent demands and aims. Besides, eight or nine out of ten pieces of information we get every day are from hearsay. How practical is it to verify every single one of them?

Employing the common sense, common knowledge, and reason of the wise as the main tool to verify hearsay is also quite subjective. Wang Chong's summary of pre-Qin classics, schools of thought, and historical writings was this: even those as cautious as the sages, those as virtuous as the exponents of the various schools of thought, and writings as unalterable as Confucian classics were not immune to exaggerations and errors. The many false and erroneous narratives and arguments that were criticized in *Critical Essays* were all products of the common sense, common knowledge, and reason of "the wise" in the early imperial period. Although Wang Chong might have been a little extreme in his conclusion, he was not completely wrong. Therefore, stopping rumors with common sense, common knowledge, and reason may not always work.

The biggest problem with "rumors stopping when they reach the wise" is that it is a boast by those who subscribe to the notion. In a society like ancient

China, where the ownership of information was extremely unbalanced, many originators and instigators of rumors were in fact "the wise." Many of those who employed rumors as a political weapon were also "the wise." The government, which possessed the fullest information and refuted rumors most strongly, was often the most enthusiastic agency in concealing information and hiding the truth. If members of disadvantaged groups, who were the weakest in creating and spreading information, totally rejected hearsay-type information, how could they know what their circumstances were and understand where their interests lay? How could they vent their emotions and proclaim their demands?

What Makes Rumors Come True?

It was discussed in Chapter 4 of this book that the rumor-type expressions of the early imperial period, such as unverifiable talk, portentous talk, and children's rhymes, were cloaked in a kind of mysticism. Unverifiable talk, portentous talk, children's rhymes, and so on might have been unfulfilled *chen* prophecies and prophetic rhymes, while *chen* prophecies and prophetic rhymes were unverifiable talk, portentous talk, and children's rhymes that had come to pass.

The psychological acceptance of its adherents is essential for any belief system, and all popular beliefs must be founded on widely accepted customs and a deeply embedded psychological core. Every belief system develops a set of symbols whose meanings and sanctity are given to them by their believers. When their meanings are revoked by the very people who vouchsafed them, these symbols become nonsensical images. The belief in the supernatural was strong in the early imperial period. Belief in *chen* prophecies was deep seated, and detailed discourses on mystical beliefs such as the Five Agents, *chen* prophecies and apocrypha, and talismanic writings pervaded the whole of society. It engendered a unique historical and cultural milieu where people believed that the destinies of individuals, society, and the state were determined or manipulated by supernatural forces. Whenever there was an epidemic spread of emotions like doubt, anger, fear, or hopelessness among the people, the psychological need for divine revelation would appear as a result. The people hoped to receive prophecies about their fates and comforting assurances that there would be a better tomorrow. For this reason, the Chinese language and script were seen as mysterious symbols with the ability to disclose "strange, coded prophecies that foretold good or ill fortune" and accommodate information revealed by Heaven. "Unusual speech" such as unverifiable talk, portentous talk, children's rhymes, and so on were conferred the power to symbolically reveal signs that were sent from Heaven. Li Xun's suggestion that it was "not impossible for unverifiable talk to have prophetic qualities" and Pei Songzhi's assertion that "the words in all children's songs would come to pass" were inevitable products of such a historical and cultural milieu.

Another mental mechanism for rumors coming true is wishful thinking. Some sociologists classify rumors into three types based on different mentalities: the Wish-Fulfillment type that expresses the wishes and hopes of its propagators; the Anxiety type that expresses the fear of its propagators; and the Divisive type that is informed by its propagators' aggressiveness, prejudices, and hate. In real life, these three types of rumors are sometimes entwined and hard to separate into neat boxes. For example, many *chen* prophecies and prophetic rhymes originated as curses.[105] Curse-type rumors vented anger by wishing for death and ruin for their targets, which in fact expressed a form of aggressive hope. Some rumors that were curses or commented on current politics were able to reflect the emotions and voices of a great many people. "A healthy person dies when a thousand people point their fingers at him." Such rumors "carried an irresistible social force that reflected a historical trend, which made their fulfillment possible and inevitable."[106]

Naturally, the "decoding" of the more typical coded *chen* prophecies and prophetic rhymes, whether it was before or after the events, expressed the wishes and hopes of their propagators. The ability of widely propagated and accepted rumors to guide public opinion; the collective wishes, demands, and consensus that they encapsulated; and the popular belief in their mysterious powers could make them become self-suggesting and self-fulfilling prophecies. At times, they could even influence the development of events and shape the future.

"Self-fulfilling prophecy" is a concept that social psychologists use to describe a mass psychological phenomenon: if people see a situation as real, then the outcome of that situation is also real. The situation may be fictional in the beginning or not based on reality, but the prophecy motivates or coalesces with the hopes of an individual or a group, inspiring effort and action. Under the right circumstances, these hopes come to fruition and the prophecy comes to pass. "Self-fulfilling prophecy" generally means that when a person has a certain hope for another, this hope will become a become true for the latter. In other words, when one hopes that another will succeed, the latter will succeed; when one hopes that another will fail, the latter will fail.

A person's hopes for himself may also be endorsed by the group and become a self-fulfilling prophecy. Several examples can be seen in the founding myth of the Western Han Dynasty, which is covered in Chapter 5

105 Examples included "after the First Emperor dies, his territory will be divided"; "the people of Chu hated Qin so much that even if there were three households left among them, they would destroy Qin"; "a thousand *li* of grass"; and so on.

106 Xie Gui'an (1998), pp.54–61.

of this book. When Liu Bang was still living in humble circumstances, he already had quite a high opinion of himself. When he was serving as corvée labor in Xianyang and he witnessed the pomp of the carriage of First Emperor of the Qin Dynasty, he made a promise to himself: "Ha! A great man should be like this!"[107] Later, when he was hiding among the swamps and rocks of Mount Mang and Mount Dang, and heard that the mother of a deity wept over his slaying of the white snake, he was secretly pleased with himself; when there was talk of "a Son of Heaven air current in the southeast," he thought he was the reason for the air current; when there were "clouds and air currents above where he stayed," he was pleased. Liu Bang had overwhelming self-confidence and always assumed that strange occurrences and portentous talk were about him. These "prophecies" that he assumed were about him became widespread among his followers, who increasingly respected him, and the "young men in Pei heard about this and many wanted to follow him." All his followers had high hopes for Liu Bang, which made the prophecy come true.[108]

Liu Xiu, Emperor Guangwu of the Eastern Han Dynasty, also claimed multiple times that his name fulfilled the *chen* prophecies, using the claim as proof of the legitimacy of claiming the throne and founding his dynasty.

Gongsun Shu and Yuan Shu, both of whom had blind faith in *chen* prophecies, also assumed they were the objects of rumors, but they failed spectacularly in this regard. Although they also had a high level of self-assurance, their confidence was not shared by the people. Despite their ability to manipulate auguries and *chen* prophecies to reassure themselves, their not being the repositories of the people's hopes meant that their failures were inevitable.

How to Offset the Negative Effects of Rumors: "Marvel Not at the Strange, and the Strange Will Cease to Be"

Human history is a history filled with rumors, and human society is a society filled with rumors. Whenever society is overwhelmed by anxiety, fear, helplessness, and a sense of crisis, rumors help the people vent their emotions, explain their predicament, "rationalize" their what they have imagined, and satisfy their psychological needs. Whenever there are conflicts of interest between different blocs, classes, and groups, rumors serve the purpose of probing and guiding public opinion, declaring demands, and even forming collective solutions. At times, they do reflect the people's will, using public opinion to supervise a society and expurgate its evils. What is strange is that

[107] *The Grand Scribe's Records*, *juan* 8, "Basic Annals of Emperor Gaozu," p.344.
[108] *Ibid.*, pp.347–348.

the manifestations of rumor-type expressions, and the manner in which they resolve problems, are sometimes dark, ambiguous, devious, and deleterious. They are sometimes more destructive than constructive. How to properly understand the nature, characteristics, social functions, and limitations of rumors with the help of historical experience and lessons, and how to unleash the positive effects such expressions have on society and politics, even as their negative effects are diluted, resolved, and even expunged, have become important issues in the creation of a harmonious society. What rumors were like in the society and politics of the early imperial period, and their effects and functions, provide many useful pointers in the exploration of this issue.

Rumor-type expressions were often synonymous with the people's opinion in the early imperial period. Within the social, political, and cultural contexts of the time, political thinkers adopted a unique discourse strategy. From their high ground of people-oriented Confucian concepts and political morality, supplemented by the discourse strategy of historical narrative and mysticism, they deconstructed the authorities' stigmatization and demonization of the people's opinion or rumor-type expressions. The authorities, for their part, treated with extreme caution rumor-type expressions and information like disseminated talk, unverifiable talk, portentous talk, and so on, which they could not easily control. On one hand, the powers that be persisted with harsh measures and punishments, swiftly attacking rumor-type expressions that obstructed the ruling order. On the other hand, they were careful not to dismiss the psychological effects rumor-type expressions had on the people, nor ignore their function as bearers of public opinion and divine warning. They attempted to create institutions to open up avenues for the people's opinion. By responding to the people's opinion in an appropriate and timely fashion, and by improving their governance, they sought to maintain social harmony and stability.[109]

In addition to those in authority meting out harsh punishments and opening up channels for the people's voices, the psychological strategy to counter the effects of rumors, according to traditional Chinese political wisdom, was to seize the ethical high ground in the first instance, for example, demonize disseminated talk as "the same crime as that committed by Guan and Cai," and attack it relentlessly. The next step was to seize the intellectual high ground, that is, invoking the mantra that "rumors stop when they reach the wise." These two strategies have been discussed earlier and will not be elaborated here.

[109] These attempts did produce positive outcomes during certain periods in history, but they were limited by the totalitarian political system of the time. As they lacked sustained and consistent institutional support and checks, good systems and policies such as these often differed according to personalities and time. Sometimes, they died with those who initiated them.

There was yet another strategy that took a low-key and evasive attitude, a strategy that was later summarized as "marvel not at the strange, and the strange will cease to be."[110] Rumors were neither sought out nor denied; they were simply allowed to fade away from the spotlight on their own.

The low-key strategy agreed with the classical Confucian attitude toward rumor-type expressions. It was recorded in "Counsels of Great Yu" in *Book of Documents*: "Do not listen to unsubstantiated words; do not follow plans about which you have not sought counsel."[111] When one did not listen to unsubstantiated words, one naturally did not seek the source of disseminated talk. By not listening, not seeking their source, and not asking, rumors would disappear on their own. When one did not hear rumors, one's mind would be at peace and one's work would not be disrupted. Therefore, Confucius told his students: "To tell, as we go along, what we have heard on the way, is to cast away our virtue."[112]

One advantage of the "marvel not at the strange" strategy is that time will tell if one is patient. With a few exceptions, rumor-type expressions do not enjoy longevity. "A rumor constitutes testimony concerning a certain context; if the latter changes, the rumor loses its *raison d'être* and immediately ceases. It no longer has any relevance."[113]

In the case of the unverifiable talk about a great flood just after Emperor Cheng of the Western Han Dynasty ascended to the throne, the court and the people went into a panic. Only General of the Left Wang Shang insisted on a different view – that it was a piece of unverifiable talk. He believed that inaction was better than action. "Shortly afterward, when Chang'an was calm, enquiries were made and it had indeed been unverifiable talk."[114]

This strategy has its limitations because "certain rumors seem, however, to defy time's corrosive action."[115] Some resilient rumors and issues would reappear in a different time and place, for example, the *chen* prophecies about "the grandson of a lord" (*Gongsun*), "Dangtu Gao," and the "one with the surname Liu shall be King." Some general rumors were not limited by time and space and eventually became myths, legends, and even collective historical memories.[116]

110 The phrase "marvel not at the strange" first appeared in *Records of Yijian, Part III, Section Ji, juan* 2, "The Domesticated Hogs of Jiang Qi," written by Hong Mai (1123–1202) of the Southern Song Dynasty: "How could one believe in the words of an animal? I have known about it for several months. Marvel not at the strange, and the strange will cease to be." (p.1314) However, such an approach had existed since ancient times.

111 *Annotations and Explanations of the Thirteen Classics: Book of Documents, juan* 4, p.136.

112 *Annotations and Explanations of the Thirteen Classics: The Analects, juan* 17, "Yang Huo," p.2525.

113 Kapferer (1990), p.109.

114 *History of the Former Han, juan* 82, p.3370.

115 Kapferer (1990), p.110.

116 See Chapter 5 of this book for details.

Even if people "marvel not at the strange," the strange may not always cease to be. Ying Shao's *Comprehensive Meaning of Customs and Habits* recorded many folk cults of the Han periods that had sprung forth through misunderstandings, miscommunication, and even jokes. In spite of their origins, these cults grew rapidly and attracted large numbers of believers. They only ceased to exist when the original source of these misunderstandings came forth to burst the bubble. Many rumors could not even be controlled by their originators once they were disseminated, so how could they cease to exist on their own? It is as Wang Chong feared, that the sages "do not seek a good reputation and will not avoid any harm that comes their way. Their blemishes and faults are given wide airing, but their virtues and strengths are hidden. They care not for the wrongs they suffer and will not put a stop to the rumors about themselves. Even when they are besmirched and slandered, they do not seek to redeem their spotless reputations." For this reason, "ugliness is exposed and the beautiful concealed; faults are revealed and virtuous acts hidden." The evildoers and hypocrites, however, "disguise their true selves to seek favor with the world, and practice deceit to please the people." Therefore, "the world does not see their flaws and praise them in unison, while leaders do not hear their evil deeds and employ them in high places." Seen in this light, "those whom the world hails as virtuous could well be evil; and those who are condemned as evil could well be good."[117] If the strange does not cease to be, how can the negative effects of rumors be eliminated?

The abovementioned strategy of Wang Shang's response to the unverifiable talk about a great flood could be quite successful. When the frightened people started to spread the rumor, the authorities "marveled not at the strange" and maintained a calm exterior to counter the chaos. The rumor then fizzled out on its own. However, if the political situation continued to be unstable, and the people's lives and social conditions continued to worsen, then the warning and symbolic meaning of such rumors would not become irrelevant, and similar incidents would come one after another. Eventually, portentous talk, disseminated talk, unverifiable talk, and rhymes would turn into *chen* prophecies, and it would be too late for regrets!

In the first year of the Yongchu reign period of Emperor An of the Eastern Han Dynasty, "the people were frightening one another because of unverifiable talk. They left their original homes with their elderly and children and became destitute." Emperor An ordered the Metropolitan Commandant and the Inspectors of Jizhou Region and Bingzhou Region to (1) have local government officials directly explain to the people; (2) provide the necessary documentation for the refugees, who had become frightened and dispossessed by

[117] *Critical Essays: Expositions, juan* 1, "Annoyances and Vexations," p.17.

unverifiable talk, to return to their homes; and (3) allow those who were still frightened to remain and not return home.[118] This was in fact a strategy similar to "marvel not at the strange, and the strange will cease to be." The difference was that instead of not listening, not asking, and not acting, Emperor An's officials responded to the situation proactively and provided the people with the necessary assistance. The outcome was much better.

During the reign of Emperor Cheng of the Western Han Dynasty, the Emperor's affinal relative Wang Feng, the Commander-in-Chief and General-in-Chief cum Intendant of the Masters of Writing, arrogated the power of the throne, causing much resentment at court. Taking advantage of a solar eclipse, the Governor of the Capital Wang Zhang asked to see the Emperor, "saying that Wang Feng was guilty of overshadowing his lord by arrogating the powers of the throne, and should be dismissed in response to the strange occurrence in the sky." Emperor Cheng ordered the Master of Writing to impeach Wang Zhang, who later died in prison.[119]

Following Wang Zhang's death, the people felt that he had been wronged and hated Wang Feng even more. Disseminated talk that poured scorn on the government began to spread. Du Qin, Prefect of the Arsenal under the General-in-Chief and one of Wang Feng's trusted men, gave this piece of advice to Wang Feng:

> The conviction of the Governor of the Capital Wang Zhang was highly confidential. As the officials and people were of the view that since Wang Zhang had always spoken up for the people, he would not be convicted of any crime that could get him dismissed. His conviction was therefore connected to the solar eclipse and what he had said about it. Even if Wang Zhang had committed a crime for other reasons and was convicted of it, if the matter was not uncovered, no one in the capital would know, let alone people in faraway places. I fear that everyone in the empire does not know that Wang Zhang was truly guilty, but believes that he committed a crime because he spoke up about something. If so, the channels of remonstrance and criticism would be blocked, and the magnanimity and virtue of Your Grace would be damaged. I am of the humble opinion that, with the opportunity afforded by the Wang Zhang affair, outspoken remonstrance should be allowed and encouraged, and Gentlemen and Attendant Officials should be allowed to submit memorials as often as they wish. Broadening the avenues of communication, announcing it near and far, all under Heaven will know Your Grace's sagacity and that Your Grace will not convict a subordinate because of what he says. In so doing, the disseminated talk will cease and all doubts will be cleared.[120]

This piece of advice was quite tactfully given, but it told Wang Feng in no uncertain terms that convicting a person based on what he had said would

118 *History of the Later Han*, *juan* 5, "Annals of Emperor An," p.209.
119 *History of the Former Han*, *juan* 60, "Biography of Du Qin," pp.2676–2677.
120 *Ibid.*, p.2678.

prevent people from speaking their minds and would be damaging to his image. Even if Wang Zheng were found guilty of committing an actual crime, and he deserved his punishment, other officials and the people found it hard to understand "the truth." They also lacked faith in the court, insisting on believing that Wang Zheng had been condemned for what he had said. The only way to eliminate the effects of disseminated talk and the negative sentiments the officials and people had of the court was to further open up the channels for feedback and make policy discussions more transparent. This would show "Your Grace's sagacity and that Your Grace will not convict a subordinate because of what he says."

Such a strategy could be referred to as "removing the firewood from under the cauldron," where both the root and symptoms are eliminated. Any germ that may start a rumor outbreak is destroyed. If the rulers of that period could see rumor-type expressions as a symptom of society's ills and a reflection of the people's discontent; if they could conduct a proper diagnosis and nurse the body politic back to health; if they could subscribe to the notion that prevention was better than cure, then even if they could not totally eradicate rumors, they could mitigate the negative and destructive effects of rumors on the state, society, and the people to a tolerable level. It would have been good for the creation of a harmonious society.

Epilogue

In the summer of 2001, I was busy at work on the banks of Clear Water Bay in Hong Kong, deep in my research into the belief in *chen* prophecies during the Western Jin, Eastern Jin, and the Northern and Southern dynasties. The fruit of my labor was the book *Power of the Words:* Chen *Prophecy in Chinese Politics, AD265–618*, published in 2003.

Ten years later, I was once again ensconced in my retreat. The dazzling sun and gentle breeze were still the same, but I had been transplanted to the banks of Peking University's Weiming Lake to enjoy my sabbatical leave, thanks to the kind arrangements made by Professor James Z. Lee, Dean of The Hong Kong University of Science and Technology's School of Humanities and Social Science, and Peking University's Office of International Relations. Jian Zhai 健斋, located on the northern bank of Weiming Lake, was an excellent place to study and write. When one needed a break or a distraction, the beautiful lake proffered delightful walks and enchanting views. Shortly after I arrived there, my first cousin once removed Zong Nian 宗年 visited me there and told me something quite incredible. More than half a century ago, my uncle Zong Baihua 宗白华, who was my mother's eldest brother, transferred from Nanjing to teach at Peking University. He, too, found temporary lodgings in Jian Zhai. He had stayed in Room 204 and I was in Room 203! Was this mere coincidence or something else, a kind of cosmic connection even? Of course, Jian Zhai is now the David Packard International Faculty Residence Pavilion in honor of the American entrepreneur's donation. It may look similar, even after the retrofitting, but in essence it is not quite the same now.

It was in the course of my research into the political and social effects of *chen* prophecies and prophetic rhymes in Chinese history between the third and seventh centuries, that I noticed the intimate connection between *chen* prophecies and prophetic rhymes and rumors. "Even a senior general like Hulü Guang was felled by the rhyme about a hundred *sheng* and the bright moon."[1]

[1] *Records of Daily Recognitions: Collected Expositions*, *juan* 3, p.163. The "hundred *sheng*" referred to the character *hu* in Hulü Guang's name (100 *sheng* was equivalent to 1 *hu*, *sheng* and *hu* being units of measure) and the "bright moon" (*mingyue*) referred to Hulü Guang's courtesy

The rhyme was deliberately disseminated by Northern Zhou's spies within the borders of Northern Qi. After its circulation as a children's song among the young, Hulü Guang's political foes within Northern Qi "decoded" it as a prophetic rhyme, bringing about the fall of the great general and his family. After Hulü Guang's death, Northern Qi's military power weakened vis-à-vis Northern Zhou, and its root cause was the "fearsome rumors."[2] After I came across this historical episode, I started to take an interest in the discussion of rumors in Western or Chinese scholarly works on social psychology, sociology, communication studies, public opinion studies, and history.

Examining the historical sources of the early imperial period from the perspectives of psychology and sociology, I found that the disseminated talk, unverifiable talk, rhymes, *chen* prophecies, prophetic rhymes, myths, legends, and so on of that period were very similar to what modern social psychologists and sociologists define as "rumors." Although these rumor-type historical sources have been dismissed as unimportant in historical research, they actually played very significant roles in the society, politics, and culture of the early imperial period. As sociologist Tamotsu Shibutani argued, rumors were a collective way of finding solutions, a recurrent method of communication in human groups and societies. Through this communication method, people in uncertain and unstable social circumstances pool their intellectual resources together to construct an interpretation of their circumstances that has meaning for them.[3]

Under the kind aegis of professors and editors like Song Chao 宋超, Peng Wei 彭卫, Shang Yongqi 尚永琪, and Sun Jiulong 孙久龙, I began in 2003 to publish the following journal articles on rumors: "Disseminated Talk and Unverifiable Talk of the Han Period" (in *Historical Studies*, 2003); "Examining the 'Portentous Talk' of the Han Period" (in *Chinese Historical Studies*, 2006); "A Brief Discussion of the Political Function of Folk Rhymes in the Han Periods and Related Myths" (in *Social Science Battlefront*, 2008); "The Construct and Context of Dynastic Founding Myths of the Western Han" (in *Collected Works of History*, 2010); and so on. Chapters 1, 2, and 3, and the first half of Chapter 5 of this book are reorganized and expanded versions of these works. Chapter 4 ("*Chen* Prophecy and Prophetic Rhymes") and the second half of Chapter 5 ("Popular Legends") are the fruits of later research.

name Mingyue. The rhyme suggested that Hulü Guang would rise and usurp the throne of the Northern Qi Dynasty.

[2] *History of Northern Qi*, *juan* 17, "Biography of Hulü Guang": "The Hulü family has for generations produced great generals. [Hulü Guang] enjoyed fame over the entire West of the Pass and [his brother Hulü Xian] wielded power over the Turks. They have daughters who were Empresses and sons who married Princesses. How fearsome rumors can be!" (p.225)

[3] Shibutani (1966), p.17.

Working intermittently, I have taken ten years to complete this book. I also extend my gratitude to my colleague Professor Li Bozhong 李伯重, who recommended my work on rumors to Zhejiang University Press and its editor Ms. Zhao Qiong 赵琼. Ms. Zhao's encouragement and stupendous efficiency had contributed to my decision to become a hermit for several months to eventually finish writing the manuscript in the summer of 2011 on the banks of Weiming Lake.

I am particularly grateful to the initiative of Professor Li Bozhong and Dr. Lucy Rhymer (Senior Commissioning Editor of Cambridge University Press), the enthusiasm of Dr. Ye Min 叶敏 (Editor of Zhejiang University Press), and the valuable reviews and comments by Professors Wang Zijin 王子今, Pu Mu-chou 蒲慕州, and Chen Lidan 陈力丹, as well as other anonymous reviewers who were invited by Cambridge University Press. It is their support and efforts that have made the English translation of this work and the sponsorship from the National Social Science Fund of China possible.

As the author of this book, I have had the great pleasure to work together with Mr. Wee Kek Koon黄克群, the translator of this work. In addition to his professional expertise and experience in Chinese-to-English translation, Mr. Wee is well versed in and has a profound knowledge of Chinese history and the classics. I look forward to critiques and comments from readers of this work. Mr. Wee should be credited for any positive feedback.

My deepest gratitude to Qinghua, my beloved wife, and Erdene, my darling son, for their immeasurable support all these years.

Lu Zongli
2019
On the northern bank of Victoria Harbour, Hong Kong

Glossary

Chinese terms are romanised in the Pinyin system

Ai Zhang	哀章
Anding	安定
Anhan	安汉
Anhui	安徽
Anping	安平
Anyang	安阳
Ao Ying	敖英
Ba	巴
Ba	霸
Bashang	霸上
Ba Shu	巴蜀
Baxi	巴西
Baideng	白登
Bai gong	白公
Baihu	白虎
Bai Juyi	白居易
Baiqu	白渠
Bai tie	白帖
Ban Biao	班彪
Ban Gu	班固
Ban Zhi	班穉
Ban Ziru	班子孺
Bao Xuan	鲍宣
Beidi	北狄
Beidi	北地
Beihai	北海
Beimang	北邙
Beiye	北掖
Bifang	毕方

Biming	毕命
Biyang	辟阳
Bian Que	扁鹊
bianshi	辩士
bingchen	丙辰
Bing Ji	邴吉
bingxu	丙戌
Bingyi	病已
bingyin	丙寅
Bingzhou	并州
Bohai	勃海
Bo	薄
Boyi	伯夷
Bozhou	亳州
bu	布
buci	卜辞
bu xiang	卜相
Cai Shaogong	蔡少公
Cai Shu	蔡叔
Cai Yong	蔡邕
Cai Zhi	蔡质
can	粲
Cangjie	仓颉
Cangwu	苍梧
Cao Cao	曹操
Cao Pi	曹丕
Cao San	曹参
Cao Zhi	曹植
ce	策
ce ci	筴辞
Cen Gongxiao	岑公孝
Cen Xi	岑熙
Cen Zhi	岑晊
chanyan	谗言
Chang'an	长安
Changdi	昌帝
Chang jiang	长江
Changping	长平
Chang Qu	常璩
Changsha	长沙
Changshan	常山
Changxin	长信

Changxing	昌兴
Changyang	长杨
Changyi	昌邑
Chao Cuo	晁错
Che Qianqiu	车千秋
chen	谶
chen	陈
Chenyang	辰阳
Chen Chigong	陈持弓
Chen Chong	陈崇
Chen Dan	陈耽
Chen Fan	陈蕃, 陈藩
Chen Feng	陈丰
Chen Guangchong	陈光崇
Chen Huan	陈奂
Chen Huang	陈晃
chenji	谶记
Chen Ji	陈级
Chen Jing	陈景
Chen Jun	陈俊
Chenliu	陈留
Chen Ping	陈平
Chen Sheng	陈胜
chenwei	谶纬
chenyao	谶谣
Chen Zhongju	陈仲举
Chen Zun	陈遵
Chengdu	成都
Cheng Jiyou	成季友
Cheng Jin	成瑨
Chengyang	城阳
Chifufu	赤伏符
Chi Jian	郗俭
Chijingzi	赤精子
chijiu	赤九
Chimei	赤眉
Chisong	赤松
Chiyang	池阳
Chiyi zipi	鸱夷子皮
Chongling	舂陵
Chongye	重壄
Chu	楚

Chuqiu	楚丘
Chu Shaosun	褚少孙
Chunqiu	春秋
Chunyu Yue	淳于越
Cui Bao	崔豹
Cui Fa	崔发
Cui Shi	崔寔
Cui Shi	崔适
cun	寸
Daji	妲己
Dayu	大禹
Dayuan	大宛
Daze	大泽
Dai	代
Dai Changle	戴长乐
Dai Ping	戴凭
Dai Yi	戴异
Danyang	丹阳
Danzhu	丹朱
Dangshan	砀山
Dangtu	当涂
dangtu gao	当涂高
dao	刂(刀)
Daojiang	导江
Deyang	德阳
Deng Chen	邓晨
Deng Li	邓鲤
Deng Sui	邓绥
Deng Tong	邓通
Deng Yu	邓禹
Deng Zhi	邓骘
di	翟
di	狄
Diwu Lun	第五伦
Diao Kui	刁逵
Ding	丁
Ding Guangshi	丁广世
dingmao	丁卯
Ding Yuanzhi	丁原植
Dong Anyu	董安于
Dong Ba	董巴
Dongfang Shuo	东方朔

Dong Fu 董扶
Donghai 东海
Dongjing 东井
Dongjun 东郡
Dongling 东陵
Dongping 东平
Dong Shaoping 董少平
dongtao 董逃
Dong Teng 董腾
Dong Xian 董贤
Dong Xuan 董宣
Dong Zhong 董忠
Dong Zhongshu 董仲舒
Dong Zhuo 董卓
dou 斗
Dou Miao 窦妙
Dou Rong 窦融
Dou Wu 窦武
Dou Xian 窦宪
Dou Ying 窦婴
Du Du 杜笃
Du Jiang 杜姜
Du Mi 杜密
Du Qiao 杜乔
Du Qin 杜钦
Du Qiong 杜琼
Du Shi 杜诗
Du Yannian 杜延年
Du Ye 杜邺
Du You 杜佑
Du Yu 杜预
Duan Gui 段珪
eyan 讹言
eyao 讹谣
Er yan 迩言
Fa yan 法言
Fan Chong 樊崇
Fan Kuai 樊哙
Fan Kui 范魁
Fan Li 范蠡
Fan Mengbo 范孟博
Fan Pang 范滂

Fan Ye	范晔
Fan Zeng	范增
Fang Bowu	房伯武
fangshi	方士
Fang Wang	方望
Fang Zhi	房植
Feng Bao	冯豹
Feng Guang	冯光
Feng Li	冯立
Feng Meng	逢萌
fengshui	风水
Feng Tong	冯同
Fengxi	丰西
Feng Xian	冯羡
Feng Yewang	冯野王
Feng Zhongwen	冯仲文
Fu Bao	附宝
Fuchai	夫差
Fu fei	宓妃
Fufeng	扶风
Fu Jian	傅坚
fu la	伏腊
Fuling	阜陵
Fuping	富平
Fu Sheng	伏胜
Fusu	扶苏
Fuxi	伏羲
Fu Zhen	傅镇
Gai Deng	盖登
Gaixia	垓下
Gangu	甘谷
Gan Ji	干吉
Ganling	甘陵
Ganquan	甘泉
Gansu	甘肃
Gan Zhongke	甘忠可
gangmao	刚卯
Gaochang	高昌
Gaodu	高都
Gao Jianli	高渐离
Gao Qi	高起
Gaoxin	高辛

Gaoyang 高阳
Gaoyao 皋陶
Gao You 高诱
ge 歌
Ge Kuanrao 盖宽饶
Geng Jian 耿建
gengshen 庚申
Gengshi 更始
gengyin 庚寅
geyao 歌谣
Gong Chong 宫崇
Gong Liu 公刘
Gonglu 公路
Gong Sheng 龚胜
Gongsun Du 公孙度
Gongsun Shu 公孙述
Gongsun Zan 公孙瓒
Gongsun Zhi 公孙支
Gongyang 公羊
Gong Yu 贡禹
gongzi 公子
Gongzi You 公子友
Goujian 勾践
Gouyi 钩弋
Gouzhang 句章
Gugong Danfu 古公亶父
Gukou 谷口
Gu Yanwu 顾炎武
Gu Yong 谷永
Gu Ziyun 谷子云
Guan Bo 管伯
Guan Fu 灌夫
Guan Longfeng 关龙逢
Guan Shu 管叔
Guantao 馆陶
Guan Zhong 管仲
Guanghan 广汉
Guangling 广陵
Guangrao 广饶
Guangyi 广义
Guangzong 广宗
guisi 癸巳

Guizhou	贵州
Gun	鲧
Guo Chang	郭昌
Guo He	郭贺
Guo Huai	郭淮
Guo Ji	郭伋
Guo Pu	郭璞
Guo Qiaoqing	郭乔卿
Guo Qin	郭钦
Guo Rang	郭穰
Guo Shengtong	郭圣通
Guo Tai	郭泰
Guo Zhongchan	郭仲产
Guo Zun	郭遵
Han	汉, 韩
Handan	邯郸
Hangu	函谷
hanhanzi	汉含孳
Han Lang	寒朗
Han Xin	韩信
Han Yanshou	韩延寿
Han Zhong	韩众
Hanzhong	汉中
Haocheng	鄗城
Haochi	滈池
He	何
Hebei	河北
Hedong	河东
Hegu	河鼓
Hejian	河间
He Jin	何进
Henan	河南
Hexi	河西
He Xiu	何休
Hengcheng	横城
Heng'e	姮娥
Hengshan	衡山
Hong Gong	弘恭
Hongnong	弘农
Hongyang	红阳
Hou Ji	后稷
Hou Lan	侯览

Hou Sen	侯参
Hou Sheng	侯生
Hu	胡
Hubei	湖北
Hu Hai	胡亥
Hulü Guang	斛律光
Hulü Xian	斛律羡
Humu Sheng	胡母生
Hunan	湖南
Hu Tu	狐突
Hu Yin	胡寅
Huze	护泽
Hua Jiao	华峤
Hua Meng	华孟
Huayin	华阴
Huai	淮
Huainan	淮南
Huaiyang	淮阳
Huan Rong	桓荣
Huan Tan	桓谭
Huangfu Mi	皇甫谧
Huangfu Song	皇甫嵩
Huanghuang	黄皇
Huangping	黄平
Huangshan	黄山
Huang Wan	黄琬
Huang Wu	黄武
Huang Xiang	黄香
Hui De	惠得
Huo Guang	霍光
Huoquan	货泉
Huo Xian	霍显
Ji	冀
Ji An	汲黯
Jibei	济北
Ji Huanzi	季桓子
Ji Kang	嵇康
Jisun	季孙
Jiyang	济阳
Jiyin	济阴
Jizhou	冀州
Ji Zi	箕子

jia	甲
Jia Biao	贾彪
Jia Juanzhi	贾捐之
Jia Kui	贾逵
Jia Xu	贾诩
Jia Yan	贾延
Jia Yi	贾谊
jiayin	甲寅
jiazi	甲子
Jiangdu	江都
Jiangsu	江苏
Jiang Taigong	姜太公
Jiangzhong	江中
Jiaodong	胶东
Jiao Kuang	焦贶
Jiao	角
Jie	桀
Jiedu	解犊
jin	金
Jin	晋
Jin Midi	金日磾
Jin Wangsun	金王孙
Jing	泾
Jingchu	荆楚
Jing Dachun	井大春
Jing Dan	井丹
Jing Fang	京房
Jing Ke	荆轲
Jingzhou	荆州
Jiujiang	九江
Jiuquan	酒泉
Julu	巨鹿
jue	玃
Jun Buyi	隽不疑
Kang Shu	康叔
Kong Anguo	孔安国
Kong Guang	孔光
Kong Ning	孔宁
Kong Rong	孔融
Kongsang	空桑
Kong Yingda	孔颖达
Kuaiji	会稽

Kuang Ding	匡鼎
Kuang Heng	匡衡
Kui	夔
Kunlun	昆仑
Kunyang	昆阳
Laiwu	莱芜
Langling	朗陵
Langya	琅邪
Langzhong	阆中
Lao Dan	老聃
Lao Liang	牢梁
Lao Zi	老子
Lechang	乐昌
Lei Yi	雷义
li	里
Li	李, 醴, 栗
Li Chen	李棽
Li Chunfeng	李淳风
Li Daoyuan	郦道元
Li Gu	李固
Li Guang	李广
Li Han	李翰
Li Jue	李傕
Li Ling	李陵
Li Shan	李善
Li Shou	李守
Li Si	李斯
Liwu	蠡吾
Li Xian	李贤
Li Xun	李寻
Li Yan	李焉
Liyang	历阳
Li Yi	李轶
Li Ying	李膺
Lian Dan	廉丹
Lian Fan	廉范
Lian Shudu	廉叔度
Liang	梁
Liang Boxia	梁伯夏
Liang Buyi	梁不疑
Liang Ji	梁冀
Liangqiu Ci	梁丘赐

Liangqiu He 梁丘贺
Liangzhou 凉州
Liaoning 辽宁
Linzi 临淄
Ling Zhilong 凌稚隆
Liu 刘（劉）
liu 流, 六
Liu Ai 刘艾
Liu An 刘安
Liu Anguo 刘安国
Liu Anyan 刘安彦
Liu Ao 刘骜
Liu Ban 刘班
Liu Bang 刘邦
Liu Bao 刘保
Liu Bei 刘备
Liu Bi 刘濞
Liu Bian 刘辩
Liu Biao 刘表
Liu Bingyi 刘病已
Liu Bo 刘髆
Liu Bo 刘伯
Liu Che 刘彻
Liu Da 刘炟
Liu Dan 刘旦
Liu Duan 刘端
Liu Fuling 刘弗陵
Liu Gen 刘根
Liu Gong 刘龚
Liu He 刘贺
Liu Heng 刘恒
Liu Hong 刘宏, 刘闳
Liu Hu 刘祜
Liu Ji 刘基, 刘季
Liu Jinu 刘寄奴
Liu Jian 刘建
Liu Jie 刘节
Liu Jin 刘进
Liu Jing 刘京
Liu Jingshu 刘敬叔
Liu Ju 刘矩, 刘据
Liu Kai 刘开

Liu Kan 刘衎
Liu Li 刘悝
Liu Long 刘隆
Liu Mao 刘茂
Liu Meng 刘猛
Liu Min 刘闵
Liu Piao 刘嫖
Liu Qi 刘启
Liu Qian 刘迁
Liu Qin 刘钦
Liu Qing 刘庆
Liu Rong 刘荣
Liu Ruyi 刘如意
Liu Shang 刘尚
Liu Sheng 刘胜
Liu Shi 刘奭
Liu Shu 刘儵
Liu Suan 刘蒜
Liu Tao 刘陶
Liu Tui 刘蜕
Liu Wei 刘鲔
Liu Wen 刘文
Liu Wu 刘武
Liu Xi 刘喜
Liu Xiang 刘向
Liu Xie 刘协
Liu Xin 刘欣, 刘歆, 刘信
Liu Xiu 刘秀
Liu Xu 刘胥
Liu Xuan 刘玄
Liu Xun 刘询
Liu Yan 刘焉, 刘延
liuyan 流言
Liu Yang 刘扬
Liu Yin 刘縯
Liu Ying 刘婴, 刘英, 刘盈
Liu Yu 刘瑜, 刘虞, 刘宇, 刘裕
Liu Ze 刘泽
Liu Zhang 刘章, 刘长
Liu Zhao 刘昭, 刘肇
Liu Zhi 刘志
Liu Zhiji 刘知几

Liu Zhijia	刘执嘉
Liu Zhong	刘仲
Liu Zhuang	刘庄
Long	陇
Long Shang	龙尚
Longxi	陇西
Lu	鲁, 卢
lu	戮
Lu Fu	禄父
Lu Jia	陆贾
Lulin	绿林
Lu Wenshu	路温舒
Lu Yun	陆云
Lu Zhonglian	鲁仲连
Lü	吕
Lü Bu	吕布
Lü Kuan	吕宽
Lü Zhi	吕雉
Luan Ba	栾巴
Luoyang	洛阳
Luo Yao	骆曜
Ma Liao	马廖
Ma Mian	马勉
Ma Yan	马严
Ma Yuan	马援
Mang	芒
mao	卯
Meng Tong	孟通
Meng Xi	孟喜
Meng Yao	孟姚
Meng Zi	孟子
Mingguang	明光
Modu	冒顿
Mo Xi	末喜
mu	亩, 牧
Nandun	南顿
Nangong	南公, 南宫
Nanjun	南郡
Nanyang	南阳
Ni Kuan	儿宽
nie	孽
ou	偶

Ouyang	欧阳
ouyu	偶语
Pangu	盘古
Pei	沛
Pei Songzhi	裴松之
Pei Yin	裴骃
Pei You	裴优
Peng Yue	彭越
Peng Zu	彭祖
Pingcheng	平城
Pinglin	平林
Pingshu	平舒
Pingtong	平通
Pingyuan	平原
Puban	蒲反
Qi	齐, 启, 戚
qilin	麒麟
Qiang	羌
Qiang Hua	强华
Qiao	谯
Qiao Xuan	谯玄
Qiao Xuan	桥玄
Qiao Zhou	谯周
Qin	秦
qin	琴
Qin Bo	秦伯
Qinchuan	秦川
Qin Yueren	秦越人
qing	顷
Qinghe	清河
Qing Zhongliao	卿仲辽
Qingzhou	青州
Qu	屈
Qucheng	曲成
Quyang	曲阳
qun	群
Rang	穰
Raoyang	饶阳
Ren An	任安
renwu	壬午
Ren Yan	任延
renzi	壬子

Ru Chun	如淳
Runan	汝南
Ruyang	汝阳
Rui Liangfu	芮良夫
sanhu	三户
Sang Hongyang	桑弘羊
se	瑟
Shalu	沙麓
Shaqiu	沙丘
Shan Chen	单臣
Shandong	山东
Shaanxi	陕西
Shanyang	山阳
Shan Yang	单飏
Shang	商, 上
Shangcai	上蔡
Shangguan	上官
Shangguan An	上官安
Shangguan Jie	上官桀
Shao Yong	邵雍
Shen	参
Shenhu	神虎
Shentu Gang	申屠刚
Shentu Jia	申屠嘉
Shen Yiji	审食其
Shen Yue	沈约
sheng	升
Sheng	圣
shi	石
Shi Dan	史丹
Shi Qi	史祈
Shisun Rui	士孙瑞
Shi Xian	石显
Shouyang	首阳
Shu	蜀
Shuqi	叔齐
Shu Xiang	叔向
Shuyang	沭阳
Shuihudi	睡虎地
Shun	舜
Shunyang	顺阳
si	巳

Sima Biao	司马彪
Sima Guang	司马光
Sima Qian	司马迁
Sima Ru	司马如
Sima Tan	司马谈
Sima Xiangru	司马相如
Sima Zhen	司马贞
Sishang	虒上
Song	宋
Song Jun	宋均
Song	嵩
Song Yi	宋义
Song Yu	宋玉
Song Zhongzi	宋仲子
Su Bo'a	苏伯阿
Su Lang	苏郎
Su Qin	苏秦
Sui	隋
Sui Hong	眭弘
Sui Meng	眭孟
Suixiang	隧乡
Sun Bao	孙宝
Sun Chong	孙宠
Sun Kuang-Teh	孙广德
Sun Huizong	孙会宗
Sun Jin	孙禁
Sun Quan	孙权
Sun Shou	孙寿
Sun Xian	孙咸
Sun Xiu	孙休
Tai	太, 泰
Tang	汤, 唐
Tang Shuyu	唐叔虞
Tang Yao	唐尧
Tian Dan	田单
Tian Fen	田蚡
Tianjin	天津
Tianshui	天水
Tian Yannian	田延年
Tongyang	鲖阳
Wan	皖
Wancheng	宛城

Wang 王
Wang Chang 王长, 王畅
Wang Cheng 王成
Wang Chong 王充
Wang Feng 王凤
Wang Fu 王符, 王甫
Wang Gen 王根
Wang Hanshi 王含始
Wang He 王贺
Wang Huan 王涣
Wang Huang 王黄
Wang Jia 王嘉
Wang Kuang 王匡, 王况
Wang Lang 王郎
Wang Li 王立
Wang Liang 王梁
Wang Ling 王陵
Wanglu 王路
Wang Mang 王莽
Wang Ping 王平
Wang Qi 王奇
Wang Qiao 王乔
Wang Shang 王商
Wang She 王涉
Wang Sheng 王盛
Wang Shumao 王叔茂
Wang Shun 王舜
Wang Shuo 王朔
Wang Wengru 王翁孺
Wang Wu 王武
Wang Xing 王兴
Wang Xu 王盱
Wang Xun 王寻
Wang Yi 王邑
Wang Yu 王宇
Wang Yun 王允, 王恽
Wang Zhang 王章
Wang Zhengjun 王政君
Wang Zhi 王娡
Wang Ziqiao 王子乔
Wang Zun 王尊
Wei 魏, 卫, 渭

Wei Bao 魏豹
weidou 威斗
Wei Qing 卫青
Wei Si 维汜
Weisu 委粟
Wei Xiao 隗嚣
Wei Xuancheng 韦玄成
Wei Zhao 韦昭
Wei Zifu 卫子夫
Wenchang 文昌
Wen Jiang 文姜
Wen Qin 文钦
Wenshui 温水
Wu 乌, 吴
Wuan 武安
Wu Bei 伍被
wuchen 戊辰
Wuchengzi 务成子
Wudu 武都
Wugong 武功
Wu Guang 吴广
Wu Han 吴汉
Wuhuan 乌桓
Wuliang 武梁
Wulu 五鹿
Wulu Chongzong 五鹿充宗
Wu Rui 吴芮
Wusun 乌孙
Wuwei 武威
Wuyang 舞阳
Wu Zhang 吴章
wuzi 戊子
Wu Zi 吴子
Wu Zixu 伍子胥
Wuzuo 五柞
Xi 戏
Xifu Gong 息夫躬
Xi Guang 锡光
Xihe 西河
Xi Hu 郄縠
Ximen Junhui 西门君惠
Xiping 西平

Xia 夏
Xia Heliang 夏贺良
Xiahou Jian 夏侯建
Xiahou Sheng 夏侯胜
Xiahou Shichang 夏侯始昌
Xiamen 夏门
Xianbei 鲜卑
Xianyang 咸阳
Xianyu Wangren 鲜于妄人
Xiang 襄, 项
Xiang Kai 襄楷
Xiang Liang 项梁
Xiang Yu 项羽
Xiao 萧
Xiao He 萧何
Xiao 崤
Xiao Wangzhi 萧望之
Xie Guang 解光
Xie Xiao 谢嚣
Xie Ye 泄冶
Xincai 新蔡
Xincheng 新城
Xin Dang 辛当
Xindu 信都
xinyou 辛酉
Xin Yuanping 新垣平
Xing 邢
Xingping 兴平
Xiong 雄
Xiong Xin 熊心
Xu 徐, 许
Xu Feng 徐凤
Xu Fu 徐市, 许负
Xu Guang 徐广
Xu Jing 徐经
Xu Ren 徐仁
Xu Shang 许商
Xu Shen 许慎
Xu Shuzhong 许叔重
Xu Yang 许杨
Xu Yu 许鹹
Xu Zhao 许昭

Xu Zheng 徐整
Xu Zhi 许芝
Xuzhou 徐州
Xuanshi 宣室
Xuantu 玄菟
Xuan Yan 玄晏
Xue Han 薛汉
Xun Yue 荀悦
Xun Zi 荀子
Yan 燕, 严
Yan Anle 颜安乐
Yan Guang 燕广
Yanmen 雁门
Yan Pengzu 严彭祖
Yan Shigu 颜师古
Yanxiang 严乡
Yan Zhong 颜忠
Yanzhou 兖州
yang 阳
Yang Biao 杨彪
Yang Bing 杨秉
Yang Boqi 杨伯起
Yang Chang 杨敞
Yang'e 阳阿
Yang Fu 杨孚
Yang Hou 杨厚
Yang Quan 杨泉
Yang Shen 杨慎
Yang Tan 杨谭
Yang Xiong 扬雄
Yang Xu 羊续
Yang Xunji 杨循吉
Yang Yun 杨恽
Yang Zhen 杨震
Yang Zheng 杨政
Yangzhou 扬州
Yang Zixing 杨子行
yao 妖, 谣, 尧, 姚
Ye 叶
Yewang 野王
Yi 易, 翼
yi 乙

yi da zi	一大子
Yi Jia	伊嘉
Yi Jiang	邑姜
yi liu zi	一六子
Yinan	沂南
yiwei	乙未
Yixing	宜兴
Yi Xingfu	仪行父
Yi Yin	伊尹
Yizhou	益州
yin	阴
Yin	殷, 尹
Yin Deng	殷登
Yinling	阴陵
Yin Min	尹敏
Yin Shang	尹赏
yinyang	阴阳
Ying	嬴, 颍
Ying Bu	英布
Ying Chang	应玚
Yingchuan	颍川
Ying Gong	嬴公
Ying Shao	应劭
Yingshi	营室
Yingtao	嬰陶
Ying Zheng	嬴政
Yong	雍
You	友
Youping	游平
Youzhou	幽州
Yu	虞, 禹
Yu Dingguo	于定国
Yu Huan	鱼豢
Yu Shun	虞舜
Yuyang	渔阳
Yu Yue	俞樾
Yuzhou	豫州
Yuan An	袁安
Yuan Ang	袁盎
Yuancheng	元城
Yuan Hong	袁宏
Yuan Shao	袁绍

Yuan Shu 袁术
Yuan Tiangang 袁天纲
Yuanwu 原武
Yue 越
Yunmeng 云梦
Yunzhong 云中
Zang Er 臧儿
Zang Gong 臧宫
Zangke 牂牁
Zang Tu 臧荼
Zang Xin 臧信
Zeng 鄫
Zhai Fangjin 翟方进
Zhai Yi 翟义
Zhai Ziwei 翟子威
Zhai Zun 祭遵
zhang 长, 丈
Zhang Anshi 张安世
Zhang Ang 张卬
Zhang Ao 张敖
Zhang Chang 张敞
Zhang Chu 张楚
Zhang Fang 张放
Zhang Gang 张纲
Zhang Han 章邯
Zhang He 章河
Zhang Heng 张衡
Zhang Hua 张华
Zhang Ji 张济
Zhang Jiao 张角
Zhang Liang 张良
Zhang Lin 张临
Zhang Man 张满
Zhang Meng 张猛
Zhang Rang 张让
Zhang Shoujie 张守节
Zhang Shouwang 张寿王
Zhang Tang 张汤
Zhang Xiu 张修
Zhang Xuan 张玄
Zhang Yan 张晏
Zhang Yanshou 张延寿

Zhang Yi 张揖
Zhang Yong 张永
Zhang You 张攸
Zhang Yu 张禹
Zhang Zhu 张助
Zhang Zijiao 张子蟜
Zhao 赵, 召
Zhao Feiyan 赵飞燕
Zhao Gao 赵高
Zhao Guanghan 赵广汉
Zhao Hede 赵合德
Zhao Jianzi 赵简子
Zhao Li 赵利
Zhao Tuo 赵佗
Zhao Xi 赵熹
Zhao Yang 赵鞅
Zhao Yi 赵翼
Zhao Yu 赵语
Zhejiang 浙江
Zhen 轸
Zhending 真定
Zhen Feng 甄丰
Zhen Fu 甄阜
Zhen Xun 甄寻
Zheng 郑
Zheng Hong 郑弘
Zheng Kuanzhong 郑宽中
Zheng Qiao 郑樵
Zheng Sa 郑飒
Zheng Xing 郑兴
Zheng Xuan 郑玄
Zhi Yun 郅恽
zhong 众
Zhong Li 重黎
Zhongli Yi 钟离意
Zhou 周, 纣
Zhou Bo 周勃
Zhou Changshan 周长山
Zhou Fu 周福
Zhou Ju 周举
Zhou Kan 周堪
Zhou Qun 周群

Zhou Shu	周舒
Zhou Xie	周燮
Zhou Xu	周栩
Zhou Xuanguang	周宣光
Zhou Yafu	周亚夫
Zhou Ze	周泽
Zhou Zhang	周章
Zhou Zhongjin	周仲进
zhu	筑
Zhu Fu	朱浮
Zhuge Lang	诸葛亮
Zhuliang	诸梁
Zhu Maichen	朱买臣
Zhu Tian	祝恬
Zhu Wei	朱鲔
Zhu Wengzi	朱翁子
Zhu Xi	朱熹
Zhuya	珠厓
Zhuyun	朱云
Zi Chan	子产
Zi Gao	子高
Zi Yu	子舆
Zong Zi	宗资
Zou Yan	邹衍
Zuo	左
Zuo Ci	左慈
Zuo Da'e	左大娥
Zuo Sheng	左圣
Zuo Wu	左吴
Zuo Xiao'e	左小娥

Bibliography

Reference Books

Bielenstein, Hans Henrik August. *The Bureaucracy of Han Times*. Cambridge: Cambridge University Press. 1980.

Boyer, Paul. *When Time Shall Be No More: Prophecy Belief in Modern American Culture*. Cambridge, MA: Harvard University Press. 1992.

Dull, Jack L. *Official Titles of the Han Dynasty: A Tentative List Compiled for the Han Dynasty History Project*. Seattle: University of Washington, 2006;

https://oregondigital.org/sets/easia/oregondigital:df72rs71t#page/68/mode/1up

Hucker, Charles O. *A Dictionary of Official Titles in Imperial China.* Stanford: Stanford University Press, 1985.

http://www2.iath.virginia.edu/saxon/servlet/SaxonServlet?source=xwomen/texts/hanshu.xml&style=xwomen/xsl/dynaxml.xsl&chunk.id=tpage&doc.view=tocc&doc.lang=bilingual) <How should we cite this kind of reference?>

Legge, James. *The Chinese Classics: With a Translation, Critical and Exegetical Notes, Prolegomena, and Copious Indexes*, 5 vols. London: Trubner, 1861–1872; https://ctext.org/.

Luo Zhufeng 罗竹风, editor-in-chief. *Hanyu da cidian* 汉语大词典 [Comprehensive Dictionary of Chinese Phrases]. Shanghai: Hanyu dacidian chubanshe, 1986–1994.

Nienhauser, William H. Jr., editor and translator. *The Grand Scribe's Records*, vols. 1, 5, 6, 7, and 8. Bloomington: Indiana University Press, 1994–2008.

Xia Zhengnong 夏征农, editor-in-chief. *Cihai* 辞海 [Cihai]. Shanghai: Shanghai cishu chubanshe, 1999.

Xu Zhongshu 徐中舒, editor-in-chief. *Hanyu da zidian* 汉语大字典 [Comprehensive Dictionary of Chinese Words]. Chengdu: Sichuan cishu chubanshe, Wuhan: Hubei cishu chubanshe, 1986–1990.

Zhongguo shehui kexueyuan yuyan yanjiusuo cidian bianji shi 中国社会科学院语言研究所词典编辑室, editor. *Xiandai hanyu cidian* 现代汉语词典 [Dictionary of Modern Chinese] 5th ed. Beijing: Shangwu yinshuguan, 2005.

Primary Sources

Bai Juyi 白居易. *Bai Juyi ji* 白居易集 [Collected Works of Bai Juyi]. Collated and edited by Gu Xuejie 顾学颉. Beijing: Zhonghua shuju, 1979.

Ban Gu 班固. *Han shu* 汉书 [History of the Former Han]. Beijing: Zhonghua shuju, 1964.

Ban Gu 班固. *Han shu buzhu* 汉书补注 [History of the Former Han: Additional Annotations]. Annotated by Wang Xianqian 王先谦. Beijing: Zhonghua zhuju, 1983.

Ban Gu 班固 et al. *Baihutong shuzheng* 白虎通疏证 [Collected Discussions at the White Tiger Hall: Explanations and Verifications]. Explained and verified by Chen Li 陈立. Beijing: Zhonghua shuju, 1994.

Cangjie pian 仓颉篇 [Book of Cangjie]. In *Congshu jicheng chubian* 丛书集成初编 [Complete Collection of Books from Various Collectanea, the First Series]. Shanghai: Shangwu yinshuguan, 1935–1937.

Cao Zhi 曹植. *Cao Zijian ji pingzhu* 曹子建集评注 [Commentaries and Annotations on the Collected Works of Cao Zijian]. Edited by Ding Yan 丁晏, annotated by Huang Jie 黄节. Taipei: Shijie shuju, 1998.

Chang Qu 常璩. *Huayang guozhi jiaobu tuzhu* 华阳国志校补图注 [Record of States South of Mount Hua: A Collated, Illustrated, and Annotated Edition]. Collated and annotated by Ren Naiqiang 任乃强. Shanghai: Shanghai guji chubanshe, 1987.

Chen Huan 陈奂. *Shi maoshi zhuanshu* 诗毛氏传疏 [Explaining the Mao Commentary on Book of Odes]. Taipei: Shijie shuju, 1957.

Chen Shou 陈寿. *San guo zhi* 三国志 [Records of the Three Kingdoms]. Annotated by Pei Songzhi 裴松之. Beijing: Zhonghua shuju, 1971.

Chen Songchang 陈松长. "Boshu *xingde yipian* shiwen" 帛书《刑德》乙篇释文 [Transcription of the silk text of *Punishment and Grace*, Volume II]. Collected in Ting Yuan-Chih 丁原植, editor-in-chief. *Mawangdui boshu xing de yanjiu lungao* 马王堆帛书《刑德》研究论稿 [Essays on the Silk Text *Punishment and Grace* Unearthed at Mawangdui]. Taipei: Taiwan guji chuban youxian gongsi, 2001.

Chen Zhi 陈埴. *Mu zhong ji* 木钟集 [Collection of the Wood and Bell]. In *Siku quanshu* 四库全书 [The Complete Library in Four Sections]. Shanghai: Shanghai guji chubanshe, 1987.

Cui Shi 崔适. *Shiji tanyuan* 史记探源 [Finding the Sources of the Grand Scribe's Records]. Beijing: Zhonghua shuju, 1986.

Ding Fubao 丁福保. *Shuo wen jie zi gulin* 说文解字诂林 [An Explication of Written Characters: Elucidations]. Beijing: Zhonghua shuju, 1988.

Du Wenlan 杜文澜, editor. *Gu yao yan* 古谣谚 [Ancient Rhymes and Adages]. Collated and edited by Zhou Shaoliang 周绍良. Beijing: Zhonghua shuju, 2000.

Du You 杜佑. *Tong dian* 通典 [Comprehensive Institutions]. In *Xu xiu siku quanshu* 续修四库全书 [Complete Library in Four Sections Continued]. Shanghai: Shanghai guji chubanshe, 1987.

Duan Yucai 段玉裁. *Shuo wen jie zi zhu* 说文解字注 [An Explication of Written Characters: Annotations]. Shanghai: Shanghai guji chubanshe, 1981.

Fan Ye 范晔. *Hou han shu* 后汉书 [History of the Later Han]. Beijing: Zhonghua shuju, 1965.

Fang Xuanling 房玄龄 et al. *Jin shu* 晋书 [History of Jin]. Beijing: Zhonghua shuju, 1974.

Gu Yanwu 顾炎武. *Ri zhi lu jishi* 日知录集释 [Records of Daily Recognitions: Collected Expositions]. Explicated by Huang Rucheng 黄汝成, collated and edited by Luan Baoqun 栾保群 and Lu Zongli 吕宗力. Shanghai: Shanghai guji chubanshe, 2006.

Guan zi 管子. *Guan zi zhu yi* 管子注译 [Guan Zi: Annotations and Interpretations]. Annotated and interpreted by Zhao Shouzheng 赵守正. Nanning: Guangxi renmin chubanshe, 1982.

Guo Maoqian 郭茂倩, editor. *Yuefu shiji* 乐府诗集 [Collection of Music Bureau Poems]. Beijing: Zhonghua shuju, 1983.

He Jianzhang 何建章. *Zhanguo ce zhushi* 战国策注释 [Strategies of the Warring States: Annotations and Explications]. Beijing: Zhonghua shuju, 1990.

Hong Mai 洪迈. *Yi jian zhi* 夷坚志 [Records of Yijian]. Collated and edited by He Zhuo 何卓. Beijing: Zhonghua shuju, 1981.

He Qinggu 何清谷. *Sanfu huangtu jiaozhu* 三辅黄图校注 [Yellow Maps of the Three Metropolitan Areas: Annotations]. Xian: Sanqin chubanshe, 1998.

Hsiao Kung-Ch'üan. 萧公权. *Zhongguo zhengzhi sixiang shi (shang)* 中国政治思想史（上）[History of Chinese Political Thought, Volume I]. Taipei: Lianjing chubanshe, 1982.

Hu Yin 胡寅. *Zhi tang du shi guanjian* 致堂读史管见 [Zhitang's Humble Opinions on History]. In *Xu xiu siku quanshu* 续修四库全书 [Complete Library in Four Sections Continued]. Shanghai: Shanghai guji chubanshe, 2002.

Huan Kuan 桓宽. *Yantie lun jiaozhu* 盐铁论校注 [Discourses on Salt and Iron: Annotations]. Beijing: Zhonghua shuju, 1992.

Jia Yi 贾谊. *Jia yi ji* 贾谊集 [Collected Works of Jia Yi]. Shanghai: Shanghai renmin chubanshe, 1976.

Jia Yi 贾谊. *Xin shu jiaozhu* 新书校注 [New Writings: Annotations]. Annotated by Yan Zhenyi 阎振益 and Zhong Xia 钟夏. Beijing: Zhonghua shuju, 2000.

Knechtges, David R. and Tong Xiao. *Wen Xuan or Selections of Refined Literature,* vols. I, II. Princeton: Princeton Legacy Library, 2014.

Knoblock, John. *Xunzi: A Translation and Study of the Complete Works*, vol. 1, Books 1–6. Stanford: Stanford University Press, 1988.

Li Daoyuan 郦道元. *Shui jing zhu jiaozheng* 水经注校证 [Annotated Water Classic: Collation and Verifications]. Annotated and verified by Chen Qiaoyi 陈桥驿. Beijing: Zhonghua shuju, 2007.

Li Yanshou 李延寿. *Nan shi* 南史 [History of the Southern Dynasties]. Beijing: Zhonghua shuju, 1975.

Liang Yusheng 梁玉绳. *Shiji zhi yi* 史记志疑 [Records of Questions about *The Grand Scribe's Records*]. Beijing: Zhonghua shuju, 1981.

Lie Zi 列子. *Lie zi jishi* 列子集释 [Lie Zi: Collected Expositions]. Explicated by Yang Bojun 杨伯峻. Beijing: Zhonghua shuju, 1979.

Liu An 刘安. *Huainan honglie jijie* 淮南鸿烈集解 [The Great and Bright of Huainan: Collected Expositions]. Explicated by Liu Wendian 刘文典. Beijing: Zhonghua shuju, 1989.

Liu tao 六韬 [Six Secret Teachings]. In *Zhongguo bingshu jicheng di yi ce* 中国兵书集成第*1*册 [Compendium of Chinese Military Treatises, Volume I]. Beijing: Jiefangjun chubanshe, Shenyang: Liaoshen shushe, 1987.

Liu Tui 刘蜕. *Liu tui ji* 刘蜕集 [Collected Works of Liu Tui]. In *Sibu congkan chubian* 四部丛刊初编 [First Series of the Collectanea of the Four Categories]. Compact edition. Taipei: Taiwan shangwu yinshuguan, 1965.

Liu Xi 刘熙. *Shi ming* 释名 [Explanation of Names]. In *Sibu congkan chubian* 四部丛刊初编 [First Series of the Collectanea of the Four Categories]. Shanghai: Shangwu yinshuguan, 1929.

Liu Xiang 刘向. *Xin xu* 新序 [New Order]. In *Siku quanshu* 四库全书 [The Complete Library in Four Sections]. Shanghai: Shanghai guji chubanshe, 1990.

Liu Xiang 刘向. *Lienü zhuan buzhu* 列女传补注 [Biographies of Exemplary Women: Additional Annotations]. Annotated by Wang Zhaoyuan 王照圆. In *Xu xiu siku quanshu* 续修四库全书 [Complete Library in Four Sections Continued]. Shanghai: Shanghai guji chubanshe, 2002.

Liu Xiang 刘向. *Shuo yuan jiaozheng* 说苑校证 [Garden of Tales: Collations and Verifications]. Annotated and verified by Xiang Zonglu 向宗鲁. Beijing: Zhonghua shuju, 1987.

Liu Yan 刘炎. *Er yan* 迩言 [Shallow words]. In *Siku quanshu* 四库全书 [The Complete Library in Four Sections]. Shanghai: Shanghai guji chubanshe, 1987.

Liu Zhen 刘珍 et al. *Dongguan han ji jiaozhu* 东观汉记校注 [Eastern Library's Records of Han: Collations and Annotations]. Collated and annotated by Wu Shuping 吴树平. Beijing: Zhonghua shuju, 2008.

Liu Zhiji 刘知几. *Shi tong tongshi* 史通通释 [Generality of Historiography: General Expositions]. Explicated by Pu Qilong 浦起龙. Shanghai: Shanghai guji chubanshe, 1978.

Loewe, Michael, editor. *Early Chinese Texts: A Bibliographical Guide.* Berkeley: The Society for the Study of Early China and the Institute of East Asian Studies, University of California, 1993.

Lu Jia 陆贾. *Xin yu jiaozhu* 新语校注 [New Words: Collations and Annotations]. Collated and annotated by Wang Liqi 王利器. Beijing: Zhonghua shuju, 1986.

Lu Qinli 逯钦立, edited and collated by. *Xianqin han weijin nanbeichao shi* 先秦汉魏晋南北朝诗 [Poems of the Pre-Qin, Han, Wei, Jin, and the Northern and Southern Dynasties]. Beijing: Zhonghua shuju, 1983.

Lü Buwei 吕不韦. *Lüshi Chunqiu xin jiaoshi* 吕氏春秋新校释 [Master Lü's Spring and Autumn Annals: New Expositions]. Explicated by Chen Qiyou 陈其猷. Shanghai: Shanghai guji chubanshe, 2002.

Ma Chengyuan 马承源, editor-in-chief. *Shanghai bowuguan cang zhanguo chu zhushu er* 上海博物馆藏战国楚竹书二 [Bamboo Scrolls from Chu during the Warring States Period in the Shanghai Museum Collection, Volume II]. Shanghai: Shanghai guji chubanshe, 2002.

Meng Zi 孟子. *Meng zi zhengyi* 孟子正义 [Mencius: Standard Interpretation]. Standard interpretation by Jiao Xun 焦循, collated and edited by Shen Wenzhuo 沈文倬. Beijing: Zhonghua shuju, 1987.

Miao Wenyuan 缪文远. *Zhanguo ce xin jiaozhu* 战国策新校注 [Strategies of the Warring States: New Annotations]. Chengdu: Bashu shushe, 1987.

Pi Xirui 皮锡瑞. *Jinwen shangshu kaozheng* 今文尚书考证 [The "New Text" of the *Book of Documents*: Verifications]. Collated and edited by Sheng Dongling 盛冬铃 and Chen Kang 陈抗. Beijing: Zhonghua shuju, 1989.

Ruan Yuan 阮元, editor. *Shisan jing zhushu* 十三经注疏 [Annotations and Explanations of the Thirteen Classics]. Beijing: Zhonghua shuju, 1980.

Shanghai shifan daxue guji zhengli zu 上海师范大学古籍整理组. *Guoyu* 国语 [Discourses of the States]. Shanghai: Shanghai guji chubanshe, 1978.

Shen Yue 沈约. *Song shu* 宋书 [History of Song]. Beijing: Zhonghua shuju, 1974.

Shuihudi qin mu zhujian zhengli xiaozu 睡虎地秦墓竹简整理小组. *Shuihudi qin mu zhujian* 睡虎地秦墓竹简 [Bamboo Slips from the Qin Tomb in Shuihudi]. Beijing: Wenwu chubanshe, 1990.

Sima Guang 司马光. *Zi zhi tong jian* 资治通鉴 [Comprehensive Mirror in Aid of Governance]. Beijing: Zhonghua shuju, 1956.

Sima Qian 司马迁. *Shiji* 史记 [The Grand Scribe's Records]. Beijing: Zhonghua shuju, 1959.

Sima Qian 司马迁. *Shiji huizhu kaozheng fu jiaobu* 史记会注考证附校补 [The Grand Scribe's Records: Collected Annotations and Verifications, with Additional Annotations]. Collectively annotated and verified by Takigawa Kametaro 泷川资言, collated and additionally annotated by Mizusawa Toshitada 水沢 利忠. Shanghai: Shanghai guji chubanshe, 1986.

Song Yanshen, editor. *Zhongguo shixueshi gangyao* 中国史学史纲要 [Outline of the History of Chinese Historiography]. Changchun: Dongbei shifa daxue chubanshe, 1992.

Sun Xingyan 孙星衍 et al., editors. *Han guan liu zhong* 汉官六种 [Six Works about Han Officials]. Collated and edited by Zhou Tianyou 周天游. Beijing: Zhonghua shuju, 1990.

Sun Yirang 孙诒让. *Mo zi jian gu* 墨子閒诂 [Mo Zi: Annotations]. Collated and edited by Sun Qizhi 孙启治. Beijing: Zhonghua shuju, 2001.

Tao Zongyi 陶宗仪, editor. *Shuo fu* 说郛 [Collection of Tales and Short Stories]. Reprint of 1927 Hanfenlou edition. Beijing: Zhongguo shudian, 1986.

Wang Chong 王充. *Lun heng jiao shi* 论衡校释 [Critical Essays: Expositions]. Explicated by Huang Hui 黄晖. Beijing: Zhonghua shuju, 1990.

Wang Fu 王符. *Qian fu lun jian* 潜夫论笺 [Disquisitions of the Hidden Scholar: Annotations]. Annotated by Wang Jipei 汪继培, edited by Peng Ze 彭泽. Beijing: Zhonghua shuju, 1979.

Wei Shou 魏收. *Wei shu* 魏书 [Book of Wei]. Beijing: Zhonghua shuju, 1974.

Wei Zheng 魏征 et al. *Sui shu* 隋书 [History of Sui]. Beijing: Zhonghua shuju, 1973.

Wu Qi 吴起. *Wu Zi* 吴子 [Wu Zi]. In *Sibu congkan chubian* 四部丛刊初编 [First Series of the Collectanea of the Four Categories]. Compact edition. Taipei: Taiwan shangwu yinshuguan, 1965.

Wu Xiaoqiang 吴小强. *Qin jian ri shu jishi* 秦简日书集释 [Almanacs on Qin Bamboo Slips: Collected Expositions]. Changsha: Yuelu shushe, 2000.

Xiao Tong 萧统, editor. *Wen xuan* 文选 [Selections of Refined Literature]. Annotated by Li Shan 李善. Beijing: Zhonghua shuju reprint of the Hu Kejia 胡克家 imprint, 1977.

Xu Dong 许洞. *Hu qian jing* 虎钤经 [The Tiger Military Treatise]. In *Congshu jicheng chubian* 丛书集成初编 [First Series of Complete Collection of Books from Various Collectanea]. Shanghai: Shangwu yinshuguan, 1935–1937.

Xu Shen 许慎. *Shuo wen jie zi* 说文解字 [An Explication of Written Characters]. Reprint of the Song-period edition collated by Xu Xuan 徐铉. Shanghai: Hanfenlou, 1919.

Xu Shen 许慎. *Shuo wen jie zi* 说文解字 [An Explication of Written Characters]. Reprint of the Song-period edition collated by Xu Xuan 徐铉 and re-collated by Sun Xingyan 孙星衍. Beijing: Zhonghua shuju, 1985.

Xu Weiyu 许维遹, explicated by. *Han shi waizhuan jishi* 韩诗外传集释 [Exoteric Traditions of the Han Version of the Odes: Collected Expositions]. Beijing: Zhonghua shuju, 1980.

Xu Yuangao 徐元诰. *Guoyu jijie* 国语集解 [Discourses of the States: Collected Expositions]. Collated and edited by Wang Shumin 王树民 and Shen Changyun 沈长云. Beijing: Zhonghua shuju, 2002.

Xun Yue 荀悦. *Qianhan ji* 前汉纪 [Annals of the Former Han]. In *Sibu congkan chubian* 四部丛刊初编 [First Series of the Collectanea of the Four Categories]. Shanghai: Shangwu yinshuguan, 1929.

Xun Yue 荀悦. *Lianghan ji* 两汉纪 [Annals of the Two Han Dynasties]. Collated and edited by Zhang Lie 张烈. Beijing: Zhonghua shuju, 2002.

Xun Zi 荀子. *Xun zi jijie* 荀子集解 [Xun Zi: Collected Explications]. Explicated by Wang Xianqian 王先谦. Beijing: Zhonghua shuju, 1988.

Yan Kejun 严可均, editor. *Quan shanggu sandai qinhan sanguo liuchao wen* 全上古三代秦汉三国六朝文 [Complete Writings of High Antiquity, the Three Eras, Qin, Han, the Three Kingdoms, and the Six Dynasties]. Beijing: Zhonghua shuju, 1958.

Yang Bojun 杨伯峻. *Chunqiu zuozhuan zhu* 春秋左传注 [Commentary of Zuo on the Spring and Autumn Annals: Annotations]. Beijing: Zhonghua shuju, 1990.

Yasui Kōzan 安居 香山 and Nakamura Shōhachi 中村 璋八, compilers and editors. *Weishu jicheng* 纬书集成 [Compendium of Apocryphal Books]. Shijiazhuang: Hebei renmin chubanshe, 1994.

Ying Shao 应劭. *Fengsu tong yi jiaozhu* 风俗通义校注 [Comprehensive Meaning of Customs and Habits: Annotations]. Annotated by Wang Liqi 王利器. Beijing: Zhonghua shuju, 1981.

Yong Rong 永瑢, Ji Yun 纪昀, et al., compilers. *Siku quanshu zongmu* 四库全书总目 [Catalog of the Complete Library in Four Sections]. Beijing: Zhonghua shuju, 1965.

Yuan Hong 袁宏. *Houhan ji jiaozhu* 后汉纪校注 [Annals of the Later Han: Collations ans Annotations]. Collated and annotated by Zhou Tianyou 周天游. Tianjin: Tianjin guji chubanshe, 1987.

Yuan Kang 袁康. *Yue jue shu jiao shi* 越绝书校释 [The Glory of Yue: Expositions]. Explicated by Li Bujia 李步嘉. Wuhan: Wuhan daxue chubanshe, 1992.

Yuan Ke 袁珂, collated and annotated by. *Shanhai jing jiaozhu* 山海经校注 [Classic of Mountains and Seas: Collations and Annotations]. Shanghai: Shanghai guji chubanshe, 1980.

Zeng Gongliang 曾公亮, Ding Du 丁度, et al. *Wujing zongyao qianji* 武经总要前集 [Military Classic: Precis, Volume I]. In *Zhongguo bingshu jicheng, di 3–5 ce* 中国兵书集成，第3–5册 [Compendium of Chinese Military Treatises, Volumes 3–5]. Beijing: Jiefangjun chubanshe, Shenyang: Liaoshen shushe, 1988.

Zhangjiashan hanmu zhujian er si qi hao hanmu zhengli xiaozu 张家山汉墓竹简二四七号汉墓整理小组. *Zhangjiashan hanmu zhujian (er si qi hao mu)* 张家山汉墓竹简（ 二四七号墓 ）[Bamboo Slips from the Zhangjiashan Han-Period Tomb (Tomb No. 247)]. Beijing: Wenwu chubanshe, 2001.

Zhangsun Wuji 长孙无忌 et al. *Tanglü shuyi* 唐律疏议 [Laws of the Tang: Explanations and Definitions]. Collated and edited by Liu Junwen 刘俊文. Beijing: Zhonghua shuju, 1983.

Zhao Yi 赵翼. *Nianer shi zhaji jiaozheng* 廿二史札记校证 [Collected Notes on the Twenty-Two Histories: Collations and Verifications]. Collated and verified by Wang Shumin 王树民. Beijing: Zhonghua shuju, 1984.

Zheng Qiao 郑樵. *Tongzhi ershi lue* 通志二十略 [Comprehensive History: Twenty Treatises]. Collated and edited by Wang Shumin 王树民. Beijing: Zhonghua shuju, 1995.

Zhou Tianyou 周天游, edited and annotated by. *Bajia houhan shu jizhu* 八家后汉书辑注 [Collections and Annotations of the Eight Versions of the History of the Later Han]. Shanghai: Shanghai guji chubanshe, 1986.

Zhu Xi 朱熹. *Shiji zhuan* 诗集传 [Collected Commentaries on the Book of Odes]. Beijing: Zhonghua shuju, 1958.

Zhu Zugeng 诸祖耿. *Zhanguo ce jizhu huikao (zengbu ben)* 战国策集注汇考（增补本）[Strategies of the Warring States: Collected Annotations and Authentications (Supplementary Edition)]. Nanjing: Fenghuang chubanshe, 2008.

Zhuang Zi 庄子. *Zhuang zi jishi* 庄子集释 [Zhuang Zi: Collected Expositions]. Explicated by Guo Qingfan 郭庆藩. Beijing: Zhonghua shuju, 1961.

Secondary Sources

Aberbach, David. *Imperialism and Biblical Prophecy, 750–500 BCE*. London: Routledge, 1993.

Allport, Gordon W. and Leo Postman. *The Psychology of Rumor*. Reissued. New York: Russell & Russell, Inc., 1965. (Copyright 1947 by Henry Holt and Company).

Aune, David Edward. *Prophecy in Early Christianity and the Ancient Mediterranean World*. Grand Rapids: William B. Eerdmans Publishing Company, 1983.

Bai Shouyi白寿彝. *Bai shouyi shixue lunji (xia)* 白寿彝史学论集（下）[Collected Essays on Historiography by Bai Shouyi, Volume II]. Beijing: Beijing shifan daxue chubanshe, 1994.

Bai Shouyi白寿彝 et al., editor-in-chief. *Zhongguo tongshi di 4 juan* 中国通史第4卷 [General History of China, Volume IV]. Shanghai: Shanghai renmin chubanshe, 1995.

Bold, Alan. *The Ballad*. New York: Methuen & Co. Ltd., 1979.

Borden, Diane and Kerric Harvey, editors. *The Electronic Grapevine: Rumor, Reputation, and Reporting in the New On-Line Environment*. Mahwah: Lawrence Erlbaum Associates, 1998.

Bronner, Stephen Eric. *A Rumor about the Jews: Reflections on Antisemitism and the Protocols of the Learned Elders of Zion*. New York: St. Martin's Press, 2000.

Cahill, Suzanne E. *The Queen Mother of the West in Medieval China*. Stanford: Stanford University Press, 1993.

Chao Fulin 晁福林. *Zhou taishi dan chenyu kao* 周太史儋谶语考 [A Study of the *Chen* Prophetic Expressions of Grand Scribe Dan of the Zhou Period]. In *Shixue yuekan* 史学月刊 [History Monthly]. 1993, 6 21–27.

Chen Guangchong 陈光崇. *Guanyu fan ye houhan shu de san ge wenti* 关于范晔《后汉书》的三个问题 [Thee Problems with Fan Ye's *History of the Later Han*]. In *Zhongguo shixueshi luncong* 中国史学史论丛 [Collected Essays in the History of Chinese Historiography]. Shenyang: Liaoning renmin chubanshe, 1984.

Chen Hsueh-Ping 陈雪屏. *Yaoyan de xinli* 谣言的心理 [The Psychology of Rumors]. Changsha yiwen congshu bianjibu, 1939.

Chen, Jack W. and David Schaberg, editors. *Idle Talk: Gossip and Anecdote in Traditional China*. Berkeley: University of California Press, 2014.

Chen Lidan 陈力丹. *Yulun xue–yulun daoxiang yanjiu* 舆论学—舆论导向研究 [Public Opinion Studies: A Study on Directing Public Opinion]. Beijing: Zhongguo guangbo dianshi chubanshe, 1999.

Chen Yexin 陈业新. "Liang hanshu wuxing zhi guanyu ziran zaihai de jiazi yu renshi" 两《汉书》"五行志"关于自然灾害的记载与认识 [Records and Understanding of Natural Disasters in the "Treatises on the Five Agents" in *History of the Former Han* and *History of the Later Han*]. In *Shixueshi yanjiu* 史学史研究 [Historiographal Research]. 2002, 3: 43–48.

Chen Zhi 陈直. *Shiji xinzheng* 史记新证 [The Grand Scribe's Records: New Verifications]. Tianjin: Tianjin renmin chubanshe, 1979.

Cho, Hyunyi. "Public Opinion as Personal Cultivation: A Normative Notion and a Source of Social Control in Traditional China." In *International Journal of Public Opinion Research*. 2000, 12 (3): 299–323.

Chou Ying-hsiung. "The Wooden-tongued Bell: The Uses of Literature and Poetry-collecting in Han China." Unpublished Ph.D. dissertation. University of California, San Diego, 1977.

Cohen, Paul A. *History in Three Keys: The Boxers as Event, Experience, and Myth*. New York: Columbia University Press, 1997.

Davis, Thomas J. *A Rumor of Revolt: The "Great Negro Plot" in Colonial New York*. New York: Free Press, 1985.

DeBendittis, Peter. *Guam's Trial of the Century: News, Hegemony, and Rumor in an American Colony*. Westport: Praeger, 1993.

DiFonzo, Nicholas and Prashant Bordia. *Rumor Psychology: Social and Organizational Approaches*. Washington, DC: American Psychological Association, 2007.

Dumont, Jean-Paul. "Rumor and Tremor in a Visayan Community: Some Anthropological Reflections on Symbolic Power." In *Silliman Journal* (Dumaguete City, Philippines). 1980, 27 (4): 258–264.

Farber, Seth. *Madness, Heresy, and the Rumor of Angels: The Revolt against the Mental Health System*. Chicago: Open Court, 1993.

Farge, Arlette and Jacques Revel. *The Vanishing Children of Paris: Rumor and Politics before the French Revolution*. Cambridge, MA: Harvard University Press, 1991.

Fine, Gary Alan. *Whispers on the Color Line: Rumor and Race in America*. Berkeley: University of California Press, 2001.

Frye, Northrop. *Words with Power*. San Diego: Harcourt Brace Jovanovich, , 1990.

Gao Dianshi 高殿石. *Zhongguo lidai tongyao jizhu* 中国历代童谣辑注 [Children's Songs in Chinese History: Edited and Annotated]. Jinan: Shandong daxue chubanshe, 1990.

Glynn, Carroll J., editor. *Public Opinion*. Boulder: Westview Press, 1999.

Goode, Erich and Nachman Ben-Yehuda. *Moral Panics: The Social Construction of Deviance*. Cambridge, MA: Blackwell, 1994.

Gross, Kenneth. *Shakespeare's Noise*. Chicago: University of Chicago Press, 2001.

Gu Jiegang 顾颉刚. *Zhongguo shanggushi yanjiu jiangyi* 中国上古史研究讲义 [Lectures on the Study of Chinese Archaic History]. Beijing: Zhonghua shuju, 1989.

Gu Jiegang 顾颉刚. "Wude zhongshi shuo xia de zhengzhi he lishi" 五德终始说下的政治和历史 [Politics and History According to the Theory of the Rise and Fall of the Five Powers]. In *Gushi bian di wu ce* 古史辨第五册 [Authenticating Archaic History, Volume V]. Shanghai: Shanghai guji chubanshe, 1982.

Guan Yanchun 关雁春. "Gongzhong yulun, shimin shehui yu fazhi" 公众舆论、市民社会与法治 [Public Opinion, Civil Society, and Rule of Law]. In *Xueshu jiaoliu* 学术交流 [Academic Exchange]. 2003, 11: 35–39.

Harris, Richard Jackson. *A Cognitive Psychology of Mass Communication*. Hillsdale: Lawrence Erlbaum Associates, 1989.

Hou Jian 侯健. "Sanzhong quanli zhiyue jizhi jiqi bijiao" 三种权力制约机制及其比较 [Three Types of Checks on Power and the Comparisons between Them]. In *Fudan xuebao* 复旦学报 [Fudan Journal]. 2001, 3: 100–106.

Hu Shouwei 胡守为. "'Ju yaoyan' yu donghan lizheng" 举谣言"与东汉吏政 ["Rhymes Reporting" and Administration of the Eastern Han]. In *Zhongshan daxue xuebao* 中山大学学报 [Journal of Sun Yat-sen University]. 2004, 6: 64–69.

Huang Zhenyun 黄震云. "Handai shenhua de duotaixing yu zhengzhi" 汉代神话的多态性与政治 [The Polymorphism and Politics of Han-Period Myths]. In *Wenxue pinglun* 文学评论 [Literary Criticism]. 2010, 2: 98–104.

Jenkins, Henry. *Textual Poachers: Television Fans & Participatory Culture*. New York: Routledge, 1992.

Jiang Wanxiu 江万秀, Lei Caiming 雷才明, and Jiang Fengxian 江凤贤. *Yaoyan toushi* 谣言透视 [Insight on Rumors]. Beijing: Qunzhong chubanshe, 1991.

Kapferer, Jean-Noël. *Rumors: Uses, Interpretations, and Images*. New Brunswick: Transaction Publishers, 1990.

Knopf, Terry Ann. *Rumors, Race, and Riots*. New Brunswick: Transaction Books, 1975.

Koenig, Fredrick. *Rumor in the Marketplace: The Social Psychology of Commercial Hearsay*. Dover: Auburn House Publishing Company, 1985.

Kuhn, Philip A. *Soulstealers: The Chinese Sorcery Scare of 1768*. Cambridge, MA: Harvard University Press, 1990.

Kushida Hisaharu 串田 久治. *Chūgoku kodai no "yō" to "yogen"* 中国古代の"谣"と"予言" [Ancient "Rhymes" and "Prophecies" in China]. Tokyo: Sōbunsha, 1999.

Le Bon, Gustave. *The Crowd: A Study of the Popular Mind*. With a new introduction by Robert A. Nye. New Brunswick: Transaction Publishers, 1995.

Lei Qunming 雷群明 and Wang Longdi 王龙娣. *Zhongguo gudai tongyao shangxi* 中国古代童谣赏析 [Appreciating Ancient Chinese Children's Songs]. Changsha: Hunan wenyi chubanshe, 1988.

Leng Dexi 冷德熙. *Chaoyue shenhua–weishu zhengzhi shenhua yanjiu* 超越神话—纬书政治神话研究 [Beyond Myths: A Study of Political Myths in Apocryphal Writings]. Beijing: Dongfang chubanshe, 1996.

Li Ling 李零. *Changsha zidanku zhanguo chu boshu yan jiu* 长沙子弹库战国楚帛书研究 [Research on Silk Text from the State of Chu in the Warring States Period Unearthed at Zidanku, Changsha]. Beijing: Zhonghua shuju, 1985.

Li Ling 李零. *Zhongguo fangshu zhengkao* 中国方术正考 [A Proper Study of Chinese Alchemy]. Beijing: Zhonghua shuju, 2006.

Li Zhonghua 李中华. "Wenziyu: xuan zai wenren toushang de lijian" 文字狱：悬在文人头上的利剑 [Literary Inquisition: The Sword that Hangs above the Heads of Intellectuals]. In *Xun gen* 寻根 [Finding Roots]. 2003, 2: 26.

Lin Jianming 林剑鸣, Yu Huaqing 余华青, Zhou Tianyou 周天游, and Huang Liuzhu 黄留珠. *Qinhan shehui wenming* 秦汉社会文明 [The Culture of Qin and Han Society]. Xian: Xibei daxue chubanshe, 1985.

Lin Yutang. *A History of the Press and Public Opinion in China*. Chicago: The University of Chicago Press, 1936.

Lippmann, Walter. *Public Opinion*. New York: Harcourt, Brace and Company, Inc., 1922.

Liu Anyan 刘安彦. *Shehui xinlixue di 5 ban* 社会心理学第5版 [Social Psychology, 5th ed.]. Taipei: Sanmin shuju, 1993.

Liu Jianming 刘建明. *Yulun chuabo* 舆论传播 [Transmission of Public Opinion]. Beijing: Qinghua daxue chubanshe, 2001.

Liu Jie 刘节. *Zhongguo shixue shigao* 中国史学史稿 [A Draft History of Chinese Historiography]. Zhengzhou: Zhongzhou shuhuashe, 1982.

Liu Kaiyang 刘开扬. *Shiyelou cungao* 柿叶楼存稿 [Manuscript of the Persimmon Leaf House]. Shanghai: Shanghai guji chubanshe, 1983.

Liu Pak-yuen 廖伯源. *Qinhan shi luncong* 秦汉史论丛 [Collected Essays on History of the Qin and Han]. Taipei: Wunan tushu chuban gongsi, 2003.

Liu Zehua 刘泽华, editor-in-chief. *Zhongguo gudai zhengzhi sixiangshi* 中国古代政治思想史 [History of Ancient Chinese Political Thought]. Tianjin: Nankai daxue chubanshe, 1992.

Loewe, Michael. *Ways to Paradise: The Chinese Quest for Immortality*. London, Boston: Allen & Unwin, 1979.

Lu Xun 鲁迅. *Lu xun quanji* 鲁迅全集 [Complete Works of Lu Xun]. Beijing: Renmin wenxue chubanshe, 1987.

Lu Yao-Tung 逯耀东. *Weijin shixue ji qita* 魏晋史学及其他 [Wei-Jin Historiography and Others]. Taipei: Dongda tushu gongsi, 1998.

Lü Simian 吕思勉. *Qinhan shi* 秦汉史 [History of the Qin and Han]. Shanghai: Shanghai guji chubanshe, 1983.

Lu Zongli 吕宗力. "Donghan beike yu chenwei shenxue" 东汉碑刻与谶纬神学 [Tombstone Inscriptions of the Eastern Han and the Theology of Apocryphal-Prophetic Discourse]. In *Yanjiusheng lunwen xuanji: zhongguo lishi fence* 研究生论文选集：中国历史分册 [Collection of Postgraduate Dissertations: Chinese History]. Nanjing: *Jiangsu guji chubanshe*, 1984: 67–88.

Lu Zongli 吕宗力. "Gansheng shenhua yu handai huangquan zhengdangxing de lunzheng" 感生神话与汉代皇权正当性的论证 [On the Myth of Miraculous Birth and the Legitimation of Han Imperial Power]. In *Qinhan shi luncong di 8 ji* 秦汉史论丛第8辑 [Collected Essays on History of the Qin and Han, Volume VIII]. Kunming: Yunnan daxue chubanshe, 2001: 415–434.

Lu Zongli吕宗力. *Power of the Words: Chen Prophecy in Chinese Politics, 265–618*. Oxford: Peter Lang AG, 2003.

Lu Zongli 吕宗力. "Handai de liuyan yu eyan" 汉代的流言与讹言 [Disseminated Talk and Unverifiable Talk of the Han Period]. In *Lishi yanjiu* 历史研究 [Historical Studies]. 2003, 2: 14–31.

Lu Zongli 吕宗力. "Handai "yaoyan" tantao" 汉代"妖言"探讨 [Examining the "Portentous Talk" of the Han Period]. In *Zhongguo shi yanjiu* 中国史研究 [Chinese Historical Studies]. 2006, 4: 39–58.

Lu Zongli 吕宗力. "Luelun minjian geyao zai handai de zhengzhi zuoyong ji xiangguan misi" 略论民间歌谣在汉代的政治作用及相关迷思 [A Brief Discussion of the Political Function of Folk Rhymes in the Han Period and Related Myths]. In *Shehui kexue zhanxian* 社会科学战线 [Social Science Battlefront]. 2008, 9: 106–124.

Lu Zongli 吕宗力. "Handai kaiguo zhi jun shenhua de jian'gou yu yujing" 汉代开国之君神话的建构与语境 [The Construct and Context of Dynastic Founding Myths of the Han Period]. In *Shixue jikan* 史学集刊 [Collected Works of History]. 2010, 2: 11–18.

Lu Zongli 吕宗力 and Luan Baoqun 栾保群. *Zhongguo minjian zhushen* 中国民间诸神 [Chinese Folk Deities]. Shijiazhuang: Hebei renmin chubanshe, 2000.

Ma Xin 马新. "Shizheng yaoyan yu lianghan minzhong canyu yishi" 时政谣谚与两汉民众参与意识 [Rhymes and Adages Commenting on Current Politics and the Concept of Participation of People during the Han Dynasties]. In *Qilu xuekan* 齐鲁学刊 [Qilu Journal]. 2001, 6: 82–88.

Matthews, George Tennyson. *News and Rumor in Renaissance Europe: The Fugger Newsletters*. New York: Capricorn Books, 1959.

Meng Xiangcai 孟祥才. *Zhongguo zhengzhi zhidu tongshi di 3 juan* 中国政治制度通史第3卷 [General History of Chinese Political Systems, Volume III]. Beijing: Renmin chubanshe, 1996.

Neubauer, Hans-Joachim. *The Rumor: A Cultural History*. Translated by Christian Braun. London: Free Association Books, 1999.

Ono Shinji. "A Deliberate Rumor: National Anxiety in China on the Eve of the Xinhai Revolution." In Eto Shinkichi and Harold Z. Schiffrin, editors. *China's Republican Revolution*. Tokyo: University of Tokyo Press, 1994, 25–40.

Ostrander, Michael E. "The Meaning of Sennacherib's Rumor in Isaiah 37:7." Unpublished M.Div. thesis. Grace Theological Seminary, 1970.

Overholt, Thomas W. *Prophecy in Cross-Cultural Perspective: A Sourcebook for Biblical Researchers*. Atlanta: Scholars Press, 1986.

Oyanagi Shigeta 小柳 司気太. *Dōyō, toshin, kyōhi* 童謠　図讖　教匪 [Children's Songs and Rhymes, *Chen* Diagrams, and Religious Bandits]. In *Tōyō shisō no kenkyū* 東洋思想の研究 [The Study of Oriental Thought]. Tokyo: Seki shoin, 1934.

Palmer, Roy. *The Sound of History: Songs and Social Comment*. Oxford: Oxford University Press, 1988.

Peng Ya-Ling 彭雅玲. *"Shitong de lishi xushu lilun"* 《史通》的历史叙述理论 [The Historical Narrative Theory of Generality of Historiography]. Taipei: Wenshizhe chubanshe, 1993.

Qian Zhongshu 钱钟书. *Guanzhui bian* 管锥编 [Limited Views] Beijing: Shenghuo dushu xinzhi sanlian shudian, 2001.

Qiu Yongming 邱永明. *Zhongguo jiancha zhidu shi* 中国监察制度史 [History of the Censorate System in China]. Shanghai: Huadong shifan daxue chubanshe, 1992.

Ramsay, Clay. *The Ideology of the Great Fear: The Soissonnais in 1789*. Baltimore: Johns Hopkins University Press, 1992.

Reumaux, Françoise. *Heiguafu: yaoyan de shiyi ji chuanbo* 黑寡妇：谣言的示意及传播 [*La veuve noire: message et transmission* de la rumeur]. Translated by Tang Jialong 唐家龙. Beijing: Shangwu yinshuguan, 1999.

Rogers, Francis Millet. *The Quest for Eastern Christians: Travels and Rumor in the Age of Discovery*. Minneapolis: University of Minnesota Press, 1962.

Rosnow, Ralph L. and Gary Alan Fine. *Rumor and Gossip: The Social Psychology of Hearsay*. New York: Elsevier, 1976.

Roth, Michael S. and Charles G. Salas. *Disturbing Remains: Memory, History, and Crisis in the Twentieth Century*. Los Angeles: Getty Research Institute, 2001.

Schwartz, Benjamin I. *The World of Thought in Ancient China*. Cambridge, MA: Belknap Press of Harvard University Press, 1985.

Shibutani, Tamotsu. *Improvised News: A Sociological Study of Rumor*. Indianapolis: Bobbs-Merrill Company, 1966.

Shibutani, Tamotsu and Kian M. Kwan. *Individuality and Social Control: Essays in Honor of Tamotsu Shibutani* (Contemporary Studies in Sociology, Volume 13). Greenwich: JAI Press, 1996.

Shive, Glenn. "Policy Debates and Rumor Mills: China Considers Restrictions on Study Abroad." In *China Exchange News* (Washington, DC). 18 (1), 1990: 3–7.

Song Su 宋衍申, editor-in-chief. *Zhongguo shixueshi gangyao* 中国史学史纲要 [An Outline of the History of Chinese Historiography]. Changchun: Dongbei shifan daxue chubanshe, 1992.

Strauss, Botho. *Rumor*. Translated by Michael Hulse. Manchester: Carcanet Press, 1984.

Su Ping 苏萍. *Yaoyan yu jindai jiao'an* 谣言与近代教案 [A Study of Rumors in Religious Cases in Modern China]. Shanghai: Yuandong chubanshe, 2001.

Sun Jiazhou 孙家洲. "Handai 'yingyan' chenyan lishi" 汉代"应验"谶言例释 [Examples and Explanations for Han-era *Chen* Prophecies that "Came True"]. In *Zhongguo zhexueshi* 中国哲学史 [History of Chinese Philosophy]. 1997, 2: 82–88.

Sun Kuang-Teh 孙广德. "Woguo zhengshi zhong de zhengzhi shenhua" 我国正史中的政治神话 [Political Myths in China's Official Histories]. In Tu Wei-Yün 杜维运, Wang Teh-Yi 王德毅, and Li Yun-Han 李云汉, editors. *Zhongguo shixue lunwen xuanji di 6 ji* 中国史学论文选集第6辑 [Selected Dissertations on Chinese Historiography, Volume VI]. Taipei: Youshi wenhua shiye gongsi, 1986: 51–125.

Sun Xupei 孙旭培. *Huaxia chuanbo lun* 华夏传播论 [Theory of Transmission in China]. Beijing: Renmin chubanshe, 1997.

Tang Linghui 汤凌慧. "Hanwendi 'yuefa shengxing' lueshu" 汉文帝"约法省刑"略述 [A Brief Account of Emperor Wen of the Western Han Dynasty's "Reduction of Laws and Punishments"]. In *Liaoning shizhuan xuebao* 辽宁师专学报 [Journal of Liaoning Teachers College]. 2000, 1: 112–114.

ter Haar, B.J. *Telling Stories: Witchcraft and Scapegoating in Chinese History*. Leiden, Boston: Brill, 2006.

Tian Beihu 田北湖. "Lun wenzhang yuanliu (2)" 论文章源流（ 2 ）[On the Sources of Essays (2)]. In *Guocui xuebao* 国粹学报 [Journal of National Culture]. 1904, 2: 1–6.

Tian Ying 天鹰. *Zhongguo gudai geyao sanlun* 中国古代歌谣散论 [Essays on Ancient Songs and Rhymes in China]. Shanghai: Zhonghua shuju shanghai bianjisuo, 1959.

Tong Xigang 仝晰纲. "Handai fengyao yu juyaoyan" 汉代风谣与举谣言 [Rhymes and Rhymes Reporting of the Han Period]. In *Renwen zazhi* 人文杂志 [Humanities Magazine]. 1999, 4: 110–111.

Truman, David B. *The Governmental Process: Political Interests and Public Opinion*. Westport: Greenwood Press, 1981.

Turner, Patricia A. *I Heard It through the Grapevine: Rumor in African-American Culture*. Berkeley: University of California Press, 1993.

Van Buren, John. *The Young Heidegger: Rumor of the Hidden King*. Bloomington: Indiana University Press, 1994.

Victor, Jeffrey S. *The Creation of a Contemporary Legend*. Chicago: Open Court, 1993.

Wang Meifang 王梅芳. "Yulun jiandu yu shehui zhengyi" 舆论监督与社会正义 [Public Opinion Supervision and Social Justice]. Wuhan: Wuhan daxue chubanshe, 2005.

Wang Qing 王青. "Hanchao de bentu zongjiao yu shenhua" 汉朝的本土宗教与神话 [The Indigenous Religions and Myths of the Han Dynasty]. Taipei: Hongye wenhua, 1998.

Wang Xiong 王雄. *Xinwen yulun yanjiu* 新闻舆论研究 [A Study of Public Opinion in the News]. Beijing: Xinhua chubanshe, 2002.

Wang Zijin 王子今. *Qinhan shehuishi lunkao* 秦汉社会史论考 [A Study of the Social History of the Qin and Han]. Beijing: Shangwu yinshuguan, 2006.

White, Luise. *Speaking with Vampires: Rumor and History in Colonial Africa*. Berkeley: University of California Press, 2000.

Wu Chengxue 吴承学. "Lun yaochen yu shichen" 论谣谶与诗谶 [Studies on *Chen* Rhymes and *Chen* Poetry]. In *Wenxue pinglun* 文学评论 [Literary Criticism]. 1996, 2: 103–112.

Xia Mingzhao 夏明钊. *Yaoyan zhe dongxi* 谣言这东西 [This Thing Called Rumor]. Shenzhen: Haitian chubanshe, 1999.

Xie Gui'an 谢贵安. *Zhongguo chenyao wenhua* 中国谶谣文化 [A Study of the Culture of *Chen* and Rhymes of China]. Haikou: Hainan chubanshe, 1998.

Xie Gui'an 谢贵安. "Gudai zhengzhi minyao ji qi shehui yulun gongneng" 古代政治民谣及其社会舆论功能 [Ancient Political Folk Ballads and Their Functions in Society and Public Opinion]. In *Hubei xingzheng xueyuan xuebao* 湖北行政学院学报 [Journal of Hubei Administration Institute]. 2002, inaugural issue: 81–84.

Xu Hualong 徐华龙. *Zhongguo geyao xinlixue* 中国歌谣心理学 [The Psychology of Chinese Songs and Rhymes]. Urumqi: Xinjiang renmin chubanshe, 1990.

Yan Buke 阎步克. *Chaju zhidu bianqian* 察举制度变迁 [Changes in the Civil Service Recruitment System]. Shenyang: Liaoning daxue chubanshe, 1997.

Yan Xinheng 阎心恒. "Minyi de xingcheng yu fazhan" 民意的形成与发展 [Formation and Development of the People's Will]. In Tseng Hsü-Pai 曾虚白,

editor-in-chief. *Zhongguo xinwen shi* 中国新闻史 [History of Chinese Journalism]. Taipei: Sanmin shuju, 1984.

Yang Mingpin 杨明品. *Xinwen yulun jiandu* 新闻舆论监督 [Supervision by Public Opinion in the News]. Beijing: Zhongguo guangbo Dianshi chubanshe, 2001.

Yang Yanqi 杨燕起, Chen Keqing 陈可青, and Lai Changyang 赖长扬, editors. *Lishi mingjia ping shiji* 历史名家评《史记》 [Commentaries on *The Grand Scribe's Records* by Famous Persons in History]. Beijing: Beijing shifan daxue chubanshe, 1986.

Ye Changlin 叶常林 and Li Ruihua 李瑞华. "Gonggong quanli jiandu moshi de lishi yanjiu" 公共权力监督模式的历史研究 [A Historical Study of the Model of Public Supervision of Power]. In *Anhui gongye daxue xuebao* 安徽工业大学学报 [Journal of Anhui University of Technology]. 2006, 1: 15–18.

Yen Keng-Wang 严耕望. *Zhongguo difang xingzheng zhidu shi (jiabu): qinhan difang zhidu* 中国地方行政制度史（ 甲部 ）：秦汉地方制度 [History of Chinese Local Administrative Systems (Part A): Local Systems in the Qin and Han]. Taipei: Lishi yuyan Yanjiusuo zhuankan zhi 45A, 1990.

Yu Guoming 喻国明. *Jiegou minyi–yige yulun xuezhe de shizheng yanjiu* 解构民意:一个舆论学者的实证研究 [Deconstructing the People's Will: Empirical Research Conducted by a Scholar of Public Opinion]. Beijing: Huaxia chubanshe, 2001.

Yu Jiaxi 余嘉锡. *Siku tiyao bianzheng* 四库提要辨证 [Dialectical Discourse on the Summary of the Complete Library in Four Sections]. Beijing: Zhonghua shuju, 1980.

Zhang Renxi 张仁玺. "Qinhan jiazu Chengyuan lianzuo kaolue" 秦汉家族成员连坐考略 [A Brief Study of Implicative Punishment among Family Members in the Qin and Han]. In *Sixiang zhanxian* 思想战线 [Ideological Battlefront]. 2003, 6: 97–102.

Zhang Taiyan 章太炎. *Zhang taiyan juan: geming zhi daode* 章太炎卷：革命之道德 [Volume on Zhang Taiyan: The Morality of Revolution]. In Jiang Deming 姜德铭, editor-in-chief. *Zhongguo xiandai mingjia mingzuo wenku* 中国现代名家名作文库 [Anthology of Famous Works by Renowned Modern Chinese Scholars]. Beijing: Zhongguo xiju chubanshe, 2001.

Zhang Tiemin 张铁民. *Yaoyan he liuyan: cuowei de xintai* 谣言和流言：错位的心态 [Rumors and Hearsay: Dislocated Mentalities]. Nanjing: Jiangsu jiaoyu chubanshe, 1997.

Zhang Xiaofeng 张晓峰. "Zhengzhi chuanbo yu zhengzhi xiangzheng lilun pingjie" 政治传播与政治象征理论评介 [A Review of the Theories of Political Communications and Political Symbolism]. In *Xiandai chuanbo shuangyuekan* 现代传播双月刊 [Modern Communications Bimonthly]. 2004, 6: 25–29.

Zhao Shiyu 赵世瑜. "Yaoyan yu xinshixue – zhang shouchang zhongguo jinshi yaoyan duhou" 谣谚与新史学—张守常《中国近世谣谚》读后 [Rhymes and Adages, and New Historiography: Some Thoughts on Zhang Shouchang's *Rhymes and Adages in Early Modern China*]. In *Lishi yanjiu* 历史研究 [Historical Studies]. 2002, 5: 166–171.

Zheng Changgan 郑昌淦. *Zhongguo zhengshi xueshuo shi* 中国政治学说史 [History of Chinese Political Theories]. Taipei: Wenjin chubanshe, 1995.

Zhong Zhaopeng 钟肇鹏. *Chenwei lunlue* 谶纬论略 [A Brief Summary of Apocryphal-Prophetic Discourse]. Shenyang: Liaoning jiaoyu chubanshe, 1991.
Zhou Changshan 周长山. *Handai difang zhengzhi shilun* 汉代地方政治史论 [Historical Review of Provincial Politics]. Beijing: Zhongguo shehui kexue chubanshe, 2006.
Zhou Xiaohong 周晓虹. *Xiandai shehui xinlixue–duowei shiye zhong de shehui xingwei yanjiu* 现代社会心理学—多维视野中的社会行为研究 [Modern Social Psychology: Study of Social Behavior from Multi-Dimensional Perspectives]. Shanghai: Shanghai renmin chubanshe, 1997.
Zhu Chuanyu朱传誉. *Zhongguo minyi yu xinwen ziyou fazhanshi* 中国民意与新闻自由发展史 [The History of the Development of Public Opinion and Press Freedom in China]. Taipei: Zhengzhong shuju, 1974.
Zhu Ziqing 朱自清. *Zhongguo geyao* 中国歌谣 [Chinese Songs and Rhymes]. Taipei: Kaijin wenhua, 1994.
Zou Xianjun 邹贤俊. *Zhongguo gudai shixue shigang* 中国古代史学史纲 [An Outline of the History of Ancient Chinese Historiography]. Wuhan: Huazhong shifan daxue chubanshe, 1989.

Index

For EU product safety concerns, contact us at Calle de José Abascal, 56–1°,
28003 Madrid, Spain or eugpsr@cambridge.org.

www.ingramcontent.com/pod-product-compliance
Ingram Content Group UK Ltd.
Pitfield, Milton Keynes, MK11 3LW, UK
UKHW020114190126
467120UK00020B/718

* 9 7 8 1 1 0 8 7 4 9 5 3 4 *